C000260156

Old parish boundaries of Staffordshire

Volume One: Pirehill

Copyright Tim Cockin 2005
All rights reserved. No part of this publication may be reproduced, stored in a retrieval system,
transmitted in any form by any means electrical or mechanical, photographed, recorded or otherwise without the prior permission of the publisher.

Published 2005

Printed and bound by MPG Books Ltd
Victoria Square, Bodmin
Cornwall PL31 1EG

Published by Malthouse Press
Grange Cottage
Malthouse Lane, Barlaston
Stoke-on-Trent ST12 9AQ
01782 372067
Timcockin@yahoo.com

ISBN 0-9539018-1-5

Old parish boundaries of Staffordshire
Volume One: Pirehill

A guide to the administrative units of Staffordshire

Tim Cockin

Malthouse Press

CONTENTS

FOREWORD

What better time than this - a general election year - to publish a much needed book on political and local government boundary changes. I say much needed because there have been so many alterations that it is quite likely the reader's home is not now in the parish it once was. Small parishes have been gobbled up, and new ones created; boundaries everywhere have been altered. Administrators, planners, and family historians need an easy reference, which is lacking at present.

The author is publishing in volumes because to map and comprehensibly gazeteer the ancient County of Stafford would take decades. Each volume focuses on a Hundred. These original divisions of a shire evolved into the more recent - though now defunct - Petty Sessional Divisions. They were created in Anglo-Saxon times, and possibly pre-date shires. They comprise vills (roughly equalling a manor). These vills or manors largely became the townships of the 18th and 19th centuries. In turn, townships were divisions of a parish, which could levy a separate Poor Rate and appoint a constable. The author has taken special care, therefore, to trace township boundaries.

By way of annotation he gives a flavour of civil and ecclesiastical records, which for years have lain gathering dust in parish chests, and are now at Stafford Record Office. In his own words the idea is "a sort of humble attempt to localise W. E. Tate's classic work 'The Parish Chest': It may help some starting on family history to consider material other than censuses."

The volume concludes with a comprehensive roll of M.Ps for all Staffordshire constituencies from the Middle Ages to the present.

Bill Cash, M.P. for Stone, Cheadle, Eccleshall,
Madeley, Hixon, Gnosall

PREFACE

This book is the result of trying to right a small deficiency of my earlier work *The Staffordshire Encyclopaedia* (2000) of not all places being assigned to a specific township, ward, ecclesiastical and civil parish. It is an aid to the administrative units of Staffordshire for family historians and local people.

Old Parish Boundaries of Staffordshire relied heavily on First/ Old Series Ordnance Survey, tithe, estate and municipal maps and I should especially like to thank all the Staffordshire Record Office staff, without whose help it would have been impossible:- Matthew Blake, Joan Capstrick, Joanne Evans, Paul Ford, Tim Groom, Mary Howes, Ruth Humphreys, Rebecca Jackson, Louise Martin, Malinda Law, Helen Legge, Catherine Nichols, Liz Street, Graham Surman, Hazel Tatlow, Joanne Terry, and Wendy Tolly. The unsung heroes are thosewho brought all the maps and vestry books to and from the strongroom:- Beryl Bentley, Strongroom Supervisor, and Jenny Hudson, Strongroom Assistant. In addition, staff at LRO (Diane Challenor, Nicola Crews, Ruth Hanslow, Joanne Peck, Robert Vaughan), SCA and Keele (JL Bailey) deserve a big thank you. In later stages the research was WSL-orientated and there I should like to thank Margaret Heath, Archive Assistant, Dominic Farr, Assistant Librarian (for his advise and labour marshalling Staffordshire Views onto a CD), and The Librarian (and County Archivist) Thea Randall, for her support and encouragement. In addition, Martin Elkes, Community Librarian ICT at Stafford Library, was so helpful, and SRRC (Shropshire Archives) for permission to publish the abbreviated list of Drayton-in-Hales parish records from their catalogue, and individuals such as Kerry Dickins, Jen Smith and others.

With photography and graphics Garry Gatensbury, again worked wonders. Many necessary images were kindly lent, and permission given for reproduction, by Roy Lewis, Michael Raven, Randle Knight, Chris Rushton and Sentinel Newspapers, Staffordshire Newspapers Ltd and The Trustees of The William Salt Library.

Many thanks also to Paul Anderton, Dr Anne Andrews, Robin Ansall, Joan Ansow, Malcolm Austen, Joan Barstow, Liz Bedford, George Beecham, Peter Bickerstaff, Steve Birks, Alaister Bishop, Mr J Blount, Lloyd Boardman, Mary Booth, Sharon Brown, Elaine Challinor, Patrick Corness, Gerald D' Arcy, Hilary Davies, Geoff Edwards, Marion Edwards, Dr DW Eyre-Walker, Keith Farr, Robert Farrell, Mrs EA Ford, Dudley Fowkes, Angela Graham, Michael Greenslade, Ernest J Hawkins, John Heath, Mrs C Heelis, Ms L Hembrough, Peter W Jones, Rhoda King, Charlotte Littlejones, Russell & Jane Maingay, Keith Meeson, Monica Moreton, Clive Read, Richard Plant, Robert Stones, Kate Thacker, Pauline Trantrum, David Tyler, Brian Walker, Carol Wedgwood, Lori Weinstein, Rev John Williams, Martin Windmill, Richard Wisker, and, members of my family, and anyone else omitted,.

INTRODUCTION

To reach the public sooner rather than later the work is split into volumes, hundred by hundred. Each volume is a guide to the civil administrative units of a Staffordshire hundred, with supplements focusing on the County's ecclesiastical, legal and welfare divisions: This volume focuses on parliamentary divisions. Each chapter focuses on an ancient parish, with an abstract on community history, using the hundred as the area of study.

In a sense the abstracts are pieces of the overall local history jigsaw. Parishes emerged as ecclesiastical units in Anglo-Saxon times (Chebsey); perhaps as a block of vills (Madeley); their boundaries sometimes failed to correspond with those of the county (Drayton-in-Hales, Mucklestone); in an age before maps knowledge of boundaries needed to be retained with annual perambulations (Milwich): Manorial tenants had rights to common land (Colwich, Weston-on-Trent), and other untamed waste later became conserved in reserves (Norton in the Moors, Stowe by Chartley, Tixall): For various reasons settlements succeeded (Newcastle-under-Lyme) whilst others were deserted (Marston): The demise of the manor, isolating demesne, together with dissolution of the Monasteries resulted in lands parochially-disenfranchised (Chartley Holme, Ranton, Yarlet), and social welfare left in the hands of individuals (Biddulph) and parishes (Whitmore), controlled by vestries (Abbots Bromley, Adbaston, Barlaston, Ranton): A gentry and mercantile class emerged leaving records of their family and estate affairs (Trentham), notes about their wider community (Audley, Barthomley), symbols of personal aggrandisement (Ashley, Sandon, Swynnerton), and testaments (Chartley Holme, Eccleshall, Ellenhall, Ingestre). The Church's dominance through register-keeping (Maer, Seighford, Stoke-upon-Trent), rights (Creswell), seating arrangements (Stone), bells (High Offley) and dues (Gayton, Keele, Tillington, Worston) diminished with social progression, growth of population leading to municipal cemeteries (Wolstanton), technological advance and shared-information for the general population (Audley, Barthomley, Betley, Colton, Gayton, Swynnerton).

The origin of the modern civil parish is the ancient parish, an entirely ecclesiastical unit. So the original CPs used the AP boundaries. With the Highway Act of 1555 the AP started to take on civil responsibilities. The Act placed responsibility for parish road maintenance on parishioners, supervised by a parish officer, the Surveyor of the Highways. By mandate, from 1538, the parish was the unit for registration of baptism, marriage and burial, in as much as the Church had dominance over most inhabitants. Over the next centuries statutes gave more and more civil responsibility to the AP. Most parish business was administered through a council in the church vestry. Other Acts followed:- 1563 (relating to institutional alms collecting), 1572 (office of Overseer of the Poor created), 1597/8 (a poor rate could be levied), 1601 (establishment of an integrated administrative system for poor relief), 1662 (parish right to expel unemployed immigrants), 1697 (parish right to see immigrants' bond certificates guaranteeing return to their home parish in case they become in need of poor relief), 1723 (parishes empowered to build workhouses if they wish - see Whitmore chapter). From the 1830s some parish powers passed to local boards, the forerunners of district councils. The most notable local board was the body of guardians governing each Union of parishes under the Poor Law Amendment Act 1834. Sanitary and Highway districts - the LBs - emerged from Acts of 1848, 1858, 1863, 1878, which in some instances were councils run parallel with the PLU. Under The Births and Deaths Registration Act of 1837, registration of births, marriages and deaths was introduced, creating Registration districts based on the PLU (and later on district councils, metropolitan boroughs and unitary authorities). The formal acknowledgement of the AP as an entirely civil unit, a tier of local government lower than these districts, seems to come in the Poor Law Amendment Act, 1866, cap 113, section 18 - 'the word 'parish' shall signify a place for which a separate Poor Rate is or can be made, or for which a separate Overseer is or can be appointed.' Qualifying for CP status (extra-parochial liberties qualified earlier, in 1858) were Cold Norton, Chapel and Hill Chorlton, and Whitgreave. So by the same token, from this time all APs could be designated CPs. Vestries or parish meetings continued until December 1894, when under the Local Government Act, 1894, they decided to become a newly-regulated Parish Council or a Parish Meeting. Not all CPs, eligible to form a PC, chose to do so, and CP status does not necessarily equate with having a PC. Even the PM of a CP can lapse, and still the CP area remains (Ellenhall). However a CP can be lost if its area is wholly carved up between other CPs (Trentham). For council purposes a CP can be grouped with another (a pg), and still the respective CP areas remain (Ingestre with Tixall). In CP areas hitherto without a PC, new PCs can be established, with the necessary Order (Creswell). New CP areas are still created, though inevitably they come hand in hand with a newly-created PC (Silverdale, Doxey).

ABBREVIATIONS

AP	Ancient Parish
B	Borough
BOR	The Book of Ranton: The Story of a Staffordshire Village. Frank Foden. 1993
BPBBP	Burslem People and Buildings, Buildings and People. Carmel Dennison. 1996
BPL	Birmingham Public Library
BSTAFFS	Buildings of Staffordshire. Staffs County Planning & Development Dept 1982
C	County
CB	County Borough
CC	County Council, County Constituency
CCW	Corresponding City Ward. Stoke-on-Trent City District (hitherto a CB) used its wards as electoral divisions in Staffordshire CC 1974-96.
CED	County Electoral District, for CC seats
Con	Conservative
Court	essentially a Royalist (MP)
Country	essentially a Parliamentarian (MP)
CP	Civil Parish
CRO	Cheshire Record Office
D	District, Division
DPB	Discovering Parish Boundaries. Angus Winchester. 1990
dem	demolished
E	East
EC	Euro Constituency
EP	Ecclesiastical Parish
GTS	Guide to Sources by Staffordshire and Stoke on Trent Archive Service. No 1 = Parish registers and Bishops' Transcripts 2000.
KUL	Keele University Library
No.	Number
L	Liberty
Lab	Labour
LB	Local Board (of Health)
LG	Local Government at district level
Lib	Liberal
PARL	Parliamentary constituencies
PB	Parliamentary Borough
PC	Parish Council

PD	Polling District
pg	parish grouping
PLU	Poor Law Union
PM	Parish Meeting
poss	possibly
prob	probably
PW	Parish Ward
MB	Municipal Borough
MTM	A Meander Through Milwich: Celebrating the New Millennium. Milwich Millennium Working Group. 2000.
N	North
NCB	National Coal Board
RD	Rural District
RSD	Rural Sanitary District
S	South
SCA	Stoke-on-Trent City Archives
SI	Statutory Instruments
	No. 152 = The Newcastle-u-Lyme (Parishes) Order 1984
	No. 223 = The West Midland Counties Order 1965
SIAS	Stafford Industrial Archaeological Society
SIASJ	Journal of the Staffordshire Industrial Archaeology Society
SPRS	Staffordshire Parish Register Society
SRDOG	Stone Rural District: The Official Guide (fifth edition c1958)
SRRC	Shropshire Record & Research Centre, alias Shropshire Archives
T	contested election (stated to 1841)
T	Township
TC	Town Council
TCTH	Trentham: A Church Through History. June Speed. 1994
UA	Unitary Authority
UD	Urban District
W	West, Ward (probably in a CB or MB)
WITP	Workhouses in the Potteries. Diane Baker. City of Stoke-on-Trent Historic Buildings Survey. n.d. 1984?
*	contested election

Also consult **The Staffordshire Encyclopaedia** (2000), Malthouse Press, copies in most libraries covering the old County of Stafford. An invaluable source and further reading (not featured in the list) is the Staffordshire and Stoke on Trent Archive Service's *Family History Pack* available at £8.00 from:- **Staffordshire Record Office**, Eastgate Street, Stafford ST16 2LZ (Tel. 01785 278379) E mail: staffordshire.record.office@staffordshire.gov.uk. **Lichfield Record Office**, Lichfield Library, The Friary, Lichfield WS13 6QG (Tel. 01543 510720) E mail: lichfield. record.office@staffordshire.gov.uk. **Burton-upon-Trent Family & Local History Centre**, Burton-upon-Trent Library, Riverside, High Street, Burton-upon-Trent DE14 1AH (Tel. 01283 239556). **Stoke on Trent City Archives**, Hanley Library, Bethesda Street, Hanley, Stoke on Trent ST1 3RD (Tel. 01782 238420) E mail: stoke.archives@stoke.gov.uk. **Service** website is www.staffordshire.gov.uk/archives/

Scale for parish maps 1 mile = 3.3r cm

The Abbots Bromley Horn Dance, Abbots Bromley

Abbots Bromley

'Abbots Bromley, once a flourishing market borough, has long since descended to the status of a village in which the main occupation, apart from the work occasioned of late years by the Woodard Schools, is agriculture.'   Marcia Alice Rice. Abbots Bromley. 1939

By 1801 the townships supported their poor cojointly (SRO QS/B Michaelmas Term 1817); each had a surveyor of highways in 1832: In 1834 a surgeon to attend the poor, and a deputy overseer of the poor were elected (D1209/5/1).
PLU. Uttoxeter 1838-1930. Abbots Bromley W by1910.
SEE ALSO pages 2, 6, 10, 21, 30, 34, 49, 78, 84, 93, 100, 116, 125, 130, 140, 142, 186, 207, 211, 213

ABBOTS BROMLEY TOWNSHIP
Abbots Bromley
Abbots Bromley CP 1866-. PC 1894- (as population in excess of 300): An item at a 1913 meeting was to audit the parochial charities' accounts; they were passed as satisfactory (SA March 22 1913 p6).
LG. East Staffordshire D(B) 1974-. No. 18 W Feb 1976-9. Bagots W Feb 1979-2002, 2002-
CED. Uttoxeter 1889-1911. Uttoxeter Rural Sept 1911-2005, 2005-
Abbots Bromley Borough
Abbots Bromley CP 1866-.

LG. East Staffordshire D(B) 1974-. No. 18 W Feb 1976-9. Bagots W Feb 1979-2002, 2002-
CED. Uttoxeter 1889-1911. Uttoxeter Rural Sept 1911-2005, 2005-

BAGOTS BROMLEY TOWNSHIP
Bagots Bromley
Abbots Bromley CP 1866-.
LG. East Staffordshire D(B) 1974-. No. 18 W Feb 1976-9. Bagots W Feb 1979-2002, 2002-
CED. Uttoxeter 1889-1911. Uttoxeter Rural Sept 1911-2005, 2005-

Abbots Bromley

BROMLEY HURST TOWNSHIP
Birchwood Farm

Abbots Bromley CP 1866-1991. Hoar Cross CP 1991-
LG. East Staffordshire D(B) 1974-. No. 18 W Feb
1976-9. Bagots W Feb 1979-2002, 2002-
CED. Uttoxeter 1889-1911. Uttoxeter Rural Sept 1911-
2005, 2005-

Bromley Hurst

Abbots Bromley CP 1866-.
LG. East Staffordshire D(B) 1974-. No. 18 W Feb
1976-9. Bagots W Feb 1979-2002, 2002-
CED. Uttoxeter 1889-1911. Uttoxeter Rural Sept 1911-
2005, 2005-

Vestry meeting notices

Notice is hereby given

----

*That the Select vestry and overseers of the poor
will lay their half yearly accounts, ending at
Michaelmas, before their fellow parishioners
on Friday the fifth day of October next
and the inhabitants are requested to assemble
in general vestry at the parish church __
at ~~eleven~~ (sic) twelve o' clock in the forenoon to examine
the same from whence it is proposed
to adjourn to the house of Mr John Bamford
where a dinner will be provided for the
occasion ___*

Vestry Clarks office}	*Francis Cope*
September 23 1832 }	*Vestry Clark.*

Notices of vestry meetings had to be displayed in townships/ parishes or in places where a separate poor rate was levied, or which had a separate overseer by the Vestries Act 1818 cap. 69 section VII. By the same Act (cap. 69 section I) notice had to be given of a vestry meeting at least three days prior to it verbally during Sunday morning service in church and by written notice pinned to the church/ chapel door. Anyone was prohibited from announcing civil matters after Sunday morning service in church by the Parish Notices Act 1837 cap. 45 section IV. By the same Act (cap. 45 section II) the notice had to be 'reduced into writing' and copies put on the doors of all churches and chapels in the parish. However, as Tate notes in The Parish Chest, this practice had begun in some parishes much earlier. From 1774 it was required proposed enclosure schemes be announced with a written posted notice. Posted notices then became popular perhaps because everyone wanted to go home to their dinners that much sooner! (Tate p152). Numerous vestry notices from 1832 survive in Abbots Bromley parish records. A general vestry meeting was held at The Cock Inn, Rudgley Street in 1832. The meeting for November 19 1849 was held in the National School Room (D1209/5/1). The above notice is an early one.

The vestry meeting notice had to be signed by either churchwarden, or rector/ vicar/ curate, or overseer by the 1837 Act (cap. 45 section III); interestingly - for it comes before the Act - this one is signed by, who I take to be, the parish clerk. Ashley began putting up public notices for vestry meetings in Aug 1838 (D44/A/PV/1). At **Barlaston** notice was given in church 'Sunday last' - presumably verbally - for the vestry meeting June 2 1831 (D3538/9). **Madeley** has vestry notices 1850s-1870s (D3412/4/1-21). In **Ranton** parish records are C19 notices of vestry meetings (D4305/1/2/1-

UTTOXETER: UTTOXETER
WOODLANDS

SK 0600 SK 0700 SK 0800 SK 0900 SK 1000 SK 1100 SK 12002900

Broomfields
Farm

HANBURY:
MARCHINGTON
WOODLANDS

KINGSTONE

Marlpit
House Farm

High Trees
Farm

Parkstile

— SK 2800

BAGOT FOREST

Heatley
Bank Farm

Park Lodge

BAGOTS BROMLEY BAGOT'S PARK

— SK 2700

Heatley
Green
Farm

Heatley
Hall Farm

Whitecross
Pits

Parkside

HANBURY:
NEWBOROUGH

BAGOT FOREST

Little Heatley
Green Farm

Squitch
House

Marsh Farm

Moors

Park Farm

— SK 2600

Bagots
Bromley

Dunstal

Fieldhouse
Farm

BROMLEY PARK

ABBOTS BROMLEY

Bromley Park
Farm

Gapstile

Radmore
Wood

Parkgate

SK 2500

ABBOTS BROMLEY
BOROUGH

Radmore
Farm

Duckley
Plantation

Leafields
Farm

Bagot Arms
Inn

Bromley
Wood Farm

† butter cross

Yeatsall
Cottages

Hall Hill

Coach and
Horses Inn

Church View
Farm

Yeatsall

○ pinfold

Bromley
Wood

Birchwood
Farm

SK 2400

BLITHFIELD RESERVOIR

Portfields

Yenbrook

Bentilee

Mill Green

Seedcroft

Hurst Farm

Bentilee
Park

YOXALL

SK 2300

BROMLEY HURST

Forge
Farm

Cross of the Hand

BLITHFIELD:
BLITHFIELD

Gilleon's
Hall

SK 2200

COLTON

SK 2200

HAMSTALL
RIDWARE

MAVESYN
RIDWARE

The Hurst

SK 07002100 SK 0800 SK 0900 SK 1000 SK 1100 SK 13002100

12). **Stone** has one 1868 (D4605/4/2). At **Ashley** vestry meetings were invariably held at either the Farmyard Public House, the Meynell Arms Inn, or the School room between 1837 to at least 1855 (D44/A/PV/1).

Map of Abbots Bromley

Division of Bagot's Bromley clearly shown on Tithe award map at Lichfield (D3470/21/1). Division of Bromley Hurst worked out using White's dir (1851) and tithe app.

3

Batchacre Park House engraving 1802. Stebbing Shaw. SV. 1. 127. Courtesy of Trustees of WSL

Adbaston

'Dear, native Adbaston! - remote from care,
Thy tranquil fields would mitigate despair;
In thy sweet vales a balsam I could find,
When naught on earth could calm my troubled mind'

Charles Bowker Ash in Adbaston, or the Days of Youth. Early C19

By 1851 the five townships of Adbaston supported their poor cojointly.

PLU. Newport 1836-1930. Adbaston W by1894-.

SEE ALSO pages 6-7, 10, 21, 24, 50, 73-4, 78, 93, 96, 100, 106, 124, 125, 131, 142, 207, 211, 233

ADBASTON TOWNSHIP

Adbaston CP 1866-. PC from 1894.

LG. Gnosall RD 1894-1934. Adbaston W 1894-. Stafford RD 1934-74, D(B) 1974-. Woodseaves W 1974-2002. Eccleshall W 2002-.

CED. Eccleshall 1889-1911. Gnosall Sept 1911-73. Stone Rural 1973-81. Gnosall 1981-2005. Eccleshall 2005-

BATCHACRE TOWNSHIP

Adbaston CP 1866-1934. High Offley 1934- (1934 Review Order C/C/O/36/2 map No. 5).

LG. Gnosall RD 1894-1934. Adbaston W 1894-. Stafford RD 1934-74, D(B) 1974-. Woodseaves W 1974-2002, Gnosall & Woodseaves W 2002-.

CED. Eccleshall 1889-.1911. Gnosall Sept 1911-73.

Stafford Rural No. 1 1973-81. Gnosall 1981-2005. Gnosall 2005-.

BISHOP'S OFFLEY TOWNSHIP

Adbaston CP 1866-.

LG. Gnosall RD 1894-1934. Adbaston W 1894-. Stafford RD 1934-74, D(B) 1974-. Woodseaves W 1974-2002. Eccleshall W 2002-.

CED. Eccleshall 1889-1911. Gnosall Sept 1911-73. Stone Rural 1973-81. Gnosall 1981-2005. Eccleshall 2005-.

FLASHBROOK TOWNSHIP

Adbaston CP 1866-.

LG. Gnosall RD 1894-1934. Adbaston W 1894-. Stafford RD 1934-74, D(B) 1974-. Woodseaves W 1974-

Map of Adbaston

Townships from OS 1" (1st ed). Boundary of Haberdashers estate from C/C/O/7/E parcel 3 no. 46.

2002. Eccleshall W 2002-.

CED. Eccleshall 1889-1911. Gnosall Sept 1911-73. Stone Rural 1973-81. Gnosall 1981-2005. Eccleshall 2005-

TUNSTALL TOWNSHIP
Tunstall

Adbaston CP.

LG. Gnosall RD 1894-1934. Adbaston W 1894-. Stafford RD 1934-74, D(B) 1974-. Woodseaves W 1974-2002. Eccleshall W 2002-.

CED. Eccleshall 1889-1911. Gnosall Sept 1911-73. Stone Rural 1973-81. Gnosall 1981-2005. Eccleshall 2005-

Lonco Brook (4)

Adbaston CP -1934. High Offley CP 1934-.

LG. Gnosall RD 1894-1934. Stafford RD 1934-74, D(B) 1974-. Woodseaves W 1974-2002. Gnosall & Woodseaves W 2002-.

CED. Eccleshall 1889-1911. Gnosall Sept 1911-73. Stafford Rural No. 1 1973-81. Gnosall 1981-2005. Gnosall 2005-.

Adbaston

Early churchwardens' accounts

Dr DW Eyre-Walker, current Adbaston Churchwarden, peruses document M64

Adbaston churchwardens' accounts 1478-88 (WSL M64) are one of only 70 or so surviving English C15 churchwardens' accounts, and Staffordshire's earliest (apart from All Saints', Walsall). The Ms is an irregular-shaped thin roll, which may have been longer. The transcription and an annotation by Dr Philip Morgan of Keele University (SHC 1999 pp83-96) throws light on pre-Reformation parochial life in Adbaston and consequently on contemporary rural parishes (WSL M. 64; it came to be in William Salt's collection because probably a Thomas Salt is mentioned).

The other Pirehill churchwardens' accounts, all post-Reformation, are:-

Abbots Bromley 1833-4 constables' accts (D1209/7/2), 1833-c1877 (D1709/9/3), 1855-6 (D1209/ 10/4).

Bagnall 1801-67 (D3381/2/1)

Barlaston 1821-2 (D3538/8/1), 1893-1901 (D3538/8/2).

Betley (memoranda from) 1726-63 (WSL SMS 420).

Biddulph 1609-1703 (D3539/2/1), 1705-20 (D3539/2/2), 1720-34 (D3539/2/3).

Blithfield 1621, 1623-4, 1631-2 (D1386/2/1), 1662-3, 1683-4, 1694-5 (D1386/2/1/4).

Blurton 1781-1822 constables' & headboroughs' accts (D3366/8/1).

Burslem 1784-94 (D3571/3/1).

Colton 1733 (D4613/3/1; unfit for production). 1755 (D4613/3/12; unfit for production). 1780 (D4613/ 3/32). 1783-4 (D4613/3/42). 1788-9 (D4613/3/50-1). 1795-8 (D4613/3/59). 1726, 1729, 1742, 1771, 1773-4, 1776-7, 1781-, 1783, 1793, 1801 overseers' accts (D4613/6/1-83). 1716, 1720, 1729, 1732-3, 1738, 1746, 1748, 1752-3, 1758, 1761-2, 1770-1 constables' accts (disbursements) (D4613/ 5/1-74).

Colwich 1753-1854 (D24/A/PC/1-64). 1774-1855 bills & accounts (D24/A/PC/65-901). 1762-75 abstracts of churchwardens' accts (D24/A/PV/ 1). 1752-63 overseers accts & bills (D24/A/PO/1-2162). 1768-84 abstracts of overseers' accts (D24/A/PV/1). 1777 overseers' accts (D874/7/3). 1753-1835 constables' accts (D24/A/PK/1-142). 1785-1827 headborough accts' (D24/A/PK/ 231-6). **Fradswell** 1717-55~6 very fragmentary (D3033/4/1/1). 1796 (D3033/4/1/2). 1821- (D4582/4/1). 1802-21 overseers' accts? (13/A/PZ/1-8). 1711-60 constables' accts (13/A/PK/1-30). 1757-9, 1773-1823, 1835-6 (with gaps) constables' accts (D3033/5/1). 1702-1866 surveyors' accts (13/A/PS/2-11). 1745 surveyors' accts (13/A/PK/1-30). 1774 surveyors' accts (13/A/PS/1). 1783, 1812-4 surveyors' accts (D3033/6/1). 1818 surveyors' accts (D3033/6/2).

Eccleshall. Chapel Chorlton 1741-85, 1810-2 chapelwardens' & overseers' accts (D3636/4/1). 1854-1914 (D3636/4/3). overseers' accts (D3636/4/2). **Cotes** (Cotes Heath) 1847-1925 (D3393/11). **Eccleshall** 1631-88 (WSL 236/27).

Gayton 1813-34 overseers' accts (D705/PO/1). 1812-3 constables'/ surveyors' accts (D705/PO/1). 1813-31 hsurveyors' accts (D705/PS/ 1/1). 1837-8 surveyors' accts (D705/PS/ 1/2). 1853-75 surveyors' accts (D705/PS/ 1/3).

High Offley 1784-1868 (D4035/2/1). 1793-1825 overseers' accts (D4035/4/1). 1871-9 surveyors' accts (D4035/5/1).

Keele 1698-1710, 1712-21 (D3514/2/1). 1840-1902 (D3514/2/3). 1744-6 constables' accts (D3514/2/2).

Madeley 1679-1731, 1733-46, 1766-91, 1794-1812, 1810-31, 1831-50 churchwardens' & overseers' accts (D3412/3/1-8). 1695-1927 loose accts, fragmentary (D3412/3/16-30). 1814-5, 1816-7, 1817-9 overseers' acct bks (D3412/5/19-21). 1848-68 overseers' acct bk (D3412/5/23). 1800-23 loose overseers' accts D3412/5/30-53). 1794-1810 constables' & surveyors' accts (D3412/6/1). 1812-25 loose constables' accts (intermittent) (D3412/6/2-14). 1806-18 loose surveyors' accts (D3412/7/1-9).

Maer 1728-1810 churchwardens' & overseers accts (D3635/4/1).

Marston 1792-1836 general accts (D53/A/PZ/1).

Milwich 1671-1753 incomplete (D917/5/1). 1766-1837 loose sheets (D917/4/1). Easter 1794 (D4029/3/2). 1794-5 (D4029/3/3). 1842-1930 (D917/4/2). 1795-1847 vouchers & receipts (D917/4/3). 1766-7 overseers' accts (D917/5/1). 1729-96 overseers' accts loose sheets (D917/6/1). 1828-38 overseers' accts (D917/6/2). 1861-8 overseers' accts (D917/6/3). 1737-66 constables' accts (D917/5/1).

Mucklestone 1818-1932 (D5725/3/1). 1817-36 overseers' accts (D5725/3/3).

Newcastle 1826-55 (D3251/4/1).

Sandon 1763-1787 general accts (D1048/3/2). 1787-1826 general accts (D1048/3/3). 1838-41 (D1048/3/4). 1839-46 (D1048/3/5). 1846-1914 (D1048/3/6). 1827-45 overseers' bills & accts (D22/A/PO/1-2). 1841-6 surveyors' accts (D22/A/PS/1).

Seighford 1620-1770 (WSL M. 600). 1805-1900 (D731/11). 1779-1828 overseers' accts (D731/12).

Stafford. St Bertelins (from Town Account Book) 1528-9, 1529-48 (WSL SMS 366/1). **St Mary** (from Town Account Book) 1529-1611, 1615, 1628 (WSL SMS 366/1), (from churchwardens' accts) 1726-75 (WSL Salt MS. 365). May 1852-Dec 1874 (D834/2/1). **St Bertelins/ Chad/ Mary** 1528-9 (WSL SMS 402), 1611-44 (WSL SMS 402). **Stafford?** 1573 (WSL SMS 366/1).

Standon 1696, 1719 (D1026/2/1). 1745-73 churchwardens' & overseers' accts (D1026/2/2).

Stoke-upon-Trent. Hanley 1791-1838 chapelwardens' accts (D3723/6/1). 1839-77 chapelwardens' accts (D3723/6/2). Longton 1810, 1812, 1818 chapelwardens' accts (D3276/4/2). 1828 surveyors' balance sheet (D3276/5/1). 1831,1833 highway surveyors' rate books (D3276/5/2). Stoke-upon-Trent 1596-1702 (WSL 13-14/46). 1589-1702 (NSFCT 1944 p259 as transcribed by A Hilton John). 1606, 1610 (x2), 1697 (D1188/14).

Stone. Fulford 1821- (D4582/4/1). **Stone** 1634-84 copied from originals as repaired in the SRO (Jan 1968) 939 1 vol; the original is D4605/2/1.

Stowe 1671-1828 (D14/A/PC/1). 1828-87 (D14/A/PC/2). 1670-1782 overseers' accts (D14/A/PO/1). 1783-1808 overseers' accts (D14/A/PO/2). 1811-32 overseers' accts (D14/A/PO/3). 1671-1760 constables' accts (D14/A/PO/1).

Swynnerton 1853-91 (D4870/2/1).

Tixall 1846-73 (D4907/1).

Weston-on-Trent 1827-36 churchwardens' & overseers' acc bk (D5328/2/1).

Whitmore 1802-37 (D159/A/PZ/1). 1803-37 overseers' accts (D3332/6/1). 1802-35 constables' accts (D159/A/PZ/1).

Wolstanton. Newchapel April 1791-Jan 1794 (D3544/5/31). 1804-09 (D3544/5/32). 1792-4, 1802-13, 1817-9 churchwardens' vouchers (D3544/5/1-16).

Churchwardens' accounts unless otherwise stated.

The Gerard tomb in Ashley Church. Drawing by the author, 2004

Ashley

'The more pastoral bits about Ashley proper contrast well with the woods and park of Willoughbridge, and the more bold and bracing tableland of Ashley Heath.'

Weston E Vernon-Yonge. Bye-paths of Staffordshire. 1911

PLU. Market Drayton soon after 1836-1930.

LG. Newcastle-u-Lyme RD 1894-1974, D(B) 1974-. No. 17 W Feb 1973-9. Loggerheads W 1979-2002. Loggerheads & Whitmore 2002-.

CED. Keele 1889-1934. Madeley 1934-81. Newcastle Rural 1981-2005, 2005-

SEE ALSO pages 2, 9-11, 21, 24, 50, 78, 116, 125, 130, 140, 142, 207, 211, 213, 233

ASHLEY

Ashley

Ashley CP 1866-1984. PC from 1894. Minutes from 1894 at SRO. Loggerheads CP 1984-. Ashley PW 1984-

Loggerheads

Ashley CP -1984. Loggerheads CP 1984-. Loggerheads PW 1984-.

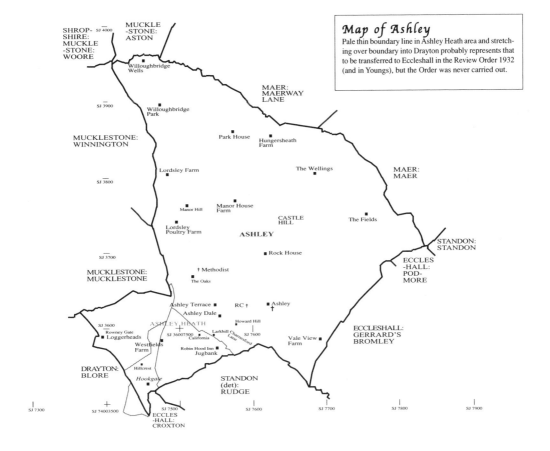

Map of Ashley

Pale thin boundary line in Ashley Heath area and stretching over boundary into Drayton probably represents that to be transferred to Eccleshall in the Review Order 1932 (and in Youngs), but the Order was never carried out.

Monumental inscriptions A-St

Ashley's spectacular alabaster Renaissance 'machine' tomb to Sir Gilbert Gerard (d1592~3), Attorney General 1558-81, and Master of the Rolls 1581-93, is the most impressive in a Pirehill church. It is an 'extraordinary monument' says Sidney A Jeavons in The Monumental Effigies of Staffordshire part III in BAST vol 71 (1953) pp15-17. But was it right for Sir Gilbert and his successors (the Meynells) at Gerard's Bromley Old Hall, to overcrowd the church with huge monuments, especially as Gerard's Bromley is outside the parish? But as manorial lords of part of Ashley and holders of the advowson their behaviour was only to be expected. It also shows that the lord's chief seat could be

Ashley

without the parish, yet close enough for the church there to be considered the demesne church; invariably the most impressive monuments inside a church are those of the manorial lords.

Listed below, and under Swynnerton, are the monument surveys of Pirehill churchyards deposited at SRO, WSL or on the internet, indicating the earliest surviving grave.

BMSGH = Birmingham & Midland Society for Genealogy & Heraldry
IND = Independent
INT = Internet (The GEUKI Staffordshire Pages - memorial inscription collection)
SMI = Survey of Monumental Inscriptions
SRO = Staffordshire Record Office
WSL = William Salt Library
p/s = part survey

Abbots Bromley St Nicholas - Elizabeth Walker d1737 aged 11 (SMI 1967 - SRO c/p/12). (GENUKI 2003 p/s).

Adbaston St Michael - Mary Tildesly of Bishops Offley d1711 (SMI 1967, BMSGH - SRO c/p/12).

Ashley St John Baptist - (GENUKI 2004 p/s).

Audley Audley St James - early grave is Thomas Vernon of the Church Style d1675 (AFHS 1995 - WSL). Bignall End Central Methodist Cem, Chapel Street - Leslie Brough of Ravens Lane d1904 (AFHS 1996 - WSL. BMSGH 1990 - SRO). Halmer End St John, Alsagers Bank - Minnie Pit disaster victims (1918), Elijah Poole d1919, grave to those who died in the Apedale Footrill disaster April 25 1923 (AFHS 1996 & BMSGH c1992 - WSL). The Independent Chapel - Frances Richardson of the Carr House d1824 (AFHS 1996 - WSL). Talke St Martin - internal mem James Caldwell d1838; external mem Elizabeth Cooper of Martin's Bank d1860 (AFHS 1995 - WSL).

Barlaston St John - John Willott d1707 (SMI 1967 - SRO c/p/12. BMSGH c1982 - WSL).

Betley St Margaret - Marmaduke Jolley d1726 aged 7_? (SMI 1967 - SRO c/p/12).

Biddulph St Lawrence - (GENUKI 2004).

Burslem St John the Baptist - John Stevenson of Burslem d1672 & wife Mary d1668 (BMSGH c1989 -WSL. GENUKI 2004). St Paul - graves from 1817 (BMSGH n.d.- WSL).

Colton St Mary - Samson Webb of the Old Wood d1686 (SMI 1969 - SRO c/p/12. BMSGH & Colton WI 1982 - WSL).

Colwich Colwich, St Michael & All Angels - Anthony Horden d1670 (BMSGH 2002 - SRO). Great Haywood, St Stephen - Thomas Addison d1855 (BMSGH 1997 - SRO, WSL). St John the Baptist RC - William Astley d1846 (Nick Gray & BMSGH 2001 - SRO, WSL).

Eccleshall Croxton St Paul - no graves pre-date 1853 (BMSGH & Offley Hay WI 1982 - SRO D4459,

WSL). <u>Chorlton</u> St Lawrence - Elizabeth Bot__ill d16__? no others from C17 then 1750s (BMSGH & Maer + District WI 1982 - SRO).

Keele St John - William Rowley of Knutton Heath d1736 (BMSGH & Staffs WI 1982 - SRO, WSL).

Madeley All Saints - Richard Bloor d1686 (SMI 1967 - SRO c/p/12. GENUKI 2004 p/s).

Milwich All Saints - William Lisett of Day Hills d1729 (SMI 1967 - SRO c/p/12. GENUKI 2003 p/s).

Mucklestone St Mary - Thomas Latham d1799 (SMI 1967 p/s - SRO c/p/12).

Newcastle-under-Lyme St Giles - John Smith, 2nd son of John Smith, Alderman d1614; tombstone is in cast iron; but most from 1720s onwards (IND 1880 - SRO D3251/3/4/1. SMI 1967 - SRO c/p/12. BMSGH c1983 - SRO, WSL). St George - John Drewry Mort d1799 (BMSGH n.d. - SRO, WSL).

Sandon All Saints - (GENUKI 2003 p/s).

Seighford St Chad - William Sands of Marston d1723 (SMI 1967 - SRO, c/p/12).

Stafford St Mary - Thomas Wollich d1703 (BMSGH 1991 - SRO 3866, WSL. A survey of 1915 - SRO D834/13/7). Christ Church - Ralph Bourne d1839 (SMI 1967 - SRO c/p/12. BMSGH 1984 - SRO D4780/4, WSL. IND 1984 - WSL). <u>Salt</u> St James - (GENUKI 2003 p/s).

Stoke-upon-Trent - <u>Bucknall</u> St Mary - (GENUKI 2004 p/s). <u>Hanley</u> St John - 1789 (BMSGH 1987 - SRO, WSL). Bethesda Methodist Chapel - 1814 (BMSGH 1976 - SRO, WSL). The Tabernacle (dem 1985, reinterred Burslem) - about 18 mems including John Forsyth d1786 (BMSGH - SRO). <u>Longton</u> St John - Anne Weston d1768 (BMSGH 1973 - SRO, WSL, also at SRO D5676/8/2). St James - Sarah Steele d1835 (BMSGH 1983 - SRO, WSL). <u>Penkhull</u> St Thomas - Elizabeth Cartlidge d1844 (BMSGH c1982 - SRO, WSL). Holy Trinity, Hartshill - Adolphus Fielding d1845, the murder victim (BMSGH 2000 - WSL. GENUKI 2003 p/s). St Peter Ad Vincula, Stoke-upon-Trent - Sybil & Henry Clark, dated 1684 (BMSGH & Elizabeth Bass 1984-7 - WSL. IND c1987 - WSL). Wesley Methodist Chapel, Epworth St - internal mem plaques from 'David Bostock Iron Founder of this town' d1820 (BMSGH c1984 - SRO, WSL). <u>Shelton</u> St Jude - graves from 1904 (BMSGH 1987 - SRO, WSL). St Matthew, Etruria - graves from 1840 and no later than 1855 (BMSGH n.d. - WSL).

Stone - <u>Aston</u> St Saviour (GENUKI 2005 p/s). <u>Hilderstone</u> Christ Church - John Bentley d1834 (SMI 1967 p/s & only pre-1850 - SRO c/p/12. GENUKI 2003 p/s). <u>Fulford</u> St Nicholas - William Simns of Cross Gate d1815 (SMI 1967 - SRO c/p/12, 6046/1. GENUKI 2003 p/s). <u>Moddershall</u> All Saints - Godfrey Wedgwood d1905. But earlier still is James Smith d1890 (BMSGH 2002 - WSL). <u>Oulton</u> St John the Evangelist - Hannah Goodwin of Knenhall d1890 (BMSGH n.d. - SRO, WSL). <u>Stone</u> St Michael - Thomas Crompton d1673 (IND Sept 1963 - copy of 1999 in church; the accompanying plan is lost. SMI 1967 - SRO c/p/12; levelled 1965, declared disused Aug 1970; mems surround churchyard wall).

Audley (Audley)

Part of the protest against reorganisation to schools in Audley in 1938: Mr Bowers, headmaster of the Ravens Lane junior school (formerly a senior school), taking names of senior scholars, who presented themselves at their former school, but were refused admission. From The Staffordshire Weekly Sentinel Sept 3 1938 p12 col 3. Courtesy of Sentinel Newspapers

Audley

'Situated on a southern spur of the Pennine Chain, the village (Alsagers Bank) enjoys a view unrivalled for miles. To the west the fertile plains of Cheshire, bisected by the M6.'

Staffordshire Federation of Women's Institutes. The Staffordshrie Village Book. 1988

By 1851 the seven townships of Audley supported their poor cojointly.
LG. Audley AP/ LB -1932.
PLU. Newcastle-u-Lyme 1838-1930. Audley W by1910.
SEE ALSO pages 10, 20-1, 23, 30, 50, 54, 78, 82, 84, 94, 96, 100, 103, 124, 129, 142, 182, 187, 207, 211 ,213

AUDLEY TOWNSHIP
Audley
Audley Rural CP 1932-. Audley PW 1948-, 2003-.
LG. Audley UD 1894-1932. Audley W 1906-32. Newcastle-u-Lyme RD 1932-74, D(B) 1974-. No. 18 W Feb 1973-4. No. 19 W Feb 1974-9. Audley & Bignall End W 1979-2002, 2002-.
CED. Audley 1889-1981. Audley & Chesterton 1981-2005, 2005-.

Audley (1)
Audley Rural CP 1932-. Bignall End W 1948-, 2003-.
LG. Audley UD 1894-1932. Audley W 1906-32. Newcastle-u-Lyme RD 1932-74, D(B) 1974-. No. 19 W Feb 1973-4. No. 20 W Feb 1974-9. Audley & Bignall End W 1979-2002, 2002-.
CED. Audley 1889-1981. Audley & Chesterton 1981-2005, 2005-.

Audley (2)
Audley Rural CP 1932-. Bignall End PW 1948-, Audley PW 2003-.
LG. Audley UD 1894-1932. Audley W 1906-32. Newcastle-u-Lyme RD 1932-74, D(B) 1974-. No. 19 W Feb 1973-4. No. 20 W Feb 1974-9. Audley & Bignall End W 1979-2002, 2002-.
CED. Audley 1889-1981. Audley & Chesterton 1981-2005, 2005-.

Audley (3)
Audley Rural CP 1932-. Bignall End PW 1948-, Audley PW 2003-.
LG. Audley UD 1894-1932. Bignall End W 1906-32. Newcastle-u-Lyme RD 1932-74, D(B) 1974-. No. 19 W Feb 1973-4. No. 20 W Feb 1974-9. Audley & Bignall End W 1979-2002, 2002-.
CED. Audley 1889-1981. Audley & Chesterton 1981-2005, 2005-.

Boyles Hall

Audley Rural CP 1932-. Bignall End PW 1948-, 2003-
LG. Audley UD 1894-1932. Bignall End W 1906-32.
Newcastle-u-Lyme RD 1932-74, D(B) 1974-. No. 19
W Feb 1973-4. No. 20 W Feb 1974-9. Audley &
Bignall End W 1979-2002, 2002-.
CED. Audley 1889-1981. Audley & Chesterton 1981-
2005, 2005-.

Burgess's Wood flank (det)

Audley Rural CP 1932-. Halmerend PW 1948-, 2003-
LG. Audley UD 1894-1932. Halmerend W 1906-32.
Newcastle-u-Lyme RD 1932-74, D(B) 1974-. No. 21
W Feb 1973-4. No. 22 W Feb 1974-9. Halmerend W
1979-2002, 2002-.
CED. Audley 1889-1981. Newcastle Rural 1981-2005.
Audley & Chesterton 2005-.

Carr House

Audley Rural CP 1932-. Audley PW 1948-, Halmerend
PW 2003-.
LG. Audley UD 1894-1932. Audley W 1906-32. New-
castle-u-Lyme RD 1932-74, D(B) 1974-. No. 18 W
Feb 1973-4. No. 19 W Feb 1974-9. Audley & Bignall
End W 1979-2002. Halmerend W 2002-.
CED. Audley 1889-1981. Audley & Chesterton 1981-
2005, 2005-.

Dean Brook

Audley Rural CP 1932-. Audley PW 1948-, Halmerend
PW 2003-.
LG. Audley UD 1894-1932. Audley W 1906-32. New-
castle-u-Lyme RD 1932-74, D(B) 1974-. No. 18 W
Feb 1973-4. No. 19 W Feb 1974-9. Audley & Bignall
End W 1979-2002, Halmerend W 2002-.
CED. Audley 1889-1981. Audley & Chesterton 1981-
2005, 2005-.

Hougher Wall

Audley Rural CP 1932-. Bignall End PW 1948-,
Halmerend PW 2003-.
LG. Audley UD 1894-1932. Bignall End W 1906-32.
Newcastle-u-Lyme RD 1932-74, D(B) 1974-. No. 19
W Feb 1973-4. No. 20 W Feb 1974-9. Audley &
Bignall End W 1979-2002, Halmerend W 2002-.
CED. Audley 1889-1981. Audley & Chesterton 1981-
2005, 2005-.

Oakdene Farm (det)

Audley Rural CP 1932-. Bignall End PW 1948-, 2003-
LG. Audley UD 1894-1932. Audley W 1906-32. New-
castle-u-Lyme RD 1932-74, D(B) 1974-. No. 19
Feb 1973-4. No. 20 W Feb 1974-9. Audley & Bignall
End W 1979-2002, 2002-.
CED. Audley 1889-1981. Audley & Chesterton 1981-
2005, 2005-.

Ryehill Farm

Audley (Bignall End)

Audley Rural CP 1932-. Bignall End PW 1948-,
Halmerend W 2003-.
LG. Audley UD 1894-1932. Audley W 1906-32. New-
castle-u-Lyme RD 1932-74, D(B) 1974-. No. 19 W
Feb 1973-4. No. 20 W Feb 1974-9. Audley & Bignall
End W 1979-2002, Halmerend W 2002-.
CED. Audley 1889-1981. Audley & Chesterton 1981-
2005, 2005-.

White House Farm

Audley Rural CP 1932-. Bignall End PW 1948-, 2003-
LG. Audley UD 1894-1932. Bignall End W 1906-32.
Newcastle-u-Lyme RD 1932-74, D(B) 1974-. No. 19
W Feb 1973-4. No. 20 W Feb 1974-9. Audley &
Bignall End W 1979-2002, 2002-.
CED. Audley 1889-1981. Audley & Chesterton 1981-
2005, 2005-.

BIGNALL END TOWNSHIP
Audley (4)

Audley Rural CP 1932-. Bignall End PW 1948-,
Audley PW 2003-
LG. Audley UD 1894-1932. Bignall End W 1906-32.
Newcastle-u-Lyme RD 1932-74, D(B) 1974-. No. 19
W Feb 1973-4. No. 20 W Feb 1974-9. Audley &
Bignall End W 1979-2002, 2002-.
CED. Audley 1889-1981. Audley & Chesterton 1981-
2005, 2005-.

Audley (5)

Audley Rural CP 1932-. Audley PW 1948-, 2003-
LG. Audley UD 1894-1932. Audley W 1906-32. New-
castle-u-Lyme RD 1932-74, D(B) 1974-. No. 18 W
Feb 1973-4. No. 19 W Feb 1974-9. Audley & Bignall
End W 1979-2002, 2002-.
CED. Audley 1889-1981. Audley & Chesterton 1981-
2005, 2005-

Audley Road

Newcastle unparished 1932-.
LG. Audley UD 1894-1932. Bignall End W 1906-32.
Newcastle-u-Lyme MB 1932-74, D(B) 1974-. No. 10
W 1932-79. Audley & Bignall End W 1979-2002.
Chesterton W 2002-
CED. Audley 1889-1934. Newcastle No. 5 1934-67.
Newcastle No. 6 Feb 1967-81. Audley & Chesterton
1981-2005, 2005-.

Bignall End

Audley Rural CP 1932-. Bignall End PW 1948-, 2003-
LG. Audley UD 1894-1932. Audley W 1906-32. New-
castle-u-Lyme RD 1932-74, D(B) 1974-. No. 19 W
Feb 1973-4. No. 20 W Feb 1974-9. Audley & Bignall
End W 1979-2002, 2002-.
CED. Audley 1889-1981. Audley & Chesterton 1981-
2005, 2005-.

Audley (Audley)

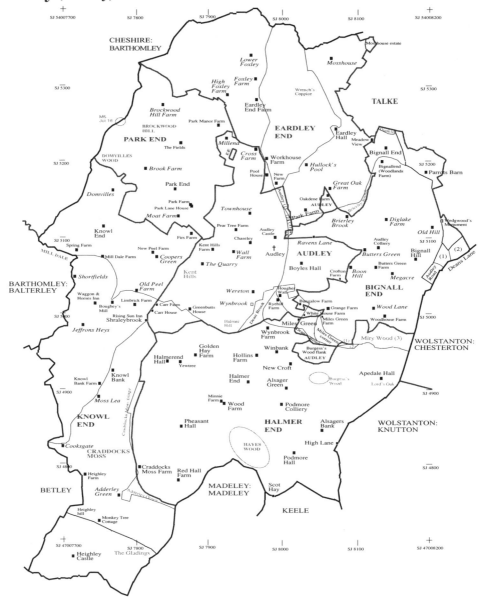

SJ 54007700   SJ 7800   SJ 7900   SJ 8000   SJ 8100   SJ 54008200

CHESHIRE: BARTHOMLEY

Lower Foxley

Mosshouse estate

Mosshouse

High Foxley Farm

Foxley Farm

Wrench's Coppice

TALKE

Brockwood Hill Farm

Park Manor Farm

Eardley End Farm

EARDLEY END

Eardley Hall

Meadow View

Bignall End

M6 Jct 16

BROCKWOOD HILL

PARK END

The Fields

Millend

Cross Farm

Workhouse Farm

Hullock's Pool

Bignallend (Woodlands Farm)

Parrots Barn

DOMVILLES WOOD

Brook Farm

Park End

Pool House

New Farm

Great Oak Farm

Domvilles

Park Farm
Park Lane House

Townhouse

Oakdene Farm

AUDLEY

Brierley Brook

Diglake Farm

Old Hill

Wedgwood's Monument

Moat Farm

Pear Tree Farm

Audley Castle

Park Farm

Audley Colliery

Bignall Hill

(1) (2)

Deans Lane

Knowl End

Firs Farm

Chaseley

Ravens Lane

Butters Green

Spring Bank

New Peel Farm

Kent Hills Farm

Wall Farm

Audley

AUDLEY

Butters Green Farm

Megacre

MILL DALE

Mill Dale Farm

Coopers Green

The Quarry

Boyles Hall

Crofton Farm

Boon Hill

Shortfields

Kent Hills

Old Peel Farm

Wereton

Hougher Wall

BIGNALL END

BARTHOMLEY: BALTERLEY

Waggon & Horses Inn

Limbrick Farm

Carr Farm

Greenbutts House

Wynbrook

Ryehill Farm

Bungalow Farm

Grange Farm

Wood Lane

Boughey's Mill

Rising Sun Inn
Shraleybrook

Carr House

Halmer Hill

Dean Brook

Miles Green

White House Farm

Miles Green Farm

Woodhouse Farm

Jeffrons Heys

Wynbrook Farm

Miles Green corner

Miry Wood (3)

WOLSTANTON: CHESTERTON

Golden Hay Farm

Hollins Farm

Winbank

Burgess's Wood flank

AUDLEY

Halmerend Hall

Yewtree

Halmer End

Alsager Green

New Croft

Apedale Hall

Burgess's Wood

Lord's Oak

Knowl Bank Farm

Knowl Bank

Minnie Farm

Wood Farm

Podmore Colliery

KNOWL END

Pheasant Hall

HALMER END

Alsagers Bank

WOLSTANTON: KNUTTON

Cooksgate

CRADDOCKS MOSS

HAYES WOOD

High Lane

Podmore Hall

Heighley Farm

Craddocks Moss Farm

Red Hall Farm

MADELEY: MADELEY

Scot Hay

BETLEY

Adderley Green

KEELE

Heighley hill

Monkey Tree Cottage

SJ 47007700   SJ 7800   The Gladings   SJ 7900   SJ 8000   SJ 8100   SJ 47008200

Heighley Castle

Bignall Hill

Audley Rural CP 1932-. Bignall End PW 1948-, 2003-

LG. Audley UD 1894-1932. Bignall End W 1906-32. Newcastle-u-Lyme RD 1932-74, D(B) 1974-. No. 19 W Feb 1973-4. No. 20 W Feb 1974-9. Audley & Bignall End W 1979-2002, 2002-.

CED. Audley 1889-1981. Audley & Chesterton 1981-2005, 2005-.

Bungalow Farm

Audley Rural CP 1932-. Bignall End PW 1948-, Halmerend PW 2003-.

LG. Audley UD 1894-1932. Bignall End W 1906-32. Newcastle-u-Lyme RD 1932-74, D(B) 1974-. No. 19 W Feb 1973-4. No. 20 W Feb 1974-9. Audley & Bignall End W 1979-2002, Halmerend W 2002-.

CED. Audley 1889-1981. Audley & Chesterton 1981-2005, 2005-.

Dean Brook

Audley Rural CP 1932-. Halmerend W 1948-, 2003-

14

LG. Audley UD 1894-1932. Halmerend W 1906-32. Newcastle-u-Lyme RD 1932-74, D(B) 1974-. No. 21 W Feb 1973-4. No. 22 W Feb 1974-9. Halmerend W 1979-2002, 2002-.
CED. Audley 1889-1981. Newcastle Rural 1981-2005. Audley & Chesterton 2005-.

Deans Lane (1)

LG. Audley UD 1894-1932. Bignall End W 1906-32. Newcastle-u-Lyme MB 1932-74, D(B) 1974-. No. 10 W 1932-79, Chesterton W 1979-2002, 2002-.
CED. Audley 1889-1934. Newcastle No. 5 1934-67. Newcastle No. 6 Feb 1967-81. Audley & Chesterton 1981-2005, 2005-.

Deans Lane (2)

LG. Audley UD 1894-1932. Talke W 1906-32. Newcastle-u-Lyme MB 1932-74, D(B) 1974-. No. 10 W 1932-79, Chesterton W 1979-2002, 2002-.
CED. Audley 1889-1934. Newcastle No. 5 1934-67. Newcastle No. 6 Feb 1967-81. Audley & Chesterton 1981-2005, 2005-.

Dunkirk

Audley Rural CP 1932-. Bignall End PW 1948-, 2003-
LG. Audley UD 1894-1932. Talke W 1906-32. Newcastle-u-Lyme RD 1932-74, D(B) 1974-. No. 19 W Feb 1973-4. No. 20 W Feb 1974-9. Audley & Bignall End W 1979-2002, 2002-.
CED. Audley 1889-1981. Audley & Chesterton 1981-2005, 2005-

Miles Green

Audley Rural CP 1932-. Bignall End PW 1948-. Halmerend PW 2003-.
LG. Audley UD 1894-1932. Halmerend W 1906-32. Newcastle-u-Lyme RD 1932-74, D(B) 1974-. No. 19 W Feb 1973-4. No. 20 W Feb 1974-9. Audley & Bignall End W 1979-2002, Halmerend W 2002-.
CED. Audley 1889-1981. Audley & Chesterton 1981-2005, 2005-.

Miles Green corner

Audley Rural CP 1932-. Bignall End PW 1948-, 2003-.
LG. Audley UD 1894-1932. Halmerend W 1906-32. Newcastle-u-Lyme RD 1932-74, D(B) 1974-. No. 19 W Feb 1973-4. No. 20 W Feb 1974-9. Audley & Bignall End W 1979-2002, 2002-.
CED. Audley 1889-1981. Audley & Chesterton 1981-2005, 2005-

Parrots Barn

Talke CP 1932-74. Kidsgrove CP 1974-. Talke PW 1974-
LG. Audley UD 1894-1932. Talke W 1906-32. Kidsgrove UD 1932-74. Newcastle-u-Lyme D(B) 1974-. No. 16 W Feb 1973-7. No. 16 W Feb 1977-9. Talke W 1979-2002, 2002-.

Audley (Eardley End)

CED. Audley 1889-1934. Kidsgrove 1934-73. Talke 1973-2005. Kidsgrove & Talke 2005-.

Wedgwood's Monument

Talke CP 1932-74. Kidsgrove CP 1974-. Talke PW 1974-.
LG. Audley UD 1894-1932. Talke W 1906-32. Kidsgrove UD 1932-74. Newcastle-u-Lyme D(B) 1974-. No. 16 W Feb 1973-7. No. 16 Feb 1977-9. Talke W 1979-2002, 2002-.
CED. Audley 1889-1934. Kidsgrove 1934-73. Talke 1973-2005. Kidsgrove & Talke 2005-.

EARDLEY END TOWNSHIP
Brierley Brook

Audley Rural CP 1932-. Bignall End PW 1948-, 2003-
LG. Audley UD 1894-1932. Bignall End W 1906-32. Newcastle-u-Lyme RD 1932-74, D(B) 1974-. No. 19 W Feb 1973-4. No. 20 W Feb 1974-9. Audley & Bignall End W 1979-2002, 2002-.
CED. Audley 1889-1981. Audley & Chesterton 1981-2005, 2005-.

Eardley End Farm

Audley Rural CP 1932-. Audley PW 1948-, 2003-.
LG. Audley UD 1894-1932. Audley W 1906-32. Newcastle-u-Lyme RD 1932-74, D(B) 1974-. No. 18 W Feb 1973-4. No. 19 W Feb 1974-9. Audley & Bignall End W 1979-2002, 2002-.
CED. Audley 1889-1981. Audley & Chesterton 1981-2005, 2005-.

Eardley Hall

Audley Rural CP 1932-. Bignall End PW 1948-, 2003-
LG. Audley UD 1894-1932. Audley W 1906-32. Newcastle-u-Lyme RD 1932-74, D(B) 1974-. No. 19 W Feb 1973-4. No. 20 W Feb 1974-9. Audley & Bignall End W 1979-2002, 2002-.
CED. Audley 1889-1981. Audley & Chesterton 1981-2005, 2005-.

Mosshouse estate

Audley Rural CP 1932-84. Bignall End PW 1948-84. Kidsgrove CP 1984-
LG. Audley UD 1894-1932. Talke W 1906-32. Newcastle-u-Lyme RD 1932-74, D(B) 1974-. No. 19 Feb 1973-4. No. 20 W Feb 1974-9. Audley & Bignall End W 1979-84. Talke W 1984-2002, 2002-.
CED. Audley 1889-1981. Audley & Chesterton 1981-4. Talke 1984-2005. Kidsgrove & Talke 2005-.

Park Farm

Audley Rural CP 1932-. Bignall End PW 1948-, 2003-
LG. Audley UD 1894-1932. Bignall End W 1906-32. Newcastle-u-Lyme RD 1932-74, D(B) 1974-. No. 19 W Feb 1973-4. No. 20 W Feb 1974-9. Audley & Bignall End W 1979-2002, 2002-.

Audley (Knowl End)

CED. Audley 1889-1981. Audley & Chesterton 1981-2005, 2005-.

Workhouse Farm
Audley Rural CP 1932-. Bignall End PW 1948-, Audley PW 2003-.
LG. Audley UD 1894-1932. Audley W 1906-32. Newcastle-u-Lyme RD 1932-74, D(B) 1974-. No. 19 W Feb 1973-4. No. 20 W Feb 1974-9. Audley & Bignall End W 1979-2002, 2002-.
CED. Audley 1889-1981. Audley & Chesterton 1981-2005, 2005-.

HALMER END TOWNSHIP
Halmer End
Audley Rural CP 1932-. Halmerend PW 1948-, 2003-
LG. Audley UD 1894-1932. Halmerend W 1906- 32. Newcastle-u-Lyme RD 1932-74, D(B) 1974-. No. 21 W Feb 1973-4. No. 22 W Feb 1974-9. Halmerend W 1979-2002, 2002-.
CED. Audley 1889-1981. Newcastle Rural 1981-2005. Audley & Chesterton 2005-.

Miles Green
Audley Rural CP 1932-. Bignall End PW 1948-, Halmerend PW 2003-.
LG. Audley UD 1894-1932. Audley W 1906-32. Newcastle-u-Lyme RD 1932-74, D(B) 1974-. No. 19 W Feb 1973-4. No. 20 W Feb 1974-9. Audley & Bignall End W 1979-2002, Halmerend W 2002-.
CED. Audley 1889-1981. Audley & Chesterton 1981-2005, 2005-.

Miry Wood (1)
Audley Rural CP 1932-. Bignall End PW 1948-, 2003-
LG. Audley UD 1894-1932. Bignall End W 1906-32. Newcastle-u-Lyme RD 1932-74, D(B) 1974-. No. 19 W Feb 1973-4. No. 20 W Feb 1974-9. Audley & Bignall End W 1979-2002, 2002-.
CED. Audley 1889-1981. Audley & Chesterton 1981-2005, 2005-.

Miry Wood (2)
Audley Rural CP 1932-. Halmerend PW 1948-, 2003-
LG. Audley UD 1894-1932. Bignall End W 1906-32. Newcastle-u-Lyme RD 1932-74, D(B) 1974-. No. 21 W Feb 1973-4. No. 22 W Feb 1974-9. Halmerend W 1979-2002, 2002-.
CED. Audley 1889-1981. Newcastle Rural 1981-2005. Audley & Chesterton 2005-.

Miry Wood (3)
Audley Rural CP 1932-. Bignall End PW 1948-, 2003-.
LG. Audley UD 1894-1932. Bignall End W 1906-32. Newcastle-u-Lyme RD 1932-74, D(B) 1974-. No. 19 W Feb 1973-4. No. 20 W Feb 1974-9. Audley & Bignall End W 1979-2002, 2002-.

CED. Audley 1889-1981. Audley & Chesterton 1981-2005, 2005-.

KNOWL END TOWNSHIP
Adderley Green
Audley Rural CP 1932-. Halmerend PW 1948-, 2003-.
LG. Audley UD 1894-1932. Halmerend W 1906-32. Newcastle-u-Lyme RD 1932-74, D(B) 1974-. No. 21 W Feb 1973-4. No. 22 W Feb 1974-9. Halmerend W 1979-2002, 2002-.
CED. Audley 1889-1981. Newcastle Rural 1981-2005. Audley & Chesterton 2005-.

Craddocks Moss fringe
Audley Rural CP 1932-. Halmerend PW 1948-, 2003-
LG. Audley UD 1894-1932. Halmerend W 1906-32. Newcastle-u-Lyme RD 1932-74, D(B) 1974-. No. 21 W Feb 1973-4. No. 22 W Feb 1974-9. Halmerend W 1979-2002, 2002-.
CED. Audley 1889-1981. Newcastle Rural 1981-2005. Audley and Chesterton 2005-.

Heighley Castle
Madeley CP 1932-.
LG. Audley UD 1894-1932. Audley W 1906-32. Newcastle-u-Lyme RD 1932-74, D(B) 1974-. No. 23 W Feb 1973-4. No. 24 W Feb 1974-9. Madeley W 1979-2002, 2002-.
CED. Audley 1889-1934. Madeley 1934-81. Newcastle Rural 1981-2005, 2005-.

Knowl Bank
Audley Rural CP 1932-. Halmerend PW 1948, 2003-
LG. Audley UD 1894-1932. Audley W 1906-32. Newcastle-u-Lyme RD 1932-74, D(B) 1974-. No. 21 W Feb 1973-4. No. 22 W Feb 1974-9. Halmerend W 1979-2002, 2002-.
CED. Audley 1889-1981. Newcastle Rural 1981-2005, Audley and Chesterton 2005-.

Knowl End
Audley Rural CP 1932-. Audley PW 1948-, 2003-.
LG. Audley UD 1894-1932. Audley W 1906-32. Newcastle-u-Lyme RD 1932-74, D(B) 1974-. No. 18 W Feb 1973-4. No. 19 W Feb 1974-9. Audley & Bignall End W 1979-2002, 2002-.
CED. Audley 1889-1981. Audley and Chesterton 1981-2005, 2005-.

Shraleybrook
Audley Rural CP 1932-. Audley PW 1948-, Halmerend PW 2003-.
LG. Audley UD 1894-1932. Audley W 1906-32. Newcastle-u-Lyme RD 1932-74, D(B) 1974-. No. 18 W Feb 1973-4. No. 19 W Feb 1974-9. Audley & Bignall End W 1979-2002, Halmerend W 2002-.

CED. Audley 1889-1981. Audley and Chesterton 1981-2005, 2005-.

PARK END TOWNSHIP

Audley Rural CP 1932-. Audley PW 1948-, 2003-
LG. Audley UD 1894-1932. Audley W 1906-32. Newcastle-u-Lyme RD 1932-74, D(B) 1974-. No. 18 W Feb 1973-4. No. 19 W Feb 1974-9. Audley & Bignall End W 1979-2002, 2002-.
CED. Audley 1889-1981. Audley and Chesterton 1981-2005, 2005-.
PLU. Newcastle-u-Lyme 1838-1930. Audley W by1910.

TALKE TOWNSHIP
Ashenough Farm

Hardings Wood CP 1894-1974. Kidsgrove TC 1974-. Talke PW 1974-.
LG. Kidsgrove UD 1894-1974. Kidsgrove W by1910-. Talke W 1934-74. Newcastle-u-Lyme D(B) 1974-. No. 16 W Feb 1973-7. No. 16 W Feb 1977-9. Talke W Feb 1979-2002, 2002-.
CED. Kidsgrove 1889-1968. Talke 1968-2005. Kidsgrove and Talke 2005-.
PLU. Newcastle-u-Lyme 1838-1930. Hardings Wood W by1910.

Bath Pool

Hardings Wood CP 1894-1974. Kidsgrove TC 1974-. Talke PW 1974-
LG. Kidsgrove UD 1894-1974. Kidsgrove W by1910-67/8. Talke W Feb 1968-74. Newcastle-u-Lyme D(B) 1974-. No. 16 W Feb 1973-7. No. 16 W Feb 1977-9. Talke W 1979-2002, 2002-.
CED. Kidsgrove 1889-1968. Talke 1968- 2005. Kidsgrove and Talke 2005-.
PLU. Newcastle-u-Lyme 1838-1930. Hardings Wood W by1910.

Bathpool Valley (1)

Hardings Wood CP 1894-1974. Kidsgrove TC 1974-. Kidsgrove PW 1974-
LG. Kidsgrove UD 1894-1974. Kidsgrove W by1910-74. Newcastle-u-Lyme D(B) 1974-. No. 13 W Feb 1973-7. No. 14 W Feb 1977-9. Kidsgrove W 1979-2002. Ravenscliffe W 2002-.
CED. Kidsgrove 1889-2005. Kidsgrove and Talke 2005-.
PLU. Newcastle-u-Lyme 1838-1930. Hardings Wood W by1910.

Bathpool Valley (4)

Hardings Wood CP 1894-1974. Kidsgrove TC 1974-. Kidsgrove PW 1974-

Audley (Talke)

LG. Kidsgrove UD 1894-1974. Kidsgrove W by1910-74. Newcastle-u-Lyme D(B) 1974-. No. 13 W Feb 1973-7. No. 14 W Feb 1977-9. Kidsgrove W 1979-2002. Ravenscliffe W 2002-.
CED. Kidsgrove 1889-2005. Kidsgrove and Talke 2005-.
PLU. Newcastle-u-Lyme 1838-1930. Hardings Wood W by1910.

Butt Lane

Talke CP 1932-74. Butt Lane PW 1932-74. Kidsgrove TC 1974-. Butt Lane PW 1974-.
LG. Audley UD 1894-1932. Butt Lane W 1906-32. Kidsgrove UD 1932-74. Talke W 1934-67/8. Butt Lane W Feb 1968-74. Newcastle-u-Lyme D(B) 1974-. No. 15 W Feb 1973-7. No. 13 W Feb 1977-9. Butt Lane W 1979-2002, 2002-.
CED. Audley 1889-1934. Kidsgrove 1934-1968. Talke 1968-2005. Kidsgrove and Talke 2005-.
PLU. Newcastle-u-Lyme 1838-1930. Audley W by1910.

Clough Hall

Hardings Wood CP 1894-1974. Kidsgrove TC 1974-. Butt Lane PW 1974-.
LG. Kidsgrove UD 1894-1974. Kidsgrove W by1910-67/8. Butt Lane W Feb 1968-74. Newcastle-u-Lyme D(B) 1974-. No. 15 W Feb 1973-7, No. 13 W Feb 1977-9. Butt Lane W 1979-2002, 2002-.
CED. Kidsgrove 1889-1968. Talke 1968-2005. Kidsgrove and Talke 2005-.
PLU. Newcastle-u-Lyme 1838-1930. Hardings Wood W by1910.

Dunkirk

Audley Rural CP 1932-. Bignall End PW 1948-, 2003-
LG. Audley UD 1894-1932. Talke W 1906-32. Newcastle-u-Lyme RD 1932-1974, D(B) 1974-. No. 19 W Feb 1973-4. No. 20 W Feb 1974-9. Audley & Bignall End W 1979-2002, 2002-.
CED. Audley 1889-1981. Audley and Chesterton 1981-2005, 2005-.
PLU. Newcastle-u-Lyme 1838-1930. Audley W by1910.

Dunkirk Farm

Audley Rural CP 1932-. Bignall End PW 1948-, 2003-
LG. Audley UD 1894-1932. Audley W 1906-32. Newcastle-u-Lyme RD 1932-1974, D(B) 1974-. No. 19 W Feb 1973-4. No. 20 W Feb 1974-9. Audley & Bignall End W 1979-2002, 2002-.
CED. Audley 1889-1981. Audley and Chesterton 1981-2005, 2005-.
PLU. Newcastle-u-Lyme 1838-1930. Audley W by1910.

Hardings Wood Road

Audley (Talke)

Hardings Wood CP 1894-1974. Kidsgrove TC 1974-. Kidsgrove PW 1974-2002. Butt Lane PW 2002-
LG. Kidsgrove UD 1894-1974. Kidsgrove W by1910-74. Newcastle-u-Lyme D(B) 1974-. No. 13 W Feb 1973-7. No. 14 W Feb 1977-9. Kidsgrove W 1979-2002. Butt Lane W 2002-.
CED. Kidsgrove 1889-2005. Kidsgrove and Talke 2005-.
PLU. Newcastle-u-Lyme 1838-1930. Hardings Wood W by1910.

Hollin's Wood Colliery (1)

Talke CP 1932-74. Butt Lane PW 1932-74. Kidsgrove TC 1974-. Talke PW 1974-. Butt Lane PW 2002-
LG. Audley UD 1894-1932. Butt Lane W 1906-32. Kidsgrove UD 1932-74. Talke W 1934-67/8. Butt Lane W Feb 1968-74. Newcastle-u-Lyme D(B) 1974-. No. 15 W Feb 1973-7. No. 13 W Feb 1977-9. Butt Lane W 1979-2002, 2002-.
CED. Audley 1889-1934. Kidsgrove 1934-68. Talke 1968-2005. Kidsgrove and Talke 2005-.
PLU. Newcastle-u-Lyme 1838-1930. Audley W by1910.

Hollin's Wood Colliery (2)

Hardings Wood CP 1894-1974. Kidsgrove TC 1974-. Butt Lane PW 1974-. Talke PW 2002-
LG. Kidsgrove UD 1894-1974. Kidsgrove W by1910-67/8. Butt Lane W Feb 1968-74. Newcastle-u-Lyme D(B) 1974-. No. 15 W Feb 1973-7. No. 13 W Feb 1977-9. Butt Lane W 1979-2002. Talke W 2002-.
CED. Kidsgrove 1889-1968. Talke 1968-2005. Kidsgrove and Talke 2005-.
PLU. Newcastle-u-Lyme 1838-1930. Hardings Wood W by1910.

Hollin's Wood Colliery (3)

Hardings Wood CP 1894-1974. Kidsgrove TC 1974-. Talke PW 1974-. Butt Lane PW 2002-
LG. Kidsgrove UD 1894-1974. Kidsgrove W by1910-34. Talke W 1934-74. Newcastle-u-Lyme D(B) 1974-. No. 16 W Feb 1973-7. No. 16 W Feb 1977-9. Talke W 1979-2002. Butt Lane W 2002-.
CED. Kidsgrove 1889-1968. Talke 1968-2005. Kidsgrove and Talke 2005-.
PLU. Newcastle-u-Lyme 1838-1930. Hardings Wood W by1910.

Hollinwood

Talke CP 1932-74. Butt Lane PW 1932-74. Kidsgrove TC 1974-. Butt Lane PW 1974-.
LG. Audley UD 1894-1932. Butt Lane W 1906-32. Kidsgrove UD 1932-74. Kidsgrove W 1934-67/8. Butt Lane W Feb 1968-74. Newcastle-u-Lyme D(B) 1974-. No. 15 W Feb 1973-7, No. 13 W Feb 1977-9. Butt Lane W 1979-2002, 2002-.

CED. Audley 1889-1934. Kidsgrove 1934-1968. Talke 1968-2005. Kidsgrove and Talke 2005-.
PLU. Newcastle-u-Lyme 1838-1930. Audley W by1910.

Kidsgrove Central Station

Hardings Wood CP 1894-1974. Kidsgrove TC 1974-. Kidsgrove PW 1974-. Ravenscliffe PW 2002-.
LG. Kidsgrove UD 1894-1974. Kidsgrove W by1910-74. Newcastle-u-Lyme D(B) 1974-. No. 13 W Feb 1973-7. No. 14 W Feb 1977-9, Kidsgrove W 1979-2002. Ravenscliffe W 2002-.
CED. Kidsgrove 1889-2005. Kidsgrove and Talke 2005-.
PLU. Newcastle-u-Lyme 1838-1930. Hardings Wood W by1910.

Lower Ash Road (1)

Hardings Wood CP 1894-1974. Kidsgrove TC 1974-. Butt Lane PW 1974-.
LG. Kidsgrove UD 1894-1974. Kidsgrove W by1910-61. Talke W 1961-67/8. Butt Lane W Feb 1968-74. Newcastle-u-Lyme D(B) 1974-. No. 15 W Feb 1973-7, No. 13 W Feb 1977-9. Butt Lane W 1979-2002, 2002-.
CED. Kidsgrove 1889-1968. Talke 1968-2005. Kidsgrove and Talke 2005-.
PLU. Newcastle-u-Lyme 1838-1930. Hardings Wood W by1910.

Lower Ash Road (2)

Talke CP 1932-74. Butt Lane PW 1932-74. Kidsgrove TC 1974-. Butt Lane PW 1974-.
LG. Audley UD 1894-1932. Butt Lane W 1906-32. Kidsgrove UD 1932-74. Talke W 1934-61. Kidsgrove W 1961-67/8. Butt Lane W Feb 1968-74. Newcastle-u-Lyme D(B) 1974-. No. 15 W Feb 1973-7. No. 13 W Feb 1977-9. Butt Lane W 1979-2002, 2002-.
CED. Audley 1889-1934. Kidsgrove 1934-1968. Talke 1968-2005. Kidsgrove and Talke 2005-.
PLU. Newcastle-u-Lyme 1838-1930. Audley W by1910.

New Road

Talke CP 1932-74. Butt Lane PW 1932-74. Kidsgrove TC 1974-. Butt Lane PW ?1974-, by1992-.
LG. Audley UD 1894-1932. Butt Lane W 1906-32. Kidsgrove UD 1932-74. Talke W by1955-74. Newcastle-u-Lyme D(B) 1974-. No. ?15 W Feb 1973-7. No. ?13 W Feb 1977-9. Butt Lane W ?1979-2002, 2002-.
CED. Audley 1889-1934. Kidsgrove 1934-68. Talke 1968-2005. Kidsgrove and Talke 2005-.
PLU. Newcastle-u-Lyme 1838-1930. Audley W by1910.

New Springs

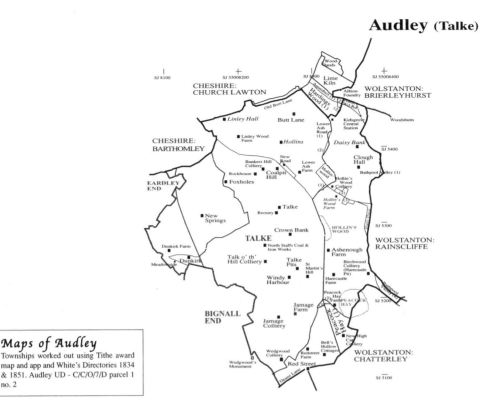

Maps of Audley
Townships worked out using Tithe award map and app and White's Directories 1834 & 1851. Audley UD - C/C/O/7/D parcel 1 no. 2

Audley Rural CP 1932-1984. Bignall End PW 1948-84. Kidsgrove TC 1984-. Talke PW 1984-
LG. Audley UD. Talke W 1906-32. Newcastle-u-Lyme RD 1932-1974, D(B) 1974-. No. 19 W Feb 1973-4, No. 20 W Feb 1974-9, Audley & Bignall End W 1979-84. Talke W 1984-2002, 2002-.
CED. Audley 1889-1981. Audley & Chesterton 1981-4. Talke 1984-2005. Kidsgrove and Talke 2005-.
PLU. Newcastle-u-Lyme 1838-1930. Audley W by1910.

Peacock's Hay (1)
LG. Audley UD 1894-1932. Talke W 1906-32. Newcastle-u-Lyme MB 1932-1974, D(B) 1974-. No. 9 W 1932-79, Bradwell & Porthill W 1979-, Bradwell W by1992-, 2002-.
CED. Audley 1889-1934. Newcastle No. 5 1934-81. Bradwell & Porthill 1981-2005, 2005-.
PLU. Newcastle-u-Lyme 1838-1930. Audley W by1910.

Peacock's Hay (2)
Newcastle unparished 1932-84. Kidsgrove TC 1984-. Talke PW 1984-
LG. Audley UD 1894-1932. Talke W 1906-32. Newcastle-u-Lyme MB 1932-1974, D(B) 1974-. No. 9 W 1932-79. Bradwell & Porthill W 1979-84, Talke W 1984-2002, 2002-

CED. Audley 1889-1934. Newcastle No. 5 1934-81. Bradwell & Porthill 1981-4. Talke 1984-2005. Kidsgrove & Talke 2005-
PLU. Newcastle-u-Lyme 1838-1930. Audley W by1910.

Peacock's Hay (3)
Newcastle unparished 1932-84. Kidsgrove TC 1984-. Talke PW 1984-
LG. Audley UD 1894-1932. Talke W 1906-32. Newcastle-u-Lyme MB 1932-1974, D(B) 1974-. No. 10 W 1932-79. Chesterton W 1979-84, Talke W 1984-2002, 2002-
CED. Audley 1889-1934. Newcastle No. 5 1934-67. Newcastle No. 6 Feb 1967-81. Audley & Chesterton 1981-4. Talke 1984-2005. Kidsgrove & Talke 2005-.
PLU. Newcastle-u-Lyme 1838-1930. Audley W by1910.

Red Street
Newcastle unparished 1932-
LG. Audley UD 1894-1932. Talke W 1906-32. Newcastle-u-Lyme MB 1932-1974, D(B) 1974-. No. 10 W 1932-79. Chesterton W 1979-2002, 2002-.
CED. Audley 1889-1934. Newcastle No. 5 1934-67. Newcastle No. 6 Feb 1967-81. Audley & Chesterton 1981-2005, 2005-.
PLU. Newcastle-u-Lyme 1838-1930. Audley W

Audley (Talke)

by1910.

Talke

Talke CP 1932-74. Talke PW 1932-74. Kidsgrove TC 1974-. Talke PW 1974-

LG. Audley UD 1894-1932. Talke W 1906-32. Kidsgrove UD 1932-74. Talke W by1955-74. Newcastle-u-Lyme D(B) 1974-. No. 16 W Feb 1973-4. No. 16 W Feb 1974-9. Talke W 1979-2002, 2002-.

CED. Audley 1889-1934. Kidsgrove 1934-68. Talke 1968-2005. Kidsgrove & Talke 2005-.

PLU. Newcastle-u-Lyme 1838-1930. Audley W by1910.

CHESHIRE

CHURCH LAWTON CP

Aquaduct (1)

Church Lawton CP -1965. Hardings Wood CP 1965-74. Kidsgrove TC 1974-. Kidsgrove PW 1974-2002. Butt Lane PW 2002-.

LG. Kidsgrove UD 1965-74. Talke W 1965-67/8. Kidsgrove W Feb 1968-74. Newcastle-u-Lyme D(B) 1974-. No. 13 W Feb 1973-7. No. 14 W Feb 1977-9. Kidsgrove W 1979-2002. Butt Lane W 2002-.

CED. Kidsgrove 1965-2005. Kidsgrove and Talke 2005-.

Aquaduct (2)

Church Lawton CP -1965. Hardings Wood CP 1965-74. Kidsgrove TC 1974-. Kidsgrove PW 1974-2002. Butt Lane PW 2002-.

LG. Kidsgrove UD 1965-74. Kidsgrove W 1965-74. Newcastle-u-Lyme D(B) 1974-. No. 13 W Feb 1973-7. No. 14 W Feb 1977-9. Kidsgrove W 1979-2002. Butt Lane W 2002-.

CED. Kidsgrove 1965-2005. Kidsgrove and Talke 2005-.

Hardings Wood (1)

Church Lawton CP -1965. Hardings Wood CP 1965-74. Kidsgrove TC 1974-. Butt Lane PW 1974-2002, 2002-.

LG. Kidsgrove UD 1965-74. Talke W 1965-67/8. Butt Lane W Feb 1968-74. Newcastle-u-Lyme D(B) 1974-. No. 15 W Feb 1973-7. No. 13 W Feb 1977-9. Butt Lane W 1979-2002, 2002-.

CED. Kidsgrove 1965-8. Talke 1968-2005. Kidsgrove and Talke 2005-.

Hardings Wood (2)

Church Lawton CP -1965. Hardings Wood CP 1965-74. Kidsgrove TC 1974-. Butt Lane PW 1974-2002, 2002-.

LG. Kidsgrove UD 1965-74. Kidsgrove W 1965-74. Newcastle-u-Lyme D(B) 1974-. No. 15 W Feb 1973-7. No. 13 W Feb 1977-9. Butt Lane W 1979-2002, 2002-.

Lime Kiln

Church Lawton CP -1965. Kidsgrove CP 1965- (TC 1974-). Kidsgrove PW 1974-2002. Butt Lane PW 2002-.

LG. Kidsgrove UD 1965-74. Kidsgrove W 1965-74. Newcastle-u-Lyme D(B) 1974-. No. 13 Feb 1973-7. No. 14 Feb 1977-9. Kidsgrove W 1979-2002. Butt Lane W 2002-.

CED. Kidsgrove 1965-2005. Kidsgrove and Talke 2005-.

Old Butt Lane

Church Lawton CP -1965. Talke CP 1965-74. Kidsgrove TC 1974-. Butt Lane PW 1974-2002, 2002-

LG. Kidsgrove UD 1932-74. Talke W 1965-67/8. Butt Lane W Feb 1968-74. Newcastle-u-Lyme D(B) 1974-. No. 15 W Feb 1973-7. No. 13 W Feb 1977-9. Butt Lane W 1979-2002, 2002-.

CED. Kidsgrove 1965-1968. Talke 1968-2005. Kidsgrove and Talke 2005-

Woodlands

Church Lawton CP -c1990. Kidsgrove TC c1990-. Kidsgrove PW c1990-2002. Butt Lane PW 2002-.

LG. Newcastle-u-Lyme D(B) c1990-. Kidsgrove W c1990-2002. Butt Lane W 2002-.

CED. Kidsgrove c1990-2005. Kidsgrove and Talke 2005-.

Personal testimony A-Ba

Personal testimony's importance in local history was championed by Prof WG Hoskins, father of Modern English Local History, when he lectured on 'History of Myddle' (1700~6) by Richard Gough (1634-1723), and later introduced the 1968 reprint.Gough's book is a remarkable and scandalous portrayal of the personalities in his Shropshire parish. 'Gossip,' said Hoskins 'is one of the most important sources for the historian who has any imaginative insight into the past. Gossip can be serious historical evidence.' Staffordshire's equivalent is 'An Accountt Who Hath Enjoyed the Severall

Estates in the Parish of **Audley** and Hamlett of Talk in the County of Stafford for 200 Years last past' (1733) by Richard Parrott (b1662) of Bignall Hill; the family name giving rise to Parrot's Barn and Parrot's Drumble in that area. The book is a survey of the religious beliefs of Audley people, their property and their characters.

With the growth of mining in the C19 Audley hamlets swelled and a lot of small schools serving each community consequently sprung up. As part of school rationalisation promoted by the Hadlow Report, by which elementary schools were organised into age-segregated units, redesignated as infant, junior and senior schools, Staffs CC tried to rationalise Audley schools in 1938. Bignall End senior children at Ravens Lane school (later Ravens Lane Primary) were transferred to Halmerend school (later Sir Thomas Boughey High School), and junior children at Halmerend school were transferred to Alsagers Bank, Wood Lane, or Audley schools. But there was horrendous parental opposition because of the new walking distances to school, considering the children were malnourished in this economically-deprived mining area. Championed by Col Wedgwood parents processed through Audley, Ryehills and Miles Green to Halmerend, and some, boycotting the schools until the following year, were prosecuted by Staffs CC (SA Aug 27 1938) (Hooligans or Rebels?: An oral History of Working Class Childhood and Youth 1889-1939. Stephen Humphries. 1st ed 1981, revised 1995 pp114-5).

However, no personal testimony in Audley Historian, Audley & District Family History Society' journal, touches on the story. Yet in No. 9 Jack Meads (b1919) says 'both the Alsagers Bank Junior School and the Halmerend Infants' School were out of date, worn out buildings', and Sarah Ward (b1916) in No. 3 says she hated Halmerend school. Also in that issue are extracts of Alsagers Bank School log books 1870-1929. On an entirely separate subject Tom Smith reminiscences in 'A Night to Remember in 1942'; in No. 4 Gertrude Evans in 'Halmer End ... And Away'; George Dobson (1865-1946) in 'An Audley Life: The Autobiography of George Dobson'; Jack Meads about Wolstanton Grammar School in 'A Grammar School Education between the Wars' ; in No. 5 John F Brown (interviewed by Ian Bailey in 1997) in 'Life in a Mining Village: Market Gardening, Rats, Pits'; in No. 6 Jack Cross in 'Memories of a Miles Green Man'; in No. 7 'Home Life In and Around Audley 1914-39' Frederick Taylor interviewed by Ian Bailey; in No. 9 Shirley McQuinn in 'My Mother's Words'; in Nos. 9 & 10 Jack Meads in 'Memories of Miles Green Between the Wars'.

In addition, there is Village Characters and Customs described from letters by a resident 1830-31 (WSL FAC 191). 'Owd Charlie' (1975, Halmerend Central Methodist Chapel) is really a memoir of the life of Charles Haywood Methodist preacher at Halmerend. In 'Staffordshire Within Living Memory' (1992) compiled by the Staffordshire Federation of Women's Institutes from notes sent by county Institutes, are stories of **Abbots Bromley**, **Adbaston**, Blithfield (the Home Guard), Burslem, Colton, Eccleshall, Madeley, Milwich, Norton-in-the-Moors, Seighford, Stafford, Stoke-upon-Trent (Hanley), Stone, Swynnerton, Wolstanton (Chesterton, Fegg Hayes). Adbaston, **Ashley**, Eccleshall, Mucklestone all figure in 'Bye-Paths of Staffordshire' by Rev Weston E. Vernon Yonge (1849-1914) remarkable for its 'folklore and entertainment value' (1911, reprinted 1991). Former Stoke-on-Trent Parks Supervisor Ernest Hawkins (b1916) produced 750 copies each of 'Memories of my life 1920-46 **Barlaston** School and Village' (2000), and 'More Memories of Barlaston' (2002). They were distributed free at the author's expense and went all over the world (WSL). As Mr Hawkins' friend, I can testify there are many more stories he has declined to publish. Nor is he pipped at the post by 'Now That Was Them Days: a selection of the memories of Barton Land Home, Barlaston' (c1980) because those residents' memories are mostly about Stoke-on-Trent (WSL pbox 5/7/3/2).

Personal testimony Ba-Z continued on pp26-27.

Barlaston

The Barlaston Parish Book (right, closed) by Barlaston researcher, Mr EJ Hawkins. Watercolour by the author, 2005

Barlaston

'Barlaston is a pleasant village which is fortunate enough to have retained, in spite of Inclosure Acts, its village green.'

Charles Masefield. Staffordshire. 1930

PLU. Stone 1838-1930. Barlaston W by1910-.
SEE ALSO pages 2, 6, 10, 21, 23-4, 30, 50, 78, 82, 96, 103, 116, 124, 130, 142, 182, 186, 187, 207, 211, 213, 230

BARLASTON TOWNSHIP
Barlaston
Barlaston CP 1866-. PC 1894-. Minutes 1894-1972 at SRO. Barlaston East PW 2003-
LG. Stone RD 1894-1974. Stafford D(B) 1974-.
Barlaston W 1974-2002, Barlaston & Oulton W 2002-
CED. Stone 1889-1911. Stone Rural Sept 1911-. Stone Rural 1955-2005. Barlaston & Fulford 2005-
Barlaston Common
Barlaston CP 1866-1988. Stone Rural CP 1988-2003. Fulford CP 2003-. Rough Close PW 2003-
LG. Stone RD 1894-1974. Stafford D(B) 1974-.
Fulford W 1974-2002, 2002-.
CED. Stone 1889-1911. Stone Rural Sept 1911-. Stone Rural 1955-2005. Barlaston & Fulford 2005-

Barlaston Park
Barlaston CP 1866-. Barlaston Park PW 2003-
LG. Stone RD 1894-1974. Stafford D(B) 1974-.
Barlaston W 1974-2002. Barlaston & Oulton W 2002-
CED. Stone 1889-1911. Stone Rural Sept 1911-. Stone Rural 1955-2005. Barlaston & Fulford 2005-
'Cocknage'
Barlaston CP 1866-1922. Stoke unparished 1922-65. Barlaston CP 1965-. Barlaston East PW 2003-.
LG. Stone RD 1894-1922. S-o-T CB 1922-65. No. 23 W 1922-55. No. 24 W 1955-65. Stone RD 1965-74. Stafford D(B) 1974-. Barlaston W 1974-2002, 2002-.
CED. Stone 1889-1911. Stone Rural Sept 1911-. Stone Rural 1965-2005. Barlaston & Fulford 2005-
PLU. Stone 1838-1922. Stone Rural W by1910-. Stoke

1922-30.

Parkfields

Barlaston CP 1866-. Barlaston West PW 2003-
LG. Stone RD 1894-1974. Stafford D(B) 1974-.
Barlaston W 1974-2002. Barlaston & Oulton W 2002-
CED. Stone 1889-1911. Stone Rural Sept 1911-. Stone
Rural 1955-2005. Barlaston & Fulford 2005-.

Sewage Works

Barlaston CP 1866-1929. Stoke unparished 1929-.
LG. Stone RD 1894-1929. S-o-T CB 1929-74, D(C)
1974-97, UA 1997-. No. 23 W 1929-55. No. 18 W
1955-65. No. 18 W 1965-79. Trentham Park W 1979-
2002. Trentham & Hanford W 2002-
CED. Stone 1889-1911. Stone Rural Sept 1911-. CCWs
1974-97.
PLU. Stone 1838-1929. Stone Rural W by1910-. Stoke

1929-30.

Wedgwood

Barlaston CP 1866-1997. Stoke unparished 1997-
LG. Stone RD 1894-1974. Stafford D(B) 1974-.
Barlaston W 1974-1996. S-o-T UA 1997-. Blurton W
1997-2002. Blurton W 2002-
CED. Stone 1889-1911. Stone Rural Sept 1911-. Stone
Rural 1955-97.

Woodend Farm

Barlaston CP 1866-1988. Stone Rural CP 1988-2003.
Fulford CP 2003-. Rough Close PW 2003-
LG. Stone RD 1894-1974. Stafford D(B) 1974-.
Barlaston W 1974-2002. Fulford W 2002-.
CED. Stone 1889-1911. Stone Rural Sept 1911-. Stone
Rural 1955-2005. Barlaston & Fulford 2005-

Parish books

Vestry minute books containing a miscellany of parish information have been called 'Parish books' by SRO in their Parish Record catalogue index. **Barlaston**'s, bound with clips for locking in 1840 and measuring 38cm by 15.5cm, includes:- lists of surveyors 1792-1832, constables 1775-1839, overseers of the poor 1793-1841; notes on parish history and details of incumbents 1598-1834; perambulations of parish boundaries; confirmation lists 1732-1766; notes of alterations to church fabric 1736-1828; resolutions on ancient church ways 1729; survey of estate sold to increase the Living 1730; list of benefactions to the poor of Barlaston 1729; resolution to pull down and rebuild the church 1762; collection for Society for Propogation of the Gospel 1779; an 'account of the seats and the houses to which they belong' 1749; minutes of vestry meetings 1823-1885 (D3538/9) (D3538/5/

Barlaston

1; Barlaston churchwarden accts bk 1821-76, telling payment made March 1840 'for binding Parish Book £0, 15s, 0d'). Others are: **Audley** (x1), **Biddulph** (several), **Blithfield** (several & one entitled 'Parson Roades Diary' c1719), **Keele** (1693-1770 - records the register, midsummer, Easter, marriage license/ banns, burial dues expected by the minister, and another 1690-1841, neither are long ledger style books), **Milwich** (1678-1823), **Sandon** (D1048/3/1 covering 1657-1945, not shaped like a ledger, more rectangular). **Trentham** (1632-1884), about which it was resolved at an (open?) vestry meeting April 3 1839 'That the ancient parish book from the year 1632 be substantially bound in Russia (a type of binding) & placed in the parish church (sic) chest' (D4480/2/2). But perhaps any vestry book was a potential Parish Book. Indeed, they are all considered as such in contemporary notes. I came across one (D3472/2/1) with this at the front:-'The Parish Book of **Standon** in the County of Stafford. Anno Domini 1829'. But it contained only vestry minutes 1829-1957. Similiarly, **Whitmore** overseers' accounts has for 1806 'To Mr Smith for Parish Books £1, 12s, 0d' (D3332/6/1), and accounts for **Weston-on-Trent** 1828 'paid for this and another parish book £0, 19s, 0d' (D5328/2/1). In the front of a **Blithfield** churchwardens' and overseers' accounts book 1760-1802(D1386/5/2) is written 'An Old Parish Book left at Oak Field by Mr William Bakewell at Lady Day 1838 and taken by Mr Will'm Lees Church warden to be put in the church coffer.' And these vestry minute books appear like 'Parish books':- **Adbaston**, **Ashley** (D44/A/PV/1), **Burslem** (St John) (D3571/3/1), Colton (D4613/1/1), Seighford (D731/10). There are no vestry minutes at SRO for **Biddulph, Eccleshall, Ellenhall, Ingestre, Marston, Norton-in-the-Moors, Stoke-upon-Trent, Stone, Swynnerton** (very little, and nothing pre 1843, and nothing in the parish chest in 1860!).

Hall o' the' Wood, Balterley, 1980s. Photograph by, and courtesy of Michael Raven

Barthomley in Staffordshire

'Here is neither church, nor chapel, nor school.'

Rev Edward Hinchliffe. Barthomley: In Letters from a former Rector to his eldest son. 1856

The other Barthomley townships, all in Ches, were Alsager, Barthomley, Crewe, and Haslington.
PLU. Newcastle-u-Lyme by1910-1930. Balterley W by1910.
SEE ALSO pages 26-27, 49, 125, 130, 186, 187, 207, 213

BALTERLEY TOWNSHIP
Balterley
Balterley CP 1866-1965. PC July 1959-. Weston, Ches 1965- (SI No. 223).
LG. Newcastle-u-Lyme RD 1894-1965.
CED. Keele 1889-1934. Madeley 1934-65.
Balterley Green
Balterley CP 1866-. In late 1894 the parish (with a population of less than 100) could obtain an Order to form a PC if the parish meeting requested one, and if the CC consented. The meeting did not vote to form a PC, nor did it wish Balterley to be grouped with a neighbouring parish. George Glover was voted chairman of parish meetings for the coming year (SA Dec 8 1894 p6). PC July 1959-. Betley and Balterley PC (a pg) May 1973-. Balterley PW May 1973-.
LG. Newcastle-u-Lyme RD 1894-1974, D(B) 1974-.

No. 18 W Feb 1973-9. Halmerend W 1979-2002, 2002-CED. Keele 1889-1934. Madeley 1934-81. Newcastle Rural 1981-2005, 2005-.
West Heath
Balterley CP 1866-1965. PC July 1959-. Chorlton, Ches 1965- (SI No. 223)
LG. Newcastle-u-Lyme RD 1894-1965.
CED. Keele 1889-1934. Madeley 1934-65.

CHESHIRE
WESTON
Gorstyhill Farm
Balterley CP 1965- (SI No. 223). Betley and Balterley PC (a pg) May 1973-. Balterley PW May 1973-.
LG. Newcastle-u-Lyme RD 1965-74, D(B) 1974-. No. 18 W Feb 1973-9. Halmerend W 1979-2002, 2002-

Barthomley in Staffordshire

CED. Madeley 1965-81. Newcastle Rural 1981-2005, 2005-.

Personal testimony Ba-Z

Balterley's answer to Parrott (see chapter on Audley) is William Kelsall (fl 1703) of Hall o' th' Wood. He produced a 700-page ms, dated 1703, on the kinship of people of Balterley and Audley, based entirely on the parish registers (private collection of Mrs John Morris of Aqualate 1944) (SHC 1944). There are lots of current reminiscences from the elderly at the back of 'Portrait of a community - **Betley**, Balterley (**Barthomley**) and Wrinehill' (1999) Mavis Smith. 'Times Remembered... Growing up in a Farming Community' are memories of Thomas Geoffrey Brassington, born Fields Farm, Betley, 1911, and his wife Evelyn Brassington, born Coopers Green Farm, Audley, 1912 (WSL pbox B/1/2). There are the diaries (1775-1810) of Rev Jonathan Wilson, curate (1775-) and vicar (1783-) of **Biddulph** (BALH) (SHC series 4 xiii pp125-35). On the restoration of Biddulph Grange gardens Major Tom Gardner's 'Memories of an early life at the Grange' appeared in SLM June/ July 1988 p15. **Burslem**: 'Childhood Memories of Burslem' by Arthur Breeze (Staffordshire Magazine Aug 1973 p21; copy in WSL CB/ COLTON/4). 'Memories of Westport Lake part 1: The beginnings' by Ernest R Fuller (STM March 1968 p33). The diary of Henry White, vicar of **Chebsey** (1785-1836), covering 1799-1800 is in the Guildhall Library, Aldermanbury, London; 34 letters of his to Mrs Parker 1803-08 and literary mss are in the Huntington Library. 'Scenes from village life, church and education at the turn of the century, in Staffordshire' (1986) by Miss Myfanwy Howells is about her mother, born in 'a cottage in the village of Chebsey' 1892 (WSL CB Howells/1). 'A Hearsay History of The Haywoods and **Colwich** 1900-39' (1997) by The Haywood Society, is based on memories. Perhaps, spurred on by this Syd Ball published in 1998 'Just Hopping over The Hedge: some recollections of life in Great Haywood between the 1920's and the 1940's'. Clifford John Lawson (b1921), Vicar of **Eccleshall** 1957-71, Chaplain of HM Prison Drake Hall 1958-, Rural Dean of Eccleshall 1965-, Prebend of Lichfield Cathedral 1970-, has left a copy of his typewriter notes at WSL:- 'Eccleshall Curates Go and Come', 'Reminiscences of Eccleshall' and 'Memoirs of Prebendary CJ Lawson' (WSL CB/Eccleshall/28, 31). But only sample pages of Isaac Richardson's life and experience (reminiscences of Croxton) 1993 have reached the WSL. 'Woodseaves (**High Offley**) Village Memories 1922-82' was produced by Woodseaves Women's Institute (WSL pbox W/5/3). An extensive collection of oral history of **Keele** parish and university - 'Off the Record: A People's History of Keele' (1998) - was compiled by Angela Drakakis-Smith. '**Madeley** in Living Memory' compiled by Vicky Moss (2000) is another well researched work, mainly based on personal testimony (Keele Uni, local coll. DA 690.M13M6). At the back of MTM are chapters for the **Milwich** memoirs of Mrs 'Doll' Eaton (aged 94), 'Bruv' Nicholls, Mrs Nellie Knight and others. 'My Boyhood in Smallthorne (**Norton-in-the-Moors**) in the 1920s' is by FWR Baddeley (n.d.) (WSL xpbox/Stoke-on-Trent/33). On the 50th anniversary of **Seighford** Airfield appeared 'The Seighford Experience: The Story of a Wartime Airfield' (1993). There are recollections on an array of topics in 'Stafford Remembered' Local History Source Book L.40 (1982) by Staffs CC Education Dept. However, 'Reminiscences of an Old Stafford Resident' (of c1840-c1890) (OSST 1932 pp43-49), is brief and not particularly revealing. The extraordinary 'Miss Garbett's memoranda and notebook' is handwritten notes made in the mid 1920s by WSL Librarian, Miss Garbett. They are brief recollections, legends and observations recounted to her about the Stafford area. 'Some of the information' says the WSL index card 'should be treated with caution unless verifiable but the book is a fascinating collection of local facts, fiction and fantasy' (WSL 7/90). Enson & Salt: 'Memories of Tinkerboro'' by Albert E Anslow appear in SA Feb 10 1950. Bertha Christina Burne was born 1884 at Cliff Bank House, **Stoke-upon-Trent**. Her 'Memories of my Victorian Childhood' (c1960s) photocopied handwritten notes are in WSL. Elizabeth W Bass's 'Bucknall: A Hole wears longer than a Patch' (1989), and 'From Wetley Moor to Bucknall

Sands' (1997) have all kinds of early C20 village reminiscences, as well as her drawings. 'A Street in Memoriam' (n.d.) is about author, Fred Leigh's childhood in Hanley (WSL CB/Hanley/2). Recollections of a visit to a Longton pottery and coal mine 1833 appear in Peter Orlando's journal (NSFCT 1914-5 pp56-63). The memories of George Hamnett, a Longton brickmaker, first appeared in Longton Sunday School Chronicle, then in HOLB (1999 ed. pp93-4). 'Longton as I first knew it' by JA Webberley appears in SLM Feb 1950 pp103-4. 'Back alley 'Neck End'' (in The Potters Rot series) (1998) is the biography of Roy Whitfield, and tells of his growing up in the Green Dock area of Longton, National Service in the RAF, and working in a pottery factory (SCA S192). 'Cinder Dip for Breakfast: a Collection of Memories' (1982) came out of a creative writing project led by Joyce Cheeseman at the Beth Johnson Day Centre in Bentilee. T Hawley's 'Pottery Life & Character sixty years ago' (c1900) (WSL sub pbox A/1/3). 'A Sociological History of Stoke-on-Trent' (1960) by photographer EJD Warrilow (1909-2000) is a tome interwoven with vast first and second-hand knowledge. 'Surviving the Slump: An oral history of Stoke-on-Trent between the Wars' by Angus McInnes in MH vol xviii (1993) pp121-140, is, as one would expect, a rather academic essay drawing on oral testimony. A general Potteries testimony is:- 'Old Times in the Potteries' (1906) by William Scarratt. And in the foreword to her 'Seven Pillars of Happiness' (1988) Joan Baggaley (b1931) writes 'The history of the Potteries district from the Ice Age to the National Garden Festival was portrayed in my first book 'The City of the Six Towns - Stoke-on-Trent.' So when I decided to write another book I thought that it should be of our present history. This time I didn't have to do any research but I have endeavoured to write about the true facts as far as my memory has allowed.' 'Memories of **Stone**' (1981) is by George Pearson, born Church Street, Stone, 1902. In the earlier 1970s Cicely Hall composed a 22-verse poem about the shops and their keepers in High Street (The Stone Gazette magazine Feb 2005 p 32). 'Grandma: A Portrait of a Staffordshire Lady' (1992) by Leslie Bishop is about his grandmother, Adelaide Bishop (nee Coghill) of Oulton House, Oulton. Famously, often straying further a field than Tittensor, is 'History of Tittensor and its Inhabitants' (1909, 3 vols) by farmer Thomas Deaville (b1851), transcribed by R Simms, author of Bibliotheca Staffordiensis (WSL). For **Stowe** is 'Memories of Hixon, recollected by Edmund Craik' edited by Malcolm Garner (WSL PN 4246) (2nd ed 2002, published by Hixon Local History Society). Edmund Craik (b1920) moved to Hixon with his family aged one; later working for English Electric. 'An Octogenarian description of boyish days at **Trentham**' by John Chadwick of Healey Hall, Lancs, appears in GM 1799. An interesting letter of 1894 in the collection of Thomas Kirkby (1824-1890) describes activities at Trentham (WSL 92/3/64). Thirty people reminisce in Chapter 9: Memories of 'Butterton Folk: A Social History' (2002) by Butterton Millennium Committee. The diary of a National Fire Service Officer 1941 briefly comments on **Whitmore** cricket club and local life (WSL M1070). **Wolstanton**: - 'Childhood Memories of Wolstanton' by Eva Beech appears in Staffordshire Magazine July 1973 p23 (WSL CB/WOLSTANTON/1). 'When I was a Child' (1903) by Methodist minister Charles Shaw (1832-1906) tells of an impoverished Tunstall childhood, labouring in a pottery, and time in Chell workhouse. 'Potteries Lad' (2004) is Bill Ridgway's collection of 1950s Chell childhood stories, which first appeared in the Sentinel journal 'The Way We Were'. 'The Lighter Side of a Parson's Life' (n.d.) by Rev FG Llewellin, vicar of Kidsgrove from 1922 to at least 1930 (WSL pbox K/2). 'Most Splendid of Men: Life in a Mining Community 1917-25' (1981) is Harold Brown's autobiography; he was born in Victoria Street, Knutton (Silverdale), 1906. 'Life and Times on the Dale: Stories and Photographs of Silverdale' (1998) by B Williams. 'Phoenix Village and other accounts of Silverdale life' (c1999) and 'Further accounts of Silverdale life' (c2001) are by Silverdale History Group (to be deposited in WSL and Newcastle Lib).

Betley Hall glass. SV. 1. 1776. Courtesy of Trustees of WSL

MORRIS DANCERS,
m an Ancient Window in the House of GEORGE TOLLET Esq.r at BETLEY in STAFFORDSHI

Betley

'this town is halfe in Staffordshire and halfe in Cheshire one side of the streete in the one and the other in the latter, so that they often jest on it in travelling one wheele goes in Staffordshire the other wheele in Cheshire:'

Celia Fiennes. Diary. 1698

PLU. Newcastle-u-Lyme 1838-1930. Betley W by1910.

SEE ALSO pages 6, 10, 26, 30, 50, 54, 78, 82, 84, 96, 124, 129, 142, 182, 186, 211, 213

BETLEY TOWNSHIP
Betley
Betley CP 1866-. PC 1894-. Betley and Balterley PC (a pg) May 1973-. Betley PW May 1973-.

LG. Newcastle-u-Lyme RD 1894-1974, D(B) 1974-. No. 18 W Feb 1973-9. Halmerend W 1979-2002, 2002-

CED. Keele 1889-1934. Madeley 1934-81. Newcastle Rural 1981-2005, 2005-.

Wrinehill
Betley CP 1866-. Betley and Balterley PC (a pg) May 1973-. Wrinehill PW May 1973-

LG. Newcastle-u-Lyme RD 1894-1974, D(B) 1974. No. 18 W Feb 1973-9. Halmerend W 1979-2002, 2002-

CED. Keele 1889-1934. Madeley 1934-81. Newcastle Rural 1981-2005, 2005-.

CHESHIRE
WYBUNBURY
BLAKENHALL CP
Frog Cottages
Betley CP 1965- (SI No. 223). Betley and Balterley PC (a pg) May 1973-. Wrinehill PW 1973-.

LG. Newcastle-u-Lyme RD 1965-74, D(B) 1974-. No. 18 W Feb 1973-9. Halmerend W 1979-2002, 2002-

CED. Madeley 1965-81. Newcastle Rural 1981-, 2005-.

WYBUNBURY
CHECKLEY CUM WRINEHILL CP
Dairy Farm
Betley CP 1965- (SI No. 223). Betley and Balterley PC (a pg) May 1973-. Wrinehill PW 1973-.

LG. Newcastle-u-Lyme RD 1965-74, D(B) 1974-. No. 18 W Feb 1973-9. Halmerend W 1979-2002, 2002-

CED. Madeley 1965-81. Newcastle Rural 1981-2005, 2005-.

Map of Balterley in Barthomley

Map of Betley
Wards - C/C/O parcel 42 no. 9.

Betley

Websites

The Betley Window, a piece of stained glass depicting eleven dancers of the Post-Medieval period, long belonged to the Tollets of **Betley**. In the C19 it awakened the public's interest in Morris dancing, which brought the glass notoriety. Patrick Corness' website 'Sources for Betley History' (launched 2000) at www.betley.net, has a colour photograph of it. In addition he has posted information on:- Ancient & early records 975-1793; Parish registers 1538-1812; Index of Betley Wills 1518-1857; Wilton Estate, Wrinehill, Auction 1918; Betley Hall Estate, Auction 1947; Bibliography; Picture Gallery. Another webmaster serving the public's appetite for local history is Steve Birks who launched 'The Local history of Stoke-on-Trent' at thepotteries.org in 1998. Steve says:- 'I created the site and I keep it updated - it's my hobby!'

During the course of this research I visited most parish and local authority sites. I have decided to record them because, by their nature, websites are ethereal and ephemeral, and documentation might aid future histories.

The above two sites, along with Stoke-on-Trent City Council (online by 1997), are currently unaffiliated to The Community Council of Staffordshire (1954) but the rest are. Affiliation means CCS's own site (1997) has a link to the site, or the site is partly CCS grant-funded, or it is on a site leased from CCS for a nominal annual sum:- **Abbots Bromley** Village Web Pages (2000) is at www.abbotsbromley.com/pc. **Audley**.net (1999), began because the village was competing in the World in Bloom competition, thanks to an organisation called Friends of Audley. youth4Audley.ik.com (2003) has an interesting history: It began out of the Citizens Online's Everybody Online Project which between Nov 2002 and Oct 2004 chose Audley and seven other UK places in which to promote the internet (having deemed them deprived in this regard): Another spin-off from the project was the hardcopy Audley Community News (July 2003) by Ernie Moulton of Bignall End. **Barlaston** on-line (Nov 2001), is at www.barlaston.org.uk. **Biddulph** Community Website (1998), at www.biddulph.co.uk, was created by Nigel Machin; The Community Website for the Parish of **Chebsey** (1997), appeared on the original CCS website, with Hilary Davies as volunteer webmaster; Hilary hopes to update the site, which has been dormant (Hilary Davies, 2005). Councillor Peter Jones initiated both **Eccleshall** Parish Council Web Site (2001), and Eccleshall Guide (2000) at www.eccleshallguide.com, for which he produces an annual paper copy. **Madeley**'s first site was by Philip Shaw; in 2000 he pooled his information with AT Finney to create the present Madeley Web Pages. **Newcastle** Borough Web Site (1996) is believed to be the UK's first district authority site, coming as part of a software package (info Tim Bevington the site's originator). **Stafford** Borough Council Web Site (April 1998), was started on their behalf by Staffordshire University (when it focused on economic development and tourism). Stafford Town: A guide for locals and visitors of the county town of Staffordshire (1998) is at www.staffordtown.co.uk. **Stoke-upon-Trent**: The Sentinel, the region's newspaper, run the principal site - ThisisStaffordshire (1997). Bagnall Village Web Site (post-1999) at www.bagnallvillage.com focuses on the Bagnall surname for genealogists. **Stone**:- into-stone.co.uk (March 2001) was founded by Lee Denny and others. The Hilderstone Website (1998) at www.hilderstone-staffs.co.uk was set up by Jenny and Douglas Crump, who say it was at no expense to the community "we have hits from all over the world and it is interesting to learn of people who lived in the village in the past." The subdivision of **Stowe** gives rise to these PC sites - www.hixon.gov.uk (2000), www.stowe-by-chartley-pc.gov.uk (2004). **Weston**, Staffordshire Website (Sept 2002) at www.westonstaffs.org.uk. **Wolstanton** - Welcome to Kidsgrove (?1995) has a local history page. In addition, there are:- Betley, **Balterley** and Wrinehill Parish Council on the Web (ES Oct 12 1998 p3), **Colton** Parish Council Web Site (post-1999), The Community Website for The Parish of **Colwich** (1999), **Ingestre**-Tixall Main Index (May 2001), and **Swynnerton** Website (Feb 2000).

Biddulph Old Hall ruins

Biddulph

'Its most prominent features are the millstone grit ridges which run on either side of the valley. To the South, high ground at Knypersley forms one of the major watersheds of England.'

Joseph Kennedy. Biddulph A Local History. 1980

Biddulph 'consists of but one township' Jonathan Wilson. 1791.
PLU. Congleton 1837-93. Leek 1893-1930.
SEE ALSO pages 6, 10, 21, 23, 24, 26, 30, 34, 44, 50, 54, 78, 93, 100, 124, 130, 186, 207, 213

BIDDULPH TOWNSHIP

Biddulph CP 1866-94. 1974-.
LG. Congleton RSD 1875-82. Biddulph USD 1882-1894. Biddulph UD 1894-1974. Staffordshire Moorlands D 1974-.

KNYPERSLEY LORDSHIP
Braddocks Hay

LG. East W 1895-1934, 1934-66, Biddulph East W Sept 1966-2002/3, 2002/3-.
CED. Biddulph 1889-1973. Biddulph No. 2 1973-81. Biddulph Town 1981-2005. Biddulph South & Endon 2005-.
Brown Lees
LG. West W 1895-1934, 1934-66, Biddulph South W Sept 1966-2002/3, Biddulph West W 2002/3-.
CED. Biddulph 1889-1973. Biddulph No. 1 1973-81.

Biddulph (Middle Biddulph)

Biddulph-Endon 1981-2005. Biddulph North 2005-.

Hayhill

LG. North W 1895-1934, West W 1934-66, Biddulph West W Sept 1966-2002/3, 2002/3-.
CED. Biddulph 1889-1973. Biddulph No. 2 1973-81. Biddulph Town 1981-2005. Biddulph North 2005-.

Knowle Style

LG. East W 1895-1934, 1934-66, Biddulph South W 1966-2002/3, Biddulph East W 2002/3-.
CED. Biddulph 1889-1973. Biddulph No. 1 1973-81. Biddulph-Endon 1981-2005. Biddulph South & Endon 2005-.

Knypersley Hall

LG. East W 1895-1934, 1934-66, Biddulph South W Sept 1966-2002/3, 2002/3-.
CED. Biddulph 1889-1973. Biddulph No. 1 1973-81. Biddulph-Endon 1981-2005. Biddulph South & Endon 2005-.

Moodystreet

LG. West W 1895-1934, 1934-66, Biddulph West W Sept 1966-2002/3, 2002/3-.
CED. Biddulph 1889-1973. Biddulph No. 2 1973-81. Biddulph Town 1981-2005. Biddulph North 2005-.

Rock End

LG. East W 1895-1934, 1934-66, Biddulph Moor W Sept 1966-2002/3, 2002/3-.
CED. Biddulph 1889-1973. Biddulph No. 1 1973-81. Biddulph-Endon 1981-2005. Biddulph North 2005-.

swimming pool

LG. East W 1895-1934, 1934-66, Biddulph East W Sept 1966-2002/3, Biddulph North W 2002/3-.
CED. Biddulph 1889-1973. Biddulph No. 2 1973-81. Biddulph Town 1981-2005. Biddulph North 2005-.

Town Hall

LG. East W 1895-1934, 1934-66, Biddulph West W Sept 1966-2002/3, Biddulph East W 2002/3-.
CED. Biddulph 1889-1973. Biddulph No. 2 1973-81. Biddulph Town 1981-2005. Biddulph South & Endon 2005-.

Whitehouse End

LG. North W 1895-1934, West W 1934-66, Biddulph South W Sept 1966-2002/3, Biddulph West W 2002/3-.
CED. Biddulph 1889-1973. Biddulph No. 1 1973-81. Biddulph-Endon 1981-, Biddulph North 2005-.

LOWER BIDDULPH LORDSHIP
The Falls

LG. North W 1895-1934, West W 1934-66, Biddulph West W Sept 1966-2002/3, 2002/3-.
CED. Biddulph 1889-1973. Biddulph No. 2 1973-81.

Biddulph Town 1981-2005. Biddulph North 2005-.

Gillow Heath

LG. North W 1895-1934, 1934-66, Biddulph North W 1966-2002/3, 2002/3-.
CED. Biddulph 1889-1973. Biddulph No. 2 1973-81. Biddulph Town 1981-2005. Biddulph North 2005-.

Gillow Heath Station

LG. West W 1895-1934, 1934-66, Biddulph West W Sept 1966-2002/3, 2002/3-.
CED. Biddulph 1889-1973. Biddulph No. 2 1973-81. Biddulph Town 1981-2005. Biddulph North 2005-.

Mow Lane

LG. North W 1895-1934, 1934-66, Biddulph North W Sept 1966-2002/3, Biddulph West W 2002/3-.
CED. Biddulph 1889-1973. Biddulph No. 2 1973-81. Biddulph Town 1981-2005. Biddulph North 2005-.

playing field

LG. North W 1895-1934, 1934-66, Biddulph West W Sept 1966-2002/3, 2002/3-.
CED. Biddulph 1889-1973. Biddulph No. 2 1973-81. Biddulph Town 1981-2005. Biddulph North 2005-.

Pot Bank

LG. North W 1895-1934, 1934-66, Biddulph West W Sept 1966-2002/3, 2002/3-.
CED. Biddulph 1889-1973. Biddulph No. 2 1973-81. Biddulph Town 1981-2005. Biddulph North 2005-.

MIDDLE BIDDULPH LORDSHIP
Biddulph Arms Inn

LG. West W 1895-1934, 1934-66, Biddulph North W Sept 1966-2002/3, 2002/3.
CED. Biddulph 1889-1973. Biddulph No. 2 1973-81. Biddulph Town 1981-2005. Biddulph North 2005-.

Christ Church

LG. North W 1895-1934, 1934-66, Biddulph Moor W Sept 1966-2002/3, 2002/3-.
CED. Biddulph 1889-1973. Biddulph No. 1 1973-81. Biddulph-Endon 1981-2005. Biddulph North 2005-.

Clough House

LG. North W 1895-1934, 1934-66, Biddulph Moor W Sept 1966-2002/3, Biddulph North W 2002/3-.
CED. Biddulph 1889-1973. Biddulph No. 1 1973-81. Biddulph-Endon 1981-2005. Biddulph North 2005-.

Greenway Hall

LG. North W 1895-1934, 1934-66, Biddulph North W Sept 1966-2002/3, 2002/3-.
CED. Biddulph 1889-1973. Biddulph No. 2 1973-81. Biddulph Town 1981-2005. Biddulph North 2005-.

The Nursery

LG. East W 1895-1934, 1934-66, Biddulph East W Sept 1966-2002/3, 2002/3.

CED. Biddulph 1889-1973. Biddulph No. 2 1973-81. Biddulph Town 1981-2005. Biddulph South & Endon 2005-.

Ox Hay

LG. East W 1895-1934, 1934-66, Biddulph North W Sept 1966-2002/3, 2002/3.
CED. Biddulph 1889-1973. Biddulph No. 2 1973-81. Biddulph Town 1981-2005. Biddulph North 2005-.

Biddulph (Upper Biddulph)
Robin Hill

LG. East W 1895-1934, 1934-66, Biddulph Moor W Sept 1966-2002/3, 2002/3-.
CED. Biddulph 1889-1973. Biddulph No. 1 1973-81. Biddulph-Endon 1981-2005. Biddulph North 2005-.

UPPER BIDDULPH LORDSHIP
Troughstone Farm

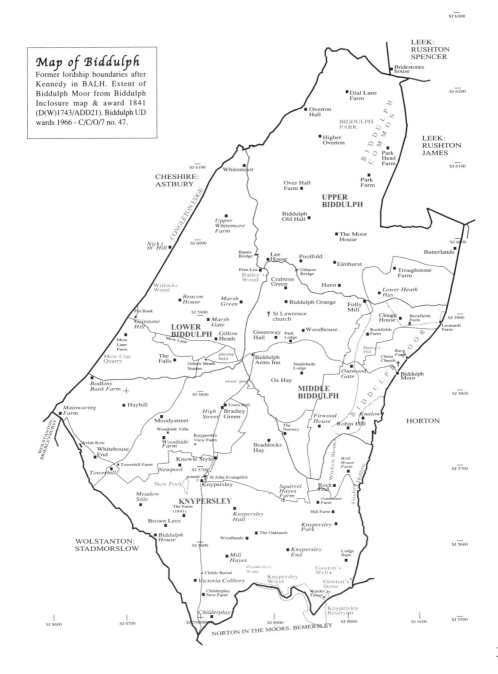

Map of Biddulph
Former lordship boundaries after Kennedy in BALH. Extent of Biddulph Moor from Biddulph Inclosure map & award 1841 (D(W)1743/ADD21). Biddulph UD wards 1966 - C/C/O/7 no. 47.

Biddulph (Upper Biddulph)

LG. North W 1895-1934, 1934-66, Biddulph Moor W Sept 1966-2002/3, Biddulph North W 2002/3-.
CED. Biddulph 1889-1973. Biddulph No. 1 1973-81. Biddulph-Endon 1981-2005. Biddulph North 2005-.

Upper Biddulph

LG. North W 1895-1934, 1934-66, Biddulph North W Sept 1966-2002/3, 2002/3-.
CED. Biddulph 1889-1973. Biddulph No. 2 1973-81. Biddulph Town 1981-2005. Biddulph North 2005-.

Early population lists

Biddulph has an early census made by Rev Jonathan Wilson, curate, on 5th, 6th, 7th & 8th of April 1779. It is in a little booklet (9.5cm x 15cm), laid out like this:-

name/ approx abode/ No. males/ No. fem/ total (SRO D3539/1/48) (WSL CB/Biddulph/6).

Also Wilson recorded the number of inhabitants of Biddulph 1779-1801 and of births, marriages, deaths 1700-79 (WSL CB/Biddulph/6); also there is his response to Dr James Falconer's question-naire to incumbents (1791), for Falconer's history of Staffordshire, which was never published (but the response survives, passing through Stebbing Shaw into the Salt Collection) (WSL SALT ms. 478/W) (SHC series 4 xiii pp125-35); also his diaries (see Balterley chapter). **Abbots Bromley** Tythes 1811-21 (D5748/2/12) - 'a list of all those who paid tithes and the type of tithe that they paid. Also contains a list of everyone living in Abbots Bromley in 1812' says the accession note in the parish record index; but a reader (a woman?) has written in brackets '?not all residents - very few women listed!' In **Colwich** parish records is the 1811 census returns (taken on May 27), showing 702 people in Great Haywood Division; 740 in Wolseley Division; 226 in Fradswell chapelry. But only for Wolseley and Fradswell have the name lists survived, laid out like this:-

Names/ Inhabited houses/ Number of Families/ Houses, buildings/ Houses unoccupied/ Families employed in agriculture/ Families employed in trade/ All other families/ Males/ Females/ Total (D24/A/PO/3362-3365).

Eccleshall has alphabetical lists of inhabitants of the manor 1626-37 (LRO Ex D & C B/A/21/1/24), another of tenants/ householders c1693-98 (LRO ...../25. SRO transcripts), another of the parish 1693 (LRO ..../48), another of houses, owners & occupiers in the town 1697 (LRO ..../28). There is an account of the **Marston** population 1801 (D53/A/PZ/1). In association with the 1811 census is a list of male and female **Newcastle-under-Lyme** inhabitants giving the names of housekeeper, number of inhabited houses, by how many families occupied, how employed, whether in agriculture, or trade, number of males and females (D3251/9/1). Population statistics for **Seighford** are in front of D731/11 for censuses 1811, 1821, 1831, 1861, 1871. The **Stoke-upon-Trent** Parish Listing, dated 2 June 1701 lists 1,629 individuals residing in 373 families in the six townships of Penkhull, Clayton, Seabridge, Shelton, Hanley, and Fenton Culvert (D(W)1742/55) (SHC 194 pp171-225; gives the listing).

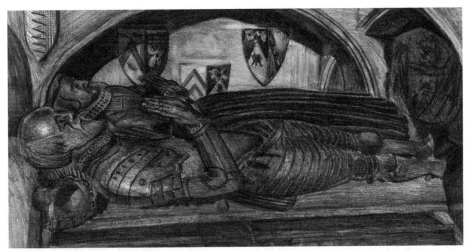

Recumbent effigies on tomb of Sir Richard Bagot (d1596) and wife, chancel N side, Blithfield Church. Drawing by the author, 2004

Blithfield

'No matter from which direction the Hall at Blithfield is approached, the low grey house always appears unexpectedly, emerging from the landscape like a ship from fog. Built in a hollow, but a hollow on high ground, it lies stretched out, seeming to cling to the soil where it has stood for so many centuries.'

Lady Bagot. Staffordshire Life. October 1948

There were separate overseers for the townships of Blithfield (alias Blithfield Side 1797) and Newton (alias Newton Side 1797) by at least 1751, and these were separate constablewicks in 1794 (D1386/5/2). By 1817 the Poor, Church, and Constable's Rates were kept separate (QS/B Michaelmas Term 1817).
PLU. Uttoxeter 1838-1930. Blithfield W by1910.
SEE ALSO pages 6, 36, 49, 78, 93, 100, 124, 129, 186, 207, 213-4

BLITHFIELD TOWNSHIP
Blithfield CP 1866-. In late 1894 the parish had the option to have parish meetings or a PC. It was entitled to an Order to form a PC without consent of the CC (as it had a population between 100 and 300). The parish meeting voted against forming a PC. It was chaired by Rev C Murray, and voted Lord Bagot chairman of future parish meetings for the coming year (SA Dec 8 1894 p6).
LG. East Staffordshire D(B) 1974-. No. 18 W Feb 1976-9. Bagots W Feb 1979-2002, 2002-
CED. Uttoxeter 1889-1911. Uttoxeter Rural Sept 1911-2005, 2005-

NEWTON TOWNSHIP
Newton
Blithfield CP 1866-.
LG. East Staffordshire D(B) 1974-. No. 18 W Feb 1976-9. Bagots W Feb 1979-2002, 2002-
CED. Uttoxeter 1889-1911. Uttoxeter Rural Sept 1911-2005, 2005-

Newton Bridge
Blithfield CP 1866-1991. Kingstone CP 1991-
LG. East Staffordshire D(B) 1974-. No. 18 W Feb 1976-9. Bagots W Feb 1979-2002, 2002-
CED. Uttoxeter 1889-1911. Uttoxeter Rural Sept 1911-2005, 2005-

Blithfield

Charity and rate accounts

Finding an ancestor in past accounts can throw light on their status, depending on the nature of the accounts. These form part of **Blithfield** parish records at SRO:- An account book of the disbursement of Sir Walter Bagot's legacy for the poor of Blithfield. It also contains offertory accounts, very detailed, giving names of parishioners to c1820 (D1386/7/1).

A Book of Easter Dues, for Blithfield, Admaston, and Newton. Includes annual lists of inhabitants and dues paid. Clearly set out in tables from 1575-92, and again from 1604-c1640: Another covering 1659-1722: Another covering 1723-49 (D1386/2/1/1).

In **Colton** PR there is an account of money collected at the Brief for Woolwich church. There is a list of 50 parishioners 1711, servants are named; £0, 19s, 0d was raised. Another account list of names for another Brief of 1709? or 1719, and another of 1716, another of 1732/3, and others (F 4613/1/1).

Forming part of **Madeley**'s records is Accounts of cash and cloth given away on St Thomas' Day which show 157 poor recipients for 1817, and 155 for 1818. Although they are named, along with the cloth and quanity, and amount of cash, their residence is not (D3412/2/25).

Sandon PR starts with a list of persons in the parish liable to pay a church rate as assessed 26 Feb 1636. Stoke charities accounts (1 vol) - detailed disbursements and receipts 1814-58 (S1188/17).

Stone Vestry Order Book includes lists of pensioners in the townships of Stone, Hilderstone, Beech and Kibblestone 1745-72 (D4605/4/1).

In the front of **Swynnerton** general register 1558-1737 is a list of inhabitants owing church rate (leawne or lewne) n.d. (D4870/1/1).

Wolstanton - List of poor inhabitants in Tunstall township who received donation from Smith Child Esq, paid out by Samuel Cartlich 1804 (D3544/5/34). Church rate assessment for the 'north side' of the parish giving names for Oldcote, Tunstall, Ravenscliff, and Stadmonslow 7 April 1768 (D3534/3/2).

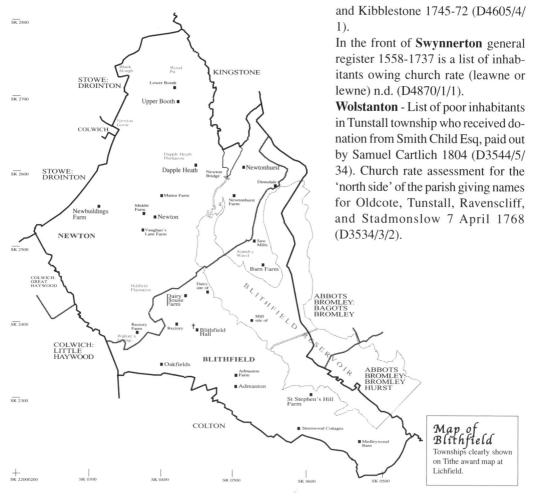

Map of Blithfield
Townships clearly shown on Tithe award map at Lichfield.

Burslem Town Hall

Burslem

'Bursley has the honours of antiquity in the Five Towns. No industrial development can ever rob it of its superiority in age, which makes its absolutely sure in its conceit..'

Arnold Bennett. The Old Wives' Tale. 1908

PLU. Wolstanton and Burslem 1838-1922. Stoke and Wolstanton 1922-30.
SEE ALSO pages 10, 24, 26, 44, 51, 54, 78, 93, 96, 124, 131, 142, 186, 207, 214, 230

BURSLEM TOWNSHIP

LG. Burslem Commissioners district (policing powers all, but lighting Burslem town only) 1825-50, LB 1850-78, MB 1878-1910 (VCH vol 8 p125). S-o-T CB 1910-74, D(C) 1974-96, UA 1996-
CED. CCWs 1974-96.
PARL. Stoke-upon-Trent PB 1832-85. Hanley PB 1885-1918. Burslem D of S-o-T PB 1918-48. S-o-T North BC 1948-

Brownhills

LG. North W 1878-1910. No. 4 W 1910-55. No. 4 W 1955-65. No. 2 W 1965-79. Tunstall North W 1979-2002. Tunstall 2002-
CED. Burslem North 1889-1910.

Dalehall

LG. North W 1878-1910. No. 4 W 1910-55. No. 4 W 1955-65. No. 4 W 1965-79. Burslem Central W 1979-2002. Burslem South W 2002-
CED. Burslem North 1889-1910.

Furlong

LG. North W 1878-1910. No. 4 W 1910-55. No. 6 W 1955-65. No. 6 W 1965-79. Burslem Grange W 1979-2002. Burslem South W 2002-
CED. Burslem North 1889-1910.

Hot Lane

LG. East W 1878-1910. No. 8 W 1910-55. No. 6 W 1955-65. No. 6 W 1965-79. Burslem Grange W 1979-2002. Burslem South W 2002-
CED. Burslem East 1889-1910.

Jenkins

Burslem (Cobridge)

LG. North W 1878-1910. No. 5 W 1910-55. No. 5 W 1955-65. No. 4 W 1965-79. Burslem Central W 1979-2002. Burslem North W 2002-.
CED. Burslem North 1889-1910.

Ladywell

LG. North W 1878-1910. No. 4 W 1910-55. No. 2 W 1955-65. No. 2 W 1965-79. Tunstall North W 1979-2002. Tunstall 2002-
CED. Burslem North 1889-1910.

Longport

LG. South W 1878-1910. No. 4 W 1910-55. No. 4 W 1955-65. No. 4 W 1965-79. Burslem Grange W 1979-2002. Burslem South W 2002-
CED. Burslem South 1889-1910.

Longport Cottage

LG. North W 1878-1910. No. 4 W 1910-55. No. 4 W 1955-65. No. 4 W 1965-79. Burslem Grange W 1979-2002. Burslem South W 2002-
CED. Burslem North 1889-1910.

Market

LG. North W 1878-1910. No. 4 W 1910-55. No. 6 W 1955-65. No. 6 W 1965-79. Burslem Central W 1979-2002. Burslem South W 2002-
CED. Burslem North 1889-1910.

Middleport

LG. South W 1878-1910. No. 6 W 1910-55. No. 4 W 1955-65. No. 4 W 1965-79. Burslem Grange W 1979-2002. Burslem South W 2002-
CED. Burslem South 1889-1910.

Navigation (1)

LG. South W 1878-1910. No. 6 W 1910-55. No. 6 W 1955-65. No. 6 W 1965-79. Burslem Grange W 1979-2002. Burslem South W 2002-
CED. Burslem South 1889-1910.

Navigation (2)

LG. South W 1878-1910. No. 6 W 1910-55. No. 4 W 1955-65. No. 6 W 1965-79. Burslem Grange W 1979-2002. Burslem South W 2002-
CED. Burslem South 1889-1910.

Navigation (3)

LG. South W 1878-1910. No. 6 W 1910-55. No. 4 W 1955-65. No. 6 W 1965-79. Burslem Grange W 1979-2002. Burslem South W 2002-
CED. Burslem South 1889-1910.

Newport

LG. South W 1878-1910. No. 6 W 1910-55. No. 4 W 1955-65. Burslem Grange W 1979-2002. Hanley West & Shelton W 2002-
CED. Burslem South 1889-1910.

Newport House

LG. South W 1878-1910. No. 6 W 1910-55. No. 4 W 1955-65. No. 6 W 1965-79. Burslem Grange W 1979-2002. Burslem South W 2002-
CED. Burslem South 1889-1910.

Pinnox Street

LG. North W 1878-1910. No. 4 W 1910-55. No. 2 W 1955-65. No. 4 W 1965-79. Tunstall North W 1979-2002. Tunstall 2002-
CED. Burslem North 1889-1910.

Saint John

LG. South W 1878-1910. No. 7 W 1910-55. No. 6 W 1955-65. No. 6 W 1965-79. Burslem Grange W 1979-2002. Burslem South W 2002-
CED. Burslem South 1889-1910.

Scotia

LG. North W 1878-1910. No. 4 W 1910-55. No. 4 W 1955-65. No. 4 W 1965-79. Burslem Central W 1979-2002. Tunstall W 2002-
CED. Burslem North 1889-1910.

Swan

LG. East W 1878-1910. No. 8 W 1910-55. No. 6 W 1955-65. No. 6 W 1965-79. Burslem Central W 1979-2002. Burslem South W 2002-
CED. Burslem East 1889-1910.

Waterloo

LG. East W 1878-1910. No. 7 W 1910-55. No. 6 W 1955-65. No. 6 W 1965-79. Burslem Grange W 1979-2002. Burslem South W 2002-
CED. Burslem East 1889-1910.

Westport

LG. South W 1878-1910. No. 6 W 1910-55. No. 4 W 1955-65. No. 4 W 1965-79. Burslem Grange W 1979-2002. Tunstall W 2002-
CED. Burslem South 1889-1910.

COBRIDGE TOWNSHIP/ VILL OF RUSHTON GRANGE

LG. Burslem Commissioners district (policing powers only) 1825-50, LB 1850-78, MB 1878-1910 (VCH vol 8 p125). S-o-T CB 1910-74, D(C) 1974-96, UA 1996-.
PARL. Stoke-upon-Trent PB 1832-85. Hanley PB 1885-1918. Burslem D of S-o-T PB 1918-48. S-o-T North BC 1948-

Canal

LG. South W 1878-1910. No. 7 W 1910-55. No. 6 W 1955-65. No. 6 W 1965-79. Burslem Grange W 1979-2002. Hanley West & Shelton W 2002-
CED. Burslem South 1889-1910.
PARL. S-o-T Central BC by1989-

Cobridge

LG. East W 1878-1910. No. 8 W 1910-55. No. 6 W 1955-65. No. 6 W 1965-79. Burslem Grange W 1979-

2002. Burslem South W 2002-
CED. Burslem East 1889-1910.
PARL. S-o-T North BC by1989-

Elder
LG. East W 1878-1910. No. 8 W 1910-55. No. 6 W 1955-65. No. 6 W 1965-79. Burslem Grange W 1979-2002. Burslem South W 2002-
CED. Burslem East 1889-1910.
PARL. S-o-T North BC by1989-

Elm
LG. East W 1878-1910. No. 7 W 1910-55. No. 6 W 1955-65. No. 6 W 1965-79. Burslem Grange W 1979-2002. Burslem South W 2002-
CED. Burslem East 1889-1910.
PARL. S-o-T North BC by1989-

Fowlea (A)
LG. South W 1878-1910. No. 6 W 1910-55. No. 4 W 1955-65. No. 6 W 1965-79. Burslem Grange W 1979-2002. Hanley West & Shelton W 2002-
CED. Burslem South 1889-1910.
PARL. S-o-T North BC by1989-

Fowlea (B)
LG. South W 1878-1910. No. 6 W 1910-55. No. 6 W 1955-65. No. 6 W 1965-79. Burslem Grange W 1979-2002. Hanley West & Shelton W 2002-
CED. Burslem South 1889-1910.
PARL. S-o-T North BC by1989-

Grange Bridge
LG. South W 1878-1910. No. 6 W 1910-55. No. 6 W 1955-65. No. 6 W 1965-79. Burslem Grange W 1979-2002. Burslem South W 2002-.
CED. Burslem South 1889-1910.
PARL. S-o-T North BC by1989-

Granville Town (1)
LG. East W 1878-1910. No. 8 W 1910-55. No. 9 W 1955-65. No. 9 W 1965-79. Shelton W 1979-2002. Burslem South W 2002-
CED. Burslem East 1889-1910.
PARL. S-o-T Central BC by1989-

Granville Town (2)
LG. East W 1878-1910. No. 8 W 1910-55. No. 9 W 1955-65. No. 9 W 1965-79. Shelton W 1979-2002. Burslem South W 2002-
CED. Burslem East 1889-1910.
PARL. S-o-T Central BC 1948-, S-o-T Central BC by1989-

Island
LG. South W 1878-1910. No. 7 W 1910-55. No. 6 W 1955-65. No. 6 W 1965-79. Shelton W 1979-2002. Hanley West & Shelton W 2002-
CED. Burslem South 1889-1910.
PARL. S-o-T Central BC by1989-

Burslem(Hulton)
Line
LG. South W 1878-1910. No. 6 W 1910-55. No. 6 1955-65. No. 6 W 1965-79. Shelton W 1979-2002. Hanley West & Shelton W 2002-
CED. Burslem South 1889-1910.
PARL. S-o-T Central BC by1989-

Rushton Grange
LG. South W 1878-1910. No. 7 W 1910-55. No. 6 W 1955-65. No. 6 W 1965-79. Burslem Grange W 1979-2002. Burslem South W 2002-
CED. Burslem South 1889-1910.
PARL. S-o-T North BC by1989-

Saint Augustine's House
LG. South W 1878-1910. No. 7 W 1910-55. No. 6 W 1955-65. No. 6 W 1965-79. Shelton W 1979-2002. Burslem South W 2002-
CED. Burslem South 1889-1910.
PARL. S-o-T Central BC by1989-

Sneyd Street
LG. East W 1878-1910. No. 8 W 1910-55. No. 8 W 1955-65. No. 6 W 1965-79. Burslem Grange W 1979-2002. Burslem South W 2002-
CED. Burslem East 1889-1910.
PARL. S-o-T North BC by1989-

Vale A
LG. East W 1878-1910. No. 8 W 1910-55. No. 8 W 1955-65. No. 6 W 1965-79. Shelton W 1979-2002. Burslem South W 2002-
CED. Burslem East 1889-1910.
PARL. S-o-T Central BC by1989-

Vale B
LG. East W 1878-1910. No. 8 W 1910-55. No. 8 W 1955-65. No. 10 W 1965-79. Shelton W 1979-2002. Burslem South W 2002-
CED. Burslem East 1889-1910.
PARL. S-o-T Central BC by1989-

Valley
LG. South W 1878-1910. No. 7 W 1910-55. No. 6 W 1955-65. No. 9 W 1965-79. Shelton W 1979-2002. Hanley West & Shelton W 2002-
CED. Burslem South 1889-1910.
PARL. S-o-T Central BC by1989-

HULTON LORDSHIP
LG. Burslem AP for poor relief and highway maintenance by1700- (VCH vol 8 p125).
PARL. Northern D of Staffordshire 1832-67. North D of Staffordshire 1867-85. North Western D of Staffordshire 1885-1918. Leek D of Staffordshire 1918-48 (unless otherwise). Leek CC 1948-83. Staffordshire Moorlands CC 1983-97. Staffordshire Moorlands CC 1997-present.

Burslem (Hulton)

Birches

Milton CP 1894-1905.

LG. Wolstanton RD (det) 1894-1904. Smallthorne UD 1904-05. Hanley MB 1905-10. S-o-T CB 1910-74, D(C) 1974-96, UA 1996-. No. 10 W 1910-55. No. 10 W 1955-65. No. 10 W 1965-79. Hanley Green W 1979-2002. Northwood & Birches Head W 2002-

CED. Bucknall 1889-1905. CCWs 1974-96.

PARL. Hanley D of S-o-T PB 1918-48. S-o-T North CB 1948-. S-o-T Central BC by1967-.

The Birches

Milton CP 1894-1905.

LG. Wolstanton RD (det) 1894-1904. Smallthorne UD 1904-05. Hanley MB 1905-10. S-o-T CB 1910-74, D(C) 1974-96, UA 1996-. No. 10 W 1910-55. No. 10 W 1955-65. No. 10 W 1965-79. Hanley Green W 1979-2002. Northwood & Birches Head W 2002-

CED. Bucknall 1889-1905. CCWs 1974-96.

PARL. Hanley D of S-o-T PB 1918-48. S-o-T Central CB 1948-

Birches Farm

Milton CP 1894-1922.

LG. Wolstanton RD (det) 1894-1904. Smallthorne UD 1904-22. Milton W by1907-22. S-o-T CB 1922-74, D(C) 1974-96, UA 1996-. No. 28 W 1910-55. No. 10 W 1955-65. No. 10 W 1965-79. Hanley Green W 1979-2002. Northwood & Birches Head W 2002-

CED. Bucknall 1889-1922. CCWs 1974-96.

PARL. S-o-T Central BC 1948-.

Birches Head

Milton CP 1894-1905.

LG. Wolstanton RD (det) 1894-1904. Smallthorne UD 1904-05. Hanley MB 1905-10. S-o-T CB 1910-74, D(C) 1974-96, UA 1996-. No. 9 W 1910-55. No. 8 W 1955-65. No. 6 W 1965-79. Hanley Green W 1979-2002. Northwood & Birches Head W 2002-

CED. Bucknall 1889-1905. CCWs 1974-96.

PARL. Hanley D of S-o-T PB 1918-48. S-o-T North CB 1948-

Birches Mead

Milton CP 1894-1922.

LG. Wolstanton RD (det) 1894-1904. Smallthorne UD 1904-22. Milton W by1907-22. S-o-T CB 1922-74, D(C) 1974-96, UA 1996-. No. 28 W 1922-55. No. 8 W 1955-65. No. 8 W 1965-79. East Valley W 1979-2002. Northwood & Birches Head W 2002-

CED. Bucknall 1889-1922. CCWs 1974-96.

PARL. S-o-T Central BC 1948-. S-o-T North BC by1967-.

Birch Green (N)

Milton CP 1894-1905.

LG. Wolstanton RD (det) 1894-1904. Smallthorne UD 1904-05. Hanley MB 1905-10. S-o-T CB 1910-74, D(C) 1974-96, UA 1996-. No. 9 W 1910-55. No. 8 W 1955-65. No. 6 W 1965-79. East Valley W 1979-2002. Northwood & Birches Head W 2002-

CED. Bucknall 1889-1905. CCWs 1974-96.

PARL. Hanley D of S-o-T PB 1918-48. S-o-T North CB 1948-

Birch Green (S)

Milton CP 1894-1905.

LG. Wolstanton RD (det) 1894-1904. Smallthorne UD 1904-05. Hanley MB 1905-10. S-o-T CB 1910-74, D(C) 1974-96, UA 1996-. No. 10 W 1910-55. No. 10 W 1955-65. No. 10 W 1965-79. Hanley Green W 1979-2002. Northwood & Birches Head W 2002-

CED. Bucknall 1889-1905. CCWs 1974-96.

PARL. Hanley D of S-o-T PB 1918-48. S-o-T North CB 1948-

Brookfield

LG. Burslem MB 1891-. East W 1891-1910. S-o-T CB 1910-74, D(C) 1974-96, UA 1996-. No. 8 W 1910-55. No. 8 W 1955-65. No. 9 W 1965-79. Burslem Grange W 1979-2002. Burslem South W 2002-

CED. Bucknall 1889-91. Burslem East 1891-. CCWs 1974-96.

PARL. Stoke-upon-Trent PB 1832-85. Hanley PB 1885-1918. Burslem D of S-o-T PB 1918-48. S-o-T North BC 1948-

Caldon (a)

Milton CP 1894-1922.

LG. Wolstanton RD (det) 1894-1904. Smallthorne UD 1904-22. Milton W by1907-22. S-o-T CB 1922-74, D(C) 1974-96, UA 1996-. No. 28 W 1922-55. No. 10 W 1955-65. No. 10 W 1965-79. Abbey W 1979-2002. Abbey Green W 2002-

CED. Bucknall 1889-1922. CCWs 1974-96.

PARL. S-o-T Central BC 1948-.

Caldon (b)

Milton CP 1894-1922.

LG. Wolstanton RD (det) 1894-1904. Smallthorne UD 1904-22. Milton W by1907-22. S-o-T CB 1922-74, D(C) 1974-96, UA 1996-. No. 28 W 1922-55. No. 10 W 1955-65. No. 11 W 1965-79. Abbey W 1979-2002. Abbey Green W 2002-

CED. Bucknall 1889-1922. CCWs 1974-96.

PARL. S-o-T Central BC 1948-.

Carmounthead

Milton CP 1894-1922. Norton-in-the-Moors CP 1922-65. South PW Nov 1949-1965.

LG. Wolstanton RD (det) 1894-1904. Smallthorne UD 1904-22. Milton W by1907-22. Leek UD 1922-65. S-o-T CB 1965-74, D(C) 1974-96, UA 1996-. No. 11 W 1965-79. Abbey W 1979-2002. Abbey Green W 2002-

CED. Bucknall 1889-1922. CCWs 1974-96.
PARL. S-o-T Central BC 1961-.

Daisy Bank

Milton CP 1894-1922.

LG. Wolstanton RD (det) 1894-1904. Smallthorne UD 1904-22. Milton W by1907-22. S-o-T CB 1922-74, D(C) 1974-96, UA 1996-. No. 27 W 1922-55. No. 7 W 1955-65. No. 8 W 1965-79. East Valley W 1979-2002. East Valley 2002-

CED. Bucknall 1889-1922. CCWs 1974-96.

PARL. S-o-T North BC 1948-.

Holden Lane

Milton CP 1894-1922.

LG. Wolstanton RD (det) 1894-1904. Smallthorne UD 1904-22. Milton W by1907-22. S-o-T CB 1922-74, D(C) 1974-96, UA 1996-. No. 28 W 1922-55. No. 8 W 1955-65. No. 8 W 1965-79. East Valley W 1979-2002. East Valley W 2002-

CED. Bucknall 1889-1922. CCWs 1974-96.

PARL. S-o-T Central BC 1948-. S-o-T North BC by1967-.

Holden Viaduct

Milton CP 1894-1922.

LG. Wolstanton RD (det) 1894-1904. Smallthorne UD 1904-22. Milton W by1907-22. S-o-T CB 1922-74, D(C) 1974-96, UA 1996-. No. 27 W 1922-55. No. 7 W 1955-65. No. 5 W 1965-79. Burslem Grange W 1979-2002. East Valley 2002-

CED. Bucknall 1889-1922. CCWs 1974-96.

PARL. S-o-T North BC 1948-.

The Hollows

LG. Burslem MB 1891-. East W 1891-1910. S-o-T CB 1910-74, D(C) 1974-96, UA 1996-. No. 8 W 1910-55. No. 8 W 1955-65. No. 10 W 1965-79. Burslem Grange W 1979-2002. Burslem South W 2002-

CED. Bucknall 1889-91. Burslem East 1891-. CCWs 1974-96.

PARL. Stoke-upon-Trent PB 1832-85. Hanley PB 1885-1918. Burslem D of S-o-T PB 1918-48. S-o-T North BC 1948-

Hulton Abbey

Milton CP 1894-1922.

LG. Wolstanton RD (det) 1894-1904. Smallthorne UD 1904-22. Milton W by1907-22. S-o-T CB 1922-74, D(C) 1974-96, UA 1996-. No. 28 W 1922-55. No. 11 W 1955-65. No. 11 W 1965-79. Abbey W 1979-2002. Abbey Green W 2002-

CED. Bucknall 1889-1922. CCWs 1974-96.

PARL. S-o-T Central BC 1948-.

Kingston (a)

Milton CP 1894-1922.

LG. Wolstanton RD (det) 1894-1904. Smallthorne UD

Burslem (Hulton)

1904-22. Milton W by1907-22. S-o-T CB 1922-74, D(C) 1974-96, UA 1996-. No. 28 W 1922-55. No. 8 W 1955-65. No. 6 W 1965-79. Burslem Grange W 1979-. Northwood & Birches Head W 2002-

CED. Bucknall 1889-1922. CCWs 1974-96.

PARL. S-o-T Central BC 1948-. S-o-T North BC by1967-.

Kingston (b)

Milton CP 1894-1922.

LG. Wolstanton RD (det) 1894-1904. Smallthorne UD 1904-22. Milton W by1907-22. S-o-T CB 1922-74, D(C) 1974-96, UA 1996-. No. 28 W 1922-55. No. 8 W 1955-65. No. 8 W 1965-79. Burslem Grange W 1979-2002. Northwood & Birches Head W 2002-

CED. Bucknall 1889-1922. CCWs 1974-96.

PARL. S-o-T Central BC 1948-. S-o-T North BC by1967-.

Mill

Milton CP 1894-1922.

LG. Wolstanton RD (det) 1894-1904. Smallthorne UD 1904-22. Milton W by1907-22. S-o-T CB 1922-74, D(C) 1974-96, UA 1996-. No. 28 W 1922-55. No. 10 W 1955-65. No. 11 W 1965-79. Abbey W 1979-2002. Northwood & Birches Head W 2002-

CED. Bucknall 1889-1922. CCWs 1974-96.

PARL. S-o-T Central BC 1948-.

Milton Road (N)

Milton CP 1894-1922.

LG. Wolstanton RD (det) 1894-1904. Smallthorne UD 1904-22. Milton W by1907-22. S-o-T CB 1922-74, D(C) 1974-96, UA 1996-. No. 28 W 1922-55. No. 8 W 1955-65. No. 6 W 1965-79. Burslem Grange W 1979-2002. East Valley W 2002-

CED. Bucknall 1889-1922. CCWs 1974-96.

PARL. S-o-T Central BC 1948-. S-o-T North BC by1967-.

Milton Road (S)

Milton CP 1894-1905.

LG. Wolstanton RD (det) 1894-1904. Smallthorne UD 1904-05. Hanley MB 1905-10. S-o-T CB 1910-74, D(C) 1974-96, UA 1996-. No. 9 W 1910-55. No. 8 W 1955-65. No. 6 W 1965-79. Burslem Grange W 1979-2002. Northwood & Birches Head W 2002-

CED. Bucknall 1889-1922. CCWs 1974-96.

PARL. Hanley D of S-o-T PB 1918-48. S-o-T North CB 1948-

Mornington Road

Milton CP 1894-1922.

LG. Wolstanton RD (det) 1894-1904. Smallthorne UD 1904-22. Milton W by1907-22. S-o-T CB 1922-74, D(C) 1974-96, UA 1996-. No. 28 W 1922-55. No. 8 W 1955-65. No. 8 W 1965-79. Burslem

Burslem (Hulton)

Grange W 1979-2002. East Valley W 2002-
CED. Bucknall 1889-1922. CCWs 1974-96.
PARL. S-o-T Central BC 1948-. S-o-T North BC
by1967-.

Northam

Milton CP 1894-1905.
LG. Wolstanton RD (det) 1894-1904. Smallthorne UD
1904-05. Hanley MB 1905-10. S-o-T CB 1910-74,
D(C) 1974-96, UA 1996-. No. 9 W 1910-55. No. 8 W
1955-65. No. 6 W 1965-79. Shelton W 1979-2002.
Northwood & Birches Hill W 2002-
CED. Bucknall 1889-1905. CCWs 1974-96.
PARL. Hanley D of S-o-T PB 1918-48. S-o-T North
CB 1948-

Pool

LG. Burslem Commissioners district (policing pow-
ers only) 1825-50 (VCH vol 8 p125), MB 1891-1910.
East W 1891-1910. S-o-T CB 1910-74, D(C) 1974-
96, UA 1996-. No. 8 W 1910-55. No. 9 W 1955-65.
No. 6 W 1965-79. Burslem Grange W 1979-2002.
Burslem South W 2002-
CED. Bucknall 1889-91. Burslem East 1891-. CCWs
1974-96.
PARL. Stoke-upon-Trent PB 1832-85. Hanley PB
1885-1918. Burslem D of S-o-T PB 1918-48. S-o-T
North BC 1948-

Sneyd

LG. Burslem Commissioners district (policing pow-
ers only) 1825-50 (VCH vol 8 p125), MB 1891-1910.
East W 1891-1910. S-o-T CB 1910-74, D(C) 1974-
96, UA 1996-. No. 8 W 1910-55. No. 8 W 1955-65.
No. 6 W 1965-79. Burslem Grange W 1979-2002.
Burslem South W 2002-
CED. Bucknall 1889-91. Burslem East 1891-. CCWs
1974-96.
PARL. Stoke-upon-Trent PB 1832-85. Hanley PB
1885-1918. Burslem D of S-o-T PB 1918-48. S-o-T
North BC 1948-. S-o-T North BC by1989-

Sneyd Green

LG. Burslem Commissioners district (policing pow-
ers only) 1825-50 (VCH vol 8 p125), MB 1891-1910.
East W 1891-1910. S-o-T CB 1910-74, D(C) 1974-
96, UA 1996-. No. 8 W 1910-55. No. 8 W 1955-65.
No. 6 W 1965-79. Burslem Grange W 1979-2002.
Burslem South W 2002-
CED. Bucknall 1889-91. Burslem East 1891-. CCWs
1974-96.
PARL. Stoke-upon-Trent PB 1832-85. Hanley PB
1885-1918. Burslem D of S-o-T PB 1918-48. S-o-T
North BC 1948-. S-o-T Central BC by1989-

Sneyd Hill Park

LG. Burslem Commissioners district (policing pow-

ers only) 1825-50 (VCH vol 8 p125), MB 1891-1910.
East W 1891-1910. S-o-T CB 1910-74, D(C) 1974-
96, UA 1996-. No. 8 W 1910-55. No. 6 W 1955-65.
No. 6 W 1965-79. Burslem Grange W 1979-2002.
Burslem South W 2002-
CED. Bucknall 1889-91. Burslem East 1891-. CCWs
1974-96.
PARL. Stoke-upon-Trent PB 1832-85. Hanley PB
1885-1918. Burslem D of S-o-T PB 1918-48. S-o-T
North BC 1948-

Willdale

Milton CP 1894-1905.
LG. Wolstanton RD (det) 1894-1904. Smallthorne UD
1904-05. Hanley MB 1905-10. S-o-T CB 1922-74,
D(C) 1974-96, UA 1996-. No. 10 W 1922-55. No. 10
W 1955-65. No. 10 W 1965-79. Abbey W 1979-2002.
Abbey Green W 2002-
CED. Bucknall 1889-1905. CCWs 1974-96.
PARL. Hanley D of S-o-T PB 1918-48. S-o-T Central
CB 1948-

Woodhead

Milton CP 1894-1922. Norton-in-the-Moors CP 1922-
65. Bagnall CP 1965-.
LG. Wolstanton RD (det) 1894-1904. Smallthorne UD
1904-22. Milton W by1907-22. Leek UD 1922-74.
Staffordshire Moorlands D 1974-. Endon & Stanley
W 1974-2002/3. Bagnall & Stanley W 2002/3-.
CED. Bucknall 1889-1922. Cheddleton 1922-73.
Cheadle No. 1 1973-81. Biddulph-Endon 1981-2005.

42

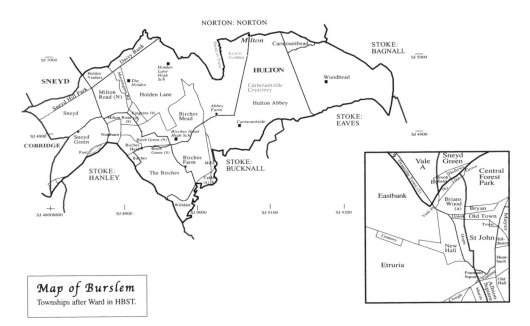

NORTON: NORTON

Milton

Carmounthead

STOKE: BAGNALL

SJ 5000

Easters Gardens

HULTON

Woodhead

SJ 5000

Daisy Bank

SNEYD

Holden Viaduct

Holden Lane High Sch

The Holden

Carmountside Cemetery

Milton Road (N)

Holden Lane

Hulton Abbey

STOKE: EAVES

Sneyd

Kingston (b)

Birches Mead

Abbey Farm

SJ 4900

Carmountside

SJ 4900

COBRIDGE

Sneyd Green

Northam

Milton Road (S)

Birches Head High Sch

Birch Green (N)

Pool

Birch Green (S)

Birches Head

Birches

Birch Green (S)

Birches Farm

Mill

STOKE: BUCKNALL

STOKE: HANLEY

The Birches

Calds (a)

Willdale

SJ 48008800

SJ 8900

SJ 9000

SJ 9100

SJ 9200

Vale A

Sneyd Green

Eastbank

Central Forest Park

Brook

Hollow

Grove

Brians Wood (a)

Bryan

Old Town

Century

Union

Town

Hope

St John

Hut. Church

New Hall

Hunt-bach

Etruria

Fountain Square

Old Hall

Clough

Albion Square

Marsh

Map of Burslem
Townships after Ward in HBST.

Biddulph South & Endon 2005-.

SNEYD TOWNSHIP

LG. Burslem Commissioners district (policing powers only) 1825-50, LB 1850-78, MB 1878-1910 (VCH vol 8 p125). S-o-T CB 1910-74, D(C) 1974-96, UA 1996-.
CED. CCWs 1974-96.
PARL. Stoke-upon-Trent PB 1832-85. Hanley PB 1885-1918. Burslem D of S-o-T PB 1918-48. S-o-T North BC 1948-.

Bycars
LG. North W 1878-1910. No. 5 W 1910-55. No. 5 W 1955-65. No. 4 W 1965-79. Burslem Central W 1979-2002. Burslem North W 2002-
CED. Burslem North 1889-1910.

Greenbank
LG. North W 1878-1910. No. 5 W 1910-55. No. 1 W 1955-65. No. 2 W 1965-79. Burslem Central W 1979-2002. Burslem North W 2002-
CED. Burslem North 1889-1910.

Hamil
LG. North W 1878-1910. No. 5 W 1910-55. No. 5 W 1955-65. No. 5 W 1965-79. Burslem Central W 1979-2002. Burslem North W 2002-
CED. Burslem North 1889-1910.

Hanley Road
LG. East W 1878-1910. No. 5 W 1910-55. No. 7 W 1955-65. No. 5 W 1965-79. Burslem Grange W 1979-2002. East Valley W 2002-
CED. Burslem East 1889-1910.

High Lane
LG. North W 1878-1910. No. 5 W 1910-55. No. 5 W 1955-65. No. 5 W 1965-79. Norton & Bradeley W 1979-2002. Burslem North 2002-
CED. Burslem North 1889-1910.

Moorland (1)
LG. East W 1878-1910. No. 8 W 1910-55. No. 6 W 1955-65. No. 6 W 1965-79. Burslem Central W 1979-2002. Burslem South W 2002-
CED. Burslem East 1889-1910.

Moorland (2)
LG. East W 1878-1910. No. 5 W 1910-55. No. 6 W 1955-65. No. 6 W 1965-79. Burslem Central W 1979-2002. Burslem South W 2002-
CED. Burslem East 1889-1910.

Moorland (3)
LG. East W 1878-1910. No. 8 W 1910-55. No. 6 W 1955-65. No. 6 W 1965-79. Burslem Grange W 1979-2002. Burslem South W 2002-
CED. Burslem East 1889-1910.

Moorland (4)
LG. East W 1878-1910. No. 5 W 1910-55. No. 6 W 1955-65. No. 6 W 1965-79. Burslem Grange W 1979-2002. Burslem South W 2002-
CED. Burslem East 1889-1910.

Burslem (Sneyd)

Melstone
LG. North W 1878-1910. No. 5 W 1910-55. No. 5 W 1955-65. No. 5 W 1965-79. Burslem Central W 1979-2002. Tunstall W 2002-
CED. Burslem North 1889-1910.

Sneyd Farm
LG. East W 1878-1910. No. 8 W 1910-55. No. 6 W 1955-65. No. 6 W 1965-79. Burslem Grange W 1979-2002. Burslem South W 2002-
CED. Burslem East 1889-1910.

Stanfield
LG. North W 1878-1910. No. 5 W 1910-55. No. 5 W 1955-65. No. 5 W 1965-79. Burslem Central W 1979-2002. Burslem North W 2002-
CED. Burslem North 1889-1910.

A recent social indicator

On April 10 2003 the Chancellor announced exemption for certain places from payment of Stamp Duty to encourage the housing market in those places. Perhaps historians will use the list as an indicator of social deprivation? In these wards of Stoke-on-Trent UA Stamp Duty is totally abolished:- Abbey, Berryhill, Blurton, Brookhouse, Burslem Central, Burslem Grange, Chell, Fenton Green, Great Fenton, Longton South, Meir Park, Norton & Bradeley, Shelton, Tunstall North: In Newcastle-under-Lyme B these wards:- Cross Heath, Holditch, Silverdale: In Staffordshire Moorlands:- Biddulph East ward.

Chartley Castle (n.d. 1813) Beauties of England & Wales . SV. X. 486. Courtesy of Trustees of WSL

Chartley Holme

'Ther is a mighty large parke. The olde castel is now yn ruine;'   John Leland. The Itinerary. c1540

PLU. Stafford 1858-1930. Stowe with Chartley Holme W by1910.
SEE ALSO pages 45-46, 50, 100, 120, 231-232

CHARTLEY HOLME LIBERTY

Chartley Holme CP 1858-1934. Regarding the forma-tion a PC in late 1894 Chartley Holme fell into the same category as Balterley. Stowe CP 1934-. Stowe PW Feb 1991-2000.

LG. Stafford RD 1894-1974, D(B) 1974-. Chartley W 1974-2002, 2002-.
CED. Stafford Rural 1889-1911. Stafford Rural East Sept 1911-34. Stafford Rural 1934-73. Stafford Rural No. 2 1973-81. Stafford Trent Valley 1981-2005, 2005-

The Prerogative Court of Canterbury probate holdings

If a testator's estate extended over more than one diocese then their Will would have to be proved in the highest probate court. This was the Prerogative Court of Canterbury (PCC: if the diocese lay in the Province of Canterbury). If the testator's estate did not extend over more than one diocese, then it could be proved in the Consistory Court of Lichfield. There are 8,372 PCC wills relating to Stafford-shire at the National Archives. Its DocumentsOnline service (www. documentsonline. pro.gov.uk) database threw up these for Pirehill in the first instance:-

Chartley Holme

Map of Chartley Holme
Tithe map of Stoweby Chartley
(1850) (D3716/2/1, 3)

Will of Charles Kenderdine, Gentleman of Stafford 4 April 1850 (PROB 11/2111)
Will of William Phillipps, yeoman of Mucclestone 4 Aug 1653 (PROB 11/228)
Sentence of Sir Thomas Wolseley of Colwich 19 June 1630 (PROB 11/157)
Will of Rev John Stevenson Catt low, Clerk of Madeley 12 Oct 1833 (PROB 11/1822)
Will of Rev Joseph Shaw, Clerk of Stafford 7 Dec 1825 (PROB 11/1706)
Will of Rev Daniel Gabriel Giberne, Clerk of Ashley 15 Sept 1749 (PROB 11/773)
Will of Sir Walter Chetwinde of Ingestre 29 May 1641 (PROB 11/186)
Will of Sir Walter Wagstaffe Bagot of Blithfield 27 Feb 1768 (PROB 11/936)
Will of Sir Edmund Windesor of Swynnerton 9 Feb 1638 (PROB 11/176).

An extra-parochial place was an extra-diocesan place and extra-parochial testators would have had their Will proved at the PCC. These are listed for Pirehill extra-parochial places (clearly, some would have estates in several dioceses, anyway):-

Chartley Holme
Will of Robert Earl Ferrars Viscount Tamworth and Lord Ferrars of Chartley 17 Jan 1718 (PROB 11/562)
Will of Robert Earle of Essex & Ewe Viscount Hereford & Bourchier Lord Ferrers of Chartley or Earl of Essex 15 Dec 1646 (PROB 11/198)
Creswell
Will of Rev Edward Whitby, Clerk of Creswell Hall 26 June 1854 (PROB 11/2194)
Will of John Cosens of Creswell Hall 18 Dec 1799 (PROB 11/1333)
Ranton Abbey
Will of Robert Harecourte of Ranton Abbey 26 June 1588 (PROB 11/72)
Will of Jonathon Cope of Ranton Abbey 23 Feb 1683 (PROB 11/372)
Tillington
Will of Symon Hering of Tillington 19 Nov 1561 (PROB 11/44)
Sentence of Richard Warde of Tillington 29 Jan 1555 (PROB 11/37)
Worston
Will of Ralphe Evison, Husbandman of Worston, perhaps not Staffs? 26 Nov 1655 (PROB 11/251)
Yarlet
None

Anglo-Saxon cross shaft, Chebsey churchyard. Drawing by the author, 2003

Chebsey

'Chebsey is an ancient village situate in the narrow valley near the confluence of the Eccleshall brook with the river Sow...'

Horne & Bennion's 'Advertiser' Almanack 1895. Stone & Eccleshall edition

PLU. Stone 1838-1930. Chebsey W by1910-.

CED. Eccleshall 1889-2005, 2005-.

Chebsey

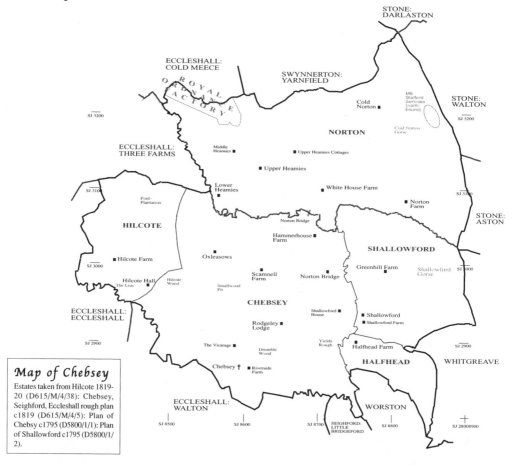

STONE:
DARLASTON

ECCLESHALL:
COLD MEECE

SWYNNERTON:
YARNFIELD

ROYAL ORDNANCE FACTORY

Cold
Norton ■

M6
Stafford
Services
(north-
bound)

STONE:
WALTON

SJ 3200

NORTON

Cold Norton
Gorse

SJ 3200

ECCLESHALL:
THREE FARMS

Middle
Heamies ■

■ Upper Heamies Cottages

SJ 310

Pool-
Plantation

Lower
Heamies ■

■ Upper Heamies

■ White House Farm

SJ 310

■ Norton
Farm

STONE:
ASTON

HILCOTE

Norton Bridge

Hammerhouse ■
Farm

■ Hilcote Farm

SJ 3000

Oxleasows ■

Hilcote Hall ■
The Leas

Hilcote
Wood

Smallwood
Pit

Scamnell ■
Farm

Norton Bridge

SHALLOWFORD

Greenhill Farm ■

Shallowford
Gorse

SJ 3000

CHEBSEY

Shallowford ■
House

■ Shallowford

ECCLESHALL:
ECCLESHALL

Rodgeley ■
Lodge

■ Shallowford Farm

SJ 2900

The Vicarage ■

Drumble
Wood

Yields
Rough

■ Halfhead Farm

SJ 2900

Chebsey † ■ Riverside
Farm

HALFHEAD

WHITGREAVE

ECCLESHALL:
WALTON

WORSTON

SJ 8500

SJ 8600

SJ 8700

SEIGHFORD:
LITTLE
BRIDGEFORD

SJ 8800

SJ 28008900

Map of Chebsey
Estates taken from Hilcote 1819-20 (D615/M/4/38): Chebsey, Seighford, Eccleshall rough plan c1819 (D615/M/4/5): Plan of Chebsy c1795 (D5800/1/1): Plan of Shallowford c1795 (D5800/1/2).

CHEBSEY TOWNSHIP
Chebsey estate
Chebsey CP 1866-. PC from 1894. At the first PC meeting held on January 5 1895 Mr Holland the manager of the District Bank, Eccleshall, was appointed treasurer, and Mr James Ibbs, assistant-overseer, took the office of clerk, as the council did not appoint one of themselves. At a 1904 PC meeting chaired by Rev CMS Patterson, the accounts of the Mason and Walker charities were read and approved (SA Jan 12 1895 p5. March 12 1904 p7 col 2). Minutes 1910-88 in SRO.
Stone RD 1894-1974. Stafford D(B) 1974-. Eccleshall W 1974-2002, 2002-

Halfhead estate
Chebsey CP 1866-.
LG. Stone RD 1894-1974. Stafford D(B) 1974-. Eccleshall W 1974-2002, 2002-

Hilcote estate
Chebsey CP 1866-.
LG. Stone RD 1894-1974. Stafford D(B) 1974-. Eccleshall W 1974-2002, 2002-

Shallowford hamlet
Chebsey CP 1866-.
LG. Stone RD 1894-1974. Stafford D(B) 1974-. Eccleshall W 1974-2002, 2002-

COLD NORTON TOWNSHIP
Cold Norton CP 1866-1932. Regarding the formation a PC in late 1894 it fell into the same category as Balterley and Chartley Holme. A parish meeting is not recorded in late 1894. Chebsey CP 1932-.
LG. Stone RD 1894-1974. Stafford D(B) 1974-. Eccleshall W 1974-2002, 2002-

The origin of parishes

The Anglo-Saxon preaching cross in Chebsey churchyard begs the question - how old is Chebsey ancient parish?; how old are the other Pirehill parishes?

This is an extremely conjectural aspect of local history. It may always be, due to lack of documentary evidence. However, studies show in the late C10 blocks of neighbouring estates in the same ownership invariably comprise a large parish. Abbots Bromley estate therefore, may have been in a huge parish with the lands of the later APs of Alrewas, Burton, Rolleston and Tatenhill, which were all part of a land grant of 941. Amazingly, estates have been revealed to be conterminous with parishes and townships of the same name a thousand years later: Abbots Bromley, Darlaston, and Madeley were: Each appear in separate grants by the Crown to noblemen in 956, 996, and 975, respectively.

With consolidation at its peak perhaps Pirehill consisted of only two or so original giant parochia. Taking into account some clues - etymology, detached portions of parishes, priests mentioned in Domesday Book, church masonry, land ownership, tradition, and past theories, it is possible to offer a tentative chronology of parish creation (The Landscape of Anglo-Saxon Staffordshire: The Charter Evidence. Della Hooke. 1983. plans, 3, 4,10) (DPB).

c1291 = the time of the Taxatio Ecclesiastica
1534~5 = date of Valor Ecclesiasticus

PARISHES (entirely ecclesiastical)

POSSIBLE PAROCHIA IN PIREHILL BY 800

'Burton': perhaps containing Abbots Bromley, as mentioned above.

Eccleshall: focus of a southern parochia, based on a British Christian community; ecles = church; ?an early endowment to See of Lichfield (SSE 1987 p30); priest - DB; c1291; 1534~5

'Trentham': focus of a northern parochia, based on upper Trent uplands; royal Mercian holding; ham = an appellation given to an estate of some importance (SSE 1987 p32); discovery of Saxon masonry; priest - DB; 1534~5

POSSIBLE PAROCHIA BY 1000

'Colwich-Stowe': size of envisaged original parochial block; name = holy place; perhaps carved out of Eccleshall - Haywood in bishop's fee - DB.

Stafford: a pre-Conquest collegiate church parochia (SSE 1987 p31); 1534~5

Stoke: size of later parish; name = holy place; Anglo-Saxon cross fragments; church in Caverswall entry - DB; perhaps carved out of Trentham, which would explain Trentham's det pts and Newcastle in Stoke - in a way following Robin Studd (SSE 1990-1 pp1-17); c1291; 1534~5

Stone: size of later parish; legend; perhaps carved out of Eccleshall; priest in Walton entry - DB; c1291

Wolstanton: tradition (HBST pp110,117); perhaps carved out of Stoke, which would explain Whitmore (det from Stoke); traditions (NSFCT 1908 p106); c1291; 1534~5

PARISHES EMERGING 1000-1179

Abbots Bromley: priest - DB; c1291

Barthomley (Ches): priest - DB (DB Cheshire. Phillimore 1978); possibly emerged earlier.

Blithfield: priest - DB; perhaps carved out of 'Colwich-Stowe' also containing Colton; whole or pt of Blithfield and Colton were in same fee - DB; c1291; 1534~5

Chebsey: priest - DB; perhaps carved out of Eccleshall; but possibly separate at an early date be-

Chebsey

cause cross shaft reputedly dates from C8 (SSE 1987 p31); parochia de Chebeseia 1185 (SHC 1924 p123); c1291; 1534~5

Colton: priest - DB; perhaps carved out of 'Colwich-Stowe'; Colwich has det pts in it and along its boundary; the ending tun signifies a small estate in a larger economic unit - SHC 1999 p8.

Colwich: created out of 'Colwich-Stowe'; it and Stowe's reciprocal det pts result from C18-19 formalisation of the division of once shared tithable lands (DPB p15).

Drayton-in-Hales (Shrops): priest - DB; Tyrley and Drayton in same DB fee (DB Shropshire. Phillimore 1986); possibly emerged earlier.

Milwich: c1140 advowson granted to Stone Priory; same fee as Stone in c1140 (SPRS); perhaps carved out of Stone (SHC 1916 p195); c1291; 1534~5

Mucklestone: priest - DB; perhaps carved out of Eccleshall as this would explain Radwood, a det pt of Eccleshall; c1291; 1534~5

Ranton Priory: probably carved out of Eccleshall when the priory was founded c1150; had extra-parochial status after 1536

Seighford: date of church is 1100 (SPRS); circumspect theory (SHC 1916 p196); carved out of Eccleshall (SL p47); c1291; 1534~5

Standon: priest - DB; perhaps carved out of Eccleshall as this would explain Rudge, a det pt of Standon; c1291; 1534~5

Stowe: created out of 'Colwich-Stowe'; it and Colwich's reciprocal det pts result from C18-19 formalisation of the division of once shared tithable lands (DPB p15); c1291; 1534~5

PARISHES EMERGING 1179-1291

Adbaston: c1291; carved out of Eccleshall; separate status 1192~1260 (SL p47) (SHC 1999 pp86-7)

Audley: c1291; perhaps carved out of Wolstanton - SHC 1916 pp192,195; separate status c1170~1223; 1534~5

Barlaston: separate status after c1225 - BAH p8; perhaps carved out of Stone as in same fee - DB; also ending tun signifies a small estate in a larger economic unit - SHC 1999 p8; 1534~5.

Biddulph: c1291; carved out of Wolstanton (SHC 1916 pp192,195); 1534~5

High Offley: parson by 1240-1 (SHC 1916 pp192, 196, 199-200. 1924 p191); carved out of Eccleshall, as in original prebend of Eccleshall; 1534~5

Madeley: c1291; perhaps carved out of Wolstanton (SHC 1916 pp192,195); 1534~5

Maer: c1291; perhaps carved out of Mucklestone (SHC 1916 p192); 1534~5

Newcastle: borough c1179, but remained ecclesiastically in Stoke until 1807 (VCH vol 8 p16).

Sandon: c1291; perhaps carved out of Stone (SHC 1916 p195); 1534~5

Swynnerton: c1291; perhaps carved out of Stone (SHC 1916 p195); 1534~5

Weston-on-Trent: c1291; probably carved out of Stowe (NSFCT 1913 p60) (SHC 1916 p192); 1534~5

PARISHES EMERGING 1291-1534~5

Ashley: 1534~5; perhaps carved out of Eccleshall; the Bishop, lord of Eccleshall, expected a service from Ashley tenants when hunting in Bishop's Wood; 1534~5.

Betley: borough by 1299, but remained ecclesiastically in Audley until 1717 (GLAUE p403)

Chartley Holme: as Ferrers chief demesne from C13 (SHC 1885 I p241) they carved it out of Stowe; thereafter, unclaimed, it had extra-parochial status.

Creswell: (GLAUE p409); carved out of Stafford; its church being redundant by 1633 it became extra-parochial.

Ellenhall: still a vill ?c1250~c1260 (SHC 1924 pp66,105); carved out of Eccleshall (SL p47).

Gayton: 1534~5; perhaps carved out of Stowe (held in DB with Amerton (itself in Stowe); the ending tun signifies a small estate in a larger economic unit - SHC 1999 p8; 1534~5

Ingestre: 1534~5; carved out of Stafford.

Keele: separate by1308-1540 with its own parish guild, and deemed a Peculiar; although technically ecclesiastically in Wolstanton until 1774 reincorporation into the mother parish was never complete (HOK pp9,40) (GLAUE p414).

Marston: known separate civil status, most parochial rights by 1548, except burial, otherwise ecclesiastically in Stafford St Mary until 1777 (GLAUE p417)

Ranton: seemingly out of Seighford (SHC 1916 p196); 1534~5.

Tixall: 1534~5; carved out of Stafford.

PARISHES (ecclesiastical/ civil) and Places (civil)

PARISHES/ PLACES 1534~5-Mid 1830s (ie: all those with a chapter in this book)
Parishes
All the aforementioned parishes

Burslem: own churchwardens by 1553; separate for poor relief by late C16 (VCH vol 8 pp198, 121); remained ecclesiastically in Stoke until 1809.

Norton-in-the-Moors: separate for poor relief by late C16 (VCH vol 8 p198); ecclesiastically in Stoke until at least 1807, technically to 1826.

Whitmore: separate for poor relief by late C16 (VCH vol 8 p198); remained ecclesiastically in Stoke until at least 1807

Places
Tillington: carved out of Stafford; deemed extra-parochial probably by 1750

Worston: carved out of Stafford; deemed extra-parochial probably by 1750

Yarlet: carved out of Stafford; deemed extra-parochial probably by 1750

Colton Local History fair, 2004

Colton

this early 'account is chiefly taken up with details of some interest perhaps to Colton people, but of little or no importance to their neighbours, it must be pleaded that few public events can be connected with a country village, particularly when it stands retired from a main road, and when, as in the present instance, it has not been the home of any one historical family,'

Rev FP Parker. Some Account of Colton and of the De Wasteneys family. 1897

John Taylor usually elected one of the two churchwardens himself from when curate 1708, and then as rector 1709 to 1765, whilst the parish elected the other. Both were selected by a house rota system. From Colton Vestry Meetings 1647-1767 (D4613/1/1) I also learnt three women had served as church-warden - Widow Bridge for Mr Webb's House, elected by the parish 1740; Widow Harvey for Jordans House & Farm, 1752; and Mrs Clarke for Mr Webb's Hamly House, elected by the rector 1762. By 1817 the Church Rate and Highway Rate were collected separately, and the Constable was paid out of the Poor Rate (QS/B Michaelmas Term 1817).

SEE ALSO pages 6, 10, 21, 24, 30, 36, 50, 53-4, 73-4, 78, 100, 116, 124, 125, 131, 182, 208, 214

COLTON TOWNSHIP

Colton CP 1866-. PC from 1894. Minutes 1894-1980 at SRO.
LG. Lichfield RD 1894-1974, D 1974-. Colton and Mavesyn Ridware W at 2002

CED. Rugeley 1889-1934. Armitage 1934-73. Lichfield Rural No. 1 Feb 1973-81. Lichfield Rural North 1981-2005. Lichfield Rural West 2005-
PLU. Lichfield 1836-1930.

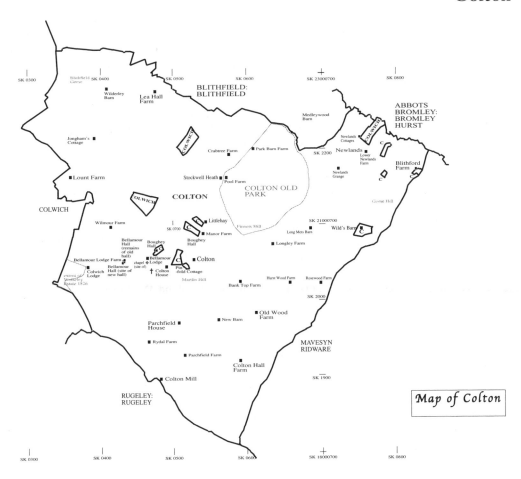

Map of Colton

COLWICH (det portions)
Colwich CP 1866-83/5. Colton CP 1883/5-.

SAME AS ABOVE

Historical societies

In Aug 2004 I attended Colton History Society's first fair. It was held in the village hall, like the one I had been to a few years earlier hosted by Hixon LHS. Both were well attended, provided excellent networking opportunities, and fascinating displays. There were old photographs, maps, documents and memorabilia. At Colton there was part of a German parachute mine which exploded in Mr G Collier's field, alongside Blithbury Rd close to the Trent Valley; a cutting from Rugeley Times Feb 6 1960 telling of the Colton floods; a cutting from the same paper? June 28 1958 telling of a forced landing in a field near Hamley House for a Chipmunk (the next day farmworkers prepared a runway for its take off by removing a hedge); and, of course, copies of the Society's own News Letter (Nov 2003, 2nd ed) telling of its first meeting in Sonia Jenkinson's home in Oct 2002: Lady Bagot became President and a committee was formed. Another fair (Oct 2005) and a website are planned.

Whilst Colton HS was born, another - the father of all local history societies - died. The North Staffordshire Field Club, held its last meeting in Dec 2002. It was founded in April 1865 for the professional class of the area to further knowledge in local history and natural sciences in an age

Colton

before these subjects became the preserve of academics. With the emergence of universities, greater mobility, and television, it and others gradually lost their appeal in the later C20. In 1923, however, it was made up of as many as ten sections - Archaeology, Botany, Entomology, Geology, History, Meteorology, Microscopy, Photography, Sketching, and Zoology. Today these have been replaced by the archaeology forum, camera club, extramural class, and wildlife trust; even the NSFC conversazione has a successor in the local history society fair. As Thelma Lancaster put it in the last transactions 'The Field Club has been like a great tree whose spreading branches gave protection to all sorts of small saplings which are strong and healthy now, but which began their lives safely only because the tree that has been the Field Club was there' (NSFCT New Series vol 28, 2003).

Stafford Borough Heritage Group

Some parish-focused local history societies affiliated to this group, founded 1994, are:- **Colton** History Society. **Colwich**'s The Haywood Society (1974), is an amenity group with a local history branch. **Eccleshall** Historical Society (1991), founded by Jan Baker, has deposited notes of Eccleshall churchyard inscriptions at SRO. **Ingestre** and **Tixall** Local History Group (1997). Old **Stafford** Society (1924) published transactions and was antecedent of Stafford Historical and Civic Society (1960). **Stone** Historical and Civic Society (1995) host lectures. **Stowe-by-Chartley**'s Hixon Local History Society (1990) publishes and holds fairs. The driving force behind **Weston** Local History Group (1998-2002) was author Jim Foley. **Wolstanton** - Tunstall History Society (by1996).

The Border History Group

Local history societies affiliated to this North Staffordshire and South Cheshire group, which is an informal, mediating and fair-holding association (www.borderhistory.co.uk), founded late 1990s, are or have been:- **Audley** & District Family History Society (May 1986), have produced journals from 1995. **Betley** and District Local History Society (Sept 1998) seems to have been preceded by Betley Local History Society (1980), founded out of a Keele University extramural class led by Robert Speake. **Biddulph** & District Genealogy & Historical Society (2002), founded by Irene Turner, was preceded by Biddulph Historical Society (1967), a transaction publisher, which deceased c1976. **Burslem** History Group (2000), continue to hold monthly meetings at The Saggarmakers Bottom Knockers Inn, Burslem; Fred Hughes, local historian, was a founder. **Wolstanton**: Silverdale History Group (Jan 1997) founded out of an uninspiring Newcastle College course whose participants were spurred on to band together and share their knowledge. In addition, there are a number of individuals and organisations such as The North Staffordshire Historians' Guild (Sept 2000) which hold informal, ad hoc meetings with a North Staffordshire focus; Apedale Heritage Trust (1997), which run a museum at former Apedale Colliery, Chesterton, housing mining artifacts, some salvaged from Chatterley-Whitfield Colliery/ Museum; The North Staffordshire Branch of BMSGH; and SPRS.

Other groups

Audley: Halmerend Village Association (Oct 1998). **Eccleshall**: Ecclian Society (1992) is a civic group. **Madeley** Conservation Group (by1990) produced 'Uncovering The Madeley Landscape' 1999, and by 2000 there was Madeley and District Community Association. **Seighford**'s Doxey Community Association (1996), a civic group, helped to make Doxey a CP. **Stoke-upon-Trent**: Bagnall Conservation Society (April 1970) (B p133). **Trentham**'s Shooters Hills and Lightwood Heritage Group existed by 2003.

Cottage on Fradswell Heath. By TP Wood. SV. IV. 207b. Courtesy of Trustees of WSL

Flowers on the grave of C19 philanthropist Charlotte Sparrow (d1874) for an annual ceremony to celebrate her life

Colwich

'It lies in beauty by the Trent, with the lofty hills of Cannock Chase splendid in the distance.'

Arthur Mee. The King's England: Staffordshire. 1937

The main part of Colwich was divided into the two sides or divisions of Great Haywood and Wolseley between at least 1759 and 1811. Each side had its own overseer. Wolseley division seems to have covered Little Haywood and Wolseley; whilst Great Haywood covered Great Haywood, Bishton, Shugborough and Oakedge (D879/5/1; using red dotted lines dated 1858, 1861) (D24/A/PV/1) (D24/A/PO/3362-65). Fradswell had a separate Poor Rate by 1754 and separate Supervisor of Highways by 1774 (D13/A/PO 17-19).

SEE ALSO pages 6, 10, 26, 30, 34, 49, 50, 54, 59, 78, 93, 100, 103, 116, 124, 125, 130, 140, 142, 182, 186, 187, 208, 211, 214

BISHTON HAMLET

Colwich CP 1866-. PC from 1894. Minutes 1894-1948, -1977 at SRO. Little Haywood PW Aug 1972-.
LG. Stafford RD 1894-1974, D(B) 1974-. Haywood & Hixon W -2002, 2002-
CED. Stafford Rural 1889-1911. Stafford Rural East Sept 1911-34. Stafford Rural 1934-73. Stafford Rural No. 2 1973-81. Stafford Trent Valley 1981-2005, 2005-
PLU. Stafford 1836-1930. Colwich W by1910.

DROINTON & HIXON HAMLETS
Colwich. 13,15,17,25

Colwich CP 1866-83~86. Stowe CP 1883? 1884? 1885? 1886?-. Stowe PW Feb 1991-2000.
LG. Stafford RD 1894-1974, D(B) 1974-. Chartley W 1974-2002, 2002-.
CED. Stafford Rural 1889-1911. Stafford Rural East Sept 1911-34. Stafford Rural 1934-73. Stafford Rural No. 2 1973-81. Stafford Trent Valley 1981-2005, 2005-
PLU. Stafford 1836-1930. Stowe with Chartley Holme W by1910.

Colwich

Colwich. 2-7,11,12

Colwich CP 1866-83~86. Stowe CP 1883?,1885?1885?,1886?-2000. Hixon PW Feb 1991-2000. Hixon CP April 1 2000-.

LG. Stafford RD 1894-1974, D(B) 1974-. Chartley W 1974-2002, Haywood & Hixon W 2002-.

CED. Stafford Rural 1889-1911. Stafford Rural East Sept 1911-34. Stafford Rural 1934-73. Stafford Rural No. 2 1973-81. Stafford Trent Valley 1981-2005, 2005-

PLU. Stafford 1836-1930. Stowe with Chartley Holme W by1910.

Colwich 16,18-24

Colwich CP 1866-83~86. Stowe CP 1883?,1885?1885?,1886?-. Stowe PW Feb 1991-2000.

LG. Stafford RD 1894-1974, D(B) 1974-. Chartley W -2002, 2002-.

CED. Stafford Rural 1889-1911. Stafford Rural East Sept 1911-34. Stafford Rural 1934-73. Stafford Rural No. 2 1973-81. Stafford Trent Valley 1981-2005, 2005-

PLU. Stafford 1836-1930. Stowe with Chartley Holme W by1910.

Colwich 8-10,14,26

Colwich CP 1866-83~86. Stowe CP 1883?,1885?1885?,1886?-. Stowe PW Feb 1991-2000.

LG. Stafford RD 1894-1974, D(B) 1974-. Chartley W 1974-2002, Haywood & Hixon W 2002-.

CED. Stafford Rural 1889-1911. Stafford Rural East Sept 1911-34. Stafford Rural 1934-73. Stafford Rural No. 2 1973-81. Stafford Trent Valley 1981-2005, 2005-

PLU. Stafford 1836-1930. Stowe with Chartley Holme W by1910.

FRADSWELL TOWNSHIP

Fradswell CP 1866-. With a population between 100 and 300 Fradswell was entitled to an Order to form a PC without consent of the CC. At a parish meeting in late 1894 it was decided not to form a PC; Rev Thomas Worthington, rector, was voted chairman of parish meetings for the coming year (SA Dec 8 1894 p6). Parish meeting minutes 1895-1979 at SRO. Weston-with-Gayton-with-Fradswell PC (a pg) 1979-2003. Milwich-with-Fradswell PC (a pg) 2003-.

LG. Stafford RD 1894-1974, D(B) 1974-. Milwich W 1974-2002, 2002-.

CED. Stafford Rural 1889-1911. Stafford Rural East Sept 1911-34. Stafford Rural 1934-73. Stafford Rural No. 2 1973-81. Stone Rural 1981-2005. Barlaston & Fulford 2005-

PLU. Stafford 1836-1930. Fradswell W by1910.

GREAT HAYWOOD HAMLET
C. 1, Great Haywood

Colwich CP 1866-. Great Haywood PW Aug 1972-.

LG. Stafford RD 1894-1974, D(B) 1974-. Haywood & Hixon W -2002, 2002-

CED. Stafford Rural 1889-1911. Stafford Rural East Sept 1911-34. Stafford Rural 1934-73. Stafford Rural No. 2 1973-81. Stafford Trent Valley 1981-2005, 2005-

PLU. Stafford 1836-1930. Colwich W by1910.

C. 27

Colwich CP 1866-. Little Haywood PW Aug 1972-.

LG. Stafford RD 1894-1974, D(B) 1974-. Haywood & Hixon W -2002, 2002-

CED. Stafford Rural 1889-1911. Stafford Rural East Sept 1911-34. Stafford Rural 1934-73. Stafford Rural No. 2 1973-81. Stafford Trent Valley 1981-2005, 2005-

PLU. Stafford 1836-1930. Colwich W by1910.

LITTLE HAYWOOD HAMLET
The Cliffs

Colwich CP 1866-. Great Haywood PW Aug 1972-

LG. Stafford RD 1894-1974, D(B) 1974-. Haywood & Hixon W -2002, 2002-

CED. Stafford Rural 1889-1911. Stafford Rural East Sept 1911-34. Stafford Rural 1934-73. Stafford Rural No. 2 1973-81. Stafford Trent Valley 1981-2005, 2005-

PLU. Stafford 1836-1930. Colwich W by1910.

Little Haywood

Colwich CP 1866-. Little Haywood PW Aug 1972-

LG. Stafford RD 1894-1974, D(B) 1974-. Haywood & Hixon W -2002, 2002-

CED. Stafford Rural 1889-1911. Stafford Rural East Sept 1911-34. Stafford Rural 1934-73. Stafford Rural No. 2 1973-81. Stafford Trent Valley 1981-2005, 2005-

PLU. Stafford 1836-1930. Colwich W by1910.

Little Tixall Lane

Colwich CP 1866-. Great Haywood PW Aug 1972-

LG. Stafford RD 1894-1974, D(B) 1974-. Haywood & Hixon W -2002, 2002-

CED. Stafford Rural 1889-1911. Stafford Rural East Sept 1911-34. Stafford Rural 1934-73. Stafford Rural No. 2 1973-81. Stafford Trent Valley 1981-2005, 2005-

PLU. Stafford 1836-1930. Colwich W by1910.

Tithebarn Farm

Colwich CP 1866-. Great Haywood PW Aug 1972-

LG. Stafford RD 1894-1974, D(B) 1974-. Haywood & Hixon W -2002, 2002-

CED. Stafford Rural 1889-1911. Stafford Rural East Sept 1911-34. Stafford Rural 1934-73. Stafford Rural No. 2 1973-81. Stafford Trent Valley 1981-2005, 2005-

Colwich

PLU. Stafford 1836-1930. Colwich W by1910.

SHUGBOROUGH HAMLET
Cannock Chase, Coalpit Lane Covert, Oakedge Park

Colwich CP 1866-. Little Haywood PW Aug 1972-.
LG. Stafford RD 1894-1974, D(B) 1974-. Haywood & Hixon W -2002, 2002-
CED. Stafford Rural 1889-1911. Stafford Rural East Sept 1911-34. Stafford Rural 1934-73. Stafford Rural No. 2 1973-81. Stafford Trent Valley 1981-2005, 2005-
PLU. Stafford 1836-1930. Colwich W by1910.

Shugborough

Colwich CP 1866-. Great Haywood PW Aug 1972-.
LG. Stafford RD 1894-1974, D(B) 1974-. Haywood & Hixon W -2002, 2002-
CED. Stafford Rural 1889-1911. Stafford Rural East Sept 1911-34. Stafford Rural 1934-73. Stafford Rural No. 2 1973-81. Stafford Trent Valley 1981-2005, 2005-
PLU. Stafford 1836-1930. Colwich W by1910.

Maps of Colwich

Townships shown on Tithe award map (1839, but drawn in later in 1858) at Stafford (D874/2/15, D1274/2/1). Division of Wolseley estate from Shugborough from D(W)1781/11/1 (1826). Detached portions identified on Land in Manor of Haywood etc c1720 (D603/H/3/9). Wards - C/C/O parcel 45 no. 1

Colwich

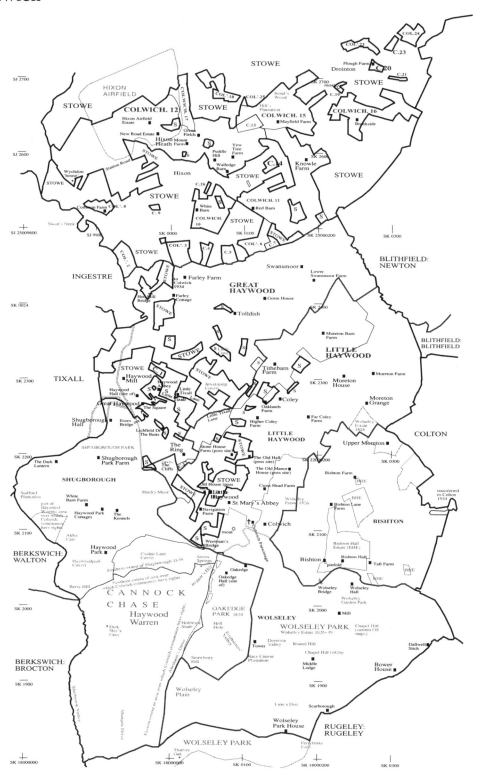

Commoners rights by property qualification

In Colwich Parish Office is correspondence about the rights of Colwich freeholders and copyholders to Commons on Cannock Chase as settled by a Decree of Chancery 1606. In WSL are documents of 1828-67 (112/37. 40. 47/41). In 1903 the Earl of Lichfield specified to the PC clerk the rights were: 1) to turn on in the summer as many sheep as they can keep during the winter on their enclosed lands. 2) to get heath, ridging turf, fern, clay, sand, marl and gravel to and for their own use to be spent upon their own land and not elsewhere. Under the Commons Registration Act 1965 the Commons area (Haywood Warren and Satnall Hills) and commoner qualification were finally settled (effective from 1968); the latter on the basis of owning one of these properties:- At **Little Haywood**: 'The Hollies'; Heather Brae; 1 Canal Cottages; Chase View; Higher Cliffs; Yew Trees, London Rd; The Post Office; 'Yeldcote', The Yeld Drive; Sunny Brae, Highfield Drive; 23 & 27 Haywood Grange; 'Seven Springs', 15 Tylecote Crescent. **The Cliffs**: 'Parklands'; 'Eldnar'. **Coley Lane**: 3 Pinfold Terrace; 'The Firs'; 'Roserie'; Peter Neale's property; 'Red Earth'. **Meadow Lane**: The Cliffs; Twixt Bridges; Deers Leap; 'Sternen'. At **Colwich**: 'Alverstone'. **Wolseley Bridge**: 'The Old House'; Moreton Farm. **Bishton**: St Bedes School (Bishton Hall); The Heritage. **In addition** all the Registration district itself (owned by Staffordshire CC 1968): some land in that district (owned by Ministry of Agriculture, Fisheries, and Food 1968): Tolldish Lane, Abbeyfields, The Uplands, Dobtree Close, Wolseley Close, and Bishton Lane (owned by Stafford RD 1968). It is not known whether commoners still exercise their rights. But in 1979 some asked for assistance to obtain a key for the barriers which were blocking certain access points, and wanted clarity on whether rights passed to new houses built on the site of one of the listed properties, lately demolished.

Window Tax

A window tax was levied 1696-1851. The only records of this tax relating to Pirehill, held by the County, are Fradswell 1785-87 (SRO D3033/5/3), and Colwich 1730 (WSL 90/25).

Creswell

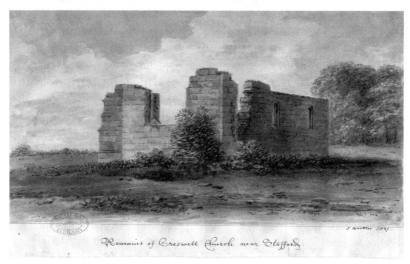

Creswell chapel ruins. By J Buckler. SV. IX. 104a. Courtesy of Trustees of WSL

Creswell

'The little church has been a ruin for centuries: fragments of the chancel survive in a field.'

Henry Thorold. Staffordshire: A Shell Guide. 1978

PLU. Stafford 1858-1930. Tillington with Creswell W by1910.
SEE ALSO pages 46, 50, 61, 78, 86, 100, 120, 195

CRESWELL
Creswell

Creswell CP 1858-. PC from 1962-. Regarding the formation of a PC in late 1894 Creswell fell into the same category as Balterley, Chartley Holme and Cold Norton. A parish meeting is not recorded in late 1894. PC from 1962-. Minutes from 1963 at SRO.

LG. Stafford RD 1894-1974, D(B) 1974-. Seighford W 1974-2002, 2002-.

CED. Stafford Rural 1889-1911. Stafford Rural West Sept 1911-34. Stafford Rural 1934-73. Stafford Rural No. 2 1973-81. Eccleshall 1981-2005. Gnosall & Doxey 2005-.

The Darling (a)

Creswell CP 1858-2002. Stafford unparished 2002-.

LG. Stafford RD 1894-1974, D(B) 1974-. Seighford W 1974-2002, Tillington W 2002-.

CED. Stafford Rural 1889-1911. Stafford Rural West Sept 1911-34. Stafford Rural 1934-73. Stafford Rural No. 2 1973-81. Eccleshall 1981-2005. Stafford North 2005-.

The Darling (b)

Creswell CP 1858-2002. Stafford unparished 2002-.

LG. Stafford RD 1894-1974, D(B) 1974-. Seighford W 1974-2002, Tillington W 2002-.
CED. Stafford Rural 1889-1911. Stafford Rural West Sept 1911-34. Stafford Rural 1934-73. Stafford Rural No. 2 1973-81. Eccleshall 1981-2005. Gnosall & Doxey 2005-.

Creswell church rights

Creswell parish was subordinate to Stafford St Mary in medieval times. It was without burial rights by the earlier C15, when it was burying its dead at St Bertelin's, Stafford, in St Mary's parish (VCH vol 6 p238). But it appears to have obtained rights later; all rights were 'restored' in 1550: 'On 6 Feb 1549-50 Creswell church was removed from the status of a chantry belonging to the king, and the patron - then Sir Nich. Hare knt - and the inhabitants had all their rights as a parish church restored' (SHC 1915 p78). Also there are hardly any Creswell entries in St Mary's PR; only one family appear showing Creswell must have been able to bury its dead:-

1574/5 Feb 19 Isabel, d of Thomas Bullock, of Creswell...bap
1578 Dec 15 William s Thomas Bullock, of Creswell & his wife... bur
1580 May 2 Arthur s Thomas Bullocke, of Creswell & his wife ... bap

Perhaps Creswell had a register from 1550. But 83 years later on the church had become redundant and register-making may never have started.
The Stafford St Mary royal free chapels, Ingestre and Tixall, were also burying their dead at St Bertelin's in the earlier C15. But they frequently appear in St Mary's PR, suggesting they did not obtain burial rights until c1590~1600.

1559 Oct 19 buried Joan Hutton, of Tixall' '1565 Nov 24 Walter, S Thom Riley, of Tixall, buried'
1568 March 28 James s Walter Aston, of Tyxall, knt buried
1570/1 Feb 18 Joan Hudsonne, of Ingestrie... buried
1572 Sept 6 Frances, illeg. d Mary, p. of Ingestrie ... bur
1573 Oct 12 Joan Ray, of Ingestrie, widow ... bur
1574 July 13 Thom. Jackson, of Ingestrie ... bur
1576/7 Jan 4 John Shelley, senex, p. of Ingestrie ... bur
1580 Sept 28 Joan, d Margaret Parrishe, of Tixall que obitt mortem imediate post partum ... bur
1582 Dec 4 Jane, d Thomas Ausbason, of Ingestrie ... bur
1583 Oct 4 Agnes, w John Parrise, of Ingestrie ... bur

Entries of inhabitants from extra-parochial places Tillington, Worston, and Yarlet show they were nominally served by Stafford St Mary's:-

1571 Sept 11 Walter, s John Heathe & Helen his wife, of Tyllington ... bap
1623 April 10 Joan Collyer of Yarlett...bur
1656/7 Nov 7 buried Mr Roe from Worston (? -transcribers note) farm

I wonder whether registers for Ingestre and Tixall started c1600: after all, their BTs (at LRO) pre-date parish registers, so implying register books have been lost (the earliest entries of those lost books may have been of c1600?).

Re-enactment of the Battle of Blore Heath (1459), September 2002

Drayton-in-Hales in Staffordshire

'Prehistory and history have left their mark in this corner of Staffordshire which presses to within ten miles of Wales.'   Vivian Bird. Staffordshire. 1973

By 1756 Drayton-in-Hales parish was divided into quarters. Betton Quarter contained Betton township; Drayton Quarter - Great and Little Drayton townships; Sutton Quarter - Longslow township, with Woodseaves and Sutton townships in Stoke-upon-Tern parish. All quarters had a separate church-warden; Drayton had two; Tyrley, at least, supported its poor separately (SRRC P97/2997/2/1).

LG. Newcastle-u-Lyme RD 1894-1974, D(B) 1974-. No. 24 W Feb 1973-4. No. 25 W Feb 1974-9. Loggerheads W 1979-2002. Loggerheads & Whitmore W 2002-.

CED. Keele 1889-1934. Madeley 1934-81. Newcastle Rural 1981-2005, 2005-

PLU. Market Drayton 1836-1930.

SEE ALSO pages 50, 63-65, 78, 93, 100, 124, 130, 140, 182, 187, 208, 214

TYRLEY QUARTER
ALMINGTON 'TOWNSHIP'
**Almington, Almington (1), Almington (2),
Johnson's Wood Farm, Oakley Lodge**

Tyrley CP 1866-1984. PC from 1894. Minutes from 1894 at SRO. Loggerheads CP 1984-. Tyrley PW 1984-

BLORE 'TOWNSHIP'
Blore, Blore (1), (2), (3)

Tyrley CP 1866-1984. Loggerheads CP 1984-. Tyrley PW 1984-.

'chapel'

Tyrley CP 1866-1932. 1932-1984 Ashley CP. Loggerheads CP 1984-. Loggerheads PW 1984-.

Rowney Farm

Tyrley CP 1866-1984. Loggerheads CP 1984-. Loggerheads PW 1984-.

Tern (1)

Original Tyrley vill? Tyrley CP 1866-1932. Market Drayton CP, Shrops 1932-.

Tern (2)

Original Tyrley vill? Tyrley CP 1866-1965. Market Drayton CP, Shrops 1965-.

Tyrley Castle Farm

Original Tyrley vill? Tyrley CP 1866-1965. Sutton upon Tern CP, Shrops 1965-.

Tyrley Wharf

Original Tyrley vill? Tyrley CP 1866-1984. Loggerheads CP 1984-. Tyrley PW 1984-.

BLORE HALL 'AREA'
Blore Farm

Tyrley CP 1866-1984. Loggerheads CP 1984-. Tyrley PW of Loggerheads CP.

'Rowney Farm'

Tyrley CP 1866-1984. Loggerheads CP 1984-. Loggerheads PW 1984-.

BROOMHALL GRANGE 'AREA'
Broomhall Grange

Tyrley CP 1866-1984. Loggerheads CP 1984-. Tyrley PW 1984-.

Tern (3)

Tyrley CP 1866-1965. Sutton upon Tern CP, Shrops 1965-.

'COAL BROOK' 'AREA'

Tyrley CP 1866-1984. Loggerheads CP 1984-. Tyrley PW 1984-.

CROOKFORD 'AREA'
Crookford

Tyrley CP 1866-1984. Loggerheads CP 1984-. Tyrley PW 1984-.

HALES 'TOWNSHIP'
Almington Hall

Tyrley CP 1866-1984. Loggerheads CP 1984-. Tyrley PW 1984-

The Brodder Spring

Tyrley CP 1866-1984. Loggerheads CP 1984-. Tyrley PW 1984-.

Dairy House

Tyrley CP 1866-1984. Loggerheads CP 1984-. Tyrley PW 1984-.

Hales (1), (2), (3), Hales Hall

Tyrley CP 1866-1984. Loggerheads CP 1984-. Tyrley PW 1984-.

The Hollings

Original Tyrley vill? Tyrley CP 1866-1965. Sutton upon Tern CP, Shrops 1965-.

Peatswood Hall

Tyrley CP 1866-1984. Loggerheads CP 1984-. Tyrley PW 1984-.

Pell Wall

Original Tyrley vill? Tyrley CP 1866-1965. Sutton upon Tern CP, Shrops 1965-.

PARSONS & WOOD MEADOW 'AREA'

Tyrley CP 1866-1984. Loggerheads CP 1984-. Tyrley PW 1984-

ROUGH LEASOW 'AREA'

Tyrley CP 1866-1984. Loggerheads CP 1984-. Tyrley PW 1984-

SHIFFORD'S GRANGE 'AREA'
Shifford's Grange Farm

Tyrley CP 1866-1984. Loggerheads CP 1984-. Tyrley PW 1984-

TYRLEY HEATH 'AREA'
The Fouralls

Original Tyrley vill? Tyrley CP 1866-1965. Sutton upon Tern CP, Shrops 1965-.

WITHY MEADOW 'AREA'

Tyrley CP 1866-1984. Loggerheads CP 1984-. Tyrley PW 1984-

WITHYNHURST 'AREA'

Tyrley CP 1866-1984. Loggerheads CP 1984-. Tyrley PW 1984-

Records of a parish divided between two counties

Since Drayton-in-Hales mother church lies in Shropshire the records for Tyrley Quarter are at Shropshire Archives, Castle Gates, Shrewsbury, SY1 2AQ (Tel: 01743 255350, email: archives@shropshire-cc.gov.uk, website: www.shropshirearchives.co.uk. The accession numbers beginning with four digits will shortly be revised:-

<u>REGISTERS (for St Mary's)</u>
General Register 1558-1787 (P97/11/1/1-4: transcript for 1659-61 (2997/14/4)). Register of bap & bur 1788-1812 (P97A/1/5), of bap 1813-31 (P97A/2/1), of bap 1831-65 (P97A/2/2). Register of bur 1813-41 (P97A/4/1). Transcript of bur 1841-. Register of banns & mar 1754-89 (P97/A/3/1), of mar 1789-1812 (P97/A/3/2), of mar 1813-37 (P97/A/3/3), of mar 1837-62 (P97/A/3/4). Banns books 1838-53 (P97/A/5/1), 1853- (P97/A/5/2).

<u>Elsewhere:-</u>
No printed transcript of registers except that from 1841.

Drayton-in-Hales in Staffordshire

At LRO:-

BTs 1681-1876 except 1756-9, 1797-1805, C 1873-6, B 1856-62; Hales bap included 1857-65, 1868

CHURCHWARDEN ACCOUNTS

1756-78 (2997/2/1), 1792-1810 (2997/2/2), 1810-7 including disbursement to the poor (2997/2/3), 1818-26 with similar disbursement (2997/2/4), 1826-33 with similar disbursement (2997/2/5).

VESTRY MINUTE BOOKS

1769-96 (2997/3/1), 1797-1818 (PL7/1-5), 1818-38 (2997/3/1a), 1838-67 (2997/3/2).

OVERSEERS OF THE POOR

Account Books 1768-1774 (2997/4/1), 1774-82 (2997/4/2). Vestry order book 1797-1818, Assessments 1825-6, Receipts & disbursements 1826-34 (PL7/1-5). Minute book 1834 (2997/9/1).

TITHE

Tithe map of the Staffordshire part of Drayton parish (SRRC - 'SRO' 2885/1-5, new reference will be P97....), Apportionment for this part of the parish, agreement 23 June 1838, confirmed 17 March 1843, copy attested 4 May 1843 (SRRC - 'SRO' 2885/1-5).

CHURCH

List of subscribers and account of receipts and disbursements, presentation of salver, set of pocket communion plate, silver tea service and purse of 100 sovereigns, presented to the Revd James Lee, Vicar of Market Drayton, 8 September 1836 (2997/6/1).

Allotment of seats, pews and sittings in Drayton in Hales Parish Church (printed, fragile) 1787 (4675/ch/4).

Plan of pews 'Old church' Market Drayton, n.d. C19 (2997/8/279).

DEEDS & ENDOWMENTS

Nearly 45 separate accessions in eight bundles. Few obvious Staffordshire references, except - Bargain and sale for creation of a rent charge (copy) 20th May 1622 concerning John Chetwood of Oakley, relating to a bread charity at Mucklestone (2997/10/40).

CHARITY

Account book 1836-67 (2997/10/61). Correspondence re Wright's charity (bread for the poor of Drayton and Tyrley) 1908-17 (2997/10/101), Stretch's legacy (for organists of Drayton & Madeley) 1902-12 (2997/10/

SHROP-SHIRE: DRAYTON-IN-HALES: BETTON

SHROPSHIRE: ADDERLEY

SJ 3600

MUCKLE -STONE: OAKLEY
Drayton Spinney

Shifford's Grange Farm

SHROPS: DRAYTON-IN-HALES: LONGSLOW

SHROPS: DRAYTON-IN-HALES: GREAT DRAYTON

SJ 3500

Shifford's Bridge

Clod Hall

Broomhall Grange

Tern (3)

BROOMHALL GRANGE

HALES. 1

SHROPS: DRAYTON-IN-HALES: LITTLE DRAYTON

Tern (1)

SJ 3400

old mill

The Hills

Tern (2)

Tyrley Castle Farm

Peatswood Hall

SHROPSHIRE: MORETON SAY

Walkmill Bridge

HALES

Victoria Mill

Pell Wall

HALES

SJ 3300

BLORE

SALISBURY HILL

Home Farm

TYRLEY HEATH

Meiklejohn Farm

Stoneyford

SHROPSHIRE: STOKE-UPON-TERN: SUTTON

mission church

Tyrley Wharf

The Fouralls

Upper Castle Farm

SJ 3200

SHROPSHIRE: STOKE-UPON-TERN: WOODSEAVES

The Hollings

SJ 6700

SJ 31006800

SJ 6900

Map of Drayton-in-Hales
C16 revised township boundaries/ estates after Twemlow (SHC 1945/6). Drayton tithe map at SRRC

64

107), April-Oct 1913 (2997/10/140-154).

Charity Commission Scheme for Adams Charity in the parishes of Adderley, Drayton in Hales, and Mucklestone. 12 March 1907 (4675/Cty/2).

BURIAL GROUND

Office copy, sentence of consecration - additional burial ground at Tyrley Heath 17 Nov. 1904 (2997/8/277). Faculty reserving to Lt. Col. Francis Twemlow or the owner for the time being of 'Peatswood' the consecration burial ground at Tyrley Heath as a private burial ground 28 Dec 1904 (2997/8/278).

PAROCHIAL CHURCH COUNCIL

'Canvass plan' for the parish of St Mary's, Market Drayton including Betton and Tyrley. Fund raising project. n.d. (?1960) (2997/11/13).

Eccleshall (Cotes Quarter, Aspley)

The badge of Eccleshall PC

Eccleshall

'One mile byond Pershall the river (Sow) reaches its first town, and what an historicial town it is.'

Bruce Braithwaite. Ripples of Time. 1987

Eccleshall was divided into quarters apparently as early as the later C12. Each quarter had church-wardens, separate overseers, and surveyor of highways. The parish was co-ordinated centrally for poor rates.

SEE ALSO pages 6, 10, 21, 26, 30, 34, 49, 54, 73-4, 78, 84, 93, 96, 100, 116, 106, 124, 125, 130, 142, 182, 186, 187, 208, 211, 214, 233

ECCLESHALL

Eccleshall CP 1866-. PC 1894-. Described as a District Council when the results from the PC elections were published in SA Dec 22 1894 p6. Minutes 1952-84, Accts 1909- at SRO.

LG. Stone RD 1894-1974. Stafford D(B) 1974-.

CED. Eccleshall 1889-2005, 2005-.

PLU. Stone 1838-1930. The meetings of Stone Union Board of Guardians and the Stone RD council ran one after another on Tuesday 19 March 1907; at the Stone RD meeting Eccleshall was constituted a special drainage area (SA March 23 1907 p5 col 1).

COTES QUARTER
ASPLEY TOWNSHIP
Aspley

Map of Cotes Quarter

Eccleshall CP. Cotes PW 1895-
LG. Eccleshall W 1974-2002, 2002-.
PLU. Cotes W by1910-.

Midley Pits

Eccleshall CP. Croxton PW 1895-. Croxton PD by1931.
LG. Eccleshall W 1974-2002, 2002-.
PLU. Croxton W by1910-.

CHATCULL TOWNSHIP
C.1

Eccleshall CP. Croxton PW 1895-. Wetwood PD by1931.
LG. Eccleshall W 1974-2002, 2002-.
PLU. Croxton W by1910-.

C.2

Eccleshall CP. Croxton PW 1895-. Croxton PD by1931.
LG. Eccleshall W 1974-2002, 2002-.

Eccleshall (Cotes Quarter, Cotes)

PLU. Croxton W by1910-.

COLD MEECE TOWNSHIP

PLU. Cotes W by1910-

Cold Meece

Eccleshall CP -1988. Cotes (called Slindon 1988-) PW 1895-. Swynnerton CP 1988-. Yarnfield PW 1988-
LG. Eccleshall W 1974-2002, 2002-.

Royal Ordnance Factory

Eccleshall CP. Cotes (called Slindon from 1988) PW 1895-
LG. Eccleshall W 1974-2002, 2002-.

COTES TOWNSHIP

PLU. Cotes W by1910-.

Cotes

Eccleshall CP -1988. Cotes PW 1895-1988. Standon CP 1988-.
LG. Eccleshall W 1974-2002, 2002-.

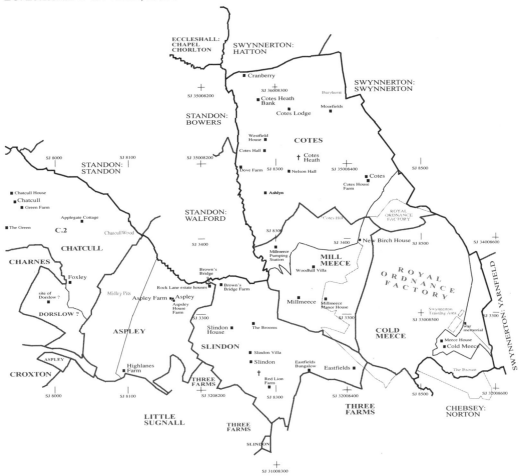

Eccleshall (Horsley Quarter, Pershall)

Royal Ordnance Factory

Eccleshall CP. Cotes (called Slindon from 1988) PW 1895-

LG. Eccleshall W 1974-2002, 2002-

MILL MEECE TOWNSHIP

PLU. Cotes W by1910-.

Mill Meece

Eccleshall CP. Cotes (called Slindon 1988-) PW 1895-

LG. Eccleshall W 1974-2002, 2002-.

Millmeece Pumping Station

Eccleshall CP -1988. Cotes PW 1895-1988. Standon CP 1988-.

LG. Eccleshall W 1974-2002, 2002-.

SLINDON TOWNSHIP

PLU. Stone 1838-1930. Cotes W by1910-.

Slindon

Eccleshall CP. Cotes (called Slindon 1988-) PW 1895-

LG. Eccleshall W 1974-2002, 2002-.

ECCLESHALL QUARTER
ECCLESHALL TOWNSHIP
Cat's Hill, E.1-3

Eccleshall CP. Cotes (called Slindon 1988-) PW 1895-

LG. Eccleshall W 1974-2002, 2002-

PLU. Cotes W by1910-.

Cotesfield, E.4-7

Eccleshall CP. Horsley PW 1895-

LG. Eccleshall W 1974-2002, 2002-

PLU. Eccleshall W by1910-.

Eccleshall

Eccleshall CP. Eccleshall PW 1895-

LG. Eccleshall W 1974-2002, 2002-

PLU. Eccleshall W by1910-.

HORSLEY QUARTER
HORSLEY TOWNSHIP
Cross Butts

Eccleshall CP. Eccleshall PW 1895-

LG. Eccleshall W 1974-2002, 2002-.

PLU. Eccleshall W by1910-.

Horsley

Eccleshall CP. Horsley PW 1895-

LG. Eccleshall W 1974-2002, 2002-.

PLU. Horsley W by1910-.

PERSHALL TOWNSHIP
P.1

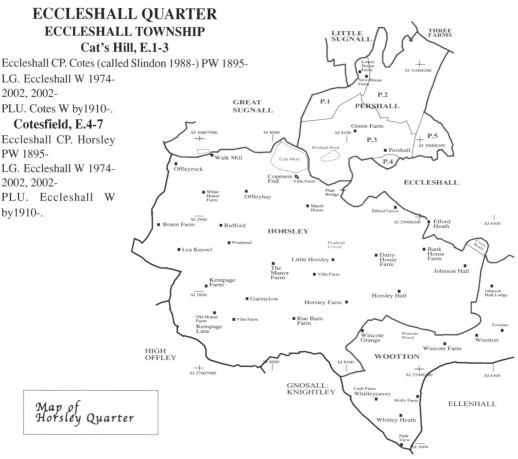

Map of Horsley Quarter

Eccleshall (Horsley Quarter, Wootton)

Map of Eccleshall Quarter

1895-.
LG. Eccleshall W 1974-2002, 2002-.
PLU. Cotes W by1910-.

P.3
Eccleshall CP. Horsley PW 1895-
LG. Eccleshall W 1974-2002, 2002-.
PLU. Horsley W by1910-.

P.4-5
Eccleshall CP. Eccleshall PW 1895-
LG. Eccleshall W 1974-2002, 2002-.
PLU. Eccleshall W by1910-.

WALTON TOWNSHIP
PLU. Horsley W by1910-.

Walton
Eccleshall CP. Horsley PW 1895-
LG. Eccleshall W 1974-2002, 2002-.

WOOTTON TOWNSHIP
Acton Hill
Eccleshall CP. Eccleshall PW 1895-
LG. Eccleshall W 1974-2002, 2002-.
PLU. Stone 1838-1930. Eccleshall W by1910-.

Wootton
Eccleshall CP. Horsley PW 1895-
LG. Eccleshall W 1974-2002, 2002-.
PLU. Horsley W by1910-.

Eccleshall CP. Croxton PW 1895-. Croxton PD by1931.
Eccleshall W 1974-2002, 2002-.
PLU. Croxton W by1910-.

P.2
Eccleshall CP. Cotes (called Slindon from 1988) PW

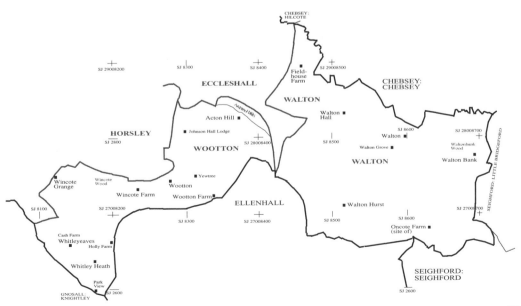

Eccleshall (Woodland Quarter, Charnes)

WOODLAND QUARTER
BROUGHTON TOWNSHIP
Broughton

Eccleshall CP. Croxton PW 1895-. Wetwood PD by1931.

LG. Eccleshall W 1974-2002, 2002-.

PLU. Croxton W by1910-.

CHARNES TOWNSHIP
Charnes

Eccleshall CP. Croxton PW 1895-. Wetwood PD by1931.

LG. Eccleshall W 1974-2002, 2002-.

PLU. Croxton W by1910-.

Whittington

Eccleshall CP. Croxton PW 1895-. Croxton PD by1931.

LG. Eccleshall W 1974-2002, 2002-.

PLU. Croxton W by1910-.

70

Eccleshall (Woodland Quarter, Great Sugnall)

CROXTON TOWNSHIP

PLU. Croxton W by1910-.

Croxton

Eccleshall CP. Croxton PW 1895-. Croxton PD by1931.

LG. Eccleshall W 1974-2002, 2002-.

Fairoak

Eccleshall CP. Croxton PW 1895-. Wetwood PD by1931.

LG. Eccleshall W 1974-2002, 2002-.

Jackson's Coppice

Eccleshall CP. Horsley PW 1895-.

LG. Eccleshall W 1974-2002, 2002-.

PLU. Horsley W by1910-.

Wood Farm

Eccleshall CP -1988. Croxton PW 1895-1988. Wetwood PD by1931. Adbaston CP 1988-.

LG. Woodseaves W 1974-2002. Eccleshall W 2002-.

CED. Eccleshall 1889-1988. Gnosall 1988-2005. Eccleshall 2005-.

GERRARD'S BROMLEY TOWNSHIP

PLU. Croxton W by1910-.

G.B.1

Eccleshall CP. Croxton PW 1895-. Wetwood PD by1931.

LG. Eccleshall W 1974-2002, 2002-.

G.B.2

Eccleshall CP. Croxton PW 1895-. Croxton PD by1931.

LG. Eccleshall W 1974-2002, 2002-.

GREAT SUGNALL TOWNSHIP

Great Sugnall

Eccleshall CP. Croxton PW 1895-

LG. Eccleshall W 1974-2002, 2002-.

PLU. Croxton W by1910-.

Sugnall Park

Eccleshall CP. Horsley PW 1895-

LG. Eccleshall W 1974-2002, 2002-.

PLU. Horsley W by1910-.

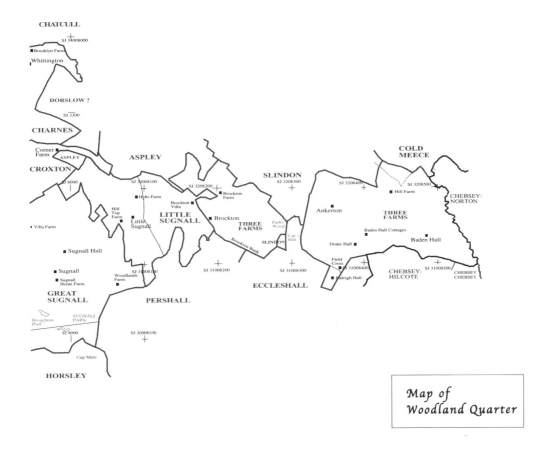

Map of Woodland Quarter

Eccleshall (Chorlton Chapelry, Radwood)

PLU. Newcastle-u-Lyme 1838-1930. Chorlton W by1910.

CHAPEL CHORLTON TOWNSHIP
Chapel Chorlton
Chapel and Hill Chorlton CP 1866-.

HILL CHORLTON TOWNSHIP
Berry Hill
Chapel and Hill Chorlton CP 1866-1984. Maer CP 1984- (unofficially styled Maer and Aston 1996-).

LITTLE SUGNALL
Brockton Villa
Eccleshall CP. Cotes (called Slindon 1988-) PW 1895-
LG. Eccleshall W 1974-2002, 2002-.
PLU. Cotes W by1910-.

Little Sugnall
Eccleshall CP. Croxton PW 1895-. Croxton PD by1931.
LG. Eccleshall W 1974-2002, 2002-.
PLU. Croxton W by1910-.

PODMORE TOWNSHIP
Podmore
Eccleshall CP. Croxton PW 1895-. Wetwood PD by1931.
LG. Eccleshall W 1974-2002, 2002-.
PLU. Croxton W by1910-

THREE FARMS TOWNSHIP
Raleigh Hall
Eccleshall CP. Eccleshall PW 1895-
Eccleshall W 1974-2002, 2002-.
PLU. Eccleshall W by1910-.

Three Farms
Eccleshall CP. Cotes (called Slindon 1988-) PW 1895-
LG. Eccleshall W 1974-2002, 2002-.
PLU. Cotes W by1910-.

CHORLTON CHAPELRY
Chapel and Hill Chorlton CP 1866-. PC from 1894.
LG. Newcastle-u-Lyme RD 1894-1974, D(B) 1974-.
No. 20 W Feb 1973-4. No. 21 W Feb 1974-9. Whitmore W 1979-2002. Loggerheads & Whitmore W 2002-
CED. Keele 1889-1934. Madeley 1934-81. Newcastle Rural 1981-2005, 2005-.

Hill Chorlton
Chapel and Hill Chorlton CP 1866-.
Maerfield
Chapel and Hill Chorlton CP 1866-1984. Maer 1984- (unofficially styled Maer and Aston CP 1996-).

RADWOOD 'TOWNSHIP'
Radwood Copse
Chapel and Hill Chorlton CP 1866-1932. Maer CP 1932-84. Madeley CP 1984-.
Radwood Hall Farm
Chapel and Hill Chorlton CP 1866-1932. Maer CP 1932-84. Whitmore CP 1984-.

Peculiar probate jurisdictions

Parishes not under the jurisdiction of the bishop or archdeacon, but of the dean or chapter of a cathedral, were called Peculiars. Eccleshall was one. Peculiars operated their own courts, known as peculiar courts. Testators in peculiar parishes had their wills proved there and not at the archdeaconry or consistory courts.

The court of the Dean of Lichfield Cathedral had jurisdiction over **Adbaston** AP.

The court of the Prebendary of **Colwich** in the Chapter of Lichfield Cathedral had jurisdiction over Colwich AP (including Fradswell). The court of the Prebendary of **Eccleshall** in the Cathedral Chapter had jurisdiction over Eccleshall AP (including Chorlton chapelry). The court of the Prebendary of Offley and Flixton in the Cathedral Chapter had jurisdiction over **High Offley** AP. From January 12 1858 (under the Court of Probate Act 1857) the business of Peculiar and Consistory Courts was transferred to the newly-created civil District Probate Registry courts.

Both Peculiar and Consistory Court records are held at LRO, where the only differences are Peculiar wills start later than Ordinary wills and the indexing is slightly different. For the Peculiar researcher there are two separate index books - Peculiar Calendars A-J, 1510-1858, and Peculiar Calendars K-Z 1510-1858, with a parish index aid 'Probate Place Name Index: Peculiars' (PPNI:P); it is split into two parts within one book to accommodate the two Calendar books.

The PPNI:P shows just how many wills relate to each peculiar:-

Peculiar	Total wills for 1510-1858	Earliest surviving will	Additional info
Adbaston	217 +?39	Elizabeth Salt Mar 25 1595	
Colwich	451 +?41 (mindful of an Haywood in Bakewell, Derbys)	Humprey Wright Nov 26 1614	Fradswell Probate inventories 1659-1759 transcribed by Janice V. Cox (WSL TS. 81).
Eccleshall	1276 +?49 +?179 for Whittington, but these are most likely to be mostly Whittington near Lichfield	Lettice Gervice or Jerves Aug 5 1603 (administration papers only), George Broughton Oct 10 1606 (70, vol 2)	
High Offley	138 +?39	Thomas Cherrington Oct 21 1662	

And the PPNI:P shows some wills catalogued in the Peculiar Calendars which relate to Ordinary parishes:-

Parish	No. of wills
Ashley	1
Audley	1
Burslem	1
Colton	7
Drayton	3
Gayton	1
Keele	1
Madeley (unspecified)	1
Mucklestone	1
Newcastle-u-Lyme	1

Eccleshall

Sandon	1
Stafford	86
Stoke-on-Trent	3
Stoke, Stoke Hall (unspecified)	2
Stone	5
Stowe	26 for Hixon, but could be Colwich?
Swynnerton	1
Weston-on-Trent (unspecified)	2
Wolstanton	2 +?9

There were other sorts of peculiar probate court, too. For instance, those of Royal Free Chapels (but there are none in Pirehill) and some manorial courts, for instance Tyrley (SRO 828; MF32).

Procession to village fete below Granny! Cartwrights Cottage (since demolished) at corner to Ellenhall Park 1961. Courtesy of the Heath family

Ellenhall

'Modernism has had but little welcome here, and the hand of time has fallen gently, bestowing a pleasing mellowness on the stonework cottages that fit so naturally with the surroundings.'

Goronwy Harnaman. Six Towns Magazine. August 1965

SEE ALSO pages 51, 75-79, 96, 100, 129, 208, 214, 233

ELLENHALL TOWNSHIP

Ellenhall CP 1866-. Option to form a PC in 1894 (with a population between 100 and 300). But the parish meeting in late 1894 decided unanimously against forming one; it voted Rev WH Stamper chairman of parish meetings for the coming year (SA Dec 8 1894 p6). There were parish meetings -?1950s; parish meetings revived c1985-.

LG. Stafford RD 1894-1974, D(B) 1974- Gnosall W 1974-2002, Seighford W 2002-

CED. Stafford Rural 1889-1911. Stafford Rural West Sept 1911-34. Gnosall 1934-73. Stafford Rural No. 1 1973-81. Gnosall 1981-2005. Gnosall & Doxey 2005-

PLU. Stafford 1836-1930. Ellenhall W by1910.

Earliest surviving proved wills

To help someone interested in parish history gage the time-scale and volume of the early wills relating to a parish, listed below are the earliest surviving Pirehill wills which were proved at the Consistory Court of Lichfield. Compiling the list was difficult due to a confusing system of indexing at LRO. For the topographer rather than the genealogist (who would look no further than the Consistory

Ellenhall

Map of Ellenhall

Court Calendars) the first port of call is the Probate Place Name Indexes. These are really the indexes to CCCs, themselves indexes to wills. But using either type of index is somewhat problematic.

<u>Consistory Court Calendars</u>
CCCs cover 1472-1860, and span a series of 10 volumes
Calendars 1 & 2 1472-1650
Calendars 3 1650-1700
Calendars 4 & 5 1700-1750
Calendars 6 & 7 1751-1800
Calendars 8 & 9 1801-1840
Calendars 10 1841-1858

Calendars 1 & 2 1472-1650, which I was interested in, is in two parts, and stretches, annoyingly, over three books. Book 1 Part 1 begins with 82 pages of surnames beginning with 'A', laid out, chronologically and then alphabetically, like this:-

year of will proved day/month	testator's name	parish	whether ad(ministration) or inv(entory) papers survive, or designation
1523/4 Mar 22	Eliz. Alsoppe	Audley	
1556 May 7	✓ Richard Ansell	Trentham	ad
1556 May 7	✓ John Ashe	Sandon	
1611/2 Feb 15	✓ Thomas Abnell	Edgmond	inv
1649 July 4	✓ James Abnett	Kinver	vol 7 ii

'B' surnames begin on p91 (page numbers appear in pencil on top left and right respectively); with 'C' on p376; and so on up to 'M' on p1286. 'N' surnames begin Part 2 Book 2 (2A), with page numbering starting again; 'Swanne' begins Part 2 Book 3 (2B), with page numbers continuing, so that 'Y' begins on p933. Calendars 1 & 2 have a red or black (photocopy) tick before the testators name which indicate that the will survives: Note, above, the will of the imaginary Eliz. Alsoppe of Audley is now missing.

Probate Place Name Indexes

So back to the PPNI and cross-referencing to CCCs. Each CCCs volume has its corresponding PPNI. These list wills by diocesan ancient parish alphabetically, irrespective of county. To accommodate Calendars 1 & 2 in two parts (and three books!) the corresponding PPNI CALENDARS 1 & 2 1472-1650 has to contain two separate A-Z parish lists (in fact, it has two more lists for other places in parishes which have had specific reference in a will). So we turn to the first parish list, or headed, VOLUME 1 1472-1650 A-M: PARISHES WITHIN THE DIOCESE and find Ellenhall. Just for example it will look something like this:-

This tells that we have indeed Ellenhall, Staffs and not Ellenhall, Shrops (if there was such a place).

These are other places in Ellenhall parish, mentioned specifically in a will: if you are interested in one, you should look further on in the Parish Index under the section entitled VOLUME 1 1472-1650 A-M: LOCATIONS (NOT PARISHES) IN THE DIOCESE.

ELLENHALL, STAFFS
SEE ALSO BROAD HEATH, LAWNHEAD, SEGGERSLEY

This is the main body of Ellenhall wills, and wills which only mention Ellenhall.

66.4, 117.8, 154.16, 337.2, 519.9, 702.13, 1086.7, 1249.21

This is a page number in Part 1 Book 1 of CCCs (1472-1650), and because you know this, you know the surnames of the testators will be 'A' to 'M'.

This is the line on that page where the Ellenhall reference can be found.

Now we turn to the second parish list with the heading VOLUME 2 1472-1650 N-Z: PARISHES WITHIN THE DIOCESE and find Ellenhall again, for example:-

This is another place in Ellenhall parish, mentioned specifically in a will, and it appears further on under the heading entitled (you've guessed it!) VOLUME 2 1472-1650 N-Z: LOCATIONS (NOT PARISHES) IN THE DIOCESE.

ELLENHALL
SEE ALSO SPURLEY BROOK

10.5, 97.18, 143.13, 889.17

This is a page number in Part 2 Book 3 (2B), and because you know this, you know the surnames of the testators will be 'Swanne' to 'Z'.

However, with later CCCs and their corresponding PPNIs the system is slightly different. PPNI of Calendars 3 1650-1700 has no separate section for locations (not parishes) in the diocese. Whilst Calendars 4 & 5 onwards are broken into separate parts based on time periods.

Due to difficult handwriting there are mistakes in translation - and many, judging from corrections. Often a will does not designate the testators' home to a parish (or even a parish to a county), so there is ambiguity whether Wrinehill, Betley, Staffs, or Wrinehill, Wrinehill, or Wrinehill, Wybunbury, both Ches is being referred to; hence, four wills could be added to Betley's total; sometimes the will does not state any home for the testator.

Adbaston, Colwich, Eccleshall, High Offley have few wills because they were all Peculiars. Abbots

Ellenhall

Bromley (Bagots Bromley, a separate manor) and Barlaston wills only appear from 1541 and 1581, respectively, because before then wills were proved in their respective manorial courts of Burton Abbey, and Lord Stafford.

The total number of wills appear after the parish heading.

Parish	1472-1650	1651-1700	1701-1725	1726-1750	1751-1775	1776-1800	Earliest surviving will
Abbots Bromley	285	134	72	85	51	50	Thomas Preson of Bagots Bromley July7 1535. William Dickenson Oct 19 1541. Ellen Alcoke Oct 19 1541. Roger Hyre Oct 19 1541.
Adbaston	2+?1	0	1	1+?1	0	2+?2	John Parcar 1536.
Ashley	66	35	23	23	6	10	John Haley May 9 1541.
Audley	318	189	78	94	34	41	Alice Abnett Oct 22 1524 (lost), Elizabeth Snede Nov 22 1535.
Barlaston	76+?2	24	15	18	15	5	William Amberye July 15 1581.
Betley	63+?4	66	35	31	25	21	Alice Warner April 30 1538.
Biddulph	151	70	41	39	16	28	John Bann the elder May 12 1533.
Blithfield	56+?5	47	25	26	10+?2	14	Lewis Meverell (Gent) July 20 1532.
Burslem	104	73	90	71	49	78	Ralph Addams Jan 26 1534.
Chebsey	94	27	24	28	8	16	William Shaw Oct 7 1533/4.
Colton	59	54	22	34	12	12	Hugh Averill March 2 1551/2.
Colwich	4+?7	0	0	1	1	0	John Edwards July 25 1549.
Colwich or Stowe	7	1	4	0	0	1	
Creswell	4	4	2	4	2	0	William Minors Aug 13 1573.
Drayton-in-Hales	?	?	?	?	1	?	these relate probably to Shrops: Richard Bramley Feb 11 1532/3 (lost). Thomas Lummans May 20 1533.
Eccleshall	10	2+?1	0	5	3+?3	4	Margaret Bushoppe Sept 10 1579.
Ellenhall	43	31	13	9	8	8	Humphrey Huntbach Feb 7 1540/1.
Gayton	55	28	13	14	8	11	James Aspre Jan 26 1534/5.
High Offley	?2	1	1	2+?1	0	0	
Ingestre	32	25	6	6	3	8	John Lyon Oct 1553.
Keele	89	48	28	25	15	7	John Symson July 31 1536 (lost), possibly Keele - Roger Burgess April 1537.
Madeley	149	69	35	46	26	18	John Malpas May 12 1533.
Maer	63	32	27*	21	12	9	Thomas Cocke or Corke July 2 1532.
Marston 'parish' (unspecified Derbys, Staffs or Shrops)	36	?	?	?	?	?	William Prynce Nov 17 1536.
Marston 'place' (near Stafford)	18	1	0	0	2	0	William Coke Oct 7 1557.
Milwich	(88+?1	43	24	37	9	19	Isabell Alyn Oct 24 1534.

Parish	1472-1650	1651-1700	1701-1725	1726-1750	1751-1775	1776-1800	Earliest surviving will
Mucklestone (excluding Woore)	207+?2	123+?1	58	55+?2	48+?1	22	Margery Barne Feb 2 1532/3.
Newcastle-u-Lyme	188	209	147	168	87	119	John Pateson May 15 1536.
Norton (unspecified, Staffs)	4	?	?	?	?	?	
Norton (unspecified, Staffs or Shrops)	59	21	?	?	?	?	
Norton-in-the-Moors	145	56	40	35	22	15	Robert Grene April 1532.
Ranton	62	28	25	12	8	11	John Unton June 26 1532 (lost). Thomas Baylie Oct 27 1533.
Sandon	64	16	20	19	17	9	John Ashe May 7 1556.
Seighford	163+?2	79	40	39	33+?1	17	Margery Cotten Feb 7 1533/4.
Stafford St Mary	380+?1	287	193	221	139	125+?3	Joan Allehell Oct 8 1556.
Standon	64	39	25	19	8	10	Richard Lovatt Jan 8 1532/3.
Stoke-upon-Trent	449+?1		113		108+?7		Thomas Dawson April 1532
		202+?3		148+?28		176+?28	(lost).
Stone	605+?2		166+?1		123		John Dekyn 1524 (lost).
		299+?2		220+?5		133	George Lauder of Hilderstone 1529.
Stowe	162+?1	67+?1	33	43	16	16	Richard Mason April 24 1532.
Swynnerton	140	62+?1	31+?1	36+?1	22+?1	15	John Swinnerton 1521 (lost). Thomas Walton Sept 25 1538.
Tixall	37	12	6	10	6	3	John Hatton April 18 1554.
Trentham	185+?80		67+?23		35+?11		John Colyer 1537.
		95+?36		44+?25		33+?13	
Weston-on-Trent	14	1	0	0	0	2	George Boghey Nov 3 1540.
Weston-upon-Trent (unspecified, Staffs or Derbys)	81	46	33	27	23	18	Alice & Hugh Gretwych Oct 25 1536.
Weston (unspecified)	?	13	20	13	7	6	
Whitmore	48	23	12	13	7	8	Roger Beche Nov 26 1532.
Wolstanton	402	174	95	70	48	56+?2	William Salmon 1530 (lost). Thomas Colclozghe July 2 1532.
Worston	2	1	0	1	0	0	Robert Dean March 16 1611/12.
Yarlet	1	2	0	0	0	0	Thomas Allett June 22 1637.

For more guidance on wills, such as probate (diocesan, peculiar, civil) courts, court procedures, the nature of a will, letters of administration, administration bonds, inventories, registers of wills, probate act books, bishops' registers, and consistory court cause records see Staffordshire and Stoke-on-Trent Archive Service's 'Family History Leaflet No. 9' (2004) which has a further reading list.

* some unspecified

Gayton church. By J. Buckler 1841. SV. IV. 214a. Courtesy of Trustees of WSL

Gayton

'Gayton is a quiet village which had the essentials of life - a church, an inn and a mill.'

Joan P Alcock. Discovering Staffordshire.1973

In 1974 parish councillor John Sherratt feared that the village was dying. There was a lack of people to warrant a proper bus service and the lack of a sewerage system meant lack of new housing; Gayton, he claimed, had once been a thriving community (SN Nov 18 2004 p8).
PLU. Stafford 1836-1930.
SEE ALSO pages 6, 51, 78, 81-82, 130, 142, 208, 214

GAYTON TOWNSHIP
Gayton

Gayton CP 1866-. With a population between 100 and 300 Gayton was entitled to an Order to form a PC without consent of the CC. At the late 1894 Gayton parish meeting 'A proposition was then made that the affairs of the parish be conducted by a meeting, and this was carried. A rider was then proposed that there should be a parish council, but this was lost. No poll was asked for' (SA Dec 8 1894 p6). Parish meeting minutes 1894-1943 (D4562), 1959-71, 1969-73 at SRO. Weston-with-Gayton PC (a pg) June 1 1973-9. Weston-with-Gayton-with-Fradswell PC (a pg) 1979-2003. Weston-with-Gayton PC (a pg) 2003-.
LG. Stafford RD 1894-1974, D(B) 1974-. Chartley W

1974-2002, 2002-.
CED. Stafford Rural 1889-1911. Stafford Rural East Sept 1911-34. Stafford Rural 1934-73. Stafford Rural No. 2 1973-81. Stafford Trent Valley 1981-2005, 2005-
Parkside Lane

Gayton CP 1866-1988. Weston-with-Gayton PC (a pg) June 1 1973-9. Weston-with-Gayton-with-Fradswell PC (a pg) 1979-88. Stowe CP 1988-.
LG. Stafford RD 1894-1974, D(B) 1974-. Chartley W 1974-2002, 2002-.
CED. Stafford Rural 1889-1911. Stafford Rural East Sept 1911-34. Stafford Rural 1934-73. Stafford Rural No. 2 1973-81. Stafford Trent Valley 1981-2005, 2005-
.

The usefulness of Tithe maps post-commutation, and indexices to the Staffordshire Advertiser

It was inevitable as the largest-scaled maps of their day tithe maps would be used for land purchase as well as tithe commutation. In SA Feb 16 1867 p3 col 3 is a Notice of exchange of lands between Dudley, Earl of Harrowby with Sewallis-Edward Shirley, Earl of Ferrers and Viscount Tamworth, and Niven Ralston, receiver (of Pirehill House), together with the tithe-rent charges, witnessed 31 Jan 1867, which uses tithe maps to identify the property involved.

> LAND LORD HARROWBY is interested in
> .... in **Gayton** (numbers relate to tithe map):- 73, 75, 77, 67, 69, 84, 91, 95, 97, 103-05, 133-37, 139, 174.
> ... in **Stowe**:- 2095, 2099, 2100, 2109, 2112-19, 2122-23, 2126-27, 2136, 2145-49, 2152-53, 2157, 2163, 2166, 2167, 2452-53, 2456, 2460-61, 2462-63, 2527-32, 2556-59.
> LAND EARL FERRERS is interested in
> .... in **Gayton**:- 6-8, 12, 15-18, 20, 23, 24, 26, 31A, 33A, 37, 39B, 270-71, 307-11, 313A, 314-16, 318-22, 324, 326, 328, 329-32, 332A, 333, 337, 341-42, 344, 346-52, 364, 367-71, 375, 377, 381-2, 384, 386-89, 391-96, 398B, 399, 401, 403, 405-08, 410, 412-13, 415-16, 418, 420, 422, 429, 430-31.
> .... in **Weston**:- 47, 47A, 48, 50-52, 161c, 161e, w162.

Using Gayton (1850) and Stowe tithe maps and Chartley Castle estate sale catalogue (1904) (WSL 3301/3) I found the fields still in the hands of the respective parties; so no exchange had taken place. Incidentally, the Notice is not indexed in The Staffordshire Advertiser Card Index 1848-79; a small oversight perhaps considering that project's magnitude!

The value of old newspapers as a source for local history was noted by Prof WG Hoskins (see Audley chapter) in Local History in England (1959) pp28-30. He went on to note in that work 'one of the greatest obstacles to their use is the lack of any index to their contents, and to search them blindly is

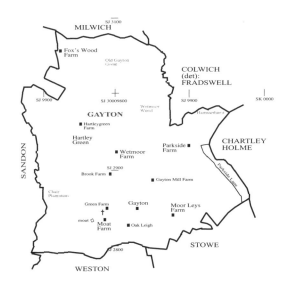

MILWICH
SJ 3100

Fox's Wood Farm

Old Gayton Goose

COLWICH (det): FRADSWELL

SJ 9900

SJ 30009800

Wetmoor Wood

SJ 9900

SK 0000

GAYTON

Hartleygreen Farm

Hartley Green

Wetmoor Farm

Parkside Farm

CHARTLEY HOLME

SANDON

SJ 2900

Brook Farm

Gayton Mill Farm

Parkside Lane

Chair Plantation

Green Farm

Gayton

Moor Leys Farm

moat

Moat Farm

Oak Leigh

STOWE

2800

WESTON

Map of Gayton

81

Gayton

a formidable task'pp162-3. When the Government's Manpower Services Commission programme agreed to fund staff to build an SA index, VCH editor, Michael Greenslade, seized the chance. He set up and supervised the scheme. It would be a great aid to future volumes in the VCH series and local history research, generally. Between 1985-88 staff (sets of two, in six-monthly spells) produced cards filling 30 box trays, which are in the Trustees Room at the WSL. They used a list of Master Headings of subjects to be indexed, compiled by Michael, himself drawing on a list given in Local History in England pp162-3. The period from the late 1840s was chosen because prior to then SA was mainly concerned with national news. The starting date 1848 was chosen because RS Hampson had already produced an Index for 1847. A perfatory note to Hampson's index (in WSL) by DG Stuart says he began it in connection with the Local History Certificate at Keele University 1973. When funding ended the staff had reached the year 1879 (VCH vol 14 pxiii, addition info from M Greenslade) (Hampson's 1847 Index book is placed by the 1848-79 Index chest of boxes). In addition, Ian Bailey has indexed SA 1840-69 (WSL Misc 360), 1870-84 (WSL 360 (ii)), 1910-19 (Alsager Lib, Ches) for **Audley**, **Balterley**, **Betley** and **Wolstanton** (SW townships only) parishes; somebody else has indexed references to C19 **Stafford** (WSL CB Stafford/165); and someone else has assembled cuttings regarding the changing face of Stafford town (WSL CB Stafford/ 149). There is an index to births, marriages and deaths in the SA1795-1820 (SHC 1968), and another 1821-1840 (SHC 1986, facsimile reproduction of indexes in WSL).

Catching pewits at Shebdon Pool in the later C17. SV. IV. 324 b. Courtesy of Trustees of WSL

High Offley

'When approached from the W it has the appearance of a medieval hill town with the church a landmark for several miles around.'

Michael Raven. Staffordshire and the Black Country. 1988

In the later C18 there appear to have been the townships of High Offley (with its own overseer), and Outparts of the parish (for which the churchwarden served as overseer) (D4035/2/1). This may be identifiable with Pitt's Woodseaves township (Pitt 1817). The boundary of Outparts is uncertain. In 1666 in the Staffs Hearth Tax assessment there is no mention of a second township/ constablewick. John Yeomans is the only overseer (SHC 1921 p121).

PLU. Newport 1836-1930. High Offley W by1894-.

SEE ALSO pages 6, 26, 50, 73-4, 84, 90, 94, 96, 100, 106, 124, 131, 208, 214, 233

HIGH OFFLEY/ OUTPARTS
TOWNSHIPS
High Offley

High Offley CP 1866-. PC ?1894-
LG. Gnosall RD 1894-1934. High Offley W 1894-.
Stafford RD 1934-74, D(B) 1974-. Woodseaves W 1974-2002. Gnosall & Woodseaves W 2002-.
CED. Eccleshall 1889-1911. Gnosall Sept 1911-73. Stafford Rural No. 1 1973-81. Gnosall 1981-2005. Gnosall 2005-.

Lonco Brook (1)

High Offley CP 1866-1934. Adbaston CP 1934-.
LG. Gnosall RD 1894-1934. High Offley W 1894-.
Stafford RD 1934-74, D(B) 1974-. Woodseaves W 1974-2002. Eccleshall W 2002-.
CED. Eccleshall 1889-1911. Gnosall Sept 1911-73. Stone Rural 1973-81. Gnosall 1981-2005. Eccleshall 2005-

Lonco Brook (2)

Adbaston AP by1855-, CP 1866-.
LG. Gnosall RD 1894-1934. High Offley W 1894-.
Stafford RD 1934-74, D(B) 1974-. Woodseaves W 1974-2002. Eccleshall W 2002-.
CED. Eccleshall 1889-1911. Gnosall Sept 1911-73. Stone Rural 1973-81. Gnosall 1981-2005. Eccleshall 2005-

Lonco Brook (3)

High Offley CP 1866-1934. Adbaston CP 1934-.
LG. Gnosall RD 1894-1934. High Offley W 1894-.
Stafford RD 1934-74, D(B) 1974-. Woodseaves W 1974-2002. Eccleshall W 2002-.
CED. Eccleshall 1889-1911. Gnosall Sept 1911-73. Stone Rural 1973-81. Gnosall 1981-2005. Eccleshall 2005-

Lonco Brook (5)

Adbaston AP by1889-, CP 1866-.
LG. Gnosall RD 1894-1934. High Offley W 1894-.
Stafford RD 1934-74, D(B) 1974-. Woodseaves W 1974-2002. Eccleshall W 2002-.

High Offley

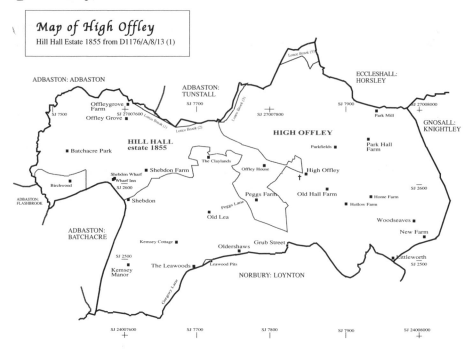

Map of High Offley
Hill Hall Estate 1855 from D1176/A/8/13 (1)

CED. Eccleshall 1889-1911. Gnosall Sept 1911-73.   Stone Rural 1973-81. Gnosall 1981-2005. Eccleshall 2005-

Bell ringing

High Offley has a list of persons appointed for ringing the parish church bells 1836 (D4035/1/19). Names of ringers 1702 appear in **Keele** Parish Book (D3514/2/1). GUNPOWDER TREASON failure was a favourite occasion for bell ringing in many parishes, nationally (Tate), and in Pirehill: **Standon** overseers' accounts (D1026/2/2) show ringers paid in 1738, 1741, 1743-5 for ringing on Nov 5. Churchwarden's accounts for **High Offley** show ringers paid for Nov 5 between 1789-99, 1804-15, 1824-7, 1831, '33-34, '52, '55, '58, '61 (D4035/2/1); at **Milwich** for 1673 (D917/5/1); at Seighford 1809-11, 1813-4, 1852(D731/11); at **Weston-on-Trent** for 1827 (D5328/2/1). CHRISTMAS was another time for bell ringing as the Parish Book of **Keele**, and **Betley** churchwarden's accounts show, for 1721 and 1787. ON OTHER OCCASIONS bells were rung at Betley for his 'Majesty's recovery' 1789, and the King's coronation day Sept 22 1801, and at **Weston-on-Trent** for the Duke of York's funeral 1827 (D5328/2/1). At **Stone** the rising bell was rung on week days at 6.00am, on Sundays at 7.00am, after which the day of the month was tolled. Also at Stone the parson's bell was rung on Sundays at 1.00pm for ten minutes, perhaps for when the parson distributed loaves of bread to the poor (RHPS p66). The LEGACY of Samuel Stretch (d1804) of Shropshire, endowed a bell to be rung at **Madeley** each evening to aid travellers; the custom ceased in the 1970s (Staffordshire Encyclopaedia) (D3412/2/25). The CURFEW bell tolled from the Monday after old Michaelmas to Shrove Tuesday at **Abbots Bromley** (GNHSS p17) (SCSF p160); at 8 o' clock every night until 1939 at **Audley** (AHJ 1995 p112); in the C19 at **Eccleshall** (SCSF p161); each night from Lady day to Michaelmas at 8.00pm, and for six months an hour earlier, at **Stone** (RHPS p66); to within a few years of 1886 at **Stowe** (NSFCT 1886 p39).

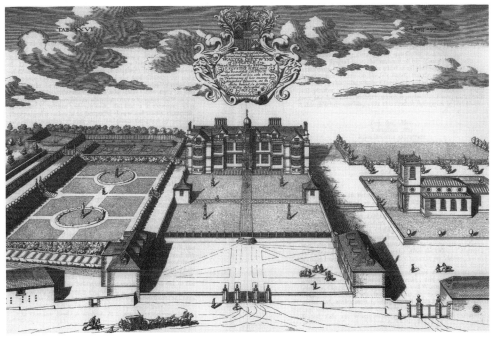

Ingestre Hall in the 17th Century from Plot's History of Staffordshire, 1686

Ingestre

'Near to Hopton, on the same side of Trent, lyeth Ingestre, which Hugo held of Rob. de Stafford, 20 Conq., but whether he were paternall ancester to ye Muttons, who not long after possest it, is hard to be determined.'

Walter Chetwynd. History of Pirehill Hundred. 1679

PLU. Stafford 1836-1930. Ingestre W by1910.
SEE ALSO pages 30, 51, 54, 61, 78, 86, 124, 131, 208

INGESTRE TOWNSHIP
Deer Park Farm

Hopton & Coton T in Stafford AP by1839-66, CP 1866-, PC Nov 1951-.
LG. Stafford RD 1894-1974, D(B) 1974-. Beaconside W 1974-2002. Milton W 2002-.
CED. Stafford Rural 1889-1911. Stafford Rural East Sept 1911-34. Stafford Rural 1934-73. Stafford Rural No. 2 1973-81. Stafford Trent Valley 1981-2005, 2005-
PLU. Stafford 1836-1930. Hopton & Coton W by1910.

Ingestre

Ingestre CP 1866-. With a population between 100 and 300 Ingestre was entitled to an Order to form a PC without consent of the CC. It is not known whether it decided to become a PC in late 1894; nor is a parish meeting recorded then; nor is any PC known of to 1979. Ingestre with Tixall PC (a pg) 1979-. Minutes 1979- at SRO. Ingestre PW 1979-
LG. Stafford RD 1894-1974, D(B) 1974-. Milford W 1974-2002, 2002-.
CED. Stafford Rural 1889-1911. Stafford Rural East Sept 1911-34. Stafford Rural 1934-73. Stafford Rural No. 2 1973-81. Stafford Trent Valley 1981-2005, 2005-.

'Ingestre Heath'

Salt & Enson T in Stafford AP by1802~39-66, CP 1866-, PC 1894-.
LG. Stafford RD 1894-1974, D(B) 1974-. Beaconside

Ingestre

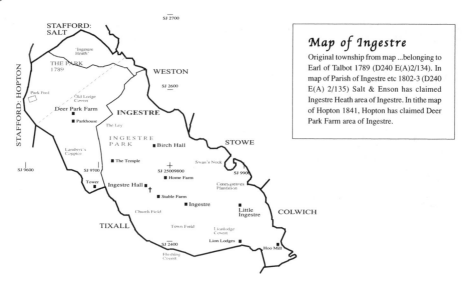

STAFFORD: SALT

'Ingestre Heath'

THE PARK 1789

WESTON

SJ 2700

SJ 2600

STAFFORD: HOPTON

Park Pool

Old Lodge Covert

Deer Park Farm

■ Parkhouse

INGESTRE

The Ley

INGESTRE PARK

■ Birch Hall

STOWE

Lambert's Coppice

SJ 9600

SJ 9700

■ The Temple

Swan's Nook

SJ 25009800

■ Home Farm

SJ 9900

Tower

Ingestre Hall ■

■ Stable Farm

Conleygreaves Plantation

■ Ingestre

Little Ingestre

COLWICH

Church Field

TIXALL

Town Field

Lionlodge Covert

SJ 2400

Lion Lodges ■

Hoo Mill

Flushing Covert

> **Map of Ingestre**
> Original township from map ...belonging to Earl of Talbot 1789 (D240 E(A)2/134). In map of Parish of Ingestre etc 1802-3 (D240 E(A) 2/135) Salt & Enson has claimed Ingestre Heath area of Ingestre. In tithe map of Hopton 1841, Hopton has claimed Deer Park Farm area of Ingestre.

W 1974-2002. Chartley W 2002-.
CED. Stafford Rural 1889-1911. Stafford Rural East

Sept 1911-34. Stafford Rural 1934-73. Stafford Rural No. 2 1973-81. Stafford Trent Valley 1981-2005, 2005-

Ambiguity concerning the probate records of Stafford's satellite prebendal estates and subordinate parishes

The dean of Lichfield diocese exercised peculiar jurisdiction over Stafford, St Mary's, and wills would have been proved in his peculiar court. So all wills from **Creswell**, **Ingestre** and **Tixall**, a chantry chapel and royal free chapels, respectively, subordinate to St Mary's, would have been proved there, too. However, probate records of peculiar courts within Lichfield diocese do not start until the 1600s and the dean's jurisdiction over St Mary's lapsed at the dissolution of St Mary's collegiate church (1548). So the Consistory Court of Lichfield proved Creswell, Ingestre and Tixall wills, after all, and they are at LRO beginning, like everywhere else, from 1521. The wills of extra-parochial places **Tillington**, **Yarlet** and **Worston**, presumably nominally in St Mary's parish, were also proved at the Consistory Court of Lichfield, and are in the main sequence of wills under St Mary's parish at LRO (VCH vol 6 p238).

Graduation Day at the University of Keele, 1999

Keele

'I am in such beauty that I am drawn like a double tooth. My beauty indeed entails some inconvenience, for people flock from all quarters to see the red Rhododendrons which are a perfect conflagration (I really never saw a more *splendid* sight) and I am headed by beards and crinolines on every gravel walk.'

Ralph Sneyd to HW Vincent 9 May 1862 (S RS/HWV. 432)

PLU. Newcastle-u-Lyme 1838-1930. Keele W by1910-.

Keele

KEELE TOWNSHIP
Bogs Cottages
Keele CP 1866-1932. PC from 1894. Newcastle unparished 1932-?1984. Keele CP ?1984-
LG. Newcastle-u-Lyme RD 1894-1932, MB 1932-74, D(B) 1974-. No. 12 W 1932-79. Silverdale W 1979-?84. Keele W ?1984-2002, 2002-
CED. Keele 1889-1934. Newcastle No. 1 1934-81. Keele & Silverdale 1981-2005. Keele & Westlands 2005-.

Bogs Wood
Keele CP 1866-1932. Newcastle unparished 1932-
LG. Newcastle-u-Lyme RD 1894-1932, MB 1932-74, D(B) 1974-. No. 12 W 1932-79. Silverdale W 1979-2002. Keele W 2002-
CED. Keele 1889-1934. Newcastle No. 1 1934-81. Keele & Silverdale 1981-2005. Keele & Westlands 2005-.

Bromley Green
Keele CP 1866-1984. Whitmore CP 1984- (SI No. 152).
LG. Newcastle-u-Lyme RD 1894-1974, D(B) 1974-. No. 22 W Feb 1973-4. No. 23 W Feb 1974-9. Keele W 1979-84. Whitmore W 1984-2002. Loggerheads & Whitmore W 2002-.

CED. Keele 1889-1934. Madeley 1934-81. Newcastle Rural 1981-2005, 2005-.

Crackley Gates (1)
Keele CP 1866-1932. Newcastle unparished 1932-
LG. Newcastle-u-Lyme RD 1894-1932, MB 1932-74, D(B) 1974-. No. 12 W 1932-79. Halmerend W 1979-2002. Silverdale & Parksite W 2002-.
CED. Keele 1889-1934. Newcastle No. 1 1934-81. Newcastle Rural 1981-2005. Audley & Chesterton 2005-.

Crackley Gates (2)
Keele CP 1866-1932. Newcastle unparished 1932-2002. Silverdale CP May 2002-
LG. Newcastle-u-Lyme RD 1894-1932, MB 1932-74, D(B) 1974-. No. 12 W 1932-79. Halmerend W 1979-2002. Silverdale & Parksite W 2002-.
CED. Keele 1889-1934. Newcastle No. 1 1934-81. Newcastle Rural 1981-2005. Cross Heath & Silverdale 2005-.

Crackley Gates (3)
Keele CP 1866-1932. Newcastle unparished 1932-2002. Silverdale CP May 2002-
LG. Newcastle-u-Lyme RD 1894-1932, MB 1932-74, D(B) 1974-. No. 12 W 1932-79. Halmerend W 1979-2002. Silverdale & Parksite W 2002-.

CED. Keele 1889-1934. Newcastle No. 1 1934-81. Newcastle Rural 1981-2005. Cross Heath & Silverdale 2005-.

Crackley Gates (4)

Keele CP 1866-1932. Newcastle unparished 1932-. Silverdale CP May 2002-
LG. Newcastle-u-Lyme RD 1894-1932, MB 1932-74, D(B) 1974- No. 12 W 1932-79. Keele W 1979-2002. Silverdale & Parksite W 2002-.
CED. Keele 1889-1934. Newcastle No. 1 1934-81. Keele & Silverdale 1981-2005. Keele & Westlands 2005-

Home Farm

Keele CP 1866-1932. Newcastle unparished 1932-.
LG. Newcastle-u-Lyme RD 1894-1932, MB 1932-74, D(B) 1974-. No. 3 W 1932-79. Keele W 1979-2002, 2002.
CED. Keele 1889-1934. Newcastle No. 2 1934-81. Keele & Silverdale 1981-2005. Keele & Westlands 2005-.

Keele

Keele CP 1866-.
LG. Newcastle-u-Lyme RD 1894-1974, D(B) 1974-. No. 22 W Feb 1973-4. No. 23 W Feb 1974-9. Keele W 1979-2002, 2002-
CED. Keele 1889-1934. Madeley 1934-81. Keele & Silverdale 1981-2005. Keele & Westlands 2005-.

Penfields

Keele CP 1866-1984. Whitmore CP 1984- (SI No. 152).
LG. Newcastle-u-Lyme RD 1894-1974, D(B) 1974-. No. 22 W Feb 1973-4. No. 23 W Feb 1974-9. Keele W 1979-84. Whitmore W 1984-2002. Loggerheads & Whitmore W 2002-
CED. Keele 1889-1934. Madeley 1934-81. Newcastle Rural 1981-2005, 2005-.

Rosemary Hill

Keele CP 1866-1927. Newcastle unparished 1927-. Silverdale CP May 2002-
LG. Newcastle-u-Lyme RD 1894-1927, MB 1927-74, D(B) 1974-. West W 1927-32. No. 2 W 1932-79. Silverdale W 1979-2002. Silverdale & Parksite 2002-
CED. Keele 1889-1928. Newcastle West 1928-34. Newcastle No. 1 1934-81. Keele & Silverdale W 1981-

2005. Cross Heath & Silverdale 2005-

Rosemary Hill Wood

Keele CP 1866-1927. Newcastle unparished 1927-.
LG. Newcastle-u-Lyme RD 1894-1927, MB 1927-74, D(B) 1974-. West W 1927-32. No. 3 W 1932-79. Keele W 1979-2002, 2002-.
CED. Keele 1889-1928. Newcastle West 1928-34. Newcastle No. 2 1934-81. Keele & Silverdale W 1981-2005. Keele & Westlands 2005-.

Scot Hay

Keele CP 1866-1932. Audley Rural CP 1932-. Halmerend PW 1948-, 2003-
LG. Newcastle-u-Lyme RD 1894-1974, D(B) 1974-. No. 21 W Feb 1973-4. No. 22 W Feb 1974-9. Halmerend W 1979-2002, 2002-
CED. Keele 1889-1934. Audley 1934-81. Newcastle Rural 1981-2005. Audley & Chesterton 2005-

Silverdale

Keele CP 1866-1932. Newcastle unparished 1932-2002. Silverdale CP May 2002-
LG. Newcastle-u-Lyme RD 1894-1932, MB 1932-74, D(B) 1974-. No. 12 W 1932-79. Silverdale W 1979-2002. Silverdale & Parksite W 2002-.
CED. Keele 1889-1934. Newcastle No. 1 1934-81. Keele & Silverdale 1981-2005. Cross Heath & Silverdale 2005-.

Silverdale House

Keele CP 1866-1932. Newcastle unparished 1932-2002. Silverdale CP May 2002-.
LG. Newcastle-u-Lyme RD 1894-1932, MB 1932-74, D(B) 1974-. No. 12 W 1932-79. Keele W 1979-2002. Silverdale & Parksite W 2002-.
CED. Keele 1889-1934. Newcastle No. 1 1934-81. Keele & Silverdale 1981-2005. Cross Heath & Silverdale 2005-.

Silverdale Ironworks

Keele CP 1866-1932. Newcastle unparished 1932-.
LG. Newcastle-u-Lyme RD 1894-1932, MB 1932-74, D(B) 1974-. No. 12 W 1932-79. Halmerend W 1979-2002, 2002-.
CED. Keele 1889-1934. Newcastle No. 1 1934-81. Newcastle Rural 1981-2005. Audley & Chesterton 2005-.

Parish service

Lists of those bound to do a parish duty or make good a financial pledge might also throw light on an ancestor's activities. There are lists of people liable to maintain **Keele** churchyard fence at sometime in later C17 (names & residences are mentioned but residences are vague - 'for his house in Keel', 'Venables house','Sarah Sneyd's house', 'Francis Beech house in Keel'), in 1706 (D3514/2/1), and

Keele

in 1732, with 42 names and their residences mentioned (D3514/2/2). At **Wolstanton** sections of the churchyard fence were staked out with markers bearing the initials of the person liable to mend that particular stretch of fence; however, in 1783 the incumbent sought diocesan advice on whether ecclesiastical law could be brought to bear on shirkers (D3534/1/14). The breakdown of this type of arrangement at **High Offley** led to the levying of a rate for churchyard fence repair as a memorandum in the Churchwardens' Acct Bk dated Nov 20 1786 recalls (D4035/2/1). There is a list of subscribers toward enlarging the Free School at **Milwich**, late C18 (D917/9/5). An assessment made on the inhabitants of **Stafford** borough for erecting a workhouse for keeping and maintaining the poor that are or shall become chargeable to the fore said inhabitants at a vestry, held by adjournment Dec 1735, removed from an old ledger and inserted into St Chad's Stafford overseers accounts (D(w)08/18). In **Stoke-upon-Trent** AP a trustees' account book includes the subscribers for a new chapel at Longton 1795-1801; perhaps over 200 people are named (D3276/4/1A-B).

Incised slab to John Egerton d1518 and wife in Madeley Church. Etching. SV. VII. 57c. Courtesy of Trustees of WSL

Madeley

'First to the wood or clearing of the witan. From the wood or clearing of the witan to the eardel, from the eardel to wriman ford, from wriman ford along the brook to Hedena's moss, from Hedena's moss around hawk batch, from the batch to the hedge, from the hedge to Wilburh's way, from Wilburh's way to the watercress spring, from the spring to the dyke, from the dyke to the great marsh, from the marsh to the watercourse, from the watercourse to wierdes ford, from wierdes ford to the reedy marsh, from the marsh to the heathy leah, from the clearing to the wooded hillock, to the the great oak, from the oak to the watercourse, from the watercourse again to the wood or clearing of the witan.'

King Edgar to Bishop Æthelwold. Grant of 3 manæ at Madeley. 975. Translated by Della Hooke

In 1851 Madeley and Onneley townships supported their poor cojointly.
PLU. Newcastle-u-Lyme 1838-1930. Madeley W by1910-.
SEE ALSO pages 2, 6, 11, 26, 30, 36, 50, 54, 78, 93-4, 96,103, 125, 131, 140, 142, 187, 208, 214, 230

MADELEY TOWNSHIP
Madeley

Madeley CP 1866-. Madeley was described as a District Council when the results from the PC elections were published in SA Dec 22 1894 p6. Accounts from 1926 at SRO.
LG. Newcastle-u-Lyme RD 1894-1974, D(B) 1974-. No. 23 W Feb 1973-4. No. 24 W Feb 1974-9. Madeley W 1979-2002, 2002-
CED. Keele 1889-1934. Madeley 1934-81. Newcastle Rural 1981-2005, 2005-.

Madeley Great Park

Madeley CP 1866-1984. Whitmore CP 1984- (SI No. 152).
LG. Newcastle-u-Lyme RD 1894-1974, D(B) 1974-. No. 23 W Feb 1973-4. No. 24 W Feb 1974-9. Madeley W 1979-2002, 2002-
CED. Keele 1889-1934. Madeley 1934-81. Newcastle Rural 1981-2005, 2005-.

ONNELEY TOWNSHIP

Madeley CP 1866-.

Madeley

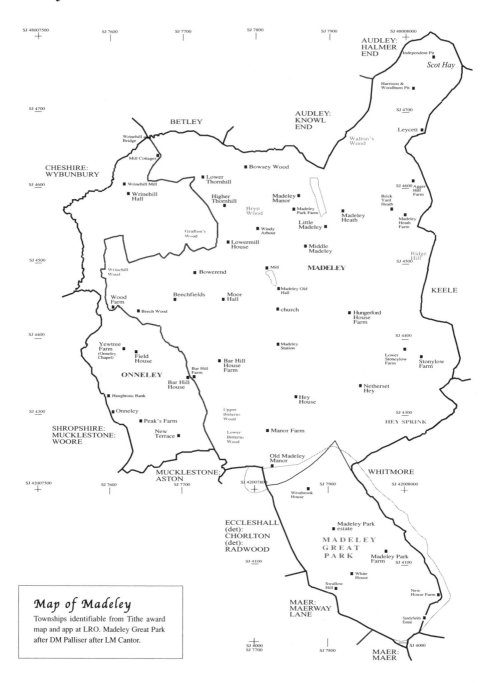

Map of Madeley

Townships identifiable from Tithe award map and app at LRO. Madeley Great Park after DM Palliser after LM Cantor.

LG. Newcastle-u-Lyme RD 1894-1974, D(B) 1974-. No. 23 W Feb 1973-4. No. 24 W Feb 1974-9. Madeley W 1979-2002, 2002-

CED. Keele 1889-1934. Madeley 1934-81. Newcastle Rural 1981-2005, 2005-.

Madeley

Troublesome township boundaries

A principal aim of this book is to show township boundaries - subdivisions of the ancient parish. These were a unit of civil administration before the ancient parish began to have responsibility for civil affairs in Tudor times. They continued as an administrative unit until the creation of civil parishes in 1866. A separate Poor Rate could be levied in a township and it could have its own constable (making it a constablewick). Township boundaries had remained largely unaltered from the C15, and invariably they are coterminous with vill, liberty and manorial boundaries. Information about boundaries comes from various sources, starting with the most accessible and reliable:-

OS NEW SERIES (1870s-90s) (a set in SRO, as well as BL) for those townships that became CPs in 1858 and 1866. For instance, Cold Norton (Chesbey).

OS OLD/ FIRST SERIES (1801-70s) (SRO & BL) for Adbaston, and some of Eccleshall in SE quarter of sheet 73, for Trentham and some of Stoke-upon-Trent in NW quarter of sheet 72 (David & Charles edition sheets 33 and 34). But detail is poor, and one would be better looking at....

TITHE MAPS. Those for Abbots Bromley (Bagot's Bromley only), Blithfield, Colwich (hamlets, drawn on later), Eccleshall, Marston, Mucklestone, Stone, Swynnerton, and Trentham, show township boundaries. But not all tithe maps do, and another source is...

ESTATE MAPS. Those for Chebsey (estates & hamlets of) (D615/M/4/38) (D615/M/4/5) (D5800/1/1) (D5800/1/2), Chorlton (D593/H/3/112), Colwich (D(W)1781/11/1) (D603/H/3/9), Ingestre 1789 (D240 E(A)2/134), Maer (D952/5/1/33), Ranton Abbey (D615/M/4/22), Stafford (D240/E (A) 2/221) (D240/E (A) 2/221) (D240/E (A) 2/233) (D240/E (A)/ 2/ 230) (D240/E (A) 2/221), Standon (D1026/3/2). When these are exhausted problems start; and the next option is to resort to...

SECONDARY SOURCES. For Biddulph lordships I looked at Kennedy in BALH; Tyrley townships (Drayton-in-Hales) at Twemlow in SHC 1945/6 (himself unable to plot the original townships); Burslem and Stoke-upon-Trent townships at Ward in HBST; Foregate Liberty (Marston) at VCH vol 6. However, when this avenue is exhausted, one might resort to...

SELF-PLOTTING, CROSS-REFERENCING SOURCES. Even if a tithe map does not show township boundaries occasionally the apportionment might list owners and occupiers of land under separate township headings. This is helpful, allowing you to plot the boundary. But I think no Pirehill apportionments fell into this category. And I had to resort to another option: - cross-reference farmers listed in the directories of W White (1834, 1851) - as there they are, invariably, placed under township headings - with the same-named farmers in the apportionment. I appreciate this method has flaws. However, Madeley, Norton-in-the-Moors, and Wolstanton, have documents partly validating findings. **Norton** parish map c1840 (1176/A/13/2), I think, showing estate/manorial boundaries, showed an identical detached portion centred on Bradley. Whilst Holditch emerged as a detached portion of Chatterley township in **Wolstanton**. This was realised by the apportionment method and suggested by White. In addition, David Dyble's A History of Apedale and Chesterton (2002) pp6-7 concludes some of Dimsdale manor lay in Chatterley township and so formed a detached portion.

In other respects Wolstanton townships were horrendously troublesome. A whole army of sources failed to agree: Tithe map/ apportionment; White; census; new CP/ EP boundaries; key to OS 25" plans in Hanley Ref Lib; and Wolstanton-Burslem Highway District plan - bundle Q/SB Midsummer Sessions 1879. In the end I reluctantly used 1894 CP boundaries which were said to be coterminous with those of former townships (VCH vol 8 pp81, 95); so Wedgwood's northern flank followed Chell CP boundary etc.

However, the apportionment method for Wolstanton threw up a picture of many detached portions: of Ravenscliffe portions at Aldery Lane, Brownlees, Harriseahead, White Hill; of small parcels of Chatterley throughout Tunstall; of a Chesterton portion N of Liverpool Rd, Kidsgrove; of a frag-

Madeley

mented Knutton interspersed with Chatterley and Brierleyhurst; of Oldcote interspersed in Ravenscliffe and Tunstall; of Tunstall protruding to Mill Farm; of Chesterton protruding in a block to Silverdale; of Chesterton village and Harriseahead both covered by numerous townships' detached portions, perhaps suggesting once intercommoned woodland and waste there. And who is to say this is not a truer picture of the original township layout, or of a C18 or earlier rationalisation of that layout, which was quite undefined? Then, subsequent rationalisation produced the wholly-consolidated C19 townships.

Returning to the notion townships are successors of vills: Dyble speculated whether Brierleyhurst, Stadmorslow, Wedgwood, Oldcote, Ravenscliffe, Tunstall, and Chatterley formed seven of the eight plough areas of the king's manor of Wolstanton in DB; with Chesterton hidden, as the missing one. I was happiest with evidence which unexpectedly turned up to validate **Madeley**. The apportionment method produced a human embryo-shaped Onneley township, which included Wrinehill Hall. A 'Copy Grant of Great Tithes' relating to Madeley, which read '...Tithes yearly or otherwise arising, renewing, growing, happening and coming within such part or parts of the said Township of Wrinehill and Onniley,' proved Onneley had formed a township with Wrinehill (D3412/1/77-80, 84-106). Also the two townships of Madeley and Onneley are mentioned in Rev JW Dalrey's tithe rent charge for 1841, 1842, '43, '44, '45, '46 in the same SRO bundle. As an aside, the extended title of 'Copy Grant' was in error and read 'Copy Grant of Great Tithes in the Townships of Wrinehill and Onniley within the parish of Madeley etc' 1827; understandably, SRO had repeated this; proving it's always important to read a document, not just go by the title in the catalogue! For **Audley** and **Seighford** I found no validation, but I am confident plausible township layouts emerged. For **Standon**, I went with Salt's four townships - Bowers, Rudge, Standon, Walford - in HOPS p5, reconciling this with the 1745 organisation by suspecting Bowers was successor to Standon hamlet; Standon to Standon Hall hamlet; Weston hamlet had been Weston estate with Shortwood, which had later merged with Bowers; Walford and Rudge, no changes. By 1851 the subdivisions of **Stowe** were hamlets Amerton, Drointon, Grindley, Hixon, Great Haywood, Little Haywood and Stowe. I suspect, they were the former liberties. Amerton is perhaps identifiable with 'Amerton Liberty' appearing on the border in Stowe parish on Gayton tithe map. There are references to a Hixon liberty/ township in the Account book of Surveyor of the Highway of Hixon township (D3717/6/1). But this area must have covered all Stowe as many ratepayers for Feb/ March 1852 in the document matched parishioners listed in White's directory 1851.

NOT ATTEMPTED. High Offley (see chapter).

Newcastle Superintendent Registrar Judy Tomkinson with the original register containing Charles Darwin's marriage certificate. Judy called in the marriage register so it could be replaced by a modern one. She said "I blew the dust of it and started indexing and this was the second entry. I was astonished." Rev Dr Martin Yould of St Peter's said a copy of the document had been on display in the foyer for years (ES 14 May 1997 p?). Courtesy of Sentinel Newspapers

Maer

'Between Stableford and Blackbrook the A51 passes through a beautiful valley of curving wooded hills. These are the Maer Hills.'

Michael Raven. Staffordshire and the Black Country. 1988

In 1839 vestry meetings were chaired by Rev JA Wedgwood and attended by Josiah II Wedgwood of Maer Hall. In 1846 Maer and Maerway Lane townships each had three constables (D3635/4/2); Still separate townships in 1880 (D3635/4/2).
PLU. Newcastle-u-Lyme 1838-1930. Maer W by1910-.
SEE ALSO pages 7, 50, 78, 93, 96, 125, 130, 142, 186, 208

MAER TOWNSHIP
Haddon

Maer CP 1866-1984. PC 1894-. Chapel & Hill Chorlton CP 1984-
LG. Newcastle-u-Lyme RD 1894-1974, D(B) 1974-.
No. 20 W Feb 1973-4. No. 21 W Feb 1974-9. Whitmore W 1979-2002. Loggerheads & Whitmore W 2002-.
CED. Keele 1889-1934. Madeley 1934-81. Newcastle Rural 1981-2005, 2005-.

Maer

Maer CP 1866- (unofficially styled Maer and Aston 1996-).
LG. Newcastle-u-Lyme RD 1894-1974, D(B) 1974-.
No. 20 W Feb 1973-4. No. 21 W Feb 1974-9. Whitmore W 1979-2002. Loggerheads & Whitmore W 2002-.
CED. Keele 1889-1934. Madeley 1934-81. Newcastle Rural 1981-2005, 2005-.

MAERWAY LANE TOWNSHIP

Maer CP 1866- (unofficially styled Maer and Aston 1996-).
LG. Newcastle-u-Lyme RD 1894-1974, D(B) 1974-.
No. 20 W Feb 1973-4. No. 21 W Feb 1974-9. Whitmore W 1979-2002. Loggerheads & Whitmore W 2002-.
CED. Keele 1889-1934. Madeley 1934-81. Newcastle Rural 1981-2005, 2005-.

Maer

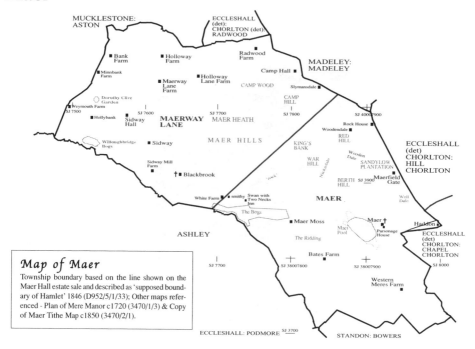

Map of Maer

Township boundary based on the line shown on the Maer Hall estate sale and described as 'supposed boundary of Hamlet' 1846 (D952/5/1/33); Other maps referenced - Plan of Mere Manor c1720 (3470/1/3) & Copy of Maer Tithe Map c1850 (3470/2/1).

Printed Parish Registers

Parish Registers are kept at SRO. Readers are expected to use microfiche copies. In exceptional circumstances the original register might be produced. Handwriting of PRs is often hard to decipher, even illegible to the untrained eye. In addition, ink has faded, there may be damage, or writing can be in Latin. **The Staffordshire Parish Register Society** (SPRS) have striven since 1902 to alleviate these problems by publishing transcriptions using the original register where they can or else Bishop's Transcripts at LRO. Their latest publication (2004) is Maer registers 1558-1746. The others for Pirehill are:- Barlaston (1905), Betley (1916), Bucknall-cum-Bagnall (St Mary) (1920), Burslem Parts 1-3 (1913), Chebsey (1964/5), Eccleshall Parts 1 (1907) Part 2 (1910), Ellenhall (1944/5), Keele (1949/50), Madeley Pt 1 (1960/1), Milwich Pt 1 (1904), Pt 2 & index (1996), Mucklestone Pt 1 (1929), Newcastle-under-Lyme Pt 1 (1931), Pt 2 (1939), Pt 3 (1981), Norton-in-the-Moors Pt 1 (1924), Pt 2 (1942/3), Ranton (1953/4), Seighford (1977/8), Stafford St Chad (1935/6), Stafford St Mary (with St Chad) (1935/6), Standon (1902), Stoke-upon-Trent Pt 1 (1914), Pt 2 (1918), Pt 3 (1925), Pt 4 (1926/7), Stowe (1909), Trentham Pt 1 (1923), Pt 2 (1906), Wolstanton Pts 1 & 2 (1990). SPRS work closely with **The Birmingham & Midland Society for Genealogy & Heraldry** (1963), who sometimes print SPRS publications or else have them on microfiche. Those published under their own imprint are: Adbaston Pts 1 & 2 (1979), Audley (1981), High Offley (1979), Madeley Pt 2, Mucklestone Pt 2, Stone & Fulford Chapel, Swynnerton. The Society of Genealogists (1911) publish the National Index of Parish Registers: 'Volume 6: North and East Midlands Part 1: Staffordshire' by Peter D Bloore (1982, revised ed. 1992); 'Volume 5: Part 1: Shropshire' by Dr Sylvia Watts (2002): and the County Sources series - 'Shropshire & Staffordshire' (2000).

Gaol Square in Foregate Liberty. Courtesy of Roy Lewis

Marston

'Marston is a village and liberty in the parish of St Mary Stafford about three miles to the north of that town, upon a good loamy soil, excellent both for corn and pasture.'

Staffordshire General and Commercial Directory. 1818

PLU. Stafford 1836-1930.

SEE ALSO pages 7, 34, 51, 78, 93, 99-101, 116, 130, 142, 186

FOREGATE LIBERTY
Brook House

St Mary and St Chad T 1807-.
LG. Stafford B 1807-1974, D(B) 1974-. West W 1835-1960. Tillington W 1960-c1981. Common W c1981-2002. Common W 2002-.
CED. Stafford West 1889-1957. Stafford North 1957-77. Stafford North Gate 1977-2005. Stafford North 2005-

County Industrial Home

St Mary and St Chad T 1807-.
LG. Stafford B 1807-1974, D(B) 1974-. East W 1835-1960. Coton W 1960-c1981. Common W c1981-2002. Common W 2002-.
CED. Stafford East 1889-1977. Stafford North Gate 1977-2005. Stafford North 2005-

Foregate

St Mary and St Chad T 1807-.

LG. Stafford B 1807-1974, D(B) 1974-. West W 1835-1960. Tillington W 1960-c1981. Forebridge W c1981-2002. Forebridge W 2002-.
CED. Stafford West 1889-1957. Stafford North 1957-77. Stafford East Gate 1977-2005. Stafford Central 2005-

Foregate Street a

St Mary and St Chad T 1807-.
LG. Stafford B 1807-1974, D(B) 1974-. West W 1835-1960. Tillington W 1960-c1981. Common W c1981-2002. Common W 2002-
CED. Stafford West 1889-1957. Stafford North 1957-77. Stafford North Gate 1977-2005. Stafford North 2005-

Foregate Street b

St Mary and St Chad T 1807-.
LG. Stafford B 1807-1974, D(B) 1974-. West W 1835-1960. Tillington W 1960-c1981. Forebridge W c1981-

Marston (Foregate)

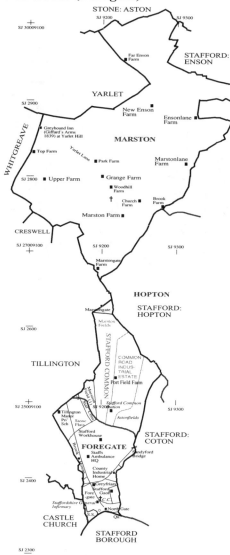

2002. Common W 2002-

CED. Stafford West 1889-1957. Stafford North 1957-77. Stafford North Gate 1977-2005. Stafford North 2005-

Greyfriars

St Mary and St Chad T 1807-.

LG. Stafford B 1807-1974, D(B) 1974-. East W 1835-1960. Coton W 1960-c1981. Common W c1981-2002. Forebridge W 2002-.

CED. Stafford East 1889-1977. Stafford North Gate 1977-2005. Stafford Central 2005-.

North Gate

St Mary and St Chad T 1807-.

LG. Stafford B 1807-1974, D(B) 1974-. East W 1835-1960. Coton W 1960-c1981. Common W c1981-2002. Forebridge W 2002-.

CED. Stafford East 1889-1977. Stafford East Gate 1977-2005. Stafford Central 2005-.

Queensway

St Mary and St Chad T 1807-.

LG. Stafford B 1807-1974, D(B) 1974-. East W 1835-1960. Forebridge W 1960-2002. Forebridge W 2002-.

CED. Stafford East 1889-1977. Stafford East Gate 1977-2005. Stafford Central 2005-.

S.S. (Sainsbury Supermarket)

St Mary and St Chad T 1807-. Tillington PH 1807-35.

LG. Stafford B 1835-1974, D(B) 1974-. West W 1835-1960. Tillington W 1960-c1981. Forebridge W c1981-2002. Forebridge W 2002-.

CED. Stafford West 1889-1957. Stafford North 1957-77. Stafford East Gate 1977-2005. Stafford Central 2005-

Sandyford Bridge

St Mary and St Chad T 1807-.

LG. Stafford B 1807-1974, D(B) 1974-. East W 1835-1960. Common W 1960-2002. Common W 2002-.

CED. Stafford East 1889-1957. Stafford North 1957-77. Stafford East Gate 1977-2005. Stafford Central 2005-.

Stafford Common

St Mary and St Chad T 1807-.

LG. Stafford B 1807-1974, D(B) 1974-. East W 1835-1924. North W 1924-60. Common W 1960-c1981. Holmcroft W c1981-2002. Common W 2002-.

CED. Stafford East 1889-1957. Stafford North 1957-77. Stafford North Gate 1977-2005. Stafford North 2005-.

Stafford Gaol

St Mary and St Chad T 1807-.

LG. Stafford B 1807-1974, D(B) 1974-. East W 1835-1960. Coton W 1960-c1981. Common W c1981-2002. Littleworth W 2002-.

Map of Marston

Marston township shown on tithe map (1839) (D834/14/15/4), and for easy reference Foregate Liberty appears in VCH vol VI

CED. Stafford East 1889-1977. Stafford North Gate 1977-2005. Stafford Central 2005-.

Stafford Workhouse
St Mary and St Chad T 1807-.
LG. Stafford B 1807-1974, D(B) 1974-. East W 1835-1924. North W 1924-60. Common W 1960-2002. Common W 2002-.
CED. Stafford East 1889-1957. Stafford North 1957-77. Stafford North Gate 1977-2005. Stafford North 2005-.

Stone Flats
St Mary and St Chad T 1807-.
LG. Stafford B 1807-1974, D(B) 1974-. East W 1835-1924. North W 1924-60. Holmcroft W 1960-2002. Holmcroft W 2002-.
CED. Stafford East 1889-1957. Stafford North 1957-77. Stafford North Gate 1977-2005. Stafford North 2005-.

Tillington Manor Primary School
St Mary and St Chad T 1807-.
LG. Stafford B 1807-1974, D(B) 1974-. West W 1835-1960. Holmcroft W 1960-2002. Holmcroft W 2002-.
CED. Stafford West 1889-1957. Stafford North 1957-77. Stafford North Gate 1977-2005. Stafford North 2005-.

MARSTON TOWNSHIP
Marston CP 1866-. With a population between 100 and 300 Marston was entitled to an Order to form a PC without consent of the CC. Marston decided not to become a PC in late 1894. Parish meeting minutes 1894-1937 (D3405/1) at SRO.
LG. Stafford D(B) 1974-. Beaconside W 1974-2002. Seighford W 2002-.
CED. Stafford Rural 1889-1911. Stafford Rural East Sept 1911-34. Stafford Rural 1934-73. Stafford Rural No. 2 1973-81. Stafford Trent Valley 1981-2005, 2005-

Marston (Marston)
MARSTON (detached)
Marston Fields (1)
Marston CP 1866-84. Tillington CP 1884-1917.
LG. Stafford B 1917-74, D(B) 1974-. East W 1917-24. North W 1924-60. Common W 1960-2002. Common W 2002-.
CED. Stafford Rural 1889-1911. Stafford Rural East Sept 1911-9. Stafford East 1919-57. Stafford North 1957-77. Stafford North Gate 1977-2005. Stafford North 2005-.

Marston Fields (2)
Marston CP 1866-84. Tillington CP 1884-1917.
LG. Stafford B 1917-74, D(B) 1974-. East W 1917-24. North W 1924-60. Holmcroft W 1960-2002. Holmcorft W 2002-.
CED. Stafford Rural 1889-1911. Stafford Rural East Sept 1911-9. Stafford East 1919-1957. Stafford North 1957-77. Stafford North Gate 1977-2005. Stafford North 2005-.

Marstongate
Marston CP 1866-84. Tillington CP 1884-1917. Stafford unparished 1917-88. Creswell CP 1988-
LG. Stafford B 1917-74, D(B) 1974-. East W 1917-24. North W 1924-60. Common W 1960-1988.
CED. Stafford Rural 1889-1911. Stafford Rural East Sept 1911-9. Stafford East 1919-1957. Stafford North 1957-77. Stafford North Gate 1977-2005. Stafford Trent Valley 2005-

Port Field Farm
Marston CP 1866-84. Tillington CP 1884-1917.
LG. Stafford B 1917-74, D(B) 1974-. East W 1917-24. North W 1924-60. Common W 1960-2002. Common W 2002-.
CED. Stafford Rural 1889-1911. Stafford Rural East Sept 1911-9. Stafford East 1919-1957. Stafford North 1957-77. Stafford North Gate 1977-2005. Stafford North 2005-.

Deserted villages
The now clearly-evident deserted medieval village in Pirehill, Marston, is a fairly recent discovery: An air photograph of it from the Cambridge University Collection appears in SPJD (1994) p48p but alludes the early lists of the Medieval Village Research Group. In 1955 MVRG listed 18 sites in Staffordshire, four were in Pirehill - Blithfield, Chartley, Deanslow, and Shugborough. Sandon was added in MVRG's 12th Annual Report 1964; on that document someone pencilled in Swynnerton and Marston. By the early 1970s however Marston was still absent from the 39 suspected lost villages identified for Pirehill and listed alphabetically in SSAHST vol 12 1970-1 p31. I have rearranged this list (incidentally, based on documentary evidence) into a parish gazetteer and added a few others (incidentally, based on archaeological evidence). Whilst the subject is mainly of interest to demographers, inhabitant lists associated with lost villages in some of the documentary evidence

Marston

may interest genealogists.

Abbots Bromley Bagot's Bromley at SK065260, deserted C18 (4), and must be one of the last occasions a village was deserted (WSL 125/375). Bromley Hurst at SK 088225? probably deserted in C18 (7).

Adbaston Adbaston at SJ 761279, probably deserted 1379-1524 (1); Francis Braddocke enclosed 20 acres of arable land for pasture 1511, perhaps depopulating a settlement to do so (11). Flashbrook Manor at SJ 746253, or Flashbrook Grange at SJ 744244 (1).

Audley Park End at SJ 786516 (6).

Biddulph Richard Biddulph enclosed 30 acres of arable land into his park 1489, perhaps depopulating a settlement to do so (11).

Blithfield at SK 045240, probably deserted 1539-? (1).

Chartley Holme Chartley Hall at SK 088285 probably deserted 1524-1666 (1).

Chebsey Cold Norton Farm at SJ 878322, or Norton Farm at SJ 882308, probably deserted 1332-1539 (4).

Colton perhaps at Littlehay if identified with unidentified DB berewick Colt (1).

Colwich Colwich Moreton House at SK 023231, or Upper Moreton at SK 029221, probably deserted 1334-1524? (1). Shugborough at SJ 990217 deserted between 1737-73 (8). Humphrey Stanley enclosed 30 acres of arable land into his park 1505, perhaps at Haywood, perhaps depopulating a settlement to do so (11). Fradswell Hall at SJ 992312 or Sun Farm at SJ 998315 (1).

Creswell at SJ 896261, probably deserted 1334-1539 (1).

Drayton-in-Hales Tyrley at Hales at SJ 715342 (1).

Eccleshall Broughton at SJ767338 probably deserted 1327-1524 (1). Dorslow or Dorveslau or Dawsley alias Deanslow at SJ 800333 (1). **Chorlton** Chapel Chorlton Haddon Lane at SJ 801385 (?). Radwood Hall Farm at SJ 773412 (4). Eccleshall at Little Ankerton at SJ 832312 or Three Farms Ankerton at SJ 836317 probably deserted 1332-1524 (4). Gerrard's Bromley at SJ 775348 probably deserted 1332-1666 (1), and possibly because of the Black Death (Inquistions Post Mortem 1349) (WSL 125/3/75). Horsley Garmelow at SJ 797279 (?). Horsley Hall at SJ 817280 (4).

Ellenhall Frankwell at SJ 84762550, probably deserted in C16 (?).

High Offley - shrunken village here, air photos of it have been taken by Dr St Joseph, and it is listed by MVRG (WSL 125/3/75) (not on SSAHST list).

Marston about Marston Farm at SJ 922274.

Mucklestone Mucklestone - possible shrunken village here (125/3/75) (not on SSAHST list). Oakley at SJ 700369 (1).

Norton-in-the- Moors perhaps at Bradley if identified with unidentified DB vill Bradelie (1)

Sandon Great Sandon at SJ 955296 probably deserted 1539-1666 (1) (SPJD p47p).

Seighford Coton Clanford at SJ 874237 (1). Bridgford Simon Harcourt enclosed 40 acres of arable land into pasture 1511, perhaps depopulating a settlement to do so (11).

Stafford Enson & Salt at Enson at SJ 941289, probably deserted 1377-1524 (1). Herberton there is little doubt the lost village of Orberton was in Herberton (?) (SHC new series vol 12 p145).

Standon The Rudge at SJ 761350 (1). Standon Swinchurch (Swines Head) at SJ 810371 (1). Weston at SJ 805367, probably deserted 1327-1524? (1).

Stone Oulton Kibblestone at SJ 914363 probably deserted in C18 (3).

Tillington Tillington Hall at SJ 910250 probably deserted 1334-1524 (1).

Tixall John Aston enclosed 100 acres of arable land, perhaps at Tixall 1501, perhaps depopulating a settlement to do so (11).

Worston at SJ 879278 (?)

Yarlet at SJ 913293 probably deserted 1154-89 (1).
Unknown Chaveldon 1539-? (4).

(1) = DB
(2) = Hundred rolls (1255-75)
(3) = Nomina Villarum (1316) - printed in Feudal Aids (Record Commissioners) v
(4) = Lay subsidy returns (1327 & 1332) - SHC1886 & 1889
(6) = Poll tax returns (1377) - courtesy of Miss LM Midgley
(1379) - SHC 1896
(7) = Lay subsidy (1524-5) - J Sheail 'The Regional Distribution of Wealth in England as indicated
in the 1524-5 Lay subsidy Returns' unpublished London Phd thesis 1968
(8) = Muster rolls (1539) - SHC 1901, 1902, 1903
(11) = (WSL 125/3/75) transcribed list from a Lansdowne Mss, a record of early enclosure in Staffordshire

In Nov 1986 Medieval Village Research Group, founded 1952, amalgamated with the Moated Sites
Research Group, founded 1971, to form the Medieval Settlement Research Group. The MVRG archive, compiled 1952-87, principally by Prof MW Beresford, JG Hurst and others, is on permanent
loan to the National Monuments Record. It is available for public consultation, and pre-1974 county
reports can be requested at a nominal charge from NMR, National Monuments Record Centre, Great
Western Village, Kemble Drive, Swindon, SN2 2GZ, Tel: (01793) 414600, email: info@rchme.co.uk

Perambulating Milwich parish boundary at Beacon Bank May 7 1995. Courtesy RW Knight

Milwich

'I have ministered in many parts of England.... But nowhere have I experienced such universal kindness and real regard as at Milwich and such as I cannot forget.'

Rev Joseph White, curate of Milwich 1836-42. letter 1849 (NSFCT 1980-1 p18)

Milwich had a system between 1660s and 1770s at least for appointing a constable from Coton, for one year, then one from Garshall for another, then one from Milwich, in rotation (D917/5/1).
PLU. Stone 1838-1930. Milwich W by1910-.
SEE ALSO pages 7, 11, 23, 26, 50, 78, 84, 90, 96, 102-103, 124, 125, 130, 142, 208, 214

MILWICH TOWNSHIP
Milwich CP 1866-. PC 1894-. Minutes 1894-1973 at SRO. Milwich-with-Fradswell PC (a pg) 2003-.
LG. Stone RD 1894-1974. Stafford D(B) 1974-.

Milwich W 1974-2002, 2002-.
CED. Stone 1889-1911. Stone Rural Sept 1911-2005. Barlaston & Fulford 2005-.

Perambulating boundaries
Of all Pirehill parishes **Milwich** has documented its boundary perambulations well; possibly because the custom still continues there. There were walks in 1684 and 1685, when walkers took two days, 1686-8, 1713, 1737, as the accounts and disbursements of John Featherstone and Joseph Philips churchwardens tell 'Spent when we went the Boundaries etc' £0, 5s, 4d (D917/5/1), 1868, 1895, 1921, 1948, 1977, 1979, 1985, 1995 and May 20 2000, when 23 walkers assembled at 10.00am at the top of Cromer Hill for the 12 mile walk (MTM pp48-9). **Stoke-upon-Trent** parish boundary was

perambulated in 1689 (NSFCT 1910 p176). Beating of **Audley** bounds occurred in Nov 1913 (Staffordshire Encyclopaedia). The south and west **Barlaston** boundary was perambulated on Ascension day 1729, and the north and east boundary on Ascension day 1730 (D3538/9). The boundaries of **Madeley** parish were walked on May 27 1717, Nov 14 1837, and Oct 22 & 23 1874 (M pp29-30). On August 3 1963 and July 20 1980 J Harri Davies rector and others perambulated **Mucklestone** EP boundary. The 1963 walk commenced at Tjarm, Napley; the 1980 started at 10.30am at Field House, Willoughbridge, after a church service at 9.45am, and finished at The Field Farm, Pipegate, at about 4.45pm (a distance of 11-12 miles): Four stewards led 73 walkers. Their signatures and those of the 1963 walkers appear in a little red log book at SRO (D3433/4/1). In 1887 the bounds of **Newcastle-u-Lyme** were perambulated not in Rogation week but in March (Staffordshire Encyclopaedia). Beating **Sandon** bounds was advertised in the local press, and by large specially-printed posters in 1830. It took two days and a detailed account of it is given in Edward Thomas' diary (MTM pp48-9). In the front of **Trentham** Minutes of Parish Committee of 35 (D4480/2/2) a newpaper cutting dated May 12 1858 (probably SA) tells of a perambulation of Trentham parish, taking 3 days. **Wolstanton**. On May 24 1895 the boundaries of Silverdale parish were perambulated which necessitated the closure of local schools for the afternoon (SA June 1 1895 p5 col 1). In addition, manor boundaries were perambulated, for instance Haywood (**Colwich**) in 1787 and Bucknall (**Stoke-upon-Trent**) in 1803 (WSL 101/41, 33/43) (WJ p24).

Map of Milwich

The Devil's Ring and Finger, the remains of a megalithic chambered tomb, N of Oakley. Watercolour by the author, 1999

Mucklestone in Staffordshire

'Anyway, Winnington Glen is a fair valley, picturesque enough to repay those who may not know of it. And under the fostering care of the Meynell Family it is never likley to lose its charms of tree and shrub, of bud and blossom.'

Weston E Vernon-Yonge. Bye-paths of Staffordshire. 1911

In 1830 there were overseers for the township of Mucklestone, another for Winnington, another for Aston, another for Oakley and Knighton (D5725/3/2). In 1851 there were said to be separate overseers for each of Mucklestone's nine townships, but they supported their poor cojointly. The Shropshire townships were Bearstone, Dorrington, Gravenhunger and Woore. At the Mucklestone vestry Decemeber 26 1823 it was resolved to appoint a surveyor to value property throughout the parish with a view to equalising the Poor Rates (D5725/3/2). The Mucklestone ledger covering 1817-1982 is incredibly detailed with names of ratepayers for each township, and overseers accounts, weekly pensioners' allowances/ disbursements (D5725/3/3).

Mucklestone in Staffordshire

LG. Newcastle-u-Lyme RD 1894-1974, D(B) 1974-. No. 24 W Feb 1973-4. No. 25 W Feb 1974-9.
Loggerheads W 1979-2002. Loggerheads & Whitmore W 2002-.
CED. Keele 1889-1934. Madeley 1934-81. Newcastle Rural 1981-2005, 2005-
PLU. Market Drayton 1836-1930.
SEE ALSO pages 7, 11, 21, 50, 79, 93, 96, 100, 103, 106, 124, 130, 140, 142, 208, 214

ASTON TOWNSHIP

Mucklestone CP 1866-1932. PC 1894-. Maer CP 1932-
(unofficially styled Maer and Aston 1996-).

KNIGHTON TOWNSHIP

Mucklestone CP 1866-1984. Loggerheads CP 1984-.
Mucklestone PW 1984-.

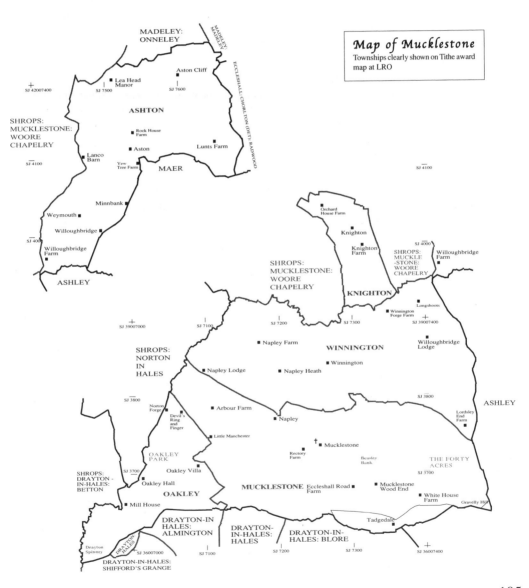

Map of Mucklestone
Townships clearly shown on Tithe award map at LRO

Mucklestone in Staffordshire

MUCKLESTONE TOWNSHIP
Gravelly Hill
Mucklestone CP 1866-1984. Loggerheads CP 1984-. Loggerheads PW 1984-.
Mucklestone
Mucklestone CP 1866-1984. Loggerheads CP 1984-. Mucklestone PW 1984-.
Tadgedale
Mucklestone CP 1866-1984. Loggerheads CP 1984-.

Loggerheads PW 1984-.

OAKLEY TOWNSHIP
Mucklestone CP 1866-1984. Loggerheads CP 1984-. Mucklestone PW 1984-.

WINNINGTON TOWNSHIP
Mucklestone CP 1866-1984. Loggerheads CP 1984-. Mucklestone PW 1984-.

Some Shropshire records at the Staffordshire Record Office and visa versa

Parishes divided between two counties illustrate that parishes predate counties and remind one of the potential of other counties' records, especially for parishes close to the border. At SRO, found loose between pages of D4610/1 (Mucklestone PR 1555-1666) is baptisms & burials 1677-1679 (D4610/14) - these entries are not recorded in the register D4610/2; they are possibly entries from its Woore chapel in Shropshire. Whilst, Shropshire Archives has a Woore index, Gravenhunger Moss Inclosure map and award 1867 is at SRO (D3433/11/1). A visit to Shropshire Archives revealed some interesting finds: In Norton-in-Hales parish records there is a map of M.H. Griffin's estate, essentially Knighton township, Mucklestone, 1868 (P210/v/1/2). Whilst its PR shows nearly everyone from Norton Forge chose to hop across the border to St Chad's. Between 1700-1812 Edgmond PR records at least 75 baptisms and burials of people from Mow Cop; 23 different family names are involved. No marriages are recorded, and it has been deduced that the people were nomads or travelling tinkers with their own form of marriage (TTTD p175). In Cheswardine records is the exchange of Glebe (22 Sept 1864) between the vicar, Rev John Healey Bromby, and Egerton William Harding of Old Springs, Tyrley - done by the Tithe Commissioners, with schedule of property exchanged and plan (the vicar had land adjoining the vicarage and castle croft, in return for the Upper and Lower Marsh Field) (P58/F/1/1/6). Cheswardine is rich in records of the Poor. A number of settlement examinations show migration to Staffordshire (to: **Adbaston**, **Eccleshall**, **High Offley**, **Mucklestone**, Norbury, and Wolverhampton). To Cheswardine came Elizabeth Ward of Whittington, Eccleshall, 1740 (P58/ fiche 267), and Thomas Sansom of Gnosall (P58/ fiche 272). Removal Orders show Alice Roberts from Cheswardine removed to High Offley 1699 (P58/ fiche 279), Richard Roberts to Maer (P58/ fiche 279), and others to Adbaston, **Ashley**, Caverswall, **Chebsey**, Church Eaton, Eccleshall and Chapel Chorlton, Gnosall, Rushall and Goscote, **Standon**, and **Swynnerton**. Whilst Edward Bate, his wife, and one child from Tyrley were removed to Cheswardine 1708 (P58/ fiche 281). There are hardly any bastardy bonds or orders which refer to Staffordshire people (fathers). Apprenticeship indentures tell of hardly anyone serving an apprentice across the border: Wolverhampton is mentioned once, Eccleshall twice. In an apprentice bond, settler in **Eccleshall**, James Scutt, binds himself not to take any apprentice 1749 (P58/ fiche 246). In vagrants' examinations and passes Margaret Wright, and rouge and vagabond Sarah Stokes, are apprehended in **Stone** in 1714 and 1807 respectively, and conveyed to Cheswardine (P58/ fiche 299. P58/ fiche 300).

The Queen on walk-about at Newcastle's Octocentenary celebrations, 1973. Courtesy of Sentinel Newspapers

Newcastle-under-Lyme

'The dignified, red brick and stone Guildhall in the High Street has presided over the busy market-place for more than 200 years and provides a fitting expression of the growth of Newcastle.'

Neville Malkin. A Grand Tour. 1976

LG. Newcastle B by1172~3-, burghal, guild and manorial autonomy 1369-1835, Improvement Commissioners district 1819-35, MB 1835-1974, D(B) 1974-.
PLU. Newcastle-u-Lyme 1838-1930. Newcastle W (with 7 seats) by1910.
PARL. Newcastle PB medieval-
SEE ALSO pages 7, 11, 30, 34, 50, 79, 96, 103, 109-110, 130, 140, 142, 167-168, 182, 208, 214, 230, 233

NEWCASTLE BOROUGH
Ash Field
West W 1835-1932. No. 1 W 1932-79. Town W 1979-2002. Cross Heath W 2002-
CED. Newcastle West 1889-1934. Newcastle No. 1 1934-81. Westlands 1981-2005. Cross Heath & Silverdale 2005-
Barracks
East W 1835-1932. No. 4 W 1932-79. Town W 1979-2002, 2002-.
CED. Newcastle East 1889-1934. Newcastle No. 2 1934-81. Westlands 1981-2005. Newcastle South 2005-

Blackfriars
West W 1835-1932. No. 3 W 1932-79. Westlands W 1979-2002, 2002-.
CED. Newcastle West 1889-1934. Newcastle No. 2 1934-81. Westlands 1981-2005. Keele & Westlands 2005-
The Brampton
East W 1835-1932. No. 5 W 1932-79. Cross Heath W 1979-2002. May Bank W 2002-
CED. Newcastle East 1889-1934. Newcastle No. 3 1934-81. Cross Heath 1981-2005. Wolstanton 2005-
Brook Lane
West W 1835-1932. No. 3 W 1932-79. Town W 1979-

Newcastle-under-Lyme

Map of Newcastle-under-Lyme
Map of borough by Malabar c1860 (735 4/6/6/1)

2002, 2002-.
CED. Newcastle West 1889-1934. Newcastle No. 2 1934-81. Westlands 1981-2005. Newcastle South 2005-

Derwent House
East W 1835-1932. No. 6 W 1932-79. Cross Heath W 1979-2002. May Bank W 2002-.
CED. Newcastle East 1889-1934. Newcastle No. 4 1934-81. Cross Heath 1981-2005. Wolstanton 2005-

Drill Hall
East W 1835-1932. No. 6 W 1932-79. Cross Heath W 1979-2002, 2002-.
CED. Newcastle East 1889-1934. Newcastle No. 4 1934-81. Cross Heath 1981-2005. Cross Heath & Silverdale 2005-

High Street
West W 1835-1932. No 2 W 1932-79. Town W 1979-2002, 2002-
CED. Newcastle West 1889-1934. Newcastle No. 1 1934-81. Westlands 1981-2005. Newcastle South 2005-

Iron Market
East W 1835-1932. No. 6 W 1932-79. Town W 1979-2002, 2002-.
CED. Newcastle East 1889-1934. Newcastle No. 4 1934-81. Westlands 1981-2005. Newcastle South 2005-
Globe Commerical Hotel Red Lion Square (ES Your Week. Aug 28 2004 p9p).

Liverpool Road
West W 1835-1932. No. 6 W 1932-. Cross Heath W 1979-2002, 2002-.

CED. Newcastle West 1889-1934. Newcastle No. 4 1934-81. Cross Heath 1981-2005. Cross Heath & Silverdale 2005-

London Road
West W 1835-1932. No. 4 W 1932-79. Town W 1979-2002, 2002-.
CED. Newcastle West 1889-1934. Newcastle No. 2 1934-81. Westlands 1981-2005. Newcastle South 2005-

Lower Green (1)
West W 1835-1932. No. 1 W 1932-79. Town W 1979-2002, 2002-.
CED. Newcastle West 1889-1934. Newcastle No. 1 1934-81. Westlands 1981-2005. Newcastle South 2005-

Lower Green (2)
West W 1835-1932. No. 1 W 1932-79. Thistleberry W 1979-2002, 2002-
CED. Newcastle West 1889-1934. Newcastle No. 1 1934-81. Westlands 1981-2005. Keele & Westalnds 2005-

The Marsh
East W 1835-1932. No. 5 W 1932-79. Town W 1979-2002, 2002-.
CED. Newcastle East 1889-1934. Newcastle No. 3 1934-81. Westlands 1981-2005. Newcastle South 2005-

Poolfields
West W 1835-1932. No 2 W 1932-79. Thistleberry W 1979-2002, 2002-.
CED. Newcastle West 1889-1934. Newcastle No. 1 1934-81. Thistleberry 1981-2005. Keele & Westlands 2005-

Thistleberry
West W 1835-1932. No 3 W 1932-79. Thistleberry W 1979-2002, 2002-
CED. Newcastle West 1889-1934. Newcastle No. 2 1934-81. Thistleberry 1981-2005. Keele & Westlands 2005-

Upper Green (1)
West W 1835-1932. No. 1 W 1932-79. Cross Heath W 1979-2002, 2002-.
CED. Newcastle West 1889-1934. Newcastle No. 1 1934-81. Cross Heath 1981-2005. Cross Heath & Silverdale 2005-

Upper Green (2)
West W 1835-1932. No. 1 W 1932-79. Town W 1979-2002, 2002-.
CED. Newcastle West 1889-1934. Newcastle No. 1 1934-81. Cross Heath 1981-2005. Newcastle South 2005-

Municipal records

Below is a list of some records and newspapers to be met with when researching an important ancient parliamentary borough such as Newcastle-under-Lyme. A similar one could be compiled for Stafford. But not, probably, for the sparsely-populated, unprosperous boroughs of Abbots Bromley (having borough status between 1222-1606), Betley (1299-1407), Eccleshall (1199-1697), Stone (1364-1536), which generated little documentation beyond that of any other community.

1166~7, 1168~9, 1172~3, 1187, 1191, 1192, 1195, 1199, 1205, 1206, 1214, 1235, 1251 some of the royal taxation, fine, aid, tallage, rent (Pipe Rolls) lists and charters

1327 Exchequer subsidy roll (SHC vol vii, pt 1, 1886 pp205-6).

1332~3 Subsidy roll of Edward III (SHC vol x, pt 1, 1889, pp81-2)

1369-1411, 1491-1855 Corporation minute books (presumably after 1835 called Borough council minute books) together with order books (Newcastle Borough Museum) (NTS)

1608 a rental (NTS pp236-42)

1620-1906 admissions of freemen (SRO microfiche copies)

1640 Subsidy roll (SHC 1941 pp155-168)

1641 Protestation return; list of male inhabitants over age of 18 (photocopy of original in House of Lords Record Office)

1664-1890 Borough Quarter Sessions minute books (Newcastle Borough Museum)

1666 Staffordshire hearth tax (SHC 1921).

1675 accounts of Thomas Smith, agent at Trentham Hall regarding Newcastle by-election expenses (SRO D593/F/2/7)

1703 rate assessment for levy in war against France & Spain; list of names and rate assessed (WSL 49/50/44)

1724 A Rentall for Newcastle Under Lyme 1734 - Poll book (SRO D593/S/16/6/1. SCA)

1747 Land Tax, and Window Tax assessments (WSL 12/41; latter is unfit for use).

1774 Poll book (SCA)

1782 Newcastle-under-Lyme Marsh Inclosure Act c. 29

1782 assessment of rate on property for raising volunteers to serve in the militia; names, some description of lands, amount of assessment (SRO D3251/7/1)

1783 Newcastle-under-Lyme Marsh Inclosure Act (Amending) c. 10

1790, 1792, 1793 Poll books (SRO. SCA)

1795 list of those summonsed for none payment of poor rate; 211 names in vestry meeting order book 1783-1810 (SRO D3251/5/1)

1802, 1807 Poll books (SRO. SCA)

1811 list of male and female ...inhabitants; lists 'housekeepers', and for each gives details of housing, occupations, etc

1812, 1815 Poll books (WSL. SCA)

1813-4 The Staffordshire Gazette

1814-9 Staffordshire Gazette and Newcastle and Pottery Advertiser

1815 Plan of Newcastle-under-Lyme by S Jackson

1816 Newcastle Inclosure Act c. 33

1816 poor rate assessment; gives names of owners & occupiers of property, street by street (2/A/G/12)

1818, 1820, 1823 Poll books (SRO. SCA)

1819-34 Newcastle and Pottery Gazette and Staffordshire Advertiser

1819-50 Improvement Commissioners minute and order books (really the business of the reformed

Newcastle-under-Lyme

Borough council after 1835) (Newcastle Borough Museum).

1822-3 Newcastle and Pottery Directory. Allbut

1827-37 admissions of burgesses (SRO microfiche copies)

1830, 1831, 1832, 1835, 1837 Poll books (WSL. SCA)

1836, 1839 Cotterill's Police Directories of the Borough of Newcastle-under-Lyme. Contain an alphabetical lists of the whole of the inhabitants householders with a classification of trades etc (WSL).

1837 rate & tax towards paying the interest on the money borrowed for purchasing the site of St George's church etc; list of inhabitants, street by street (N-u-L churchwardens)

1838-1948 Newcastle Poor Law Union minute books (SRO, together with ledgers 1843-1927)

1841 Tithe file, appointment and map

1841, 1842 Poll books (WSL. SCA)

1843 rate & tax for necessary repairs of the church; list of inhabitants, street by street, together with description of property (N-u-L churchwardens)

1859 Newcastle-under-Lyme Burgess Lands Act c. 103

c1860 Plan of Newcastle-under-Lyme by R Malabar

1861 Newcastle-under-Lyme Marsh Lands Act c. 43

1870 rate collection book; covers whole town, street by street (N-u-L)

1871, 1881 Historical records and directory of Newcastle-under-Lyme. J Ingamells. 1871 (WSL PN 4246 NEW 16 RR), 1881 (WSL PN 4246 NEW 18)

1874 Newcastle-under-Lyme Almanack

1874/5 The Staffordshire Daily Times (Newcastle-under-Lyme's only daily paper)

1881-1909 The Newcastle Guardian and Silverdale, Chesterton and Audley Chronicle

See also Family Papers, under Trentham chapter

Actors in an open-air Shakespeare production at Ford Green Hall, 2004. Courtesy of Chris Rushton

Norton in the Moors

'The village of Norton is situated on an eminence between two of the upper branches of the river Trent; the land in its vicinity is cold, and the country hilly.'

Staffordshire General and Commercial Directory. 1818

BEMERSLEY TOWNSHIP
Ball Hayes
Norton-in-the-Moors CP 1866-94. Smallthorne CP 1894-1922. PC 1894-. Stoke unparished 1922-.
LG. Smallthorne UD 1894-1922. Smallthorne W by1907-22. S-o-T CB 1922-74, D(C) 1974-97, UA 1997-. No. 27 W 1922-55. No. 7 W 1955-65. No. 7 W 1965-79. Norton & Bradeley W 1979-2002. Norton & Bradeley W 2002-
CED. Smallthorne 1889-1922. CCWs 1974-97.
PARL. S-o-T North BC 1948-.

Barn Hays
Norton-in-the-Moors CP 1866-94. Smallthorne CP 1894-1922. Stoke unparished 1922-.
LG. Smallthorne UD 1894-1922. Smallthorne W by1907-22. S-o-T CB 1922-74, D(C) 1974-97, UA 1997-. No 27 W 1922-55. No. 3 W 1955-65. No. 5 W

1965-79. Norton & Bradeley W 1979-2002. Norton & Bradeley W 2002-
CED. Smallthorne 1889-1922. CCWs 1974-97.
PARL. S-o-T North BC 1948-.

Bemersley
Norton-in-the-Moors CP 1866-1922. PC 1894-. Stoke unparished 1922-.
LG. Leek RD 1894-1922. S-o-T CB 1922-74, D(C) 1974-97, UA 1997-. No 27 W 1922-55. No. 3 1955-65. No. 3 W 1965-79. Chell W 1979-2002. Chell & Packmoor W 2002-.
CED. Smallthorne 1889-1922. CCWs 1974-97.
PARL. S-o-T North BC 1948-.

Bradeley
Norton-in-the-Moors CP 1866-94. Smallthorne CP 1894-1922. Stoke unparished 1922-.
LG. Smallthorne UD 1894-1922. Smallthorne W by1907-22. S-o-T CB 1922-74, D(C) 1974-97, UA

Norton in the Moors (Bemersley)

1997-. No 27 W 1922-55. No. 3 W 1955-65. No. 5 W 1965-79. Norton & Bradeley W 1979-2002. Norton & Bradeley W 2002-
CED. Smallthorne 1889-1922. CCWs 1974-97.
PARL. S-o-T North BC 1948-.

Catharine Fields

Norton-in-the-Moors CP 1866-94. Smallthorne CP 1894-1922. Stoke unparished 1922-.
LG. Smallthorne UD 1894-1922. Smallthorne W by1907-22. S-o-T CB 1922-74, D(C) 1974-97, UA 1997-. No 27 W 1922-55. No. 3 W 1955-65. No. 3 W 1965-79. Chell W 1979-2002. Chell & Packmoor W 2002-
CED. Smallthorne 1889-1922. CCWs 1974-97.
PARL. S-o-T North BC 1948-.

Greenway Bank

Norton-in-the-Moors CP 1866-1965. Brown Edge PW Nov 1949-1965. Brown Edge CP 1965-.
LG. Leek RD 1894-1974. Staffordshire Moorlands D 1974-. Brown Edge W 1974-2002/3. Brown Edge & Endon W 2002/3-.
CED. Smallthorne 1889-1922. Cheddleton 1922-73. Biddulph No. 1 1973-81. Biddulph-Endon 1981-2005. Biddulph South & Endon 2005-.

Hartland (1)

Norton-in-the-Moors CP 1866-94. Smallthorne CP 1894-1922. Stoke unparished 1922-.
LG. Smallthorne UD 1894-1922. Smallthorne W by1907-22. S-o-T CB 1922-74, D(C) 1974-97, UA 1997-. No 27 W 1922-55. No. 3 W 1955-65. No. 3 W 1965-79. Chell W 1979-2002. Norton & Bradeley W 2002-
CED. Smallthorne 1889-1922. CCWs 1974-97.
PARL. S-o-T North BC 1948-.

Hartland (2)

Norton-in-the-Moors CP 1866-94. Smallthorne CP 1894-1922. Stoke unparished 1922-
LG. Smallthorne UD 1894-1922. Smallthorne W by1907-22. S-o-T CB 1922-74, D(C) 1974-97, UA 1997-. No 27 W 1922-55. No. 7 W 1955-65. No. 7 W 1965-79. Chell W 1979-2002. Norton & Bradeley W 2002-
CED. Smallthorne 1889-1922. CCWs 1974-97.
PARL. S-o-T North BC 1948-.

Heath Fields

Norton-in-the-Moors CP 1866-94. Smallthorne CP 1894-1922. Stoke unparished 1922-
LG. Smallthorne UD 1894-1922. Smallthorne W by1907-22. S-o-T CB 1922-74, D(C) 1974-97, UA 1997-. No 27 W 1922-55. No. 3 W 1955-65. No. 5 W 1965-79. Norton & Bradeley W 1979-2002. Norton & Bradeley W 2002-

CED. Smallthorne 1889-1922. CCWs 1974-97.
PARL. S-o-T North BC 1948-.

New Hayes (a)

Norton-in-the-Moors CP 1866-94. Smallthorne CP 1894-1922. Stoke unparished 1922-.
LG. Smallthorne UD 1894-1922. Smallthorne W by1907-22. S-o-T CB 1922-74, D(C) 1974-97, UA 1997-. No 27 W 1922-55. No. 7 W 1955-65. No. 5 W 1965-79. Norton & Bradeley W 1979-2002. Burslem North W 2002-
CED. Smallthorne 1889-1922. CCWs 1974-97.
PARL. S-o-T North BC 1948-.

New Hayes (b)

Norton-in-the-Moors CP 1866-94. Smallthorne CP 1894-1922. Stoke unparished 1922-.
LG. Smallthorne UD 1894-1922. Smallthorne W by1907-22. S-o-T CB 1922-74, D(C) 1974-97, UA 1997-. No 27 W 1922-55. No. 7 W 1955-65. No. 5 W 1965-79. Norton & Bradeley W 1979-2002. Norton & Bradeley W 2002-
CED. Smallthorne 1889-1922. CCWs 1974-97.
PARL. S-o-T North BC 1948-.

New Hayes Colliery (1)

Norton-in-the-Moors CP 1866-94. Smallthorne CP 1894-1922. Stoke unparished 1922-.
LG. Smallthorne UD 1894-1922. Smallthorne W by1907-22. S-o-T CB 1922-74, D(C) 1974-97, UA 1997-. No. 27 W 1922-55. No. 7 W 1955-65. No. 5 W 1965-79. East Valley 1979-2002. Burslem North W 2002-
CED. Smallthorne 1889-1922. CCWs 1974-97.

New Hayes Colliery (2)

Norton-in-the-Moors CP 1866-94. Smallthorne CP 1894-1922. Stoke unparished 1922-.
LG. Smallthorne UD 1894-1922. Smallthorne W by1907-22. S-o-T CB 1922-74, D(C) 1974-97, UA 1997-. No 27 W 1922-55. No. 7 W 1955-65. No. 5 W 1965-79. East Valley 1979-2002. Norton & Bradeley W 2002-
CED. Smallthorne 1889-1922. CCWs 1974-97.
PARL. S-o-T North BC 1948-.

Outclough

Norton-in-the-Moors CP 1866-1922. Stoke unparished 1922-
LG. Leek RD 1894-1922. S-o-T CB 1922-74, D(C) 1974-97, UA 1997-. No 27 W 1922-55. No. 3 W 1955-65. No. 3 W 1965-79. Norton & Bradeley W 1979-2002. Norton & Bradeley W 2002-
CED. Smallthorne 1889-1922. CCWs 1974-97.
PARL. S-o-T North BC 1948-.

Ridgeway

Norton-in-the-Moors CP 1866-1965. Norton Green

Norton in the Moors (Bemersley)

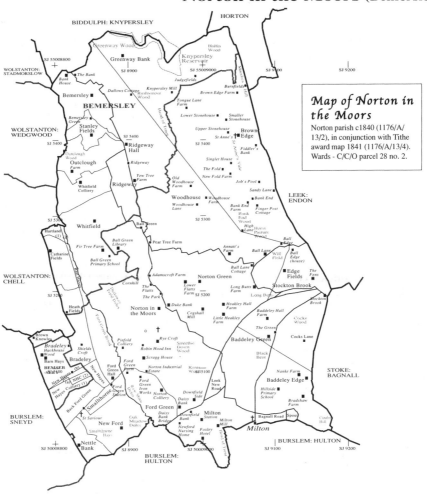

Map of Norton in the Moors

Norton parish c1840 (1176/A/13/2), in conjunction with Tithe award map 1841 (1176/A/13/4). Wards - C/C/O parcel 28 no. 2.

PW Nov 1949-1965. Stoke unparished 1965-.
LG. Leek RD 1894-1965. S-o-T CB 1965-74, D(C) 1974-97, UA 1997-. No 7 W 1965-79. Norton & Bradeley W 1979-2002. Norton & Bradeley W 2002-
CED. Smallthorne 1889-1922. Cheddleton 1922-65. CCWs 1974-97.

Ridgeway Hall

Norton-in-the-Moors CP 1866-1965. Norton Green PW Nov 1949-1965. Brown Edge CP 1965-.
LG. Leek RD 1894-1974. Staffordshire Moorlands D 1974-. Brown Edge W 1974-2002/3. Brown Edge & Endon W 2002/3-.
CED. Smallthorne 1889-1922. Cheddleton 1922-73. Biddulph No. 1 1973-81. Biddulph-Endon 1981-2005. Biddulph South & Endon 2005-.

Stanley Fields

Norton-in-the-Moors CP 1866-1922. Stoke unparished 1922-.
LG. Leek RD 1894-1922. S-o-T CB 1922-74, D(C) 1974-97, UA 1997-. No 27 W 1922-55. No. 3 W 1955-65. No. 3 W 1965-79. Norton & Bradeley W 1979-2002. Chell & Packmoor W 2002-
CED. Smallthorne 1889-1922. CCWs 1974-97.
PARL. S-o-T North BC 1948-.

Whitfield

Norton-in-the-Moors CP 1866-1922. Stoke unparished 1922-.
LG. Leek RD 1894-1922. S-o-T CB 1922-74, D(C) 1974-97, UA 1997-. No 27 W 1922-55. No. 7 W 1955-65. No. 7 W 1965-79. Norton & Bradeley W 1979-2002. Norton & Bradeley W 2002-
CED. Smallthorne 1889-1922. CCWs 1974-97.
PARL. S-o-T North BC 1948-.

Whitfield Colliery

Norton in the Moors (Norton)

Norton-in-the-Moors CP 1866-1922. Stoke unparished 1922-.

LG. Leek RD 1894-1922. S-o-T CB 1922-74, D(C) 1974-97, UA 1997-. No 27 W 1922-55. No. 3 W 1955-65. No. 7 W 1965-79. Norton & Bradeley W 1979-2002. Norton & Bradeley W 2002-

CED. Smallthorne 1889-1922. CCWs 1974-97.

PARL. S-o-T North BC 1948-.

NORTON TOWNSHIP
Baddeley Edge

Norton-in-the-Moors CP 1866-1965. PC 1894-. South PW Nov 1949-1965. Stoke unparished 1965-.

LG. Leek RD 1894-1965. S-o-T CB 1965-74, D(C) 1974-1997, UA 1997-. No. 11 W 1965-79. Abbey W 1979-2002. Abbey Green W 2002-

CED. Smallthorne 1889-1922. Cheddleton 1922-65. CCWs 1974-97.

Baddeley Green

Norton-in-the-Moors CP 1866-1965. East PW Nov 1949-1965. Stoke unparished 1965-.

LG. Leek RD 1894-1965. S-o-T CB 1965-74, D(C) 1974-97, UA 1997-. No 8 W 1965-79. East Valley W 1979-2002. East Valley W 2002-

CED. Smallthorne 1889-1922. Cheddleton 1922-65. CCWs 1974-97.

Back Ford Green

Norton-in-the-Moors CP 1866-94. Smallthorne CP 1894-1922. PC 1894-. Stoke unparished 1922-.

LG. Smallthorne UD 1894-1922. Smallthorne W by1907-22. S-o-T CB 1922-74, D(C) 1974-97, UA 1997-. No. 27 W 1922-55. No. 7 W 1955-65. No. 5 W 1965-79. East Valley 1979-2002. Burslem North W 2002-

CED. Smallthorne 1889-1922. CCWs 1974-97.

Bagnall Road

Norton-in-the-Moors CP 1866-96. Milton CP 1896-1922. PC 1896-. Stoke unparished 1922-.

LG. Leek RD 1894-6. Wolstanton RD (det) 1896-1904. Smallthorne UD 1904-22. Milton W by1907-22. S-o-T CB 1922-74, D(C) 1974-97, UA 1997-. No 28 W 1922-55. No. 11 W 1955-65. No. 11 W 1965-79. Abbey W 1979-2002. Abbey Green W 2002-

CED. Bucknall 1889-1922. CCWs 1974-97.

PARL. S-o-T Central BC 1948-.

Ball Green

Norton-in-the-Moors CP 1866-1965. Norton Green PW Nov 1949-65. Stoke unparished 1965-.

LG. Leek RD 1894-1965. S-o-T CB 1965-74, D(C) 1974-97, UA 1997-. No 7 W 1965-79. Norton & Bradeley W 1979-2002. Norton & Bradeley W 2002-

CED. Smallthorne 1889-1922. Cheddleton 1922-65. CCWs 1974-97.

Ball Hayes

Norton-in-the-Moors CP 1866-94. Smallthorne CP 1894-1922.

LG. Smallthorne UD 1894-1922. Smallthorne W by1907-22. S-o-T CB 1922-74, D(C) 1974-97, UA 1997-. No. 27 W 1922-55. No. 3 W 1955-65. No. 3 W 1965-79. Chell W 1979-2002. Chell & Packmoor W 2002-

CED. Smallthorne 1889-1922. CCWs 1974-97.

PARL. S-o-T North BC 1948-.

Black Bent

Norton-in-the-Moors CP 1866-1965. South PW Nov 1949-1965. Stoke unparished 1965-.

LG. Leek RD 1894-1965. S-o-T CB 1965-74, D(C) 1974-97, UA 1997-. No 8 W 1965-79. East Valley W 1979-2002. East Valley W 2002-

CED. Smallthorne 1889-1922. Cheddleton 1922-65. CCWs 1974-97.

Bradeley

Norton-in-the-Moors CP 1866-94. Smallthorne CP 1894-1922. Stoke unparished 1922-.

LG. Smallthorne UD 1894-1922. Smallthorne W by1907-22. S-o-T CB 1922-74, D(C) 1974-97, UA 1997-. No 27 W 1922-55. No. 3 W 1955-65. No. 5 W 1965-79. Norton & Bradeley W 1979-2002. Norton & Bradeley W 2002-

CED. Smallthorne 1889-1922. CCWs 1974-97.

PARL. S-o-T North BC 1948-.

Brown Edge

Norton-in-the-Moors CP 1866-1965. Brown Edge PW Nov 1949-1965. Brown Edge CP 1965-.

LG. Leek RD 1894-1974. Staffordshire Moorlands D 1974-. Brown Edge W 1974-2002/3. Brown Edge & Endon W 2002/3-.

CED. Smallthorne 1889-1922. Cheddleton 1922-73. Biddulph No. 1 1973-81. Biddulph-Endon 1981-2005. Biddulph South & Endon 2005-.

Brown Knowles

Norton-in-the-Moors CP 1866-94. Smallthorne CP 1894-1922. Stoke unparished 1922-

LG. Smallthorne UD 1894-1922. Smallthorne W by1907-22. S-o-T CB 1922-74, D(C) 1974-97, UA 1997-. No 27 W 1922-55. No. 3 W 1955-65. No. 5 W 1965-79. Norton & Bradeley W 1979-. Norton & Bradeley W 2002-

CED. Smallthorne 1889-1922. CCWs 1974-97.

PARL. S-o-T North BC 1948-.

Cocks Lane

Norton-in-the-Moors CP 1866-1965. East PW Nov 1949-1965. Stoke unparished 1965-

LG. Leek RD 1894-1965. S-o-T CB 1965-74, D(C) 1974-97, UA 1997-. No. 11 W 1965-79. Abbey W 1979-2002. Abbey Green W 2002-
CED. Smallthorne 1889-1922. Cheddleton 1922-65. CCWs 1974-97.

Edge Fields
Norton-in-the-Moors CP 1866-1965. East PW Nov 1949-1965. Brown Edge CP 1965-?1997. Endon & Stanley CP ?1997-.
LG. Staffordshire Moorlands D 1974-. Brown Edge W 1974-2002/3, Bagnall & Stanley W 2002/3-.
CED. Smallthorne 1889-1922. Cheddleton 1922-73. Biddulph No. 1 1973-81. Biddulph-Endon 1981-2005. Biddulph South & Endon 2005-.

Ford Green
Norton-in-the-Moors CP 1866-1922. Stoke unparished 1922-.
LG. Leek RD 1894-1922. S-o-T CB 1922-74, D(C) 1974-97, UA 1997-. No 27 W 1922-55. No. 7 W 1955-65. No. 8 W 1965-79. East Valley W 1979-2002. East Valley W 2002-
CED. Smallthorne 1889-1922. CCWs 1974-97.
PARL. S-o-T North BC 1948-.

Ford Green Hall
Norton-in-the-Moors CP 1866-94. Smallthorne CP 1894-1922. Stoke unparished 1922-.
LG. Smallthorne UD 1894-1922. Smallthorne W by1907-22. S-o-T CB 1922-74, D(C) 1974-97, UA 1997-. No 27 W 1922-55. No. 7 W 1955-65. No. 7 W 1965-79. Norton & Bradeley W 1979-2002. Norton & Bradeley W 2002-
CED. Smallthorne 1889-1922. CCWs 1974-97.
PARL. S-o-T North BC 1948-.

Leek New Road
Norton-in-the-Moor CP 1866-1922. Stoke unparished 1922-.
LG. Leek RD 1894-1922. S-o-T CB 1922-74, D(C) 1974-97, UA 1997-. No 27 W 1922-55. No. 7 W 1955-65. No. 8 W 1965-79. East Valley W 1979-2002. East Valley W 2002-
CED. Smallthorne 1889-1922. CCWs 1974-97.
PARL. S-o-T North BC 1948-.

Long Butts
Norton-in-the-Moors CP 1866-1965. East PW Nov 1949-65. Stoke unparished 1965-.
LG. Leek RD 1894-1965. S-o-T CB 1965-74, D(C) 1974-97, UA 1997-. No 7 W 1965-79. Norton & Bradeley W 1979-2002. Norton & Bradeley W 2002-
CED. Smallthorne 1889-1922. Cheddleton 1922-65. CCWs 1974-97.

Milton
Norton-in-the-Moors CP 1866-96. Milton CP 1896-

Norton in the Moors (Norton)
1922. Stoke unparished 1922-.
LG. Leek RD 1894-6. Wolstanton RD (det) 1896-1904. Smallthorne UD 1904-22. Milton W by1907-22. S-o-T CB 1922-74, D(C) 1974-97, UA 1997-. No 28 W 1922-55. No. 8 W 1955-65. No. 8 W 1965-79. East Valley W 1979-2002. East Valley W 2002-
CED. Bucknall 1889-1922. CCWs 1974-97.
PARL. S-o-T Central BC 1948-.

Nettle Bank
Norton-in-the-Moors CP 1866-94. Smallthorne CP 1894-1922. Stoke unparished 1922-.
LG. Smallthorne UD 1894-1922. Smallthorne W by1907-22. S-o-T CB 1922-74, D(C) 1974-97, UA 1997-. No 27 W 1922-55. No. 7 W 1955-65. No. 5 W 1965-79. East Valley W 1979-2002. East Valley W 2002-
CED. Smallthorne 1889-1922. CCWs 1974-97.
PARL. S-o-T North BC 1948-.

New Ford
Norton-in-the-Moors CP 1866-94. Smallthorne CP 1894-1922. Stoke unparished 1922-.
LG. Smallthorne UD 1894-1922. Smallthorne W by1907-22. S-o-T CB 1922-74, D(C) 1974-97, UA 1997-. No 27 W 1922-55. No. 7 W 1955-65. No. 8 W 1965-79. East Valley W 1979-2002. East Valley W 2002-
CED. Smallthorne 1889-1922. CCWs 1974-97.
PARL. S-o-T North BC 1948-.

New Hayes Colliery
Norton-in-the-Moors CP 1866-94. Smallthorne CP 1894-1922. Stoke unparished 1922-.
LG. Smallthorne UD 1894-1922. Smallthorne W by1907-22. S-o-T CB 1922-74, D(C) 1974-97, UA 1997-. No 27 W 1922-55. No. 7 W 1955-65. No. 5 W 1965-79. Norton & Bradeley W 1979-2002. Norton & Bradeley W 2002-
CED. Smallthorne 1889-1922. CCWs 1974-97.
PARL. S-o-T North BC 1948-.

Norton
Norton-in-the-Moors CP 1866-1922. Stoke unparished 1922-.
LG. Leek RD 1894-1922. S-o-T CB 1922-74, D(C) 1974-97, UA 1997-. No 27 W 1922-55. No. 7 W 1955-65. No. 7 W 1965-79. Norton & Bradeley W 1979-2002. Norton & Bradeley W 2002-
CED. Smallthorne 1889-1922. CCWs 1974-97.
PARL. S-o-T North BC 1948-.

Norton Green
Norton-in-the-Moors CP 1866-1965. Norton Green PW Nov 1949-1965. Stoke unparished 1965-.
LG. Leek RD 1894-1965. S-o-T CB 1965-74, D(C) 1974-97, UA 1997-. No 7 W 1965-79. Norton &

Norton-in-the-Moors (Norton)

Bradeley W 1979-2002. Norton & Bradeley W 2002-CED. Smallthorne 1889-1922. Cheddleton 1922-65. CCWs 1974-97.

Pear Tree Farm

Norton-in-the-Moors CP 1866-1965. Norton Green PW Nov 1949-65. Stoke unparished 1965-.
LG. Leek RD 1894-1965. S-o-T CB 1965-74, 1974-97, UA 1997-. No 7 W 1965-79. Norton & Bradeley W 1979-2002. Norton & Bradeley W 2002-CED. Smallthorne 1889-1922. Cheddleton 1922-65. CCWs 1974-97.

Smallthorne

Norton-in-the-Moors CP 1866-94. Smallthorne CP 1894-1922. Stoke unparished 1922-.
LG. Smallthorne UD 1894-1922. Smallthorne W by1907-22. S-o-T CB 1922-74, D(C) 1974-97, UA 1997-. No 27 W 1922-55. No. 7 W 1955-65. No. 5 W 1965-79. East Valley W 1979-2002. East Valley W 2002-
CED. Smallthorne 1889-1922. CCWs 1974-97.
PARL. S-o-T North BC 1948-.

Spout

Norton-in-the-Moors CP 1866-96. Milton CP 1896-1922. Norton-in-the-Moors CP 1922-65. South PW Nov 1949-1965. Stoke unparished 1965-.
LG. Leek RD 1894-6. Wolstanton RD (det) 1896-1904. Smallthorne UD 1904-22. Milton W by1907-22. Leek RD 1922-65. S-o-T CB 1965-.74, D(C) 1974-97, UA 1997- No 11 W 1965-79. Abbey W 1979-2002. Abbey Green W 2002-
CED. Bucknall 1889-1922. Cheddleton 1922-65. CCWs 1974-97.

Register of Common land

Squatters on Norton manor common land made Brown Edge village. There, Bank End (2), Marshes Hill (3), and Edgefields (4) are still common land (in Brown Edge CP ownership), designated such under the Commons Registration Act 1965. Registration (in Pirehill) took place from 1967, was approved 1970-2, and for some ownership was not finalised until 1981. At the time coal under each common was claimed by the NCB (under the Coal Acts 1938, 1943, and Coal Industry Nationalisation Act 1946). The Register itself was held by the County Clerk's office to c2002, and then Land Charges in Development Services. The number in brackets is the registration number. The other ancient parishes featured are:- **Adbaston** - Offley Marsh Common (60) owned by Adbaston CP. **Ashley** - Heathgrove, Loggerheads (122a), W side of Church Rd (122b), E side of Ashley church (122c) owned by Loggerheads CP. **Barlaston** Common (21, 75) owned by Stafford B. **Colton** - Stockwell Health Pool (73), land on the E bank of Moreton Brook (74) originally owned by the Gardiner family of 'The Farm House' Longdon Green, Longdon, later by Colton CP. **Colwich** - some of Cannock Chase (89), owned by Staffs CC, and Haywood Warren and Satnall Hills (17), many owners, see Colwich. **Eccleshall** - Elford Heath (29), Podmore Green (30), Fairoak Green (31) originally owned by Church Commissioners for England, later by Stafford B. Elford Heath (107), owned by Church Commissioners for England. The Waste, Chapel Chorlton (121 - the rights owner is entitled to graze five cattle there), Gravel Hole, Copmere (108 - the rights owner is entitled to extract marl, clay, and gravel there) both subject to protection under Section 9 of the Act. **Marston** - Stafford Common (1) owned by Stafford Common Land Trustees. **Stoke-upon-Trent** (**Bagnall**) - The Quarry, Springs Bank (101) owned by Bagnall CP. Harthill Quarry, Bagnall (102), The Quarry, Salters Well (104), Liberty Quarry, at Stanley (103), The Quarry, Thorneyedge Rd (100), all subject to protection under Section 9 of the Act. Bagnall CP have pedestrian rights in connection with the rights of Bagnall CP inhabitants to extract stone from the last two. (**Clayton**) - Clayton Green (40) owned by Newcastle B. **Stone** - Fulford Green (32), Saverley Green Common (35), Walton Heath Common (33) owned by Stafford B. **Swynnerton** - Yarnfield Green (34), 325 Sq metres of land to W of No. 2 The Furlong, Yarnfield (34a), 161 Sq metres of land to the N of No. 2 The Furlong (36 - ceased to be common land on Sept 6 1983) owned by Stafford B. **Wolstanton** Marsh (49) owned by the Duchy of Lancaster.

Ranton church. By TP Wood. SV. VIII. 53b. Courtesy of Trustees of WSL

Ranton

'Rustic little Ranton'

Henry Thorold. Staffordshire: A Shell Guide. 1978

With a population between 100 and 300 Ranton was entitled to an Order to form a PC without consent of the CC. It decided to have one at its parish meeting in late 1894.

PLU. Stafford 1836-1930. Ranton W by1910.
SEE ALSO pages 2, 51, 79, 96, 117-118, 125, 131, 142, 208, 214

RANTON TOWNSHIP
Ranton CP 1866-. PC May 1954-
LG. Stafford D(B) 1974-. Gnosall W 1974-2002,
Seighford W 2002-.

CED. Stafford Rural 1889-1911. Stafford Rural West
Sept 1911-34. Gnosall 1934-73. Stafford Rural No. 1
1973-81. Gnosall 1981-2005. Gnosall & Doxey 2005-

Ratepayers and vestry meetings

Male ratepayers were eligible to attend open vestries. But rarely do Pirehill vestry minute books list ratepayers; but such lists appear for Fradswell (**Colwich**) 1754, 1757, 1767, 1768 (D13/A/PO 17-19), and a list appears at the front of **Ranton** Vestry Book 1830-94 (D4305/1/1): 'Rate Payers in the parish of Ranton. Viscount Anson, Francis Eld Esq, William Hall, William Addison ___ Ronton Hall,

Ranton

Thomas Deakin ___ Woodside Farm, Thomas Robinson ___ Park nook Farm, James Beafvington ___ Ronton, Joseph Glover ___ Ronton, Wiliam Tricket ___ The Gate, James Fernihough ___ Brough Hall, Peter Bailey ___ Extol Farm, Major Dain ___ Long Compton, William Cork ___ Ditto, Thomas Hart ___ Long Compton, Willm Chapman ___ Ditto, Thos Ford ___, Hart ___ Ronton, John Perkin ___ Ronton, William Davies ___ The Vicarage Farm.' Many turn up at meetings in 1831, 1834, 1835, 1837.

Ranton Abbey

Ranton Abbey

'considerable remains of this abbey are still standing. They consist principally of a lofty well built tower; and the outer walls of the church, which are extremely low; together with a small portion of the cloisters.'
White's Directory of Staffordshire. 1834

PLU. Stafford 1858-1930. Ellenhall W by1910.
SEE ALSO pages 46, 50, 93, 119-120, 231-232

RANTON ABBEY TOWNSHIP
Ranton Abbey CP 1858-84. Ellenhall CP 1884-.
LG. Stafford RD 1894-1974, D(B) 1974-. Gnosall W 1974-2002, Seighford W 2002-

CED. Stafford Rural 1889-1911. Stafford Rural West Sept 1911-34. Gnosall 1934-73. Stafford Rural No. 1 1973-81. Gnosall 1981-2005. Gnosall & Doxey 2005-

Extra-parochial places made parishes for Poor Law purposes

By the Local Government Act 1858 c. 98 extra-parochial places were made civil parishes for the purpose of joining a PLU under the clause LXXVII 'Incorporation of any place into a Local Board.' Thereafter they elected a Guardian of the Poor for their Union - in each case this was Stafford PLU. Their overseers also became enfranchised in the system. Three of the six Pirehill extra-parochial places were relieving their poor before this, by 1817, as shown by Poor Law expenditure returns for

Ranton Abbey

Creswell, Ranton Monastery, and Tillington in the Pirehill South bundle (QS/B Michaelmas Term 1817).

As was often the case, and for whatever reason, the Act was not implemented immediately. No Guardians were elected for the extra-parochial places in 1858, nor 1859, and perhaps not in 1860 (SA April 10 1858 p4 col 5). Since SRO has no meeting minutes for these 'new' civil parishes (if any meetings were held), the only way to find overseers of this period (perhaps the earliest record of officers for these places), is in Petty Session records or in SA.

GUARDIANS (elected locally by rate payers)
Chartley Holme - no returns 1860, Charles Babb 1862, J Deavall 1863
Creswell - no returns 1860, John Kenderdine 1862-3
Ranton Monastery - no returns 1860, George Hall 1862, Jno Hall 1863
Tillington - no returns 1860, Edward Marsh 1862-3
Worston - no returns 1860, no one 1862-3
Yarlet - no returns 1860, no one 1862-3
(SA April 21 1860 p4 col 4. April 12 1862 p4 col 6. April 11 1863 p4 col 4)

OVERSEERS (paid officers, appointed at the Stafford Division Petty Sessional Court)
Chartley Holme - C Babb 1861, ? 1862, C Babb 1863, JM Meikan 1865, no one 1866, William Ball 1867
Creswell - no one 1861, ? 1862, Henry Marsh 1863, 1865-7
Ranton Monastery - no one 1861, ? 1862, P Rochell 1863, James Bellingham 1865-7,
Tillington - no one 1861, ? 1862, H Woodhouse 1863, W Lees 1865, Edward Marsh 1866, W Jennings 1867
Worston - no one 1861, ? 1862, W Milner 1863, Cornelius Scott Devey 1865-6, W Milner 1867
Yarlet - no one 1861, ? 1862, William S Woolfe, jun 1863, 1865-7
(SA April 13 1861 p4 col 4. April 11 1863 p4 col 4. April 8 1865 p4 col 6. April 14 1866 p4 col 6. April 13 1867 p4)

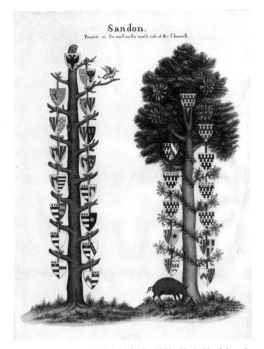

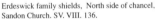

Erdeswick family shields, North side of chancel, Sandon Church. SV. VIII. 136.

Erdeswick family shields, South side of chancel. SV. VIII. 135. Both courtesy of Trustees of WSL

Sandon

'If you drive up the narrow lane leading off the A51 at Sandon, north-east of Stafford and head towards All Saints Church you will quickly find yourself transported away from the hubbub of the 20th century back over 600 years. For in this quiet backwater of Staffordshire can be found wonderfully preserved evidence of the medieval landscape.'

John Darlington. Stafford Past. 1994

At a Sandon 'vestry meeting (1815) held other day Sam: Hodgson applying for relief was offered 12/ half? week if he would be the pinner for the parish & work on the Roads when required' (D1048/3/9). PLU. Stone 1838-1930. Sandon W by1910-.

SEE ALSO pages 7, 11, 23, 36, 50, 79, 100, 103,123-125, 131, 208, 214

SANDON TOWNSHIP
Bridgend

Sandon CP 1866-1934. PC 1894-. Minutes from 1894 at SRO. Salt & Enson CP 1934-.
LG. Stone RD 1894-1934. Stafford RD 1934-74, D(B) 1974-. Beaconside W 1974-2002. Chartley W 2002-.
CED. Stone 1889-1911. Stone Rural Sept 1911-73. Stafford Rural No. 2 1973-81. Stafford Trent Valley 1981-2005, 2005-.

Sandon

Sandon CP 1866- (PC styled Sandon and Burston Sept 1989-).
LG. Stone RD 1894-1974. Stafford D(B) 1974-. Milwich W 1974-2002, 2002-.
CED. Stone 1889-1911. Stone Rural Sept 1911-2005. Barlaston & Fulford 2005-

Tollgate Farm

Sandon CP 1866-1934. Salt & Enson CP 1934-88.

Sandon

STONE: HILDERSTONE

Warren Farm   Hatherton Farm
Little Hardiwick
Hollywood
+ SJ 33009300   SJ 9400   SJ 9500   SJ 9600   + SJ 33009700

Common Farm ■

Twerlow Farm ■

Hardiwick Grove ■

SJ 3200

SANDON
Smallrice   Shaw Wood Farm   **MILWICH**   SJ 3200
Kiplass Lane Farm ■
■ Hardiwick Farm   Smallrice Farm   The Moors
Golding's Well
Joel Pool
Kiplass Slip   Cramer Hill
SANDON
SJ 3100
Iron Bridge   Romer Farm ■
Sandy Leys Farm ■
Lander's Wood ■ Farm   SJ 3100
Sandon Wood Farm

STONE: ASTON
Lane Farm ■   Kendrick's Barn ■

■ Burston Cottage Farm
SJ 3000   Black Hill   SJ 3000
Stonehouse Farm ■

Sandon ■ Stonebench Farm   † Sandon Old Hall site of   Sandon Wood   **GAYTON**
■ Dog Farm
Sandon Station ■   Dog and Doublet Inn
SANDON PARK
SJ 2900   ■ Mill Farm   Vicarswood ■   SJ 2900
STAFFORD: ENSON
■ Sandon Hall

■ Sandon Home Farm
Stocking Brook
STAFFORD: SALT   Salt Bridge ■ Bridgend   ■ Pitt's Column
+ SJ 28009300   SJ 9400   SJ 9500   SJ 9600   Tollgate Farm ■   + SJ 28009700
WESTON ON TRENT

Map of Sandon

Weston CP 1988-.
LG. Stone RD 1894-1934. Stafford RD 1934-74, D(B) 1974-. Beaconside W 1974-88. Chartley W 1988-2002, 2002-.
CED. Stone 1889-1911. Stone Rural Sept 1911-73. Stafford Rural No. 2 1973-81. Stafford Trent Valley 1981-2005, 2005-.

SANDON (det in Stone)
North
Sandon CP (det) 1866-?1894. Stone Rural CP 1894-. Meaford and Aston PW 1968-.
LG. Stone RD 1894-1974. Stafford D(B) 1974-. Oulton W 1974-2002. Milwich W 2002-.
CED. Stone 1889-1911. Stone Rural Sept 1911-2005. Barlaston & Fulford 2005-.

South
Sandon CP (det) 1866-?1894. Stone Rural CP 1894-1932. Sandon CP 1932- (PC styled Sandon and Burston Sept 1989-).
LG. Stone RD 1894-1974. Stafford D(B) 1974-. Milwich W 1974-2002, 2002-.
CED. Stone 1889-1911. Stone Rural Sept 1911-2005. Barlaston & Fulford 2005-.

Some Pirehill families in Staffordshire visitation records, qualified to bear a coat of arms

On Sandon church chancel walls Staffordshire's first antiquary, Sampson Erdeswick (c1539-1603), author of 'A Survey of Staffordshire' (c1593, published 1717), painted two trees hung with his ancestors' shields, such was his fascination with heraldry. He also he had his tomb and the E window decorated with ancestral shields, even creating fake windows in the chancel for more arms because the E window could not carry enough. He also embellished the gallery of his house, the long-lost Sandon Old Hall, with Staffordshire gentlemen's coats of arms (a later Staffordshire antiquary, Walter Chetwynd made a list of them).

By Erdeswick's time armorial bearings had become hereditary, and there was a need for a College of Arms (set up in 1485) to grant, control, and confirm them. From 1529/30 the College sent out its heralds on visits (or **visitations**) to every county to investigate new applications; the last visitation was in 1686; arms granted since then to 1898 appear in lists published by the Harleian Society.

Erdeswick was so impressed by Robert Glover (1543/4-1588), Somerset Herald, who made the 1583 Staffordshire visitation, he called him 'the only sufficient man in his time for armorye and descents in this land'. The DNB describes Glover as the heralds' heraldist, going on to say he had a vision of what needed to be done for heraldic and genealogical studies. Between 1578-8 he located and copied most of the medieval English rolls of arms; he also made innumerable drawings of medieval armorial seal impressions and other medieval coats of arms, and then he arranged these in the heraldists' order, as ordinary of arms.

For the genealogist the point to all this is, if there is a coat of arms there is invariably a ready-made pedigree which can be consulted at the WSL (eg:- the pedigree of Macclesfield of Chesterton by Tony Dunn 1995, WSL).

Dates that may appear after Pirehill families eligible to bear arms and what they refer to

1272-C16 Not a visitation date, but to as far back as Col. Wedgwood (in SHC 1913) could trace the family arms.

1528-9 A visitation by Bernolte, Clarencieux. (College of Arms) (BL - Harleian Collection Ms f76-90v is part of a visitation apparently earlier than that of 1583, and perhaps original). *Sadly, there was no time to reference this for the list below.*

1563 A visitation by William Flower, Norroy King of Arms (College of Arms, several copies) (BL - Harleian Collection Ms f54v) (Queen's College library, Oxon). *Sadly, no time to reference this for the list.*

1566 The date erroneously assigned in the Harleian Collection catalogue (of the C19) to the 1563 visitation.

1583 The family had their arms confirmed in the 1583 Visitation by Robert Glover, Somerset Herald, for W. Flower, Norroy. If 'i' before date the family were deemed by Glover to be of low birth and not noble enough to bear arms. If 'dt' the arms are doubtful (BL - Harleian Collection, several copies) (SHC 1883).

1614 A visitation by Richard St. George, Norroy (College of Arms) (BL - Harleian Collection, several copies) (SHC 1885). *No time to reference this; however, those confirmed in 1663-4 have pedigrees starting with those confirmed in 1614 - so, if 1663-4 then most likely 1614 also.*

1663-4 The family had their arms confirmed in the 1663-4 Visitation by William Dugdale, Norroy, who was accompanied by Gregory King, later Lancaster Herald (several copies at College of Arms) (BL - Harleian Collection) (SHC 1885).

1682 Whether or not proved in earlier sited visitations, the family have their arms depicted on Robert Plot's map (accompanying NHS 1686, but the map is dated 1682).

Sandon

post-1687 The Harleian Society (founded 1869) has printed lists of those who received grants of arms from 1687 to 1898.

Abnet of Audley 1663-4, 1682.

Allen of Fulford 1663-4

Anson of Shugborough 1663-4

Aston of Tixall 1583, 1682.

Aston of Bishton 1682.

Aston of Milwich 1663-4, 1682.

Audley of Heighley by 1273, 1583

Lord Audley of Audley 1583

Bagnall of Barlaston 1682

Bagnall of Stoke 1583

Bagot of Hyde 1272

Bagot of Blithfield 1583, 1663-4, 1682

Barbour of Flashbrook i1583, 1663-4

Barbour (Edward) of Eccleshall 1583

Bertram of Cocknage/ London

Bedle of Old Park (?) i1583

Beduley of Ellerton Grange 1682

Beek of Hopton 1324

Biddulph of Biddulph 1583, 1682

Biddulph of Bucknall 1583

Biddulph of Fenton 1583

Bosvill of Byanna 1682

Botiler of Tyrley 1308

Bowier of Hethhouse Grange, and Broadheath (Seighford?/Ellenhall?) 1583

Bowyer of Madeley 1583

Bowyer of Knypersley 1583, 1663-4, 1682

Braddock of Adbaston 1583, 1663-4

Bradock (Edmund) of Adbaston dt1583

Brereton of Beech 1663-4, 1682

Brett (Edward) of Keele dt1583

Brett of Keele 1583

Brett of Dimsdale 1663-4

Brocke of Hanley i1583

Broughton of Broughton 1663-4, 1682

Bucknall of Ubberley i1583

Busby of Kibblestone 1583

Chetwood of Oakley 1663-4, 1682

Chetwynd of Chetwynd, Shrops (progenitors of the Staffs Chetwynds) 1308

Chetwynd of Rudge 1682

Chetwynd of Ingestre 1583, 1663-4, 1682

Cleyton of Aston Cliff C16

Colclough of Stoke-upon-Trent 1583

Colclough of Burslem 1663-4

Collyer of Darlaston 1583, 1682

Collyer of Yarlet 1663-4, 1682

Cope of Ranton Abbey 1663-4, 1682

Corbett of Hanford 1583

Cotton of Booth 1583

Cradock of Stafford (formerly of Cheshire) 1614

Crompton of Stone Park i1583 (slightly different to later arms), 1663-4, 1682

Cumberlege of Stoke 1682

Degge of Colton 1682

Digby of Sandon 1663-4

Dorrington of Cotton (Coton Clanford?) i1583

Eardley of Eardley 1583

Egerton of Betley 1583, 1682

Egerton of Wrinehill 1583, 1682

Eld of Seighford from 1574, 1614, 1663-4, 1682

Erdeswick of Sandon 1583, 1663-4

Erdeswick of Heatley Green 1682

Feake of Stafford 1663-4

Ferrers of Chartley temp Edward I

Lord Ferrers of Chartley C16, 1682

Fitton of Trentham 1583

Fitzherbert of Swynnerton 1682

Foley of Longton 1682

Fowden/ Foden of Fulford i1583, 1663-4

Fowler of St Thomas Priory 1583, 1682

Gamble of Hardwicke i1583

Gamul of Oulton c1662

Gaywood of Bishops Offley i1583, 1663-4

Gaywood of Podmore i1583

Gerard of Gerards Bromley c1662

Lady Gerard of Sandon 1682

Giffard of High Offley 1682

Gresley of Colton 1583

Grovensnor of Whitmore 1583

Harcourt of Ellenhall by 1278, 1583, 1682

Harcourt of Ranton 1583

Hastang of Chebsey temp Edward I

Heveningham of Aston-by-Stone 1583, 1682

Hinkeley of Stoke-by-Stone 1324

De Hopton of Tyrley 1272

Jervis of Chatcull i1583, 1682
Justice of Knighton 1682
Leveson of Trentham 1583, 1682
Mere of Maer 1272
Macclesfield of Maer 1583
Macclesfield of Chesterton 1682
Mainwaring of Whitmore 1583, 1682
Marshall of Colton 1324
Needham of Ashley? 1583
Noel of Hilcote 1583, 1682
Offley of Madeley 1583
Orcharde of Garshall i1583
Pershall of Pershall 1583, 1682
Pettit of Hextall i1583
Pettyt of Bagot's Bromley i1583
Pulesdon of Flashbrook 1308
Road of Flashbrook 1682
Roos (Peter) of Swineshead dt1583
Russ/ Rosse of Eccleshall 1583
 Rowley of Heakley i1583
Short of Oulton 1682
Short of Meaford 1682
Skrymsher of Hillhouse 1682
Skrymsher of Johnson Hall 1583, 1682
Smith of Newcastle-u-Lyme 1583
Sneyd of Bradwell 1682
Sneyd of Keele 1682
Stafford of Weston Hall 1682
Standon of Standon temp Edward I

Swynnerton (Edward) of Eccleshall dt1583
  Swynnerton of Swynnerton temp Edward I,
  1583
Terrick of Clayton 1682
Thickness of Balterley 1583, 1682
Touchet of Markeaton 1308
Trussell of Kibblestone 1324
Underwood of Beech 1682
Unwin of Chatterley/ London 1583
Unwin of Clough (Hall) 1583
Vyse of Standon 1583, 1682
Walkden of Walton 1583
Walker of Weston i1583
Wastney of Colton 1272
Whitby of Great Haywood 1682
Whitemore of Madeley i1583
Whitgreave of Bridgeford 1583
Whitworth of Adbaston 1682
Wilmot of Eardley 1682
Wolseley of Wolseley 1682
Wolseley (Erasmus) of Chebsey 1583
Yonge of Charnes i1583

(Catalogue of the Heralds' Visitations with reference to etc .... in the BM. 1825. 2nd ed) (GM Sept 1829 p213) (SOS 1844 preface lxix) (SHC 1982 pp25-6) (The Local Historian's Encyclopedia. J. Richardson. 1993).

Seighford (Aston)

Tomb of William (d1593) and Mercy Bowyer, Seighford Church. SV. VIII. 158a. Courtesy of Trustees of WSL

Seighford

'The village of Seighford consists of a few scattered houses well thatched. The general face of the country is level, and in a high state of cultivation.'

Staffordshire General and Commercial Directory. 1818

'...John Haywood dog whipper...' paid £2,5s, 0d 1814-15, 1816-19 (D731/11).
PLU. Stafford 1836-1930. Seighford with Worston W by1910.
SEE ALSO pages 11, 24, 26, 34, 50, 54, 79, 84, 94, 96, 100, 124, 125, 129-131, 208, 211, 214

SEIGHFORD

PLU. Stafford 1836-1930. Seighford with Worston W by1910.

ASTON LIBERTY
Aston Bank

Seighford CP 1866-1917. Stafford unparished 1917-2005. Doxey CP April 2005-.
LG. Stafford RD 1894-1917, B 1917-74, D(B) 1974-. West W 1917-60. Highfields W 1960-c1981. Tillington W c1981-2002. Tillington W 2002-.
CED. Stafford Rural 1889-1911. Stafford Rural West

Sept 1911-9. Stafford West 1919-57. Stafford North 1957-77. Stafford North Gate 1977-2005. Gnosall & Doxey 2005-

Aston Bank Farm

Seighford CP 1866-2002. PC 1894-. Minutes from 1894 at SRO. Doxey PW 1972-2002. Stafford unparished 2002-5. Doxey CP April 2005-.
LG. Stafford RD 1894-1974, D(B) 1974-. Seighford W 1974-2002. Tillington W 2002-
CED. Stafford Rural 1889-1911. Stafford Rural West Sept 1911-34. Gnosall 1934-73. Stafford Rural No. 1 1973-81. Eccleshall 1981-2005. Gnosall & Doxey

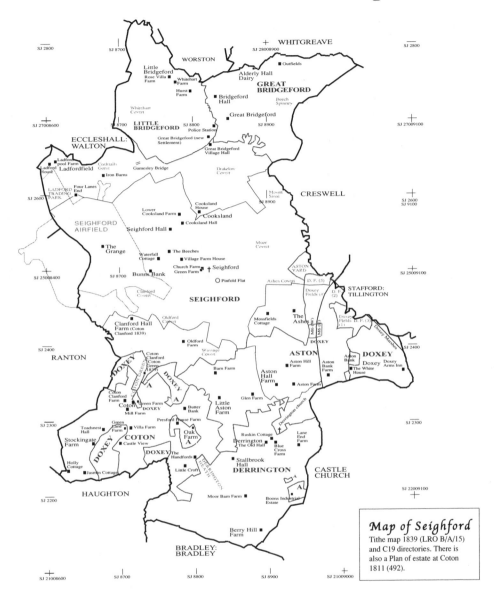

Map of Seighford
Tithe map 1839 (LRO B/A/15)
and C19 directories. There is
also a Plan of estate at Coton
1811 (492).

2005-.

Aston Hall Farm

Seighford CP 1866-. Doxey PW 1972-.
LG. Stafford RD 1894-1974, D(B) 1974-. Seighford
W 1974-2002, 2002-.
CED. Stafford Rural 1889-1911. Stafford Rural West
Sept 1911-34. Gnosall 1934-73. Stafford Rural No. 1
1973-81. Eccleshall 1981-2005. Gnosall & Doxey
2005-.

Boons Industrial Estate, Derrington church,

Little Aston Farm, Oak Farm

Seighford CP 1866-. Derrington PW 1972-.
LG. Stafford RD 1894-1974, D(B) 1974-. Seighford
W 1974-2002, 2002-.
CED. Stafford Rural 1889-1911. Stafford Rural West
Sept 1911-34. Gnosall 1934-73. Stafford Rural No. 1
1973-81. Eccleshall 1981-2005. Gnosall & Doxey
2005-.

Doxey Fields (2)

Seighford CP 1866-2002. Doxey Fields PW 1972-

Seighford (Derrington)

2002. Stafford unparished 2002-.
LG. Stafford RD 1894-1974, D(B) 1974-. Seighford 1974-2002. Tillington W 2002-.
CED. Stafford Rural 1889-1911. Stafford Rural West Sept 1911-34. Gnosall 1934-73. Stafford Rural No. 1 1973-81. Eccleshall 1981-2005. Gnosall & Doxey 2005-.

Doxey Fields (4)

Seighford CP 1866-. Doxey PW 1972-
LG. Stafford RD 1894-1974, D(B) 1974-. Seighford W 1974-2002, 2002-.
CED. Stafford Rural 1889-1911. Stafford Rural West Sept 1911-34. Gnosall 1934-73. Stafford Rural No. 1 1973-81. Eccleshall 1981-2005. Gnosall & Doxey 2005-.

Doxey Fields (5)

Seighford CP 1866-. Seighford PW 1972-.
LG. Stafford RD 1894-1974, D(B) 1974-. Seighford W 1974-2002, 2002-.
CED. Stafford Rural 1889-1911. Stafford Rural West Sept 1911-34. Gnosall 1934-73. Stafford Rural No. 1 1973-81. Eccleshall 1981-2005. Gnosall & Doxey 2005-.

DOXEY LIBERTY
Coton Green, Green Farm, Green Lane Farm

Seighford CP 1866-. Derrington PW 1972-.
LG. Stafford RD 1894-1974, D(B) 1974-. Seighford W 1974-2002, 2002-.
CED. Stafford Rural 1889-1911. Stafford Rural West Sept 1911-34. Gnosall 1934-73. Stafford Rural No. 1 1973-81. Eccleshall 1981-2005. Gnosall & Doxey 2005-.

Doxey

Seighford CP 1866-1917. Stafford unparished 1917-2005. Doxey CP April 2005-.
LG. Stafford RD 1894-1917, B 1917-74, D(B) 1974-. West W 1917-60. Highfields W 1960-c1981. Tillington W c1981-2002. Tillington W 2002-.
CED. Stafford Rural 1889-1911. Stafford Rural West Sept 1911-9. Stafford West 1919-57. Stafford North 1957-77. Stafford North Gate 1977-2005. Gnosall & Doxey 2005-

Doxey Fields (1)

Seighford CP 1866-2002. Doxey Fields PW 1972-2002. Stafford unparished 2002-5. Doxey CP April 2005-.
LG. Stafford RD 1894-1974, D(B) 1974-. Seighford 1974-2002. Tillington W 2002-.
CED. Stafford Rural 1889-1911. Stafford Rural West Sept 1911-34. Gnosall 1934-73. Stafford Rural No. 1

1973-81. Eccleshall 1981-2005. Gnosall & Doxey 2005-.

Doxey Fields (3)

Seighford CP 1866-2002. Doxey PW 1972-2002. Stafford unparished 2002-.
LG. Stafford RD 1894-1974, D(B) 1974-. Seighford W 1974-2002. Tillington W 2002-
CED. Stafford Rural 1889-1911. Stafford Rural West Sept 1911-34. Gnosall 1934-73. Stafford Rural No. 1 1973-81. Eccleshall 1981-2005. Gnosall & Doxey 2005-.

Doxey Marshes

Seighford CP 1866-1917. Stafford unparished 1917-.
LG. Stafford RD 1894-1917, B 1917-74, D(B) 1974-. West W 1917-60. Tillington W 1960-2002. Tillington W 2002-.
CED. Stafford Rural 1889-1911. Stafford Rural West Sept 1911-9. Stafford West 1919-57. Stafford North 1957-77. Stafford North Gate 1977-2005. Gnosall & Doxey 2005-

M6 (E)

Seighford CP 1866-2002. Doxey PW 1972-2002. Stafford unparished 2002-5. Doxey CP April 2005-.
LG. Stafford RD 1894-1974, D(B) 1974-. Seighford 1974-2002. Tillington W 2002-.
CED. Stafford Rural 1889-1911. Stafford Rural West Sept 1911-34. Gnosall 1934-73. Stafford Rural No. 1 1973-81. Eccleshall 1981-2005. Gnosall & Doxey 2005-.

M6 (W)

Seighford CP 1866-. Doxey PW 1972-
LG. Stafford RD 1894-1974, D(B) 1974-. Seighford W 1974-2002, 2002-.
CED. Stafford Rural 1889-1911. Stafford Rural West Sept 1911-34. Gnosall 1934-73. Stafford Rural No. 1 1973-81. Eccleshall 1981-2005. Gnosall & Doxey 2005-.

COTON LIBERTY

Seighford CP 1866-. Derrington PW 1972-.
LG. Stafford RD 1894-1974, D(B) 1974-. Seighford W 1974-2002, 2002-.
CED. Stafford Rural 1889-1911. Stafford Rural West Sept 1911-34. Gnosall 1934-73. Stafford Rural No. 1 1973-81. Eccleshall 1981-2005. Gnosall & Doxey 2005-.

DERRINGTON LIBERTY

Seighford CP 1866-. Derrington PW 1972-.
LG. Stafford RD 1894-1974, D(B) 1974-. Seighford W 1974-2002, 2002-.

CED. Stafford Rural 1889-1911. Stafford Rural West Sept 1911-34. Gnosall 1934-73. Stafford Rural No. 1 1973-81. Eccleshall 1981-2005. Gnosall & Doxey 2005-.

GREAT BRIDGEFORD LIBERTY

Seighford CP 1866-. Great Bridgeford PW 1972-.
LG. Stafford RD 1894-1974, D(B) 1974-. Seighford W 1974-2002, 2002-
CED. Stafford Rural 1889-1911. Stafford Rural West Sept 1911-34. Gnosall 1934-73. Stafford Rural No. 1 1973-81. Eccleshall 1981-2005. Gnosall & Doxey 2005-.

LITTLE BRIDGEFORD LIBERTY

Seighford CP 1866-. Great Bridgeford PW 1972-.
LG. Stafford RD 1894-1974, D(B) 1974-. Seighford W 1974-2002, 2002-
CED. Stafford Rural 1889-1911. Stafford Rural West Sept 1911-34. Gnosall 1934-73. Stafford Rural No. 1 1973-81. Eccleshall 1981-2005. Gnosall & Doxey 2005-.

SEIGHFORD LIBERTY
The Ashes

Seighford CP 1866-. Doxey PW 1972-
LG. Stafford RD 1894-1974, D(B) 1974-. Seighford W 1974-2002, 2002-.
CED. Stafford Rural 1889-1911. Stafford Rural West Sept 1911-34. Gnosall 1934-73. Stafford Rural No. 1

Seighford (Seighford)

1973-81. Eccleshall 1981-2005. Gnosall & Doxey 2005-.

Clanford Hall Farm

Seighford CP 1866-. Derrington PW 1972-.
LG. Stafford RD 1894-1974, D(B) 1974-. Seighford W 1974-2002, 2002-.
CED. Stafford Rural 1889-1911. Stafford Rural West Sept 1911-34. Gnosall 1934-73. Stafford Rural No. 1 1973-81. Eccleshall 1981-2005. Gnosall & Doxey 2005-.

Ladfordfield

Seighford CP 1866-. Great Bridgeford PW 1972-.
LG. Stafford RD 1894-1974, D(B) 1974-. Seighford W 1974-2002, 2002-.
CED. Stafford Rural 1889-1911. Stafford Rural West Sept 1911-34. Gnosall 1934-73. Stafford Rural No. 1 1973-81. Eccleshall 1981-2005. Gnosall & Doxey 2005-.

Seighford

Seighford CP 1866-. Seighford PW 1972-.
LG. Stafford RD 1894-1974, D(B) 1974-. Seighford W 1974-2002, 2002-.
CED. Stafford Rural 1889-1911. Stafford Rural West Sept 1911-34. Gnosall 1934-73. Stafford Rural No. 1 1973-81. Eccleshall 1981-2005. Gnosall & Doxey 2005-.

MANY LIBERTIES
Aston Yard

Aston, Doxey, Seighford liberties all had dole field strips in Aston Yard.
Same as Seighford.

Parish registers

Seighford PR's peculiar starting date (1560) is puzzling. It is neither very early or late, or one of the 1558 band. But put in the context of parish register history along with others, perhaps it can be explained.

The earliest registers

The mandatory registering of baptisms, marriages and burials begins in 1538. To 1598 registers were made on paper or loose sheets. In accordance with an Order of 1598 the parishes below transcribed all their loose sheet registers into a parchment book.

1538-   Audley (SRO). Talke St Martin Bap 1830- (SRO).
1538-   Betley (SRO)
1538-   Blithfield Mar 1539- (SRO).

The next earliest registers

By the Order of 1598 Ellenhall and Keele made the necessary transcriptions. But their parchment books do not start from 1538 because 1). there were no entries for 1538-9, or 2). the parish did not comply with the Order to start with, or 3). the earliest sheet(s) was lost.

1539-   Ellenhall Mar 1563-; Bap 1599- (SRO)

Seighford

1540-   Keele (SRO)

Other early registers

By the Order of 1598 these parishes made transcriptions. But the first book starts after 1538, because 1). the parish did not comply with the Order to start with, or 2). the earliest sheet(s) was lost.

1551-   Ashley (SRO); The signatures of Ashley churchwardens Edward Craddock and William Rowe appear where sheets ended Oct 1558, Oct 1563, March 1564, May 1567, June 1571, Feb 1573 and so on, certifying that the parchment register was a true copy from the sheets.

1551-   Barlaston Bap 1573-; Mar 1598- (SRO).

1555-   Mucklestone (SRO)

Lazy transcribers

These parishes transcribed only their loose sheet registers from 1558 because the Order of 1598 had implied it was only necessary to transcribe from 'the first year of her Majesty's reign'.

1558-   Abbots Bromley (SRO)

1558-   Biddulph (SRO)

1558-   Drayton-in-Hales (SRC)

1558-   Maer (SRO)

1558-   Standon (SRO)

1558-   Swynnerton (SRO)

1558-   Trentham (SRO). Blurton Mar 1754- (SRO), Bap 1813-, Bur 1828- (SRO). Hanford Bap & Bur 1828-, Mar 1843- (SRO)

1558-   Whitmore (SRO)

Many years of loose sheets lost

These parishes must have lost a wad(s) of early paper registers; so that their first parchment book starts with these peculiar dates.

1559-   Stafford St Mary (SRO, where another register which apparently does not duplicate the overlapping years). St Chad 1636 (SRO, where a register of baptisms 1648-51 which apparently does not duplicate the overlapping years).

1560-   Seighford (SRO)

1562-   Barthomley (CRO)

1563-   Newcastle St Giles (SRO). St George Bur 1829-, Bap 1832-, Mar 1837- (SRO)

1564-   Eccleshall (Chorlton) (SRO). Eccleshall 1573- (SRO)

1565-   Marston (SRO)

1568-   Stone, St Michael (SRO). Hilderstone Bap 1830-, Bur 1833-, Mar 1841- (SRO). Fulford Mar 1800-, Bur 1815- (SRO), Bap 1809- (LRO).

1573-   Milwich (SRO). Regarding BTs at LRO: A letter of 1776 exists (SRO D917/2/6) to Rev J Knight from T Buckeridge, Lichfield Registrars' Office stating that the register of Bishop Meuland was no longer in existence; Buckeridge suggests that it may have been destroyed in the Civil War.

1575-   Stowe-by-Chartley (SRO)

1576-   Norton-in-the-Moors (SRO)

1583-   Weston-on-Trent (SRO)

1590-   Colwich (SRO)

1593-   Gayton (SRO)

The first parchment book is lost

Having probably transcribed loose sheet or paper registers into a book (1598), these parishes subsequently lost it; the start date then is the earliest entry in the second or even third book.

1600-	Adbaston (SRO)
1628-	Wolstanton (SRO). Newchapel Bap 1723-, Bur 1724-, Mar 1741- (SRO). Tunstall Christ Church Bap & Bur 1832, Mar 1838- (SRO)
1629-	Stoke-upon-Trent St Peter (SRO). Bucknall Bap 1758-(SRO), Bur & Mar 1762- (LRO). Hanley St John Bap 1789-, Mar & Bur 1791- (SRO, part are BTs for as a memorandum in chapelwarden's accounts says 'The books and registers etc. were destroyed by fire in August 1842; the time of the Chartist riots'). Longton St James the Less Bap & Bur 1834, Mar 1837- (SRO). Shelton St Mark Bur & Bap 1834, Mar 1839- (SRO)
1636-	Burslem (SRO); an earlier book, 1578-, was burnt in the fire of 1717; a surviving transcript of it was made in 1701 (VCH vol 8 p123).
1636-	Sandon (SRO). The book starts in 1636 (although in fact there are some mar and bur from 1635), and was probably preceded by earlier books.
1647-	Colton (SRO). The book (in English) starts in 1647, and was probably preceded by earlier books.
1655-	Ranton (SRO); 'from their size it would appear that there existed originally at least two earlier parish volumes' (SPRS 1953-4). A fire at the Smithy in WW2 destroyed a strong box containing most of the parish papers then being kept in the attic of the adjoining cottage (BOR p39).
1659-	High Offley (LRO). The book begins in 1689, and with the existence of earlier BTs, clearly there was at least one earlier book (SPRS 1979).
1660-	Chebsey (LRO); the books covering 1538 to 1713 have long ago disappeared and the parish one containing bap and bur 1732-1812 and mar to 1754 was lost when one of the safes in the church was stolen in recent years (SPRS 1964/5)
1663-	Tixall (LRO)
1676-	Ingestre (LRO)
1678-	Madeley (SRO); two earlier books going back to 1567 existed in the earlier C18. They were seen by antiquary William Kelsall of Balterley who completely copied them; his mss formed part of the Aqualate collection, and the collection may have been at WSL (SPRS Pt 1 1960/1)

Izaak Walton's House, Eastgate Street

Stafford St Chad

'The parishioners I should think about 500 people, but it is in the midst of a thickly populated and destitute district.'

Samuel Gilson, Perpetual Curate in Returns of the Religious Census. 1851

The parish's most famous native may be Izaak Walton (1593-1683), author and angler. His house in Eastgate Street (plaque by the entrance to the Police Station in Eastgate Street) may have stood within the parish boundary. He gave £22 to build a stone wall round the graveyard of St Chad, and in 1672 he assigned rent which could be used by the churchwardens to maintain the church wall (VCH vol 6).

PLU. Stafford 1836-1930. (Stafford) East W by1910.

ST CHAD TOWNSHIP
St Chad's
St Mary and St Chad T by1728- (VCH vol 6 p230).
LG. Stafford B by1206-1835, MB 1835-1974, D(B) 1974-. East W 1835-1960. Forebridge W 1960-2002. Forebridge W 2002-
CED. Stafford East 1889-1977. Stafford East Gate 1977-2005. Stafford Central 2005-

Map of Stafford St Chad

St Chad's parish is shown on Map of the Borough of Stafford 1838 (D593/H/3/277)

Procession of Judges at one of the last Assizes, Market Square, Stafford (SA 175th Anniversary Souvenir 1970 p47 - courtesy of Roy Lewis). Courtesy of Staffordshire Newspapers Limited

Stafford St Mary

''tis an old and indeed ancient town, and gives name to the county, but we thought to have found something more worth going so much out of the way in it'

Daniel Defoe. A Tour Through The Whole Island of Great Britain. 1724-6

The wards of Stafford borough in 1735 were Green Gate ward, East Gate ward, and Goal Gate ward (D(w)08/18).

PLU. Stafford 1836-1930.

SEE ALSO pages 11, 26, 30, 49, 54, 79, 82, 86, 90, 93, 96, 100, 124, 125, 130, 139-140, 142, 208, 211, 214, 230

ST MARY TOWNSHIP
Broad Eye

St Mary and St Chad T by1728-1807. Forebridge T in Castle Church AP 1807-35 (VCH vol 6 pp185, 230). Stafford unparished 1835-.

LG. Stafford B by1206-1807, MB 1835-1974, D(B) 1974-. West W 1835-1960. In 1919 Mrs South was one of three who were the first women elected to a municipal council in Staffordshire. Returned for West Ward she was the first to sit on Stafford borough council. She was the wife of Mr CF South auctioneer of Leecroft, Rowley Park, Stafford, and nominated by the Women's Citizen's Association (SA Nov 8 1919 p7p). Tillington W 1960-c1981. Forebridge W c1981-2002. Forebridge W 2002-

CED. Stafford West 1889-1957. Stafford North 1957-77. Stafford East Gate 1977-2005. Stafford Central 2005-

PLU. (Stafford) West W by1910.

East Gate

St Mary and St Chad T by1728- (VCH vol 6 p230).

LG. Stafford B by1206-1835, MB 1835-1974, D(B) 1974-. East W 1835-1960. Forebridge W 1960-2002. Forebridge W 2002-

CED. Stafford East 1889-1977. Stafford East Gate 1977-2005. Stafford Central 2005-

PLU. (Stafford) East W by1910.

Pearl Brook (3)

St Mary and St Chad T by1728- (VCH vol 6 p230).

LG. Stafford B by1206-1835, MB 1835-1974, D(B) 1974-. East W 1835-1960. Forebridge W 1960-2002. Littleworth W 2002-

CED. Stafford East 1889-1977. Stafford East Gate 1977-2005. Stafford Central 2005-

Stafford St Mary (Hopton and Coton, Coton)

PLU. (Stafford) East W by1910.

Pennicrofts

St Mary and St Chad T by1728- (VCH vol 6 p230).
LG. Stafford B by1206-1835, MB 1835-1974, D(B) 1974-. East W 1835-1960. Littleworth W 1960-2002. Littleworth W 2002-
CED. Stafford East 1889-1977. Stafford East Gate 1977-2005. Stafford Central 2005-
PLU. (Stafford) East W by1910.

St Mary's

St Mary and St Chad T by1728- (VCH vol 6 p230).
LG. Stafford B by1206-1835, MB 1835-1974, D(B) 1974-. West W 1835-1960. Tillington W 1960-c1981. Forebridge W c1981-2002. Forebridge W 2002-
CED. Stafford West 1889-1957. Stafford North 1957-77. Stafford East Gate 1977-2005. Stafford Central 2005-
PLU. (Stafford) West W by1910.

HOPTON AND COTON TOWNSHIP

Hopton T and Coton T (?and Herberton and Sow liberties) united by 1801 (SRO QS/B Michaelmas Term 1817).

COTON TOWNSHIP (D834/14/15/8)

Armstrong

Hopton & Coton CP 1866-1917. PC 1894-? Stafford unparished 1917-.
LG. Stafford RD 1894-1917, MB 1917-74, D(B) 1974-. East W 1917-60. Coton W 1960-c1981. Littleworth W c1981-2002. Coton W 2002-.
CED. Stafford Rural 1889-1911. Stafford Rural East Sept 1911-9. Stafford East 1919-77. Stafford East Gate 1977-2005. Stafford Central 2005-
PLU. Hopton & Coton W by1910.

Beaconside

Hopton & Coton CP 1866-1917. Stafford unparished 1917-88. Hopton & Coton CP 1988-
LG. Stafford RD 1894-1917, MB 1917-74, D(B) 1974-. East W 1917-60. Coton W 1960-88. Beaconside W 1988-2002. Milford W 2002-
CED. Stafford Rural 1889-1911. Stafford Rural East Sept 1911-9. Stafford East 1919-77. Stafford East Gate 1977-88. Stafford Trent Valley 1988-2005, 2005-
PLU. Hopton & Coton W by1910.

Coton

Hopton & Coton CP 1866-76. Stafford unparished 1876-.
LG. Stafford MB 1876-1974, D(B) 1974-. East W 1876-1960. Coton W 1960-2002. Littleworth W 2002-

Coton Farm

Hopton & Coton CP 1866-1917. Stafford unparished 1917-.
LG. Stafford RD 1894-1917, MB 1917-74, D(B) 1974-. East W 1917-60. Coton W 1960-2002. Coton W 2002-
CED. Stafford Rural 1889-1911. Stafford Rural East Sept 1911-9. Stafford East 1919-77. Stafford East Gate 1977-2005. Stafford Central 2005-
PLU. Hopton & Coton W by1910.

Coton Field

Hopton & Coton CP 1866-76. Stafford unparished 1876-.
LG. Stafford MB 1876-1974, D(B) 1974-. East W 1876-1960. Coton W 1960-2002. Coton W 2002-.
CED. Stafford East 1889-1977. Stafford East Gate 1977-2005. Stafford Central 2005-
PLU. (Stafford) East W by1910.

Coton Hill

Hopton & Coton CP 1866-1917. Stafford unparished 1917-.
LG. Stafford RD 1894-1917, MB 1917-74, D(B) 1974-. East W 1917-60. Littleworth W 1960-2002. Littleworth W 2002-.
CED. Stafford Rural 1889-1911. Stafford Rural East Sept 1911-9. Stafford East 1919-77. Stafford East Gate 1977-2005. Stafford Central 2005-
PLU. Hopton & Coton W by1910.

Harris

Hopton & Coton CP 1866-1917. Stafford unparished 1917-.
LG. Stafford RD 1894-1917, MB 1917-74, D(B) 1974-. East W 1917-60. Littleworth W 1960-c1981. Coton W c1981-2002. Littleworth W 2002-.
CED. Stafford Rural 1889-1911. Stafford Rural East Sept 1911-9. Stafford East 1919-77. Stafford East Gate 1977-2005. Stafford Central 2005-
PLU. Hopton & Coton W by1910.

Haybarn

Hopton & Coton CP 1866-2002, PC 1894-?, Nov 1951-. Stafford unparished 2002-.
LG. Stafford RD 1894-1974, D(B) 1974-. Beaconside W 1974-2002. Common W 2002-.
CED. Stafford Rural 1889-1911. Stafford Rural East Sept 1911-34. Stafford Rural 1934-73. Stafford Rural No. 2 1973-81. Stafford Trent Valley 1981-2005. Stafford North 2005-
PLU. Hopton & Coton W by1910.

Kingston Brook

Hopton & Coton CP 1866-2002, PC 1894-?, Nov 1951-

Stafford St Mary (Hopton and Coton, Coton)

. Stafford unparished 2002-.

LG. Stafford RD 1894-1974, D(B) 1974-. Beaconside W 1974-2002, Littleworth W 2002-.

CED. Stafford Rural 1889-1911. Stafford Rural East Sept 1911-34. Stafford Rural 1934-73. Stafford Rural No. 2 1973-81. Stafford Trent Valley 1981-2005. Stafford Central 2005-

PLU. Hopton & Coton W by1910.

Kingston Hill

Hopton & Coton CP 1866-1917. Stafford unparished 1917-.

LG. Stafford RD 1894-1917, MB 1917-74, D(B) 1974-. East W 1917-60. Littleworth W 1960-2002. Littleworth W 2002-.

CED. Stafford Rural 1889-1911. Stafford Rural East Sept 1911-9. Stafford East 1919-77. Stafford East Gate 1977-2005. Stafford Central 2005-

PLU. Hopton & Coton W by1910.

Lammascote

Hopton & Coton CP 1866-76. Stafford unparished 1917-.

LG. Stafford MB 1876-1974, D(B) 1974-. East W 1876-1960. Forebridge W 1960-2002. Forebridge W 2002-

CED. Stafford East 1889-1977. Stafford East Gate 1977-2005. Stafford Central 2005-

PLU. (Stafford) East W by1910.

Littleworth

Hopton & Coton CP 1866-76. Stafford unparished 1876-.

LG. Stafford B 1876-1974, D(B) 1974-. East W 1876-1934. South W 1934-60. Littleworth W 1960-2002. Littleworth W 2002-.

CED. Stafford East 1889-1934. Stafford West 1934-1957. Stafford East 1957-77. Stafford East Gate 1977-2005. Stafford Central 2005-

PLU. (Stafford) East W by1910.

Oxford Gardens

Hopton & Coton CP 1866-1917. Stafford unparished 1917-.

LG. Stafford RD 1894-1917, MB 1917-74, D(B) 1974-. East W 1917-60. Coton W 1960-2002. Common W 2002-.

CED. Stafford Rural 1889-1911. Stafford Rural East Sept 1911-9. Stafford East 1919-77. Stafford East Gate 1977-2005. Stafford North 2005-

PLU. Hopton & Coton W by1910.

Pearl Brook (1)

LG. Stafford B perhaps from 1206, certainly by1546-1835, MB 1835-1974, D(B) 1974-. East W 1835-1960. Forebridge W 1960-2002. Littleworth W 2002-

CED. Stafford East 1889-1977. Stafford East Gate

1977-2005. Stafford Central 2005-

PLU. (Stafford) East W by1910.

Pearl Brook (2)

LG. Stafford B perhaps from 1206, certainly by1546-. Stafford B 1807-35, MB 1835-1974, D(B) 1974-. East W 1835-1960. Forebridge W 1960-2002. Forebridge W 2002-

CED. Stafford East 1889-1977. Stafford East Gate 1977-2005. Stafford Central 2005-

PLU. (Stafford) East W by1910.

Portal

Hopton & Coton CP 1866-2002, PC 1894-?, PC Nov 1951-. Stafford unparished 2002-.

LG. Stafford RD 1894-1974, D(B) 1974-. Beaconside W 1974-2002, Coton W 2002-.

CED. Stafford Rural 1889-1911. Stafford Rural East Sept 1911-34. Stafford Rural 1934-73. Stafford Rural No. 2 1973-81. Stafford East Gate 1981-2005. Stafford Central 2005-

PLU. Hopton & Coton W by1910.

RAF Stafford

Hopton & Coton CP 1866-, PC 1894-?, PC Nov 1951-

LG. Stafford RD 1894-1974, D(B) 1974-. Beaconside W 1974-2002. Milford W 2002-

CED. Stafford Rural 1889-1911. Stafford Rural East Sept 1911-34. Stafford Rural 1934-73. Stafford Rural No. 2 1973-81. Stafford Trent Valley 1981-2005, 2005-

PLU. Hopton & Coton W by1910.

St George's Hospital

Coton L perhaps by1807-66, and so Hopton & Coton CP 1866-76. Stafford unparished 1876-.

LG. Stafford B by1546-; perhaps reverts to Coton T, but certainly Stafford MB 1876-1974, D(B) 1974-. East W 1876-1960. Coton W 1960-2002. Littleworth W 2002-

CED. Stafford East 1889-1977. Stafford East Gate 1977-2005. Stafford Central 2005-

PLU. (Stafford) East W by1910.

St John

Hopton & Coton CP 1866-76. Stafford unparished 1876-.

LG. Stafford MB 1876-1974, D(B) 1974-. East W 1876-1960. Littleworth W 1960-2002. Littleworth W 2002-.

CED. Stafford East 1889-1977. Stafford East Gate 1977-2005. Stafford Central 2005-

PLU. Stafford 1836-1930. (Stafford) East W by1910.

Sandon Road

Hopton & Coton CP 1866-1917. Stafford unparished 1917-.

LG. Stafford RD 1894-1917, MB 1917-1974, D(B)

135

Stafford St Mary (Hopton and Coton, Coton)

1974-. East W 1917-24. North W 1924-60. Common W 1960-2002. Common W 2002-.

CED. Stafford Rural 1889-1911. Stafford Rural East Sept 1911-9. Stafford East 1919-1957. Stafford North 1957-77. Stafford North Gate 1977-2005, 2005-

PLU. Hopton & Coton W by 1910.

Sandyford

Hopton & Coton CP 1866-76. Stafford unparished 1876-.

LG. Stafford MB 1876-1974, D(B) 1974-. East W 1876-1960. Coton W 1960-2002. Coton W 2002-

CED. Stafford East 1889-1977. Stafford North Gate 1977-2005. Stafford Central 2005-

PLU. (Stafford) East W by 1910.

Smallman

Hopton & Coton CP 1866-76. Stafford unparished 1876-.

LG. Stafford MB 1876-1974, D(B) 1974-. East W 1876-1960. Coton W 1960-2002. Coton W 2002-

CED. Stafford East 1889-1977. Stafford East Gate 1977-2005. Stafford Central 2005-.

PLU. (Stafford) East W by 1910.

Thieves Ditch Meadows a

St Mary & St Chad APs/ Castle Church AP. Coton T/ Forebridge T -1807.

LG. Stafford B 1807-35, MB 1835-1974, D(B) 1974-. East W 1835-1960. Forebridge W 1960-2002. Forebridge W 2002-

CED. Stafford East 1889-1977. Stafford East Gate 1977-2005. Stafford Central 2005-.

PLU. (Stafford) East W by 1910.

Thieves Ditch Meadows b

St Mary & St Chad APs/ Castle Church AP. Coton T/ Forebridge T -1807.

LG. Stafford B 1807-35, MB 1835-1974, D(B) 1974-. East W 1835-1924. South W 1924-60. Forebridge W 1960-2002. Forebridge W 2002-.

CED. Stafford East 1889-1925. Stafford West 1925-1957. Stafford East 1957-77. Stafford East Gate 1977-2005. Stafford Central 2005-.

PLU. (Stafford) East W by 1910.

Thieves Ditch Meadows c

St Mary & St Chad APs/ Castle Church AP. Coton T/ Forebridge T -1807.

LG. Stafford B 1807-35, MB 1835-1974, D(B) 1974-. East W 1835-1960. Littleworth W 1960-2002.

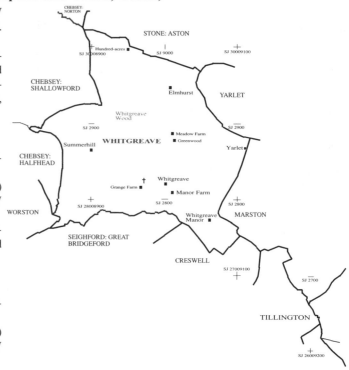

Littleworth W 2002-.

CED. Stafford East 1889-1977. Stafford East Gate 1977-2005. Stafford Central 2005-.

PLU. (Stafford) East W by 1910.

Thieves Ditch Meadows d

St Mary & St Chad APs/ Castle Church AP. Coton T/ Forebridge T -1807.

LG. Stafford B 1807-35, MB 1835-1974, D(B) 1974-. East W 1835-1924. South W 1924-60. Littleworth W 1960-2002. Littleworth W 2002-.

CED. Stafford East 1889-1925. Stafford West 1925-1957. Stafford East 1957-77. Stafford East Gate 1977-2005. Stafford Central 2005-.

PLU. (Stafford) East W by 1910.

Tithe Barn

Coton T perhaps by 1807-66, and so Hopton & Coton CP 1866-76. Stafford unparished 1876-.

LG. Stafford B by 1546-; perhaps reverts to Coton T, but certainly Stafford MB 1876-1974, D(B) 1974-. East W 1876-1960. Littleworth W 1960-2002. Littleworth W 2002-.

CED. Stafford East 1889-1977. Stafford East Gate 1977-2005. Stafford Central 2005-

PLU. Stafford 1836-1930. (Stafford) East W by 1910.

Stafford St Mary (Hopton and Coton, Hopton)

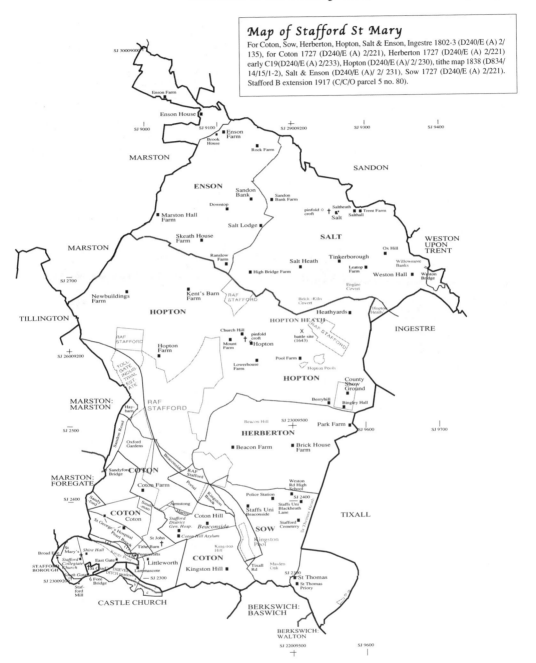

HERBERTON LIBERTY

Hopton & Coton CP 1866-, PC 1894-?, PC Nov 1951-
LG. Stafford RD 1894-1974, D(B) 1974-. Beaconside
W 1974-2002. Milton W 2002-.
CED. Stafford Rural 1889-1911. Stafford Rural East
Sept 1911-34. Stafford Rural 1934-73. Stafford Rural

No. 2 1973-81. Stafford Trent Valley 1981-2005, 2005-
PLU. Hopton & Coton W by1910.

HOPTON TOWNSHIP
Hopton

Hopton & Coton CP 1866-, PC 1894-?, PC Nov 1951-

Stafford St Mary (Hopton and Coton, Sow)

Whitgreave chapel. By TP Wood. SV. IX. 109b. Courtesy of Trustees of WSL

LG. Stafford RD 1894-1974, D(B) 1974-. Beaconside W 1974-2002. Milton W 2002-.

CED. Stafford Rural 1889-1911. Stafford Rural East Sept 1911-34. Stafford Rural 1934-73. Stafford Rural No. 2 1973-81. Stafford Trent Valley 1981-2005, 2005-

PLU. Hopton & Coton W by1910.

Tollgate Industrial Estate

Hopton & Coton CP 1866-2002. Stafford unparished 2002-

LG. Stafford RD 1894-1974, D(B) 1974-. Beaconside W 1974-2002. Common W 2002-.

CED. Stafford Rural 1889-1911. Stafford Rural East Sept 1911-34. Stafford Rural 1934-73. Stafford Rural No. 2 1973-81. Stafford Trent Valley 1981-2005. Stafford North 2005-.

PLU. Hopton & Coton W by1910.

SOW LIBERTY

Deemed extra-parochial in 1766 (Castle Church PR)

Kingston Pool

Hopton & Coton CP 1866-2002, PC 1894-?, PC Nov 1951-. Stafford unparished 2002-.

LG. Stafford RD 1894-1974, D(B) 1974-. Beaconside W 1974-2002, Littleworth W 2002-.

CED. Stafford Rural 1889-1911. Stafford Rural East Sept 1911-34. Stafford Rural 1934-73. Stafford Rural No. 2 1973-81. Stafford Trent Valley 1981-2002. Stafford Central 2002-5, 2005-.

PLU. Hopton & Coton W by1910.

Sow

Hopton & Coton CP 1866-.

LG. Stafford RD 1894-1974, D(B) 1974-. Beaconside W 1974-2002, Milford W 2002-.

CED. Stafford Rural 1889-1911. Stafford Rural East Sept 1911-34. Stafford Rural 1934-73. Stafford Rural No. 2 1973-81. Stafford Trent Valley 1981-2005, 2005-
PLU. Hopton & Coton W by1910.

St Thomas
Hopton & Coton CP 1866-1988. Tixall CP 1988-, Ingestre with Tixall PC (a pg) 1988-. Tixall PW 1988-
LG. Stafford RD 1894-1974, D(B) 1974-. Milford W 1974-2002, Milford W 2002-.
CED. Stafford Rural 1889-1911. Stafford Rural East Sept 1911-34. Stafford Rural 1934-73. Stafford Rural No. 2 1973-81. Stafford Trent Valley 1981-2005, 2005-
PLU. Hopton & Coton W by1910.

Tixall Road
Hopton & Coton CP 1866-?1997. Stafford unparished ?1997-
LG. Stafford RD 1894-1974, D(B) 1974-. Littleworth W 1974-2002, 2002-.
CED. Stafford Rural 1889-1911. Stafford Rural East Sept 1911-34. Stafford Rural 1934-73. Stafford Rural No. 2 1973-81. Stafford Trent Valley 1981-?1997. Stafford East Gate ?1997-2005. Stafford Central 2005-.
PLU. Hopton & Coton W by1910.

SALT AND ENSON TOWNSHIP
A union early temp Elizabeth I of chapels of Enson and Salt (GLAUE p421).

ENSON CHAPELRY
Salt & Enson CP 1866-, PC 1894-. Minutes 1894-1990 at SRO.
LG. Stafford RD 1894-1974, D(B) 1974-. Beaconside W 1974-2002. Chartley W 2002-.
LG. Stafford RD 1894-1974, D(B) 1974-.
CED. Stafford Rural 1889-1911. Stafford Rural East Sept 1911-34. Stafford Rural 1934-73. Stafford Rural No. 2 1973-81. Stafford Trent Valley 1981-2005-, 2005-
PLU. Salt & Enson W by1910.

SALT CHAPELRY
Salt
Salt & Enson CP 1866-, PC 1894-. Minutes from 1894 at SRO.
LG. Stafford RD 1894-1974, D(B) 1974-. Beaconside

Stafford St Mary (Whitgreave)
W 1974-2002. Chartley W 2002-.
CED. Stafford Rural 1889-1911. Stafford Rural East Sept 1911-34. Stafford Rural 1934-73. Stafford Rural No. 2 1973-81. Stafford Trent Valley 1981-2005, 2005-
PLU. Salt & Enson W by1910.

'Hopton Heath'
Hopton & Coton T in Stafford AP by1802-66, CP 1866-, PC Nov 1951-.
LG. Stafford RD 1894-1974, D(B) 1974-. Beaconside W 1974-2002. Milton W 2002-.
CED. Stafford Rural 1889-1911. Stafford Rural East Sept 1911-34. Stafford Rural 1934-73. Stafford Rural No. 2 1973-81. Stafford Trent Valley 1981-2005, 2005-
PLU. Stafford 1836-1930. Hopton & Coton W by1910.

Weston Bridge
Weston on Trent AP by1802-66, CP 1866-, PC 1894-, PC styled Weston 1961-. Weston-with-Gayton PC (a pg) June 1 1973-9. Weston-with-Gayton-with-Fradswell PC (a pg) 1979-2003. Weston-with-Gayton PC (a pg) 2003-.
LG. Stafford RD 1894-1974, D(B) 1974-. Chartley W 1974-2002, 2002-.
CED. Stafford Rural 1889-1911. Stafford Rural East Sept 1911-34. Stafford Rural 1934-73. Stafford Rural No. 2 1973-81. Stafford Trent Valley 1981-2005, 2005-

WHITGREAVE TOWNSHIP
Separate for Poor relief by 1801 (SRO QS/B Michaelmas Term 1817). Whitgreave CP 1866-. With a population between 100 and 300 Whitgreave was entitled to an Order to form a PC without consent of the CC. But the parish meeting in late 1894 voted against forming one. It was chaired by GH Tunnicliffe (SA Dec 8 1894 p6). There was a parish meeting in 1917 (SA March 24 1917 p7 col 6). PC Jan 1928-.
LG. Stafford RD 1894-1974, D(B) 1974-. Beaconside W 1974-2002. Seighford W 2002-.
CED. Stafford Rural 1889-1911. Stafford Rural West Sept 1911-34. Stafford Rural 1934-73. Stafford Rural No. 2 1973-81. Stafford Trent Valley 1981-2005. Gnosall & Doxey 2005-.
PLU. Whitgreave & Yarlet W by1910.

Select vestries
The vestry, the precursor of the PC, was a meeting which carried out the civil affairs of a parish. Meeting in the vestry (see Abbots Bromley), it had control over the Church and Poor Rates, examined the churchwardens accounts (see Adbaston), elected (at the Easter meeting) at least one of the churchwardens (see Colton), perhaps oversaw the conduct of overseers and constables, and minuted its business in what have become known as Parish Books (see Barlaston). There were two types of

Stafford St Mary

vestry: An Open vestry (see Standon) for any male ratepayer that wished to attend (see Ranton), or Select vestry, a committee of the incumbent, parish officers and others (often the wealthier parishioners) acting on behalf of the parish. Select vestries evolved because:- there had been one by custom; one was established in the C17 by a Bishop's Faculty; one was part and parcel of particular Church Building Acts (not really applicable in Pirehill); the parish had become too populous to be governed by Open vestry; or one was set up under the Sturges Bourne Act 1819, and was really a Parish Committee, dealing with Poor Relief, but known as a Select Vestry. Judging from minute preambles these were Select for at least the period stated: **Abbots Bromley** by Sept 1832 to March 1834, except for general Easter meetings 1833 (D1209/5/1). **Ashley** 1824 (with Open Easter vestries), 1835, 1836 to Aug 1838, thereafter Open (D44/A/PV/3-4); **Colwich** Aug 1833 to Aug 1836; **Drayton-in-Hales**; in 1834 there was a committee to deal with poor relief (SRRC P97/2997/9/1). **Keele** from/ by May 1823 to Oct 1824; **Madeley** from 1819, one of the new Parish Committees under the 1819 Act (MHSP p62), and in the period Sept 29 1831 to April 12 1832; **Mucklestone** from/ by Oct 30 1823 to Dec 2 1824, April 10 1832 to at least June 21 1832 (for poor purposes only & only for Staffs side of parish); **Newcastle-u-Lyme** St Giles, perhaps from Dec 4 1806 when the vestry comprised a 'committee' or 'general committee' - although it appears to have been appointed at the annual Easter meeting by an Open vestry to April 19 1838 (with the creation of Newcastle PLU), thereafter there were Open vestries; **Stafford** Stafford St Mary ?1735-, ?1742 (when a Select committee was set up for conducting, inspecting, implementing the management of the workhouse), ?1763-83 (D1323/K/ 1) because minutes not signed, a monthly inspector(s) appointed; list of 68 names in front may represent the committee?; Stafford a populous place; things are 'ordered' to be done, not resolved by vote; **Stoke-upon-Trent** from 1816- (VCH vol 8 p194); **Trentham** Feb 1834- March 1838 described as a committee meeting. **Whitmore** on account of a certain mention of 'Rates uncollected and allowed by the select vestry on the 9th day of July 1823 £12.19s.8d' (D3332/6/1). **Wolstanton** regular (though not annual/ Easter) meetings from May 6 1835 to 1838.

Standon Post Office in Standon village, from an old postcard

Standon

'The village straggles up the hill from Cotes Heath and the ugly gantries of the electrified main line railway.'   Michael Raven. Staffordshire and the Black Country. 1988

Standon overseers' accounts (D1026/2/2) show in 1745 there were separate districts of Standon hamlet, Standon Hall hamlet, Walford hamlet, Ridge hamlet and Weston hamlet for the assessment of or/ and collection of poor rate.
PLU. Stone 1838-1930. Standon W by1910-.
SEE ALSO pages 24, 79, 84, 93, 94, 96, 100, 106, 124, 125, 130, 142, 208, 214

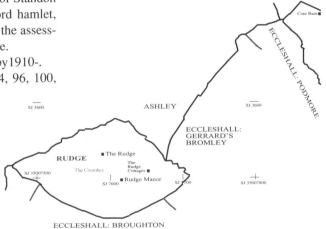

Maps of Rudge and Standon (overleaf)
For division of townships 1838 tithe map in WSL S.MS 417/150. For Weston estate - 1838 consolidated Weston manor/ estate identifiable from tithe map award and app (D1026/3/2).

RUDGE (det) TOWNSHIP

Standon CP 1866-1932. PC 1894-. Minutes from 1894 at SRO. Eccleshall CP 1932-. Cotes PW 1932-5. Croxton PW April 1935-

LG. Stone RD 1894-1974. Stafford D(B) 1974-. Eccleshall W 1974-2002, 2002-.
CED. Eccleshall 1889-2005, 2005-.

Standon

BOWERS, STANDON, WALFORD TOWNSHIPS

Standon CP 1866-.

LG. Stone RD 1894-1974. Stafford D(B) 1974-.
Eccleshall W 1974-2002, 2002-.
CED. Eccleshall 1889-2005, 2005-.

Open vestries

Judging from minute preambles these parishes had an Open vestry for at least the period stated, as opposed to a Select vestry (see Stafford): **Abbots Bromley** general Easter meetings 1833 only, April 1834- (D1209/5/1); **Adbaston** 1726-1863 (D4183/3/1); **Ashley** Oct 1838- (D44/A/PV/1) (D44/A/PV/3-4); **Audley** 1729-, 1742-; **Barlaston** 7 Feb 1762 only, 11 June 1823- (D3538/9); **Betley** 1787-; **Blithfield**,1850s onwards (D1386/1/6); **Burslem** 1791-; **Chebsey** 1789-1874; **Colwich** 1807-33, 1837-, **Eccleshall** Chorlton 1850s-; **Gayton** 1 meeting in 1832 only; **Keele** 1725 only, 1738, 1790, from Oct 1824-77; **Maer** 1830-97; **Marston** 1820 only; **Madeley** Sept 15 1831, April 24 1832 (annual general meeting to decide who will sit on the select vestry), May 3 1832-54; **Milwich** 1790-1820; **Mucklestone** Jan 6 1825-May 5 1831, then in 1845, 1850; **Newcastle-u-Lyme** St Giles, perhaps to Nov 20 1806, & perhaps from Oct 8 1846 when 'general vestry meetings were held' to 1928 at least; **Ranton** 1830-94; **Sandon** 1799, 1811-27, 1828-41, 1842-90. **Seighford** 1847-1920; ? **Stafford** St Chad 1838-1870s; **Standon** 1815-8, 1825, 1829-1957. **Stoke-upon-Trent** Fenton Christ Church 1869-; **Stowe** 1754, 1855-1939 probably open, but a committee formed in 1860s to allocate pews; **Swynnerton** 1843-C20; **Trentham** March 1838-; **Wolstanton** Newchapel 1839-. Wolstanton April 7 1835 one meeting only, 1836 April 5 annual meeting only, same for 1837 to 1838, thereafter an open vestry.

S.W VIEW OF BUCKNALL CHURCH.

Bucknall Chapel. By TP Wood. SV. VII. 173b. Courtesy of Trustees of WSL

Stoke-upon-Trent

'May Stoke-on-Trent, a real city, spacious and gay, fit for good craftsmen to live in, rise high and white; and may the blanket of smoke, the sooty dolls' houses, the blackened fields, soon be nothing but a memory, a tale of the old pioneers.'

JB Priestley. English Journey. 1933

SEE ALSO for Stoke generally, pages 26, 30, 34, 36, 44, 79, 93, 96, 103, 120, 140, 167-8, 214, 233: for Bagnall, 6, 54, 96, 116, 208, 211: for Botteslow,186: for Bucknall11, 96, 124, 131,167-8, 208: for Clayton,116: for Fenton, 120,142, 208, 230: for Hanley, 7, 11, 124, 131, 182, 208, 230: for Longton, 7, 11, 90, 131, 208, 230: for Penkhull 7, 131, 182,11,186, 208, 230: for Shelton 11,131

BAGNALL, BUCKNALL, EAVES QUARTER

A union of Bucknall (with Eaves) and Bagnall districts for Poor Relief in early C17. The quarter had its own overseer (VCH vol 8 p198).

BAGNALL CHAPELRY

PLU. Stoke-upon-Trent 1836-1922, Stoke-upon-Trent and Wolstanton 1922-30.

Bagnall

S-u-T Rural CP 1894-5. Bagnall PW Nov 1894-5. Bagnall CP Nov 1895-. There was no contest for the first PC in 1896. It was chosen and formed (SA March 14 1896 p3). Minutes from 1896 at SRO.

LG. Stoke RD 1895-1906. Leek RD Sept 1906-1974. Staffs Moorlands D 1974-. Endon & Stanley W 1974-2002/3. Bagnall & Stanley W 2002/3-.

CED. Bucknall 1889-1922. Cheddleton 1922-1973.

143

Stoke-upon-Trent (Bagnall, Bucknall, Eaves Quarter, Bucknall)

Cheadle No. 1 1973-81. Biddulph-Endon 1981-2005. Biddulph South & Endon 2005-.

Jack Hayes

S-u-T Rural CP 1894-5. Bagnall PW Nov 1894-5. Bagnall CP Nov 1895-1965. Stoke unparished 1965-LG. Stoke RD 1895-1906. Leek RD Sept 1906-1974. S-o-T CB 1965-74, D(C) 1974-97, UA 1997-. No. 11 W 1965-79. Abbey W 1979-2002. Abbey Green W 2002-

CED. Bucknall 1889-1922. Cheddleton 1922-65. CCWs 1974-97.

BUCKNALL TOWNSHIP

PARL. Stoke-on-Trent Central BC 1948-. ?1981-
PLU. S-u-T 1836-1922. S-u-T & Wolstanton 1922-30. Bucknall & Eaves W by1894-6. Bucknall W Mar 1896-.

Abbey Hulton

S-u-T Rural CP 1894-1922. Bucknall & Eaves PW Dec 1894-6. Bucknall PW Mar 1896-1922.

LG. S-u-T RD 1894-1922. S-o-T CB 1922-74, D(C) 1974-97, UA 1997-. No. 28 W 1922-55. No. 11 W 1955-65. No. 11 W 1965-79. Abbey W 1979-2002. Abbey Green W 2002-.

CED. Bucknall 1889-1922. CCWs 1974-97.

Ash Bank

S-u-T Rural CP 1894-1922. Bucknall & Eaves PW Dec 1894-6. Bucknall PW Mar 1896-1922. Caverswall CP 1922-77. Werrington PW 1922-66. Ash Hall PW July 1966-77. Caverswall & Werrington CP Feb 1977-88. Werrington PW 1977-88. Werrington CP 1988-.

LG. S-u-T RD 1894-1922. Cheadle RD 1922-74. Staffordshire Moorlands D 1974-. Werrington W 1974-2002/3, 2002/3-

CED. Bucknall 1889-1922. Caverswall 1922-2005, 2005-

Bentilee

S-u-T Rural CP 1894-1922. Bucknall & Eaves PW Dec 1894-6. Bucknall PW Mar 1896-1922.

LG. S-u-T RD 1894-1922. S-o-T CB 1922-74, D(C) 1974-97, UA 1997-. No. 28 W 1922-55. No. 16 W 1955-65. No. 16 W 1965-79. Brookhouse W 1979-2002. Bentilee & Townsend W 2002-.

CED. Bucknall 1889-1922. CCWs 1974-97.

Big Brookhouse

S-u-T Rural CP 1894-1922. Bucknall & Eaves PW Dec 1894-6. Bucknall PW Mar 1896-1922. Caverswall CP 1922-65. Werrington PW 1922-65.

LG. S-u-T RD 1894-1922. Cheadle RD 1922-65. S-o-T CB 1965-74, D(C) 1974-97, UA 1997-. No. 11 W 1965-. No. 15 W 1965-79. Brookhouse W 1979-2002. Bentilee & Townsend W 2002-

Bucknall

S-u-T Rural CP 1894-1922. Bucknall & Eaves PW Dec 1894-6. Bucknall PW Mar 1896-1922.

LG. S-u-T RD 1894-1922. S-o-T CB 1922-74, D(C) 1974-97, UA 1997-. No. 28 W 1922-55. No. 16 W 1955-65. No. 15 W 1965-79 Berryhill W 1979-2002. Bentilee & Townsend W 2002-.

CED. Bucknall 1889-1922. CCWs 1974-97.

Bucknall Park

S-u-T Rural CP 1894-1922. Bucknall & Eaves PW Dec 1894-6. Bucknall PW Mar 1896-1922.

LG. S-u-T RD 1894-1922. S-o-T CB 1922-74, D(C) 1974-97, UA 1997-. No. 28 W 1922-55. No. 11 W 1955-65. No. 15 W 1965-79. Berryhill W 1979-2002. Berryhill & Hanley East W 2002-

CED. Bucknall 1889-1922. CCWs 1974-97.

Chapel

S-u-T Rural CP 1894-1922. Bucknall & Eaves PW Dec 1894-6. Bucknall PW Mar 1896-1922.

LG. S-u-T RD 1894-1922. S-o-T CB 1922-74, D(C) 1974-97, UA 1997-. No. 28 W 1922-55. No. 11 W 1955-65. No. 11 W 1965-79. Abbey W 1979-2002. Bentilee & Townsend W 2002-.

CED. Bucknall 1889-1922. CCWs 1974-97.

Eaves brook

S-u-T Rural CP 1894-1922. Bucknall & Eaves PW Dec 1894-6. Bucknall PW Mar 1896-1922. Caverswall CP 1922-77. Werrington PW 1922-66. Caverswall PW July 1966-77. Caverswall & Werrington CP Feb 1977-88. Werrington PW 1977-88. Werrington CP 1988-.

LG. S-u-T RD 1894-1922. Cheadle RD 1922-74. Staffordshire Moorlands D 1974-. Werrington W 1974-2002/3. Caverswall W 2002/3-.

CED. Bucknall 1889-1922. Caverswall 1922-2005, 2005-.

Eaves Lane

S-u-T Rural CP 1894-1922. Bucknall & Eaves PW Dec 1894-6. Bucknall PW Mar 1896-1922.

LG. S-u-T RD 1894-1922. S-o-T CB 1922-74, D(C) 1974-97, UA 1997-. No. 28 W 1922-55. No. 11 W 1955-65. No. 15 W 1965-79. Brookhouse W 1979-2002. Bentilee & Townsend W 2002-.

CED. Bucknall 1889-1922. CCWs 1974-97.

Fellbrook

S-u-T Rural CP 1894-1922. Bucknall & Eaves PW Dec 1894-6. Bucknall PW Mar 1896-1922.

LG. S-u-T RD 1894-1922. S-o-T CB 1922-74, D(C) 1974-97, UA 1997-. No. 28 W 1922-55. No. 11 W 1955-65. No. 15 1965-79. Berryhill W 1979-2002. Bentilee & Townsend W 2002-.

Stoke-upon-Trent (Bagnall, Bucknall, Eaves Quarter, Bucknall)

Map of Bagnall, Bucknall, Eaves Quarter

For Eaves the Bucknall & Bagnall tithe map (1846) (LRO B/A/15) together with C19 directories.

CED. Bucknall 1889-1922. CCWs 1974-96.

Field (a)

S-u-T Rural CP 1894-1922. Bucknall & Eaves PW Dec 1894-6. Bucknall PW Mar 1896-1922.
LG. S-u-T RD 1894-1922. S-o-T CB 1922-74, D(C) 1974-97, UA 1997-. No. 28 W 1922-55. No. 16 W 1955-65. No. 15 W 1965-79. Fenton Green W 1979-2002. Berryhill & Hanley East W 2002-
CED. Bucknall 1889-1922. CCWs 1974-97.
PARL. S-o-T Central BC 1948-. S-o-T South BC

?1981-

Field (b)

S-u-T Rural CP 1894-1922. Bucknall & Eaves PW Dec 1894-6. Bucknall PW Mar 1896-1922.
LG. S-u-T RD 1894-1922. S-o-T CB 1922-74, D(C) 1974-97, UA 1997-. No. 24 W 1922-55. No. 16 W 1955-65. No. 15 W 1965-79. Fenton Green W 1979-2002. Berryhill & Hanley East W 2002-
CED. Bucknall 1889-1922. CCWs 1974-97.
PARL. S-o-T Central BC 1948-. S-o-T South BC

Stoke-upon-Trent (Bagnall, Bucknall, Eaves Quarter, Bucknall)

?1981-

Field (c)

S-u-T Rural CP 1894-1922. Bucknall & Eaves PW Dec 1894-6. Bucknall PW Mar 1896-1922.

LG. S-u-T RD 1894-1922. S-o-T CB 1922-74, D(C) 1974-97, UA 1997-. No. 24 W 1922-55. No. 16 W 1955-65. No. 16 W 1965-79. Brookhouse W 1979-2002. Bentilee & Townsend W 2002-

CED. Bucknall 1889-1922. CCWs 1974-97.

PARL. S-o-T Central BC 1948-, ?1981-

Fonthill

Same as Heath Field

Heath Field

S-u-T Rural CP 1894-1922. Bucknall & Eaves PW Dec 1894-6. Bucknall PW Mar 1896-1922.

LG. S-u-T RD 1894-1922. S-o-T CB 1922-74, D(C) 1974-97, UA 1997-. No. 28 W 1922-55. No. 11 W 1955-65. No. 15 W 1965-79. Abbey W 1979-2002. Abbey Green W 2002-.

CED. Bucknall 1889-1922. CCWs 1974-97.

Hulme (1)-(3)

Caverswall CP 1883?-1977. Caverswall PW 1895-1966. Caverswall PW July 1966-77. Caverswall & Werrington CP Feb 1977-88. Caverswall PW Feb 1977-88. Werrington CP 1988-.

LG. Cheadle RD 1894-1974. Staffordshire Moorlands D 1974-. Werrington W 1974-2002/3. Caverswall W 2002/3-.

CED. Caverswall 1889-2005, 2005-.

Hulme (4)

PARL. S-o-T South BC 1948-. S-o-T Central ?1981-. Caverswall CP 1883?-1922. Caverswall PW 1895-1922.

LG. Cheadle RD 1894-1922. S-o-T CB 1922-74, D(C) 1974-97, UA 1997-. No. 24 W 1922-55. No. 23 W 1955-65. No. 23 W 1965-79. Brookhouse W 1979-2002. Bentilee & Townsend W 2002-

CED. Caverswell 1889-1922. CCWs 1974-97.

Hulme (5)

PARL. S-o-T South BC 1948-. S-o-T Central ?1981-. Caverswall CP 1883?-1922. Caverswall PW 1895-1922.

LG. Cheadle RD 1894-1922. S-o-T CB 1922-74, D(C) 1974-97, UA 1997-. No. 24 W 1922-55. No. 23 W 1955-65. No. 16 W 1965-79. Brookhouse W 1979-2002. Bentilee & Townsend W 2002-

CED. Caverswall 1889-1922. CCWs 1974-97.

Hulton Abbey Park

S-u-T Rural CP 1894-1922. Bucknall & Eaves PW Dec 1894-6. Bucknall PW Mar 1896-1922.

LG. S-u-T RD 1894-1922. S-o-T CB 1922-74, D(C) 1974-97, UA 1997-. No. 28 W 1922-55. No. 11 W

1955-65. No. 11 1965-79. Berryhill W 1979-2002. Bentilee & Townsend W 2002-.

CED. Bucknall 1889-1922. CCWs 1974-97.

Ivy House Mill

S-u-T Rural CP 1894-1922. Bucknall & Eaves PW Dec 1894-6. Bucknall PW Mar 1896-1922.

LG. S-u-T RD 1894-1922. S-o-T CB 1922-74, D(C) 1974-97, UA 1997-. No. 28 W 1922-55. No. 16 W 1955-65. No. 14 W 1965-79. Berryhill W 1979-2002. Berryhill & Hanley East W 2002-

CED. Bucknall 1889-1922. CCWs 1974-97.

Leek Road (1)

S-u-T Rural CP 1894-1922. Bucknall & Eaves PW Dec 1894-6. Bucknall PW Mar 1896-1922.

LG. S-u-T RD 1894-1922. S-o-T CB 1922-74, D(C) 1974-97, UA 1997-. No. 28 W 1922-55. No. 11 W 1955-65. No. 15 W 1965-79. Abbey W 1979-2002. Abbey Green W 2002-.

CED. Bucknall 1889-1922. CCWs 1974-97.

Leek Road (2)

S-u-T Rural CP 1894-1922. Bucknall & Eaves PW Dec 1894-6. Bucknall PW Mar 1896-1922.

LG. S-u-T RD 1894-1922. S-o-T CB 1922-74, D(C) 1974-97, UA 1997-. No. 28 W 1922-55. No. 11 W 1955-65. No. 15 W 1965-79. Berryhill W 1979-2002. Abbey Green W 2002-.

CED. Bucknall 1889-1922. CCWs 1974-97.

Little Brookhouse Farm

S-u-T Rural CP 1894-1922. Bucknall & Eaves PW Dec 1894-6. Bucknall PW Mar 1896-1922. Caverswall CP 1922-65. Werrington PW 1922-65.

LG. S-u-T RD 1894-1922. Cheadle RD 1922-65. S-o-T CB 1965-74, D(C) 1974-97, UA 1997-. No. 11 W 1965-. No. 16 W 1965-79. Brookhouse W 1979-2002. Bentilee & Townsend W 2002-

CED. Bucknall 1889-1922. Caverswall 1922-65. CCWs 1974-97.

Park

S-u-T Rural CP 1894-1922. Bucknall & Eaves PW Dec 1894-6. Bucknall PW Mar 1896-1922.

LG. S-u-T RD 1894-1922. S-o-T CB 1922-74, D(C) 1974-97, UA 1997-. No. 28 W 1922-55. No. 11 W 1955-65. No. 15 W 1965-79. Abbey W 1979-2002. Bentilee & Townsend W 2002-.

CED. Bucknall 1889-1922. CCWs 1974-97.

Pool House Farm

S-u-T Rural CP 1894-1922. Bucknall & Eaves PW Dec 1894-6. Bucknall PW Mar 1896-1922.

LG. S-u-T RD 1894-1922. S-o-T CB 1922-74, D(C) 1974-97, UA 1997-. No. 28 W 1922-55. No. 16 W 1955-65. No. 15 W 1965-79. Berryhill W 1979-2002. Berryhill & Hanley East W 2002-

Stoke-upon-Trent (Bagnall, Bucknall, Eaves Quarter, Eaves)

CED. Bucknall 1889-1922. CCWs 1974-97.

Simfields

S-u-T Rural CP 1894-1922. Bucknall & Eaves PW Dec 1894-6. Bucknall PW Mar 1896-1922. Caverswall CP 1922-77. Werrington PW 1922-66. Ash Hall PW July 1966-77. Caverswall & Werrington CP Feb 1977-88. Werrington PW Feb 1977-88. Werrington CP 1988-.

LG. S-u-T RD 1894-1922. Cheadle RD 1922-74. Staffordshire Moorlands D 1974-. Werrington W 1974-2002/3. Caverswall W 2002/3-.

CED. Bucknall 1889-1922. Caverswall 1922-2005, 2005-.

Stonehouse Farm

Caverswall CP 1883?-1977. Caverswall PW 1895-1966. Caverswall PW July 1966-77. Caverswall & Werrington CP Feb 1977-88. Caverswall PW Feb 1977-88. Werrington CP 1988-.

LG. Cheadle RD 1894-1974. Staffordshire Moorlands D 1974-. Werrington W 1974-2002/3. Caverswall W 2002/3-.

CED. Caverswall 1889-2005, 2005-.

Townsend

S-u-T Rural CP 1894-1922. Bucknall & Eaves PW Dec 1894-6. Bucknall PW Mar 1896-1922.

LG. S-u-T RD 1894-1922. S-o-T CB 1922-74, D(C) 1974-97, UA 1997-. No. 28 W 1922-55. No. 16 W 1955-65. No. 15 W 1965-79. Brookhouse W 1979-2002. Bentilee & Townsend W 2002-.

CED. Bucknall 1889-1922. CCWs 1974-97.

Ubberley

S-u-T Rural CP 1894-1922. Bucknall & Eaves PW Dec 1894-6. Bucknall PW Mar 1896-1922.

LG. S-u-T RD 1894-1922. S-o-T CB 1922-74, D(C) 1974-97, UA 1997-. No. 28 W 1922-55. No. 16 W 1955-65. No. 16 W 1965-79. Berryhill W 1979-2002. Bentilee & Townsend W 2002-.

CED. Bucknall 1889-1922. CCWs 1974-97.

W. R. (Werrington Road)

S-u-T Rural CP 1894-1922. Bucknall & Eaves PW Dec 1894-6. Bucknall PW Mar 1896-1922.

LG. S-u-T RD 1894-1922. S-o-T CB 1922-74, D(C) 1974-97, UA 1997-. No. 28 W 1922-55. No. 11 W 1955-65. No. 11 W 1965-79. Abbey W 1979-2002. Bentilee & Townsend W 2002-.

CED. Bucknall 1889-1922. CCWs 1974-97.

EAVES TOWNSHIP

PLU. S-u-T 1836-1922. S-u-T & Wolstanton 1922-30. Bucknall & Eaves W by1894-6. Eaves W Mar 1896-

Eaves

S-u-T Rural CP 1894-1922. Bucknall & Eaves PW Dec 1894-6. Eaves PW Mar 1896-1922. Caverswall CP 1922-77. Werrington PW 1922-66. Ash Hall PW July 1966-77. Caverswall & Werrington CP Feb 1977-88. Werrington PW 1977-88. Werrington CP 1988-.

LG. S-u-T RD 1894-1922. Cheadle RD 1922-74. Staffordshire Moorlands D 1974-. Werrington W 1974-2002/3, 2002/3-

CED. Bucknall 1889-1922. Caverswall 1922-2005, 2005-

Eaves Lane (N)

S-u-T Rural CP 1894-1922. Bucknall & Eaves PW Dec 1894-6. Eaves PW Mar 1896-1922.

LG. S-u-T RD 1894-1922. S-o-T CB 1922-74, D(C) 1974-97, UA 1997-. No. 28 W 1922-55. No. 11 W 1955-65. No. 15 W 1965-79. Brookhouse W 1979-2002. Bentilee & Townsend W 2002-.

CED. Bucknall 1889-1922. CCWs 1974-97.

Great Eaves

S-u-T Rural CP 1894-1922. Bucknall & Eaves PW Dec 1894-6. Eaves PW Mar 1896-1922. Caverswall CP 1922-65. Werrington PW 1922-65.

LG. S-u-T RD 1894-1922. Cheadle RD 1922-65. S-o-T CB 1965-74, D(C) 1974-97, UA 1997-. No. 11 W 1965-. No. 15 W 1965-79. Brookhouse W 1979-2002. Bentilee & Townsend W 2002-

CED. Bucknall 1889-1922. Caverswall 1922-65. CCWs 1974-97.

Greenfields

S-u-T Rural CP 1894-1922. Bucknall & Eaves PW Dec 1894-6. Eaves PW Mar 1896-1922. Caverswall CP 1922-65. Werrington PW 1922-65. Bagnall CP 1965-

LG. S-u-T RD 1894-1922. Cheadle RD 1922-65. Leek RD 1965-74. Staffordshire Moorlands D 1974-. Endon & Stanley W 1974-2002/3. Bagnall & Stanley W 2002/3-.

CED. Bucknall 1889-1922. Caverswall 1922-65. Cheddleton 1965-1973. Cheadle No. 1 1973-81. Biddulph-Endon 1981-2005. Biddulph South & Endon 2005-.

Holehouse Farm

S-u-T Rural CP 1894-1922. Bucknall & Eaves PW Dec 1894-6. Eaves PW Mar 1896-1922. Stoke unparished 1922-

LG. S-u-T RD 1894-1922. S-o-T CB 1922-74, D(C) 1974-97, UA 1997-. No. 28 W 1922-55. No. 11 W 1955-65. No. 11 W 1965-79. Abbey W 1979-2002. Abbey Green W 2002-.

CED. Bucknall 1889-1922. CCWs 1974-97.

Little Eaves

S-u-T Rural CP 1894-1922. Bucknall & Eaves PW Dec 1894-6. Eaves PW Mar 1896-1922. Caverswall CP 1922-65. Werrington PW 1922-65. Stoke unparished 1965-.

147

Stoke-upon-Trent (Botteslow, Fenton, Longton Quarter, Botteslow)

LG. S-u-T RD 1894-1922. Cheadle RD 1922-65. S-o-T CB 1965-74, D(C) 1974-97, UA 1997-. No. 11 W 1965-. No. 11 W 1965-79. Abbey W 1979-2002. Abbey Green W 2002-.

CED. Bucknall 1889-1922. Caverswall 1922-65. CCWs 1974-97.

Ringstone Farm

S-u-T Rural CP 1894-1922. Bucknall & Eaves PW Dec 1894-6. Eaves PW Mar 1896-1922. Caverswall CP 1922-77. Werrington PW 1922-66. Werrington Windmill PW July 1966-77. Caverswall & Werrington CP Feb 1977-88. Werrington PW Feb 1977-88. Werrington CP 1988-.

LG. S-u-T RD 1894-1922. Cheadle RD 1922-74. Staffordshire Moorlands D 1974-. Werrington W 1974-2002/3, 2002/3-

CED. Bucknall 1889-1922. Caverswall 1922-2005, 2005-

Washerwall

S-u-T Rural CP 1894-1922. Bucknall & Eaves PW Dec 1894-6. Eaves PW Mar 1896-1922. Caverswall CP 1922-77. Werrington Windmill PW July 1966-77. Caverswall & Werrington CP Feb 1977-88. Werrington PW Feb 1977-88. Werrington CP 1988-.

LG. S-u-T RD 1894-1922. Cheadle RD 1922-74. Staffordshire Moorlands D 1974-. Werrington W 1974-2002/3. Cellarhead W 2002/3-.

CED. Bucknall 1889-1922. Caverswall 1922-2005, 2005-.

Wetley Moor

S-u-T Rural CP 1894-5. Bagnall PW Nov 1894-5. Bagnall CP Nov 1895-.

LG. Stoke RD 1895-1906. Leek RD Sept 1906-1974. Staffs Moorlands D 1974-. Endon & Stanley W 1974-2002/3. Bagnall & Stanley W 2002/3-.

CED. Bucknall 1889-1922. Cheddleton 1922-1973. Cheadle No. 1 1973-81. Biddulph-Endon 1981-2005. Biddulph South & Endon 2005-.

PLU. Stoke-upon-Trent 1836-1922, Stoke-upon-Trent and Wolstanton 1922-30.

BOTTESLOW, FENTON, LONGTON QUARTER

A union of the three Poor Relief districts of Fenton Vivian (with Botteslow), Fenton Culvert and Longton (with Lane End) in the early C17. The quarter had its own overseer (VCH vol 8 p198).

BOTTESLOW LIBERTY

Fenton Vivian T post-medieval-. Botteslow L by1679-. S-u-T Rural CP 1894-1922. Botteslow PW Nov 1894-1922. Stoke unparished 1922-.

LG. S-u-T RD 1894-1922. S-o-T CB 1922-74, D(C) 1974-97, UA 1997-.

CED. Bucknall 1889-1922. CCWs 1974-97.

PLU. Stoke-upon-Trent 1836-1922, Stoke-upon-Trent and Wolstanton 1922-30.

PARL. North Western D. Leek D. Stoke-on-Trent Central BC 1948-

Glover's

LG. No. 28 W 1922-55. No. 16 W 1955-65. No. 15 W 1965-79. Fenton Green W 1979-2002. Berryhill & Hanley East W 2002-

PARL. S-o-T Central BC 1974-. S-o-T South BC ?1981-

Govan

LG. No. 28 W 1922-55. No. 16 W 1955-65. No. 15 W 1965-79. Berryhill W 1979-2002. Berryhill & Hanley East W 2002-

PARL. S-o-T South BC 1974-. S-o-T Central BC ?1981-

Hallhill

LG. No. 28 W 1922-55. No. 16 W 1955-65. No. 15 W 1965-79. Berryhill W 1979-2002. Berryhill & Hanley East W 2002-

PARL. S-o-T Central BC 1974-, ?1981-

Lower Botteslow

LG. No. 28 W 1922-55. No. 14 W 1955-65. No. 14 W 1965-79. Berryhill W 1979-2002. Berryhill & Hanley East W 2002-

PARL. S-o-T Central BC 1974-, ?1981-

RT (River Trent)

LG. No. 28 W 1922-55. No. 19 W 1955-65. No. 19 W 1965-79. Hartshill W 1979-2002. Hanley West & Shelton W 2002-

PARL. S-o-T South BC 1974-. S-o-T Central BC ?1981-

Shaft

LG. No. 28 W 1922-55. No. 16 W 1955-65. No. 15 W 1965-79. Fenton Green W 1979-2002. Longton North W 2002-

PARL. S-o-T Central BC 1974-. S-o-T South BC ?1981-

Upper Botteslow

LG. No. 28 W 1922-55. No. 16 W 1955-65. No. 15 W 1965-79. Berryhill W 1979-2002. Berryhill & Hanley East W 2002-

PARL. S-o-T Central BC 1974-, ?1981-

VR (Victoria Road) 1

LG. No. 19 W 1922-55. No. 19 W 1955-65. No. 19 W 1965-79. Hartshill W 1979-2002. Hanley West & Shelton W 2002-

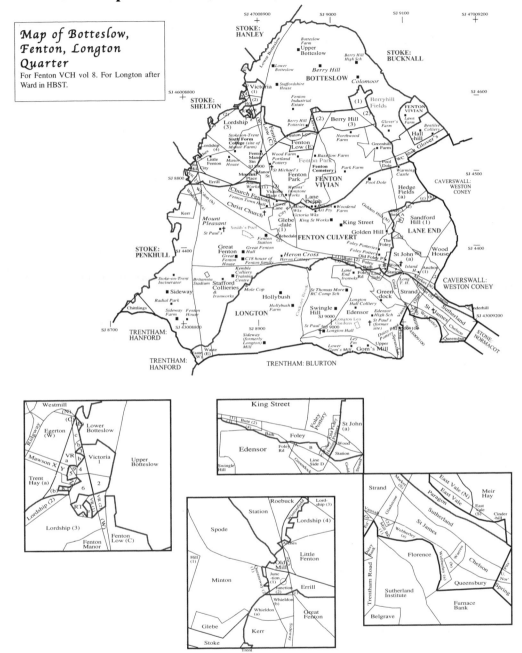

Map of Botteslow, Fenton, Longton Quarter

For Fenton VCH vol 8. For Longton after Ward in HBST.

PARL. S-o-T South BC 1974-. S-o-T Central BC ?1981-

VR (Victoria Road) 2

LG. No. 28 W 1922-55. No. 14 W 1955-65. No. 14 W 1965-79. Berryhill W 1979-2002. Berryhill & Hanley East W 2002-.

PARL. S-o-T Central BC 1974-, ?1981-

WC (Warming Castle)

LG. No. 20 W 1922-55. No. 16 W 1955-65. No. 15 W 1965-79. Fenton Green W 1979-2002. Longton North W 2002-

PARL. S-o-T Central BC 1974-. S-o-T South BC

Stoke-upon-Trent (Botteslow, Fenton, Longton Quarter, Fenton Culvert)

?1981-

FENTON CULVERT TOWNSHIP

Fenton Culvert T post-medieval-. Fenton CP 1894-1910.

LG. Fenton Commissioners district 1839-73, LB 1873-94, UD 1894-1910. S-o-T CB 1910-74, D(C) 1974-97, UA 1997-

CED. Fenton 1889-1904. Fenton No.1 or No. 2 1904-07. Fenton Southern 1907-10. CCWs 1974-97.

PARL. Stoke-upon-Trent PB 1832-1918. Stoke-upon-Trent D of Stoke-on-Trent PB 1918-48. Stoke-on-Trent South BC 1948-, 1974-, ?1981-

Bath
LG. South W 1895-1910. No. 22 W 1910-55. No. 20 W 1955-65. No. 20 W 1965-79. Longton South W 1979-2002. Longton South W 2002-

Bute (1)
LG. South W 1895-1910. No. 22 W 1910-55. No. 20 W 1955-65. No. 19 W 1965-79. Great Fenton W 1979-2002. Fenton W 2002-

Bute (2)
LG. South W 1895-1910. No. 22 W 1910-55. No. 20 W 1955-65. No. 20 W 1965-79. Great Fenton W 1979-2002. Fenton W 2002-

Bute (3)
LG. South W 1895-1910. No. 22 W 1910-55. No. 20 W 1955-65. No. 19 W 1965-79. Great Fenton W 1979-2002. Longton South 2002-

Bute (4)
LG. South W 1895-1910. No. 22 W 1910-55. No. 20 W 1955-65. No. 20 W 1965-79. Great Fenton W 1979-2002. Longton South 2002-

Chittlings
LG. South W 1895-1910. No. 22 W 1910-55. No. 19 W 1955-65. No. 19 W 1965-79. Trentham Park W 1979-2002. Trentham & Hanford W 2002-

Christ Church
LG. West W 1895-1910. No. 22 W 1910-55. No. 19 W 1955-65. No. 19 W 1965-79. Great Fenton W 1979-2002. Fenton W 2002-

Church Fenton
LG. West W 1895-1910. No. 19 W 1910-55. No. 19 W 1955-65. No. 19 W 1965-79. Great Fenton W 1979-2002. Fenton W 2002-

City Road
LG. East W 1895-1910. No. 19 W 1910-55. No. 21 W 1955-65. No. 21 W 1965-79. Fenton Green W 1979-2002. Fenton W 2002-
CED. Fenton Northern 1907-10.

Foley
LG. South W 1895-1910. No. 22 W 1910-55. No. 20 W 1955-65. No. 20 W 1965-79. Longton South W 1979-2002. Fenton W 2002-

The Foley
LG. East W 1895-1910. No. 20 W 1910-55. No. 23 W 1955-65. No. 21 W 1965-79. Fenton Green W 1979-. Fenton W 2002-
CED. Fenton Northern 1907-10.

Foley House
LG. South W 1895-1910. No. 22 W 1910-55. No. 20 W 1955-65. No. 20 W 1965-79. Longton South W 1979-2002. Longton North W 2002-

Glebedale (1)
LG. West W 1895-1910. No. 22 W 1910-55. No. 19 W 1955-65. No. 21 W 1965-79. Fenton Green W 1979-2002. Fenton W 2002-

Glebedale (2)
LG. West W 1895-1910. No. 22 W 1910-55. No. 19 W 1955-65. No. 21 W 1965-79. Great Fenton W 1979-2002. Fenton W 2002-

Goldenhill
LG. East W 1895-1910. No. 20 W 1910-55. No. 23 W 1955-65. No. 23 W 1965-79. Fenton Green W 1979-2002. Fenton W 2002-
CED. Fenton Northern 1907-10.

Goldenhill (N)
LG. East W 1895-1910. No. 20 W 1910-55. No. 23 W 1955-65. No. 21 W 1965-79. Fenton Green W 1979-2002. Fenton W 2002-
CED. Fenton Northern 1907-10.

Great Fenton
LG. South W 1895-1910. No. 22 W 1910-55. No. 19 W 1955-65. No. 19 W 1965-79. Great Fenton W 1979-2002. Fenton W 2002-

Hedge Fields (a)
LG. East W 1895-1910. No. 20 W 1910-55. No. 21 W 1955-65. No. 21 W 1965-79. Fenton Green W 1979-2002. Longton South 2002-
CED. Fenton Northern 1907-10.

Hedge Fields (b)
LG. East W 1895-1910. No. 20 W 1910-55. No. 23 W 1955-65. No. 23 W 1965-79. Fenton Green W 1979-2002. Longton South 2002-
CED. Fenton Northern 1907-10.

Hedge Fields (c)
LG. East W 1895-1910. No. 20 W 1910-55. No. 21 W 1955-65. No. 23 W 1965-79. Fenton Green W 1979-2002. Longton South 2002-
CED. Fenton Northern 1907-10.

Heron Cross
LG. South W 1895-1910. No. 22 W 1910-55. No. 19 W 1955-65. No. 19 W 1965-79. Great Fenton W 1979-

Stoke-upon-Trent (Botteslow, Fenton, Longton Quarter, Fenton Vivian)

2002. Blurton W 2002-

Kerr
LG. South W 1895-1910. No. 22 W 1910-55. No. 15 W 1955-65. No. 19 W 1965-79. Trentham Park W 1979-2002. Stoke & Trent Vale W 2002-

King Street
LG. East W 1895-1910. No. 20 W 1910-55. No. 21 W 1955-65. No. 21 W 1965-79. Fenton Green W 1979-2002. Fenton W 2002-
CED. Fenton Northern 1907-10.

Lower Lane
LG. West W 1895-1910. No. 19 W 1910-55. No. 19 W 1955-65. No. 21 W 1965-79. Fenton Green W 1979-2002. Fenton W 2002-

Old Foley Pottery
LG. East W 1895-1910. No. 20 W 1910-55. No. 23 W 1955-65. No. 21 W 1965-79. Fenton Green W 1979-2002. Longton North W 2002-
CED. Fenton Northern 1907-10.

Sideway
LG. South W 1895-1910. No. 22 W 1910-55. No. 19 W 1955-65. No. 19 W 1965-79. Trentham Park W 1979-. Stoke & Trent Vale W 2002-

Whieldon (a)
LG. South W 1895-1910. No. 22 W 1910-55. No. 15 W 1955-65. No. 19 W 1965-79. Great Fenton W 1979-2002. Stoke & Trent Vale W 2002-

Whieldon (b)
LG. South W 1895-1910. No. 22 W 1910-55. No. 19 W 1955-65. No. 19 W 1965-79. Great Fenton W 1979-2002. Stoke & Trent Vale W 2002-

Whieldon (c)
LG. West W 1895-1910. No. 22 W 1910-55. No. 19 W 1955-65. No. 19 W 1965-79. Great Fenton W 1979-2002. Stoke & Trent Vale W 2002-

FENTON VIVIAN TOWNSHIP
Fenton Vivian T post-medieval-. Fenton CP 1894-1910.
LG. Fenton Commissioners district 1839-73, LB 1873-94, UD 1894-1910. S-o-T CB 1910-74, D(C) 1974-97, UA 1997-
CED. Fenton 1889-1904. Fenton No.1 or No. 2 1904-07. Fenton Northern 1907-10. CCWs 1974-97.
PARL. Stoke-upon-Trent PB 1832-1918. Stoke-upon-Trent D of Stoke-on-Trent PB 1918-48. Stoke-on-Trent South BC 1948-

Arches
LG. West W 1895-1910. No. 19 W 1910-55. No. 19 W 1955-65. No. 13 W 1965-79. Hartshill W 1979-2002. Hanley West & Shelton W 2002-

CED. Fenton Southern 1907-10.
PARL. S-o-T South BC 1948-, 1974-. S-o-T Central BC ?1981-

Berry Hill (1)
LG. East W 1895-1910. No. 20 W 1910-55. No. 21 W 1955-65. No. 15 W 1965-79. Berryhill W 1979-2002. Berryhill & Hanley East W 2002-
PARL. S-o-T South BC 1948-. S-o-T Central BC 1974-, ?1981-.

Berry Hill (2)
LG. East W 1895-1910. No. 20 W 1910-55. No. 21 W 1955-65. No. 15 W 1965-79. Berryhill W 1979-2002. Berryhill & Hanley East W 2002-
PARL. S-o-T South BC 1948-, 1974-. S-o-T Central BC ?1981-

Berry Hill (3)
LG. East W 1895-1910. No. 20 W 1910-55. No. 21 W 1955-65. No. 21 W 1965-79. Berryhill W 1979-2002. Berryhill & Hanley East W 2002-
PARL. S-o-T South BC 1948-, 1974-. S-o-T Central BC ?1981-

City
LG. West W 1895-1910. No. 22 W 1910-55. No. 19 W 1955-65. No. 19 W 1965-79. Hartshill W 1979-2002. Fenton W 2002-
CED. Fenton Southern 1907-10.
PARL. S-o-T South BC 1948-, 1974-. S-o-T Central BC ?1981-

Errill
LG. West W 1895-1910. No. 22 W 1910-55. No. 19 W 1955-65. No. 19 W 1965-79. Great Fenton W 1979-2002. Fenton W 2002-
CED. Fenton Southern 1907-10.
PARL. S-o-T South BC 1948-, 1974-, ?1981-.

Fenton Cemetery
LG. East W 1895-1910. No. 19 W 1910-55. No. 21 W 1955-65. No. 21 W 1965-79. Fenton Green W 1979-2002. Fenton W 2002-
PARL. S-o-T South BC 1948-, 1974-, ?1981-

Fenton Low
LG. North W 1895-1910. No. 19 W 1910-55. No. 21 W 1955-65. No. 15 W 1965-79. Berryhill W 1979-2002. Berryhill & Hanley East W 2002-

Fenton Low (C)
PARL. S-o-T South BC 1948-. S-o-T Central BC 1974-, ?1981-
LG. North W 1895-1910. No. 19 W 1910-55. No. 16 W 1955-65. No. 15 W 1965-79. Berryhill W 1979-2002. Berryhill & Hanley East W 2002-
PARL. S-o-T South BC 1948-, 1974-. S-o-T Central ?1981-

Fenton Low (E)

Stoke-upon-Trent (Botteslow, Fenton, Longton Quarter, Fenton Vivian)

LG. North W 1895-1910. No. 19 W 1910-55. No. 21 W 1955-65. No. 21 W 1965-79. Berryhill W 1979-2002. Berryhill & Hanley East W 2002-
PARL. S-o-T South BC 1948-, 1974-. S-o-T Central ?1981-

Fenton Low (W)

LG. North W 1895-1910. No. 19 W 1910-55. No. 14 W 1955-65. No. 14 W 1965-79. Berryhill W 1979-2002. Berryhill & Hanley East W 2002-
PARL. S-o-T South BC 1948-. S-o-T Central BC 1974-, ?1981-

Fenton Manor Station

LG. North W 1895-1910. No. 19 W 1910-55. No. 19 W 1955-65. No. 19 W 1965-79. Great Fenton W 1979-2002. Fenton W 2002-
PARL. S-o-T South BC 1948-, 1974-. S-o-T Central BC ?1981-

Fenton Park

LG. North W 1895-1910. No. 19 W 1910-55. No. 21 W 1955-65. No. 21 W 1965-79. Fenton Green W 1979-2002. Fenton W 2002-
PARL. S-o-T South BC 1948-, 1974-, ?1981-

Greenhill Farm

LG. East W 1895-1910. No. 20 W 1910-55. No. 21 W 1955-65. No. 21 W 1965-79. Fenton Green W 1979-2002. Berryhill & Hanley East W 2002-
PARL. S-o-T South BC 1948-, 1974-, ?1981-.

Junction (1)

LG. West W 1895-1910. No. 22 W 1910-55. No. 19 W 1955-65. No. 19 W 1965-79. Great Fenton W 1979-2002. Stoke & Trent Vale W 2002-
CED. Fenton Southern 1907-10.
PARL. S-o-T Central BC 1948-, 1974-. S-o-T South BC ?1981-

Junction (2)

LG. West W 1895-1910. No. 22 W 1910-55. No. 19 W 1955-65. No. 19 W 1965-79. Great Fenton W 1979-2002. Stoke & Trent Vale W 2002-
CED. Fenton Southern 1907-10.
PARL. S-o-T South BC 1948-, 1974-, ?1981-

Lane Delph

LG. East W 1895-1910. No. 20 W 1910-55. No. 21 W 1955-65. No. 21 W 1965-79. Fenton Green W 1979-2002. Fenton W 2002-
PARL. S-o-T South BC 1948-, 1974-, ?1981-

Lawn Farm

S-u-T Rural CP 1910-1922. Botteslow PW Nov 1910-1922.
LG. Fenton UD 1894-1910. S-u-T RD 1910-1922. S-o-T CB 1922-74, D(C) 1974-97-, UA 1997-. No. 28 W 1922-55. No. 16 W 1955-65. No. 15 W 1965-79. Berryhill W 1979-2002. Berryhill & Hanley East W 2002-
CED. Fenton 1889-1904. Fenton No.1 or No. 2 1904-07. Fenton Northern 1907-10. Bucknall 1910-22. CCWs 1974-97.
PARL. S-o-T Central BC 1948-, 1974-, ?1981-

Little Fenton

LG. West W 1895-1910. No. 19 W 1910-55. No. 19 W 1955-65. No. 19 W 1965-79. Hartshill W 1979-2002. Fenton W 2002-
CED. Fenton Southern 1907-10.
PARL. S-o-T South BC 1948-, 1974-. S-o-T Central BC ?1981-

Lordship (1)

LG. North W 1895-1910. No. 19 W 1910-55. No. 13 W 1955-65. No. 9 W 1965-79. Hartshill W 1979-2002. Hanley West & Shelton W 2002-
PARL. S-o-T South BC 1948-. S-o-T Central BC 1974-, ?1981-

Lordship (2)

LG. North W 1895-1910. No. 19 W 1910-55. No. 13 W 1955-65. No. 9 W 1965-79. Hartshill W 1979-2002. Hanley West & Shelton W 2002-
PARL. S-o-T South BC 1948-, 1974-. S-o-T Central BC ?1981-

Lordship (3)

LG. North W 1895-1910. No. 19 W 1910-55. No. 19 W 1955-65. No. 19 W 1965-79. Hartshill W 1979-2002. Hanley West & Shelton W 2002-
PARL. S-o-T South BC 1948-, 1974-. S-o-T Central BC ?1981-

Lordship (4)

LG. West W 1895-1910. No. 19 W 1910-55. No. 19 W 1955-65. No. 19 W 1965-79. Hartshill W 1979-2002. Hanley West & Shelton W 2002-
CED. Fenton Southern 1907-10.
PARL. S-o-T South BC 1948-, 1974-. S-o-T Central BC ?1981-

Manor Street

LG. North W 1895-1910. No. 19 W 1910-55. No. 19 W 1955-65. No. 19 W 1965-79. Great Fenton W 1979-2002. Fenton W 2002-
PARL. S-o-T South BC 1948-, 1974-, ?1981-

Mounfield Place

LG. West W 1895-1910. No. 19 W 1910-55. No. 19 W 1955-65. No. 19 W 1965-79. Great Fenton W 1979-2002. Fenton W 2002-
CED. Fenton Southern 1907-10.
PARL. S-o-T South BC 1948-, 1974-, ?1981-

Old Mill

LG. West W 1895-1910. No. 22 W 1910-55. No. 15 W 1955-65. No. 13 W 1965-79. Hartshill W 1979-2002. Hartshill & Penkhull W 2002-

Stoke-upon-Trent (Botteslow, Fenton, Longton Quarter, Lane End)

CED. Fenton Southern 1907-10.

PARL. S-o-T Central BC 1948-, 1974-, ?1981-

Pool Dole

LG. East W 1895-1910. No. 20 W 1910-55. No. 21 W 1955-65. No. 21 W 1965-79. Fenton Green W 1979-2002. Longton North W 2002-

PARL. S-o-T South BC 1948-, 1974-, ?1981-

Queensway (1)

LG. West W 1895-1910. No. 22 W 1922-55. No. 19 W 1955-65. No. 13 W 1965-79. Great Fenton W 1979-2002. Stoke & Trent Vale W 2002-

CED. Fenton Southern 1907-10.

PARL. S-o-T Central BC 1948-, 1974-, ?1981-

Queensway (2)

LG. West W 1895-1910. No. 22 W 1922-55. No. 19 W 1955-65. No. 19 W 1965-79. Great Fenton W 1979-2002. Stoke & Trent Vale W 2002-

CED. Fenton Southern 1907-10.

PARL. S-o-T South BC 1948-, 1974-, ?1981-

Victoria (1)

LG. North W 1895-1910. No. 19 W 1910-55. No. 14 W 1955-65. No. 14 W 1965-79. Berryhill W 1979-2002. Berryhill & Hanley East W 2002-.

PARL. S-o-T South BC 1948-. S-o-T Central 1974-, ?1981-

Victoria (2)

LG. North W 1895-1910. No. 19 W 1910-55. No. 14 W 1955-65. No. 14 W 1965-79. Berryhill W 1979-2002. Berryhill & Hanley East W 2002-.

PARL. S-o-T South BC 1948-. S-o-T Central 1974-, ?1981-

Victoria (3)

LG. North W 1895-1910. No. 19 W 1910-55. No. 19 W 1955-65. No. 19 W 1965-79. Hartshill W 1979-2002. Berryhill & Hanley East W 2002-.

PARL. S-o-T South BC 1948-, 1974-. S-o-T Central BC ?1981-

Victoria (4)

LG. North W 1895-1910. No. 19 W 1910-55. No. 19 W 1955-65. No. 19 W 1965-79. Hartshill W 1979-2002. Berryhill & Hanley East W 2002-.

PARL. S-o-T South BC 1948-, 1974-. S-o-T Central BC ?1981-

Victoria (5)

LG. North W 1895-1910. No. 19 W 1910-55. No. 13 W 1955-65. No. 9 W 1965-79. Hartshill W 1979-2002. Berryhill & Hanley East W 2002-.

PARL. S-o-T South BC 1948-, 1974-. S-o-T Central BC ?1981-

Victoria (6)

LG. North W 1895-1910. No. 19 W 1910-55. No. 19 W 1955-65. No. 19 W 1965-79. Hartshill W 1979-

2002. Hanley West & Shelton W 2002-

PARL. S-o-T South BC 1948-, 1974-. S-o-T Central BC ?1981-

Victoria (7)

LG. North W 1895-1910. No. 19 W 1910-55. No. 13 W 1955-65. No. 9 W 1965-79. Hartshill W 1979-2002. Hanley West & Shelton W 2002-

PARL. S-o-T South BC 1948-, 1974-. S-o-T Central BC ?1981-

Victoria (8)

LG. North W 1895-1910. No. 19 W 1910-55. No. 13 W 1955-65. No. 9 W 1965-79. Hartshill W 1979-2002. Hanley West & Shelton W 2002-

PARL. S-o-T South BC 1948-, 1974-. S-o-T Central BC ?1981-

Victoria (9)

LG. North W 1895-1910. No. 19 W 1910-55. No. 13 W 1955-65. No. 9 W 1965-79. Hartshill W 1979-2002. Berryhill & Hanley East W 2002-.

PARL. S-o-T South BC 1948-, 1974-. S-o-T Central BC ?1981-

Victoria Place (1)

LG. West W 1895-1910. No. 19 W 1910-55. No. 19 W 1955-65. No. 19 W 1965-79. Great Fenton W 1979-2002. Fenton W 2002-

CED. Fenton Southern 1907-10.

PARL. S-o-T South BC 1948-, 1974-, ?1981-

Victoria Place (2)

LG. North W 1895-1910. No. 19 W 1910-55. No. 21 W 1955-65. No. 19 W 1965-79. Fenton Green W 1979-2002. Fenton W 2002-

PARL. S-o-T South BC 1948-, 1974-, ?1981-

Victoria Place (3)

LG. West W 1895-1910. No. 19 W 1910-55. No. 21 W 1955-65. No. 19 W 1965-79. Fenton Green W 1979-2002. Fenton W 2002-

CED. Fenton Southern 1907-10.

PARL. S-o-T South BC 1948-, 1974-, ?1981-

y, z

LG. North W 1895-1910. No. 19 W 1910-55. No. 19 W 1955-65. No. 19 W 1965-79. Hartshill W 1979-2002. Hanley West & Shelton W 2002-

PARL. S-o-T South BC 1948-, 1974-. S-o-T Central BC ?1981-

LANE END TOWNSHIP

Longton T post-medieval-, Lane End T by1679-. Longton CP 1894-1910.

LG. Longton Commissioners district 1839-58, LB 1858-65, MB 1865-1910. S-o-T CB 1910-74, D(C) 1974-97, UA 1997-

CED. Longton No.1 or No. 2 1889-98. Longton No.1

153

Stoke-upon-Trent (Botteslow, Fenton, Longton Quarter, Longton)

or No. 2 or No. 3 1898-. CCWs 1974-97.
PARL. Stoke-upon-Trent PB 1832-1918. Stoke-upon-Trent D of Stoke-on-Trent PB 1918-48. Stoke-on-Trent South BC 1948-, 1974-, ?1981-

Anchor (1)
LG. St John W 1865-95. St John W 1895-1910. No. 23 W 1910-55. In 1919 Miss Florence A Farmer was one of three who were the first women elected to a municipal council in Staffordshire. Returned unopposed she was the first woman elected to Stoke-on-Trent city council, sitting for No. 23 Ward. Her father was the late Alderman GE Farmer JP, mayor of Longton 1895-6. (SA Nov 8 1919 p7p). No. 23 W 1955-65. No. 23 W 1965-79. Weston W 1979-2002. Longton North W 2002-

Anchor (2)
LG. St John W 1865-95. Sandford Hill W 1895-1910. No. 24 W 1910-55. No. 23 W 1922-55. No. 23 W 1965-79. Weston W 1979-2002. Longton North W 2002-

Anchor (3)
LG. St John W 1865-95. St John W 1895-1910. No. 23 W 1910-55. No. 23 W 1955-65. No. 23 W 1965-79. Weston W 1979-2002. Longton North W 2002-

Anchor (4)
LG. St John W 1865-95. Sandford Hill W 1895-1910. No. 24 W 1910-55. No. 23 W 1922-55. No. 23 W 1965-79. Weston W 1979-2002. Longton North W 2002-

Cinderhill
LG. St John W 1865-95. Sutherland W 1895-1910. No. 24 W 1910-55. No. 23 W 1955-65. No. 23 W 1965-79. Weston W 1979-2002. Longton North W 2002-

Clayfield A
LG. St John W 1865-95. Sandford Hill W 1895-1910. No. 24 W 1910-55. No. 23 W 1955-65. No. 21 W 1965-79. Fenton Green W 1979-2002. Fenton W 2002-
Clayfield B
LG. St John W 1865-95. Sandford Hill W 1895-1910. No. 24 W 1910-55. No. 23 W 1955-65. No. 23 W 1965-79. Fenton Green W 1979-2002. Fenton W 2002-

Market (N)
LG. St John W 1865-95. St John W 1895-1910. No. 23 W 1910-55. No. 23 W 1955-65. No. 22 W 1965-79. Longton South W 1979-2002. Longton North W 2002-

Paragon
LG. St John W 1865-95. Sutherland W 1895-1910. No. 24 W 1910-55. No. 23 W 1955-65. No. 22 W 1965-79. Longton South W 1979-2002. Longton North W 2002-

Saint John (a)
LG. St John W 1865-1910. No. 23 W 1910-55. No. 23

W 1955-65. No. 21 W 1965-79. Fenton Green W 1979-2002. Longton North W 2002-

Saint John (b)
LG. St John W 1865-1910. No. 23 W 1910-55. No. 23 W 1955-65. No. 23 W 1965-79. Fenton Green W 1979-2002. Longton North W 2002-

Saint John (c)
LG. St John W 1865-95. Sandford Hill W 1895-1910. No. 23 W 1910-55. No. 23 W 1955-65. No. 21 W 1965-79. Fenton Green W 1979-2002. Longton North W 2002-

Sandford Hill (1)
LG. St John W 1865-95. Sandford Hill W 1895-1910. No. 24 W 1910-55. No. 23 W 1955-65. No. 23 W 1965-79. Fenton Green W 1979-2002. Longton North W 2002-

Sandford Hill (2)
LG. St John W 1865-95. Sandford Hill W 1895-1910. No. 24 W 1910-55. No. 23 W 1955-65. No. 21 W 1965-79. Fenton Green W 1979-2002. Longton North W 2002-

Sandford Hill (3)
LG. St John W 1865-95. St John W 1895-1910. No. 24 W 1910-55. No. 23 W 1955-65. No. 21 W 1965-79. Fenton Green W 1979-2002. Longton North W 2002-

Station
LG. St Paul W 1865-84. Market W 1895-1910. No. 23 W 1910-55. No. 20 W 1955-65. No. 20 W 1965-79. Longton South W 1979-2002. Longton North W 2002-

Wood
LG. St Paul W 1865-84. Market W 1895-1910. No. 23 W 1910-55. No. 23 W 1955-65. No. 21 W 1965-79. Fenton Green W 1979-2002. Longton North W 2002-

Wood House
LG. St John W 1865-95. Sandford Hill W 1895-1910. No. 24 W 1910-55. No. 23 W 1922-55. No. 23 W 1965-79. Weston W 1979-2002. Longton North W 2002-

LONGTON TOWNSHIP
Longton T post-medieval-. Longton CP 1894-1910.
LG. Longton Commissioners district 1839-58, LB 1858-65, MB 1865-1910. S-o-T CB 1910-74, D(C) 1974-97, UA 1997-
CED. Longton No.1 or No. 2 1889-98. Longton No.1 or No. 2 or No. 3 1898-. CCWs 1974-97.
PARL. Stoke-upon-Trent PB 1832-1918. Stoke-upon-Trent D of Stoke-on-Trent PB 1918-48. Stoke-on-Trent South BC 1948-, 1974-, ?1981-

Chelson
LG. St James W 1865-95. Normacot W 1895-1910.

154

Stoke-upon-Trent (Botteslow, Fenton, Longton Quarter, Longton)

No. 26 W 1910-55. No. 22 W 1955-65. No. 22 W 1965-79. Longton South W 1979-2002. Longton North W 2002-

Edensor
LG. St Paul W 1865-1910. No. 23 W 1910-55. No. 20 W 1955-65. No. 20 W 1965-79. Longton South W 1979-2002. Longton South W 2002-

Fern
LG. St Paul W 1865-84. Florence W 1884-1910. No. 25 W 1910-55. No. 20 W 1955-65. No. 20 W 1965-79. Longton South W 1979-2002. Longton South W 2002-

Foley Road
LG. St Paul W 1865-1910. No. 23 W 1910-55. No. 20 W 1955-65. No. 20 W 1965-79. Longton South W 1979-2002. Longton South W 2002-

Gladstone
LG. St James W 1865-1910. No. 23 W 1910-55. No. 20 W 1955-65. No. 20 W 1965-79. Longton South W 1979-2002. Longton North W 2002-

Gold
LG. St Paul W 1865-95. Market W 1895-1910. No. 23 W 1910-55. No. 20 W 1955-65. No. 20 W 1965-79. Longton South W 1979-2002. Longton North W 2002-

Gom's Mill
LG. St Paul W 1865-1910. No. 23 W 1910-55. No. 20 W 1955-65. No. 20 W 1965-79. Blurton W 1979-2002. Longton South W 2002-

Greendock
LG. St Paul W 1865-95. Market W 1895-1910. No. 23 W 1910-55. No. 20 W 1955-65. No. 20 W 1965-79. Longton South W 1979-2002. Longton South W 2002-

Hollybush
LG. St Paul W 1865-1910. No. 23 W 1910-55. No. 20 W 1955-65. No. 19 W 1965-79. Great Fenton W 1979-2002. Blurton W 2002-

Line Side A
LG. St Paul W 1865-1910. No. 20 W 1910-55. No. 20 W 1955-65. No. 20 W 1965-79. Longton South W 1979-2002. Fenton W 2002-

Line Side B
LG. St Paul W 1865-95. Market W 1895-1910. No. 20 W 1910-55. No. 20 W 1955-65. No. 20 W 1965-79. Longton South W 1979-2002. Fenton W 2002-

Line Side C
LG. St Paul W 1865-95. Market W 1895-1910. No. 20 W 1910-55. No. 20 W 1955-65. No. 20 W 1965-79. Longton South W 1979-2002. Longton North W 2002-

Line Side D
LG. St Paul W 1865-95. Market W 1895-1910. No. 20 W 1910-55. No. 20 W 1955-65. No. 20 W 1965-79.

Longton South W 1979-2002. Longton South W 2002-

Market (South)
LG. St John W 1865-1910. No. 23 W 1910-55. No. 23 W 1955-65. No. 22 W 1965-79. Longton South W 1979-2002. Longton North W 2002-

Millbank (1)
LG. St James W 1865-1910. No. 23 W 1910-55. No. 22 W 1955-65. No. 22 W 1965-79. Longton South W 1979-2002. Longton South W 2002-

Millbank (2)
LG. St James W 1865-1910. No. 23 W 1910-55. No. 20 W 1955-65. No. 22 W 1965-79. Longton South W 1979-2002. Longton South W 2002-

Queensbury
LG. St James W 1865-84. Florence W 1884-95. Normacot W 1895-1910. No. 26 W 1910-55. No. 22 W 1955-65. No. 22 W 1965-79. Longton South W 1979-2002. Longton South W 2002-

Saint James
LG. St James W 1865-1910. No. 25 W 1910-55. No. 22 W 1955-65. No. 22 W 1965-79. Longton South W 1979-2002. Longton North W 2002-

Spratslade
LG. St Paul W 1865-84. Florence W 1884-1910. No. 25 W 1910-55. No. 20 W 1955-65. No. 20 W 1965-79. Longton South W 1979-2002. Longton South W 2002-

Strand
LG. St James W 1865-95. Market W 1895-1910. No. 23 W 1910-55. No. 20 W 1955-65. No. 20 W 1965-79. Longton South W 1979-2002. Longton North W 2002-

Sutherland
LG. St John W 1865-95. Sutherland W 1895-1910. No. 24 W 1910-55. No. 23 W 1955-65. No. 22 W 1965-79. Longton South W 1979-2002. Longton North W 2002-

Swingle Hill
LG. St Paul W 1865-1910. No. 23 W 1910-55. No. 20 W 1955-65. No. 20 W 1965-79. Great Fenton W 1979-2002. Longton South W 2002-

Vauxall
LG. St James W 1865-95. Market W 1895-1910. No. 23 W 1910-55. No. 20 W 1955-65. No. 22 W 1965-79. Longton South W 1979-2002. Longton South W 2002-

Warren
LG. St James W 1865-1910. No. 26 W 1910-55. No. 22 W 1955-65. No. 22 W 1965-79. Longton South W 1979-2002. Longton North W 2002-

Waste (East)
LG. St Paul W 1865-1910. No. 23 W 1910-55. No. 20

W 1955-65. No. 19 W 1965-79. Blurton W 1979-2002. Blurton W 2002-

Waste (West)

LG. St Paul W 1865-1910. No. 23 W 1910-55. No. 18 W 1955-65. No. 18 W 1965-79. Trentham Park W 1979-2002. Trentham & Hanford W 2002-

Webberley (a)

LG. St James W 1865-1910. No. 25 W 1910-55. No. 22 W 1955-65. No. 22 W 1965-79. Longton South W 1979-2002. Longton South W 2002-

Webberley (b)

LG. St James W 1865-1910. No. 26 W 1910-55. No. 22 W 1955-65. No. 22 W 1965-79. Longton South W 1979-2002. Longton South W 2002-

PENKHULL QUARTER

A union of the two Poor Relief districts Penkhull with Boothen T and Clayton and Seabridge T in early C17. The quarter had its own overseer (VCH vol 8 p198).

PENKHULL TOWNSHIP

Stoke CP 1894-1910.

LG. Stoke-upon-Trent Improvement Commissioners district 1839-74, MB 1874-1910. S-o-T CB 1910-74, D(C) 1974-97, UA 1997- (VCH vol 8 p194).

CED. Stoke No. 1 or No. 2 1889-1910. CCWs 1974-97.

PARL. Stoke-upon-Trent PB 1832-1918.

Boothen

LG. South W 1874-1910. No. 21 W 1910-55. No. 17 W 1955-65. No. 17 W 1965-79. Trentham Park W 1979-2002. Stoke & Trent Vale W 2002-.

PARL. S-u-T D of S-o-T PB 1918-48. S-o-T South BC 1948-, 1974-. S-o-T South BC ?1981-.

Brisley

LG. South W 1874-1910. No. 17 W 1910-55. No. 17 W 1955-65. No. 17 W 1965-79. Stoke West W 1979-2002. Hartshill & Penkhull 2002-

PARL. S-u-T D of S-o-T PB 1918-48. S-o-T Central BC 1948-. S-o-T South BC 1974-. S-o-T Central BC ?1981-.

Campbell Road (1)

LG. South W 1874-1910. No. 21 W 1910-55. No. 19 W 1955-65. No. 19 W 1965-79. Trentham Park W 1979-2002. Stoke & Trent Vale W 2002-.

PARL. S-u-T D of S-o-T PB 1918-48. S-o-T South BC 1948-, 1974-. S-o-T South BC ?1981-.

Campbell Road (2)

LG. South W 1874-1910. No. 21 W 1910-55. No. 18 W 1955-65. No. 18 W 1965-79. Trentham Park W 1979-2002. Stoke & Trent Vale W 2002-.

PARL. S-u-T D of S-o-T PB 1918-48. S-o-T South BC 1948-, 1974-. S-o-T South BC ?1981-.

Castle (det)

LG. Newcastle MB 1875-. West W 1875-1932. No. 2 W 1932-. Thistleberry W by1981-. Town W 2002-.

CED. Newcastle West 1889-. Newcastle No. 1 1973-81. Thistleberry 1981-2005. Keele & Westlands 2005-

PARL. Newcastle PB 1832-

Castle Bank (det)

LG. Newcastle MB 1875-. West W 1875-1932. No. 2 W 1932-. Thistleberry W by1981-, 2002-.

CED. Newcastle West 1889-. Newcastle No. 1 1973-81. Thistleberry 1981-2005. Keele & Westlands 2005-

PARL. Newcastle PB 1832-

Glebe

LG. South W 1874-1910. No. 18 W 1910-55. No. 15 W 1955-65. No. 13 W 1965-79. Stoke West W 1979-2002. Stoke & Trent Vale W 2002-.

PARL. S-u-T D of S-o-T PB 1918-48. S-o-T Central BC 1948-, 1974-, ?1981-.

Grindley

LG. West W 1874-1910. No. 16 W 1910-55. No. 12 W 1955-65. No. 12 W 1965-79. Stoke West W 1979-2002. Hartshill & Penkhull W 2002-

PARL. Hanley D of S-o-T PB 1918-48. S-o-T Central BC 1948-, 1974-, ?1981-.

Hanford Bridge

LG. S-u-T B 1874-1910. South W 1874-1910. Stoke 1910-. No. 21 W 1910-55. No. 18 W 1955-65. No. 17 W 1965-79. Trentham Park W 1979-2002. Trentham & Hanford W 2002-

PARL. S-u-T D of S-o-T PB 1918-48. S-o-T South BC 1948-, 1974-, ?1981-.

Hanford Mill

LG. South W 1874-1910. No. 21 W 1910-55. No. 18 W 1955-65. No. 18 W 1965-79. Trentham Park W 1979-2002. Trentham & Hanford 2002-.

PARL. S-u-T D of S-o-T PB 1918-48. S-o-T South BC 1948-, 1974-, ?1981-.

Hartshill

LG. West W 1874-1910. No. 16 W 1910-55. No. 12 W 1955-65. No. 12 W 1965-79. Hartshill W 1979-2002. Hartshill & Penkhull W 2002-

PARL. Hanley D of S-o-T PB 1918-48. S-o-T Central BC 1948-, 1974-, ?1981-.

Hill (1)

LG. East W 1874-1910. No. 17 W 1910-55. No. 15 W 1955-65. No. 13 W 1965-79. Stoke West W 1979-2002. Stoke & Trent Vale W 2002-.

Map of Penkhull Quarter

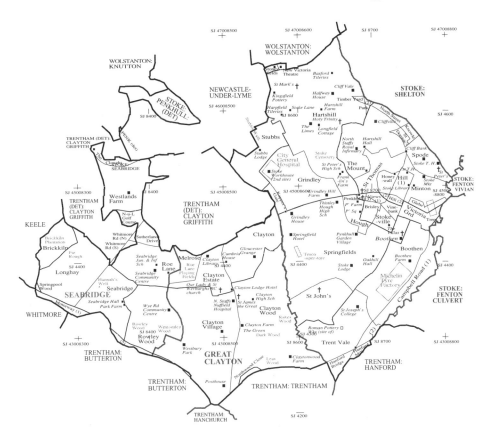

PARL. S-u-T D of S-o-T PB 1918-48. S-o-T Central BC 1948-, 1974-, ?1981-.

Hill (2)

LG. South W 1874-1910. No. 17 W 1910-55. No. 15 W 1955-65. No. 13 W 1965-79. Stoke West W 1979-2002. Stoke & Trent Vale W 2002-.
PARL. S-u-T D of S-o-T PB 1918-48. S-o-T Central BC 1948-, 1974-, ?1981-.

Honeywall

LG. East W 1874-1910. No. 17 W 1910-55. No. 15 W 1955-65. No. 13 W 1965-79. Hartshill W 1979-2002. Hartshill & Penkhull 2002-.
PARL. S-u-T D of S-o-T PB 1918-48. S-o-T Central BC 1948-, 1974-, ?1981-.

Hough

LG. South W 1874-1910. No. 21 W 1910-55. No. 17 W 1955-65. No. 17 W 1965-79. Stoke West W 1979-2002. Hartshill & Penkhull 2002-.
PARL. S-u-T D of S-o-T PB 1918-48. S-o-T South BC 1948-. 1974-. S-o-T Central BC ?1981-.

Stoke-upon-Trent (Penkhull Quarter, Penkhull)

Knapper's Gate
LG. West W 1874-1910. No. 16 W 1910-55. No. 12 W 1955-65. No. 12 W 1965-79. Stoke West W 1979-2002. Stoke & Trent Vale W 2002-
PARL. Hanley D of S-o-T PB 1918-48. S-o-T Central BC 1948-, 1974-, ?1981-.

Knowle
LG. West W 1874-1910. No. 18 W 1910-55. No. 15 W 1955-65. No. 13 W 1965-79. Hartshill W 1979-2002. Hartshill & Penkhull 2002-.
PARL. S-u-T D of S-o-T PB 1918-48. S-o-T Central BC 1948-, 1974-, ?1981-

Minton
LG. East W 1874-1910. No. 18 W 1910-55. No. 15 W 1955-65. No. 13 W 1965-79. Stoke West W 1979-2002. Stoke & Trent Vale W 2002-.
PARL. S-u-T D of S-o-T PB 1918-48. S-o-T Central BC 1948-, 1974-, ?1981-.

The Mount
LG. West W 1874-1910. No. 17 W 1910-55. No. 15 W 1955-65. No. 12 W 1965-79. Hartshill W 1979-2002. Hartshill & Penkhull 2002-
PARL. S-u-T D of S-o-T PB 1918-48. S-o-T Central BC 1948-, 1974-, ?1981-.

Newcastle Junction (2)
LG. West W 1874-1910. No. 16 W 1910-55. No. 15 W 1955-65. No. 13 W 1965-79. Hartshill W 1979-2002. Hartshill & Penkhull 2002-.
PARL. Hanley D of S-o-T PB 1918-48. S-o-T Central BC 1948-, 1974-, ?1981-.

New Victoria Theatre
LG. West W 1874-1910. No. 16 W 1910-55. No. 12 W 1955-65. Newcastle MB 1965-. No. 5 W 1965-79. May Bank W 1979-2002, 2002-.
CED. Newcastle No. 3 1965-81. Wolstanton W 1981-2005, 2005-.
PARL. Hanley D of S-o-T PB 1918-48. S-o-T Central BC 1948-. Newcastle BC 1974-

North Street
LG. West W 1874-1910. No. 17 W 1910-55. No. 15 W 1955-65. No. 13 W 1965-79. Hartshill W 1979-2002. Hartshill & Penkhull 2002-.
PARL. S-u-T D of S-o-T PB 1918-48. S-o-T Central BC 1948-, 1974-, ?1981-.

Park
LG. West W 1874-1910. No. 16 W 1910-55. No. 15 W 1955-65. No. 12 W 1965-79. Hartshill W 1979-2002. Hartshill & Penkhull 2002-.
PARL. Hanley D of S-o-T PB 1918-48. S-o-T Central BC 1948-, 1974-, ?1981-.

Penkhull
LG. South W 1874-1910. No. 17 W 1910-55. No. 17

W 1955-65. No. 17 W 1965-79. Stoke West W 1979-2002. Hartshill & Penkhull 2002-
PARL. S-u-T D of S-o-T PB 1918-48. S-o-T Central BC 1948-. S-o-T South BC 1974-. S-o-T Central BC ?1981-.

Pool Dam (det)
LG. Newcastle MB 1875-. West W 1875-1932. No. 2 W 1932-. Westlands W by1981-. Town W 1992-.
CED. Newcastle West 1889-. Newcastle No. 1 1973-81. Westlands 1981-2005. Newcastle South 2005-
PARL. Newcastle PB 1832-

Pool Side (det)
LG. Newcastle MB 1875-. West W 1875-1932. No. 1 W 1932-. Westlands W by1981-. Town W by1992-.
CED. Newcastle West 1889-. Newcastle No. 1 1973-81. Westlands 1981-2005. Newcastle South 2005-
PARL. Newcastle PB 1832-

Saint Dominic's
LG. West W 1874-1910. No. 18 W 1910-55. No. 15 W 1955-65. No. 12 W 1965-79. Hartshill W 1979-2002. Hartshill & Penkhull 2002-.
PARL. S-u-T D of S-o-T PB 1918-48. S-o-T Central BC 1948-, 1974-, ?1981-

Saint John's
LG. South W 1874-1910. No. 21 W 1910-55. No. 18 W 1955-65. No. 17 W 1965-79. Stoke West W 1979-2002. Stoke & Trent Vale W 2002-.
PARL. S-u-T D of S-o-T PB 1918-48. S-o-T South BC 1948-, 1974-. S-o-T Central BC ?1981-.

Saint Thomas
LG. West W 1874-1910. No. 17 W 1910-55. No. 15 W 1955-65. No. 13 W 1965-79. Hartshill W 1979-2002. Hartshill & Penkhull 2002-
PARL. S-u-T D of S-o-T PB 1918-48. S-o-T Central BC 1948-, 1974-, ?1981-.

Spode
LG. East W 1874-1910. No. 18 W 1910-55. No. 15 W 1955-65. No. 13 W 1965-79. Hartshill W 1979-2002. Hartshill & Penkhull 2002-
PARL. S-u-T D of S-o-T PB 1918-48. S-o-T Central BC 1948-, 1974-, ?1981-.

Springfields
LG. South W 1874-1910. No. 21 W 1910-55. No. 17 W 1955-65. No. 17 W 1965-79. Stoke West W 1979-2002. Stoke & Trent Vale W 2002-.
PARL. S-u-T D of S-o-T PB 1918-48. S-o-T South BC 1948-, 1974-. S-o-T Central BC ?1981-.

Stokeville
LG. South W 1874-1910. No. 17 W 1910-55. No. 17 W 1955-65. No. 17 W 1965-79. Stoke West W 1979-2002. Stoke & Trent Vale W 2002-.
PARL. S-u-T D of S-o-T PB 1918-48. S-o-T Central

Stoke-upon-Trent (Penkhull Quarter, Penkhull)

Clayton Hall. c1840. By T Taylor. SV. 111. 117a. Courtesy of Trustees of WSL

BC 1948-. S-o-T South BC 1974-. S-o-T Central BC ?1981-.

Stoneyfields
LG. West W 1874-1910. No. 16 W 1910-55. No. 12 W 1955-65. Newcastle MB 1965-. No. 5 W 1965-79. Cross Heath W 1979-2002. May Bank W 2002-.
CED. Newcastle No. 3 1973-81. Cross Heath 1981-2005. Wolstanton 2005-.
PARL. Hanley D of S-o-T PB 1918-48. S-o-T Central BC 1948-. Newcastle BC 1974-.

Stubbs
LG. West W 1874-1910. No 16 W 1910-55. No. 12 W 1955-65. Newcastle MB 1965-. No. 4 W 1965-79. Town W 1979-2002, 2002-.
CED. Newcastle No. 2 1973-81. Westlands 1981-2005. Newcastle South 2005-
PARL. S-u-T D of S-o-T PB 1918-48. Hanley D of S-o-T PB 1918-48. S-o-T Central BC 1948-. Newcastle BC 1974-.

Timber Yard
LG. West W 1874-1910. No. 16 W 1910-55. No. 12 W 1955-65. No. 13 W 1965-79. Hartshill W 1979-2002. Hartshill & Penkhull 2002-
PARL. Hanley D of S-o-T PB 1918-48. S-o-T Central BC 1948-, 1974-, ?1981-.

Trent
LG. South W 1874-1910. No. 18 W 1910-55. No. 15

W 1955-65. No. 19 W 1965-79. Stoke West W 1979-2002. Stoke & Trent Vale W 2002-.
PARL. S-u-T D of S-o-T PB 1918-48. S-o-T South BC 1948-, 1974-, ?1981-.

Trent Vale
LG. South W 1874-1910. No. 21 W 1910-55. No. 18 W 1955-65. No. 17 W 1965-79. Trentham Park W 1979-2002. Stoke & Trent Vale W 2002-.
PARL. S-u-T D of S-o-T PB 1918-48. S-o-T South BC 1948-, 1974-. S-o-T South BC ?1981-.

Victoria Ground
LG. South W 1874-1910. No. 18 W 1910-55. No. 15 W 1955-65. No. 13 W 1965-79. Stoke West W 1979-2002. Stoke & Trent Vale W 2002-.
PARL. S-u-T D of S-o-T PB 1918-48. S-o-T Central BC 1948-. S-o-T South BC 1974-. S-o-T Central BC ?1981-.

Views (1)
LG. South W 1874-1910. No. 17 W 1910-55. No. 15W 1955-65. No. 13 W 1965-79. Hartshill W 1979-2002. Hartshill & Penkhull 2002-.
PARL. S-u-T D of S-o-T PB 1918-48. S-o-T Central BC 1948-. S-o-T South BC 1974-. S-o-T Central BC ?1981-.

Views (2)
LG. South W 1874-1910. No. 17 W 1910-55. No. 15 W 1955-65. No. 13 W 1965-79. Hartshill W 1979-

159

Stoke-upon-Trent (Penkhull Quarter, Seabridge)

2002. Hartshill & Penkhull 2002-
PARL. S-u-T D of S-o-T PB 1918-48. S-o-T Central
BC 1948, 1974-, ?1981-.

Views (3)

LG. South W 1874-1910. No. 17 W 1910-55. No. 15
W 1955-65. No. 17 W 1965-79. Hartshill W 1979-
2002. Hartshill & Penkhull 2002-.
PARL. S-u-T D of S-o-T PB 1918-48. S-o-T Central
BC 1948-. S-o-T South BC 1974-. S-o-T Central BC
?1981-.

Vinebank

LG. South W 1874-1910. No. 17 W 1910-55. No. 15
W 1955-65. No. 13 W 1965-79. Stoke West W 1979-
2002. Stoke & Trent Vale W 2002-.
PARL. S-u-T D of S-o-T PB 1918-48. S-o-T Central
BC 1948-. S-o-T South BC 1974-. S-o-T Central BC
?1981-.

CLAYTON TOWNSHIP

Great Clayton Vill medieval-
LG. Stoke-upon-Trent Commissioners district 1839 to
at least 1874 (VCH vol 8 p194) and possibly 1894.

Clayton

S-u-T Rural CP 1894-6. Clayton & Seabridge PW Nov
1894-6. Clayton CP 1896-1927. There was an election for the first PC in 1896 (SA March 14 1896
p3). Newcastle unparished 1927-.
LG. S-u-T RD 1894-6. Newcastle-u-Lyme RD 1896-
1927, MB 1927-74, D(B) 1974-. West W 1927-32. No.
3 W 1932-79. Clayton W 1979-2002, 2002-
CED. Stone 1889-98. Keele 1898-1927. Newcastle
West 1927-34. Newcastle No. 2 1934-81. Westlands
W 1981-2005. Newcastle South 2005-.

Clayton Estate

S-u-T Rural CP 1894-6. Clayton & Seabridge PW Nov
1894-6. Clayton CP 1896-1927. Newcastle unparished
1927-.
LG. S-u-T RD 1894-6. Newcastle-u-Lyme RD 1896-
1927, MB 1927-74, D(B) 1974-. West W 1927-32. No.
3 W 1932-79. Seabridge W 1979-2002, 2002-.
CED. Stone 1889-98. Keele 1898-1927. Newcastle
West 1927-34. Newcastle No. 2 1934-81. Thistleberry
1981-2005. Newcastle South 2005-.

Clayton Village

S-u-T Rural CP 1894-6. Clayton & Seabridge PW Nov
1894-6. Clayton CP 1896-1932. Newcastle unparished
1932-.
LG. S-u-T RD 1894-6. Newcastle-u-Lyme RD 1896-
1932, MB 1932-74, D(B) 1974-. No. 3 W 1932-79.
Seabridge W 1979-2002, 2002-
CED. Stone 1889-98. Keele 1898-1934. Newcastle No.

2 1934-81. Thistleberry 1981-2005. Newcastle South
2005-.

Clayton Wood

S-u-T Rural CP 1894-6. Clayton & Seabridge PW Nov
1894-6. Clayton CP 1896-1932. Newcastle unparished
1932-.
LG. S-u-T RD 1894-6. Newcastle-u-Lyme RD 1896-
1932, MB 1932-74, D(B) 1974-. No. 3 W 1932-79.
Clayton W 1979-2002, 2002-
CED. Stone 1889-98. Keele 1898-1934. Newcastle No.
2 1934-81. Westlands 1981-2005. Newcastle South
2005-.

Melrose

S-u-T CP 1894-6. Clayton & Seabridge PW Nov 1894-
6. Clayton CP 1896-1927. Newcastle unparished 1927-
.
LG. S-u-T RD 1894-6. Newcastle-u-Lyme RD 1896-
1927, MB 1927-74, D(B) 1974-. West W 1927-32. No.
3 W 1932-79. Seabridge W 1979-2002. Westlands W
2002-
CED. Stone 1889-98. Keele 1898-1928. Newcastle
West 1928-34. Newcastle No. 2 1934-81. Thistleberry
1981-2005. Keele & Westlands 2005-

Northwood Close

S-u-T Rural CP 1894-6. Clayton & Seabridge PW Nov
1894-6. Trentham CP ?1896-. Swynnerton CP 1932-.
LG. S-u-T RD 1894-6. Stone RD ?1896-1974. Staf-
ford D(B) 1974-. Swynnerton W 1974-2002, 2002-.
CED. Stone 1889-1911. Stone Rural Sept 1911-1934.
Eccleshall 1934-2005, 2005-.

SEABRIDGE TOWNSHIP

Seabridge Vill medieval-

Brickkiln

S-u-T Rural CP 1894-6. Clayton & Seabridge PW Nov
1894-6. Clayton CP 1896-1932. Newcastle unparished
1932-.
LG. S-u-T RD 1894-6. Newcastle-u-Lyme RD 1896-
1932, MB 1932-74, D(B) 1974-. No. 3 W 1932-79.
Keele W 1979-2002, 2002-.
CED. Stone 1889-98. Keele 1898-1934. Newcastle No.
2 1934-81. Keele & Silverdale 1981-2005. Keele &
Westlands 2005-.

The Cloughs

S-u-T Rural CP 1894-6. Clayton & Seabridge PW Nov
1894-6. Clayton CP 1896-1921. Newcastle unparished
1921-.
LG. S-u-T RD 1894-6. Newcastle-u-Lyme RD 1896-
1921, MB 1921-74, D(B) 1974-. West W 1921-32. No.
2 W 1932-79. Thistleberry W 1979-2002, 2002-
CED. Stone 1889-98. Keele 1898-1921. Newcastle
West 1921-34. Newcastle No. 1 1934-81. Thistleberry

1981-2005. Keele & Westlands 2005-.

Hands Wood

S-u-T Rural CP 1894-6. Clayton & Seabridge PW Nov 1894-6. Clayton CP 1896-1932. Newcastle unparished 1932-.

LG. S-u-T RD 1894-6. Newcastle-u-Lyme RD 1896-1932, MB 1932-74, D(B) 1974-. No. 3 W 1932-79. Thistleberry W 1979-2002, 2002-

CED. Stone 1889-98. Keele 1898-1934. Newcastle No. 2 1934-81. Keele & Silverdale 1981-2005. Keele & Westlands 2005-.

Longhay

S-u-T Rural CP 1894-6. Clayton & Seabridge PW Nov 1894-6. Clayton CP 1896-1932. Newcastle unparished 1932-.

LG. S-u-T RD 1894-6. Newcastle-u-Lyme RD 1896-1932, MB 1932-74, D(B) 1974-. No. 3 W 1932-79. Thistleberry W 1979-2002, 2002-

CED. Stone 1889-98. Keele 1898-1934. Newcastle No. 2 1934-81. Thistleberry 1981-2005. Keele & Westlands 2005-.

Motorway (1)

S-u-T Rural CP 1894-6. Clayton & Seabridge PW Nov 1894-6. Clayton CP 1896-1932. Newcastle unparished 1932-84. Whitmore CP 1984- (SI No. 152).

LG. S-u-T RD 1894-6. Newcastle-u-Lyme RD 1896-1932, MB 1932-74, D(B) 1974-. No. 3 W 1932-79. Thistleberry W 1979-84. Whitmore W 1984-2002. Loggerheads & Whitmore 2002-.

CED. Stone 1889-98. Keele 1898-1934. Newcastle No. 2 1934-81. Thistleberry 1981-4. Newcastle Rural 1984-2005, 2005-.

Motorway (5)

S-u-T Rural CP 1894-6. Clayton & Seabridge PW Nov 1894-6. Clayton CP 1896-1932. Newcastle unparished 1932-84. Whitmore CP 1984- (SI No. 152).

LG. S-u-T RD 1894-6. Newcastle-u-Lyme RD 1896-1932, MB 1932-74, D(B) 1974-. No. 3 W 1932-79. Thistleberry W 1979-84. Whitmore W 1984-2002. Loggerheads & Whitmore 2002-.

CED. Stone 1889-98. Keele 1898-1934. Newcastle No. 2 1934-81. Thistleberry 1981-4. Newcastle Rural 1984-2005, 2005-.

Newcastle-u-Lyme Golf Course

S-u-T Rural CP 1894-6. Clayton & Seabridge PW Nov 1894-6. Clayton CP 1896-1927. Newcastle unparished 1927-.

LG. S-u-T RD 1894-6. Newcastle-u-Lyme RD 1896-1927, MB 1927-74, D(B) 1974-. West W 1927-32. No. 3 W 1932-79. Thistleberry W 1979-2002, 2002-.

CED. Stone 1889-98. Keele 1898-1927. Newcastle West 1927-34. Newcastle No. 2 1934-81. Thistleberry

1981-2005. Keele & Westlands 2005-.

Roe Lane

S-u-T Rural CP 1894-6. Clayton & Seabridge PW Nov 1894-6. Clayton CP 1896-1932. Newcastle unparished 1932-.

LG. S-u-T RD 1894-6. Newcastle-u-Lyme RD 1896-1932, MB 1932-74, D(B) 1974-. No. 3 W 1932-79. Seabridge W 1979-2002. Westlands W 2002-.

CED. Stone 1889-98. Keele 1898-1934. Newcastle No. 2 1934-81. Thistleberry 1981-2005. Keele & Westlands 2005-.

Rowley Wood

S-u-T Rural CP 1894-6. Clayton & Seabridge PW Nov 1894-6. Clayton CP 1896-1932. Newcastle unparished 1932-.

LG. S-u-T RD 1894-6. Newcastle-u-Lyme RD 1896-1932, MB 1932-74, D(B) 1974-. No. 3 W 1932-79. Seabridge W 1979-2002, 2002-

CED. Stone 1889-98. Keele 1898-1934. Newcastle No. 2 1934-81. Thistleberry W 1981-2005. Newcastle South 2005-.

Seabridge

S-u-T Rural CP 1894-6. Clayton & Seabridge PW Nov 1894-6. Clayton CP 1896-1932. Newcastle unparished 1932-.

LG. S-u-T RD 1894-6. Newcastle-u-Lyme RD 1896-1932, MB 1932-74, D(B) 1974-. No. 3 W 1932-79. Seabridge W 1979-2002. Westlands W 2002-

CED. Stone 1889-98. Keele 1898-1934. Newcastle No. 2 1934-81. Thistleberry 1981-2005. Keele & Westlands 2005-.

Springpool Wood

S-u-T Rural CP 1894-6. Clayton & Seabridge PW Nov 1894-6. Clayton CP 1896-1932. Newcastle unparished 1932-84. Keele CP 1984-.

LG. S-u-T RD 1894-6. Newcastle-u-Lyme RD 1896-1932, MB 1932-74, D(B) 1974-. No. 3 W 1932-79. Thistleberry W 1979-2002, 2002-.

CED. Stone 1889-98. Keele 1898-1934. Newcastle No. 2 1934-81. Thistleberry 1981-4. Keele & Silverdale 1984-2005. Keele & Westlands 2005-.

Sutherland Drive

S-u-T Rural CP 1894-6. Clayton & Seabridge PW Nov 1894-6. Clayton CP 1896-1932. Newcastle unparished 1932-.

LG. S-u-T RD 1894-6. Newcastle-u-Lyme RD 1896-1932, MB 1932-74, D(B) 1974-. Westlands W 1979-2002, 2002-.

CED. Stone 1889-98. Keele 1898-1934. Newcastle No. 2 1934-81. Westlands 1981-2005. Keele & Westlands 2005-.

Stoke-upon-Trent (Shelton Quarter, Hanley)

Westlands Farm

S-u-T Rural CP 1894-6. Clayton & Seabridge PW Nov 1894-6. Clayton CP 1896-1927. Newcastle unparished 1927-.

LG. S-u-T RD 1894-6. Newcastle-u-Lyme RD 1896-1927, MB 1927-74, D(B) 1974-. West W 1927-32. No. 3 W 1932-79. Thistleberry W 1979-2002, 2002-.

CED. Stone 1889-98. Keele 1898-1927. Newcastle West 1927-34. Newcastle No. 2 1934-81. Thistleberry 1981-2005. Keele & Westlands 2005-.

SHELTON QUARTER

The Poor Relief district of Hanley and Shelton townships became a quarter in early C17. The quarter had its own overseer (VCH vol 8 p198).

HANLEY TOWNSHIP

Hanley CP 1894-1910.

LG. Hanley Improvement Commissioners district 1825-57, MB 1857-89, CB 1889-1910. S-o-T CB 1910-74, D(C) 1974-97, UA 1997-

CED. CCWs 1974-97.

PARL. Stoke-upon-Trent PB 1832-85. Hanley PB 1885-1918. Hanley D of Stoke-on-Trent PB 1918-48.

Albion Square

LG. South W 1857-95. Eastwood W 1895-1910. No. 15 W 1910-55. No. 14 1955-65. No. 14 W 1965-79. Shelton W 1979-2002. Hanley West & Shelton W 2002-

PARL. S-o-T Central CB 1948-

Bryan

LG. East W 1857-95. Providence W 1895-1910. No. 9 W 1922-55. No. 9 W 1955-65. No. 9 W 1965-79. Shelton W 1979-2002. Burslem South W 2002-

PARL. S-o-T North CB 1948-

Bucknall Bridge

LG. East W 1857-95. Northwood W 1895-1910. No. 12 W 1910-55. No. 10 W 1955-65. No. 15 W 1965-79. Berryhill W 1979-2002. Berryhill & Hanley East W 2002-

PARL. S-o-T Central CB 1948-

Bucknall Station

LG. East W 1857-95. Wellington W 1895-1910. No. 12 W 1910-55. No. 16 W 1955-65. No. 15 W 1965-79. Berryhill W 1979-2002. Berryhill & Hanley East W 2002-

PARL. S-o-T Central CB 1948-

Caldon

LG. East W 1857-95. Northwood W 1895-1910. No. 12 W 1910-55. No. 10 W 1955-65. No. 10 W 1965-

79. Abbey W 1979-2002. Abbey Green W 2002-

PARL. S-o-T Central CB 1948-

Central Forest Park

LG. East W 1857-95. Providence W 1895-1910. No. 9 W 1910-55. No. 9 W 1955-65. No. 10 W 1965-79. Shelton W 1979-2002. Burslem South W 2002-

PARL. S-o-T North CB 1948-

Cromer

LG. East W 1857-95. Northwood W 1895-1910. No. 10 W 1910-55. No. 10 W 1955-65. No. 10 W 1965-79. Abbey W 1979-2002. Abbey Green W 2002-

PARL. S-o-T Central CB 1948-

Cromwell

LG. East W 1857-95. Providence W 1895-1910. No. 9 W 1910-55. No. 9 W 1955-65. No. 10 W 1965-79. Shelton W 1979-2002. Northwood & Birches Head W 2002-

PARL. S-o-T North CB 1948-

Eastwood

LG. South W 1857-95. Eastwood W 1895-1910. No. 15 W 1910-55. No. 14 W 1955-65. No. 14 W 1965-79. Shelton W 1979-2002. Berryhill & Hanley East W 2002-

PARL. S-o-T Central CB 1948-

Fountain Square

LG. North W 1857-95. Hope W 1895-1910. No. 11 W 1910-55. No. 9 W 1955-65. No. 9 W 1965-79. Shelton W 1979-2002. Hanley West & Shelton 2002-

PARL. S-o-T Central CB 1948-

Gilman

LG. East W 1857-95. Wellington W 1895-1910. No. 15 W 1910-55. No. 14 W 1955-65. No. 14 W 1965-79. Hanley Green W 1979-2002. Hanley West & Shelton 2002-

PARL. S-o-T Central CB 1948-

Grove

LG. East W 1857-95. Providence W 1895-1910. No. 9 W 1910-55. No. 8 W 1955-65. No. 10 W 1965-79. Shelton W 1979-2002. Burslem South W 2002-

PARL. S-o-T North CB 1948-

Hillchurch

LG. East W 1857-95. Providence W 1895-1910. No. 10 W 1910-55. No. 10 W 1955-65. No. 9 W 1965-79. Hanley Green W 1979-2002. Hanley West & Shelton W 2002-

PARL. S-o-T Central CB 1948-

Hillcrest

LG. East W 1857-95. Northwood W 1895-1910. No. 12 W 1910-55. No. 10 W 1955-65. No. 10 W 1965-79. Hanley Green W 1979-2002. Northwood & Birches Head W 2002-

PARL. S-o-T Central CB 1948-

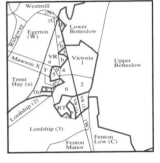

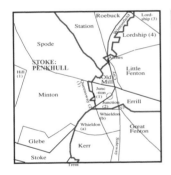

Map of
Shelton
Quarter
For Shelton and
Hanley townships see
VCH vol 8.

Huntbach

LG. East W 1857-95. Northwood W 1895-1910. No.
10 W 1910-55. No. 10 W 1955-65. No. 9 W 1965-79.
Hanley Green W 1979-2002. Hanley West & Shelton
W 2002-
PARL. S-o-T Central CB 1948-

Ivy House

LG. East W 1857-95. Wellington W 1895-1910. No.
12 W 1910-55. No. 14 W 1955-65. No. 14 W 1965-
79. Berryhill W 1979-2002. Berryhill & Hanley East
W 2002-
PARL. S-o-T Central CB 1948-

Ivy House Bridge

LG. East W 1857-95. Wellington W 1895-1910. No.
12 W 1910-55. No. 10 W 1955-65. No. 10 W 1965-

79. Berryhill W 1979-2002. Abbey Green W 2002-
PARL. S-o-T Central CB 1948-

Joiner's Square

LG. South W 1857-1895. Eastwood W 1895-1910. No.
15 W 1910-55. No. 14 W 1955-65. No. 14 W 1965-
79. Berryhill W 1979-2002. Berryhill & Hanley East
W 2002-
PARL. S-o-T Central CB 1948-

Lichfield Street

LG. South W 1857-95. Eastwood W 1895-1910. No.
14 W 1910-55. No. 14 W 1955-65. No. 14 W 1965-
79. Shelton W 1979-2002. Hanley West & Shelton
2002-
PARL. S-o-T Central CB 1948-

Mayer

LG. East W 1857-95. Providence W 1895-1910. No.
10 W 1910-55. No. 10 W 1955-65. No. 10 W 1965-
79. Hanley Green W 1979-2002. Northwood & Birches
Head W 2002-
PARL. S-o-T Central CB 1948-

Mill

LG. East W 1857-95. Wellington W 1895-1910. No.
15 W 1910-55. No. 14 W 1955-65. No. 14 W 1965-
79. Berryhill W 1979-2002. Berryhill & Hanley East
W 2002-

Stoke-upon-Trent (Shelton Quarter, Shelton)

PARL. S-o-T Central CB 1948-

Northwood

LG. East W 1857-95. Northwood W 1895-1910. No. 12 W 1910-55. No. 10 W 1955-65. No. 10 W 1965-79. Hanley Green W 1979-2002. Northwood & Birches Head W 2002-

PARL. S-o-T Central CB 1948-

Northwood Green

LG. East W 1857-95. Wellington W 1895-1910. No. 12 W 1910-55. No. 10 W 1955-65. No. 10 W 1965-79. Hanley Green W 1979-2002. Northwood & Birches Head W 2002-

PARL. S-o-T Central CB 1948-

Northwood Park

LG. East W 1857-95. Northwood W 1895-1910. No. 10 W 1910-55. No. 10 W 1955-65. No. 10 W 1965-79. Hanley Green W 1979-2002. Northwood & Birches Head W 2002-

PARL. S-o-T Central CB 1948-

Ogden

LG. South W 1857-95. Eastwood W 1895-1910. No. 15 W 1910-55. No. 14 W 1955-65. No. 14 W 1965-79. Shelton W 1979-2002. Hanley West & Shelton W 2002-

PARL. S-o-T Central CB 1948-

Old Hall

LG. East W 1857-95. Northwood W 1895-1910. No. 12 W 1922-55. No. 10 W 1955-65. No. 14 W 1965-79. Hanley Green W 1979-2002. Hanley West & Shelton W 2002-

PARL. S-o-T Central CB 1948-

Old Town

LG. East W 1857-95. Providence W 1895-1910. No. 9 W 1910-55. No. 9 W 1955-65. No. 9 W 1965-79. Shelton W 1979-2002. Northwood & Birches Head W 2002-

PARL. S-o-T North CB 1948-

Saint John

LG. North W 1857-95. Hope W 1895-1910. No. 9 W 1910-55. No. 9 W 1955-65. No. 9 W 1965-79. Shelton W 1979-2002. Hanley West & Shelton 2002-

PARL. S-o-T North CB 1948-

Tontine

LG. South W 1857-95. Eastwood W 1895-1910. No. 15 W 1910-55. No. 14 1955-65. No. 9 W 1965-79. Shelton W 1979-2002. Hanley West & Shelton W 2002-

PARL. S-o-T Central CB 1948-

Town

LG. East W 1857-95. Providence W 1895-1910. No. 9 W 1910-55. No. 9 W 1955-65. No. 9 W 1965-79. Shelton W 1979-2002. Hanley West & Shelton W 2002-

PARL. S-o-T North CB 1948-

Upper Green

LG. East W 1857-95. Providence W 1895-1910. No. 9 W 1910-55. No. 9 W 1955-65. No. 10 W 1965-79. Hanley Green W 1979-2002. Northwood & Birches Head W 2002-

PARL. S-o-T North CB 1948-

Well

LG. East W 1857-95. Wellington W 1895-1910. No. 15 W 1910-55. No. 14 W 1955-65. No. 14 W 1965-79. Hanley Green W 1979-2002. Berryhill & Hanley East W 2002-

PARL. S-o-T Central CB 1948-

Wellington

LG. East W 1857-95. Wellington W 1895-1910. No. 12 W 1910-55. No. 14 W 1955-65. No. 14 W 1965-79. Hanley Green W 1979-2002. Berryhill & Hanley East W 2002-

PARL. S-o-T Central CB 1948-

Westacre

LG. East W 1857-95. Northwood W 1895-1910. No. 12 W 1910-55. No. 11 W 1955-65. No. 15 W 1965-79. Berryhill W 1979-2002. Berryhill & Hanley East W 2002-

PARL. S-o-T Central CB 1948-

SHELTON TOWNSHIP

Hanley CP 1894-1910.

LG. Hanley Improvement Commissioners district 1825-57 (urban areas close to Hanley only - VCH vol 8 p158), MB 1857-89, CB 1889-1910. S-o-T CB 1910-74, D(C) 1974-97. UA 1997-.

CED. CCWs 1974-97.

PARL. Stoke-upon-Trent PB 1832-85. Hanley PB 1885-1918. Hanley D of Stoke-on-Trent PB 1918-48.

Brians Wood (a)

LG. North W 1857-95. Hope W 1895-1910. No. 9 W 1910-55. No. 9 W 1955-65. No. 9 W 1965-79. Shelton W 1979-2002. Burslem South W 2002-

PARL. S-o-T North CB 1948-, S-o-T Central by1989-

Brians Wood (b)

LG. North W 1857-95. Hope W 1895-1910. No. 9 W 1910-55. No. 8 W 1955-65. No. 9 W 1965-79. Shelton W 1979-2002. Burslem South W 2002-

PARL. S-o-T North CB 1948-, S-o-T Central by1989-

Brians Wood (C)

LG. North W 1857-95. Hope W 1895-1910. No. 9 W 1910-55. No. 8 W 1955-65. No. 10 W 1965-79. Shelton W 1979-2002. Burslem South W 2002-

PARL. S-o-T North CB 1948-, S-o-T Central by1989-

Broomfield
LG. North W 1857-95. Etruria W 1895-1910. No. 11 W 1910-55. No. 13 W 1955-65. No. 9 W 1965-79. Shelton W 1979-2002. Hanley West & Shelton W 2002-
PARL. S-o-T Central CB 1948-

Brunswick
LG. South W 1857-95. Eastwood W 1895-1910. No. 15 W 1910-55. No. 14 W 1955-65. No. 14 W 1965-79. Shelton W 1979-2002. Hanley West & Shelton W 2002-
PARL. S-o-T Central CB 1948-

Cauldon
LG. South W 1857-95. Cauldon W 1895-1910. No. 13 W 1910-55. No. 13 W 1955-65. No. 9 W 1965-79. Shelton W 1979-2002. Hanley West & Shelton W 2002-
PARL. S-o-T Central CB 1948-

Cauldon Road
LG. South W 1857-95. Park W 1895-1910. No. 14 W 1910-55. No. 13 W 1955-65. No. 9 W 1965-79. Shelton W 1979-2002. Hanley West & Shelton W 2002-
PARL. S-o-T Central CB 1948-

Century
LG. North W 1857-95. Etruria W 1895-1910. No. 11 W 1910-55. No. 9 W 1955-65. No. 9 W 1965-79. Shelton W 1979-2002. Burslem South W 2002-
PARL. S-o-T Central CB 1948-

Cliff Vale
LG. North W 1857-95. Etruria W 1895-1910. No. 13 W 1910-55. No. 13 W 1955-65. No. 9 W 1965-79. Shelton W 1979-2002. Hanley West & Shelton W 2002-
PARL. S-o-T Central CB 1948-

Cliff Vale Bank
LG. North W 1857-95. Etruria W 1895-1910. No. 13 W 1910-55. No. 12 W 1955-65. No. 12 W 1965-79. Hartshill W 1979-2002. Hartshill & Penkhull W 2002-
PARL. S-o-T Central CB 1948-

Cockshute
LG. South W 1857-95. Cauldon W 1895-1910. No. 13 W 1910-55. No. 15 W 1955-65. No. 13 W 1965-79. Hartshill W 1979-2002. Hartshill & Penkhull W 2002-
PARL. S-o-T Central CB 1948-

Eastbank
LG. North W 1857-95. Hope W 1895-1910. No. 11 W 1910-55. No. 9 W 1955-65. No. 9 W 1965-79. Shelton W 1979-2002. Burslem South W 2002-
PARL. S-o-T Central CB 1948-

Egerton (C)
LG. South W 1857-95. Eastwood W 1895-1910. No. 15 W 1910-55. No. 14 W 1955-65. No. 19 W 1965-79. Hartshill W 1979-2002. Berryhill & Hanley East W 2002-
PARL. S-o-T Central CB 1948-

Egerton (E)
LG. South W 1857-95. Eastwood W 1895-1910. No. 15 W 1910-55. No. 14 W 1955-65. No. 14 W 1965-79. Hartshill W 1979-2002. Berryhill & Hanley East W 2002-
PARL. S-o-T Central CB 1948-

Egerton (N)
LG. South W 1857-95. Eastwood W 1895-1910. No. 15 W 1910-55. No. 14 W 1955-65. No. 14 W 1965-79. Hartshill W 1979-2002. Berryhill & Hanley East W 2002-
PARL. S-o-T Central CB 1948-

Egerton (W)
LG. South W 1857-95. Eastwood W 1895-1910. No. 15 W 1910-55. No. 14 W 1955-65. No. 9 W 1965-79. Hartshill W 1979-2002. Berryhill & Hanley East W 2002-
PARL. S-o-T Central CB 1948-

Etruria
LG. North W 1857-95. Etruria W 1895-1910. No. 11 W 1910-55. No. 9 W 1955-65. No. 9 W 1965-79. Shelton W 1979-2002. Hanley West & Shelton W 2002-
PARL. S-o-T Central CB 1948-

Fowlhay
LG. North W 1857-95. Etruria W 1895-1910. No. 11 W 1910-55. No. 12 W 1955-65. No. 12 W 1965-79. Hartshill W 1979-2002. Hartshill & Penkhull 2002-
PARL. S-o-T Central CB 1948-

Fowlea
LG. North W 1857-95. Hope W 1895-1910. No. 11 W 1910-55. No. 6 W 1955-65. No. 9 W 1965-79. Shelton W 1979-2002. Hanley West & Shelton W 2002-
PARL. S-o-T Central CB 1948-

Hanley Park
LG. South W 1857-95. Park W 1895-1910. No. 14 W 1910-55. No. 14 W 1955-65. No. 14 W 1965-79. Shelton W 1979-2002. Hanley West & Shelton W 2002-
PARL. S-o-T Central CB 1948-

Hope
LG. North W 1857-95. Hope W 1895-1910. No. 9 W 1910-55. No. 9 W 1955-65. No. 9 W 1965-79. Shelton W 1979-2002. Hanley West & Shelton W 2002-
PARL. S-o-T North CB 1948-

Marsh
LG. South W 1857-95. Eastwood W 1895-1910. No. 14 W 1910-55. No. 14 W 1955-65. No. 14 W 1965-79. Shelton W 1979-2002. Hanley West & Shelton W

Stoke-upon-Trent (Shelton Quarter, Shelton)

2002-
PARL. S-o-T Central CB 1948-

Mawson X
LG. South W 1857-95. Park W 1895-1910. No. 14 W 1910-55. No. 13 W 1955-65. No. 9 W 1965-79. Hartshill W 1979-2002. Berryhill & Hanley East W 2002-
PARL. S-o-T Central CB 1948-

Mawson Y
LG. South W 1857-95. Park W 1895-1910. No. 14 W 1910-55. No. 13 W 1955-65. No. 9 W 1965-79. Hartshill W 1979-2002. Berryhill & Hanley East W 2002-
PARL. S-o-T Central CB 1948-. S-o-T South BC 1974-

Mawson Z
LG. South W 1857-95. Park W 1895-1910. No. 14 W 1910-55. No. 13 W 1955-65. No. 9 W 1965-79. Hartshill W 1979-2002. Hanley West & Shelton W 2002-
PARL. S-o-T Central CB 1948-. S-o-T South BC 1974-

Newcastle Junction (1)
LG. South W 1857-95. Cauldon W 1895-1910. No. 13 W 1910-55. No. 12 W 1955-65. No. 12 W 1965-79. Hartshill W 1979-2002. Hartshill & Penkhull W 2002-
PARL. S-o-T Central CB 1948-

New Hall
LG. North W 1857-95. Hope W 1895-1910. No. 11 W 1910-55. No. 9 W 1955-65. No. 9 W 1965-79. Shelton W 1979-2002. Hanley West & Shelton W 2002-
PARL. S-o-T Central CB 1948-

Pall Mall
LG. South W 1857-95. Park W 1895-1910. No. 14 W 1910-55. No. 14 W 1955-65. No. 14 W 1965-79. Shelton W 1979-2002. Hanley West & Shelton W 2002-
PARL. S-o-T Central CB 1948-

Piccadilly
South W 1857-95. Eastwood W 1895-1910. No. 14 W 1910-55. No. 14 W 1955-65. No. 9 W 1965-79. Shelton W 1979-2002. Hanley West & Shelton W 2002-.

Post
Stoke-upon-Trent glebe land in Stoke-upon-Trent Improvement Commissioners district 1839-74 (VCH vol 8 pp158,194).
LG. S-u-T MB 1874-1910. East W 1874-1910. No. 18 W 1910-55. No. 13 W 1955-65. No. 9 W 1965-79. Hartshill W 1979-2002. Hanley West and Shelton W 2002-
CED. Stoke No. 1 or No. 2 1889-. CCWs 1974-97.
PARL. Stoke PB 1885-1918. Stoke D of S-o-T PB 1918-48. S-o-T South CB 1948-

Ridge House

Ridge
LG. North W 1857-95. Hope W 1895-1910. No. 11 W 1910-55. No. 9 W 1955-65. No. 9 W 1965-79. Shelton W 1979-2002. Hanley West & Shelton W 2002-
PARL. S-o-T Central CB 1948-

Ridgway
LG. South W 1857-95. Eastwood W 1895-1910. No. 15 W 1910-55. No. 14 W 1955-65. No. 9 W 1965-79. Berryhill W 1979-2002. Hanley West & Shelton W 2002-
PARL. S-o-T Central CB 1948-

Roebuck
Stoke-upon-Trent glebe land in Stoke-upon-Trent Improvement Commissioners district 1839-74 (VCH vol 8 pp158,194).
LG. S-u-T MB 1874-1910. East W 1874-1910. No. 18 W 1910-55. No. 13 W 1955-65. No. 13 W 1965-79. Hartshill W 1979-2002. Hanley West and Shelton W 2002-
CED. Stoke No. 1 or No. 2 1889-. CCWs 1974-97.
PARL. Stoke PB 1885-1918. Stoke D of S-o-T PB 1918-48. S-o-T South CB 1948-

Shelton
LG. South W 1857-95. Park W 1895-1910. No. 14 W 1922-55. No. 13 W 1955-65. No. 14 W 1965-79. Shelton W 1979-2002. Hanley West & Shelton W 2002-
PARL. S-o-T Central CB 1948-

Snow Hill
LG. North W 1857-95. Cauldon W 1895-1910. No. 13 W 1910-55. No. 13 W 1955-65. No. 9 W 1965-79. Shelton W 1979-2002. Hanley West & Shelton W 2002-
PARL. S-o-T Central CB 1948-

Stoke Station
Stoke-upon-Trent glebe land in Stoke-upon-Trent Improvement Commissioners district 1839-74 (VCH vol 8 pp158,194).
LG. S-u-T MB 1874-1910. East W 1874-1910. No. 18 W 1910-55. No. 15 W 1955-65. No. 13 W 1965-79. Hartshill W 1979-2002. Hartshill & Penkhull W 2002-
CED. Stoke No. 1 or No. 2 1889-. CCWs 1974-97.
PARL. Stoke PB 1885-1918. Stoke D of S-o-T PB 1918-48. S-o-T South CB 1948-

Talbot
LG. South W 1857-95. Eastwood W 1895-1910. No. 15 W 1910-55. No. 14 1955-65. No. 14 W 1965-79. Shelton W 1979-2002. Berryhill & Hanley East W 2002-
PARL. S-o-T Central CB 1948-

Tinkers Clough
LG. North W 1857-95. Etruria W 1895-1910. No. 13 W 1910-55. No. 13 W 1955-65. No. 9 W 1965-79.

Shelton W 1979-2002. Hanley West & Shelton W 2002-

PARL. S-o-T Central CB 1948-

Trent Hay (a)

LG. South W 1857-95. Park W 1895-1910. No. 14 W 1910-55. No. 13 W 1955-65. No. 9 W 1965-79. Hartshill W 1979-2002. Hanley West & Shelton W 2002-

PARL. S-o-T Central CB 1948-

Trent Hay (b)

LG. Same as Trent Hay (a).

PARL. S-o-T Central CB 1948-. S-o-T South BC 1974-

Union

LG. North W 1857-95. Hope W 1895-1910. No. 9 W 1910-55. No. 9 W 1955-65. No. 9 W 1965-79. Shelton W 1979-2002. Northwood & Birches Head W 2002-

PARL. S-o-T North CB 1948-

Vale

LG. North W 1857-95. Etruria W 1895-1910. No. 13 W 1910-55. No. 9 W 1955-65. No. 9 W 1965-79. Shelton W 1979-2002. Hanley West & Shelton W 2002-

PARL. S-o-T Central CB 1948-

Vale Place

LG. North W 1857-95. Hope W 1895-1910. No. 9 W 1910-55. No. 9 W 1955-65. No. 6 W 1965-79. Shelton W 1979-2002. Burslem South W 2002-

PARL. S-o-T North CB 1948-, S-o-T Central by1989-

VR (Victoria Road) a

LG. South W 1857-95. Eastwood W 1895-1910. No. 15 W 1910-55. No. 14 W 1955-65. No. 9 W 1965-79. Hartshill W 1979-2002. Berryhill & Hanley East W 2002-

PARL. S-o-T Central CB 1948-. S-o-T South CB 1974-

VR (Victoria Road) b

LG. Hanley B 1857-89, CB 1889-1910. South W 1857-

95. Eastwood W 1895-1910. Stoke 1910-. No. 15 W 1910-55. No. 19 W 1955-65. No. 19 W 1965-79. Hartshill W 1979-2002. Berryhill & Hanley East W 2002-

PARL. S-o-T Central CB 1948-. S-o-T South CB 1974-

VR (Victoria Road) c

LG. South W 1857-95. Eastwood W 1895-1910. No. 15 W 1910-55. No. 14 W 1955-65. No. 19 W 1965-79. Hartshill W 1979-2002. Berryhill & Hanley East W 2002-

PARL. S-o-T Central CB 1948-. S-o-T South CB 1974-

Warner

LG. South 1857-95. Park W 1895-1910. No. 14 W 1910-55. No. 13 W 1955-65. No. 9 W 1965-79. Shelton W 1979-2002. Hanley West & Shelton W 2002-

PARL. S-o-T Central CB 1948-

Westmill

LG. South W 1857-95. Eastwood W 1895-1910. No. 15 W 1910-55. No. 14 W 1955-65. No. 14 W 1965-79. Berryhill W 1979-2002. Berryhill & Hanley East W 2002-

PARL. S-o-T Central CB 1948-

Winton

LG. South W 1857-95. Park W 1895-1910. No. 14 W 1922-55. No. 15 W 1955-65. No. 13 W 1965-79. Hartshill W 1979-2002. Hartshill & Penkhull W 2002-

PARL. S-o-T Central CB 1948-

Wintonfield

LG. Same as Roebuck.

PARL. S-o-T Central CB 1948-. S-o-T South BC 1974-

Woodlands

LG. North W 1857-95. Hope W 1895-1910. No. 11 W 1910-55. No. 9 W 1955-65. No. 6 W 1965-79. Shelton W 1979-2002. Hanley West & Shelton W 2002-

PARL. S-o-T Central CB 1948-

Discreet weddings so long as the curate lives!

When looking for a marriage in a large industrial parish, like Stoke-upon-Trent, be mindful, if between 1740-1837, it may be recorded in the PR of a periphery rural chapel, not in the PR of the bride or groom's own district church. When editing the PR of Norton-in-the-Moors (1942), itself a chapel of Stoke, T Roberts found a number of weddings taking place disproportionate to local population. It was the same in all Stoke-upon-Trent rural chapels. Inhabitants from Pottery districts (Burslem, Fenton, Hanley, Longton, Stoke) were exercising their right to marry in any church in the extensive parish. Roberts suggests it was a day-out to the nearest countryside in an age before honeymoons. Ward on Burslem weddings at Bucknall in HBST says the couple sought discretion in the anonymity of a church outside their neighbourhood especially regarding the publication of banns. In one respect Roberts missed a point. He noted the practice carried on after the passing of the Stoke Rectory Act, 1807 (which gave the chapels parochial status), forgetting the Act only came into force when the

Stoke-upon-Trent

existing curate died or resigned. This explains the anomalies; the reason why Norton-in-the-Moors curate, Rev Daniel Turner, continued to sign himself curate until his departure in 1826; and the decline thereafter of an abnormal number of marriages.

Periods of abnormal number of marriages
Bucknall 1805-1819, 1835-7
Newcastle 1780-1805
Norton-in-the-Moors (in this respect became known as the Gretna Green of the Potteries) 1740s-1822, 1822-6 (far less), 1826-37 (significantly less again)
Whitmore 1753-95, 1796-7 (banns only), 1797-1804 (half previous).

(Norton PR Introduction by T Roberts, 1942) (VCH vol 8 p121 note).

Stone Parish Chest in St Michael's Church, Stone. Drawing by the author, 2005

Stone

'A great parish (as in large) and market town'
Puritan Survey of the Church in Staffordshire in 1604 (English Historical Revue, vol. 26 (1911) pp38f, and SHC 1915 pp258-262)

Stone was divided into quarters - Beech, Hilderstone, Kibblestone, and Stone - apparently in or by the earlier C17 (SOK p31).
SEE ALSO pages 2, 7, 27, 30, 36, 49, 79, 84, 93, 96, 100, 116, 124, 125, 130, 182, 208-9, 214, 230

BEECH QUARTER
BEECH TOWNSHIP
PLU. Stone 1838-1930. Stone Rural W by1910-
Beech
Stone Rural CP 1894-1932. PC minutes from 1894 at SRO. 1901eSwynnerton CP 1932-. Tittensor PW Nov 1954-.
LG. Stone RD 1894-1974. Stafford D(B) 1974-. Swynnerton W 1974-2002, 2002-.
CED. Stone 1889-1911. Stone Rural Sept 1911-34.

Eccleshall 1934-2005, 2005-.
Knowl Wall
Stone Rural CP 1894-1932. Swynnerton CP 1932-. Trentham PW Nov 1954-.
LG. Stone RD 1894-1974. Stafford D(B) 1974-. Swynnerton W 1974-2002, 2002-.
CED. Stone 1889-1911. Stone Rural Sept 1911-34. Eccleshall 1934-2005, 2005-.
Sandyford
Stone Rural CP 1894-. Meaford and Aston PW

Stone (Beech Quarter, Walton)

1968-. Meaford PW 2003-.
LG. Stone RD 1894-1974. Stafford D(B) 1974-.
Oulton W 1974-2002. Barlaston & Oulton W 2002-.
CED. Stone 1889-1911. Stone Rural Sept 1911-
2005. Barlaston & Fulford 2005-.

DARLASTON TOWNSHIP
PLU. Stone 1838-1930. Stone Rural W by1910-
Darlaston Hall
Stone Rural CP 1894-. Meaford and Aston PW 1968-
2003. Meaford PW 2003-.
LG. Stone RD 1894-1974. Stafford D(B) 1974-. Oulton
W 1974-2002. Barlaston & Oulton W 2002-.
CED. Stone 1889-1911. Stone Rural Sept 1911-2005.
Barlaston & Fulford 2005-.
Filleybrooks
Stone Rural CP 1894-1932. Stone CP 1932- (TC 1973/
4-). Walton PW April 1965-2003, 2003-
LG. Stone RD 1894-1932, UD 1932-74. Walton W
April 1965-1974. Stafford D(B) 1974-. Walton W
1974-2002, 2002-.
CED. Stone 1889-1911. Stone Rural Sept 1911-34.
Stone Urban 1934-2005. Stone 2005-.
Filly Brook (2)
Stone Rural CP 1894-. Meaford and Aston PW 1968-
2003. Aston PW 2003-.
LG. Stone RD 1894-1974. Stafford D(B) 1974-. Oulton
W 1974-2002. Milwich W 2002-.
CED. Stone 1889-1911. Stone Rural Sept 1911-2005.
Barlaston & Fulford 2005-.
Trent Road
Stone Rural CP 1894-1932. Stone CP 1932- (TC 1973/
4-). Walton PW April 1965-2003. Stonefield &
Christchurch PW 2003-
LG. Stone RD 1894-1932, UD 1932-74. Walton W
April 1965-1974. Stafford D(B) 1974-. Walton W
1974-2002. Stonefield & Christchurch W 2002-.
CED. Stone 1889-1911. Stone Rural Sept 1911-34.
Stone Urban 1934-2005. Stone 2005-.

TITTENSOR TOWNSHIP
PLU. Stone 1838-1930. Stone Rural W by1910.
Tittensor
Stone Rural CP 1894-1932. Swynnerton CP 1932-.
Tittensor PW Nov 1954-.
LG. Stone RD 1894-1974. Stafford D(B) 1974-.
Swynnerton W 1974-2002, 2002-.
CED. Stone 1889-1911. Stone Rural Sept 1911-34.
Eccleshall 1934-2005, 2005-.
Tittensor Chase

Stone Rural CP 1894-. Meaford and Aston PW 1968-
2003. Meaford PW 2003-.
LG. Stone RD 1894-1974. Stafford D(B) 1974-. Oulton
W 1974-2002. Barlaston & Oulton W 2002-.
CED. Stone 1889-1911. Stone Rural Sept 1911-2005.
Barlaston & Fulford 2005-.

WALTON TOWNSHIP
PLU. Stone 1838-1930. Stone Rural W by1910.
Filly Brook (1)
Stone Rural CP 1894-. Meaford and Aston PW 1968-
2003. Meaford PW 2003-.
LG. Stone RD 1894-1974. Stafford D(B) 1974-. Oulton
W 1974-2002. Barlaston & Oulton W 2002-.
CED. Stone 1889-1911. Stone Rural Sept 1911-2005.
Barlaston & Fulford 2005-.
Stone House Hotel
Stone Rural CP 1894-1988. Meaford & Aston PW
1968-88. Stone CP 1988- (TC 1973/4-). Walton PW
1988-2003, 2003-.
LG. Stone RD 1894-1974. Stafford D(B) 1974-. Oulton
W 1974-88. Walton W 1988-2002, 2002-.
CED. Stone 1889-1911. Stone Rural Sept 1911-1988.
Stone Urban 1988-2005. Stone 2005-.
Walton
Stone Rural CP 1894-1932. Stone CP 1932- (TC 1973/
4-). Walton PW April 1965-2003, 2003-.
LG. Stone RD 1894-1932, UD 1932-74. Walton W
April 1965-74. Stafford D(B) 1974-. Walton W 1974-
2002, 2002-.
CED. Stone 1889-1911. Stone Rural Sept 1911-34.
Stone Urban 1934-2005. Stone 2005-.
Walton Heath
Stone Rural CP 1894-. Meaford and Aston PW 1968-
2003. Aston PW 2003-.
LG. Stone RD 1894-1974. Stafford D(B) 1974-. Oulton
W 1974-2002. Milwich W 2002-.
CED. Stone 1889-1911. Stone Rural Sept 1911-2005.
Barlaston & Fulford 2005-.
Walton Hill House
Stone Rural CP 1894-Oct 1955. Stone CP Oct 1955-.
Walton PW April 1965-2003, 2003-.
LG. Stone RD 1894-1955. Stone UD Oct 1955-74.
Walton W April 1965-74. Stafford D(B) 1974-. Walton
W 1974-2002, 2002-.
CED. Stone 1889-1911. Stone Rural Sept 1911-55.
Stone Urban 1955-2005. Stone 2005-.
W(est bridge) P(ark) playing fields
Stone CP 1894-. Walton PW April 1965-2003, 2003-
LG. Stone UD 1894-1974. Walton W April 1965-74.
Stafford D(B) 1974-. Walton W 1974-2002, 2002-.

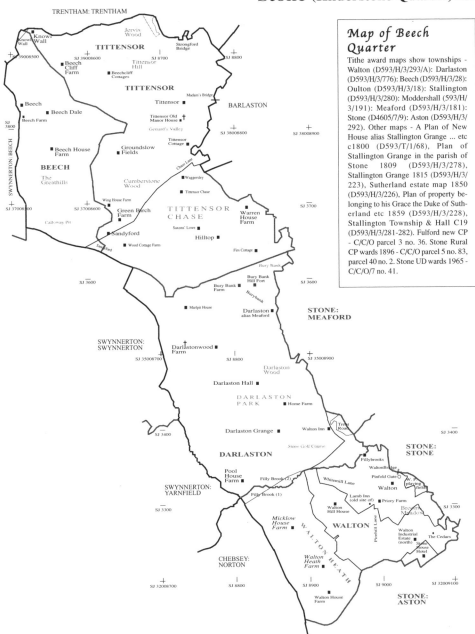

TRENTHAM: TRENTHAM

Jervis Wood

Knowl Wall

Knowl Wall

TITTENSOR

SJ 39008500

SJ 39008600

Strongford Bridge

SJ 8700

SJ 8800

Beech Cliff Farm

Tittensor Hill

Beechcliff Cottages

TITTENSOR

Madam's Bridge

Tittensor

BARLASTON

Beech

SJ 3800

Beech Dale

Beech Farm

Tittensor Old Manor House

SJ 38008800

SJ 38008900

Genard's Valley

Beech House Farm

Groundslow Fields

Tittensor Cottage

BEECH

The Greathills

SWYNNERTON: BEECH

Cumberstone Wood

Chase Lane

Waggersley

Wing House Farm

SJ 37008500

SJ 37008600

Tittensor Chase

Green Birch Farm

TITTENSOR CHASE

SJ 3700

Calloway Pit

Warren House Farm

Sandyford

Saxons' Lowe

Hilltop

Wood Cottage Farm

Firs Cottage

Bury Bank

Bury Bank Hill Fort

SJ 3600

Bury Bank Farm

Bury-bank

SJ 3600

STONE: MEAFORD

Marlpit House

Darlaston alias Meaford

SWYNNERTON: SWYNNERTON

Darlastonwood Farm

SJ 35008700

SJ 8800

SJ 35008900

Darlaston Wood

Darlaston Hall

DARLASTON PARK

Home Farm

Darlaston Grange

Walton Inn

Trent Road

SJ 3400

SJ 3400

DARLASTON

Stone Golf Course

STONE: STONE

Fillybrooks

Walton Bridge

Pool House Farm

Filly Brook (2)

Whitemill Lane

Pinfold Gate

playing field

Walton

SWYNNERTON: YARNFIELD

Filly Brook (1)

Lamb Inn (old site of)

Priory Farm

SJ 3300

SJ 3300

Micklow House Farm

Walton Hill House

Pyehill Lane

Brook Meadow

SJ 3300

WALTON

Walton Industrial Estate (north)

Stone House Hotel

The Cedars

CHEBSEY: NORTON

WALTON HEATH

Walton Heath Farm

SJ 32008700

SJ 8800

SJ 8900

SJ 9000

SJ 32009100

Walton House Farm

STONE: ASTON

Map of Beech Quarter

Tithe award maps show townships - Walton (D593/H/3/293/A): Darlaston (D593/H/3/776): Beech (D593/H/3/28): Oulton (D593/H/3/18): Stallington (D593/H/3/280): Moddershall (593/H/3/191): Meaford (D593/H/3/181): Stone (D4605/7/9): Aston (D593/H/3/292). Other maps - A Plan of New House alias Stallington Grange ... etc c1800 (D593/T/1/68), Plan of Stallington Grange in the parish of Stone 1809 (D593/H/3/278), Stallington Grange 1815 (D593/H/3/223), Sutherland estate map 1850 (D593/H/3/226), Plan of property belonging to his Grace the Duke of Sutherland etc 1859 (D593/H/3/228), Stallington Township & Hall C19 (D593/H/3/281-282). Fulford new CP - C/C/O parcel 3 no. 36. Stone Rural CP wards 1896 - C/C/O parcel 5 no. 83, parcel 40 no. 2. Stone UD wards 1965 - C/C/O/7 no. 41.

CED. Stone 1889-1911. Stone Urban Sept 1911-2005. Stone 2005-.
PLU. Stone 1838-1930. Stone W by1910.

HILDERSTONE QUARTER

ASTON, BURSTON, LITTLE STOKE TOWNSHIP

PLU. Stone 1838-1930. Stone Rural W by1910-.

Aston

Stone Rural CP 1894-. Meaford and Aston PW 1968-2003. Aston PW 2003-.
LG. Stone RD 1894-1974. Stafford D(B) 1974-. Oulton

Stone (Hilderstone Quarter)

W 1974-2002. Milwich W 2002-.
CED. Stone 1889-1911. Stone Rural Sept 1911-2005.
Barlaston & Fulford 2005-.

Aston Cricket Club (1)

Stone Rural CP 1894-1988. Meaford and Aston PW
1968-88. Stone CP 1988-. St Michaels PW 1988-2003,
2003-
LG. Stone RD 1894-1974. Stafford D(B) 1974-. Oulton
W 1974-88. St Michaels W 1988-2002, 2002-.
CED. Stone 1889-1911. Stone Rural Sept 1911-88.
Stone Urban 1988-2005. Stone 2005-.

Aston Cricket Club (2)

Stone Rural CP 1894-2003. Meaford and Aston PW
1968-2003. Stone CP 2003-. St Michaels PW 2003-.
LG. Stone RD 1894-1974. Stafford D(B) 1974-. Oulton
W 1974-2002. St Michaels W 2002-.
CED. Stone 1889-1911. Stone Rural Sept 1911-2002.
Stone Urban 2002-5. Stone 2005-.

2005-.

Burston

Stone Rural CP 1894-1932. Sandon CP 1932-(styled
Sandon and Burston CP from Sept 1989).
LG. Stone RD 1894-1974. Stafford D(B) 1974-.
Milwich W 1974-2002, 2002-.
CED. Stone 1889-1911. Stone Rural Sept 1911-2005.
Barlaston & Fulford 2005-.

Little Stoke

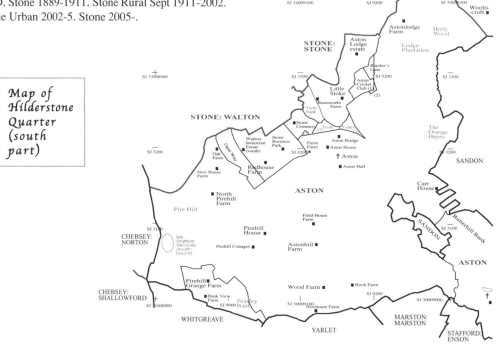

Map of
Hilderstone
Quarter
(south
part)

Blackie's Lane

Stone Rural CP 1894-1988. Meaford and Aston PW
1968-88. Stone CP 1988-2003. St Michaels PW 1988-
2003. Stone Rural CP 2003-. Aston PW 2003-
LG. Stone RD 1894-1974. Stafford D(B) 1974-. Oulton
W 1974-88. St Michaels W 1988-2002. Milwich W
2002-.
CED. Stone 1889-1911. Stone Rural Sept 1911-88.
Stone Urban 1988-2002. Barlaston & Fulford 2002-5,

Stone Rural CP 1894-1932. Stone CP 1932- (TC 1973/
4-). St Michaels PW April 1965-2003, 2003-
LG. Stone RD 1894-1932, UD 1932-74. St Michaels
April 1965-74. Stafford D(B) 1974-. St Michaels W
1974-2002, 2002-.
CED. Stone 1889-1911. Stone Rural Sept 1911-2005.
Stone 2005-.

Opal Way

Stone Rural CP 1894-2003. Meaford and Aston PW

SJ 37009400

SJ 9500

SJ 9600

SJ 37009700

STONE:
FULFORD

The Leasows ■

DRAYCOTT IN THE MOORS:

Bird In Hand
Inn

SJ 3600

SJ 3600

*S H A R P L E Y
H E A T H*

STONE:
MODDERSHALL

■ The Hurstage

Heathy Close ■

LEIGH:
LEIGH

High Elms ■

*S T O N E
H E A T H*

High Forest
Farm

Stone Heath
Farm ■

Manor House ■

Sharpley Farm ■

SJ 3500

SJ 3500

Dingle Lane

✝ Green Farm ■

■ Hilderstone Hall

Newfields ■

Crossgate
Barn ■

■ Hilderstone

Lower Bank ■
Farm

■ Dingle Wood
Farm

Alder
Wood

Wooliscroft ■

Hall Farm ■

*Peakshill
Wood*

HILDERSTONE

SJ 34009400

SJ 9500

SJ 9600

SJ 34009700

SJ 34009300

■ Peakshill Farm

STONE:
STONE

■ Wooliscroft

Whitesytch Farm ■

■ Leasows Farm

MILWICH

Astonlodge
Farm ■

Holly
Wood

STONE:
ASTON

SJ 9300

The
Orange
Hayes

SANDON

SJ 3200

Carr
House ■

SANDON

Butterhill Bank

SJ 30009000

SJ 9100

SJ 31009200

Shruggs
Farm ■

Sunnyside ■

ASTON

The
Shruggs

Burston ■

✝ Yewtree
Farm

SJ 30009000

SJ 3000

Burston Hall

MARSTON:
MARSTON

STAFFORD:
ENSON

SJ 9000

SJ 9100

SJ 29009200

1968-2003. Stone CP 2003-. Walton PW 2003-.
LG. Stone RD 1894-1974. Stafford D(B) 1974-. Oulton
W 1974-2002. Walton W 2002-.
CED. Stone 1889-1911. Stone Rural Sept 1911-2002.
Stone Urban 2002-2005. Stone 2005-.

Pirehill Grange Farm

Stone Rural CP 1894-1988. Meaford and Aston PW
1968-88. Whitgreave CP 1988-.
LG. Stone RD 1894-1974. Stafford D(B) 1974-.

Seighford W 1974-2002, 2002-.
CED. Stone 1889-1911. Stone Rural Sept 1911-88.
Stafford Trent Valley 1988-2005. Gnosall & Doxey
2005-.

Redhouse Farm

Stone Rural CP 1894-1988. Meaford and Aston PW
1968-88. Stone CP 1988-. Walton PW 1988-.
LG. Stone RD 1894-1974. Stafford D(B) 1974-. Oulton
W 1974-88. Walton W 1988-2002, 2002-.
CED. Stone 1889-1911. Stone Rural Sept 1911-88.
Stone Urban 1988-2005. Stone 2005-.

Stone Cemetery

Stone Rural CP 1894-Oct 1955. Stone CP Oct 1955-
(TC 1973/4-). Walton PW April 1965-2003, 2003-.
LG. Stone RD 1894-Oct 1955, UD Oct 1955-74.
Walton W April 1965-74. Stafford D(B) 1974-. Walton
W 1974-2002, 2002-.
CED. Stone 1889-1911. Stone Rural Sept 1911-55.
Stone Urban 1955-2005. Stone 2005-.

Trent Bank

Stone Rural CP 1894-1932. Stone CP 1932- (TC 1973/
4-). Walton PW April 1965-2003, 2003-.
LG. Stone RD 1894-1932, UD 1932-74. Walton W
April 1965-74. Stafford D(B) 1974-. Walton W 1974-
2002, 2002-.
CED. Stone 1889-1911. Stone Rural Sept 1911-34.
Stone Urban 1934-2005. Stone 2005-.

Trent Valley (1) & (2)

Stone Rural CP 1894-1988. Meaford and Aston PW
1968-88. Stone CP 1988-.
LG. Stone RD 1894-1974. Stafford D(B) 1974-. Oulton

Stone (Hilderstone Quarter, Normacot)

W 1974-88. Walton W 1988-2002, 2002-.
CED. Stone 1889-1911. Stone Rural Sept 1911-88.
Stone Urban 1988-2005. Stone 2005-.

Trent Valley (3)

Stone Rural CP 1894-1988. Meaford and Aston PW
1968-88. Stone CP 1988-.
LG. Stone RD 1894-1974. Stafford D(B) 1974-. Oulton
W 1974-88. St Michaels W 1988-2002, 2002-.
CED. Stone 1889-1911. Stone Rural Sept 1911-88.
Stone Urban 1988-2005. Stone 2005-.

FULFORD TOWNSHIP

PLU. Stone 1838-1930. Fulford & Hilderstone W
by1910-3. Fulford W 1913-.

Fulford

Stone Rural CP 1894-7. Fulford CP 1897-. Fulford
PW Nov 1949-.
LG. Stone RD 1894-1974. Stafford D(B) 1974-.
Fulford W 1974-2002, 2002-.
CED. Stone 1889-1911. Stone Rural Sept 1911-2005.
Barlaston & Fulford 2005-.

Leacroft

Stone Rural CP 1894-7. Fulford CP 1897-. Fulford PW
Nov 1949-.
LG. Stone RD 1894-1974. Stafford D(B) 1974-.
Fulford W 1974-2002, 2002-.
CED. Stone 1889-1911. Stone Rural Sept 1911-2005.
Barlaston & Fulford 2005-.

HILDERSTONE TOWNSHIP

Stone Rural CP 1894-7. At a meeting of the ratepayers of Hilderstone, convened by Mr J Browne,
on 27 February 1896, it was decided, with only
one dissentient, to petition the CC for a separate
parish (SA March 7 1896 p7 col 6). Hilderstone
CP 1897-.
LG. Stone RD 1894-1974. Fulford and Hilderstone W
1898-1913. Hilderstone W 1913-. Stafford D(B) 1974-
. Milwich W 1974-2002, 2002-.
CED. Stone 1889-1911. Stone Rural Sept 1911-2005.
Barlaston & Fulford 2005-.
PLU. Stone 1838-1930. Stone Rural W -1898. Fulford
and Hilderstone W 1898-1913. Hilderstone W 1913-.

NORMACOT TOWNSHIP

Grange End

Stone Rural CP 1894-1932. Fulford CP 1932-. Meir
Heath PW Nov 1949-, 2003-
LG. Stone RD 1894-1974. Stafford D(B) 1974-.
Fulford W 1974-2002, 2002-.
CED. Stone 1889-1911. Stone Rural Sept 1911-2005.

Barlaston & Fulford 2005-.
PLU. Stone 1838-1930. Stone Rural W by1910-.

Grindley

Stone Rural CP 1894-1932. Fulford CP 1932-. Blythe
Bridge PW Nov 1949-, 2003-
LG. Stone RD 1894-1974. Stafford D(B) 1974-.
Fulford W 1974-2002, 2002-.
CED. Stone 1889-1911. Stone Rural Sept 1911-2005.
Barlaston & Fulford 2005-.
PLU. Stone 1838-1930. Stone Rural W by1910-.

Ludwall

Stone Rural CP 1894-1922. Stoke unparished 1922-.
LG. Stone RD 1894-1922. S-o-T CB 1922-74, D(C)
1974-97, UA 1997-. No. 26 W 1922-55. No. 24 W
1955-65. No. 22 W 1965-79. Longton South W 1979-
2002. Meir Park & Sandon W 2002-
CED. Stone 1889-1911. Stone Rural Sept 1911-22.
CCWs 1974-97.
PLU. Stone 1838-1930. Stone Rural W by1910-.

Meir Green

Normacot CP 1894-6. Longton CP March 31 1896-
1910.
LG. Longton MB 1884-1910. S-o-T CB 1910-74, D(C)
1974-97, UA 1997-. Florence W 1884-95. Meir W
1895-1910. No. 26 W 1910-55. No. 22 W 1955-65.
No. 22 W 1965-79. No. 22 W 1965-79. Longton South
W 1979-. Longton South W 2002-
CED. Longton No. 1 or No. 2 1889-97. Longton No. 1
or No. 2 or No. 3 1897-1910. CCWs 1974-97.
PLU. Stone 1838-96. S-u-T 1896-1922. S-u-T &
Wolstanton 1922-30. No. 26 W 1910-.
PARL. Stoke PB 1885-1918. Stoke D of S-o-T 1918-
48. S-o-T South BC 1948-

Meir Heath

Stone Rural CP 1894-1988. Moddershall PW 1968-
88. Fulford CP 1988-. Meir Heath PW 1988-2003,
2003-
LG. Stone RD 1894-1974. Stafford D(B) 1974-.
Fulford W 1974-2002, 2002-.
CED. Stone 1889-1911. Stone Rural Sept 1911-2005.
Barlaston & Fulford 2005-.
PLU. Stone 1838-1930. Stone Rural W by1910-.

Meir Park

Stone Rural CP 1894-1932. Fulford CP 1932-65. ?Meir
Heath PW Nov 1949-. Stoke unparished 1965-.
LG. Stone RD 1894-1965. S-o-T CB 1965-74, D(C)
1974-97, UA 1997-. No. 24 W 1965-79. Meir Park W
1979-2002. Meir Park & Sandon W 2002-
CED. Stone 1889-1911. Stone Rural Sept 1911-65.
CCWs 1974-97.
PLU. Stone 1838-1930. Stone Rural W by1910-.

Normacot

Normacot CP 1894-6. Longton CP March 31 1896-

Stone (Hilderstone Quarter, Normacot)

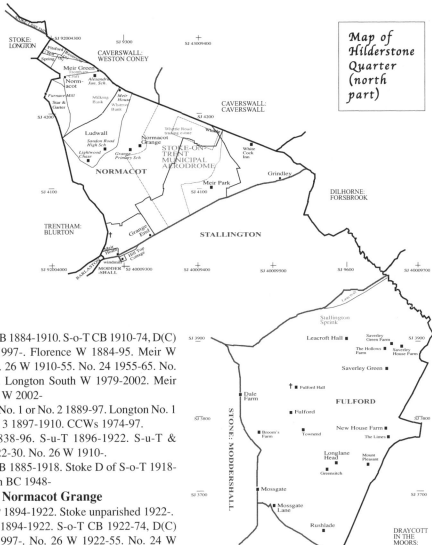

Map of
Hilderstone
Quarter
(north
part)

1910.
LG. Longton MB 1884-1910. S-o-T CB 1910-74, D(C) 1974-97, UA 1997-. Florence W 1884-95. Meir W 1895-1910. No. 26 W 1910-55. No. 24 1955-65. No. 22 W 1965-79. Longton South W 1979-2002. Meir Park & Sandon W 2002-

CED. Longton No. 1 or No. 2 1889-97. Longton No. 1 or No. 2 or No. 3 1897-1910. CCWs 1974-97.

PLU. Stone 1838-96. S-u-T 1896-1922. S-u-T & Wolstanton 1922-30. No. 26 W 1910-.

PARL. Stoke PB 1885-1918. Stoke D of S-o-T 1918-48. S-o-T South BC 1948-

Normacot Grange

Stone Rural CP 1894-1922. Stoke unparished 1922-.
LG. Stone RD 1894-1922. S-o-T CB 1922-74, D(C) 1974-97, UA 1997-. No. 26 W 1922-55. No. 24 W 1955-65. No. 24 W 1965-79. Meir Park W 1979-2002. Meir Park & Sandon W 2002-

CED. Stone 1889-1911. Stone Rural Sept 1911-22. CCWs 1974-97.

PLU. Stone 1838-1922. Stone Rural W by1910. S-u-T & Wolstanton 1922-30.

Pitsford

Normacot CP 1894-6. Longton CP March 31 1896-1910.
LG. Longton MB 1884-1910. S-o-T CB 1910-74, D(C) 1974-97, UA 1997-. Florence W 1884-95. Normacot W 1895-1910. No. 24 W 1910-55. No. 23 W 1955-65. No. 22 W 1965-79. Longton South W 1979-2002. Longton North W 2002-

CED. Longton No. 1 or No. 2 1889-97. Longton No. 1

or No. 2 or No. 3 1897-1910. CCWs 1974-97.
PLU. Stone 1838-96. S-u-T 1896-1922. S-u-T & Wolstanton 1922-30. No. 24 W 1910-.

PARL. Stoke PB 1885-1918. Stoke D of S-o-T 1918-48. S-o-T South BC 1948-

Reservoir (a)

Normacot CP 1894-6. Longton CP March 31 1896-1910.
LG. Longton MB 1884-1910. S-o-T CB 1910-74, D(C) 1974-97, UA 1997-. Florence W 1884-95. Meir W 1895-1910. No. 26 W 1910-55. No. 23 W 1955-65.

Stone (Kibblestone Quarter, Meaford)

No. 22 W 1965-79. Longton South W 1979-2002. Longton North W 2002-

CED. Longton No. 1 or No. 2 1889-97. Longton No. 1 or No. 2 or No. 3 1897-1910. CCWs 1974-97.

PLU. Stone 1838-96. S-u-T 1896-1922. S-u-T & Wolstanton 1922-30. No. 26 W 1910-.

PARL. Stoke PB 1885-1918. Stoke D of S-o-T 1918-48. S-o-T South BC 1948-

Reservoir (b)

Normacot CP 1894-6. Longton CP March 31 1896-1910.

LG. Longton MB 1884-1910. S-o-T CB 1910-74, D(C) 1974-97, UA 1997-. Florence W 1884-95. Meir W 1895-1910. No. 26 W 1910-55. No. 22 W 1955-65. No. 22 W 1965-79. Longton South W 1979-2002. Longton North W 2002-

CED. Longton No. 1 or No. 2 1889-97. Longton No. 1 or No. 2 or No. 3 1897-1910. CCWs 1974-97.

PLU. Stone 1838-96. S-u-T 1896-1922. S-u-T & Wolstanton 1922-30. No. 26 W 1910-.

PARL. Stoke PB 1885-1918. Stoke D of S-o-T 1918-48. S-o-T South BC 1948-

Spring

Normacot CP 1894-6. Longton CP March 31 1896-1910.

LG. Longton MB 1884-1910. S-o-T CB 1910-74, D(C) 1974-97, UA 1997-. Florence W 1884-95. Normacot W 1895-1910. No. 26 W 1910-55. No. 22 W 1955-65. No. 22 W 1965-79. Longton South W 1979-2002. Longton South W 2002-

CED. Longton No. 1 or No. 2 1889-97. Longton No. 1 or No. 2 or No. 3 1897-1910. CCWs 1974-97.

PLU. Stone 1838-96. S-u-T 1896-1922. S-u-T & Wolstanton 1922-30. No. 26 W 1910-.

PARL. Stoke PB 1885-1918. Stoke D of S-o-T 1918-48. S-o-T South BC 1948-

Star & Garter

Normacot CP 1894-6. Longton CP March 31 1896-1910.

LG. Longton MB 1884-1910. S-o-T CB 1910-74, D(C) 1974-97, UA 1997-. Florence W 1884-95. Normacot W 1895-1910. No. 26 W 1910-55. No. 22 W 1955-65. No. 22 W 1965-79. Longton South W 1979-2002. Longton South W 2002-

CED. Longton No. 1 or No. 2 1889-97. Longton No. 1 or No. 2 or No. 3 1897-1910. CCWs 1974-97.

PLU. Stone 1838-96. S-u-T 1896-1922. S-u-T & Wolstanton 1922-30. No. 26 W 1910-.

PARL. Stoke PB 1885-1918. Stoke D of S-o-T 1918-48. S-o-T South BC 1948-

Upper Normacot

Normacot CP 1894-6. Longton CP March 31 1896-1910.

LG. Longton MB 1884-1910. S-o-T CB 1910-74, D(C) 1974-97, UA 1997-. Florence W 1884-95. Normacot W 1895-1910. No. 26 W 1910-55. No. 22 W 1955-65. No. 22 W 1965-79. Longton South W 1979-2002. Longton North W 2002-

CED. Longton No. 1 or No. 2 1889-97. Longton No. 1 or No. 2 or No. 3 1897-1910. CCWs 1974-97.

PLU. Stone 1838-96. S-u-T 1896-1922. S-u-T & Wolstanton 1922-30. No. 26 W 1910-.

PARL. Stoke PB 1885-1918. Stoke D of S-o-T 1918-48. S-o-T South BC 1948-

Whittle

Stone Rural CP 1894-1922. Stoke unparished 1922-65. Fulford CP 1965-. Blythe Bridge PW 1965-2003, 2003-

LG. Stone RD 1894-1922. S-o-T CB 1922-65. No. 26 W 1922-55. No. 24 W 1955-65. Stone RD 1965-74. Stafford D(B) 1974-. Fulford W 1974-2002, 2002-.

CED. Stone 1889-1911. Stone Rural Sept 1911-22. Stone Rural 1965-2005. Barlaston & Fulford 2005-.

PLU. Stone 1838-1922. Stone Rural W by1910. S-u-T & Wolstanton 1922-30.

KIBBLESTONE QUARTER
MEAFORD TOWNSHIP

PLU. Stone 1838-1930. Stone Rural W by1910-.

Stone Town Field (comprising open fields Stone Field and the Sandpits) was inclosed by an Act of 1798; the Act exonerated owners from tithes. It covered areas - Common Plot (excluding Edge Hill house), Meaford Fields estate, Meaford Hall (SE corner only), Oulton Cross, Sandpits, Stonefield, Trent Wood, Whitebridge Industrial Estate.

Barlaston Golf Course

Stone Rural CP 1894-. Meaford and Aston PW 1968-2003. Meaford PW 2003-.

LG. Stone RD 1894-1974. Stafford D(B) 1974-. Barlaston W 1974-2002. Barlaston & Oulton W 2002-. CED. Stone 1889-1911. Stone Rural Sept 1911-2005. Barlaston & Fulford 2005-.

Common Plot

Stone Rural CP 1894-1932. Stone CP 1932- (TC 1973/4-). Stonefield & Christchurch PW April 1965-2003, 2003-

LG. Stone RD 1894-1932, UD 1932-74. Stonefield & Christchurch W April 1965-1974. Stafford D(B) 1974-. Stonefield & Christchurch W 1974-2002, 2002-.

CED. Stone 1889-1911. Stone Rural Sept 1911-34.

Stone Urban 1934-2005. Stone 2005-.

Downs

Stone Rural CP 1894-2003. Oulton PW 1968-2003.
Barlaston CP 2003-. Barlaston East PW 2003-
LG. Stone RD 1894-1974. Stafford D(B) 1974-. Oulton
W 1974-2002. Barlaston & Oulton W 2002-.
CED. Stone 1889-1911. Stone Rural Sept 1911-2005.
Barlaston & Fulford 2005-.

Edge Hill

Stone Rural CP 1894-. Meaford and Aston PW 1968-
2003. Meaford PW 2003-.
LG. Stone RD 1894-1974. Stafford D(B) 1974-.
Stonefield & Christchurch W 1974-2002. Barlaston &
Oulton W 2002-.
CED. Stone 1889-1911. Stone Rural Sept 1911-74.
Stone Urban 1974-2002. Stone Rural 2002-2005.
Barlaston & Fulford 2005-.

Meaford Farm

Stone Rural CP 1894-. Oulton PW 1968-2003, 2003-.
LG. Stone RD 1894-1974. Stafford D(B) 1974-. Oulton
W 1974-2002. Barlaston & Oulton W 2002-.
CED. Stone 1889-1911. Stone Rural Sept 1911-2005.
Barlaston & Fulford 2005-.

Meaford Fields estate

Stone Rural CP 1894-2003. Meaford and Aston PW
1968-2003. Stone CP 2003-. Stonefield & Christchurch
PW 2003-.
LG. Stone RD 1894-1974. Stafford D(B) 1974-.
Stonefield & Christchurch W 1974-2002, 2002-.
CED. Stone 1889-1911. Stone Rural Sept 1911-74.
Stone Urban 1974-2005. Stone 2005-.

Meafordhall Farm

Stone Rural CP 1894-1988. Meaford and Aston PW
1968-88. Barlaston CP 1988-. Barlaston West PW
2003-
LG. Stone RD 1894-1974. Stafford D(B) 1974-.
Barlaston W 1974-2002. Barlaston & Oulton W 2002-
CED. Stone 1889-1911. Stone Rural Sept 1911-2005.
Barlaston & Fulford 2005-.

Meaford Hall

Stone Rural CP 1894-. Meaford and Aston PW 1968-
2003. Meaford PW 2003-.
LG. Stone RD 1894-1974. Stafford D(B) 1974-. Oulton
W 1974-2002. Barlaston & Oulton W 2002-.
CED. Stone 1889-1911. Stone Rural Sept 1911-2005.
Barlaston & Fulford 2005-.

Oulton Cross

Stone CP 1894- (TC 1973/4-). Stonefield &
Christchurch PW April 1965-2003, 2003-
LG. Stone UD 1894-1974. Stonefield & Christchurch
W April 1965-1974. Stafford D(B) 1974-. Stonefield
& Christchurch W 1974-2002, 2002-.

Stone (Kibblestone Quarter, Meaford)

CED. Stone 1889-1911. Stone Urban Sept 1911-2005.
Stone 2005-.

Out Lanes

Stone Rural CP 1894-. Oulton PW 1968-2003. Meaford
PW 2003-.
LG. Stone RD 1894-1974. Stafford D(B) 1974-. Oulton
W 1974-2002. Barlaston & Oulton W 2002-.
CED. Stone 1889-1911. Stone Rural Sept 1911-2005.
Barlaston & Fulford 2005-.

railway (1)

Stone Rural CP 1894-1988. Oulton PW 1968-88.
Barlaston CP 1988-. Barlaston West PW 2003-.
LG. Stone RD 1894-1974. Stafford D(B) 1974-. Oulton
W 1974-2002. Barlaston & Oulton W 2002-.
CED. Stone 1889-1911. Stone Rural Sept 1911-2005.
Barlaston & Fulford 2005-.

railway (2)

Stone Rural CP 1894-1988. Oulton PW 1968-88.
Barlaston CP 1988-. Barlaston East PW 2003-.
LG. Stone RD 1894-1974. Stafford D(B) 1974-. Oulton
W 1974-2002. Barlaston & Oulton W 2002-.
CED. Stone 1889-1911. Stone Rural Sept 1911-2005.
Barlaston & Fulford 2005-.

Sandpits

Stone Rural CP 1894-1932. Stone CP 1932- (TC 1973/
4-). Walton PW April 1965-2003. Stonefield &
Christchurch PW 2003-
LG. Stone RD 1894-1932, UD 1932-74. Walton W
April 1965-1974. Stafford D(B) 1974-. Walton W
1974-2002. Stonefield & Christchurch W 2002-.
CED. Stone 1889-1911. Stone Rural Sept 1911-34.
Stone Urban 1934-2005. Stone 2005-.

Stonefield

Stone CP 1894- (TC 1973/4-). Stonefield &
Christchurch PW April 1965-2003, 2003-
LG. Stone UD 1894-1974. Stonefield & Christchurch
W April 1965-1974. Stafford D(B) 1974-. Stonefield
& Christchurch W 1974-2002, 2002-.
CED. Stone 1889-1911. Stone Urban Sept 1911-2005.
Stone 2005-.
PLU. Stone 1838-1930. Stone W by1910-.

Trent Wood

Stone Rural CP 1894-1932. Stone CP 1932- (TC 1973/
4-). Stonefield & Christchurch PW April 1965-2003.
Walton PW 2003-
LG. Stone RD 1894-1932, UD 1932-74. Stonefield &
Christchurch W April 1965-1974. Stafford D(B) 1974-
. Stonefield & Christchurch W 1974-2002. Walton W
2002-.
CED. Stone 1889-1911. Stone Rural Sept 1911-34.
Stone Urban 1934-2005. Stone 2005-.

177

Stone (Kibblestone Quarter, Moddershall)

Whitebridge Industrial Estate (1)

Stone CP 1894- (TC 1973/4-). Stonefield & Christchurch PW April 1965-2003. Walton PW 2003-

LG. Stone UD 1894-1974. Stonefield & Christchurch W April 1965-1974. Stafford D(B) 1974-. Stonefield & Christchurch W 1974-2002. Walton W 2002-.

CED. Stone 1889-1911. Stone Urban Sept 1911- 2005. Stone 2005-.

PLU. Stone 1838-1930. Stone W by1910-.

Whitebridge Industrial Estate (2)

Stone Rural CP 1894-1932. Stone CP 1932- (TC 1973/4-). Stonefield & Christchurch PW April 1965-2003, 2003-

LG. Stone RD 1894-1932, UD 1932-1974. Stonefield & Christchurch W April 1965-1974. Stafford D(B) 1974-. Stonefield & Christchurch W 1974-2002, 2002-

CED. Stone 1889-1911. Stone Rural Sept 1911-34. Stone Urban 1934-2005. Stone 2005-.

MODDERSHALL TOWNSHIP

Berry Hills

Stone Rural CP 1894-. Moddershall PW 1968-2003, 2003-

LG. Stone RD 1894-1974. Stafford D(B) 1974-. Fulford W 1974-2002. Barlaston & Oulton W 2002-.

CED. Stone 1889-1911. Stone Rural Sept 1911-2005. Barlaston & Fulford 2005-.

PLU. Stone 1838-1930. Stone Rural W by1910-.

Blacklake Plantation

Stone Rural CP 1894-7. Fulford CP 1897-. Meir Heath PW Nov 1949-, 2003-

LG. Stone RD 1894-1974. Stafford D(B) 1974-. Fulford W 1974-2002. Barlaston & Oulton W 2002-.

CED. Stone 1889-1911. Stone Rural Sept 1911-2005. Barlaston & Fulford 2005-.

PLU. Stone 1838-1930. Stone Rural W -1898. Fulford & Hilderstone W 1898-1913. Fulford W 1913-.

Black Pits

Stone Rural CP 1894-2003. Moddershall PW 1968-2003. Barlaston CP 2003-. Barlaston East PW 2003-

LG. Stone RD 1894-1974. Stafford D(B) 1974-. Oulton W 1974-2002. Barlaston & Oulton W 2002-.

CED. Stone 1889-1911. Stone Rural Sept 1911-2005. Barlaston & Fulford 2005-.

PLU. Stone 1838-1930. Stone Rural W by1910-.

Cotwalton Drumble

Stone Rural CP 1894-. Meaford and Aston PW 1968-2003. Aston PW 2003-.

LG. Stone RD 1894-1974. Stafford D(B) 1974-. Oulton W 1974-2002. Milwich W 2002-.

CED. Stone 1889-1911. Stone Rural Sept 1911-2005. Barlaston & Fulford 2005-.

PLU. Stone 1838-1930. Stone Rural W by1910-.

Crossgate

Stone Rural CP 1894-7. Fulford CP 1897-. Fulford PW Nov 1949-, 2003-

LG. Stone RD 1894-1974. Stafford D(B) 1974-. Fulford W 1974-2002. Barlaston & Oulton W 2002-.

CED. Stone 1889-1911. Stone Rural Sept 1911-2005. Barlaston & Fulford 2005-.

PLU. Stone 1838-1930. Stone Rural W -1898. Fulford & Hilderstone W 1898-1913. Fulford W 1913-.

Dale

Stone Rural CP 1894-7. Fulford CP 1897-. Blythe Bridge PW Nov 1949-, 2003-

LG. Stone RD 1894-1974. Stafford D(B) 1974-. Fulford W 1974-2002. Barlaston & Oulton W 2002-.

CED. Stone 1889-1911. Stone Rural Sept 1911-2005. Barlaston & Fulford 2005-.

PLU. Stone 1838-1930. Stone Rural -1898. Fulford & Hilderstone W 1898-1913. Fulford W 1913-.

Leadendale

Stone Rural CP 1894-2003. Moddershall PW 1968-. Fulford CP 2003-. Rough Close PW 2003-

LG. Stone RD 1894-1974. Stafford D(B) 1974-.

Stone (Kibblestone Quarter, Moddershall)

Fulford W 1974-2002, 2002-.
CED. Stone 1889-1911. Stone Rural Sept 1911-2005.
Barlaston & Fulford 2005-.
PLU. Stone 1838-1930. Stone Rural W by1910-.

Moddershall

Stone Rural CP 1894-. Moddershall PW 1968-2003, 2003-.
LG. Stone RD 1894-1974. Stafford D(B) 1974-. Oulton W 1974-2002. Barlaston & Oulton W 2002-.
CED. Stone 1889-1911. Stone Rural Sept 1911-2005.
Barlaston & Fulford 2005-.
PLU. Stone 1838-1930. Stone Rural W by1910-.

Upper Scotch Brook

Stone Rural CP 1894-. Moddershall PW 1968-2002, 2003-

LG. Stone RD 1894-1974. Stafford D(B) 1974-.
Barlaston W 1974-2002. Barlaston & Oulton W 2002-
CED. Stone 1889-1911. Stone Rural Sept 1911-2005.
Barlaston & Fulford 2005-.
PLU. Stone 1838-1930. Stone Rural W by1910-.

'Wooliscroft Dell'

Stone Rural CP 1894-. Moddershall PW 1968-2003, 2003-
LG. Stone RD 1894-1974. Stafford D(B) 1974-.
Milwich W 1974-2002. Barlaston & Oulton W 2002-.
CED. Stone 1889-1911. Stone Rural Sept 1911-2005.
Barlaston & Fulford 2005-.
PLU. Stone 1838-1930. Stone Rural W by1910-.

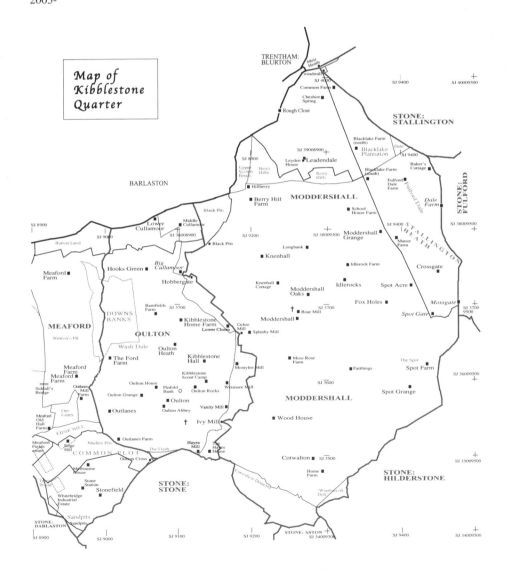

Stone (Kibblestone Quarter, Oulton)
OULTON TOWNSHIP
PLU. Stone 1838-1930. Stone Rural W by1894.

The Flash
Stone Rural CP 1894-. Oulton PW 1968-2003, 2003-.
LG. Stone RD 1894-1974. Stafford D(B) 1974-.
Stonefield & Christchurch W 1974-2002. Barlaston &
Oulton W 2002-.
CED. Stone 1889-1911. Stone Rural Sept 1911-74.
Stone Urban 1974-2002. Stone Rural 2002-5. Barlaston
& Fulford 2005-.

Hobbergate
Stone Rural CP 1894-. Moddershall PW 1968-2003,
2003-.
LG. Stone RD 1894-1974. Stafford D(B) 1974-. Oulton
W 1974-2002. Barlaston & Oulton W 2002-.
CED. Stone 1889-1911. Stone Rural Sept 1911-2005.
Barlaston & Fulford 2005-.

Ivy Mill
Stone Rural CP 1894-. Moddershall PW 1968-2003,
2003-.
Stone RD 1894-1974. Stafford D(B) 1974-. Oulton W
1974-2002. Barlaston & Oulton W 2002-.
CED. Stone 1889-1911. Stone Rural Sept 1911-2005.
Barlaston & Fulford 2005-.

Lower Cullamoor
Stone Rural CP 1894-2003. Oulton PW 1968-2003.
Barlaston CP 2003-. Barlaston East PW 2003-.
LG. Stone RD 1894-1974. Stafford D(B) 1974-. Oulton
W 1974-2002. Barlaston & Oulton W 2002-.
CED. Stone 1889-1911. Stone Rural Sept 1911-2005.
Barlaston & Fulford 2005-.

Middle Cullamoor
Stone Rural CP 1894-2003. Moddershall PW 1968-
2003. Barlaston CP 2003-.
Barlaston East PW 2003-
LG. Stone RD 1894-1974. Staf-
ford D(B) 1974-. Oulton W
1974-2002. Barlaston & Oulton
W 2002-.
CED. Stone 1889-1911. Stone
Rural Sept 1911-2005. Barlaston
& Fulford 2005-.

Oulton
Stone Rural CP 1894-. Oulton
PW 1968-2003, 2003-.
LG. Stone RD 1894-1974. Staf-
ford D(B) 1974-. Oulton W
1974-2002. Barlaston & Oulton
W 2002-.
CED. Stone 1889-1911. Stone
Rural Sept 1911-2005. Barlaston
& Fulford 2005-.

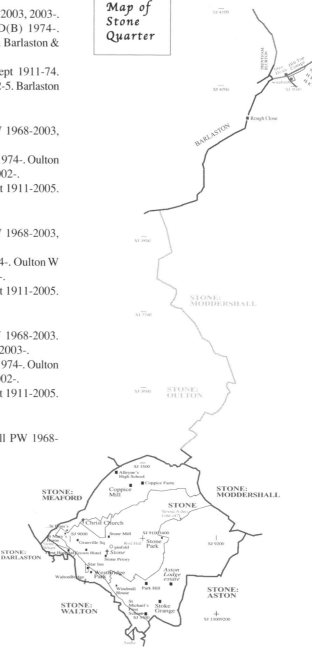

Map of
Stone
Quarter

SJ 42009400

STONE:
NORMACOT
SJ 41009300
SJ 9400

Grindley
The Farm

SJ 41009500

DILHORNE:
FORSBROOK

works

Grange Cottage
formerly Stallington Grange
(the second)

TRENTHAM: BURTON

Meir Heath

Hill Top Cottage

New House
(alias Stallington Grange c1800)

Grange House
formerly Stallington Grange

STALLINGTON

Gorstybirch

Lower Gorsty Birch

DRAYCOTT IN THE MOORS

windmill
SJ 4000

SJ 9400

SJ 40009500

SJ 40009600

SJ 39009700

Stallington Farm

Little Leacroft Farm

Stallington

STONE:
MODDERSHALL

Stallington Hall

FULFORD

SJ 39009300

SJ 9400

SJ 9500

SJ 9600

STONE QUARTER
STALLINGTON TOWNSHIP
Grange House
Stone Rural CP 1894-7. Fulford CP 1897-. Meir Heath PW Nov 1949-, 2003-
LG. Stone RD 1894-1974. Stafford D(B) 1974-. Fulford W 1974-2002, 2002-.
CED. Stone 1889-1911. Stone Rural Sept 1911-2005. Barlaston & Fulford 2005-.
PLU. Stone 1838-1930. Stone Rural -1898. Fulford & Hilderstone W 1898-1913. Fulford W 1913-.

Hill Top Cottage
Shown in Stallington T on tithe map (D593/H/3/280) but in Normacot T on other C19 maps.
The same as Grange House.

Stallington
Stone Rural CP 1894-7. Fulford CP 1897-. Blythe Bridge PW Nov 1949-, 2003-
LG. Stone RD 1894-1974. Stafford D(B) 1974-. Fulford W 1974-2002, 2002-.
CED. Stone 1889-1911. Stone Rural Sept 1911-2005. Barlaston & Fulford 2005-.
PLU. Stone 1838-1930. Stone Rural -1898. Fulford & Hilderstone W 1898-1913. Fulford W 1913-.

Stallington Hall
Stone Rural CP 1894-7. Fulford CP 1897-. Fulford PW Nov 1949-, 2003-
LG. Stone RD 1894-1974. Stafford D(B) 1974-. Fulford W 1974-2002, 2002-.
CED. Stone 1889-1911. Stone Rural Sept 1911-2005. Barlaston & Fulford 2005-.
PLU. Stone 1838-1930. Stone Rural -1898. Fulford &

Stone (Stone Quarter, Stallington)
Hilderstone W 1898-1913. Fulford W 1913-.

windmill
Shown in Stallington T on tithe map (D593/H/3/280, 281-282) but in Moddershall T on maps c1800, 1850, 1859 (D593/T/1/68) (D593/H/3/226) (D593/H/3/228).
The same as Grange House.

STONE TOWNSHIP
Andre
Stone Rural CP 1894-Oct 1955. Stone CP Oct 1955- (TC 1973/4-). Walton PW April 1965-2003, 2003-
LG. Stone RD 1894-Oct 1955. Stone UD Oct 1955-74. Walton W April 1965-1974. Stafford D(B) 1974-. Walton W 1974-2002, 2002-.
CED. Stone 1889-1911. Stone Rural Sept 1911-55. Stone Urban 1955-2005. Stone 2005-.
PLU. Stone 1838-1930. Stone Rural W by1910.

Christ Church
Stone CP 1894- (TC 1973/4-), minutes 1912-87 at SRO. St Michaels PW April 1965-Feb 1971. Stonefield & Christchurch PW Feb 1971-2003, 2003-
LG. Stone UD 1894-74. St Michaels W April 1965-Feb 1971. Stonefield & Christchurch W Feb 1971-1974. Stafford D(B) 1974-. Stonefield & Christchurch W 1974-2002, 2002-.
CED. Stone 1889-1911. Stone Urban Sept 1911-2005. Stone 2005-.
PLU. Stone 1838-1930. Stone W by1910.

Coppice Mill
Stone CP 1894- (TC 1973/4-). Stonefield & Christchurch PW April 1965-2003, 2003-
LG. Stone UD 1894-1974. Stonefield & Christchurch W April 1965-1974. Stafford D(B) 1974-. Stonefield & Christchurch W 1974-2002, 2002-.
CED. Stone 1889-1911. Stone Urban Sept 1911-2005. Stone 2005-.
PLU. Stone 1838-1930. Stone W by1910.

Star Inn
Stone CP 1894- (TC 1973/4-). Walton PW April 1965-2003. Stonefield & Christchurch PW 2003-
LG. Stone UD 1894-74. Walton W April 1965-1974. Stafford D(B) 1974-. Walton W 1974-2002. Stonefield & Christchurch W 2002-.
CED. Stone 1889-1911. Stone Urban Sept 1911-2005. Stone 2005-.
PLU. Stone 1838-1930. Stone W by1910.

181

Stone (Stone Quarter)

Stoke Grange

Stone CP 1894- (TC 1973/4-). St Michaels PW April 1965-2003, 2003-

LG. Stone UD 1894-1974. St Michaels W April 1965-1974. Stafford D(B) 1974-. St Michaels W 1974-2002, 2002-

CED. Stone 1889-1911. Stone Urban Sept 1911-2005. Stone 2005-.

PLU. Stone 1838-1930. Stone W by1910.

Stone Park

Stone CP 1894- (TC 1973/4-). St Michaels W April 1965-2003. Stonefield & Christchurch W 2003-.

LG. Stone UD 1894-1974. St Michaels PW April 1965-1974. Stafford D(B) 1974-. St Michaels W 1974-2002. Stonefield & Christchurch W 2002-.

CED. Stone 1889-1911. Stone Urban Sept 1911-2005. Stone 2005-.

PLU. Stone 1838-1930. Stone W by1910.

Stone Wharf

Stone Rural CP 1894-1932. Stone CP 1932- (TC 1973/4-). Walton PW April 1965-2003. Stonefield & Christchurch PW 2003-.

LG. Stone RD 1894-1932, UD 1932-74. Walton W April 1965-1974. Stafford D(B) 1974-. Walton W 1974-2002, Stonefield & Christchurch W 2002-.

CED. Stone 1889-1911. Stone Urban Sept 1911-2005. Stone 2005-.

PLU. Stone 1838-1930. Stone Rural W by1910.

Trent Hospital

Stone CP 1894- (TC 1973/4-). Walton PW April 1965-2003. Stonefield & Christchurch PW 2003-.

LG. Stone UD 1894-1974. Walton W April 1965-1974. Stafford D(B) 1974-. Walton W 1974-2002. Stonefield & Christchurch W 2002-.

CED. Stone 1889-1911. Stone Urban Sept 1911-2005. Stone 2005-.

PLU. Stone 1838-1930. Stone W by1910.

Westbridge Park

Stone CP 1894- (TC 1973/4-). Walton PW April 1965-2003, 2003-

LG. Stone UD 1894-1974. Walton W April 1965-1974. Stafford D(B) 1974-. Walton W 1974-2002, 2002-.

CED. Stone 1889-1911. Stone Urban Sept 1911-2005. Stone 2005-.

PLU. Stone 1838-1930. Stone W by1910.

Pews

The corner of a box pew (the pews are coeval with the C18 church) in St Michael's, Stone, made a good easel for my drawing of the old parish chest in the E aisle. Accounts or other records about pews (they were allocated freehold or rented by the churchwarden) are good indicators of social class in a community. There are records at SRO for Chapel Chorlton (**Eccleshall**) 1827; **Audley** 1794. Talke chapel (D4017/5/1); **Barlaston** (award of) 1831, (seating plans) 1809-31, (exchange of) 1814, in parish book; **Betley** (conveyance of Stubbs/ Britain) 1769; **Colton** (award of) 1853; **Colwich** (church seating) 1854; in High Offley parish records is this Release: Thomas Leech, tanner, to John Collins, yeoman, of a pew in the gallery of **Drayton-in-Hales** church, 25 Jan 1711/12 (D4035/7/2). **Newcastle-u-Lyme** St Giles (pew grants) 1721-57; **Stoke-upon-Trent** Hanley St John five title deeds of pews 1738-1871; Stoke St Peter Ad Vincula (allocation of seats) 1634 printed (D1188/16), (seating plan) 1827. **Stone** Fulford 1825 (D4582/3/3); correspondence re abolition of the 'pew rent system' of augmenting income at Hilderstone 1936-48 (D3408/1/167-173); Stone St Michael (pew owners) 1758, 1891, 1896, (amended pew allotments) 1891, (lots of title deeds). **Stowe** detailed receipts of pew rents at St Peter, Hixon 1848-1931. **Weston-on-Trent** (faculty of) 1810.

Tim Coleshaw, English Nature Site Manager Staffordshire & Cheshire NNRs leads a tour group round Chartley Moss, 2004. Courtesy of G Gatensbury

Stowe by Chartley

'There was a blacksmith's shop at Amerton on the corner of the Amerton to Shirleywich Lane run by Mr Edwards, but it was empty and derelict before the War when they started to build Hixon Aerodrome.'

Edmund Craik. Memories of Hixon. 2002: The shop was demolished and its rubble used as hard core for the Aerodrome

There is an excellent list of parish overseers in Stowe-by-Chartley overseers accounts (D14/A/PO/ 1), transcribed out of former books. There was one constable for the period 1670-1758, formerly called the constable of Chartley, later of Stowe parish. In 1851 the hamlets supported their poor co-jointly.

PLU. Stafford 1836-1930. Stowe with Chartley Holme W by1910.
SEE ALSO pages 7, 27, 30, 49, 50, 54, 79, 81, 84, 94, 96, 130, 182, 186-187, 211, 214

AMERTON HAMLET
Amerton
Stowe CP 1866-. The first PC meeting took place in Earl Ferrers School Dec 4 1894; and the last united council took place on March 22 2000 (Stafford Post March 23 2000 p11; with history of the united PC). The bid for separate PCs for Stowe-by-Chartley and Hixon had come from Stowe councillors who believed a severed parish would mean reduced precepts. Many of the old PC were surprised when the CC granted permission, believing it would result in an insufficient budget for Stowe. Mr J Blount, former clerk to the old council, and now clerk to both, says his workload for Stowe is about half that for Hixon. Minutes from 1894-1947, 1947-76 at SRO. Stowe PW Feb 1991-2000.

Stowe by Chartley (Amerton)

LG. Stafford RD 1894-1974, D(B) 1974-. Chartley W 1974-2002, 2002-.
CED. Stafford Rural 1889-1911. Stafford Rural East Sept 1911-34. Stafford Rural 1934-73. Stafford Rural No. 2 1973-81. Stafford Trent Valley 1981-2005, 2005-

Amerton Brook tributary (2)

Stowe CP 1866-1988. Weston CP 1988-
LG. Stafford RD 1894-1974, D(B) 1974-. Chartley W 1974-2002, 2002-.
CED. Stafford Rural 1889-1911. Stafford Rural East Sept 1911-34. Stafford Rural 1934-73. Stafford Rural No. 2 1973-81. Stafford Trent Valley 1981-2005, 2005-

Moorleys Lane

Stowe CP 1866-1988. Gayton CP 1988-
LG. Stafford RD 1894-1974, D(B) 1974-. Chartley W 1974-2002, 2002-.
CED. Stafford Rural 1889-1911. Stafford Rural East Sept 1911-34. Stafford Rural 1934-73. Stafford Rural No. 2 1973-81. Stafford Trent Valley 1981-2005, 2005-

Stowe. 1,7

Stowe CP 1866-, PC 1894-2000. Hixon PW Feb 1991-2000. Hixon PC April 1 2000-.

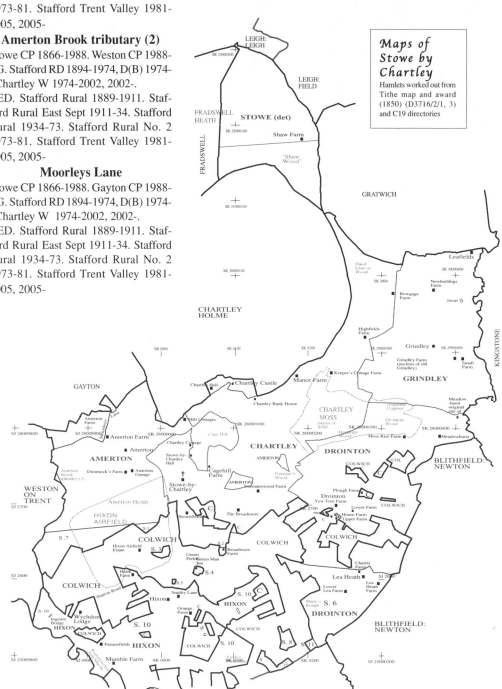

Maps of Stowe by Chartley
Hamlets worked out from Tithe map and award (1850) (D3716/2/1, 3) and C19 directories

184

LG. Stafford RD 1894-1974, D(B) 1974-. Chartley W 1974-2002, Haywood & Hixon W 2002-.
CED. Stafford Rural 1889-1911. Stafford Rural East Sept 1911-34. Stafford Rural 1934-73. Stafford Rural No. 2 1973-81. Stafford Trent Valley 1981-2005, 2005-

CHARTLEY HAMLET
Chartley Castle
Stowe AP -?1858 (1850~90). Chartley Holme CP ?1858-1934. Stowe CP 1934-.
LG. Stafford RD 1894-1974, RD 1894-1974, D(B) 1974-. Chartley W 1974-2002, 2002-.
CED. Stafford Rural 1889-1911. Stafford Rural East Sept 1911-34. Stafford Rural 1934-73. Stafford Rural No. 2 1973-81. Stafford Trent Valley 1981-2005, 2005-
PLU. Stafford 1858-1930. Stowe with Chartley Holme W by1910.

Stowe
Stowe CP 1866-. Stowe PW Feb 1991-2000.
LG. Stafford RD 1894-1974, D(B) 1974-. Chartley W 1974-2002, 2002-.
CED. Stafford Rural 1889-1911. Stafford Rural East Sept 1911-34. Stafford Rural 1934-73. Stafford Rural No. 2 1973-81. Stafford Trent Valley 1981-2005, 2005-

Stowe. 2
Stowe CP 1866-, PC 1894-2000. Hixon PW Feb 1991-2000. Hixon PC April 1 2000-.
LG. Stafford RD 1894-1974, D(B) 1974-. Chartley W 1974-2002, Haywood & Hixon W 2002-.
CED. Stafford Rural 1889-1911. Stafford Rural East Sept 1911-34. Stafford Rural 1934-73. Stafford Rural No. 2 1973-81. Stafford Trent Valley 1981-2005, 2005-

Detached portion
Shaw Farm
Stowe CP 1866- (integral from 1934). Stowe PW Feb 1991-2000.
LG. Stafford RD 1894-1974, D(B) 1974-. Milwich W 1974-2002, Chartley W 2002-.
CED. Stafford Rural 1889-1911. Stafford Rural East Sept 1911-34. Stafford Rural 1934-73. Stafford Rural No. 2 1973-81. Stafford Trent Valley 1981-2005, 2005-

'Shaw Wood'
Stowe CP 1866- (integral from 1934). Stowe PW Feb 1991-2000.
LG. Stafford RD 1894-1974, D(B) 1974-. Chartley W 1974-2002, 2002-.

Stowe by Chartley (Grindley)
CED. Stafford Rural 1889-1911. Stafford Rural East Sept 1911-34. Stafford Rural 1934-73. Stafford Rural No. 2 1973-81. Stafford Trent Valley 1981-2005, 2005-

DROINTON HAMLET
Drointon
Stowe CP 1866-. Stowe PW Feb 1991-2000.
LG. Stafford RD 1894-1974, D(B) 1974-. Chartley W 1974-2002, 2002-.
CED. Stafford Rural 1889-1911. Stafford Rural East Sept 1911-34. Stafford Rural 1934-73. Stafford Rural No. 2 1973-81. Stafford Trent Valley 1981-2005, 2005-
Stowe. 6,11
Stowe CP -2000. Hixon PW Feb 1991-2000. Hixon CP April 1 2000-.
LG. Stafford RD 1894-1974, D(B) 1974-. Chartley W 1974-2002, Haywood & Hixon W 2002-.
CED. Stafford Rural 1889-1911. Stafford Rural East Sept 1911-34. Stafford Rural 1934-73. Stafford Rural No. 2 1973-81. Stafford Trent Valley 1981-2005, 2005-

GRINDLEY HAMLET
Stowe CP 1866-. Stowe PW Feb 1991-2000.
LG. Stafford RD 1894-1974, D(B) 1974-. Chartley W

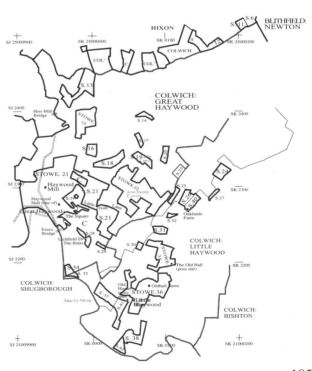

Stowe by Chartley (Little Haywood)

1974-2002, 2002-.
CED. Stafford Rural 1889-1911. Stafford Rural East Sept 1911-34. Stafford Rural 1934-73. Stafford Rural No. 2 1973-81. Stafford Trent Valley 1981-2005, 2005-

HIXON HAMLET
Stowe. 3,4,5,8,9,10,12

Stowe CP 1883?,1885?1885?,1886?-, PC 1894-2000. Hixon PW Feb 1991-2000. Hixon CP April 1 2000-.
LG. Stafford RD 1894-1974, D(B) 1974-. Chartley W 1974-2002, Haywood & Hixon W 2002-.
CED. Stafford Rural 1889-1911. Stafford Rural East Sept 1911-34. Stafford Rural 1934-73. Stafford Rural No. 2 1973-81. Stafford Trent Valley 1981-2005, 2005-

GREAT HAYWOOD HAMLET
Stowe. 13

Stowe CP 1866-1934. Colwich CP 1934-. Great Haywood PW Aug 1972-.
LG. Stafford RD 1894-1974, D(B) 1974-. Haywood & Hixon W 1974-2002, 2002-.
CED. Stafford Rural 1889-1911. Stafford Rural East Sept 1911-34. Stafford Rural 1934-73. Stafford Rural No. 2 1973-81. Stafford Trent Valley 1981-2005, 2005-
Stowe. 14-23,28,29,34,39
Colwich CP 1883? 1884? 1885? 1886?-. Great

Haywood PW Aug 1972-
LG. Stafford RD 1894-1974, D(B) 1974-. Haywood & Hixon W 1974-2002, 2002-.
CED. Stafford Rural 1889-1911. Stafford Rural East Sept 1911-34. Stafford Rural 1934-73. Stafford Rural No. 2 1973-81. Stafford Trent Valley 1981-2005, 2005-
PLU. Stafford 1836-1930. Colwich W by1910.

LITTLE HAYWOOD HAMLET
Stowe. 25, 26, 30, 35, 37

Colwich CP 1883?,1885?1885?,1886?-. Great Haywood PW Aug 1972-.
LG. Stafford RD 1894-1974, D(B) 1974-. Haywood & Hixon W 1974-2002, 2002-.
CED. Stafford Rural 1889-1911. Stafford Rural East Sept 1911-34. Stafford Rural 1934-73. Stafford Rural No. 2 1973-81. Stafford Trent Valley 1981-2005, 2005-
PLU. Stafford 1836-1930. Colwich W by1910.
Stowe. 24, 27, 31, 32, 33, 36, 38, 40, 41, 42
Colwich CP 1883?,1885?1885?,1886?-. Little Haywood PW Aug 1972-
LG. Stafford RD 1894-1974, D(B) 1974-. Haywood & Hixon W 1974-2002, 2002-.
CED. Stafford Rural 1889-1911. Stafford Rural East Sept 1911-34. Stafford Rural 1934-73. Stafford Rural No. 2 1973-81. Stafford Trent Valley 1981-2005, 2005-
PLU. Stafford 1836-1930. Colwich W by1910.

Protected nature reserves

Unsurprisingly, Chartley Moss, lying in the centre of Stowe parish, is a Site of Special Scientific Interest (SSSI), and a Ramsar site under the Ramsar Convention. It is a glacial hollow created in the Ice Age, and Britain's largest Schwingmoor bog. SSSIs are 'the best examples of our natural heritage of wildlife habitats, geological features and landforms'. They were identified by the predecessor of English Nature under the National Parks and Access to the Countryside Act 1949, and protected under the Wildlife and Countryside Act 1981, strengthened in 1992, and by the Countryside and Rights of Way Act 2000.

The Pirehill Sites of Special Scientific Interest (SSSIs) are: Goat Lodge, **Abbots Bromley**; Black Firs and Cranberry Bog, Balterley, **Barthomley** (a SWTR); **Betley** Mere; **Blithfield** Reservoir; Stafford Brook in Wolseley Park, and some of Cannock Chase, perhaps in **Colwich**; Cop Mere, **Eccleshall**; Maer Pool, **Maer**; Ford Green Reedbed, **Norton-in-the-Moors**; Pasturefields Salt Marsh (a SWTR) in **Stowe**; Doxey and **Tillington** Marshes (a SWTR); Rawbones Meadow in **Tixall**; King's and Hargreaves Woods, **Trentham**; Metallic Tileries, Park House, **Wolstanton**.

The Pirehill Local Nature Reserves (LNRs) are (dates when designated):- **Barlaston** and Rough Close Common (2000) (SJ 923396, SJ 926399) 20 acres; Whitemoor (2001) (SJ 886605) in **Biddulph** 4.4 acres; Westport Lake (2004) (SJ 855501) in **Burslem**; and Bagnall Road Wood (2004) (SJ 912501) in Hulton, 6.1 acres; Astonfields Balancing Lakes (2004) (SJ 926248) in **Marston**, 4.2 acres; in **Norton-in-the-Moors** Marshes Hill Common (2001) (SJ 905548), 6.4 acres, and Whitfield Valley (SJ 885546) (1991) 84.4 acres; in **Stoke-upon-Trent** Hartshill Park (2003) (SJ 893482), in Penkhull 13.5 acres, and Berryhill Fields (2003) (SJ 907458) in Botteslow, 63.3 acres; **Stone** Meadows (2005), behind Redwood Avenue, where Staffordshire Amphibian and Reptile Group (SARG) was launched 2005 (ES April 30 2005 p19).

The Pirehill <u>Staffordshire Wildlife Trust Reserves</u> (SWTRs) (SWT has its HQ at the Wolseley Centre, Wolseley Bridge, Colwich) are:-

Parrot's Drumble (SJ 821519) in **Audley**, a 30 acre ancient bluebell wood. Hem Heath and Newstead Woods (SJ 885411) in **Barlaston** and **Trentham**, a 100 acre wood partly owned by and leased from Wedgwood. Black Firs and Cranberry Bog (SJ 746502) in Balterley, **Barthomley**, a 15 acre peatland (a SSSI). **Colwich** Brickworks (SJ 013215), is a 10 acre former quarry. Burnt Wood (SJ 736 355) in Tyrley, **Drayton-in-Hales**, a 98 acre semi natural ancient wood managed by the Trust on an agreement with Forest Enterprise. Jackson's Coppice & Marsh (SJ 786301) in Croxton, **Eccleshall**, a 20 acre semi-natural ancient wood and marsh - leased from the Sugnall Estate. Bateswood (SJ 796471) is 61 acres of grassland and pools in **Madeley**. Pasturefields in **Stowe** is 8 acres of inland saltmarsh (a SSSI) and meadow at SJ 994248. Doxey Marshes (SJ 903250) in **Tillington** is 300 acres of wet grassland (a SSSI).

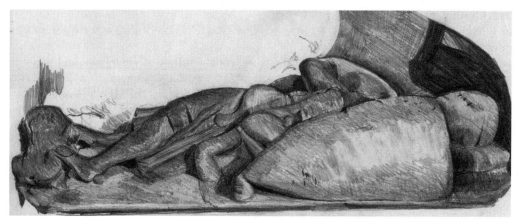

Recumbent effigy of Sir John de Swynnerton (d c1254), Swynnerton Church. Drawing by the author, 2003

Swynnerton

'Swynnerton typifies the old English village with its stately Hall standing in parkland, the churches, thatched cottages, cricket ground and inn which once incorporated a farm.'

Staffordshire Federation of Women's Institutes. The Staffordshire Village Book. 1988

Survey for equalising Swynnerton poor rate 1833 - names of owners and occupiers, reference plan (cf D4474/1) description of property, quanities, price per acre and yearly value (D4474/1). In 1851 the townships supported their poor cojointly.

SEE ALSO pages 7, 21, 30, 36, 50, 79, 93, 96, 106, 116,124, 125, 130, 142, 190-1, 209, 214, 233

ACTON TOWNSHIP
Acton
Swynnerton CP 1866-1932. PC 1894-. Minutes 1894-1950 in SRO. Whitmore CP 1932-
LG. Stone RD 1894-1932. Newcastle-u-Lyme RD 1932-74, D(B) 1974-. No. 20 W Feb 1973-4. No. 21 W Feb 1974-9. Whitmore W 1979-2002. Loggerheads & Whitmore 2002-.
CED. Eccleshall 1889-1934. Madeley 1934-81. Newcastle Rural 1981-2005, 2005-.

Hobgoblin Gate
Swynnerton CP 1866-. Trentham PW Nov 1954-
LG. Stone RD 1894-1974, Stafford D(B) 1974-.
Swynnerton W 1974-2002, 2002-.
CED. Eccleshall 1889-2005, 2005-.

Racecourse
Swynnerton CP 1866-1932. Whitmore CP 1932-84. Keele CP 1984- (SI No. 152).
LG. Stone RD 1894-1932, Newcastle-u-Lyme RD 1932-74, D(B) 1974-. No. 20 W Feb 1973-4. No. 21 W Feb 1974-9. Whitmore W 1979-84. Keele W 1984-2002, 2002-
CED. Eccleshall 1889-1934. Madeley 1934-81. Newcastle Rural 1981-4. Keele & Silverdale 1984-2005. Keele & Westlands 2005-.

'Shelton'
Swynnerton CP 1866-. Swynnerton PW Nov 1954-.
LG. Stone RD 1894-1974. Stafford D(B) 1974-.
Swynnerton W 1974-2002, 2002-.
CED. Eccleshall 1889-2005, 2005-.

Welldale
Swynnerton CP 1866-. Swynnerton PW Nov 1954-.
LG. Stone RD 1894-1974. Stafford D(B) 1974-.
Swynnerton W 1974-2002, 2002-.
CED. Eccleshall 1889-2005, 2005-.

BEECH TOWNSHIP
Beech

Swynnerton CP 1866-. Swynnerton PW Nov 1954-.
LG. Stone RD 1894-1974. Stafford D(B) 1974-.
Swynnerton W 1974-2002, 2002-.
CED. Eccleshall 1889-2005, 2005-.

The Stretters
Swynnerton CP 1866-. Tittensor PW Nov 1954-.
LG. Stone RD 1894-1974. Stafford D(B) 1974-.

Swynnerton (Swynnerton)
Swynnerton W 1974-2002, 2002-.
CED. Eccleshall 1889-2005, 2005-.

HATTON TOWNSHIP
Swynnerton CP 1866-. Swynnerton PW Nov 1954-
LG. Stone RD 1894-1974. Stafford D(B) 1974-.
Swynnerton W 1974-2002, 2002-.
CED. Eccleshall 1889-2005, 2005-.

SHELTON TOWNSHIP
Hanchurch Heath
Swynnerton CP 1866-. Trentham PW Nov 1954-
LG. Stone RD 1894-1974. Stafford D(B) 1974-.
Swynnerton W 1974-2002, 2002-.
CED. Eccleshall 1889-2005, 2005-.

Shelton
Swynnerton CP 1866-. Swynnerton PW Nov 1954-
LG. Stone RD 1894-1974. Stafford D(B) 1974-.
Swynnerton W 1974-2002, 2002-.
CED. Eccleshall 1889-2005, 2005-.

SWYNNERTON TOWNSHIP
Long Compton
Swynnerton CP 1866-. Tittensor PW Nov 1954-

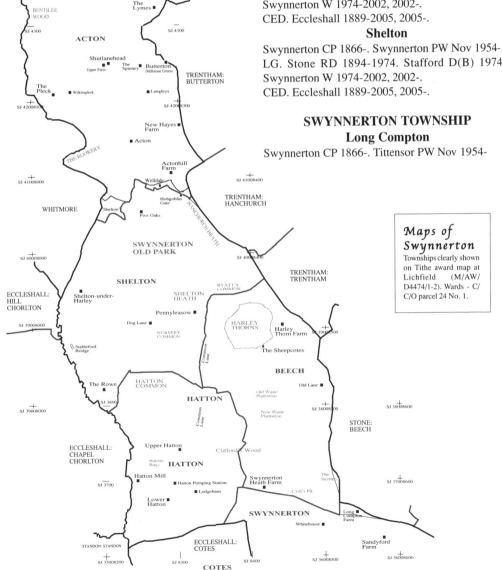

Maps of
Swynnerton
Townships clearly shown
on Tithe award map at
Lichfield   (M/AW/
D4474/1-2). Wards - C/
C/O parcel 24 No. 1.

Swynnerton (Yarnfield)

LG. Stone RD 1894-1974. Stafford D(B) 1974-.
Swynnerton W 1974-2002, 2002-.
CED. Eccleshall 1889-2005, 2005-.

Pilstones Wood
Swynnerton CP 1866-. Yarnfield PW Nov 1954-
LG. Stone RD 1894-1974. Stafford D(B) 1974-.
Swynnerton W 1974-2002, 2002-.
CED. Eccleshall 1889-2005, 2005-.

Swynnerton
Swynnerton CP 1866-. Swynnerton PW Nov 1954-
LG. Stone RD 1894-1974. Stafford D(B) 1974-.
Swynnerton W 1974-2002, 2002-.
CED. Eccleshall 1889-2005, 2005-.

YARNFIELD TOWNSHIP
Highlowbank
Swynnerton CP 1866-. Swynnerton PW Nov 1954-
LG. Stone RD 1894-1974. Stafford D(B) 1974-.
Swynnerton W 1974-2002, 2002-.

CED. Eccleshall 1889-2005, 2005-.
Yarnfield
Swynnerton CP 1866-. Yarnfield PW Nov 1954-
LG. Stone RD 1894-1974. Stafford D(B) 1974-.
Swynnerton W 1974-2002, 2002-.
CED. Eccleshall 1889-2005, 2005-.

Monumental records St-Z

Swynnerton St Mary - George Rowley d1705 (SMI 1967 - SRO c/p/12). Our Lady of Assumption RC - Emily Charlotte, wife of Basil Fitzherbert d1881 (BMSGH 2002 - SRO on open shelves with printed PRs).

Tixall, St John - Richard Biddulph d1627/8 servant of the Aston family (BMSGH & Great Haywood WI 1982 - SRO D5428/2/1; album which once contained the survey. D5428/2/2; survey).

Trentham - Blurton, St Bartholomew - graves from later 1820s (BMSGH 2003 - WSL). Dresden, Church of the Resurrection - John Tams d1855 (BMSGH 2003 - SRO open shelves). Hanford, St Matthias - internal & external mems to Anne Fenton d1830, wife of Thomas Fenton of Stoke Lodge; she was last surviving child of Josiah & Ellen Spode (BMSGH 2002 - WSL).

Whitmore, St Mary & All Saints - Elizabeth Eldershaw of the Lane House d1745 aged 16 (SMI 1967 - SRO c/p/12).

Wolstanton - <u>Chesterton</u>, Holy Trinity - no grave will pre-date 1851, WW1/ WW2 cenotaph in Chesterton Park (BMSGH c2002 - WSL). <u>Knutton</u>, St Luke, Silverdale - nothing before 1853 (IND c1995 - WSL). <u>Thursfield</u>, St James, Newchapel - Ralph Hancock d1751 aged 19 (SMI 1967 - SRO c/p/12).

The Survey of Monumental Inscriptions (SMI)

The provenance of the SMI - as suggested by its catalogue index title - is the CC Planning Department; but no one there can remember the project, as it ran such a long time ago, from 1967 to c1970. It by no means surveyed all Staffordshire churchyards, nor was each churchyard's survey complete. Local enthusiasts, some doing several churchyards, carried it out, invariably a family group, so that - judging by handwriting - children made some recordings: I was touched by one form completed by a child J Teale who had transcribed the inscription on the grave of Mary Lightfoot of Madeley Heath d1794, herself a child aged 9. Most recorders tried to write the inscription as it appeared on the monument; but Whitmore recorders went a stage further placing the inscription within a drawing of the monument. There was uniformity, too, with the standardised SMI yellow questionnaire form which recorders were expected to complete for each monument; it asked:- 1. NAME(S) OF DECEASED. 2. PARISH. 3. DENOMINATION OF CHURCH. 4. ZONE LETTER (relating to a plan). 5. NUMBER OF MEMORIAL? 6. TYPE OF MEMORIAL? 7. MATERIAL? (of mon). 8. RAILINGS? (does the monument have railings - yes/ no). 9. ORNAMENT? 10. CONDITION? 11. WORTHY OF PHOTOGRAPH? (yes/ no). 12. INSCRIPTION (space to write the inscription). 13. NAME OF RECORDER. 14. DATE OF RECORD.

Robert Sherlock (author of IAS), may have set up SMI when conservation officer for the CC (info Michael Greenslade). William Read got involved with what he believes was a Keele Uni survey of St Mary's Stafford at this time. This was through his teacher Stan Parker (Sir Graham Balfour School - 1968); in addition, no SMI survey of St Mary's Stafford exists at SRO (info William Read).

The Birmingham & Midland Society for Genealogy and Heraldry surveys (BMSGH)

These surveys by members of the Society, the principal family history society for Staffordshire, Warwickshire and Worcestershire, founded 1963, are an ongoing (1980s-). Sometimes surveys are made by other individuals or groups (mainly Women's' Institutes) working under BMSGH auspices. The surveys, as yet, do not cover all Staffordshire, although each survey is comprehensive. Four copies of each survey made are deposited at:- 1). SRO and or WSL. 2). Birmingham Reference Library. 3). Society of Genealogists, London, and 4). the BMSGH Library, Margaret St, Birmingham. In addition, SCA, holds CDRom copies.

GENealogy, United Kingdom & Ireland surveys (GENUKI)

This is the internet's GENUKI website (1995), an enormous genealogy service, and specifically its Memorial Inscription Collection in the Wishful Thinking's GENUKI: Staffordshire Pages. This is a list of monumental inscriptions recorded by individuals researching their own family history, so invariably not complete churchyard surveys. It began in 1986 with Rosemary Lockie's assembly of recordings, predominantly from the Peak District. However, others have contributed, recently. The Staffordshire collection is mainly by Alf Beard, but St Saviour, Aston-by-Stone, for example, is by Vicki Backhouse. Constantly updated, with even additions to an existing set of records, the site needs frequent checking.

Tillington

Eccleshall Road from an old postcard. Courtesy of Roy Lewis

Tillington

'the road running from Stafford to Eccleshall is now a wide, modern highway busy with traffic, but it was once a quiet country road and before that possibly little more than a track.'

Joan Rogers. A History of Eccleshall Road. 1985

SEE ALSO pages 46, 51, 61, 86, 100, 120, 186, 187, 195, 209, 230, 231-232

Berry (1)

Tillington CP 1858-1917. Tillington PC 1894-1917 was served by the same clerk for its entirety. Mr Charles Wall, painter, of Marston road, was nominated to the 1896 council but withdrew, owing to non-residence in the parish. He was cordially thanked for his services on the late council (SA March 14 1896 p3. April 7 1917 p6). Creswell CP 1917-34. Stafford unparished 1934-88. Creswell CP 1988-

LG. Stafford RD 1894-1934, B 1934-74, D(B) 1974-. West W 1934-60. Tillington W 1960-2002.

CED. Stafford Rural 1889-1911. Stafford Rural West Sept 1911-34. Stafford West 1934-1957. Stafford North 1957-77. Stafford North Gate 1977-88. Eccleshall 1988-2005. Gnosall & Doxey 2005-

PLU. Stafford 1858-1930. Tillington with Creswell W by 1910.

Berry (2)

Tillington CP 1858-1917. Creswell CP 1917-2002. PC 1962-. Stafford unparished 2002-.

LG. Stafford RD 1894-1974, D(B) 1974-. Seighford W 1974-2002. Tillington W 2002-.

CED. Stafford Rural 1889-1911. Stafford Rural West Sept 1911-34. Stafford Rural 1934-73. Stafford Rural No. 2 1973-81. Eccleshall 1981-2002. Stafford North Gate 2002-5. Stafford North 2005-

PLU. Stafford 1858-1930. Tillington with Creswell W by 1910.

Boundary Farm

Tillington CP 1858-1917. Creswell CP 1917-34. Stafford unparished 1934-.

LG. Stafford RD 1894-1934, B 1934-74 D(B) 1974-. West W 1934-60. Tillington W 1960-2002. Holmcroft W 2002-.

CED. Stafford Rural 1889-1911. Stafford Rural West

Sept 1911-34. Stafford West 1934-1957. Stafford North 1957-77. Stafford North Gate 1977-2005. Stafford North 2005-.

PLU. Stafford 1858-1930. Tillington with Creswell W by1910.

Boundary Flash

Tillington CP 1858-1917. Creswell CP 1917-34. Stafford unparished 1934-.

LG. Stafford RD 1894-1934, B 1934-74 D(B) 1974-. West W 1934-60. Tillington W 1960-2002. Tillington W 2002-.

CED. Stafford Rural 1889-1911. Stafford Rural West Sept 1911-34. Stafford West 1934-1957. Stafford North 1957-77. Stafford North Gate 1977-2005. Stafford North 2005-.

PLU. Stafford 1858-1930. Tillington with Creswell W by1910.

The Darling (1)

Tillington CP 1858-1917. Creswell CP 1917-2002. PC 1962-. Stafford unparished 2002-

LG. Stafford RD 1894-1974, D(B) 1974-. Seighford W 1974-2002. Tillington W 2002-.

CED. Stafford Rural 1889-1911. Stafford Rural West Sept 1911-34. Stafford Rural 1934-73. Stafford Rural No. 2 1973-81. Stafford Eccleshall 1981-2002. Stafford North Gate 2002-5. Gnosall & Doxey 2005-

PLU. Stafford 1858-1930. Tillington with Creswell W by1910.

The Darling (2)

Tillington CP 1858-1917. Stafford unparished 1917-.

LG. Stafford RD 1894-1917, B 1917-74 D(B) 1974-. West W 1917-60. Tillington W 1960-2002. Tillington W 2002-.

CED. Stafford Rural 1889-1911. Stafford Rural West Sept 1911-9. Stafford West 1919-1957. Stafford North 1957-77. Stafford North Gate 1977-2005. Gnosall & Doxey 2005-.

PLU. Stafford 1858-1930. (Stafford) West W by1910.

The Darling (3) & (4)

Tillington CP 1858-1917. Creswell CP 1917-2002. PC 1962-. Stafford unparished 2002-5. Doxey CP April 2005-.

LG. Stafford RD 1894-1974, D(B) 1974-. Seighford W 1974-2002. Tillington W 2002-.

CED. Stafford Rural 1889-1911. Stafford Rural West Sept 1911-34. Stafford Rural 1934-73. Stafford Rural No. 2 1973-81. Stafford Eccleshall 1981-2002. Stafford North Gate 2002-5. Gnosall & Doxey 2005-

PLU. Stafford 1858-1930. Tillington with Creswell W by1910.

Elm House

Tillington CP 1858-1917. Stafford unparished 1917-.

LG. Stafford RD 1894-1917, B 1917-74 D(B) 1974-.

West W 1917-60. Tillington W 1960-c1981. Common W c1981-2002. Common W 2002-.

CED. Stafford Rural 1889-1911. Stafford Rural West Sept 1911-9. Stafford West 1919-1957. Stafford North 1957-77. Stafford North Gate 1977-2005. Stafford North 2005-.

PLU. Stafford 1858-1930. (Stafford) West W by1910.

Motorway

Tillington CP 1858-1917. Creswell 1917-34. Stafford unparished 1934-88. Creswell CP 1988-

LG. Stafford RD 1894-1934, B 1934-74, D(B) 1974-. West W 1934-60. Tillington W 1960-88. Seighford W 1988-2002, 2002-.

CED. Stafford Rural 1889-1911. Stafford Rural West Sept 1911-34. Stafford West 1934-1957. Stafford North 1957-77. Stafford North Gate 1977-88. Eccleshall 1988-2005. Gnosall & Doxey 2005-.

PLU. Stafford 1858-1930. Tillington with Creswell W by1910.

Parkside

Tillington CP 1858-1917. Stafford unparished 1917-.

LG. Stafford RD 1894-1917, B 1917-74, D(B) 1974-. East W 1917-60. Holmcroft W 1960-2002. Holmcroft W 2002-.

CED. Stafford Rural 1889-1911. Stafford Rural West Sept 1911-9. Stafford East 1919-1957. Stafford North 1957-77. Stafford North Gate 1977-2005. Stafford North 2005-.

PLU. Stafford 1858-1930. (Stafford) East W by1910.

Premier Lodge

Tillington CP 1858-1917. Creswell CP 1917-. PC 1962-.

LG. Stafford RD 1894-1974, D(B) 1974-. Seighford W 1974-2002, 2002-.

CED. Stafford Rural 1889-1911. Stafford Rural West Sept 1911-34. Stafford Rural 1934-73. Stafford Rural No. 2 1973-81. Eccleshall 1981-2005. Gnosall & Doxey 2005-,

PLU. Stafford 1858-1930. Tillington with Creswell W by1910.

Redhill Gorse

Tillington CP 1858-1917. Creswell CP 1917-2002. PC 1962-. Stafford unparished 2002-.

LG. Stafford RD 1894-1974, D(B) 1974-. Seighford W 1974-2002. Holmcroft W 2002-.

CED. Stafford Rural 1889-1911. Stafford Rural West Sept 1911-34. Stafford Rural 1934-73. Stafford Rural No. 2 1973-81. Eccleshall 1981-2002. Stafford North Gate 2002-5. Stafford North 2005-.

PLU. Stafford 1858-1930. Tillington with Creswell W by1910.

Stafford Common

Tillington

Tillington CP 1858-1917. Stafford unparished 1917-.
LG. Stafford RD 1894-1917, B 1917-74, D(B) 1974-.
East W 1917-60. Holmcroft W 1960-2002. Common
W 2002-.
CED. Stafford Rural 1889-1911. Stafford Rural West
Sept 1911-9. Stafford East 1919-1957. Stafford North
1957-77. Stafford North Gate 1977-2005. Stafford
North 2005-.
PLU. Stafford 1858-1930. (Stafford) East W by1910.

Tillington

Tillington CP 1858-1917. Stafford unparished 1917-.
LG. Stafford RD 1894-1917, B 1917-74, D(B) 1974-.
West W 1917-60. Tillington W 1960-2002. Tillington
W 2002-.
CED. Stafford Rural 1889-1911. Stafford Rural West
Sept 1911-9. Stafford West 1919-1957. Stafford North
1957-77. Stafford North Gate 1977-2005. Stafford
North 2005-.
PLU. Stafford 1858-1930. (Stafford) West W by1910.

Tillington Drain 1

Tillington CP 1858-1917. Stafford unparished 1917-.
LG. Stafford RD 1894-1917, B 1917-74, D(B) 1974-.
West W 1917-60. Tillington W 1960-c1981. Forebridge
W c1981-2002. Common W 2002-.
CED. Stafford Rural 1889-1911. Stafford Rural West
Sept 1911-9. Stafford West 1919-1957. Stafford North
1957-77. Stafford North Gate 1977-2005. Stafford
North 2005-.
PLU. Stafford 1858-1930. (Stafford) West W by1910.

Tillington Drain 2

Tillington CP 1858-1917. Stafford unparished 1917-.
LG. Stafford RD 1894-1917, B 1917-74, D(B) 1974-.
West W 1917-60. Tillington W 1960-c1981. Forebridge
W c1981-2002. Common W 2002-.
CED. Stafford Rural 1889-1911. Stafford Rural West
Sept 1911-9. Stafford West 1919-1957. Stafford North
1957-77. Stafford East Gate 1977-2005. Stafford North
2005-
PLU. Stafford 1858-1930. (Stafford) West W by1910.

Tillington Drain 3

Tillington CP 1858-1917. Stafford unparished 1917-.
LG. Stafford RD 1894-1917, B 1917-74, D(B) 1974-.
West W 1917-60. Tillington W 1960-c1981. Forebridge
W c1981-2002. Forebridge W 2002-.
CED. Stafford Rural 1889-1911. Stafford Rural West
Sept 1911-9. Stafford West 1919- 1957. Stafford North
1957-77. Stafford East Gate 1977-2005. Stafford Cen-
tral 2005-.
PLU. Stafford 1858-1930. (Stafford) West W by1910.

Tillington Drain 4

Tillington CP 1858-1917. Stafford unparished 1917-.
LG. Stafford RD 1894-1917, B 1917-74, D(B) 1974-.

West W 1917-60. Tillington W 1960-c1981. Forebridge
W c1981-2002. Forebridge W 2002-.
CED. Stafford Rural 1889-1911. Stafford Rural West
Sept 1911-9. Stafford West 1919-1957. Stafford North
1957-77. Stafford North Gate 1977-2005. Stafford
Central 2005-.
PLU. Stafford 1858-1930. (Stafford) West W by1910.

Tillington Drain 5

Tillington CP 1858-1917. Stafford unparished 1917-.
LG. Stafford RD 1894-1917, B 1917-74, D(B) 1974-.
West W 1917-60. Tillington W 1960-c1981. Common
W c1981-2002. Common W 2002-.
CED. Stafford Rural 1889-1911. Stafford Rural West
Sept 1911-9. Stafford West 1919-1957. Stafford North
1957-77. Stafford East Gate 1977-2005. Stafford North
2005-.
PLU. Stafford 1858-1930. (Stafford) West W by1910.

Tillington Farm

Tillington CP 1858-1917. Creswell CP 1917-34. Staf-
ford unparished 1934-.
LG. Stafford RD 1894-1934, B 1934-74, D(B) 1974-.
West W 1934-60. Tillington W 1960-2002. Tillington
W 2002-.
CED. Stafford Rural 1889-1911. Stafford Rural West
Sept 1911-34. Stafford West 1934-1957. Stafford North
1957-77. Stafford North Gate 1977-2005. Stafford
North 2005-
PLU. Stafford 1858-1930. (Stafford) West W by1910.

Tillington Hall

Tillington CP 1858-1917. Stafford unparished 1917-.
LG. Stafford RD 1894-1917, B 1917-74, D(B) 1974-.
West W 1917-60. Tillington W 1960-2002. Holmcroft
W 2002-.
CED. Stafford Rural 1889-1911. Stafford Rural West
Sept 1911-9. Stafford West 1919-1957. Stafford North
1957-77. Stafford North Gate 1977-2005. Stafford
North 2005-.
PLU. Stafford 1858-1930. (Stafford) West W by1910.

Tillington Pool

Tillington CP 1858-1917. Stafford unparished 1917-.
LG. Stafford RD 1894-1917, B 1917-74, D(B) 1974-.
West W 1917-60. Tillington W 1960-2002. Tillington
W 2002-.
CED. Stafford Rural 1889-1911. Stafford Rural West
Sept 1911-9. Stafford West 1919-1957. Stafford North
1957-77. Stafford North Gate 1977-2005. Stafford
North 2005-.
PLU. Stafford 1858-1930. (Stafford) West W by1910.

Trinity Fields

Tillington CP 1858-1917. Stafford unparished 1917-.
LG. Stafford RD 1894-1917, B 1917-74, D(B) 1974-.
West W 1917-60. Holmcroft W 1960-2002. Holmcroft

W 2002-.

CED. Stafford Rural 1889-1911. Stafford Rural West Sept 1911-9. Stafford West 1919- 57. Stafford North 1957-77. Stafford North Gate 1977-2005. Stafford North 2005-

PLU. Stafford 1858-1930. (Stafford) West W by1910.

Trinity Rise

Tillington CP 1858-1917. Creswell CP 1917-34. Stafford unparished 1934-.

LG. Stafford RD 1894-1934, B 1934-74, D(B) 1974-. West W 1934-60. Tillington W 1960-c1981. Holmcroft W c1981-2002. Holmcroft W 2002-.

CED. Stafford Rural 1889-1911. Stafford Rural West Sept 1911-34. Stafford West 1934-1957. Stafford North 1957-77. Stafford North Gate 1977-2005. Stafford North 2005-.

PLU. Stafford 1858-1930. Tillington with Creswell W by1910.

Warren Lane

Tillington CP 1858-1917. Creswell CP 1917-2002. PC 1962-. Stafford unparished 2002-.

LG. Stafford RD 1894-1974, D(B) 1974-. Seighford W 1974-2002. Tillington W 2002-.

CED. Stafford Rural 1889-1911. Stafford Rural West Sept 1911-34. Stafford Rural 1934-73. Stafford Rural No. 2 1973-81. Eccleshall 1981-2002. Stafford North Gate 2002-5. Stafford North 2005-

PLU. Stafford 1858-1930. Tillington with Creswell W by1910.

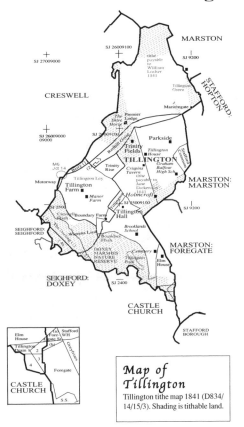

Map of Tillington
Tillington tithe map 1841 (D834/14/15/3). Shading is tithable land.

The tithes of Extra-parochial places

If an extra-parochial place had tithable land, that tithable land too was commuted to a rent-charge under the Tithe Commutation Act 1836. In four of the six Pirehill extra-parochial places this was the case. So that **Creswell**, **Tillington**, **Worston**, and **Yarlet** have tithe maps and awards; Creswell's is at LRO, the rest have copies at SRO. It is unknown whether **Chartley Holme** and **Ranton Abbey** ever had tithes to be commuted, but no awards were made. St Mary's collegiate church at Stafford had land and tithes in Creswell, Tillington, Worston, Yarlet, and on its dissolution these passed to the Crown. Subsequently, they were granted or sold off, really, to lay impropriators. I suppose, on the grounds of the church having held land and tithes in these places these places were nominally a part of St Mary's AP.

The Stafford Charities were impropriators of the Yarlet tithes (D834/14/15/6), a small parcel of land on the N boundary. William Kenderine, William Locker and Jane Dickinson were the impropriators of the Tillington tithes (D834/14/15/13), having the shaded area about Trinity Fields, the shaded area in the far north, and the shaded area about Walden Avenue, respectively. The Rector of Creswell was the impropriator of Creswell tithes. Essentially, Creswell Hall estate - owned by Rev Edward Whitby and Thomas Edward Whitby - alone was tithable, and adjoining it a small part of land, owned by the GJR, was also tithable. However, a great deal of Worston (see) was tithable; having belonged to Coton prebend in St Mary's collegiate church, Elizabeth I, granted the tithes to Stafford Corporation for the support the mother church (W p343).

Tixall

'How sweetly on that mouldering tower,
How sweetly on that ivy bower,
Whose branches through the ruins creep,
The Melancholy moon-beams sleep!'

Arthur Clifford. A Midnight Meditation Among The Ruins at Tixall. 1813

PLU. Stafford 1836-1930. Tixall W by1910.

SEE ALSO pages 7, 30, 51, 61, 54, 79, 86, 100, 120, 131, 186, 197, 209

TIXALL
Sow New Course

Tixall CP 1866-1934. Berkswich CP 1934-.
LG. Stafford RD 1894-1974, D(B) 1974-. Milford W 1974-2002, 2002-.
CED. Stafford Rural 1889-1911. Stafford Rural East Sept 1911-34. Stafford Rural 1934-73. Stafford Rural No. 2 1973-81. Stafford Trent Valley 1981-2005, 2005-
Tixall
Tixall CP 1866-. With a population between 100 and

300 Tixall was entitled to an Order to form a PC without consent of the CC. But the parish meeting in late 1894 voted against forming one (SA Dec 8 1894 p6). Minutes of annual parish meetings 1894-1925 (D3380/5/1). Ingestre with Tixall PC (a pg) 1979-. Tixall PW 1979-
LG. Stafford RD 1894-1974, D(B) 1974-. Milford W 1974-2002, 2002-.
CED. Stafford Rural 1889-1911. Stafford Rural East Sept 1911-34. Stafford Rural 1934-73. Stafford Rural No. 2 1973-81. Stafford Trent Valley 1981-2005, 2005-
.

The AONB and the CP

Exceptional landscapes can be designated Areas of Outstanding Natural Beauty (AONBs) under the National Parks and Access to the Countryside Act, 1949. To date there are 41 AONBs in England and Wales. The first was the Gower (1956); the most recent is Tamar Valley (1995). Cannock Chase, the second smallest and Staffordshire's only one, was designated in 1958. A joint advisory committee comprising members of amenity, nature and farming groups, Staffordshire CC, Stafford BC, other local authorities and PCs covering the AONB area, manage the AONB. The PCs of Tixall and Ingestre, and Colwich have representatives on the Committee, as the north end of the AONB stretches into those CPs; although in point of fact, Mary Booth, Chief Executive of Staffordshire Parish Councils' Association, represents Tixall and Ingestre. (One wonders whether the AONB was extended to cover Tixall village in 1984, when the village became a conservation area? -SN Feb 24 1984 p3). Both CPs and the AONB Committee have a reciprocal duty of care. As yet the Committee has not become a Conservation Board under section 86 of the Countryside and Rights of Way (CroW) Act 2000. But in 2004 it did publish a five-year management plan as required by section 89 of the Act.

In Cannock Chase AONB, is:- common land over which commoners have rights; a country park; Forestry Commission land; a Staffordshire Wildlife Trust reserve, a non-statutory but protected site, eg:- George's Hayes in Longdon; a Site of Special Scientific Interest (SSSI), eg:- Rawbones Meadow in Ingestre and Tixall; probably a Site of Biological Importance (SBI); they are locally important and lower than SSSI (in Staffordshire ranked into Grades 1 and 2: Staffs CC, Staffordshire Wildlife Trust and the Potteries Museum co-operate in servicing, monitoring, updating and keeping the records: Stoke-on-Trent CC has its own wildlife site system).

In the Chase AONB there could be - although there is not - a Local Nature Reserve (LNR); a Biosphere Reserve (BR), internationally recognised under UNESCO's Man and the Biosphere (MAB) programme 1971; a Marine Nature Reserve (MNR), established under the Wildlife and Countryside Act 1981; a Country Wildlife Site (CWSS), a League Against Cruel Sports creation, mainly in Somerset and Devon; a National Nature Reserve (NNR) (and one perhaps designated a Special Protection Area (SPA) under the EC Birds Directive, or a Special Area of Conservation (SAC) under the EC Habitats and Species Directive, or a Ramsar site under the Ramsar Convention).

Map of Tixall

Trentham (Blurton)

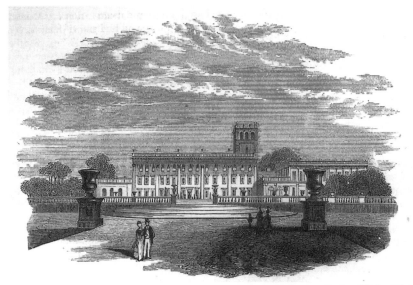

Trentham Hall, demolished 1912

Trentham

'then to Trentum and passed by a great house of Mr. Leveston Gore, and went on the side of a high hill below which the River Trent rann and turn'd its silver steame forward and backward into Ss which looked very pleasant circleing about the fine meadows in their flourishing tyme, bedecked with hay almost ripe and flowers;'

Celia Fiennes. Diary. 1698

In 1851 the township supported their poor cojointly.
SEE ALSO pages 6, 24, 27,49, 54, 79, 93, 103,124, 125, 130, 140, 186, 187, 190, 206-9, 214, 230

BLURTON TOWNSHIP
Barlaston Park
Trentham CP 1866-1932. The results of those elected to the first PC are published in SA Dec 22 1894 p6; the Duke of Sutherland was one. No poll demanded. Minutes 1917-32, and receipts and payments only for 1895 at SRO. Barlaston CP 1932-. Barlaston Park PW 2003-
Stone RD 1894-1974. Stafford D(B) 1974-. Barlaston W 1974-2002. Barlaston & Oulton W 2002-
CED. Stone 1889-1911. Stone Rural Sept 1911-2005. Barlaston & Fulford 2005-
PLU. Stone 1838-1930. Trentham W by1910.
Belgrave
Trentham CP 1866-94. Florence CP 1894-6. Longton CP March 31 1896-1910.

LG. Longton MB 1884-1910. Florence W 1884-95. Florence W 1895-1910. S-o-T CB 1910-74, D(C) 1974-97, UA 1997-. No. 25 W 1910-55. No. 22 W 1955-65. No. 22 W 1965-79. Blurton W 1979-2002. Longton South W 2002-
CED. Longton No. 1 or No. 2 1889-97. Longton No.1 or No. 2 or No. 3 1897-1910. CCWs 1974-97.
PLU. Stone 1838-96. S-u-T 1896-1922. S-u-T & Wolstanton 1922-30.
PARL. Stoke PB 1885-1918. Stoke D of S-o-T PB 1918-48. S-o-T South BC 1948-
Blurton
Trentham CP 1866-1922. Stoke unparished 1922-.
LG. Stone RD 1894-1922. S-o-T CB 1922-74, D(C) 1974-97, UA 1997-. No. 23 W 1922-55. No. 20 W 1955-65. No. 20 W 1965-79. Blurton W 1979-2002. Blurton W 2002-

CED. Stone 1889-1911. Stone Rural Sept 1911-22.
CCWs 1974-97.
PLU. Stone 1838-1922. Trentham W by1910. S-u-T
& Wolstanton 1922-1930. No. 23 W 1922-.

Blurton Road

Trentham CP 1866-1922. Stoke unparished 1922-.
LG. Stone RD 1894-1922. S-o-T CB 1922-74, D(C)
1974-97, UA 1997-. No. 23 W 1922-55. No. 20 W
1955-65. No. 20 W 1965-79. Blurton W 1979-2002.
Longton South W 2002-
CED. Stone 1889-1911. Stone Rural Sept 1911-22.
CCWs 1974-97.
PLU. Stone 1838-1922. Trentham W by1910. S-u-T
1922-1930.

Cocknage

Trentham CP 1866-1932. Barlaston CP 1932-.
Barlaston East PW 2003-
LG. Stone RD 1894-1974. Stafford D(B) 1974-.
Barlaston W 1974-2002. Barlaston & Oulton W 2002-
CED. Stone 1889-1911. Stone Rural Sept 1911-2005.
Barlaston & Fulford 2005-
PLU. Stone 1838-1930. Trentham W 1910-.

Daisy Bank

Trentham CP 1866-94. Florence CP 1894-6. Longton
CP 1896-1910. Stoke unparished 1910-.
LG. Longton MB 1884-1910. St Paul W 1884-1910.
S-o-T CB 1910-74, D(C) 1974-97, UA 1997-. No. 25
W 1910-55. No. 20 W 1955-65. No. 20 W 1965-79.
Longton South W 1979-. Longton South W 2002-
CED. Longton No. 1 or No. 2 1889-97. Longton No.1
or No. 2 or No. 3 1897-1910. CCWs 1974-97.
PLU. Stone 1838-96. S-u-T 1896-1922. S-u-T &
Wolstanton 1922-30. No. 25 W 1910-.
PARL. Stoke PB 1885-1918. Stoke D of S-o-T PB
1918-48. S-o-T South BC 1948-

Dresden

Trentham CP 1866-94. Florence CP 1894-6. Longton
CP 1896-1910.
LG. Longton MB 1884-1910. Dresden W 1884-1910.
S-o-T CB 1910-74, D(C) 1974-97, UA 1997-. No. 25
W 1910-55. No. 22 W 1955-65. No. 22 W 1965-79.
Blurton W 1979-2002. Longton South W 2002-
CED. Longton No. 1 or No. 2 1889-97. Longton No.1
or No. 2 or No. 3 1897-1910. CCWs 1974-97.
PLU. Stone 1838-96. S-u-T 1896-1922. S-u-T &
Wolstanton 1922-30. No. 25 W 1910-.
PARL. Stoke PB 1885-1918. Stoke D of S-o-T PB
1918-48. S-o-T South BC 1948-

Drubbery

Trentham CP 1866-94. Florence CP 1894-6. Longton
CP 1896-1910.
LG. Longton MB 1884-1910. Florence W 1884-95.

Trentham (Blurton)

Dresden W 1895-1910. S-o-T CB 1910-74, D(C) 1974-
97, UA 1997-. No. 25 W 1910-55. No. 20 W 1955-65.
No. 20 W 1965-79. Blurton W 1979-2002. Blurton W
2002-.
CED. Longton No. 1 or No. 2 1889-97. Longton No.1
or No. 2 or No. 3 1897-1910. CCWs 1974-97.
PLU. Stone 1838-96. S-u-T 1896-1922. S-u-T &
Wolstanton 1922-30. No. 25 W 1910-.
PARL. Stoke PB 1885-1918. Stoke D of S-o-T PB
1918-48. S-o-T South BC 1948-

Florence

Trentham 1866-94. Florence CP 1894-6. Longton CP
1896-1910.
LG. Longton MB 1884-1910. Florence W 1884-95. St
James W 1895-1910. S-o-T CB 1910-74, D(C) 1974-
97, UA 1997-. No. 25 W 1910-55. No. 22 W 1955-65.
Longton South W 1979-2002. Longton South W 2002-
CED. Longton No. 1 or No. 2 1889-97. Longton No.1
or No. 2 or No. 3 1897-1910. CCWs 1974-97.
PLU. Stone 1838-96. S-u-T 1896-1922. S-u-T &
Wolstanton 1922-30. No. 25 W 1910-.
PARL. Stoke PB 1885-1918. Stoke D of S-o-T PB
1918-48. S-o-T South BC 1948-

Furnace Bank

Trentham 1866-94. Florence CP 1894-6. Longton CP
1896-1910.
LG. Longton MB 1884-1910. Florence W 1884-95.
Normacot W 1895-1910. S-o-T CB 1910-74, D(C)
1974-97, UA 1997-. No. 26 W 1910-55. No. 22 W
1955-65. No. 22 W 1965-79. Longton South W 1979-
2002. Longton South W 2002-
CED. Longton No. 1 or No. 2 1889-97. Longton No.1
or No. 2 or No. 3 1897-1910. CCWs 1974-97.
PLU. Stone 1838-96. S-u-T 1896-1922. S-u-T &
Wolstanton 1922-30. No. 26 W 1910-.
PARL. Stoke PB 1885-1918. Stoke D of S-o-T PB
1918-48. S-o-T South BC 1948-

Lightwood

Trentham CP 1866-1922. Stoke unparished 1922-.
LG. Stone RD 1894-1922. S-o-T CB 1922-74, D(C)
1974-97, UA 1997-. No. 23 W 1922-55. No. 24 W
1955-65. No. 24 W 1965-79. Meir Park W 1979-2002.
Meir Park & Sandon W 2002-
CED. Stone 1889-1911. Stone Rural Sept 1911-22.
CCWs 1974-97.
PLU. Stone 1838-1922. Trentham W by1910. S-u-T
& Wolstanton 1922-30.

Longbrook

Trentham CP 1866-1922. Stoke unparished 1922-.
LG. Stone RD 1894-1922. S-o-T CB 1922-74, D(C)
1974-97, UA 1997-. No. 23 W 1922-55. No. 20 W
1955-65. No. 20 W 1965-79. Blurton W 1979-2002.

Trentham (Blurton)

Blurton W 2002-
CED. Stone 1889-1911. Stone Rural Sept 1911-22. CCWs 1974-97.
PLU. Stone 1838-1922. Trentham W by1910. S-u-T & Wolstanton 1922-30.

Longton Brook
Trentham CP 1866-1922. Stoke unparished 1922-.
LG. Stone RD 1894-1922. S-o-T CB 1922-74, D(C) 1974-97, UA 1997-. No. 21 W 1922-55. No. 18 W 1955-65. No. 18 W 1965-79. Trentham Park W 1979-2002. Trentham & Hanford 2002-
CED. Stone 1889-1911. Stone Rural Sept 1911-22. CCWs 1974-97.
PLU. Stone 1838-1922. Trentham W by1910. S-u-T & Wolstanton 1922-30.

Newstead
Trentham CP 1866-1932. Barlaston CP 1932-65. Stoke unparished 1965-.
LG. Stone RD 1894-1965. S-o-T CB 1965-74, D(C) 1974-97, UA 1997-. No. 18 W 1965-79. Blurton W 1979-. Blurton W 2002-
CED. Stone 1889-1911. Stone Rural Sept 1911-65. CCWs 1974-97.
PLU. Stone 1838-1930. Trentham W by1910-.

Newstead Farm
Trentham CP 1866-1922. Stoke unparished 1922-.
LG. Stone RD 1894-1922. S-o-T CB 1922-74, D(C) 1974-97, UA 1997-. No. 23 W 1922-55. No. 18 W 1955-65. No. 18 W 1965-79. Blurton W 1979-2002. Blurton W 2002-
CED. Stone 1889-1911. Stone Rural Sept 1911-22. CCWs 1974-97.
PLU. Stone 1838-1922. Trentham W by1910. S-u-T & Wolstanton 1922-30.

Newstead Plantation
Trentham CP 1866-1932. Barlaston CP 1932-1997.
LG. Stone RD 1894-1974. Stafford D(B) 1974-97. Barlaston W 1974-1997. S-o-T UA 1997-. Blurton W 1997-2002. Blurton W 2002-
CED. Stone 1889-1911. Stone Rural Sept 1911-97.
PLU. Stone 1838-1930. Trentham W by1910-.

Newstead Treatment Works
Trentham CP 1866-1932. Barlaston CP 1932-65.
LG. Stone RD 1894-1965. S-o-T CB 1965-74, D(C) 1974-97, UA 1997-. No. 18 W 1965-79. Blurton W 1979-2002. Blurton W 2002-
CED. Stone 1889-1911. Stone Rural Sept 1911-65. CCWs 1974-97.
PLU. Stone 1838-1930. Trentham W by1910-.

Newstead Treatment Works Extension
Trentham CP 1866-1932. Barlaston CP 1932-1997.
LG. Stone RD 1894-1974. Stafford D(B) 1974-97.

Barlaston W 1974-1997. S-o-T UA 1997-. Blurton W 1997-2002. Blurton W 2002-
CED. Stone 1889-1911. Stone Rural Sept 1911-97.
PLU. Stone 1838-1930. Trentham W by1910-.

Queen's Park
Trentham 1866-94. Florence CP 1894-6. Longton CP 1896-1910.
LG. Longton MB 1884-1910. Florence W 1884-95. Dresden W 1895-1910. S-o-T CB 1910-74, D(C) 1974-97, UA 1997-. No. 25 W 1910-55. No. 22 W 1955-65. No. 22 W 1965-79. Blurton W 1979-2002. Longton South W 2002-
CED. Longton No. 1 or No. 2 1889-97. Longton No.1 or No. 2 or No. 3 1897-1910. CCWs 1974-97.
PLU. Stone 1838-96. S-u-T 1896-1922. S-u-T & Wolstanton 1922-30. No. 25 W 1910-.
PARL. Stoke PB 1885-1918. Stoke D of S-o-T PB 1918-48. S-o-T South BC 1948-

Red Bank
Trentham CP 1866-94. Florence CP 1894-6. Longton CP 1896-1910. LG. Longton MB 1884-1910. Florence W 1884-95. Dresden W 1895-1910. S-o-T CB 1910-74, D(C) 1974-97, UA 1997-. No. 25 W 1910-55. No. 22 W 1955-65. No. 22 W 1965-79. Longton South W 1979-2002. Longton South W 2002-
CED. Longton No. 1 or No. 2 1889-97. Longton No.1 or No. 2 or No. 3 1897-1910. CCWs 1974-97.
PLU. Stone 1838-96. S-u-T 1896-1922. S-u-T & Wolstanton 1922-30. No. 25 W 1910-.
PARL. Stoke PB 1885-1918. Stoke D of S-o-T PB 1918-48. S-o-T South BC 1948-

Sutherland Avenue
Trentham CP 1866-94. Florence CP 1894-6. Longton CP 1896-1910.
LG. Longton MB 1884-1910. Florence W 1884-95. Dresden W 1895-1910. S-o-T CB 1910-74, D(C) 1974-97, UA 1997-. No. 25 W 1910-55. No. 20 1955-65. No. 20 W 1965-79. Blurton W 1979-2002. Longton South W 2002-
CED. Longton No. 1 or No. 2 1889-97. Longton No.1 or No. 2 or No. 3 1897-1910. CCWs 1974-97.
PLU. Stone 1838-96. S-u-T 1896-1922. S-u-T & Wolstanton 1922-30. No. 25 W 1910-.
PARL. Stoke PB 1885-1918. Stoke D of S-o-T PB 1918-48. S-o-T South BC 1948-

Sutherland Institute
Trentham CP 1866-94. Florence CP 1894-6. LG. Longton CP 1896-1910. Longton MB 1884-1910. Florence W 1884-1910. Stoke CB 1910-. No. 25 W 1910-55. No. 22 W 1955-65. Longton South W 1979-2002. Longton South W 2002-
CED. Longton No. 1 or No. 2 1889-97. Longton No.1

or No. 2 or No. 3 1897-1910.
PLU. Stone 1838-96. S-u-T 1896-1922. S-u-T & Wolstanton 1922-30. No. 25 W 1910-.
PARL. Stoke PB 1885-1918. Stoke D of S-o-T PB 1918-48. S-o-T South BC 1948-

Tilehurst
Trentham CP 1866-1922. Stoke unparished 1922-.
LG. Stone RD 1894-1922. S-o-T CB 1922-74, D(C) 1974-97, UA 1997-. No. 23 W 1922-55. No. 20 W 1955-65. No. 19 W 1965-79. Great Fenton W 1979-2002. Blurton W 2002-
CED. Stone 1889-1911. Stone Rural Sept 1911-22. CCWs 1974-97.
PLU. Stone 1838-1922. Trentham W by1910. S-u-T & Wolstanton 1922-30.

Trentham Road
Trentham CP 1866-94. Florence CP 1894-6. Longton CP 1896-1910.
LG. Longton MB 1884-1910. Florence W 1884-1910. S-o-T CB 1910-74, D(C) 1974-97, UA 1997-. No. 25 W 1910-55. No. 20 W 1955-65. No. 20 W 1965-79. Longton South W 1979-2002. Longton South W 2002-
CED. Longton No. 1 or No. 2 1889-97. Longton No.1 or No. 2 or No. 3 1897-1910. CCWs 1974-97.
PLU. Stone 1838-96. S-u-T 1896-1922. S-u-T & Wolstanton 1922-30. No. 25 W 1910-.
PARL. Stoke PB 1885-1918. Stoke D of S-o-T PB 1918-48. S-o-T South BC 1948-

Victoria
Trentham CP 1866-94. Florence CP 1894-6. Longton CP 1896-1910.
LG. Longton MB 1884-1910. Florence W 1884-1895. Meir W 1895-1910. S-o-T CB 1910-74, D(C) 1974-97, UA 1997-. No. 26 W 1910-55. No. 22 1955-65. No. 22 W 1965-79. Longton South W 1979-2002. Longton South W 2002-
CED. Longton No. 1 or No. 2 1889-97. Longton No.1 or No. 2 or No. 3 1897-1910. CCWs 1974-97.
PLU. Stone 1838-96. S-u-T 1896-1922. S-u-T & Wolstanton 1922-30. No. 26 W 1910-.
PARL. Stoke PB 1885-1918. Stoke D of S-o-T PB 1918-48. S-o-T South BC 1948-

BUTTERTON TOWNSHIP
PLU. Stone 1838-1930. Trentham W by1910-.
Butterton
Trentham CP 1866-1932. Whitmore CP 1932-.
LG. Stone RD 1894-1932. Newcastle-u-Lyme RD 1932-74, D(B) 1974-. No. 20 W Feb 1973-4. No. 21 W Feb 1974-9. Whitmore W 1979-2002. Loggerheads & Whitmore W 2002-.
CED. Stone 1889-1911. Stone Rural Sept 1911-34.

Trentham (Clayton Griffith)
Madeley 1934-81. Newcastle Rural 1981-2005, 2005-
Motorway (2)
Trentham CP 1866-1932. Whitmore CP 1932-84. Newcastle unparished 1984- (SI No. 152).
LG. Stone RD 1894-1932. Newcastle-u-Lyme RD 1932-74, D(B) 1974-. No. 20 W Feb 1973-4. No. 21 W Feb 1974-9. Whitmore W 1979-84. Seabridge W 1984-2002. Westlands W 2002-
CED. Stone 1889-1911. Stone Rural Sept 1911-34. Madeley 1934-81. Newcastle Rural 1981-4. Thistleberry 1984-2005. Keele & Westlands 2005-.

Motorway (3)
Trentham CP 1866-1932. Newcastle unparished 1932-
LG. Stone RD 1894-1932. Newcastle-u-Lyme MB 1932-74, D(B) 1974-. No. 3 W 1932-79. Seabridge W 1979-2002. Westlands W 2002-
CED. Stone 1889-1911. Stone Rural Sept 1911-34. Newcastle No. 2 1934-81. Thistleberry W 1981-2005. Keele & Westlands 2005-.

Motorway (4)
Trentham CP 1866-1932. Newcastle unparished 1932-84. Whitmore CP 1984- (SI No. 152).
LG. Stone RD 1894-1932. Newcastle-u-Lyme MB 1932-74, D(B) 1974-. No. 3 W 1932-79. Seabridge W 1979-84. Whitmore W 1984-2002. Loggerheads & Whitmore W 2002-.
CED. Stone 1889-1911. Stone Rural Sept 1911-34. Newcastle No. 2 1934-81. Thistleberry 1981-4. Newcastle Rural 1984-2005, 2005-.

Motorway (6)
Trentham CP 1866-1932. Whitmore CP 1932-84 (SI No. 152). Newcastle unparished 1984-.
LG. Stone RD 1894-1932. Newcastle-u-Lyme RD 1932-74, D(B) 1974-. No. 20 W Feb 1973-4. No. 21 W Feb 1974-9. Whitmore W 1979-84. Seabridge W 1979-2002, 2002-.
CED. Stone 1889-1911. Stone Rural Sept 1911-34. Madeley 1934-81. Newcastle Rural 1981-4. Thistleberry 1984-2005. Keele & Westlands 2005-.

Peacock Lane
Trentham CP 1866-1932. Whitmore CP 1932-?65. Swynnerton CP ?1965-. Trentham PW ?1965-.
LG. Stone RD 1894-1932. Newcastle-u-Lyme RD 1932-?65. Stone RD ?1965-74. Stafford D(B) 1974-. Swynnerton W 1974-2002, 2002-.
CED. Stone 1889-1911. Stone Rural Sept 1911-34. Madeley 1934-?65. Eccleshall ?1965-2005, 2005-.

CLAYTON GRIFFITH
Clayton Griffith Former township and manor separate to Clayton (Great Clayton) (W p236), alias Little Clayton (VCH vol 8 p77).

Trentham (Clayton Griffith)

Barker's Wood (N)

Trentham CP 1866-94. Keele CP 1894-1927. Newcastle unparished 1927-.

LG. Newcastle-u-Lyme RD 1894-1927, MB 1927-74, D(B) 1974-. West W 1927-32. No. 3 W 1932-79. Keele W 1979-2002, 2002-

CED. Stone 1889-95. Keele 1895-1927. Newcastle West 1927-34. Newcastle No. 2 1934-81. Keele & Silverdale 1981-2002. Keele & Westlands 2005-

PLU. Stone 1838-94. Newcastle-u-Lyme 1894-1930. Keele W by1910.

Barker's Wood (S)

Trentham CP 1866-94. Keele CP 1894-1932. Newcastle unparished 1932-.

LG. Newcastle-u-Lyme RD 1894-1932, MB 1932-74, D(B) 1974-. No. 3 W 1932-79. Keele W 1979-2002, 2002-

CED. Stone 1889-95. Keele 1895-1934. Newcastle No. 2 1934-81. Keele & Silverdale 1981-2005. Keele & Westlands 2005-

PLU. Stone 1838-94. Newcastle-u-Lyme 1894-1930. Keele W by1910.

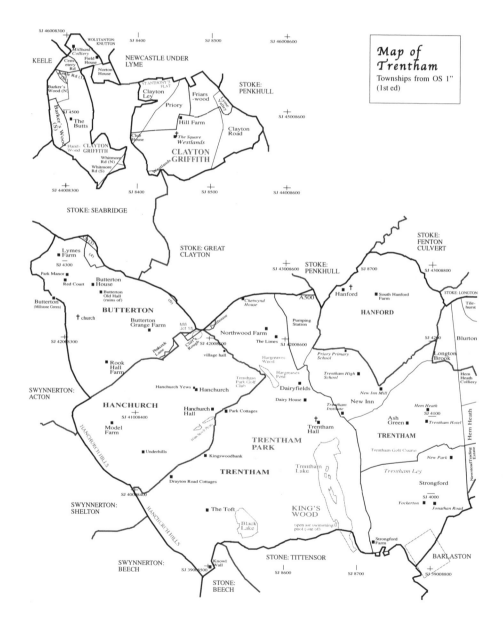

The Butts

Trentham CP 1866-94. Keele CP 1894-1927. Newcastle unparished 1927-.

LG. Newcastle-u-Lyme RD 1894-1927, MB 1927-74, D(B) 1974-. West W 1927-32. No. 3 W 1932-79. Thistleberry W 1979-2002, 2002-

CED. Stone 1889-95. Keele 1895-1928. Newcastle West 1928-34. Newcastle No. 2 1934-81. Keele & Silverdale 1981-2005. Keele & Westlands 2005-.

PLU. Stone 1838-94. Newcastle-u-Lyme 1894-1930. Keele W by1910.

Cemetery Road

Trentham CP 1866-94. Keele CP 1894-1927. Newcastle unparished 1927-2002. Silverdale CP May 2002-

LG. Newcastle-u-Lyme RD 1894-1927, MB 1927-74, D(B) 1974-. West W 1927-32. No. 2 W 1932-79. Silverdale W 1979-2002. Silverdale & Parksite W 2002-.

CED. Stone 1889-95. Keele 1895-1927. Newcastle West 1927-34. Newcastle No. 1 1934-81. Keele & Silverdale 1981-2005. Cross Heath & Silverdale 2005-

PLU. Stone 1838-94. Newcastle-u-Lyme 1894-1930. Keele W by1910.

Clayton Ley

Trentham CP 1866-96. Clayton CP 1896-1921. Newcastle unparished 1921-.

Trentham (Clayton Griffith)

LG. Stone RD 1894-96. Newcastle-u-Lyme RD 1896-1921, MB 1921-74, D(B) 1974-. West W 1921-32. No. 3 W 1932-79. Thistleberry W 1979-2002, 2002-

CED. Stone 1889-98. Keele 1898-1921. Newcastle West 1921-34. Newcastle No. 2 1934-81. Thistleberry 1981-2005. Keele & Westlands 2005-.

PLU. Stone 1838-96. Newcastle-u-Lyme 1896-1930. Clayton W by1910.

Clayton Road

Trentham CP 1866-96. Clayton CP 1896-1927. Newcastle unparished 1927-.

LG. Stone RD 1894-96. Newcastle-u-Lyme RD 1896-1927, MB 1927-74, D(B) 1974-. West W 1927-32. No. 3 W 1932-79. Clayton W 1979-2002, 2002-.

CED. Stone 1889-98. Keele 1898-1927. Newcastle West 1927-34. Newcastle No. 2 1934-81. Westlands 1981-2005. Newcastle South 2005-

PLU. Stone 1838-94. Newcastle-u-Lyme 1896-1930. Clayton W by1910.

Club House

Trentham CP 1866-96. Clayton CP 1896-1927. Newcastle unparished 1927-.

LG. Stone RD 1894-96. Newcastle-u-Lyme RD 1896-1927, MB 1927-74, D(B) 1974-. West W 1927-32. No. 3 W 1932-79. Thistleberry W 1979-2002, 2002-

CED. Stone 1889-98. Keele 1898-1927. Newcastle West 1927-34. Newcastle No. 2 1934-81. Thistleberry

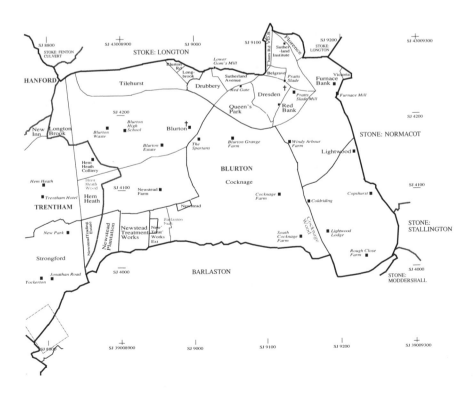

Trentham (Clayton Griffith)

1981-2005. Keele & Westlands 2005-
PLU. Stone 1838-94. Newcastle-u-Lyme 1896-1930.
Clayton W by1910.

Field House
Trentham CP 1866-94. Keele CP 1894-1927. Newcastle unparished 1927-.
LG. Newcastle-u-Lyme RD 1894-1927, MB 1927-74, D(B) 1974-. West W 1927-32. No. 2 W 1932-79. Thistleberry W 1979-2002, 2002-
CED. Stone 1889-95. Keele 1895-1927. Newcastle West 1927-34. Newcastle No. 1 1934-81. Thistleberry 1981-2005. Keele & Westlands 2005-
PLU. Stone 1838-94. Newcastle-u-Lyme 1894-1930. Keele W by1910.

Friarswood
Trentham CP 1866-77. Newcastle unparished 1877-.
LG. Newcastle-u-Lyme MB 1877-1974, D(B) 1974-. West W 1877-1932. No. 3 W 1932-79. Westlands W 1979-2002, 2002-
CED. Newcastle West 1889-1934. Newcastle No. 2 1934-81. Westlands 1981-2005. Keele & Westlands 2005-
PLU. Stone 1838-77. Newcastle-u-Lyme 1877-1930. Newcastle W by1910.

Hill Farm
Trentham CP 1866-96. Clayton CP 1896-1927. Newcastle unparished 1927-.
LG. Stone RD 1894-96. Newcastle-u-Lyme RD 1896-1927, MB 1927-74, D(B) 1974-. West W 1927-32. No. 3 W 1932-79. Westlands W 1979-2002, 2002-
CED. Stone 1889-98. Keele 1898-1927. Newcastle West 1927-34. Newcastle No. 2 1934-81. Westlands 1981-2005. Keele & Westlands 2005-
PLU. Stone 1838-96. Newcastle-u-Lyme 1896-1930. Clayton W by1910.

Keele Road (1)
Trentham CP 1866-94. Keele CP 1894-1927. Newcastle unparished 1927-.
LG. Newcastle-u-Lyme RD 1894-1927, MB 1927-74, D(B) 1974-. West W 1927-32. No. 2 W 1932-79. Thistleberry W 1979-2002, 2002-
CED. Stone 1889-95. Keele 1895-1927. Newcastle West 1927-34. Newcastle No. 1 1934-81. Thistleberry 1981-2005. Keele & Westlands 2005-
PLU. Stone 1838-94. Newcastle-u-Lyme 1894-1930. Keele W by1910.

Keele Road (2)
Trentham CP 1866-94. Keele CP 1894-1927. Newcastle unparished 1927-.
LG. Newcastle-u-Lyme RD 1894-1927, MB 1927-74, D(B) 1974-. West W 1927-32. No. 2 W 1932-79. Thistleberry W 1979-2002. Keele W 2002-

CED. Stone 1889-95. Keele 1895-1927. Newcastle West 1927-34. Newcastle No. 1 1934-81. Thistleberry 1981-2005. Keele & Westlands 2005-.
PLU. Stone 1838-94. Newcastle-u-Lyme 1894-1930. Keele W by1910.

Lyme Valley
Trentham CP 1866-77. Newcastle unparished 1877-
LG. Newcastle-u-Lyme MB 1877-1974, D(B) 1974-. West W 1877-1932. No. 3 W 1932-79. Clayton W 1979-2002, 2002-
CED. Newcastle West 1889-1934. Newcastle No. 2 1934-81. Westlands 1981-2005. Newcastle South 2005-.
PLU. Stone 1838-77. Newcastle-u-Lyme 1877-1930. Newcastle W by1910.

Norton House
Trentham CP 1866-94. Keele CP 1894-1921. Newcastle unparished 1921-.
LG. Newcastle-u-Lyme RD 1894-1921, MB 1921-74, D(B) 1974-. West W 1921-32. No. 2 W 1932-79. Thistleberry W 1979-2002, 2002-
CED. Stone 1889-95. Keele 1895-1921. Newcastle West 1921-34. Newcastle No. 1 1934-81. Thistleberry 1981-2005. Keele & Westlands 2005-.
PLU. Stone 1838-94. Newcastle-u-Lyme 1894-1930. Keele W by1910.

Priory
Trentham CP 1866-96. Clayton CP 1896-1921. Newcastle unparished 1921-.
LG. Stone RD 1894-96. Newcastle-u-Lyme RD 1896-1921, MB 1921-74, D(B) 1974-. West W 1921-32. No. 3 W 1932-. Westlands W by1981-, 2002-
CED. Stone 1889-98. Keele 1898-1921. Newcastle West 1921-34. Newcastle No. 2 1934-81. Westlands 1981-2005. Keele & Westlands 2005-
PLU. Stone 1838-96. Newcastle-u-Lyme 1896-1930. Clayton W by1910.

Westlands
Trentham CP 1866-96. Clayton CP 1896-1927. Newcastle unparished 1927-.
LG. Stone RD 1894-96. Newcastle-u-Lyme RD 1896-1927, MB 1927-74, D(B) 1974-. West W 1927-32. No. 3 W 1932-79. Thistleberry W 1979-2002. Westlands W 2002-
CED. Stone 1889-98. Keele 1898-1927. Newcastle West 1927-34. Newcastle No. 2 1934-81. Thistleberry 1981-2005. Keele & Westlands 2005-.
PLU. Stone 1838-96. Newcastle-u-Lyme 1896-1930. Clayton W by1910.

Whitmore Road (N)
Trentham CP 1866-94. Keele CP 1894-1927. Newcastle unparished 1927-.

LG. Newcastle-u-Lyme RD 1894-1927, MB 1927-74, D(B) 1974-. West W 1927-32. No. 3 W 1932-79. Westlands W 1979-2002, 2002-
CED. Stone 1889-95. Keele 1895-1927. Newcastle West 1927-34. Newcastle No. 2 1934-81. Westlands 1981-2005. Keele & Westlands 2005-
PLU. Stone 1838-94. Newcastle-u-Lyme 1894-1930. Keele W by1910.

Whitmore Road (S)
Trentham CP 1866-94. Keele CP 1894-1927. Newcastle unparished 1927-.
LG. Newcastle-u-Lyme RD 1894-1927, MB 1927-74, D(B) 1974-. West W 1927-32. No. 3 W 1932-79. Seabridge W 1979-2002. Westlands W 2002-
CED. Stone 1889-95. Keele 1895-1927. Newcastle West 1927-34. Newcastle No. 2 1934-81. Thistleberry 1981-2005. Keele & Westlands 2005-.
PLU. Stone 1838-94. Newcastle-u-Lyme 1894-1930. Keele W by1910.

HANCHURCH TOWNSHIP
PLU. Stone 1838-1930. Trentham W by1910-.
Cliff's Rough
Trentham CP 1866-1932. Whitmore CP 1932-?65 Swynnerton CP ?1965-. Trentham PW ?1965-.
LG. Stone RD 1894-1932. Newcastle-u-Lyme RD 1932-?65. Stone RD ?1965-74. Stafford D(B) 1974-. Swynnerton W 1974-2002, 2002.
CED. Stone 1889-1911. Stone Rural Sept 1911-34. Madeley 1934-?65. Eccleshall ?1965-2005, 2005-
Hanchurch
Trentham CP 1866-1932. Swynnerton CP 1932-. Trentham PW Nov 1954-.
LG. Stone RD 1894-1974. Stafford D(B) 1974-. Swynnerton W 1974-2002, 2002-.
CED. Stone 1889-1911. Stone Rural Sept 1911-34. Eccleshall 1934-2005, 2005-.
M6 Jct 15
Trentham CP 1866-1932. Whitmore CP 1932-
LG. Stone RD 1894-1932. Newcastle-u-Lyme RD 1932-74, D(B) 1974-. No. 20 W Feb 1973-4. No. 21 W Feb 1974-9. Whitmore W 1979-2002. Loggerheads & Whitmore W 2002-.
CED. Stone 1889-1934. Madeley 1934-81. Newcastle Rural 1981-2005, 2005-.

HANFORD TOWNSHIP
Trentham CP 1866-1922. Stoke unparished 1922-.
LG. Stone RD 1894-1922. S-o-T CB 1922-74, D(C) 1974-97, UA 1997-. No. 21 W 1922-55. No. 18 W 1955-65. No. 18 W 1965-79. Trentham Park W 1979-2002. Trentham & Hanford W 2002-

Trentham (Trentham)
CED. Stone 1889-1911. Stone Rural Sept 1911-22. CCWs 1974-97.
PLU. Stone 1838-1922. Trentham W by1910-. S-u-T & Wolstanton 1922-30.

TRENTHAM TOWNSHIP
A500
Trentham CP 1866-96. Clayton CP 1896-1932. Newcastle unparished 1932-65. Stoke unparished 1965-
LG. Stone RD 1894-6. Newcastle-u-Lyme RD 1896-1932, MB 1932-65. No. 3 W 1932-65. S-o-T CB 1965-74, D(C) 1974-97, UA 1997-. No. 17 W 1965-79. Trentham Park W 1979-2002. Trentham & Hanford W 2002-
CED. Stone 1889-98. Bucknall 1898-1922. Keele 1922-34. Newcastle No. 2 1934-65. CCWs 1974-97.
PLU. Stone 1838-96. Newcastle-u-Lyme 1896-1930. Clayton W by1910.
Ash Green
Trentham CP 1866-1922. Stoke unparished 1922-
LG. Stone RD 1894-1922. S-o-T CB 1922-74, D(C) 1974-97, UA 1997-. No. 23 W 1922-55. No. 18 1955-65. No. 18 W 1965-79. Trentham Park W 1979-2002. Trentham & Hanford W 2002-
CED. Stone 1889-1911. Stone Rural Sept 1911-22. CCWs 1974-97.
PLU. Stone 1838-1922. Trentham W by1910-. S-u-T & Wolstanton 1922-30.
Hem Heath
Trentham CP 1866-1922. Stoke unparished 1922-.
LG. Stone RD 1894-1922. S-o-T CB 1922-74, D(C) 1974-97, UA 1997-. No. 23 W 1922-55. No. 18 W 1955-65. No. 18 W 1965-79. Blurton W 1979-2002. Blurton W 2002-.
CED. Stone 1889-1911. Stone Rural Sept 1911-22. CCWs 1974-97.
PLU. Stone 1838-1922. Trentham W by1910-. S-u-T & Wolstanton 1922-30.
Hem Heath Colliery
Trentham CP 1866-1922. Stoke unparished 1922-.
LG. Stone RD 1894-1922. S-o-T CB 1922-74, D(C) 1974-97, UA 1997-. No. 23 W 1922-55. No. 20 W 1955-65. No. 20 W 1965-79. Blurton W 1979-2002. Blurton W 2002-.
CED. Stone 1889-1911. Stone Rural Sept 1911-22. CCWs 1974-97.
PLU. Stone 1838-1922. Trentham W by1910-. S-u-T & Wolstanton 1922-30.
New Inn
Trentham CP 1866-1922. Stoke unparished 1922-.
LG. Stone RD 1894-1922. S-o-T CB 1922-74, D(C) 1974-97, UA 1997-. No. 21 W 1922-55. No. 18 W

Trentham (Trentham)

1955-65. No. 18 W 1965-79. Trentham Park W 1979-2002. Trentham & Hanford W 2002-

CED. Stone 1889-1911. Stone Rural Sept 1911-22. CCWs 1974-97.

PLU. Stone 1838-1922. Trentham W by1910-. S-u-T & Wolstanton 1922-30.

Newstead Trading Estate

Trentham CP 1866-1932. Barlaston CP 1932-97.

LG. Stone RD 1894-1974. Stafford D(B) 1974-97. Barlaston W 1974-97. S-o-T UA 1997-. Blurton W 1997-2002. Blurton W 2002-

CED. Stone 1889-1911. Stone Rural Sept 1911-97.

PLU. Stone 1838-1930. Trentham W by1910-.

Posthouse

Trentham CP 1866-?96. Clayton CP ?1896-1932. Newcastle unparished 1932-.

LG. Stone RD 1894-1932. Newcastle-u-Lyme MB 1932-74, D(B) 1974-. No. 3 W 1932-79. Seabridge W 1979-2002, 2002-

CED. Stone 1889-98. Bucknall 1898-1922. Keele 1922-34. Newcastle No. 2 1934-81. Thistleberry W 1981-2005. Newcastle South 2005-.

PLU. Stone 1838-?96. Newcastle-u-Lyme ?1896-1930. Clayton by1910-.

Pumping Station

Trentham CP 1866-1922. Stoke unparished 1922-.

LG. Stone RD 1894-1922. S-o-T CB 1922-74, D(C) 1974-97, UA 1997-. No. 21 W 1922-55. No. 18 W 1955-65. No. 17 W 1965-79. Trentham Park W 1979-2002. Trentham & Hanford W 2002-

CED. Stone 1889-1911. Stone Rural Sept 1911-22.

CCWs 1974-97.

PLU. Stone 1838-1922. Trentham W by1910-. S-u-T & Wolstanton 1922-30.

Strongford

Trentham CP 1866-1929. Stoke unparished 1929-.

LG. Stone RD 1894-1929. S-o-T CB 1929-74, D(C) 1974-97, UA 1997-. No. 23 W 1929-55. No. 18 W 1955-65. No. 18 W 1965-79. Trentham Park W 1979-2002. Trentham & Hanford W 2002-

CED. Stone 1889-1911. Stone Rural Sept 1911-29. CCWs 1974-97.

PLU. Stone 1838-1929. Trentham W by1910-. S-u-T & Wolstanton 1929-30.

Strongford Bridge

Trentham CP 1866-1929. Stoke unparished 1929-65. Swynnerton CP 1965-. Trentham PW 1965-.

LG. Stone RD 1894-1929. S-o-T CB 1929-65. No. 23 W 1929-55. No. 18 W 1955-65. Stone RD 1965-74. Stafford D(B) 1974-. Swynnerton W 1974-2002, 2002-

CED. Stone 1889-1911. Stone Rural Sept 1911-29. Eccleshall 1965-2005, 2005-.

PLU. Stone 1838-1929. Trentham W by1910-. S-u-T & Wolstanton 1929-30.

Trentham

Trentham CP 1866-1932. Swynnerton CP 1932-. Trentham PW Nov 1954-.

LG. Stone RD 1894-1974. Stafford D(B) 1974-. Swynnerton W 1974-2002, 2002-.

CED. Stone 1889-1911. Stone Rural Sept 1911-34. Eccleshall 1934-2005, 2005-.

PLU. Stone 1838-1930. Trentham W by1910-.

Family papers

A great SRO archive is the Sutherland Collection. The largest accession of the Collection, D593, lent by the Sutherland family since 1959, is currently (2005) for sale. A smaller accession, D4092, was secured by SRO after the Sutherlands sold Trentham in the 1980s. Stafford BC has agreed to give £10,000 towards the £1.9 million needed to buy the Sutherland Collection. Items include James Brindley's 1759 prototype plan for the Trent and Mersey Canal canal, and Lancelot 'Capability' Brown's plan for the landscaping of Trentham Park. Funding applications have already been submitted to a variety of organisations, including the Heritage Lottery Fund. Cash injections have also been provided by Staffs CC, Stoke-on-Trent City C, Staffordshire Environment Fund, and Friends of the National Libraries group. Parish and district councils have also been approached for help (SN Jan 6 2005 p9). The index catalogues for D593 in SRO stretch to 20 volumes; and there is even an index to the index. There are 22 subject headings, each having a particular letter of the alphabet (and these letters appear after the main accession number). Below, are the subject headings, with, in brackets, a content example:-

A - Medieval deeds (Mucklestone 1378-1525)

B - Title deeds (Barlaston 1641-1874)

C - General deeds (marriage settlements in which George Granville, Marquis of Stafford, had a part 1814-23)

D - Draft and copy deeds (North Staffordshire Estate 1893-1914)

E - Legal (17th Century cases brought on behalf of Dame Margaret Leveson, a lunatic, widow of Admiral Sir Richard Leveson, 1611-39/40)

F - Accounts and vouchers (Newcastle accts and vouchers 1775-1812)

G - Rentals (Newcastle-under-Lyme Rentals 1804-75, 1813-96)

H - Maps, plans, surveys (Coal mining & engineering drawings of the Longton area)

I - Leases (North Staffordshire Estate 1545/6-1920)

J - Manor Court rolls and papers (Trentham 1461-1833)

K - Estate correspondence (James and George Loch, personal letters 1824-75)

L - Estate memoranda and reports (Trentham agents' memoranda 1810-1910)

M - Mining records (Foley Colliery, Hanley Colliery, Meirheath Colliery)

N - Estate agency records (Cash books, Day books and ledgers 1722-1932)

O - Other estate documents (insurance 1762-1867)

P - Personal (correspondence of George Granville, 2nd Marquis of Stafford, later 1st Duke of Sutherland, and his wife (Countess of Sutherland in her own right) 1814-32

Q - Private Secretaries letters and papers (Thomas Jackson's correspondence 1835-66)

R - Household (Duchesses' vouchers and accounts 1827-90)

S - Public Office (Newcastle-under-Lyme by-/ elections 1675-77, 1685, 1714-15, 1724, 1734-5, 1740, 1747, 1752-4, 1790, 1792, 1793, 1802, 1823)

T - Solicitors' Papers (Newcastle-under-Lyme sales of property 1781-1853, Newcastle Rentals 1776-1816)

U - Miscellaneous Personal Mss

V - Private Material (Sale catalogues of the Sutherland estates in North Staffordshire 1893-1933)

Leveson-Gower (Sutherland) or other family papers which have some link - whether deed, lease, rental, valuation, inventory, survey, estate map, account, manorial record, correspondence, diary - with a particular parish, and so might help in the writing of the history of that parish, are listed below under the parish concerned (for the comprehensive list see Staffordshire Family Collections (1992) Staffordshire Archive Service), in SRO, unless otherwise stated:

ABBOTS BROMLEY
Bagot, Legge, Littleton, Paget

ADBASTON
Whitworth (WSL)

ASHLEY
Chetwynd, Davenport, Fletcher/ Fletcher-Boughey, Aston (WSL), Chetwynd (WSL)

AUDLEY
Fletcher/ Fletcher-Boughey, Heathcote, Hill Child, Vernon-Yonge, Wedgwood of Bignall End, Aston (WSL)

BARTHOMLEY
Balterley -Twemlow/ Fletcher-Twemlow, Stafford

BARLASTON
Broughton-Adderley (CRO & SRO), **Leveson-Gower**, Stafford, Parker-Jervis (WSL)

BETLEY
Fletcher/ Fletcher-Boughey, Twemlow/ Fletcher-Twemlow, Vernon-Yonge

BIDDULPH
Mainwaring/ Cavenagh-Mainwaring papers, Heathcote, Sparrow (WSL)

BLITHFIELD
Bagot, Sneyd-Kynnersley

BURSLEM
Landor, Wedgwood (KUL), Wedgwood of Bignall End, Wood of Brownhills, Bourne of

Trentham

Newcastle (WSL), Sparrow (WSL)

Hulton - Aston (WSL)

CHEBSEY

Anson, Giffard, Anson (WSL)

COLTON

Bagot, Landor, Anson (WSL), Anson (WSL)

COLWICH

Anson, Chetwynd, Paget, Wolseley, Anson (WSL), Sparrow (WSL)

Fradswell - Ryder, Swinfen/ Swinfen-Bourn (SRO & WSL)

DRAYTON-IN-HALES

Tyrley - Anson, Broughton, Fletcher/ Fletcher-Boughey, Meynell/ Meynell-Ingram

ECCLESHALL

Philips, Pilkington, Salt, Stafford, Vernon of Hilton, Bourne of Newcastle (WSL), Sparrow (WSL), Parker-Jervis (WSL), Salt of Weeping Cross (WSL)

Aspley - Vernon-Yonge

Broughton - Delves-Broughton (CRO)

Charnes - Vernon-Yonge

Chorlton - Davenport, **Leveson-Gower**

Cotes - Cotes papers, Salt of Weeping Cross (WSL)

Croxton -Vernon-Yonge

Eccleshall - Cotes, Fletcher/ Fletcher-Boughey, Giffard

Gerards Bromley - Fletcher/ Fletcher-Boughey, Vernon-Yonge

Pershall - Broughton, Pershall (WSL), Salt of Weeping Cross (WSL)

Podmore - Whitworth (WSL)

Slindon - Salt, Pershall (WSL)

Sugnall - Chetwynd (WSL)

ELLENHALL

Anson (SRO & WSL)

GAYTON

Ryder

HIGH OFFLEY

Anson, Whitworth (WSL)

INGESTRE

Chetwynd (SRO & WSL)

KEELE

Sneyd (KUL)

MADELEY

Heathcote, Levett, Stafford, Vernon-Yonge

MAER

Davenport

MILWICH

Knight, Ryder, Vernon of Milwich, Aston (WSL)

MUCKLESTONE

Chetwode, Levett

NEWCASTLE-U-LYME

Duchy of Lancaster (PRO), Fletcher/ Fletcher-Boughey, **Leveson-Gower**, Pilkington, Bagnall (WSL), Bourne of Newcastle (WSL), Sparrow (WSL)

NORTON-IN-THE-MOORS

Adderley (BPL), Heathcote, Sparrow (SRO & WSL), Stafford, Bagnall (WSL), Chetwynd (WSL),

RANTON

Anson, Eld

SANDON

Knight, Ryder

SEIGHFORD

Eld, Sparrow, Stafford

STAFFORD

Stafford, Chetwynd (WSL), Parker-Jervis (WSL), Sneyd of Byrley Lodge (WSL)

Hopton - Chetwynd (SRO & WSL)

Salt & Enson - Chetwynd (SRO & WSL)

St Mary - Chetwynd (SRO), Dickenson (SRO & WSL), Giffard, Kenderine

Sow - Fowler (WSL)

STANDON

Chetwynd, Fletcher/ Fletcher-Boughey, Salt of Weeping Cross (WSL)

STOKE-UPON-TRENT

Sparrow (WSL)

Bagnall - Sparrow (WSL)

Bucknall - Landor, Sparrow (SRO & WSL)

Fenton - Allen-Simpkin, Broad, Fletcher/ Fletcher-Boughey

Fenton Vivian - Parker-Jervis (WSL)

Hanley - Allen-Simpkin

Longton - Heathcote, **Leveson-Gower**, Parker-Jervis (WSL)

Penkhull -Fletcher/ Fletcher-Boughey

STONE

Knight, Bagnall (WSL)

Aston (Burston) - Ryder

Beech - **Leveson-Gower**

Darlaston - Mainwaring/ Cavenagh-Mainwaring, **Leveson-Gower**

Fulford - Allen-Simpkin, Knight

Hilderstone - Bourne, Parker-Jervis (WSL)

Meaford - Bagnall (WSL), Parker-Jervis (WSL)

Moddershall - Parker-Jervis (WSL)

Normacot - **Leveson-Gower**

Oulton - Parker-Jervis (WSL)

Stallington - **Leveson-Gower**

Stone - Allen-Simpkin, Leveson-Gower, Parker-Jervis (WSL)

Tittensor - **Leveson-Gower**, Stafford, Unett

Walton - Parker-Jervis (WSL)

SWYNNERTON

Mainwaring/ Cavenagh-Mainwaring, Pilkington, Stafford

TILLINGTON

Stafford, Salt of Weeping Cross (WSL)

TIXALL

Chetwynd, Aston (WSL)

TRENTHAM

Fletcher/ Fletcher-Boughey

Blurton - **Leveson-Gower**

Butterton - Pilkington

Hanchurch - **Leveson-Gower**

Hanford - **Leveson-Gower**

Trentham - **Leveson-Gower**, Pilkington

WESTON-ON-TRENT

Chetwynd, Philips, Ryder

WHITMORE

Mainwaring/ Cavenagh-Mainwaring, Stafford

WOLSTANTON

Fletcher/ Fletcher-Boughey, Hill Child, Landor, Bagnall (WSL), Bourne of Newcastle (WSL), Sparrow (WSL)

Knutton - Fletcher/ Fletcher-Boughey

Tunstall - Sneyd papers (KUL), Antrobus, Hill Child

Wedgwood - Bagnall (WSL)

The Green at Weston on Trent in the early 20th, or late 19th Century. Courtesy of Roy Lewis

Weston-on-Trent

'Weston is a typical mid-Staffordshire village where time seems to be at standstill, and the peace and quiet is reminiscent of the 'early Sunday morning feeling,"

Weston W.I. in The Venture Magazine for Staffordshire Women. March 1948

SEE ALSO pages 7, 24, 30, 50, 54, 79, 81, 84, 125, 130, 142, 182, 209, 211

WESTON-ON-TRENT TOWNSHIP
PLU. Stafford 1836-1930. Weston-on-Trent W by1910.

Amerton Brook tributary (1)

Weston on Trent CP (styled Weston 1961-) 1866-. PC 1894-. Minutes 1894-1961, 1961-69 at SRO. Weston-with-Gayton PC (a pg) June 1 1973-1988. Stowe CP 1988-.

LG. Stafford RD 1894-1974, D(B) 1974-. Chartley W 1974-2002, 2002-.

CED. Stafford Rural 1889-1911. Stafford Rural East Sept 1911-. Stafford Rural 1934-73. Stafford Rural No. 2 1973-81. Stafford Trent Valley 1981-2005, 2005-.

Amerton Brook tributary (3)

Weston on Trent CP (styled Weston 1961-) 1866-.

Map of Weston-on-Trent

210

Weston-with-Gayton PC (a pg) June 1 1973-1988. Stowe CP 1988-.
LG. Stafford RD 1894-1974, D(B) 1974-. Chartley W 1974-2002, 2002-.
CED. Stafford Rural 1889-1911. Stafford Rural East Sept 1911-34. Stafford Rural 1934-73. Stafford Rural No. 2 1973-81. Stafford Trent Valley 1981-2005, 2005-

Weston-on-Trent

Weston on Trent CP (styled Weston 1961-) 1866-.

Weston-with-Gayton PC (a pg) June 1 1973-9. Weston-with-Gayton-with-Fradswell PC (a pg) 1979-2003. Weston-with-Gayton PC (a pg) 2003-.
LG. Stafford RD 1894-1974, D(B) 1974-. Chartley W 1974-2002, 2002-.
CED. Stafford Rural 1889-1911. Stafford Rural East Sept 1911-34. Stafford Rural 1934-73. Stafford Rural No. 2 1973-81. Stafford Trent Valley 1981-2005, 2005-

Village greens

I think the prettiest villages are Green Villages, those in which houses are grouped round a common green, as opposed to a village strung along a central road. In a letter to J Blamire Brown, clerk to the Lieutenancy, John Burke of S. Andrew's C.E. School, **Weston**, writes:- our 'Village Green is a very good example of its kind and considered to be one of the best in Staffordshire.' He is attempting to persuade Blamire Brown to secure a slight detour of Queen Elizabeth II's progress to Shugborough 25 May 1973, to pass through Weston village (Weston PC correspondence D1383/6). Between 1968-72 nine greens in Pirehill, including The Green, Weston (registration number 14, in Weston CP ownership) were registered under the Commons Registration Act 1965. Ownership for all Pirehill greens was established by 1980. The Register itself is held at Land Charges in Development Services. It was at the County Clerk's office prior to c2002. The other registered greens are (the number in brackets is the registration number): **Abbots Bromley** - The Village Green (1), owned by Abbots Bromley CP. **Ashley** - The Green (30), owned by Staffs CC. **Barlaston** - The Village Green (22), owned by Barlaston CP, has/ had a keeper; grazing rights for up to six beef cattle and bullocks (for Highfield House & Farm (redundant by 1990s), but not exercised since 1930s; and byelaws which the PC implemented 1910 (revised 1996) under section 15 of the Open Spaces Act 1906. A feature on it was an old red telephone box, removed 2004, and not replaced. **Colwich** - Fradswell Parish Field (6), owned by Fradswell Parish Meeting Trustees. **Eccleshall** - Chorlton Village Green (17), owned by Chorlton CP. **Seighford** Village Green (11), owned by Seighford CP. **Stafford (St Mary)** - The Village Green, Hopton (291), owned by Hopton CP. **Stoke-upon-Trent** - The Village Greens, Bagnall (24), owned by Bagnall CP. A non-registered green is that in the centre of **Betley**. It was created when the high wall and the Lodge to Betley Hall were demolished. In 1971 Cyril Ball gave it to the village. In 1999 it was administered by the PC, and had a keeper (Portrait of a Community: Betley, Balterley and Wrinehill. 1999. Mavis Smith and others). Millennium Greens (MGs) funded by the Millennium Commission, administered by the Countryside Agency, started to appear in 1996. A condition of a grant was that individual MG trusts owned or held the land on long lease, so that the space would have protection in perpetuity. By the end of 2001 there were 245 MGs. The only ones in Staffordshire (post-1974 county) are all in Pirehill: Bishops Offley MG in **Adbaston**; **Audley** MG; Derrington MG in **Seighford**; Hixon MG in **Stowe**; Packmoor MG in **Wolstanton**.

Whitmore

Whitmore Church (1838). By TP Wood. SV. II. 97b. Courtesy of Trustees of WSL

Whitmore

'where the village people are still the tenantry of the Mainwaring family, and where the windows of the fine Caroline house overlook a rolling landscape, all of which is part of the Mainwaring estate.'

Margaret Wilson. Staffordshire Life. October 1958

'Paid 'Mr Booth for surveying the parish in order to make a rate for the Relief of the Poor ....£16,12s,4d' 1819 (D3332/6/1).

SEE ALSO pages 7, 24, 27, 51, 79, 124, 125, 130, 140, 167-168, 190, 209, 213-214, 233

WHITMORE TOWNSHIP

PLU. Newcastle-u-Lyme 1838-1930. Whitmore W by1910-.

Meece tributary

Whitmore CP 1866-1984. The results of those elected to the first PC are published in SA Dec 22 1894 p6; it was unamimously resolved that the Rev PE Mainwaring be elected from outside the council to be chairman. Minutes 1894-1944 at SRO. Chapel and Hill Chorlton CP 1984- (SI No. 152).

LG. Newcastle-u-Lyme RD 1894-1974, D(B) 1974-. No. 20 W Feb 1973-4. No. 21 W Feb 1974-9. Whitmore W 1979-2002. Loggerheads & Whitmore W 2002-.

CED. Keele 1889-1934. Madeley 1934-81. Newcastle Rural 1981-2005, 2005-.

Racecourse

Whitmore CP 1866-1984. Keele CP 1984-.

LG. Newcastle-u-Lyme RD 1894-1974, D(B) 1974-. No. 20 W Feb 1973-4. No. 21 W Feb 1974-9. Whitmore W 1979-84. Keele W 1984-2002, 2002-

CED. Keele 1889-1934. Madeley 1934-81. Newcastle Rural 1981-4. Keele & Silverdale 1984-2005. Keele & Westlands 2005-

Whitmore

Whitmore CP 1866-.

LG. Newcastle-u-Lyme RD 1894-1974, D(B) 1974-. No. 20 W Feb 1973-4. No. 21 W Feb 1974-9. Whitmore W 1979-2002. Loggerheads & Whitmore W 2002-.

CED. Keele 1889-1934. Madeley 1934-81. Newcastle Rural 1981-2005, 2005-.

212

Workhouses of the Old Poor Law system

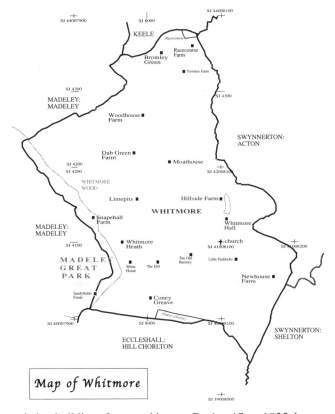

Map of Whitmore

If a parish had a workhouse it is probably referred to in parish accounts. Sometimes there is no direct reference, but shortly you get the impression the parish is paying frequently for repairs etc at a particular property, and this must be the workhouse (or called a poorhouse). Not all parishes had a workhouse, but those that did generally found it more cost effective than paying out relief. Records of early workhouses are virtually non-existent; sometimes accounts are run through the overseers accounts. At **Whitmore** 'the Clays House' 1803, 'the Clay' 1808, 'the Clays' 1810, 1833, 'Clays house' 1819, 1821, 1824, 1828 must be the workhouse. Presumably, it lay in 'Clays lane' 1806 (D3332/6/1). In March 1835 the vestry planned to take over existing buildings for a workhouse. By Aug/ Sept 1835 they considered erecting a workhouse (D3332/6/3). **Abbots Bromley** parish workhouse in Schoolhouse Lane, opposite the old Free Grammar School, operated between 1764 and 1841; horn dancing occurred outside the church every Sunday to collect alms for its upkeep (D1209/5/1) (AB pp186-7). There was an agreement for maintenance of **Ashley** poor in Audley workhouse 1773; later there was an Ashley parish workhouse, which Thomas Kinnersley had a hand in erecting; a special meeting of the vestry met June 1 1838 to discuss its dispersal (D44/A/PO/33) (D44/A/PV/1). **Audley** workhouse, Alsager Road, succeeding an earlier workhouse, built 1733, started receiving inmates from May 1734. It was held by the Trustee of the Audley Grammar School until 1900, and became known as Workhouse Farm (A pp43-46). There is no evidence for a **Barlaston** workhouse. **Barthomley** parish workhouse, existing in an unknown location by 1767, presumably housed Balterley inmates (Barthomley: The Story of an estate village. Robert Speake. 1995. pp228-9). **Betley** overseers' accts for 1748 state 'For removing the poor from Betley to Audley poorhouse 12-0'; there are references to the poorhouse (at Betley?) 1767. In 1774 approval was given and progress made in building of two houses (for the poor) at Betley Common (BVC pp127-9). **Biddulph** parish workhouse stood at Gillow Heath many years prior to 1834 (BALH p152). There is no evidence for a **Blithfield** workhouse from parish accounts 1760-1802. Perhaps, due to the Bagots philanthropic spirit they could not bring themselves to set up one, preferring out relief (in the late C18 and early C19 Lord Bagot quite often ordered the Overseer make payments to poor soldiers and sailors). Anyhow, with the absence of later accounts it is hard to conclude. In 1779 'paid the Leigh officer for Bailey's family 39 weeks pay ....£5, 17s, 0d' is a reference perhaps to out relief for a Blithfield family Blithfield is obliged to support in Leigh parish. However, payments

Whitmore

were made in 1790 to house Mary Rock of Newton township in a workhouse (D1386/5/2). There was a workhouse at **Burslem** by 1741, with a capacity of 60 in 1775. A new workhouse was built at Greenhead in 1780. Enlarged 1835 to hold up to 300, it was later a barracks, and a pottery until demolished in 1958 (VCH vol 8 pp129-30) (WITP p11 fig 8). **Chebsey**: no evidence. There were agreements for **Colton** and **Colwich** to house their poor at Rugeley workhouse 1781 (D4613/6/76) (D24/A/PO/3247-3249). Fradswell entered into an agreement to house its poor in Leigh workhouse 1785 (D3033/4/7/2). **Drayton-in-Hales** workhouse, serving Tyrley quarter, existing by 1756, stood in Shropshire Street, Market Drayton; enlarged 1839 (SRRC 2997/2/1). The old **Eccleshall** parish workhouse was dilapidated in 1810. Shortly afterwards it was rebuilt at Goal Butts, Eccleshall; later becoming Eagle House (VE p92). **Ellenhall**: no evidence. **Gayton** sent its poor to Leigh workhouse between at least 1814-32 (D705/PO/1). **High Offley**: no evidence. There was a **Keele** workhouse from 1737 (Keele Parish Book 1693-1770). **Madeley**, having used Audley workhouse (A pp43-6), set up its own in 1832 in the Holborn premises of J Cunliffe Offley. Madeley vestry committee book 1831-54 has the rules, orders and regulations, including the Bill of Fare intended for inmates (D3412/4/4). The Register Book April 7 1832 - April 30 1838, will be of the greatest interest containing 109 names. The register has these headings:- Paupers names/ Age/ When admitted/ Last residence/ Former employer/ How settled (how qualified for a settlement certificate)/ Gained discharge/ Observations (D3412/5/690). The Work Book is also of interest, with these headings:- Date/ Paupers name/ By whom employed/ His employ/ Time/ Account of/ Amount received/ Observations (D3412/5/691). **Maer**: no evidence. **Milwich** entered into agreements to house its poor in Ipstones workhouse 1793 (D917/6/23), and Leigh workhouse 1800 (D917/6/24). **Mucklestone** vestry minutes book (D5725/3/3) refer to a workhouse in 1819. In its churchwardens' accounts Easter 1826 to Easter 1827 it is recorded 'Spent at a Meeting concerning exchanging the Poors Building £0, 1s, 6d' (D5725/3/1). Property in Higherland, **Newcastle**, served as a workhouse from 1731. In 1838-9 the Union workhouse, in Keele road, was built to its E (VCH vol 8 p33). **Norton-in-the-Moors** parish workhouse, Endon Road, almost opposite to Norton Hall, was built c1798 on waste land adjoining the estate of Charles Adderley. It housed 7 inmates in 1813; 10 in 1814; only two in 1815. It closed in 1839 and later became a dwelling (WITP p6 figs 2, 3). In 1840 **Ranton** vestry voted to sell its parish workhouse; it was bought at auction at The Gate Public House by John Worthington, Boo(uc)klemaker of Seighford for £73 (D4305/1/1). **Sandon** used Leigh workhouse by an agreement of 1799 (D1048/3/3) (D22/A/PO/121). **Seighford** overseers' accounts Easter 1805-1806 mention 'Paid for mending the stairs at Poor house ...£0, 2s, 6d'; and 200 bricks costing £0, 6s, 0d for the floor were needed between 1817-18. The property, which was sold c1836 for £87, may be identifiable with the 'new house' mentioned in 1801? (D731/12) (SIAS. No. 2 p59). **Stafford** workhouse, in a building of the former Stafford Collegiate Church, on S side of St Mary's churchyard, opened 1738; it was still open in 1836 (VCH vol 6 p231). **Standon**: no evidence. **Stoke-upon-Trent** workhouse reputedly built 1735 stood at the corner of Trent Valley Road and Manor Court Street, Penkhull (WITP p5). A **Stone** parish workhouse existed by 1735. It was re-thatched in 1743 (SIS p48). **Stowe** overseers' accounts show materials were needed for the fabric of a poor house in the parish 1761; and payment was made to Crouch workhouse in 1775, and 1777 (D14/A/PO/1); whilst its churchwardens' accounts tell of payment for ale to workmen when repairing the workhouse 1804-5 (D14/A/PC/1). **Swynnerton**: no evidence. **Trentham** parish workhouse was built 1809-10 on land given by the Duke of Sutherland off Trentham Road in the Splatslade area of Blurton. It housed 56 inmates in 1813; 48 in 1839 (WITP p9 figs 6, 7). **Wolstanton** workhouse, said to have been originally a number of small cottages bought by the parish authorities, was at the NE end of the Marsh. In 1814 it housed 102 inmates (WITP p11).

Methodists celebrate at Mow Cop

Methodists gathered for the 150th Anniversary (1957) of the Primitive Methodist Revivalist camp meeting on Mow Cop 1807. Courtesy of Sentinel Newspapers

Wolstanton

'Today the scene is changed. The charm of the landscape has been ploughed into the foundations of factories, shops and dwellings which sprang up too quickly to bother about beauty.'

Tom Byrne. Tales From The Past. 1977

The parish was divided into 'north side' and 'south side' for poor relief by at least 1768; each side appears to have had its own churchwardens and overseers. The vestry meeting for the 'north side' in 1768 was held at Newchapel (D3534/3/2). In 1851 the townships supported their poor co-jointly.

The AP (excluding Tunstall T) effectively a CP between 1866 to 1894 when carved up into Chell, Chesterton, Goldenhill, Kidsgrove, Newchapel, Silverdale, Wolstanton CPs, each with their own PCs.

SEE ALSO pages 7, 27, 30, 36, 44, 49, 54, 79, 82, 90, 93-4, 96, 116, 124, 125, 131, 140, 142, 186, 191, 209, 211, 214, 230

NORTH SIDE
BRIERLEYHURST TOWNSHIP
Albion Foundry

Kidsgrove CP 1894- (TC 1974-). Kidsgrove PW 1974-2002. Butt Lane PW 2002-.
LG. Kidsgrove UD 1894-1974. Kidsgrove W by1907-74. Newcastle-u-Lyme D(B) 1974-. No. 13 Feb 1973-7. No. 14 Feb 1977-9. Kidsgrove W 1979-2002. Butt

Lane W 2002-.
CED. Kidsgrove 1889-2005. Kidsgrove and Talke 2005-.

Brierleyhurst
Newchapel CP 1894-1974. Brierleyhurst PW May 1895-. Kidsgrove TC 1974-. Newchapel PW 1974-2002, 2002-
LG. Wolstanton RD 1894-1904. Kidsgrove UD 1904-

215

Wolstanton (North Side, Chell)

74. Newchapel W by1907-74. Newcastle-u-Lyme D(B) 1974-. No. 14 W Feb 1973-7. No. 15 W Feb 1977-9. Newchapel W 1979-2002, 2002-.
CED. Kidsgrove 1889-2005. Kidsgrove and Talke 2005-.

Dove Bank

Kidsgrove CP 1894- (TC 1974-). Kidsgrove PW 1974-2002, 2002-
LG. Kidsgrove UD 1894-1974. Kidsgrove W by1907-74. Newcastle-u-Lyme D(B) 1974-. No. 13 W Feb 1973-7. No. 14 W Feb 1977-9. Kidsgrove W 1979-2002, 2002-.
CED. Kidsgrove 1889-2005. Kidsgrove and Talke 2005-.

Kidsgrove

Kidsgrove CP 1894- (TC 1974-). Kidsgrove PW 1974-2002. Ravenscliffe PW 2002-.
LG. Kidsgrove UD 1894-1974. Kidsgrove W by1907-74. Newcastle-u-Lyme D(B) 1974-. No. 13 W Feb 1973-7. No. 14 Feb 1977-9. Kidsgrove W 1979-2002. Ravenscliffe W 2002-.
CED. Kidsgrove 1889-2005. Kidsgrove & Talke 2005-

Mount Pleasant

Newchapel CP 1894-1965. Brierleyhurst PW May 1895-. Old Rode CP, Ches 1965-.
LG. Wolstanton RD 1894-1904. Kidsgrove UD 1904-74. Newchapel W by1907-65.
CED. Kidsgrove 1889-1965.

Parklands

Kidsgrove CP 1894- (TC 1974-). Kidsgrove PW 1974-2002, 2002-
LG. Kidsgrove UD 1894-1974. Kidsgrove W by1907-74. Newcastle-u-Lyme D(B) 1974-. No. 13 W Feb 1973-7. No. 14 W Feb 1977-9. Kidsgrove W 1979-2002-, 2002-.
CED. Kidsgrove 1889-2005. Kidsgrove and Talke 2005-.

The Rookery

Newchapel CP 1894-1974. Brierleyhurst PW May 1895-. Kidsgrove TC 1974-. Newchapel PW 1974-2002. Kidsgrove PW 2002-
LG. Wolstanton RD 1894-1904. Kidsgrove UD 1904-74. Newchapel W by1907-74. Newcastle-u-Lyme D(B) 1974-. No. 14 W Feb 1973-7. No. 15 W Feb 1977-9. Newchapel W 1979-2002. Kidsgrove W 2002-.
CED. Kidsgrove 1889-2005. Kidsgrove and Talke 2005-.

Tamar

Newchapel CP 1894-1974. Brierleyhurst PW May 1895-. Kidsgrove TC 1974-. Kidsgrove PW 1974-2002. Ravenscliffe PW 2002-
LG. Wolstanton RD 1894-1904. Kidsgrove UD 1904-

74. Newchapel W by1907-74. Newcastle-u-Lyme D(B) 1974-. No. 14 W Feb 1973-7. No. 15 W Feb 1977-9. Newchapel W 1979-2002. Ravenscliffe W 2002-.
CED. Kidsgrove 1889-2005. Kidsgrove and Talke 2005-.

'Whitehill Park'

Newchapel CP 1894-1974. Brierleyhurst PW May 1895-. Kidsgrove TC 1974-. Newchapel PW 1974-2002. Kidsgrove PW 2002-
LG. Wolstanton RD 1894-1904. Kidsgrove 1904-74. Newchapel W by1907-74. Newcastle-u-Lyme D(B) 1974-. No. 14 W Feb 1973-7. No. 15 W Feb 1977-9. Kidsgrove W 1979-2002, 2002-.
CED. Kidsgrove 1889-2005. Kidsgrove and Talke 2005-.

CHELL TOWNSHIP
Bank Top

Chell CP 1894-1922. Chell PW Aug 1895-1922.
LG. Wolstanton RD 1894-1904. Smallthorne UD 1904-22. Chell W by1907-22. S-o-T CB 1922-74, D(C) 1974-97, UA 1997-. No. 27 W 1922-55. No. 3 W 1955-65. No. 5 W 1965-79. Burslem Central W 1979-2002. Burslem North W 2002-
CED. Tunstall North 1889-1910. Smallthorne 1910-22. CCWs 1974-97.

Burnwood

Chell CP 1894-1922. Chell PW Aug 1895-1922.
LG. Wolstanton RD 1894-1904. Smallthorne UD 1904-22. Chell W by1907-22. S-o-T CB 1922-74, D(C) 1974-97, UA 1997-. No. 27 W 1922-55. No. 3 W 1955-65. No. 3 W 1965-79. Chell W 1979-2002. Norton & Bradeley W 2002-
CED. Tunstall North 1889-1910. Smallthorne 1910-22. CCWs 1974-97.

Burslem Golf Course (1)

Chell CP 1894-1922. Chell PW Aug 1895-1922.
LG. Wolstanton RD 1894-1904. Smallthorne UD 1904-22. Chell W by1907-22. S-o-T CB 1922-74, D(C) 1974-97, UA 1997-. No. 27 W 1922-55. No. 3 W 1955-65. No. 5 W 1965-79. Burslem Central W 1979-2002. Burslem North W 2002-
CED. Tunstall North 1889-1910. Smallthorne 1910-22. CCWs 1974-97.

Burslem Golf Course (2)

Chell CP 1894-1922. Chell PW Aug 1895-1922.
LG. Wolstanton RD 1894-1904. Smallthorne UD 1904-22. Chell W by1907-22. S-o-T CB 1922-74, D(C) 1974-97, UA 1997-. No. 27 W 1922-55. No. 5 W 1955-65. No. 5 W 1965-79. Burslem Central W 1979-2002. Burslem North W 2002-
CED. Tunstall North 1889-1910. Smallthorne 1910-

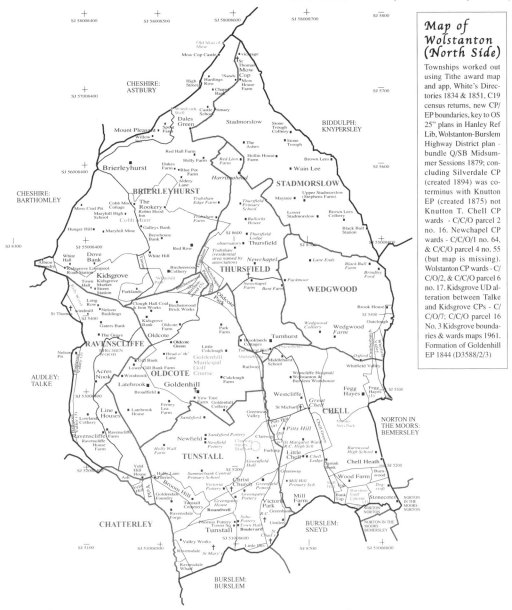

Map of Wolstanton (North Side)

Townships worked out using Tithe award map and app, White's Directories 1834 & 1851, C19 census returns, new CP/EP boundaries, key to OS 25" plans in Hanley Ref Lib, Wolstanton-Burslem Highway District plan - bundle Q/SB Midsummer Sessions 1879; concluding Silverdale CP (created 1894) was coterminus with Knutton EP (created 1875) not Knutton T. Chell CP wards - C/C/O parcel 2 no. 16. Newchapel CP wards - C/C/O/1 no. 64, & C/C/O parcel 4 no. 55 (but map is missing). Wolstanton CP wards - C/C/O/2, & C/C/O parcel 6 no. 17. Kidsgrove UD alteration between Talke and Kidsgrove CPs - C/C/O/7; C/C/O parcel 16 No. 3 Kidsgrove boundaries & wards maps 1961. Formation of Goldenhill EP 1844 (D3588/2/3)

22. CCWs 1974-97.

Chell Green

Chell CP 1894-1922. Chell PW Aug 1895-1922. LG. Wolstanton RD 1894-1904. Smallthorne UD 1904-22. Chell W by1907-22. S-o-T CB 1922-74, D(C) 1974-97, UA 1997-. No. 27 W 1922-55. No. 3 W 1955-65. No. 2 W 1965-79. Chell W 1979-2002. Chell & Packmoor W 2002-
CED. Tunstall North 1889-1910. Smallthorne 1910-22. CCWs 1974-97.

Chell Heath

Chell CP 1894-1922. Chell PW Aug 1895-1922. LG. Wolstanton RD 1894-1904. Smallthorne UD 1904-22. Chell W by1907-22. S-o-T CB 1922-74, D(C) 1974-97, UA 1997-. No. 27 W 1922-55. No. 3 W 1955-65. No. 3 W 1965-79. Chell W 1979-2002. Chell & Packmoor W 2002-
CED. Tunstall North 1889-1910. Smallthorne 1910-22. CCWs 1974-97.

Fegg Hayes

217

Wolstanton (North Side, Chell)

Chell CP 1894-1922. Fegg Hayes PW Aug 1895-1922. LG. Wolstanton RD 1894-1904. Smallthorne UD 1904-22. Chell W by1907-22. S-o-T CB 1922-74, D(C) 1974-97, UA 1997-. No. 27 W 1922-55. No. 3 W 1955-65. No. 3 W 1965-79. Chell W 1979-2002. Chell & Packmoor W 2002-

CED. Tunstall North 1889-1910. Smallthorne 1910-22. CCWs 1974-97.

Fegg Hayes (1)

Chell CP 1894-1922. Fegg Hayes PW Aug 1895-1922. LG. Wolstanton RD 1894-1904. Smallthorne UD 1904-22. Chell W by1907-22. S-o-T CB 1922-74, D(C) 1974-97, UA 1997-. No. 27 W 1922-55. No. 3 W 1955-65. No. 3 W 1965-79. Chell W 1979-2002. Norton & Bradeley W 2002-

CED. Tunstall North 1889-1910. Smallthorne 1910-22. CCWs 1974-97.

Fegg Hayes (2)

Chell CP 1894-1922. Fegg Hayes PW Aug 1895-1922. LG. Wolstanton RD 1894-1904. Smallthorne UD 1904-22. Chell W by1907-22. S-o-T CB 1922-74, D(C) 1974-97, UA 1997-. No. 27 W 1922-55. No. 7 W 1955-65. No. 7 W 1965-79. Norton & Bradeley W 1979-2002. Norton & Bradeley W 2002-

CED. Tunstall North 1889-1910. Smallthorne 1910-22. CCWs 1974-97.

Greenway

Chell CP 1894-99. Chell PW Aug 1895-99. Tunstall CP 1899-1910.

LG. Wolstanton RD 1894-9. Tunstall UD 1899-1910. Chell W 1900-10. S-o-T CB 1910-74, D(C) 1974-97, UA 1997-. No. 3 W 1910-55. No. 2 W 1955-65. No. 2 W 1965-79. Burslem Central W 1979-2002. Tunstall W 2002-

CED. Tunstall North 1889-1910. CCWs 1974-97.
PARL. Burslem D of S-o-T PB 1918-48.

Little Chell

Chell CP 1894-99. Chell PW Aug 1895-99. Tunstall CP 1899-1910.

LG. Wolstanton RD 1894-9. Tunstall UD 1899-1910. Chell W 1900-10. S-o-T CB 1910-74, D(C) 1974-97, UA 1997-. No. 3 W 1910-55. No. 3 W 1955-65. No. 2 W 1965-79. Chell W 1979-2002. Burslem North W 2002-

CED. Tunstall North 1889-1910. CCWs 1974-97.
PARL. Burslem D of S-o-T PB 1918-48.

Mill Farm

Chell CP 1894-99. Chell PW Aug 1895-99. Tunstall CP 1899-1910.

LG. Wolstanton RD 1894-9. Tunstall UD 1899-1910. Chell W 1900-10. S-o-T CB 1910-74, D(C) 1974-97, UA 1997-. No. 3 W 1910-55. No. 2 W 1955-65. No. 2

W 1965-79. Burslem Central W 1979-2002. Burslem North W 2002-

CED. Tunstall North 1889-1910. CCWs 1974-97.
PARL. Burslem D of S-o-T PB 1918-48.

Mill Hill

Chell CP 1894-1922. Chell PW Aug 1895-1922. LG. Wolstanton RD 1894-1904. Smallthorne UD 1904-22. Chell W by1907-22. S-o-T CB 1922-74, D(C) 1974-97, UA 1997-. No. 27 W 1922-55. No. 3 W 1955-65. No. 2 W 1965-79. Burslem Central W 1979-2002. Burslem North W 2002-

CED. Tunstall North 1889-1910. Smallthorne 1910-22. CCWs 1974-97.

Pitts Hill (a)

Chell CP 1894-99. Chell PW Aug 1895-99. Tunstall CP 1899-1910.

LG. Wolstanton RD 1894-9. Tunstall UD 1899-1910. Chell W 1900-10. S-o-T CB 1910-74, D(C) 1974-97, UA 1997-. No. 3 W 1910-55. No. 3 W 1955-65. No. 1 W 1965-79. Chell W 1979-2002. Chell & Packmoor W 2002-

CED. Tunstall North 1889-1910. CCWs 1974-97.
PARL. Burslem D of S-o-T PB 1918-48.

Pitts Hill (b)

Chell CP 1894-99. Chell PW Aug 1895-99. Tunstall CP 1899-1910.

LG. Wolstanton RD 1894-9. Tunstall UD 1899-1910. Chell W 1900-10. S-o-T CB 1910-74, D(C) 1974-97, UA 1997-. No. 3 W 1910-55. No. 3 W 1955-65. No. 1 W 1965-79. Chell W 1979-2002. Burslem North W 2002-

CED. Tunstall North 1889-1910. CCWs 1974-97.
PARL. Burslem D of S-o-T PB 1918-48.

Pitts Hill (c)

Chell CP 1894-99. Chell PW Aug 1895-99. Tunstall CP 1899-1910.

LG. Wolstanton RD 1894-9. Tunstall UD 1899-1910. Chell W 1900-10. S-o-T CB 1910-74, D(C) 1974-97, UA 1997-. No. 3 W 1910-55. No. 3 W 1955-65. No. 1 W 1965-79. Chell W 1979-2002. Tunstall W 2002-
CED. Tunstall North 1889-1910. CCWs 1974-97.
PARL. Burslem D of S-o-T PB 1918-48.

Saint Michael

Chell CP 1894-1904. Chell PW Aug 1895-1904.
LG. Wolstanton RD 1894-9. Tunstall UD 1904-10. Chell W 1904-10. S-o-T CB 1910-74, D(C) 1974-97, UA 1997-. No. 1 W 1910-55. No. 3 W 1955-65. No. 1 W 1965-79. Chell W 1979-2002. Burslem North W 2002-

CED. Tunstall North 1889-1910. CCWs 1974-97.
PARL. Burslem D of S-o-T PB 1918-48.

Sprink Bank

Chell CP 1894-1922. Chell PW Aug 1895-1922.
LG. Wolstanton RD 1894-1904. Smallthorne UD 1904-22. Chell W by1907-22. S-o-T CB 1922-74, D(C) 1974-97, UA 1997-. No. 27 W 1922-55. No. 3 W 1955-65. No. 3 W 1965-79. Burslem Central W 1979-2002. Chell & Packmoor W 2002-
CED. Tunstall North 1889-1910. Smallthorne 1910-22. CCWs 1974-97.

Stonecotes
Chell CP 1894-1922. Chell PW Aug 1895-1922.
LG. Wolstanton RD 1894-1904. Smallthorne UD 1904-22. Chell W by1907-22. S-o-T CB 1922-74, D(C) 1974-97, UA 1997-. No. 27 W 1922-55. No. 3 W 1955-65. No. 5 W 1965-79. Burslem Central W 1979-2002. Norton & Bradeley W 2002-
CED. Tunstall North 1889-1910. Smallthorne 1910-22. CCWs 1974-97.

Top
Chell CP 1894-1922. Chell PW Aug 1895-1922.
LG. Wolstanton RD 1894-1904. Smallthorne UD 1904-22. Chell W by1907-22. S-o-T CB 1922-74, D(C) 1974-97, UA 1997-. No. 27 W 1922-55. No. 3 W 1955-65. No. 3 W 1965-79. Burslem Central W 1979-2002. Burslem North W 2002-
CED. Tunstall North 1889-1910. Smallthorne 1910-22. CCWs 1974-97.

Westcliffe
Chell CP 1894-1904. Chell PW Aug 1895-1904.
LG. Wolstanton RD 1894-1904. Tunstall UD 1904-10. Chell W 1904-10. S-o-T CB 1910-74, D(C) 1974-97, UA 1997-. No. 1 W 1910-55. No. 3 W 1955-65. No. 1 W 1965-79. Chell W 1979-2002. Chell & Packmoor W 2002-
CED. Tunstall North 1889-1910. CCWs 1974-97.
PARL. Burslem D of S-o-T PB 1918-48.

Whitfield Valley
Chell CP 1894-1922. Chell PW Aug 1895-1922.
LG. Wolstanton RD 1894-1904. Smallthorne UD 1904-22. Chell W by1907-22. S-o-T CB 1922-74, D(C) 1974-97, UA 1997-. No. 27 W 1922-55. No. 3 W 1955-65. No. 7 W 1965-79. Norton & Bradeley W 1979-2002. Norton & Bradeley W 2002-
CED. Tunstall North 1889-1910. Smallthorne 1910-22. CCWs 1974-97.

Wood Farm
Chell CP 1894-1922. Chell PW Aug 1895-1922.
LG. Wolstanton RD 1894-1904. Smallthorne UD 1904-22. Chell W by1907-22. S-o-T CB 1922-74, D(C) 1974-97, UA 1997-. No. 1 W 1922-55. No. 3 W 1955-65. No. 3 W 1965-79. Chell W 1979-2002. Burslem North W 2002-
CED. Tunstall North 1889-1910. Smallthorne 1910-

Wolstanton (North Side, Oldcote)
22. CCWs 1974-97.

OLDCOTE TOWNSHIP
Birchenwood (2)
Goldenhill CP 1894-1904. No. 1 or Oldcott PW 1896-1904. Kidsgrove CP 1904- (TC 1974-). Kidsgrove PW 1974-?84. Newchapel PW ?1984-2002. Kidsgrove PW 2002-.
LG. Wolstanton RD 1894-1904. Kidsgrove UD 1904-74. Kidsgrove W by1907-74. Newcastle-u-Lyme D(B) 1974-. No. 13 W Feb 1973-7. No. 14 W Feb 1977-9. Kidsgrove W 1979-?1984. Newchapel W ?1984-2002, Kidsgrove W 2002-.
CED. Tunstall North 1889-1904. Kidsgrove 1904-2005. Kidsgrove and Talke 2005-.

Birchenwood (3)
Goldenhill CP 1894-1904. No. 1 or Oldcott PW 1896-1904. Kidsgrove CP 1904- (TC 1974-). Kidsgrove PW 1974-
LG. Wolstanton RD 1894-1904. Kidsgrove UD 1904-74. Kidsgrove W by1907-74. Newcastle-u-Lyme D(B) 1974-. No. 13 W Feb 1973-7. No. 14 W Feb 1977-9. Kidsgrove W 1979-2002, 2002-.
CED. Tunstall North 1889-1904. Kidsgrove 1904-2005. Kidsgrove and Talke 2005-.

Goldenhill
Goldenhill CP 1894-1904. No. 1 or Oldcott PW 1896-1904.
LG. Wolstanton RD 1894-1904. Tunstall UD 1904-10. Goldenhill W 1904-10. S-o-T CB 1910-74, D(C) 1974-97, UA 1997-. No. 1 W 1910-55. No. 1 W 1955-65. No. 1 W 1965-79. Tunstall North W 1979-2002. Tunstall W 2002-.
CED. Tunstall North 1889-1910. CCWs 1974-97.
PARL. Burslem D of S-o-T PB 1918-48. S-o-T North BC 1948-.

Latebrook
Goldenhill CP 1894-1904. No. 2 or Ravenscliffe PW 1896-1904.
LG. Wolstanton RD 1894-1904. Tunstall UD 1904-10. Goldenhill W 1904-10. S-o-T CB 1910-74, D(C) 1974-97, UA 1997-. No. 1 W 1910-55. No. 1 W 1955-65. No. 1 W 1965-79. Tunstall North W 1979-2002. Tunstall W 2002-.
CED. Tunstall North 1889-1910. CCWs 1974-97.
PARL. Burslem D of S-o-T PB 1918-48. S-o-T North BC 1948-.

Oldcote
Goldenhill CP 1894-1904. No. 1 or Oldcott PW 1896-1904. Kidsgrove CP 1904- (TC 1974-). Kidsgrove PW 1974-2002. Ravenscliffe PW 2002-.
LG. Wolstanton RD 1894-1904. Kidsgrove UD 1904-

Wolstanton (North Side, Thursfield)

74. Kidsgrove W by1907-74. Newcastle-u-Lyme D(B) 1974-. No. 13 W Feb 1973-7. No. 14 W Feb 1977-9. Kidsgrove W 1979-2002. Ravenscliffe W 2002-.
CED. Tunstall North 1889-1904. Kidsgrove 1904-2005. Kidsgrove and Talke 2005-.

Oldcote Park

Goldenhill CP 1894-1904. No. 1 or Oldcott PW 1896-1904.
LG. Wolstanton RD 1894-1904. Tunstall UD 1904-10. Goldenhill W 1904-10. S-o-T CB 1910-74, D(C) 1974-97, UA 1997-. No. 1 W 1910-55. No. 3 W 1955-65. No. 3 W 1965-79. Chell W 1979-. Chell & Packmoor W 2002-.
CED. Tunstall North 1889-1910. CCWs 1974-97.
PARL. Burslem D of S-o-T PB 1918-48. S-o-T North BC 1948-.

Railway

Goldenhill CP 1894-1904. No. 1 or Oldcott PW 1896-1904.
LG. Wolstanton RD 1894-1904. Tunstall UD 1904-10. Goldenhill W 1904-10. S-o-T CB 1910-74, D(C) 1974-97, UA 1997-. No. 1 W 1910-55. No. 3 W 1955-65. No. 1 W 1965-79. Chell W 1979-. Chell & Packmoor W 2002-.
CED. Tunstall North 1889-1910. CCWs 1974-97.
PARL. Burslem D of S-o-T PB 1918-48. S-o-T North BC 1948-.

RAVENSCLIFFE TOWNSHIP
Acres Nook

Goldenhill CP 1894-1904. No. 2 or Ravenscliffe PW 1896-1904. Kidsgrove CP 1904- (TC 1974-). Ravenscliffe PW 2002-.
LG. Wolstanton RD 1894-1904. Kidsgrove UD 1904-74. Kidsgrove W by1907-74. Newcastle-u-Lyme D(B) 1974-. No. 13 W Feb 1973-7. No. 14 W Feb 1977-9. Kidsgrove W 1979-2002. Ravenscliffe W 2002-.
CED. Kidsgrove 1889-2005. Kidsgrove & Talke 2005-

Bathpool Valley (2)

Kidsgrove CP 1894- (TC 1974-). Butt Lane PW 2002-
LG. Kidsgrove UD 1894-1974. Kidsgrove W by1907-67/8. Butt Lane W Feb 1968-74. Newcastle-u-Lyme D(B) 1974-. No. 15 W Feb 1973-7. No. 13 W Feb 1977-9. Butt Lane W 1979-2002, 2002-.
CED. Kidsgrove 1889-1968. Talke 1968-2005. Kidsgrove & Talke 2005-.

Bathpool Valley (3)

Kidsgrove CP 1894- (TC 1974-). Talke PW 1974-2002, 2002-.
LG. Kidsgrove UD 1894-1974. Kidsgrove W by1907-74. Newcastle-u-Lyme D(B) 1974-. No. 16 W Feb 1973-7. No. 16 W Feb 1977-9. Talke W 1979-2002,

2002-
CED. Kidsgrove 1889-1968. Talke 1968-2005. Kidsgrove & Talke 2005-.

Line Houses

PARL. Burslem D of S-o-T PB 1918-48. S-o-T North BC 1948-.
Goldenhill CP 1894-1904. No. 2 or Ravenscliffe PW 1896-1904.
LG. Wolstanton RD 1894-1904. Tunstall UD 1904-10. Goldenhill W 1904-10. S-o-T CB 1910-74, D(C) 1974-97, UA 1997-. No. 1 W 1910-55. No. 1 W 1955-65. No. 1 W 1965-79. Tunstall North W 1979-2002. Tunstall W 2002-.
CED. Kidsgrove 1889-1904. Tunstall North 1904-10. CCWs 1974-97.

Ravenscliffe

Kidsgrove CP 1894- (TC 1974-). Kidsgrove PW 1974-2002. Ravenscliffe PW 2002-.
LG. Kidsgrove UD 1894-1974. Kidsgrove W by1907-74. Newcastle-u-Lyme D(B) 1974-. No. 13 W Feb 1973-7. No. 14 Feb 1977-9. Kidsgrove W 1979-2002. Ravenscliffe W 2002-.
CED. Kidsgrove 1889-2005. Kidsgrove & Talke 2005-

Saint Thomas

Kidsgrove CP 1894- (TC 1974-). Butt Lane PW 1974-2002, 2002-.
LG. Kidsgrove UD 1894-1974. Kidsgrove W by1907-67/8. Butt Lane W Feb 1968-74. Newcastle-u-Lyme D(B) 1974-. No. 16 W Feb 1973-7. No. 16 W Feb 1977-9. Butt Lane W 1979-2002, 2002-.
CED. Kidsgrove 1889-1968. Talke 1968-2005. Kidsgrove & Talke 2005-.

STADMORSLOW TOWNSHIP

Newchapel CP 1894-1974. Stadmorslow PW May 1895-. Kidsgrove TC 1974-. Newchapel PW 1974-2002, 2002-.
LG. Wolstanton RD 1894-1904. Kidsgrove UD 1904-74. Newchapel W by1907-74. Newcastle-u-Lyme D(B) 1974-. No. 14 Feb 1973-77. No. 15 W Feb 1977-9. Newchapel W 1979-2002, 2002-.
CED. Kidsgrove 1889-2005. Kidsgrove and Talke 2005-.

THURSFIELD TOWNSHIP
Brooklands Cottages

Newchapel CP 1894-1922. Thursfield PW May 1895-1922.
LG. Wolstanton RD 1894-1904. Kidsgrove UD 1904-22. Newchapel W by1907-22. S-o-T CB 1922-74, D(C) 1974-97, UA 1997-. No. 27 W 1922-55. No. 1 W 1955-65. Tunstall North W 1979-2002. Tunstall W 2002-

220

CED. Kidsgrove 1889-1922. CCWs 1974-97.
PARL. S-o-T North BC 1948-.

Middlehurst

Newchapel CP 1894-1904. Thursfield PW 1895-1904.
LG. Wolstanton RD 1894-1904. Tunstall UD 1904-10. Chell W 1904-10. S-o-T CB 1910-74, D(C) 1974-97, UA 1997-. No. 1 W 1922-55. No. 3 W 1955-65. No. 1 W 1965-79. Chell W 1979-2002. Chell & Packmoor W 2002-
CED. Kidsgrove 1889-1910. CCWs 1974-97.
PARL. Burslem D of S-o-T PB 1918-48.

Newchapel

Newchapel CP 1894-1974. Thursfield PW May 1895-. Kidsgrove TC 1974-. Newchapel PW 1974-9. Kidsgrove PW 1979-2002. Newchapel PW 2002-.
LG. Wolstanton RD 1894-1904. Kidsgrove UD 1904-74. Newchapel W by1907-74. Newcastle-u-Lyme D(B) 1974-. No. 14 W Feb 1973-7. No. 15 W Feb 1977-9. Kidsgrove W 1979-2002. Newchapel W 2002-.
CED. Kidsgrove 1889-2005. Kidsgrove and Talke 2005-.

Pennyfields

Newchapel CP 1894-1974. Thursfield PW May 1895-. Kidsgrove TC 1974-. Newchapel PW 1974-9. Kidsgrove PW 1979-
LG. Wolstanton RD 1894-1904. Kidsgrove UD 1904-74. Newchapel W by1907-74. Newcastle-u-Lyme D(B) 1974-. No. 14 W Feb 1973-7. No. 15 W Feb 1977-9. Kidsgrove W 1979-2002, 2002-.
CED. Kidsgrove 1889-2005. Kidsgrove and Talke 2005-.

Trubshaw

Newchapel CP 1894-1974. Thursfield PW May 1895-. Kidsgrove TC 1974-. Newchapel PW 1974-2002. Kidsgrove PW 2002-
LG. Wolstanton RD 1894-1904. Kidsgrove UD 1904-74. Newchapel W by1907-74. Newcastle-u-Lyme D(B) 1974-. No. 14 W Feb 1973-7. No. 15 W Feb 1977-9. Newchapel W 1979-2002. Kidsgrove W 2002-.
CED. Kidsgrove 1889-2005. Kidsgrove and Talke 2005-.

Thursfield

Newchapel CP 1894-1974. Thursfield PW May 1895-. Kidsgrove TC 1974-. Newchapel PW 1974-
LG. Wolstanton RD 1894-1904. Kidsgrove UD 1904-74. Newchapel W by1907-74. Newcastle-u-Lyme D(B) 1974-. No. 14 W Feb 1973-7. No. 15 W Feb 1977-9. Kidsgrove W 1979-?84. Newchapel W 1979-2002, 2002-.
CED. Kidsgrove 1889-2005. Kidsgrove and Talke 2005-.

Turnhurst

Wolstanton (North Side, Tunstall)

Newchapel CP 1894-1922. Thursfield PW May 1895-1922.
LG. Wolstanton RD 1894-1904. Kidsgrove UD 1904-22. Newchapel W by1907-22. S-o-T CB 1922-74, D(C) 1974-97, UA 1997-. No. 27 W 1922-55. No. 3 W 1955-65. No. 3 W 1965-79. Chell W 1979-2002. Chell & Packmoor W 2002-
CED. Kidsgrove 1889-1922. CCWs 1974-97.
PARL. S-o-T North BC 1948-.

TUNSTALL TOWNSHIP

Tunstall CP 1894-1910.
LG. Tunstall LB 1855-94 (VCH vol 8 p95), UD 1894-1910. S-o-T CB 1910-74, D(C) 1974-97, UA 1997-.
PARL. Stoke-upon-Trent PB 1832-85. Newcastle PB 1885-1918. Burslem D of S-o-T PB 1918-48. S-o-T North BC 1948-.

Ash

Goldenhill CP 1894-1904. No. 2 (Ravenscliffe by1901) PW 1896-1904.
LG. Tunstall UD 1904-1910. Goldenhill W 1904-10. S-o-T CB 1910-65. No. 2 W 1910-55. No. 1 W 1955-65. Newcastle MB 1965-74, D(B) 1974-. No. 9 W 1932-79. Bradwell 1979-2002, 2002-.
CED. Tunstall North 1889-1910. Newcastle No. 5 1965-81. Bradwell & Porthill 1981-2005, 2005-

Boulevard

LG. South W 1895-1910. No. 3 W 1910-55. No. 2 W 1955-65. No. 2 W 1965-79. Tunstall North W 1979-2002. Tunstall W 2002-.
CED. Tunstall South 1889-1910. CCWs 1974-97.

Broom Hill

LG. North W 1895-1910. No. 2 W 1910-55. No. 1 W 1955-65. No. 1 W 1965-79. Tunstall North W 1979-2002. Tunstall W 2002-.
CED. Tunstall North 1889-1910. CCWs 1974-96.

Christ Church

LG. North W 1895-1910. No. 3 W 1910-55. No. 1 W 1955-65. No. 1 W 1965-79. Tunstall North W 1979-2002. Tunstall W 2002-.
CED. Tunstall North 1889-1910. CCWs 1974-97.

Clanway

LG. North W 1895-1910. No. 3 W 1910-55. No. 3 W 1955-65. No. 1 W 1965-79. Chell W 1979-2002. Chell & Packmoor W 2002-.
CED. Tunstall North 1889-1910. CCWs 1974-97.

Furlong

LG. North W 1895-1910. No. 3 W 1910-55. No. 3 W 1955-65. No. 1 W 1965-79. Chell W 1979-2002. Tunstall W 2002-.
CED. Tunstall North 1889-1910. CCWs 1974-97.

Greenbank

Wolstanton (North Side, Wedgwood)

LG. South W 1895-1910. No. 3 W 1910-55. No. 2 W 1955-65. No. 2 W 1965-79. Burslem Central W 1979-2002. Burslem North W 2002-.
CED. Tunstall South 1889-1910. CCWs 1974-97.

Greenway Valley

LG. North W 1895-1910. No. 1 W 1910-55. No. 3 W 1955-65. No. 1 W 1965-79. Chell W 1979-2002. Chell & Packmoor W 2002-.
CED. Tunstall North 1889-1910. CCWs 1974-97.

Little Pits

LG. South W 1895-1910. No. 3 W 1910-55. No. 2 W 1955-65. No. 4 W 1965-79. Tunstall North W 1979-2002. Tunstall W 2002-.
CED. Tunstall South 1889-1910. CCWs 1974-97.

Newfield

LG. North W 1895-1910. No. 1 W 1910-55. No. 1 W 1955-65. No. 1 W 1965-79. Tunstall North W 1979-2002. Tunstall W 2002-.
CED. Tunstall North 1889-1910. CCWs 1974-97.

Ravensdale

LG. South W 1895-1910. No. 2 W 1910-55. No. 2 W 1955-65. No. 2 W 1965-79. Burslem Grange W 1979-2002. Tunstall W 2002-.
CED. Tunstall South 1889-1910. CCWs 1974-97.

Ravensdale Forge

LG. North W 1895-1910. No. 2 W 1910-55. No. 1 W 1955-65. No. 2 W 1965-79. Tunstall North W 1979-2002. Tunstall W 2002-.
CED. Tunstall North 1889-1910. CCWs 1974-97.

Ravensdale Wharf

LG. South W 1895-1910. No. 2 W 1910-55. No. 2 W 1955-65. No. 4 W 1965-79. Burslem Grange W 1979-2002. Tunstall W 2002-.
CED. Tunstall South 1889-1910. CCWs 1974-97.

Roundwell

LG. North W 1895-1910. No. 2 W 1910-55. No. 2 W 1955-65. No. 2 W 1965-79. Tunstall North W 1979-2002. Tunstall W 2002-.
CED. Tunstall North 1889-1910. CCWs 1974-97.

Tunstall

LG. South W 1895-1910. No. 2 W 1910-55. No. 2 W 1955-65. No. 2 W 1965-79. Tunstall North W 1979-2002. Tunstall W 2002-.
CED. Tunstall South 1889-1910. CCWs 1974-96.

Victoria Park

LG. South W 1895-1910. No. 3 W 1910-55. No. 2 W 1955-65. No. 2 W 1965-79. Burslem Central W 1979-. Tunstall W 2002-.
CED. Tunstall South 1889-1910. CCWs 1974-96.

Yeld

LG. North W 1895-1910. S-o-T CB 1910-65. No. 2 W 1910-55. No. 1 W 1955-65. Newcastle MB 1965-74,

D(B) 1974-. No. 9 W 1965-79. Porthill W 1979-2002. Bradwell W 2002-.
CED. Tunstall North 1889-1910. Newcastle No. 5 1965-81. Bradwell & Porthill W 1981-2005, 2005-.

Yeld Hill

LG. North W 1895-1910. S-o-T CB 1910-65. No. 2 W 1910-55. No. 1 W 1955-65. Newcastle MB 1965-74, D(B) 1974-. No. 9 W 1965-79. Bradwell W 1979-2002, 2002-.
CED. Tunstall North 1889-1910. Newcastle No. 5 1965-81. Bradwell & Porthill W 1981-2005, 2005-.

WEDGWOOD TOWNSHIP

PARL. S-o-T North BC 1948-.

Brook House

Chell CP 1894-1922. Wedgwood PW Aug 1895-1922. Stoke unparished 1922-.
LG. Wolstanton RD 1894-1904. Smallthorne UD 1904-22. Chell W by1907-22. S-o-T CB 1922-74, D(C) 1974-97, UA 1997-. No. 27 W 1922-55. No. 3 W 1955-65. No. 3 W 1965-79. Norton & Bradeley W 1979-2002. Chell & Packmoor W 2002-.
CED. Kidsgrove 1889-95. Tunstall North 1895-1910. Smallthorne 1910-22. CCWs 1974-97.

Cumberbatch

Chell CP 1894-1922. Wedgwood PW Aug 1895-1922. Stoke unparished 1922-.
LG. Wolstanton RD 1894-1904. Smallthorne UD 1904-22. Chell W by1907-22. S-o-T CB 1922-74, D(C) 1974-97, UA 1997-. No. 27 W. No. 1 1922-55. No. 3 W 1955-65. No. 3 W 1965-79. Chell W 1979-2002. Norton & Bradeley W 2002-.
CED. Kidsgrove 1889-95. Tunstall North 1895-1910. Smallthorne 1910-22. CCWs 1974-97.

Outclough

Chell CP 1894-1922. Wedgwood PW Aug 1895-1922. Stoke unparished 1922-.
LG. Wolstanton RD 1894-1904. Smallthorne UD 1904-22. Chell W by1907-22. S-o-T CB 1922-74, D(C) 1974-97, UA 1997-. No. 27 W 1922-55. No. 3 W 1955-65. No. 3 W 1965-79. Norton & Bradeley W 1979-2002. Norton & Bradeley W 2002-.
CED. Kidsgrove 1889-95. Tunstall North 1895-1910. Smallthorne 1910-22. CCWs 1974-97.

Wedgwood

Chell CP 1894-1922. Wedgwood PW Aug 1895-1922. Stoke unparished 1922-.
LG. Wolstanton RD 1894-1904. Smallthorne UD 1904-22. Chell W by1907-22. S-o-T CB 1922-74, D(C) 1974-97, UA 1997-. No. 27 W. No. 1 1922-55. No. 3 W 1955-65. No. 3 W 1965-79. Chell W 1979-2002. Chell & Packmoor W 2002-.

CED. Kidsgrove 1889-95. Tunstall North 1895-1910. Smallthorne 1910-22. CCWs 1974-97.

Whitfield Valley
Chell CP 1894-1922. Wedgwood PW Aug 1895-1922. Stoke unparished 1922-.

LG. Wolstanton RD 1894-1904. Smallthorne UD 1904-22. Chell W by1907-22. S-o-T CB 1922-74, D(C) 1974-97, UA 1997-. No. 27 W 1922-55. No. 3 W 1955-65. No. 7 W 1965-79. Norton & Bradeley W 1979-2002. Norton & Bradeley W 2002-.

CED. Kidsgrove 1889-95. Tunstall North 1895-1910. Smallthorne 1910-22. CCWs 1974-97.

SOUTH SIDE
CHATTERLEY TOWNSHIP
Bathpool Valley (5)
Kidsgrove CP (and there det) 1894-1932. Hardings Wood CP 1932-74. Kidsgrove TC 1974-84. Newcastle unparished 1984-.

LG. Kidsgrove UD 1894-1974. Kidsgrove W by1907-74. Newcastle-u-Lyme D(B) 1974-. No. 16 W Feb 1973-7. No. 16 W Feb 1977-9. Talke W 1979-84. Bradwell W 1984-2002, 2002-.

CED. Kidsgrove 1889-1984. Bradwell & Porthill 1984-2005, 2005-

Bradwell
Wolstanton CP 1894-32. Central PW 1896-32.

LG. Wolstanton RD 1894-1904, United UD 1904-32. Wolstanton W by1913-. Newcastle-u-Lyme MB 1932-74, D(B) 1974-. No. 9 W 1932-79. Bradwell W 1979-2002, 2002-.

CED. Wolstanton 1889-1910. Wolstanton 1910-34. Newcastle No. 5 1934-81. Bradwell & Porthill 1981-2005, 2005-

Bradwell Lodge (a)
Wolstanton CP 1894-32. Central PW 1896-32.

LG. Wolstanton RD 1894-1904, United UD 1904-32. Wolstanton W by1913-. Newcastle-u-Lyme MB 1932-74, D(B) 1974-. No. 9 W 1932-79. Porthill W 1979-2002, 2002-.

CED. Wolstanton 1889-1910. Wolstanton 1910-34. Newcastle No. 5 1934-81. Bradwell & Porthill 1981-2005, 2005-

Bradwell Lodge (b)
Wolstanton CP 1894-1932. Longbridge Hays PW 1896-1932.

LG. Wolstanton RD 1894-1904, United UD 1904-32. Wolstanton W by1913-. Newcastle-u-Lyme MB 1932-74, D(B) 1974-. No. 9 W 1932-79. Porthill W 1979-2002, 2002-.

CED. Wolstanton 1889-1910. Wolstanton 1910-34. Newcastle No. 5 1934-81. Bradwell & Porthill 1981-

Wolstanton (South Side, Chatterley)
2005, 2005-

Chatterley
Wolstanton CP 1894-1932. Longbridge Hays PW 1896-1932.

LG. Wolstanton RD 1894-1904, United UD 1904-32. Wolstanton W by1913-. Newcastle-u-Lyme MB 1932-74, D(B) 1974-. No. 9 W 1932-79. Porthill W 1979-2002. Bradwell W 2002-.

CED. Wolstanton 1889-1910. Wolstanton 1910-34. Newcastle No. 5 1934-81. Bradwell & Porthill 1981-2005, 2005-

Fowlea Brook
Wolstanton CP 1894-1932. Longbridge Hays PW 1896-1932.

LG. Wolstanton RD 1894-1904, United UD 1904-32. Wolstanton W by1913-. Newcastle-u-Lyme MB 1932-65. No. 9 W 1932-65. Stoke CB 1965-. No. 2 W 1955-65. No. 4 W 1965-79. Burslem Grange W 1979-. Tunstall W 2002-.

CED. Wolstanton 1889-1910. Wolstanton 1910-34. Newcastle No. 5 1934-65. CCWs 1974-96.

Goldendale
Wolstanton CP 1894-. Longbridge Hays PW 1896-1932.

LG. Wolstanton RD 1894-1904, United UD 1904-32. Wolstanton W by1913-. Newcastle-u-Lyme MB 1932-65. No. 9 W 1932-65. S-o-T CB 1965-74, D(C) 1974-97, UA 1997-. No. 1 W 1955-65. No. 2 W 1965-79. Tunstall North W 1979-. Tunstall W 2002-.

CED. Wolstanton 1889-1910. Wolstanton 1910-34. Newcastle No. 5 1934-65. CCWs 1974-96.

High Carr
Chesterton CP 1894-32.

LG. Wolstanton RD 1894-1904, United UD 1904-32. Chesterton W by1913-. Newcastle-u-Lyme MB 1932-74, D(B) 1974-. No. 9 W 1932-79. Chesterton W 1979-2002, 2002-.

CED. Wolstanton 1889-1910. Chesterton 1910-34. Newcastle No. 5 1934-81. Audley & Chesterton 1981-2005, 2005-.

Holditch
Chesterton CP 1894-32.

LG. Wolstanton RD 1894-1904, United UD 1904-32. Chesterton W by1913-. Newcastle-u-Lyme MB 1932-74, D(B) 1974-. No. 11 W 1932-79. Holditch W 1979-2002, 2002-.

CED. Wolstanton 1889-1910. Chesterton 1910-34. Newcastle No. 5 1934-67. Newcastle No. 6 Feb 1967-81. Cross Heath 1981-2005. Bradwell & Porthill 2005-

Longport Station
1896-

LG. Wolstanton RD 1894-1904, United UD 1904-32.

Wolstanton (South Side, Chesterton)

Wolstanton W by1913-. Newcastle-u-Lyme MB 1932-65. No. 9 W 1932-65. S-o-T CB 1965-74, D(C) 1974-97, UA 1997-. No. 6 W 1955-65. No. 4 W 1965-79. Burslem Grange W 1979-2002. Burslem South W 2002-

CED. Wolstanton 1889-1910. Wolstanton 1910-34. Newcastle No. 5 1934-65. CCWs 1974-97.

Park House

Wolstanton CP 1894-1932. Longbridge Hays PW 1896-

LG. Wolstanton RD 1894-1904, United UD 1904-32. Wolstanton W by1913-. Newcastle-u-Lyme MB 1932-74, D(B) 1974-. No. 9 W 1932-79. Bradwell W 1979-2002, 2002-.

CED. Wolstanton 1889-1910. Wolstanton 1910-34. Newcastle No. 5 1934-81. Bradwell & Porthill 1981-2005, 2005-.

Peacock Hay

Kidsgrove CP (and there det) 1894-1932. Hardings Wood CP 1932-74. Kidsgrove CP 1974-

LG. Kidsgrove UD 1894-1974. Kidsgrove W by1907-61. Talke W Feb 1961-74. Newcastle-u-Lyme D(B) 1974-. No. 16 W Feb 1973-7. No. 16 W Feb 1977-9. Talke W 1979-2002, 2002-.

CED. Kidsgrove 1889-1968. Talke 1968-2005. Kidsgrove & Talke 2005-.

Porthill (1)

Wolstanton CP 1894-1932. Central PW 1896-

LG. Wolstanton RD 1894-1904, United UD 1904-32. Wolstanton W by1913-. Newcastle-u-Lyme MB 1932-74, D(B) 1974-. No. 9 W 1932-79. Bradwell 1979-2002. Porthill W 2002-

CED. Wolstanton 1889-1910. Wolstanton 1910-34. Newcastle No. 5 1934-81. Bradwell & Porthill 1981-2005, 2005-

Porthill (2)

Wolstanton CP 1894-1932. Longbridge Hays PW 1896-1932.

LG. Wolstanton RD 1894-1904, United UD 1904-32. Wolstanton W by1913. Newcastle-u-Lyme MB 1932-74, D(B) 1974-. No. 9 W 1932-79. Bradwell 1979-2002. Porthill W 2002-

CED. Wolstanton 1889-1910. Wolstanton 1910-34. Newcastle No. 5 1934-81. Bradwell & Porthill 1981-2005, 2005-

Ravensdale

Wolstanton CP 1894-1932. Longbridge Hays PW 1896-1932.

LG. Wolstanton RD 1894-1904, United UD 1904-32. Wolstanton W by1913-. Newcastle-u-Lyme MB 1932-65. No. 9 W 1932-65. St-o-T CB 1965-74, D(C) 1974-97, UA 1997-. No. 2 W 1955-65. No. 2 W 1965-79.

Burslem Grange W 1979-. Tunstall W 2002-.

CED. Wolstanton 1889-1910. Wolstanton 1910-34. Newcastle No. 5 1934-65. CCWs 1974-97.

Ravensdale New Forge

Wolstanton CP 1894-1932. Longbridge Hays PW 1896-1932.

LG. Wolstanton RD 1894-1904, United UD 1904-32. Wolstanton W by1913-. Newcastle-u-Lyme MB 1932-65. No. 9 W 1932-65. S-o-T CB 1965-74, D(C) 1974-97, UA 1997-. No. 2 W 1955-65. No. 2 W 1965-79. Tunstall North W 1979-. Tunstall W 2002-.

CED. Wolstanton 1889-1910. Wolstanton 1910-34. Newcastle No. 5 1934-65. CCWs 1974-97.

CHESTERTON TOWNSHIP

Chesterton CP 1894-1932.

LG. Wolstanton RD 1894-1904, United UD 1904-32. Chesterton W by1913-. Newcastle-u-Lyme MB 1932-74, D(B) 1974-.

Beasley

LG. No. 10 W 1932-79. Chesterton W 1979-2002. Holditch W 2002-

CED. Wolstanton 1889-1910. Chesterton 1910-34. Newcastle No. 5 1934-67. Newcastle No. 6 Feb 1967-81. Audley & Chesterton 1981-2005. Bradwell & Porthill 2005-.

Burley

LG. No. 10 W 1932-79. Halmerend W 1979-2002. Chesterton W 2002-.

CED. Wolstanton 1889-1910. Chesterton 1910-34. Newcastle No. 5 1934-67. Newcastle No. 6 Feb 1967-81. Audley & Chesterton 1981-2005, 2005-.

Chesterton

LG. No. 11 W 1932-79. Chesterton W 1979-2002, 2002-.

CED. Wolstanton 1889-1910. Chesterton 1910-34. Newcastle No. 5 1934-67. Newcastle No. 6 Feb 1967-81. Audley & Chesterton 1981-2005, 2005-.

Crackley

LG. No. 10 W 1932-79. Audley & Chesterton W by1981-. Chesterton W by1992-.

CED. Wolstanton 1889-1910. Chesterton 1910-34. Newcastle No. 5 1934-67. Newcastle No. 6 Feb 1967-81. Audley & Chesterton 1981-2005, 2005-.

Mount Pleasant

LG. No. 11 W 1932-79. Holditch W 1979-2002, 2002-

CED. Wolstanton 1889-1910. Chesterton 1910-34. Newcastle No. 5 1934-67. Newcastle No. 6 Feb 1967-81. Cross Heath 1981-2005. Bradwell & Porthill 2005-

The Mount

LG. No. 11 W 1932-79. Chesterton W 1979-2002. Holditch W 2002-

CED. Wolstanton 1889-1910. Chesterton 1910-34. Newcastle No. 5 1934-67. Newcastle No. 6 Feb 1967-81. Audley & Chesterton 1981-2005. Bradwell & Porthill 2005-.

Primrose Grove
LG. No. 10 W 1932-79. Chesterton W 1979-. Holditch W 2002-
CED. Wolstanton 1889-1910. Chesterton 1910-34. Newcastle No. 5 1934-67. Newcastle No. 6 Feb 1967-81. Audley & Chesterton 1981-2005. Bradwell & Porthill 2005-.

Rowhurst
LG. No. 10 W 1932-79. Audley & Bignall End W 1979-. Chesterton W 2002-
CED. Wolstanton 1889-1910. Chesterton 1910-34. Newcastle No. 5 1934-67. Newcastle No. 6 Feb 1967-81. Audley & Chesterton 1981-2005, 2005-

KNUTTON TOWNSHIP
Knutton LB 1858- . Silverdale CP 1894-1932. Wolstanton RD 1894-1904, United UD 1904-32. Silverdale W by1913-. Newcastle MB 1932-74, D(B) 1974-.

Apedale Colliery
LG. No. 11 W 1932-79. Halmerend W 1979-2002. Holditch W 2002-.
CED. Silverdale 1889-1934. Newcastle No. 5 1934-67. Newcastle No. 6 Feb 1967-81. Cross Heath 1981-2005. Bradwell & Porthill 2005-.

Black Bank
LG. No. 11 W 1932-79. Halmerend W 1979-?1984. Silverdale W ?1984-2002. Halmerend W 2002-
CED. Silverdale 1889-1934. Newcastle No. 5 1934-67. Newcastle No. 6 Feb 1967-81. Newcastle Rural 1981-2005. Audley & Chesterton 2005-.

Cross Heath
LG. No. 6 W 1932-79. Cross Heath W 1979-2002, 2002-.
CED. Silverdale 1889-1934. Newcastle No. 4 1934-81. Cross Heath 1981-2005. Cross Heath & Silverdale 2005-

Dam (1)
LG. No. 1 W 1932-79. Town W 1979-2002. Cross Heath W 2002-
CED. Silverdale 1889-1934. Newcastle No. 1 1934-81. Westlands 1981-2005. Cross Heath & Silverdale 2005-.

Dam (2)
LG. No. 1 W 1932-79. Town W 1979-2002. Knutton & Silverdale W 2002-
CED. Silverdale 1889-1934. Newcastle No. 1 1934-81. Westlands 1981-2005. Cross Heath & Silverdale

Wolstanton (South Side, Knutton)
2005-

Dam (3)
LG. No. 1 W 1932-79. Town W 1979-2002, 2002-
CED. Silverdale 1889-1934. Newcastle No. 1 1934-81. Westlands 1981-2005. Newcastle South 2005-

Dam (4)
LG. No. 2 W 1932-79. Thistleberry W 1979-2002. Town W 2002-
CED. Silverdale 1889-1934. Newcastle No. 1 1934-81. Thistleberry 1981-2005. Newcastle South 2005-.

Dam (5)
LG. No. 2 W 1932-79. Thistleberry W 1979-2002, 2002-
CED. Silverdale 1889-1934. Newcastle No. 1 1934-81. Thistleberry 1981-2005. Keele & Westlands 2005-

Duggeleys
LG. No. 2 W 1932-79. Thistleberry W 1979-2002, 2002-.
CED. Silverdale 1889-1934. Newcastle No. 1 1934-81. Thistleberry 1981-2005. Keele & Westlands 2005-

Gorsty Bank
Silverdale CP May 2002-
LG. No. 1 W 1932-79. Silverdale W 1979-2002. Silverdale & Parksite W 2002-.
CED. Silverdale 1889-1934. Newcastle No. 1 1934-81. Keele & Silverdale 1981-2005. Cross Heath & Silverdale 2005-.

Gorsty Farm
Silverdale CP May 2002-
LG. No. 12 W 1932-79. Silverdale W 1979-2002. Knutton & Silverdale W 2002-.
CED. Silverdale 1889-1934. Newcastle No. 1 1934-81. Keele & Silverdale W 1981-2005. Cross Heath & Silverdale 2005-.

Grubbers Ash
LG. No. 11 W 1932-79. Halmerend W 1979-2002, 2002-.
CED. Silverdale 1889-1934. Newcastle No. 5 1934-67. Newcastle No. 6 Feb 1967-81. Newcastle Rural 1981-2005. Audley & Chesterton 2005-.

Grubbers Ash Colliery
LG. No. 12 W 1932-79. Halmerend W 1979-2002, 2002-.
CED. Silverdale 1889-1934. Newcastle No. 1 1934-81. Newcastle Rural 1981-2005. Audley & Chesterton 2005-.

Grubbers Hill
Silverdale CP May 2002-.
LG. No. 12 W 1932-79. Halmerend W 1979-2002. Silverdale & Parksite W 2002-.
CED. Silverdale 1889-1934. Newcastle No. 1 1934-81. Newcastle Rural 1981-2005. Cross Heath &

Wolstanton (South Side, Knutton)

Silverdale 2005-.

High Lane

Audley Rural CP 1984-. Halmerend PW 1984, 2003-
LG. No. 12 W 1932-79. Halmerend W 1979-2002, 2002-.
CED. Silverdale 1889-1934. Newcastle No. 1 1934-81. Newcastle Rural 1981-2005. Audley & Chesterton 2005-.

Hooters Hall Farm

LG. No. 11 W 1932-79. Holditch W 1979-2002, 2002-
CED. Silverdale 1889-1934. Newcastle No. 5 1934-67. Newcastle No. 6 Feb 1967-81. Cross Heath 1981-2005. Bradwell & Porthill 2005-.

Knutton

LG. No. 11 W 1932-79. Silverdale W 1979-2002. Knutton & Silverdale W 2002-
CED. Silverdale 1889-1934. Newcastle No. 5 1934-67. Newcastle No. 6 Feb 1967-81. Keele & Silverdale W by1981-2005. Cross Heath & Silverdale 2005-

Knutton Heath

Silverdale CP May 2002-.
LG. No. 1 W 1932-79. Silverdale W 1979-2002. Knutton & Silverdale W 2002-.
CED. Silverdale 1889-1934. Newcastle No. 1 1934-81. Keele & Silverdale W 1981-2005. Cross Heath & Silverdale 2005-

Knutton Lane

LG. No. 1 W 1932-79. Silverdale W 1979-2002. Knutton & Silverdale W 2002-.
CED. Silverdale 1889-1934. Newcastle No. 1 1934-81. Keele & Silverdale W 1981-2005. Cross Heath & Silverdale 2005-

Lyme Brook

LG. No. 1 W 1932-79. Silverdale W 1979-2002. Cross Heath W 2002-.
CED. Silverdale 1889-1934. Newcastle No. 1 1934-81. Keele & Silverdale W 1981-2005. Cross Heath & Silverdale 2005-

Lyme Valley (2)

LG. No. 11 W 1932-79. Halmerend W 1979-2002, 2002-.
CED. Silverdale 1889-1934. Newcastle No. 5 1934-67. Newcastle No. 6 Feb 1967-81. Cross Heath 1981-2005. Audley & Chesterton 2005-.

Lyme Valley (3)

LG. No. 11 W 1932-79. Halmerend W 1979-2002, 2002-
CED. Silverdale 1889-1934. Newcastle No. 5 1934-67. Newcastle No. 6 Feb 1967-81. Keele & Silverdale W 1981-2005. Audley & Chesterton 2005-.

Lyme Valley (4)

LG. No. 11 W 1932-79. Holditch W 1979-2002. Knutton & Silverdale W 2002-
CED. Silverdale 1889-1934. Newcastle No. 5 1934-67. Newcastle No. 6 Feb 1967-81. Cross Heath 1981-2005. Cross Heath & Silverdale 2005-.

Milehouse

LG. No. 8 W 1932-79. Holditch W 1979-2002. Cross Heath W 2002-
CED. Silverdale 1889-1934. Newcastle No. 4 1934-81. Cross Heath 1981-2005. Cross Heath & Silverdale 2005-.

Milehouse Lane (1)

LG. No. 11 W 1932-79. Cross Heath W 1979-2002, 2002-
CED. Silverdale 1889-1934. Newcastle No. 5 1934-67. Newcastle No. 6 Feb 1967-81. Cross Heath 1981-2005. Cross Heath & Silverdale 2005-.

Milehouse Lane (2)

LG. No. 11 W 1932-79. Holditch W 1979-2002. Cross Heath W 2002-
CED. Silverdale 1889-1934. Newcastle No. 5 1934-67. Newcastle No. 6 Feb 1967-81. Cross Heath W 1981-2005. Cross Heath & Silverdale 2005-.

Mill Street

Silverdale CP May 2002-
LG. No. 12 W 1932-79. Silverdale W 1979-2002. Knutton & Silverdale W 2002-.
CED. Silverdale 1889-1934. Newcastle No. 1 1934-81. Keele & Silverdale W 1981-. Cross Heath & Silverdale 2005-.

New Grove Colliery

Silverdale CP May 2002-
LG. No. 11 W 1932-79. Silverdale 1979-2002. Silverdale & Parksite W 2002-.
CED. Silverdale 1889-1934. Newcastle No. 5 1934-67. Newcastle No. 6 Feb 1967-81. Keele & Silverdale W 1981-2005. Cross Heath & Silverdale 2005-

Old Grove Colliery

Silverdale CP May 2002-
LG. No. 11 W 1932-79. Silverdale W 1979-2002. Knutton & Silverdale W 2002-.
CED. Silverdale 1889-1934. Newcastle No. 5 1934-67. Newcastle No. 6 Feb 1967-81. Keele & Silverdale W 1981-2005. Cross Heath & Silverdale 2005-

Racecourse

Silverdale CP May 2002-
LG. No. 1 W 1932-79. Silverdale W 1979-2002. Silverdale & Parksite W 2002-.
CED. Silverdale 1889-1934. Newcastle No. 1 1934-81. Keele & Silverdale W 1981-2005. Cross Heath & Silverdale 2005-.

Wolstanton (South Side, Knutton)

Map of Wolstanton (South Side)

Silverdale

Silverdale CP May 2002-
LG. No. 12 W 1932-79. Silverdale W 1979-2002.
Silverdale & Parksite W 2002-.
CED. Silverdale 1889-1934. Newcastle No. 1 1934-81. Keele & Silverdale W 1981-2005. Cross Heath & Silverdale 2005-.

Spoil

Silverdale CP May 2002-
LG. No. 12 W 1932-79. Silverdale W 1979-2002.
Silverdale & Parksite W 2002-.
CED. Silverdale 1889-1934. Newcastle No. 1 1934-81. Newcastle Rural 1981-2005. Cross Heath & Silverdale 2005-.

Watermills Farm

Audley Rural CP 1984-. Halmerend PW 1984, 2003-.
LG. No. 11 W 1932-79. Halmerend W 1979-2002, 2002-.
CED. Silverdale 1889-1934. Newcastle No. 5 1934-67. Newcastle No. 6 Feb 1967-81. Newcastle Rural 1981-2005. Audley & Chesterton 2005-.

Whitebarn Colliery

LG. No. 11 W 1932-79. Silverdale W 1979-2002.
Halmerend W 2002-.
CED. Silverdale 1889-1934. Newcastle No. 5 1934-67. Newcastle No. 6 Feb 1967-81. Keele & Silverdale W 1981-2005. Audley & Chesterton 2005-.

Wolstanton (South Side, Wolstanton)

WOLSTANTON TOWNSHIP

LG. Wolstanton RD 1894-1904, United UD 1904-32. Wolstanton W by1913-. Newcastle-u-Lyme MB 1932-74, D(B) 1974-.

Ashfield Brook

Wolstanton RD 1894-1904, United UD 1904-32. Chesterton W by1913-. Chesterton CP 1894-1932.
LG. No. 11 W 1932-79. Holditch W 1979-2002. Cross Heath W 2002-
CED. Wolstanton 1889-1910. Chesterton 1910-34. Newcastle No. 5 1934-67. Newcastle No. 6 Feb 1967-81. Cross Heath 1981-2005. Cross Heath & Silverdale 2005-

Basford

Wolstanton CP 1894-1932. May Bank PW 1896-
LG. No. 5 W 1932-79. May Bank W 1979-2002, 2002-
CED. Wolstanton 1889-1910. Wolstanton 1910-34. Newcastle No. 3 1934-81. Wolstanton 1981-2005, 2005-

Beasley

Chesterton CP 1894-1932.
LG. Chesterton W by1913-. No. 10 W 1932-79. Chesterton W 1979-2002. Holditch W 2002-
CED. Wolstanton 1889-1910. Chesterton 1910-34. Newcastle No. 5 1934-67. Newcastle No. 6 Feb 1967-81. Audley & Chesterton 1981-2005. Bradwell & Porthill 2005-

Beasley House

Chesterton CP 1894-1932.
LG. Chesterton W by1913-. No. 9 W 1932-79. Chesterton W 1979-2002, 2002-.
CED. Wolstanton 1889-1910. Chesterton 1910-34. Newcastle No. 5 1934-81. Audley & Chesterton W 1981-2005, 2005-.

Bradwell Grange

Wolstanton CP 1894-1932. Central PW 1896-1932.
LG. No. 9 W 1932-79. Bradwell W 1979-2002. Porthill W 2002-
CED. Wolstanton 1889-1910. Wolstanton 1910-34. Newcastle No. 5 1934-81. Bradwell & Porthill W 1981-2005, 2005-.

Dimsdale

Wolstanton CP 1894-1932. Central PW 1896-1932.
LG. No. 9 W 1932-79. Bradwell W 1979-2002, 2002-
CED. Wolstanton 1889-1910. Wolstanton 1910-34. Newcastle No. 5 1934-81. Bradwell & Porthill W 1981-2005, 2005-.

Dimsdale Hall

Wolstanton CP 1894-1932. Central PW 1896-1932.
LG. No. 8 W 1932-79. Holditch W 1979-2002. Cross Heath W 2002-.
CED. Wolstanton 1889-1910. Wolstanton 1910-34.

Newcastle No. 4 1934-81. Cross Heath 1981-2005. Cross Heath & Silverdale 2005-.

Dimsdale Parade (1)

Wolstanton CP 1894-1932. Central PW 1896-1932.
LG. No. 8 W 1932-79. Bradwell W 1979-2002. Holditch W 2002-.
CED. Wolstanton 1889-1910. Wolstanton 1910-34. Newcastle No. 4 1934-81. Cross Heath 1981-2005. Bradwell & Porthill 2005-.

Dimsdale Parade (2)

Wolstanton CP 1894-1932. Central PW 1896-1932.
LG. No. 8 W 1932-79. Holditch W 1979-2002, 2002-
CED. Wolstanton 1889-1910. Wolstanton 1910-34. Newcastle No. 4 1934-81. Cross Heath 1981-2005. Bradwell & Porthill 2005-.

Dimsdale Parade (3)

Wolstanton CP 1894-1932. Central PW 1896-1932.
LG. No. 8 W 1932-79. Bradwell W 1979-2002, 2002-
CED. Wolstanton 1889-1910. Wolstanton 1910-34. Newcastle No. 4 1934-81. Bradwell & Porthill 1981-2005, 2005-.

Dunkirk

Wolstanton RD 1894-1904, United UD 1904-32. Chesterton W by1913-. Chesterton CP 1894-1932.
LG. No. 11 W 1932-79. Holditch W 1979-2002, 2002-
CED. Wolstanton 1889-1910. Chesterton 1910-34. Newcastle No. 5 1934-67. Newcastle No. 6 Feb 1967-81. Cross Heath 1981-2005. Bradwell & Porthill 2005-

Fowlea Valley (1)

Wolstanton CP 1894-1932. Central PW 1896-1932.
LG. No. 9 W 1932-65. S-o-T CB 1965-74, D(C) 1974-97, UA 1997-. No. 6 W 1955-65. No. 4 W 1965-79. Burslem Grange W 1979-2002. Burslem South W 2002-.
CED. Wolstanton 1889-1910. Wolstanton 1910-34. Newcastle No. 5 1934-65. CCWs 1974-97.

Fowlea Valley (2)

Wolstanton CP 1894-1932. Central PW 1896-1932.
LG. No. 7 W 1932-65. S-o-T CB 1965-74, D(C) 1974-97, UA 1997-. No. 6 W 1955-65. No. 6 W 1965-79. Burslem Grange W 1979-2002. Burslem South W 2002-.
CED. Wolstanton 1889-1910. Wolstanton 1910-34. Newcastle No. 3 1934-65. CCWs 1974-97.

Fowlea Valley (3)

Wolstanton CP 1894-1932. Central PW 1896-1932.
LG. No. 7 W 1932-65. S-o-T CB 1965-74, D(C) 1974-97, UA 1997-. No. 6 W 1955-65. No. 6 W 1965-79. Burslem Grange W 1979-2002. Burslem South W 2002-.
CED. Wolstanton 1889-1910. Wolstanton 1910-34. Newcastle No. 3 1934-65. CCWs 1974-97.

Fowlea Valley (4)

Wolstanton CP 1894-1932. May Bank PW 1896-1932. LG. No. 7 W 1932-65. S-o-T CB 1965-74, D(C) 1974-97, UA 1997-. No. 6 W 1955-65. No. 6 W 1965-79. Burslem Grange W 1979-2002. Burslem South W 2002-.

CED. Wolstanton 1889-1910. Wolstanton 1910-34. Newcastle No. 3 1934-65. CCWs 1974-97.

Fowlea Valley (5)

Wolstanton CP 1894-1932. May Bank PW 1896-1932. LG. No. 7 W 1932-65. S-o-T CB 1965-74, D(C) 1974-97, UA 1997-. No. 6 W 1955-65. No. 6 W 1965-79. Burslem Grange W 1979-2002. Hanley West & Shelton W 2002-.

CED. Wolstanton 1889-1910. Wolstanton 1910-34. Newcastle No. 3 1934-65. CCWs 1974-97.

Fowlea Valley (6)

Wolstanton CP 1894-1932. May Bank PW 1896-1932 LG. No. 5 W 1932-65. S-o-T CB 1965-74, D(C) 1974-97, UA 1997-. No. 11 W 1955-65. No. 9 W 1965-79. Shelton W 1979-2002. Hanley West & Shelton W 2002-.

CED. Wolstanton 1889-1910. Wolstanton 1910-34. Newcastle No. 3 1934-65. CCWs 1974-97.

Hassam Parade

Wolstanton CP 1894-1932. Central PW 1896-1932. LG. No. 8 W 1932-79. Wolstanton W 1979-2002, 2002- CED. Wolstanton 1889-1910. Wolstanton 1910-34. Newcastle No. 4 1934-81. Wolstanton 1981-2005, 2005-.

High Fields

Wolstanton CP 1894-1932. May Bank PW 1896-1932 LG. No. 7 W 1932-79. Wolstanton W 1979-2002. May Bank W 2002-.

CED. Wolstanton 1889-1910. Wolstanton 1910-34. Newcastle No. 3 1934-81. Wolstanton 1981-2005, 2005-.

Highfield Tileries

Wolstanton CP 1894-1932. May Bank PW 1896-1932. LG. No. 7 W 1932-79. Wolstanton W 1979-2002, 2002- CED. Wolstanton 1889-1910. Wolstanton 1910-34. Newcastle No. 3 1934-81. Wolstanton 1981-2005, 2005-.

Lyme Brook

Wolstanton CP 1894-1932. May Bank PW 1896-1932. LG. No. 6 W 1932-79. Cross Heath W 1979-2002, 2002-.

CED. Wolstanton 1889-1910. Wolstanton 1910-34. Newcastle No. 4 1934-81. Cross Heath 1981-2005. Cross Heath & Silverdale 2005-.

May Bank

Wolstanton CP 1894-1932. May Bank PW 1896-1932.

Wolstanton (South Side, Wolstanton)

LG. No. 6 W 1932-79. May Bank 1979-2002, 2002-. CED. Wolstanton 1889-1910. Wolstanton 1910-34. Newcastle No. 4 1934-81. Wolstanton 1981-2005, 2005-.

Porthill Grange

Wolstanton CP 1894-1932. Central PW 1896-1932. LG. No. 9 W 1932-79. Porthill W 1979-2002, 2002-. CED. Wolstanton 1889-1910. Wolstanton 1910-34. Newcastle No. 5 1934-81. Bradwell & Porthill W 1981-2005, 2005-.

Ridgway

Wolstanton CP 1894-1932. Central PW 1896-1932. LG. No. 7 W 1932-79. Wolstanton W 1979-2002. Porthill W 2002-.

CED. Wolstanton 1889-1910. Wolstanton 1910-34. Newcastle No. 3 1934-81. Wolstanton 1981-2005. Bradwell & Porthill 2005-.

St Georges

Wolstanton CP 1894-1932. Central PW 1896-1932. LG. No. 8 W 1932-79. Wolstanton W 1979-2002, 2002- CED. Wolstanton 1889-1910. Wolstanton 1910-34. Newcastle No. 4 1934-81. Wolstanton 1981-2005, 2005-

Sandy Lane

Wolstanton CP 1894-1932. May Bank PW 1896-1932. LG. No. 5 W 1932-79. Cross Heath W 1979-2002. May Bank W 2002-.

CED. Wolstanton 1889-1910. Wolstanton 1910-34. Newcastle No. 3 1934-81. Cross Heath 1981-2005. Wolstanton 2005-.

Sparch

Wolstanton CP 1894-1932. Central PW 1896-1932. LG. No. 8 W 1932-79. May Bank 1979-2002. Wolstanton W 2002-.

CED. Wolstanton 1889-1910. Wolstanton 1910-34. Newcastle No. 4 1934-81. Wolstanton 1981-2005, 2005-.

Templar

Wolstanton CP 1894-1932. Central PW 1896-1932. LG. No. 9 W 1932-79. Porthill W 1979-2002, 2002-. CED. Wolstanton 1889-1910. Wolstanton 1910-34. Newcastle No. 5 1934-81. Bradwell & Porthill W 1981-2005, 2005-.

Upper Marsh

Wolstanton CP 1894-1932. May Bank PW 1896-1932. LG. No. 7 W 1932-79. May Bank 1979-2002, 2002-. CED. Wolstanton 1889-1910. Wolstanton 1910-34. Newcastle No. 3 1934-81. Wolstanton W 1981-2005, 2005-.

Watlands

Wolstanton CP 1894-1932. Central PW 1896-1932. LG. No. 8 W 1932-79. Porthill W 1979-2002, 2002-.

Wolstanton (South Side, Wolstanton)

CED. Wolstanton 1889-1910. Wolstanton 1910-34. Newcastle No. 4 1934-81. Bradwell & Porthill 1981-2005, 2005-.

Wolstanton

Wolstanton CP 1894-1932. Central PW 1896-1932. LG. No. 7 W 1932-79. Wolstanton W 1979-2002, 2002-. CED. Wolstanton 1889-1910. Wolstanton 1910-34. Newcastle No. 3 1934-81. Wolstanton W 1981-2005, 2005-.

Wolstanton Marsh

Wolstanton CP 1894-1932. May Bank PW 1896-1932. LG. No. 7 W 1932-79. May Bank W 1979-2002. Wolstanton W 2002-. CED. Wolstanton 1889-1910. Wolstanton 1910-34. Newcastle No. 3 1934-81. Wolstanton W 1981-2005, 2005-.

Wulstan

Wolstanton CP 1894-1932. May Bank PW 1896-1932. LG. No. 6 W 1932-79. Cross Heath W 1979-2002. May Bank W 2002-. CED. Wolstanton 1889-1910. Wolstanton 1910-34. Newcastle No. 4 1934-81. Cross Heath 1981-2005. Wolstanton 2005-.

Municipal burial grounds

By 2004 SRO & SCA had won support from the Heritage Lottery Fund to film civil cemetery records. Stoke-on-Trent CC have allowed them to film their records: The dates of records on microfiche (and which RO houses them), appear after the opening date of the cemetery. **Barlaston** Cemetery Hartwell road, Barlaston, opened 1866. **Burslem** Cemetery, Hanley Rd, opened 1879 (1884-1969 SRO, SCA). Carmountside Cemetery, Leek Rd (1947-69 SRO, SCA). **Madeley** Cemetery, Manor Rd, opened Nov 29 1996. **Newcastle** Cemetery, Lymewood Grove, opened July 1 1866. **Norton-in-the-Moors** Smallthorne Cemetery, Ford Green Rd (1879-1969 SRO, SCA). **Stafford** Cemetery in Tixall Road, Sow, opened 1964. **Stoke-upon-Trent** - Fenton Cemetery, Bassilow Rd opened 1887 (1887-1969, SRO, SCA). Hanley Cemetery, Stoke Rd (opened 1860) (1860-1969 SRO, SCA). Longton Cemetery, Spring Garden Rd (opened 1877) (1877-1969, SRO, SCA. GENUKI 2003 p/s). Stoke Cemetery, Queen's Rd, opened 1884 (1884-1969, SRO, SCA). **Stone** Cemetery, Stafford Rd, Walton, opened Sept 5 1903. Stafford Cemetery, Eccleshall Rd, **Tillington**, opened 1856 (1856-64 LRO B/V/7/3/13/1). **Trentham** Cemetery, Stone Rd; graves from 1817; in extension from 1927; passed from PCC to Stoke-on-Trent CC in 1960 (1960-9 SRO, SCA). **Wolstanton** - Bradwell Cemetery, Chatterley Close opened Jan 1965. Chesterton Cemetery, Hollows Farm, Loomer Rd opened March 31 1915. Kidsgrove Cemetery, Attwood Rise (opened ?). Knutton Cemetery, Cotswold Ave opened Feb 18 1888. Silverdale Cemetery, Cemetery Road opened May 3 1886. Tunstall Cemetery, Broomhill St, opened 1868 (1868-1969 SRO, SCA).

Worston Mill. Etching in glass at the mill. Courtesy of Worston Mill

Worston

'The land and manorial rights belong entirely to William Milner esq. who resides at the Hall.'

Kelly's Directory of Staffordshire 1884

PLU. Stafford 1836-1930. Seighford with Worston W by1910.

SEE ALSO pages 46, 51, 61, 79, 86, 100, 103, 120, 195, 231-232

WORSTON TOWNSHIP

Worston CP 1858-1934. Worston was not eligible to form a PC in 1894 (with a population of less than 100). The parish meeting in late 1894 voted unanimously for Edward Johnson as chairman for parish meetings in the coming year (SA Dec 8 1894 p6) and evidently did not wish to make a request to form a PC. Seighford CP 1934-. Great Bridgeford PW 1972-.

LG. Stafford RD 1894-1974, D(B) 1974-. Seighford W 1974-2002, 2002-.

CED. Stafford Rural 1889-1911. Stafford Rural West Sept 1911-34. Gnosall 1934-73. Stafford Rural No. 1 1973-81. Eccleshall 1981-2005. Gnosall & Doxey 2005-.

Map of Worston

Tithe maps of extra-parochial places

Tillington, **Worston**, and **Yarlet** were nominally served by St Mary's church, Stafford (partly because the church had tithable land there?); So, at SRO, their tithe maps are indexed under the records of Stafford St Mary. On the Tillington map (1841, D834/14/15/3) fields (with names) are only shown if they are tithable (about half the liberty). On the Yarlet map (1846, D834/14/15/6) all fields (with names) are shown, but only one - Far Part of Great Aston leasow - was tithable. On the Worston map (1846, D834/14/15/5) all fields (with names) are shown, and most were tithable. In fact, Worston seems to have been troublesome to the Tithe Commissioners, seven years going by between the initial tithe file (1838) and the schedule (1845). The principal proprietor John Milner, owned nearly

Worston

all of the tithable land, whilst the proprietors of the Grand Junction Railway owned the railway line (11a, 31). The Trustees of the Stafford Charities were entitled to the tithes. Commissioner, Charles Pym, in his preamble to the apportionment, refers to disagreements, and he had 'held divers meetings in the said parish.'(NSJFS 13 1973 pp34-5).

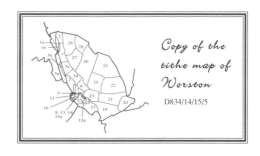

Copy of the tithe map of Worston

D834/14/15/5

John Milner occupied: - Long Meadow (1), part of Long Meadow (1a), plantation (1b), Little Brooms (2), Long Brooms (3), part of Long Brooms (3a), part of Long Brooms (3b), Shallow Ford Lane (4), Mill Meadow (5), part of Mill Meadow (5a), Mad Croft (6), Millers Croft (7), cottage & garden (8), Mill House, part of mill stream flood gate yard and flat (9), Bye Flat (11), Green Way (12), pond (12a), Farm House Buildings yard & garden (15), Pool Croft (16), Malthouse Meadow (17), Coney Greaves and Hall Pool Meadow (18), Whitgreave Meadow (20), Gospel Field (21), Ox Leasow (22), Green Croft (23), Sheep Leasow (24), Sheep and Crooked Leasow (25), Thistley Field (26), Near Shallow Ford (27), Pear tree field (28), Further Shallow Ford (29), Near Brooms (30). John Milner's tenants - John Evans (13), Aaron Fletcher (14a), William Wetton (14) - occupied cottages & gardens.

Yarlet Hall, which has housed a preparatory school since 1873. Watercolour by James Dunn, 1980s, courtesy of Yarlet School

Yarlet

'Yarlet, I recall, was built in the style of a sort of mock castle, with a square tower on the front of the house which formed the main entrance. It was covered with virginia creeper, which always seemed to be brilliant in my mind, though this really was only in autumn, I suppose.'

Ruth Plant, sister of a Yarlet School boy. The Yarlet Story. 1993

PLU. Stafford 1836-1930. Whitgreave & Yarlet W by1910.
SEE ALSO pages 46, 51, 61, 79, 86, 120, 124, 195, 231-232, 233

YARLET TOWNSHIP

Yarlet CP 1858-1934. The parish was not eligible to form a PC in 1894 (with a population of less than 100). A parish meeting is not recorded in late 1894. Marston CP 1934- (1934 Review Order C/C/O/36/2 map No. 5). LG. Stafford RD 1894-1974, D(B) 1974-. Beaconside W 1974-2002. Seighford W 2002-. CED. Stafford Rural 1889-1911. Stafford Rural East Sept 1911-34. Stafford Rural 1934-73. Stafford Rural No. 2 1973-81. Stafford Trent Valley 1981-2005, 2005-

Some errors in secondary sources

The Phillimore Atlas and Index of Parish Registers (Cecil Humphery-Smith. 1995) erroneously shows **Yarlet** as a detached portion of Weston-upon-Trent ancient parish. No mention of Yarlet is made in the Weston registers 1583- (F975/1/1) or 1681- (F975/1/2). Youngs' GLAUE is sometimes in error. For instance unaware of the Stoke Rectory Act, 1807, elevating the chapelries of **Bucknall-cum-Bagnall**, **Burslem**, **Newcastle-under-Lyme**, **Norton-in-the-Moors**, and **Whitmore** to rectories, on the deaths of the existing curates (VCH vol 8 p121 note), placing **Adbaston**, **Ashley**, **Chebsey**, **Eccleshall**, **Ellenhall**, **High Offley**, **Swynnerton** in Handsworth Parliamentary Division 1885-1918, and for **Ashley** no civil boundary change occurred in 1932.

233

Index

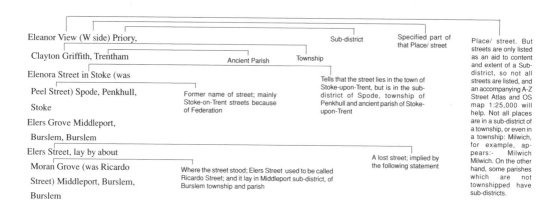

Eleanor View (W side) Priory, Clayton Griffith, Trentham

Elenora Street in Stoke (was Peel Street) Spode, Penkhull, Stoke

Elers Grove Middleport, Burslem, Burslem

Elers Street, lay by about Moran Grove (was Ricardo Street) Middleport, Burslem, Burslem

Sub-district — Township — Ancient Parish — Specified part of that Place/ street

Tells that the street lies in the town of Stoke-upon-Trent, but is in the sub-district of Spode, township of Penkhull and ancient parish of Stoke-upon-Trent

Former name of street; mainly Stoke-on-Trent streets because of Federation

Where the street stood; Elers Street used to be called Ricardo Street; and it lay in Middleport sub-district, of Burslem township and parish

A lost street; implied by the following statement

Place/ street. But streets are only listed as an aid to content and extent of a Sub-district, so not all streets are listed, and an accompanying A-Z Street Atlas and OS map 1:25,000 will help. Not all places are in a sub-district of a township, or even in a township: Milwich, for example, appears:- Milwich Milwich. On the other hand, some parishes which are not townshipped have sub-districts.

Eccleshall, Stoke-upon-Trent, Stone and Wolstanton chapters are arranged by their Quarter/ Side regions (blocks of townships for poor relief), and there is no account of them in the index - so scan the relevant chapter for the township subheading.

Key to boundary lines

———— (1 point stroke) = ancient parish boundary
———— (1 point stroke, half tone) = township, liberty boundary
———— (.5 point stroke) = Parliamentary, CP (post 1894), MB, UA boundary
———— (.5 point stroke, half tone) = liberty, lordship, estate boundary
———— (hairline stroke) = ward boundary of a UD, MB
———— (hairline stroke, pale to half tone) = reservoir, pool, wood, campus, industrial estate, nature reserve
·············· (dual hairline stroke, pale tone) = major river course

A

A50 (centre, S side) Greendock, Longton, Stoke

A50 (E end, S side) Stafford Collieries, Fenton Culvert, Stoke

A50 (interchange with Foley Road, S side) Line Side D, Longton, Stoke

A50 (interchange with Upper Normacot Road) Spring, Normacot, Stone

A50 (NW part of interchange with Foley Road) Foley, Fenton Culvert, Stoke

A50 (tiny centre part, N side) New Uttoxeter Road, Stallington, Stone

A50 (tiny centre part, S side) Grindley, Normacot, Stone

A50 (W end, N side) Great

Fenton, Fenton Culvert, Stoke

A50 Link at Fenton King Street, Fenton Culvert, Stoke

A50 Link Road (N end, S end, E side, and interchange with King Street) King Street, Fenton Culvert, Stoke

A5007/ Uttoxeter Road (centre, S side) Normacot Grange, Normacot, Stone

Abberley House Bradwell Lodge (a), Chatterley, Wolstanton

Abberley's Plantation Bagot's Bromley, Abbots Bromley

Abbey Drive Stowe 36, Little Haywood, Stowe

Abbey Farm Holden Lane, Hulton, Burslem

Abbey Hill School Abbey Hulton, Bucknall, Stoke

Abbey Hulton Abbey Hulton,

Bucknall, Stoke

Abbey Island Batchacre, Adbaston

Abbey Lane (most) Abbey Hulton, Bucknall, Stoke

Abbey Lane (S end, W side) Heath Field, Bucknall, Stoke

Abbey Road Abbey Hulton, Bucknall, Stoke

Abbey Road (S tip) W.R., Bucknall, Stoke

Abbey Street Abbey Hulton, Bucknall, Stoke

Abbey Street Silverdale, Knutton, Wolstanton

Abbey Street (E tip) Stoke Grange, Stone, Stone

Abbey Street (most) Stone Park, Stone, Stone

Abbeyfields Great Haywood, Colwich

Abbot's Drive Holden Lane,

Hulton, Burslem

Abbot's Way (centre) Friarswood, Clayton Griffith, Trentham

Abbot's Way (N end) Priory, Clayton Griffith, Trentham

Abbot's Way (S end) Hill Farm, Clayton Griffith, Trentham

Abbots Bromley Abbots Bromley borough, Abbots Bromley

Abbots Bromley Hospital Abbots Bromley borough, Abbots Bromley

Abbots Park See Bromley Park Abbots Bromley, Abbots Bromley

Abbots Road Hulton Abbey, Hulton, Burslem

Abbots Walk Stafford Workhouse, Foregate, Marston

Abbotts Court Hulton Abbey,

I

O

Romer Side

313

Index

Index

INDEX TO CHAPTER ABSTRACTS

SUPPLEMENT
A roll of Staffordshire parliamentary representation

THE HOUSE OF LORDS
The Staffordshire Peerage

1067 Earldom of Hereford (county) (Breteuil, Miles, Fitzmiles, Bohun); merged in the Crown 1399

1070 Earldom of Chester (county); merged in the Crown 1901

1074 Earldom of Shropshire or Shrewsbury (Montgomery, Bellime, Talvas, Talbot); extinct 1171

1088 Earldom of Warwick (Beaumont, Neville from 1449); forfeited 1477/8; restored 1492; forfeited 1499

1138 Earldom of Derby (Ferrers); extinct 1265

1160 Barony of Basset - progenitors of the Bassets of Drayton, Colston, Heddington, and Wycombe; extinct 1272

1198 Bishopric of Coventry; from 1208 Bishopric of Coventry and Lichfield; from 1661 Bishopric of Lichfield and Coventry; from 1836 Bishopric of Lichfield

1266 Earldom of Derby (county) (to Edmund, the King's youngest son); forfeited 1321/2

1266/7 Earldom of Lancaster (county); forfeited 1321/2

1295 Barony of Furnivall or Furnivalle (of Sheffield, Worksop); united 1442 with Earldoms of Shrewsbury & Water-

ford; abeyant 1616; revived 1654 (Howard, Earl of Arundel); abeyant 1777; revived 1913; abeyant 1968

1295 Barony of Basset (of Drayton); extinct 1390

1295 Barony of Verdun; abeyant 1316

1299 Barony of Stafford (Stafford); forfeited 1521; restored 1547; holder deprived by/ at 1640 & became extinct.

1299 Barony of Ferrers (of Chartley) (Ferrers, Devereux); extinct 1646

1299 Barony of Tuchet or Tochet; abeyant 1321/2; revived 1405 but subsequently styled Lords Audley; terminated 1420/1

1299 Barony of Grendon (of Grendon, Warws, and Shenstone, Staffs); extinct 1364/5

1308 Barony of Somery; extinct 1322

1312/3 Barony of Audley (for Nicholas Audley or Aldithley of Heighley); terminated 1405 in favour of John Tuchet who was summons to Parl. by writ as Baron Tuchet (however he was frequently styled Lord Audley). For his successor James Tuchet the Barony of Audley was revived 1420/1; abeyant 1872; revived 1942; abeyant 1997

1317 Barony of Audley (for Hugh Audley or Aldithley jnr, 2nd s of Hugh Audley (who afterwards (viz. in 1321) was also summons to Parl.); by marriage passed into the Stafford family; forfeited 1483; restored 1486; forfeited 1521.

1321 Barony of Audley of Stratton Audley, Oxon (for Hugh Audley youngest s of James Audley of Heighley (b1267)); forfeited 1322

1331/2 Barony of Talbot; united 1442 with the Earldoms of Shrewsbury and Waterford; abeyant 1616; revived 1654 (Howard, Earl of Arundel); abeyant 1777

1336/7 Earldom of Derby; abeyant 1360/1; revived 1385; merged in the Crown 1399

1337 Barony of Swynnerton (of Swynnerton); reputedly, and for 1337 only

1345 Earldom of Lancaster (county); abeyant 1360/1

1348 Barony of Bourchier (from 1570 Devereux); forfeited 1600/1; restored 1604; abeyant 1646

1350/1 Earldom of Stafford (county) (Stafford); forfeited 1521

1351 Dukedom of Lancaster (county) (the Earl

of Derby); extinct 1360/1

1357 Barony of Lisle (of Kingston Lisle, Berks); abeyant 1382; revived 1444 for John Talbot (see below)

1361 Earldom of Lancaster (for John 'of Gaunt'); merged in the Crown 1412/3

1362 Dukedom of Lancaster (for John 'of Gaunt'); merged in the Crown 1412/3

1370 Barony of Sir Richard de Stafford (d1380); abeyant 1380 (DNB)

1397 Dukedom of Hereford (Henry of Lancaster s of John 'of Gaunt'); merged in the Crown 1399

1440 Viscounty of Tartas (in Guienne, France) (for Sir Philip Chetwynd)

1440 Barony of Dudley; abeyant 1757, abeyance terminated 1916

1442 Earldom of Salop (or thereafter Earldom of Shrewsbury) (John Talbot who was also created Earl of Waterford 1442); continuing in 2000 when declared the Premier Earldom (on the Roll) in the Peerage of both England and Ireland

1444 Barony of Lisle (of Kingston Lisle, Berks) (John Talbot 4th s of John Talbot 1st Earl of

Shrewsbury); dormant 1469/70; revived 1474/5 (Grey); abeyant 1504; revived c1530 (John Dudley); extinct 1538

1445 Dukedom of Warwick (Beaumont); extinct 1446

1446 Viscounty of Bourchier (Bourchier); extinct 1539/40

1451 Viscounty of Lisle (of Kingston Lisle, Berks) (John Talbot); extinct 1469/70

1461 Earldom of Essex (Bourchier); extinct 1539/40; revived 1543; extinct 1570; recreated 1570 (for Walter Devereux); extinct 1646

1465 Barony of Mountjoy (Walter Blount of Barton Blount, Derbys d1474); extinct 1606

1483 Viscounty of Lisle (of Kingston Lisle, Berks) (Grey); extinct 1504; revived 1513; suspended 1519

1485 Earldom of Derby (Stanley); continuing in 2000

1523 Viscounty of Lisle (of Kingston Lisle, Berks) (Arthur Plantagenet); extinct 1541/2

1541/2 Viscounty of Lisle (of Kingston Lisle, Berks) (John Dudley); forfeited 1553; revived 1605 for Robert Sydney; extinct 1743

1546/7 Earldom of Warwick (John Dudley); forfeited 1553; descendants assumed title to end of C17

1547 Peers who hold the new title, Lord Lieutenant of Staffordshire, start to appear

1549 Barony of Paget; united with the Earldom of Uxbridge 1784; continuing in 2000

1549/50 Viscounty of Hereford (Devereux); forfeited 1600/1; restored 1604, and since 1643 has been premier viscounty, continuing in 2000

1551 Dukedom of Northumberland (John Dudley); forfeited 1553

& passed to his b Ambrose & became extinct on Ambrose's death 1589/90; however, John's descendants assumed title to end of C17

1561 Earldom of Warwick (Ambrose Dudley); extinct 1589/90

1564 Earldom of Leicester (Robert Dudley, 5th s of John Dudley, Duke of Northumberland); extinct 1588

1572 Earldom of Essex (Walter Devereux, Viscount Hereford, Lord Ferrers etc); extinct 1646

1572 Barony of Compton (of Compton Wynates, Warws) (Charlotte suo jure Baroness Ferrers & Baroness Compton); in abeyance from 1749; revived 1774; in abeyance from 1855

1603 Earldom of Devonshire (Charles Blount, Baron Mountjoy); extinct 1606

1603 Barony of Sydney (of Penshurst, Kent) (Robert Sydney); extinct 1743

1603 Barony of Gerard (of Gerard's Bromley) (Gerard); extinct 1733

1618 Earldom of Leicester (Robert Sydney); extinct 1743

1621 (Ireland) Viscounty of Valentia (Annesley of Arley); continuing 2000

1621 (Ireland) Viscounty of Wilmot (of Athlone) (Wilmot); Henry Wilmot was MP for Tamworth 1640-1; extinct 1681

1621/2 Viscounty of Andover (of Andover, Hants) (Thomas Howard of Charlton, Wilts); descends in the Earldom of Berkshire (1626); continuing in 2000

1621/2 Barony of Howard (of Charleton, Wilts) (Thomas Howard of Charlton, Wilts); descends in the Earldom of Berkshire (1626); continuing in 2000

1624 (Ireland) Viscount

Lecale (Thomas Cromwell, d1653); extinct 1687

1626 Earldom of Berkshire (Thomas Howard of Charlton, Wilts); united in the Earldom of Suffolk (1603) from 1745; continuing in 2000

1627 (Scotland) Lord Aston of Forfar (Aston); devolved 1751, several claimants

1628 Earldom of Stamford (of Stamford, Lincs) (Henry Grey, Baron of Groby (1603)); extinct 1976

1629 (Ireland) Barony of Mountnorris (of Mountnorris, co. Armagh) (Annesley); continuing in 2000

1640 Viscounty of Stafford (county) (Howard); forfeited 1680; extinct 1762

1640 Barony of Stafford (county) (Howard); attainted 1680; restored 1824 (Jerningham)

1640 Barony of Stafford (county) (for Mary, sister & heir to Henry Stafford); forfeited 1693/4

1643 Barony of Wilmot (of Adderbury, Oxon) (Wilmot); extinct 1681

1644 Barony of Ward (of Birmingham) (Humble Ward); merged 1860 in the Earldom of Dudley

1645 (Ireland) Earldom of Ardglass (Thomas Cromwell, d1653, m into Meverell fam of Throwley); extinct 1687

1652 Earldom of Rochester (Wilmot); Henry Wilmot was MP for Tamworth 1640-1; extinct 1681

1660 (Ireland) Barony of Loughneagh and Viscounty of Massereene (of Loughneagh and Massereene, both co. Antrim) (Clotworthy, succeeded by his son-in-law Sir John Skeffington of Fisherwick 1665); continuing in 2000

1661 Barony of Annesley of Newport Paynel, Bucks, and Earldom of Anglesey, Wales (Annesley); extinct

1761

1661 Barony of Townshend (of Lynn Regis, Norfolk) (Townshend); descends with the Marquessate of Townshend 1787

1674/5 Viscounty of Bradford (of Bradford, Shrops) (Francis Newport of High Ercall, Shrops); extinct 1762

1677 Barony of Ferrers (new creation) (Robert Shirley of Staunton Harold, Leics); abeyant 1740/1; revived 1774; abeyant 1855

1682 Viscounty of Townshend (of Raynham, Norfolk) (Townshend); descends with the Marquessate of Townshend 1787

1682 Viscounty of Weymouth (Sir Thomas Thynne); descends with the Marquessate of Bath 1789

1682 Barony of Dartmouth (of Dartmouth, Devon)(George Legge); continuing in 2000

1688 Earldom of Stafford (for Mary (nee Stafford) widow of William Howard); extinct 1693/4

1688 Earldom of Stafford (county) (Henry Stafford-Howard); extinct 1762

1694 Marquessate of Alton and Duke of Shrewsbury (Charles Talbot of Alton); extinct 1718

1694 Earldom of Bradford (of Bradford, Shrops) (Francis Newport of High Ercall, Shrops); extinct 1762

1703 Barony of Gower (of Stittenham, Yorks); descends with the Dukedom of Sutherland; continuing in 2000

1711 Earldom of Dartmouth (of Dartmouth, Devon) (William Legge); continuing in 2000.

1711 Earldom of Ferrers (Robert Shirley of Staunton Harold, Leics); continuing in 2000

1711 Viscounty of Lewisham (of Lewisham, Kent) (William Legge); continuing in 2000.

1711 Viscounty of Tamworth (Robert Shirley of Staunton Harold); descends with the Earldom of Ferrers 1711

1711/2 Barony of Foley (of Kidderminster) (for the M.P.); extinct 1766

1711/2 Barony of Burton (of Burton) (Paget); extinct 1769

1715 Dukedom of Newcastle-upon-Tyne (Thomas Pelham-Holles); replaced with the Dukedom of Newcastle-under-Line or Lyme in 1756; extinct 1768

1716 Barony of Parker (of Macclesfield, Ches) (Thomas Parker d1723); continuing in 2000

1717 (Ireland) Viscounty of Chetwynd (of Bearhaven, co. Kerry) (Walter Chetwynd d1735/6); continuing in 2000

1717 (Ireland) Barony of Rathdowne, co. Dublin (Walter Chetwynd d1735/6); continuing in 2000

1720 Barony of Ducie (of Moreton) (for Matthew Ducie Moreton of Moreton and Engleton); extinct 1771

1721 Earldom of Macclesfield (of Macclesfield, Ches) (Baron Parker); continuing in 2000

1721 (Ireland) Barony of Whitworth (of Galway, co. Galway) (Charles Whitworth d1725); extinct 1725

1721 Viscounty of Parker (of Ewelm, Oxon) (Thomas Parker); continuing in 2000

1727 (Ireland) Viscounty of Galway (John Monckton); continuing in 2000

1729 Earldom of Waldegrave (Waldegrave); John Waldegrave was M.P. for Newcastle-u-Lyme 1754-; continuing in 2000

1733 Barony of Talbot (of Hensol, co. Glamorgan) (Charles Talbot b1685); descends with the Earldom of Shrewsbury; continuing in 2000

1746 Earldom of Gower (John Leveson-Gower, Baron Gower); descends with the Dukedom of Sutherland; continuing in 2000

1746 Viscounty of Trentham (John Leveson-Gower, Baron Gower); descends with the Dukedom of Sutherland; continuing in 2000

1747 Baron Anson of Soberton (for George Anson); extinct 1762

1756 Dukedom of Newcastle-under-Line or Lyme (Thomas Pelham-Holles, passing on his death 1768 to Henry Clinton, Earl of Lincoln); extinct 1988

1756 (Ireland) Earldom of Massereene (of Massereene, co. Antrim) (Clotworthy-Skeffington); extinct 1816

1756 Barony of Hyde (of Hindon, Wilts) (Villiers); descends with the Earldom of Clarendon; continuing in 2000

1756 Barony of Lyttleton (of Frankley, Worcs) (George Lyttleton); extinct 1779; recreated 1794 (see below)

1761 Earldom of Talbot (William Talbot, son of Charles b1686, d1782); extinct 1782

1762 Barony of Vernon (of Kinderton, Ches) (Vernon of Sudbury and Houndhill); continuing in 2000

1763 Viscounty Dudley and Ward (of Dudley); extinct from 1833

1763 Barony of Ducie (of Tortworth, Glous) (for Matthew Ducie Moreton, the younger); continuing in 2000

1776 Barony of Harrowby (of Harrowby, Lincs) (Nathaniel Ryder); continuing in 2000

1776 Barony of Foley (of Kidderminster) (for the cousin of the former Baron Foley); continuing in 2000

1780 Barony of Bagot (of Bagot's Bromley) (Bagot); continuing in 2000

1780 Barony of Dinevor (of Dinevor, co. Carmarthen) (William Talbot, Baron Talbot of Hensol d1782); descends with the Earldom of Shrewsbury; continuing in 2000.

1784 Earldom of Leicester (county) (George Townshend); abeyant 1855

1784 Earldom of Uxbridge (Paget); descends with the Marquessate of Anglesey; continuing in 2000

1784 Earldom of Talbot (of Hensol, co. Glamorgan (John Talbot, later Chetwynd-Talbot d1793); descends with the Earldom of Shrewsbury; continuing in 2000

1784 Viscounty of Ingestre (John Talbot d1793); descends with the Earldom of Shrewsbury; continuing in 2000

1786 Marquessate of Stafford (county) (Granville Leveson-Gower); descends with the Dukedom of Sutherland; continuing in 2000

1787 Marquessate of Townshend (of Raynham, Norfolk) (Townshend); continuing in 2000

1789 Marquessate of Bath (Thomas Thynne, Viscount Weymouth) continuing in 2000

1790 (GB) Barony of Fisherwick (of Fisherwick, Staffs) (Arthur Chichester); descends with the Marquessate of Donegall; continuing in 2000

1791 (Ireland) Marquessate of Donegall (and (Ireland) Earldom of Belfast 1791) (Arthur Chichester); continuing in 2000

1793 (Ireland) Earldom of Mountnorris (Arthur Annesley); extinct 1844

1794 Barony of Bradford (of Bradford, Shrops) (Henry Bridgeman); descends with the Earldom of Bradford (1815); continuing in 2000

1794 Barony of Lyttleton (of Frankley, Worcs) (William Henry Lyttleton of Hagley Pk, Worcs); descends with the Viscounty of Cobham (1718) from 1889; continuing in 2000

1796 Barony of Calthorpe (of Calthorpe, Norfolk) (Gough-Calthorpe); extinct 1997

1797 Earldom of Jervis (John Jervis); expired 1823

1797 Barony of Jervis (John Jervis); expired 1823

1800 (Ireland) Barony of Gardner (of Uttoxeter) (Alan Gardner d1809); dormant 1883

1800 (Ireland) Barony of Whitworth (of Newport Pratt, co. Galway) (Charles Whitworth d1825); extinct 1825

1801 Viscounty of St Vincent (John Jervis); continuing in 2000

1806 Viscounty of Anson and Barony of Soberton (Anson); descends with the Earldom of Lichfield 1831; continuing in 2000

1806 (UK) Barony of Gardner (of Uttoxeter) (Alan Gardner d1809); dormant 1883

1806 Barony of Crewe (of Crewe, Ches) (John Crewe); extinct 1893

1809 Earldom of Harrowby (of Harrowby, Lincs) (Ryder); continuing in 2000

1809 Viscounty of Sandon (of Sandon, Staffs) (Ryder); continuing in 2000

1813 Viscounty of Whitworth (of Adbaston, Staffs) (Charles Whitworth d1825); extinct 1825

1815 Marquessate of Anglesey (of Anglesey, Wales) (Paget); continuing in 2000

1815 Earldom of Whitworth (Charles Whitworth d1825); extinct 1825

1815 Earldom of Bradford (of Bradford, Shrops) (Orlando Bridgeman); continuing in 2000

1815 Viscounty of Granville (Granville Leveson-Gower d1846); continuing in 2000

1815 Viscounty of Newport (of Newport, Shrops) (Orlando Bridgeman); continuing in 2000

1815 Barony of Adbaston (of Adbaston, Staffs) (Charles Whitworth d1825); extinct 1825

1823 Viscounty of Beresford (of Beresford, Staffs) (William Carr Beresford); extinct 1854

1826 Barony of Gower (George Granville Leveson-Gower d1861); descends with the Dukedom of Sutherland (1833); continuing in 2000

1827 Viscounty Ednam (of Ednam, Co. Roxburgh) (John William Ward); extinct 1833; revived 1860 (for William Ward); descends with the Earldom of Dudley, continuing in 2000

1831 Earldom of Lichfield (Anson); continuing in 2000

1831 Barony of Wenlock (of Wenlock, Shrops) (Lawley of Canwell); extinct 1834

1833 Dukedom of Sutherland (Leveson-Gower); continuing in 2000

1833 Earldom of Granville (Granville Leveson-Gower d1846); continuing in 2000

1833 Barony of Leveson (of Stone, Staffs) (Granville Leveson-Gower d1846); descends with the Earldom of Granville; continuing in 2000

1835 Barony of Hatherton (of Hatherton,

Staffs) (Littleton); continuing in 2000

1837 Earldom of Ducie (for Thomas Reynolds-Moreton); continuing in 2000

1838 Barony of Wrottesley (of Wrottesley, Staffs) (Wrottesley); continuing in 2000

1839 Barony of Wenlock (of Wenlock, Shrops) (Paul Beilby Lawley-Thompson, younger b of former Baron Wenlock); extinct 1932

1846 Barony of Gough (of Chinkang-Foo, China and of Maharajore and the Sutlej, East Indies) (Gough); continuing in 2000

1849 Viscounty of Gough (of Goojerat, Punjab, and of Limerick, Ireland) (Gough); continuing in 2000

1860 Earldom of Dudley (of Dudley Castle) (William Ward, Baron Ward of Birmingham); continuing in 2000

1878 Barony of Norton (of Norton-in-the-Moors, Staffs) (Adderley); continuing in 2000

1882 Barony of Wolseley (of Cairo and of Wolseley, Staffs) (Garnet Joseph Wolseley d1913); extinct 1913

1885 Viscounty of Wolseley (of Wolseley, Staffs) (Wolseley); extinct 1936

1886 Barony of Burton (of Rangemore and of Burton-on-Trent) (Bass); extinct 1909

1887 Barony of Monckton (of Serlby, Notts) (George Edmund Milnes Monckton-Arundell); extinct 1971

1895 Earldom of Crewe (of Crewe, Ches) (Robert Offley Ashburton Milnes, afterwards Crewe-Milnes, Baron Houghton); extinct 1945

1897 Baron Burton (of Burton-on-Trent and of

Rangemore) (Bass); continuing in 2000

1900 Barony of Northcote (of Exeter, Devon) (Henry Stafford Northcote b1846); extinct 1911

1903 Barony of Biddulph (of Biddulph, Staffs) (Biddulph); continuing in 2000

1908 Viscounty of Wolverhampton (Fowler); extinct 1943

1911 Marquessate of Crewe (of Crewe, Ches) (Robert Offley Ashburton Milnes, afterwards Crewe-Milnes); extinct 1945

1911 Earldom of Madeley (of Madeley, Staffs) (Robert Offley Ashburton Milnes, afterwards Crewe-Milnes); extinct 1945

1916 Barony of Anslow (of Anslow, Staffs) (Tonman Mosley); extinct 1933

1917 Barony of Annesley (Arthur Annesley); extinct 1949

1919 Barony of Swinfen (of Chetsey, Surrey) (Swinfen); at 2003 hereditary peer remaining in Lords for a transitional period

1919 Barony of Forster (of Lepe, Hants) (Henry William Forster b1866); extinct 1936

1937 Earldom of Baldwin (of Bewdley, Worcs); continuing in 2000

1942 Barony of Wedgwood (Wedgwood of Barlaston); continuing in 2000

1945 Barony of Chetwode (of Chetwode, Bucks) (Chetwode); perhaps no Staffs connection; continuing in 2000

1956 (Life) Barony of Evershed (Francis Evershed of Stapenhill, Staffs); extinct 1966

1957 Viscounty of Monckton (of Brenchley, Kent) (Monckton); continuing in 2000

1960 Barony of Nelson

(of Stafford) (Sir George Horatio Nelson); continuing in 2000

1962 Barony of Dilhorne (of Towester, Northants) (Manningham-Buller); continuing in 2000

1963 Barony of Normanbrook (of Chelsea) (Sir Norman Craven Brook, native of Wolverhampton); extinct 1967

1964 Viscounty of Dilhorne (of Green Norton, Northants) (Manningham-Buller); continuing in 2000

1966 (Life) Barony of Rowley (of Rowley Regis) (Arthur Henderson); extinct 1968

1970 (Life) Barony of Boyle (of Handsworth) (Edward Charles Gurney Boyle); extinct 1981

1970 (Life) Barony of Burntwood (of Burntwood, Staffs) (Julian Ward Snow); extinct 1982

1970 (Life) Barony of Davies (of Leek) (Harold Davies); extinct 1985

1974 (Life) Barony of Harmar-Nicholls (of Peterborough, Cambs) (Harmar Harmar-Nicholls); continuing in 2000

1981 (Life) Barony of Thomas (of Swynnerton, Staffs) (Hugh Swynnerton Thomas); continuing in 2000

1987 (Life) Barony of Wyatt (of Weeford, Staffs) (Woodrow Lyle Wyatt); extinct 1997

1992 (Life) Barony of Archer (of Sandwell) (Peter Kingsley Archer); continuing in 2000

1992 (Life) Barony of Ashley of Stoke (Jack Ashley of Widnes, Ches); continuing in 2000

1999 Barony of King (of West Bromwich) (Tarsem King); continuing in 2000

THE HOUSE OF COMMONS

COUNTY SEATS

Staffordshire 1213-1832

1213 ?

1216 ?

1258 Robert de Halghton, Adam de Brumpton, William Bagot, Payn de Wasteneys

1261 ?

1263 ?

1265 ?

1267 ?

1273 ?

1275 (1) ?

1275 (2) ?

1283 (1) ?

1283 (2) ?

1290 William de Stafford, William de Mere

1294 ?

1295 Henry de Creswall, Richard Caverswall

1296-7 ?

1297 ?

1298 William de Stafford, Henry Mauveysin

1300 Ralph Basset, Henry Mauveysin

1301 Ralph Basset of Sapecote, Henry Mauveysin

1302 Henry de Cresswall, William Tromewyne

1305 William Tromewyne, Philip de Barynton

1306 William de Stafford, William de Mere

1307 Robert de Staundon, Robert de Ditton

1307-8 William de Stafford, William de Mere

1308 ?

1309 Robert de Dutton, Robert de Tok

1311-12 William de Stafford, Robert Tok

1312 (1) ?

1312 (2) Roger Trumwyne, Robert Tok

1313 (1) Roger Trumwyne, Robert de Bures

1313 (2) Roger Tromwyne, Robert de Bures

1313 (3) William de Stafford, Richard de Caverswall

1314 (1) ? (did not meet)

1314 (2) ?

1315 Robert de Dotton, John de Perton

1316 (1) William Trumwyn, Robert de Tok

1316 (2) Thomas le Rous, John de Barre

1316 (3) Thomas le Rous, miles, William Trumwyne, miles

1318 (1) ?

1318 (2) William de Stafford, miles, Robert de Grendon

1319 Ralph de Rolleston, Robert de Dutton

1320 Robert de Grendon (sheriff), John de Hynkeleye

1321 Robert Tok, Robert de Dutton

1322 (1) John de Swynnerton, Henry de Bysshebury

1322 (2) John Gyffard, Philip de Somervill

1324 (1) Philip de Barynton, miles, Philip de Somervill

1324 (2) John Giffard of Chilinton, Richard de Hampton

1324 Exceptional Council - James de Audley (elder brother of Hugh d' Audley the younger, Earl of Gloucester), Thomas de Furnivall, jun, Thomas de Pipe, Thomas de Halghton, Philip de Barinton, Thomas de Barinton, Walter de Verdon, Ralph Basset of Weldon, Roger de Ockover, John Gifford, Ralph de Grendon, Robert de Grendon, Philip de Somervile, William de Camvile, Roger de Swynnerton, Richard de Vernon, John Hamlyn, William Trussell of Cubbleston, John de Arderne, Anselm de (le) Marshal, Hugh de Meinell, Thomas de Rideware, Nicholas de Longford, Robert Bek, Ralph de Rolleston, Robert de Stapleton, Thomas de (le) Rous, Henry de Bisshebury (sheriff), John de Swynoferton, Robert de Dutton, William de Stafford, William Wasterneys, Richard Dracot, John Hinkley, John Hasanke, John Harecourt, Robert de Burs

1325 Robert de Knyghteleye, miles, John de Hynkele, miles

1326-7 Henry de Bisshebury, John de Swynnerton

1327 Philip de Somervill,

miles, John de Swynnerton, miles

1328 (1) James de Stafford, John de Hinkeleye (sheriff)

1328 (2) John de Swynnerton, John de Hynkeleye

1328 (3) Robert de Dutton, miles, Ralph de Grendon

1328-9 Robert de Dutton, Richard de Blythefeld

1330 (1) John de Hynkele, Henry de Bysshebury (sheriff)

1330 (2) William Trussebut, Ralph de Grendon

1331 Henry de Bisshebury (sheriff), William Trussebut

1332 (1) William Trussebut, Philip de Luttleye

1332 (2) Philip de Somervill, Robert le Mareschal

1332-3 John de Aston, Richard de Falede

1334 (1) Malculm de Wasteneys, Robert de Dutton

1334 (2) John de Draycote, Richard de Peshale

1335 John de Swynnerton, John de Hynkeley

1336 (1) Philip de Somervill, John de Hynkeleye (sheriff)

1336 (2) Philip de Somervill, Robert Mauveysyn

1337 (1) Richard de

Staffordshire 1086-1099~1135

Newcastle under Lyme

CHESHIRE

DERBYSHIRE

SHROPSHIRE

Stafford

Lichfield

LEICS

Chilcote (DERBYS)

Tamworth

WARWICKSHIRE

Dudley (WORCS)

WORCESTERSHIRE

Peshale, Simon de Ruggeleye

1337 (2) (summoned by Writs) Rad. Basset le piere, Roger de Swynnerton, Thomas de Hilghton, Rad. le Botiler

1337 (2) (elected) Hugh de Meignall, John de Freford

1338 (1) Richard de Peshale, Richard de Venables

1338 (2) Richard de Peshale (sheriff), Malculm Wasteneys

1339 (1) Richard de Peshale, John de Stafford

1339 (2) Simon de Ruggeleye, William

Jarpenvill

1340 (1) ?

1340 (2) John de Stafford, Simon de Ruggeley (sheriff)

1340 (3) ?

1340 Assembly directed to attend as merchants by Writ - Roger de Neuport, Ralph Teynterel, William le Mortimer, John de Bolenhull

1341 Richard de Stafford, Adam de Peshale (sheriff)

1343 Thomas de Swynnerton, Richard de Peshale

1343 Roger de Aston, John de Draycote

1346 Simon de Ruggele, Roger Michel

1348 (1) John Bagot, Simon de Ruggeley

1348 (2) John de Draycote, Stephen de Ireton

1349 No parliament sat

1351 John de Verdon, Thomas Adam

1352 (1) John de Perton, Adam le Alblaster

1352 (2) John Trumwyn, chiv

1353 Walter de Verdon

1354 Walter de Verdon, John Musard

1355 John de Draycot, chiv, Walter Verdon, chiv

1357 ?

1358 Roger de Aston, chiv, John de Draycote, miles

1360 John Draycote, chiv, John de Perton, chiv

1361 John Musard, chiv, Robert de Grendon

1362 Robert de Grendon, chiv, Philip de Lutteleye

1363 Robert de Grendon, chiv (sheriff), Nicholas de Beck, chiv

1365 Robert de Grendon, chiv, Nicholas de Beek, chiv (both resigned due to ill health; instead John de Perton and William de Walshale sat)

1366 John de Perton, Philip de Lutteley (sheriff)

1368 John Draycot, miles, Philip de Lutteley (sheriff)

1369 John de Verdon, chiv, William del Wode

1371 John de Draycot, John de Perton (sheriff)

1372 John de Gresley (sheriff), William de Halghton

1373 John de Verdon, chiv (sheriff), John de Knightleye

1376 John de Verdon, chiv, John de Knightleye

1377 (1) Nicholas de Stafford, chiv, Adam de Peshale

1377 (2) Nicholas Stafford, chiv, Thomas de Thamenhorn, chiv

1378 Robert de Swynnerton, John de Hynkeley

1379 Nicholas de Stafford, John de Knyghteley

1380 (1) Nicholas de Stafford, chiv, Thomas de Aston, chiv

1380 (2) Adam de Peshale, William Walshale

1381-2 Adam de Peshale, chiv, John Basset, chiv

1382 (1) Thomas de Thamenhore, chiv, Thomas de Stafford, chiv

1382 (2) Richard de Pershale, chiv, John de Knightele

1383 (1) Adam de Peshale, chiv, John Knyghtley, jun

1383 (2) Nicholas de

Stafford, chiv, Richard de Peshale, chiv

1384 (1) John de Knyghtley, Thomas de Aston, chiv

1384 (2) Nicholas de Stafford, chiv, William de Walshale

1385 Nicholas de Stafford, John de Hynkeley

1386 William de Shareshull, Adomar Taverner

1388 (1) John Ipstones, chiv, Roger de Longrugg

1388 (2) Thomas de Aston, chiv, John Delves

1390 (1) Nicholas de Stafford, John Delves

1390 (2) Nicholas de Stafford, John Delves

1391 John Bagod, chiv, William Walsale

1392 (never met)

1393 Thomas de Aston, chiv, William Walsale (or John Delves)

1394 William de Walsall, John Ipstones

1395 William de Shareshull, chiv, Aylmer de Lichfield

1397 John Bagot, chiv, Robert Frauncesy, chiv

1397-8 Rustin Villenawe, John Bagot, chiv

1399 (1) ?

1399 (2) Robert Fraunceys, Thomas Aston

1400-1 Robert Fraunceys, chiv, John Bagot, chiv

1402? (1) ? probably never met

1402 (2) William Walshale, John Swynnerton

1403-4 William de Walshale, Ralf de Stafford

1404 Robert Fraunceys, chiv, John Bagot, chiv

1406 Humphrey de Stafford, jun, chiv, Thomas de Aston, chiv

1407 John Bagot, chiv, William Neuport, chiv

1410 ? possibly John Delves was an MP representing the county or a borough

1411 William Neuport, chiv, John Bagot, chiv

1413 (1) ? possibly New-

port, or Robert Bapthorpe was an MP representing the county or a borough (SHC 1917-18 p175)

1413 (2) Thomas Gresley, chiv, Hugh Erdeswick

1414 (1) John Meverel, William Walshale

1414 (2) William Neuport, John Meverel

1415 ? (no returns)

1416 (1) Humphrey de Halghton, Roger Bradshaw

1416 (2) ?

1417 ?

1419 Richard Vernon, chiv, Thomas Gresley, chiv

1420 William Lee of Aston, John Myners

1421 (1) John Bagot, chiv, Richard Lone

1421 (2) Hugh de Erdeswyk, Richard Lone

1422 John de Gresley,

miles, Thomas Stanley

1423-4 Roger Aston, miles et chiv, Richard Lone

1425 John Delves, Richard Lone

1426 Richard Lone, Thomas Arblaster

1427-8 John Gresley, chiv, Humphrey Stafford of Chebsey

1429-30 Roger Aston, miles et chiv, Ralf Egerton of Wrimehill

Staffordshire by c1166-1278

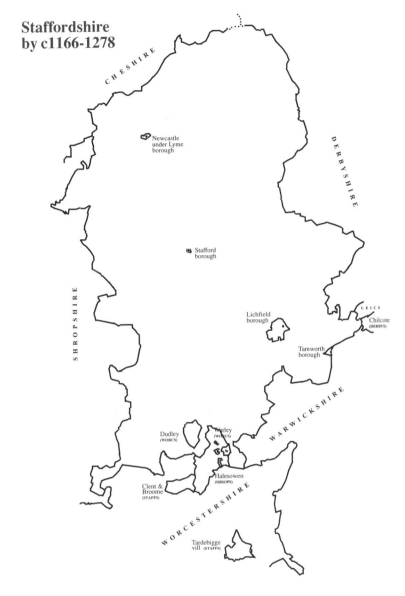

CHESHIRE

DERBYSHIRE

Newcastle under Lyme borough

Stafford borough

SHROPSHIRE

Lichfield borough

L E I C S

Chilcote (DERBYS)

Tamworth borough

WARWICKSHIRE

Dudley (WORCS)

Warley (WORCS)

Halesowen (SHROPS)

Clent & Broome (STAFFS)

WORCESTERSHIRE

Tardebigge vill (STAFFS)

325

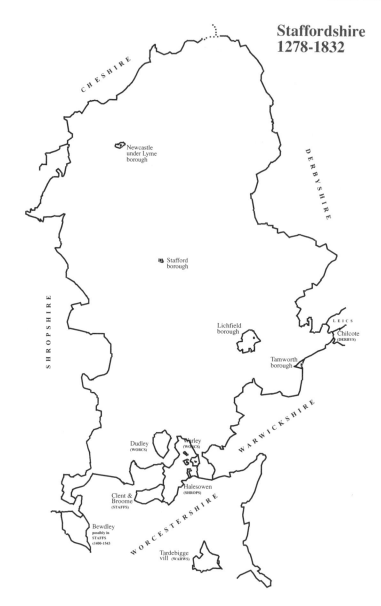

Staffordshire
1278-1832

1469 ?
1470-1 ?
1472-5 Edmund Dudley, John Stanley
1477-8 John Ferrers, armiger, John Bagot, armiger
1483 (1) ?
1483 (2) ?
1483 (3) ?
1484 ?
1485-6 ?
1487-8 ?
1489-90 ?
1491-2 Sir Humphrey Savage, Kt, Sir Humphrey Stanley, Kt
1495-6 ?
1497 County/ or a borough -?Richard Wrottesley, ?Humphrey Peshale, ?Humphrey Swynnerton, ?Thomas Welles
1504 ?Edmund Dudley
1509 ?
1512-14 ?
1515 ?
1523 ?
1529-36 John Gyfford, miles, Edward Lytilton, miles
1536 ?
1539-40 ?
1542-4 John Dudley, Kt, Philip Draycot, Kt
1545-7 George Gryffyth, miles, Thomas Fitzherbert, armiger
1547-52 William Paget, miles, KG, John Harcourt, miles
by 1552 Sir John Harcourt, miles, Sir Ralph Bagnoll, miles
1553 (1) William Devereux, armiger, Walter Aston, armiger
1553 (2) Sir Thomas Giffard, Kt, Edward Lyttleton, Esq
1554 John (rectius Philip) Draycot, miles, Thomas Gray, armiger
1554-5 ?Anthony Draycot, ?Henry Stafford
1555 Thomas Gyfford, miles, Edward Lytelton, miles
1558 Brian Fowler, armiger, Francis Meverel, armiger
1559 Sir Ralph Bagnalde, Kt, Simon Harcourt, Esq
1563-7 Simon Harcourt,

1431 John Harpur, John Mynors
1432 Thomas Arblaster, William Lee of Aston
1433 Hugh Erdeswick, Thomas Arblaster
1435 Thomas Arblaster, William Lee
1437 John Hampton, John Minours
1439-40 John Hampton, Thomas Arblaster
1442 John Hampton, Ralf Egerton
1445-6 ?
1447 John Stanley, armiger, William Mitton, armiger
1449 John Hampton, armiger, William Cumberford, gent
1449-50 John Hampton, Robert Whitgreve
1450-51 John Stanley, armiger, John Gresley, armiger
1453-4 John Gresley, miles, John Hampton, armiger
1455-6 William Vernon, miles, Humphrey Swynnerton, armiger
1459 ?
1460 ?
1461 ?
1463-5 ?
1467-8 John Stanley, miles, John Delves, armiger

Esq, John Graye, Esq

1571 John Grey Esq, Thomas Trentham

1572-83 John Fletewood, Esq, Thomas Horwood, Esq

1584-5 Edward (Dudley) (Return torn, name supplied by B. Willis), Edward Leigh, Esq

1586-7 John Grey, Esq, William Bassett, Esq

1588-9 Walter Harcourt, Esq, Thomas Gerrard, Esq

1593 * Sir Christopher Blount, Kt, Sir Walter Harcourte, Kt

1597-8 (John) Sutton alias Dudley, Sir Christopher Blount, Kt

1601 Sir Thomas Gerard, Kt, Sir John Egerton, Kt

1603 Sir Robert Stanford, Kt replaced in by-election 1607 by Sir John Egerton, Kt, Sir Edward Littleton, Kt replaced in by-election 1609 by Francis Trentham, Esq

1614 Sir Walter Chetwynd, Kt, Thomas Crompton, Esq

1621-2 Sir William Bowyer, Kt, Thomas Crompton, Esq

1624-5 Sir William Bowyer, Kt, Sir EdwardLittleton, Kt

1625 Sir Simon Weston, Kt, Richard Erdeswick, Esq

1626 Sir Simon Weston, Kt, Sir William Bowyer, Kt

1628-9 Sir Harvey Bagot, Bart, Thomas Crompton, Esq

1640 Sir Edward Littleton, Bart (Country), Sir William Bowyer, Kt (Country)

1640-53 T Sir Edward Littleton, Bart (Royalist) 1640-46, Sir William Bowyer, Kt (Parl.) 1640-41, Sir Harvey Bagot, Kt (Royalist) 1641-42, John Bowyer, Esq (Parl.) 1646-48 (when secluded), Sir Richard Skeffington, Kt (Parl.) 1646-47, Thomas Crompton Esq (Parl. and Rumper) 1647-53

1653 Convention - George Bellot, Esq, John Chetwode, Esq

1654-5 Sir Charles Wrottesley, Bart, Thomas Crompton, Esq, Thomas Whitgreve, Esq

1656-8 Sir Charles Wolseley, bart, Thomas Crompton, Esq, Thomas Whitgreve, Esq

1659 Jan - April Col Thomas Crompton, Sir Thomas Whitgreve, Kt

1659 May - Rumper, restored May 1659:- Thomas Crompton

Secluded member, returned **Feb 1660**:- John Bowyer

1660 Edward Bagot, Esq, William Sneyd, Esq

1661-79 Sir Thomas Leigh, Kt, Randolph Egerton, Esq (1661-62), Sir Edward Littleton, Bart (1663-)

1679 Sir Walter Bagot, Bart (Tory), Sir John Bowyer, Bart (Whig)

1679-81 Sir Walter Bagot, Bart (Tory), Sir John Bowyer, Bart (Whig)

1681 Sir Walter Bagot, Bart (Tory), Sir John Bowyer, Bart (Whig)

1685-7 Sir Walter Bagot, Bart (Tory), Edward Littleton, Esq (Tory)

1689-90 John Grey, Esq (Tory), Sir Walter Bagott, Bart (Tory)

1690-5 John Grey, Esq (Tory), Walter Chetwynd, Esq (Tory)(1690-93), Sir Walter Bagott, Bart (1693-95)

1695-8 John Grey, Esq (Tory), Henry Paget, Esq (Mod. Tory)

1698-1700 T Henry Paget, Esq (Tory), Edward Bagot, Esq (Tory)

1701 Henry Paget, Esq (Tory), Edward Bagott, Esq (Tory)

1701-2 Henry Paget, Esq (Tory), Edward Bagott, Esq (Tory)

1702-5 Henry Paget, Esq (Tory), Edward Bagot, Esq (Tory)

1705-8 Henry Paget, Esq (Tory), Sir Edward Bagot, Bart (Tory)

1708-10 Henry Paget, Esq (Tory), John Wrottesley, Esq (Tory)

1710-13 Henry Paget, Esq (Tory) (1710-2), William Ward, jun, Esq (Tory), Charles Bagot, jun, Esq (Tory) (1712-3)

1713-5 Ralph Sneyd, Esq (Tory), Henry Vernon of Sudbury, Esq (Tory)

1715-22 Thomas, Lord Paget (Tory), William Ward, Esq (Tory) (1715-20), William Leveson Gower, Esq (Tory) (1720-2)

1722-27 Thomas Catesby, Lord Paget (Tory), William Leveson Gower, Esq (Tory)

1727-34 William Leveson Gower, Esq (Tory), Sir Walter Wagstaff Bagot, Bart (Tory)

1734-41 William Leveson Gower, Esq (Tory), Sir Walter Bagot, Bart (Tory)

1741-7 William Leveson Gower, Esq (Tory), Sir Walter Wagstaff Bagot, Bart (Tory)

1747-54 T Sir Walter Wagstaff Bagot, Bart (Tory), William Leveson Gower, Esq (Bedford Whig)

1754-61 William Leveson Gower, Esq (Bedford Whig) (1754-6), William Bagot, Esq (Tory), Henry Frederick Thynne, Esq (Bedford Whig) (1757-61)

1761-8 George Harry, Lord Grey (Whig), William Bagot, Esq (Tory)

1768-74 George Harry, Lord Grey (Whig) (1768), Sir William Bagot, Bart (Tory), Captain John Wrottesley (Bedford Whig) (1768-74)

1774-80 Sir William Bagot, Bart (Tory), Sir John Wrottesley, Bart (Gower-Whig)

1780-4 T George Legge,

Viscount Lewisham (Tory), Sir John Wrottesley, Bart (Gower-Whig)

1784-90 Sir Edward Littleton (Tory), Sir John Wrottesley, Bart (Gower-Whig) (1784-7), George Granville Leveson Gower, Lord Trentham (Gower-Whig) (1787-90)

1790-96 Earl Gower (Gower Whig), Sir Edward Littleton, bart (Tory)

1796-1802 Earl Gower (Gower Whig) (1796-9), Sir Edward Littleton (Tory), Lord Granville Leveson Gower (Gower Whig) (1800-02)

1802-6 Sir Edward Littleton, bart (Tory), Lord Granville Leveson Gower (Gower Whig)

1806-7 Sir Edward Littleton, bart (Tory), Lord Granville Leveson Gower (Gower Whig)

1807-12 Sir Edward Littleton, bart (Tory) (1807-12), Lord Granville Leveson Gower (Canningite), Edward John Walhouse (Tory) (1812)

1812-18 Lord Granville Leveson Gower (Tory) (1812-5), Edward John Littleton (Tory), George Granville Leveson Gower, Earl Gower (Canningite) (1816-8)

1818-20 Edward John Littleton (Tory), Earl Gower (Canningite)

1820-6 Edward John Littleton (Tory), Sir John Fenton Boughey (Whig) (1820-3), Sir John Wrottesley, bart (Whig) (1823-6)

1826-30 Edward John Littleton (Canningite), Sir John Wrottesley, bart (Whig)

1830-31 Edward John Littleton (Reformer), Sir John Wrottesley (Whig)

1831-2 Edward John Littleton (Whig), Sir John Wrottesley, bart (Whig)

NORTHERN
DIVISION OF
STAFFORDSHIRE
1832-1867

Northern Division of Staffordshire
1832-1867

1832-4 T Sir Oswald Moseley, Bt (Lib), Edward Buller (Lib)

1835-7 Sir Oswald Moseley, Bt (Lib-Whig), Edward Buller (Lib-Whig)

1837-41 T Hon WB Baring (Con), Edward Buller (Lib-Whig)

1841-7 CB Adderley (Con) (unopposed), JDW Russell (Con) (unopposed)

1847-52 CB Adderley (Con), Viscount Brackley (Con) (1847-51), S Child (Con) (1851-2)

1852-7 CB Adderley (Con) (unopposed), S Child (Con) (unopposed)

1857-9 CB Adderley (Con) (1857-8) (1858-9) (unopposed), S Child (Con)

1859-65 CB Adderley (Con) (unopposed), Viscount Ingestre (Con) (unopposed)

1865-8 CB Adderley (Con), E Buller (EM Buller) (Lib)

**SOUTHERN DIVISION
OF STAFFORDSHIRE
1832-67**

Southern Division of Staffordshire
1832-1867

1832-4 Rt Hon Edward John Littleton (Lib), Sir John Wrottesley, bart (Lib)

1835-7 Rt Hon Edward John Littleton (Lib) (1835), Sir John Wrottesley, bart (Whig), Sir Francis Lyttleton Holyoake Goodricke, bart (Con) (1835-7)**T**

1837-41 **T** Col Hon George Anson (Lib), Viscount Ingestre (Con)

1841-7 Hon G Anson (Lib) (1841-6) (unopposed) (1846-7) (unopposed), Viscount Ingestre (Con)

1847-52 Hon G Anson (Lib) (unopposed), Viscount Ingestre (Con) (1847-9) (unopposed), Viscount Lewisham (Con) (1849-52) (unopposed)

1852-7 Hon G Anson (Lib) (1852-3) (unopposed), Viscount Lewisham (Con) (1852-4) (unopposed), Hon ER Littleton (Lib) (1853-7) (unopposed), Lord Paget (Earl of Uxbridge) (Lib) (1854-7)

1857-9 HJWH Foley (Lib) (unopposed), WO Foster (Lib) (unopposed)

1859-65 HJWH Foley (Lib) (unopposed), WO Foster (Lib) (unopposed)

1865-8 HJWH Foley (Lib) (unopposed), WO Foster (Lib) (unopposed)

329

NORTH DIVISION OFSTAFFORDSHIRE 1867-1885

North Division of Staffordshire 1867-1885

1868-74 CB Adderley (Con) (unopposed), Sir EM Buller Bt (Lib) (unopposed)

1874-80 Sir CB Adderley (Con) (1874) (unopposed) (1874-8) (unopposed), CM Campbell (Con) (unopposed), RW Hanbury (Con) (1878-80) (unopposed)

1880-5 WY Craig (Lib), HT Davenport (Con)

West Division of Staffordshire 1867-1885

1868-74 S Child (Con), HFM Ingram (Con) (1868-71), F Monckton (Con) (1871-74) (unopposed)

1874-80 AS Hill (Con) (unopposed), F Monckton (Con) (unopposed)

1880-5 AS Hill (Con), F Monckton (Con)

East Division of Staffordshire 1867-1885

1868-74 MA Bass (Lib), JR McClean (Lib) (1868-73), SC Allsopp (Con) (1873-4)

1874-80 MA Bass (Lib) (unopposed), SC Allsopp (Con) (unopposed)

1880-5 MA Bass (Lib), H Wiggin (Lib)

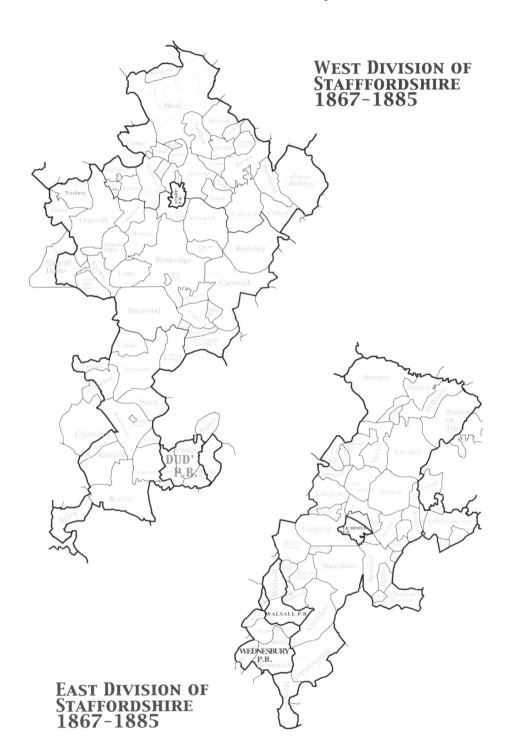

West Division of Staffordshire 1867-1885

East Division of Staffordshire 1867-1885

BURTON
DIVISION
1885-1948

Burton Division 1885-1948

1892-5 S Evershed (Gladstonian Lib) (unopposed)
1895-1900 Sydney Evershed (Gladstonian Lib) (unopposed)
1900-06 Major Robert F Ratcliff (Lib Unionist)
1906-10 Major RF Ratcliff (Lib Unionist)
1910 (Jan) Major RF Ratcliff (Con)
1910 (Dec)-1918 Lt-Col RF Ratcliff (Lib Unionist)
1918-22 Col John

Gretton (Unionist) (unopposed)
1922-3 Col J Gretton (Con) (unopposed)
1923-4 Col Rt Hon J Gretton (Con) (unopposed)
1924-9 Col Rt Hon J Gretton (Con)
1929-31 Col Rt Hon J Gretton (Con)
1931-5 Col Rt Hon J Gretton (Con)
1935- Col Rt Hon J Gretton (Con)
1945-50 W Lyne (Lab)

1885-6 Sir MA Bass (Lib)
1886-92 Sir MA Bass (Lib) (unopposed)

(1886), S Evershed (Gladstonian Lib) (1886-92)

Handsworth Division 1885-1918

1885-6 H Wiggin (Lib)
1886-92 H Wiggin ((Lib Unionist) (unopposed)
1892-5 Sir H Meysey-Thompson (Lib Unionist)
1895-1900 Sir H Meysey-Thompson (Lib

Unionist) (unopposed)
1900-06 Sir H Meysey-Thompson (Lib Unionist) (unopposed)
1906-10 Major EC Meysey-Thompson (Lib Unionist)

1910 (Jan) Major EC Meysey-Thompson (Lib Unionist)
1910 (Dec)-1918 Lt-Col EC Meysey-Thompson (Lib Unionist) (unopposed)

HANDSWORTH
DIVISION 1885-
1918

KINGSWINFORD
DIVISION 1885-1918

Kingswinford Division 1885-1918

1885-6 AS Hill (Con)
1886-92 AS Hill (Con) (unopposed)
1892-5 Rt Hon AS Hill (Con)
1895-1900 Rt Hon AS Hill (Con) (unopposed)
1900-06 Col WG Webb (Con) (unopposed)

(1900-05), Henry Staveley Hill (Con)
1906-10 HS Staveley-Hill (Con)
1910 (Jan) HS Staveley-Hill (Con) (unopposed)
1910 (Dec)-1918 HS Staveley-Hill (Con) (unopposed)

332

Leek Division 1885-1918

1885-6 C Crompton (Lib)
1886-92 HT Davenport (Con)
1892-95 C Bill (Con)
1895-1900 Charles Bill (Con)
1900-06 Robert Pearce

(Lib)
1906-10 Col AH Heath (Con)
1910 (Jan) Col AH Heath (Con)
1910 (Dec)-1918 (Sir) Robert Pearce (Lib)

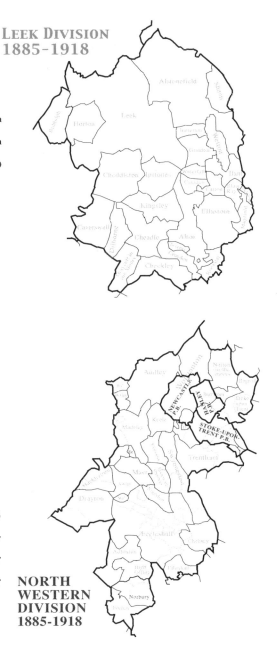

LEEK DIVISION 1885-1918

LICHFIELD DIVISION 1885-1918

Lichfield Division 1885-1918

1885-6 Sir J Swinburne (Lib)
1886-92 Sir J Swinburne (Gladstonian Lib)
1892-5 Major L Darwin (Lib Unionist)
1895-1900 HC Fulford (Gladstonian Lib) (1895-6), TCT Warner

(Gladstonian Lib) (1896-1900)
1906-10 TCT Warner (Lib)
1910 (Jan) Col (Sir) TCT Warner (Lib)
1910 (Dec)-1918 Sir TCT Warner (Lib)

NORTH WESTERN DIVISION 1885-1918

North Western Division 1885-1918

1885-6 G Leverson-Gower (Lib)
1886-92 Capt J Edwards-Heathcote (Con)
1892-5 James Heath (Con)

1895-1900 James Heath (Con)
1900-06 (Sir) J Heath (Con)
1906-10 (Sir) A Billson

(Lib) (1906-07), Albert Stanley (Lab) (1907-10)
1910 (Jan) Albert Stanley (Lab) (1910-6), Samuel Finney (Lab)

(1916-8) (unopposed)
1910 (Dec)-1918 Albert Stanley (Lab) (1910-16), S Finney (Lab) (unopposed) (1916-8)

333

Western Division 1885-1918

1885-6 HA Bass (Lib)
1886-92 Hamar A Bass (Lib Unionist) (unopposed)
1892-5 HA Bass (Lib Unionist)
1895-1900 HA Bass (Lib Unionist) (unopposed) (1895-8), A Henderson (Lib Unionist) (unopposed) (1898-1900)
1900-06 (Sir) A Henderson (Lib Unionist) (unopposed)
1906-10 Henry D McLaren (Lib)
1910 (Jan) GA Lloyd (Lib Unionist)
1910 (Dec)-1918 (Sir) GA Lloyd (Lib Unionist) (1910-18), no bye-election before dissolution

WESTERN DIVISION 1885-1918

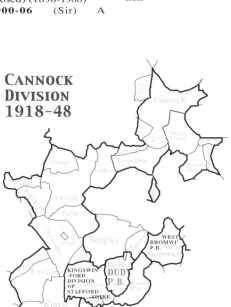

CANNOCK DIVISION 1918-48

Cannock Division 1918-48

1918-22 James Parker (Coalition Lab)
1922-3 WM Adamson (Lab)
1923-4 WM Adamson (Lab)
1924-9 WM Adamson (Lab)
1929-31 WM Adamson (Lab)
1931-5 Mrs SA Ward (Con)
1935-45 WM Adamson (Socialist)
1945-50 Miss Jennie Lee (Lab)

Kingswinford Division 1918-48

1918-22 CH Sitch (Lab)
1922-3 CH Sitch (Lab)
1923-4 CH Sitch (Lab)
1924-9 CH Sitch (Socialist)
1929-31 CH Sitch (Lab)
1931-5 ALS Todd (Con)
1935-45 A Henderson (Socialist)
1945-50 Major A Henderson (Lab)

Leek Division 1918-48

1918-22 William Bromfield (Lab)
1922-3 W Bromfield (Lab)
1923-4 W Bromfield (Lab)
1924-9 W Bromfield (Lab)

1929-31 W Bromfield (Lab)
1931-5 Arthur Ratcliffe (Con)
1935-45 W Bromfield (Socialist)
1945-50 Harold Davies (Lab)

Lichfield Division 1918-48

1918-22 Col Sir TCT Warner (Coalition Lib)
1922-3 Col Sir TCT Warner (National Lib)
1923-4 Frank Hodges (Lab)
1924-9 R Roy Wilson (Con)
1929-31 JA Lovat-Fraser

(Socialsit)
1931-5 JA Lovat-Fraser (Nationalist)
1935-45 JA Lovat-Fraser (National Lab) (1935-8), CC Poole (Socialist) (1938-)
1945-50 Capt CC Poole (Lab)

Stafford Division 1918-48

1918-22 Capt Hon WG Ormsby-Gore (Coalition Unionist)
1922-3 Capt Hon WGA Ormsby-Gore (Unionist)
1923-4 Capt Hon WGA Ormsby-Gore (Unionist)
1924-9 Capt Hon WGA Ormsby-Gore (Con)
1929-31 Capt Rt Hon

WGA Ormsby-Gore (Con)
1931-5 Rt Hon WGA Ormsby-Gore (Con)
1935-45 Rt Hon WGA Ormsby-Gore (Con) (1935-8), GEP Thorneycroft (Con) (1938-45)
1945-50 Capt S Swingler (Lab)

Stone Division 1918-48

STONE DIVISION 1918-48

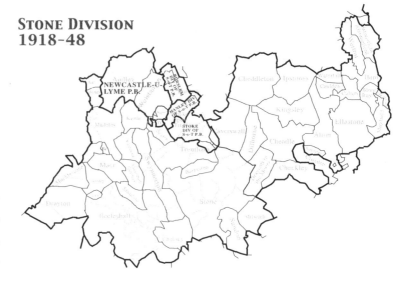

1918-22 Brig-Gen Sir S Hill Child Bt (Coalition Unionist)
1922-3 JQ Lamb (Unionist)
1923-4 JQ Lamb (Unionist)
1924-9 JQ Lamb (Con)
1929-31 Sir JQ Lamb (Con)
1931-5 Sir JQ Lamb (Con)
1935-45 Sir JQ Lamb (Con)
1945-50 Major HCP Fraser (Con)

Brierley Hill C.C. 1948-74

1950-1 CJ Simmons (Lab)
1951-5 CJ Simmons (Lab)
1955-9 CJ Simmons (Lab)
1959-64 JE Talbot (Con)

1964-6 JE Talbot (Con)
1966-70 JE Talbot (Con) (1966-7), WF Montgomery (Con) (1967-70)
1970-4 WF Montgomery (Con)

BRIERLEY HILL C.C. 1948-74

BURTON C.C. 1948-74

Burton C.C. 1948-74

1950-1 A Colegate (Con)
1951-5 A Colegate (Con)
1955-9 JC Jennings (Con)
1959-64 JC Jennings (Con)

1964-6 JC Jennings (Con)
1966-70 JC Jennings (Con)
1970-4 JC Jennings (Con)

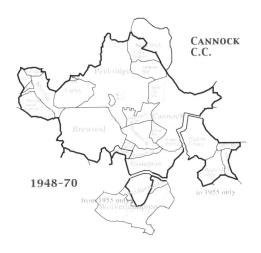

Cannock C.C. 1948-83

1950-1 Miss J Lee (Lab)
1951-5 Miss J Lee (Lab)
1955-9 Miss J Lee (Lab)
1959-64 Miss J Lee (Lab)
1964-6 Miss J Lee (Lab)
1966-70 Rt Hon J Lee (Lab)
1970-4 PT Cormack (Con)
1974-9 Gwilym E Roberts (Lab)
1979-83 GE Roberts (Lab)

Leek C.C. 1948-83

1950-1 H Davies (Lab)
1951-5 H Davies (Lab)
1955-9 H Davies (Lab)
1959-64 H Davies (Lab)
1964-6 H Davies (Lab)
1966-70 H Davies (Lab)
1970-4 David L Knox (Con)
1974-9 DL Knox (Con)
1979-83 DL Knox (Con)

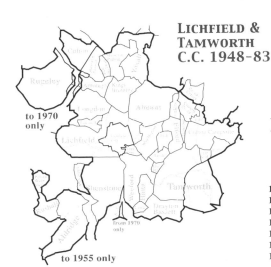

Lichfield and Tamworth C.C. 1948-83

1950-1 JW Snow (Lab)
1951-5 JW Snow (Lab)
1955-9 JW Snow (Lab)
1959-64 JW Snow (Lab)
1964-6 JW Snow (Lab)
1966-70 JW Snow (Lab)
1970-4 Maj-Gen JA d'Avigdor-Goldsmid, CB, OBE, MC (Con)
1974-9 Maj-Gen JA d'Avigdor-Goldsmid (Con)
1979-83 BJ Heddle (Con)

Newcastle-under-Lyme B.C. 1948-83

1950-1 JD Mack (Lab)
1951-5 ST Swingler (Lab)
1955-9 ST Swingler (Lab) **1959-64** ST Swingler (Lab)
1964-6 ST Swingler

(Lab)
1966-70 ST Swingler (Lab)
1970-4 John Golding (Lab)
1974-9 J Golding (Lab)
1979-83 J Golding (Lab)

NEWCASTLE-U-LYME B.C. 1948-83

1948-83

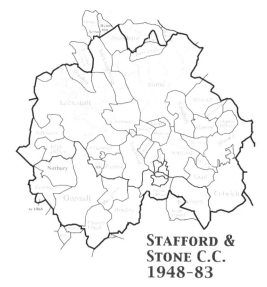

STAFFORD & STONE C.C. 1948-83

Stafford and Stone C.C. 1948-83

1950-1 Hon Hugh Charles Patrick Fraser (Con)
1951-5 HCP Fraser (Con)
1955-9 Hon HCPJ Fraser (Con)
1959-64 Hon HCPJ Fraser, MBE (Con)
1964-6 Hon HCPJ Fraser

(Con)
1966-70 Hon HCPJ Fraser (Con)
1970-4 Rt Hon HCPJ Fraser (Con)
1974-9 Rt Hon HCPJ Fraser (Con)
1979-83 Rt Hon HCPJ Fraser (Con)

Burton C.C. 1974-97

1974-9 Ivan J Lawrence (Con)
1979-83 IJ Lawrence (Con)
1983-7 IJ Lawrence

(Con)
1987-92 IJ Lawrence (Con)
1992-7 IJ Lawrence (Con)

BURTON C.C. 1974-97

Cannock & Burntwood
C.C. 1983-97

	(Con)		(Con)	
1983-7 JGD Howarth		**1987-92** JGD Howarth		**1992-7** A Wright (Lab)

Newcastle-under-Lyme B.C.
1983-present

NEWCASTLE B.C. 1983-PRESENT

1983-7 J Golding (Lab) (1983-6), Mrs Llinos Golding (Lab) (1986-7)
1987-92 Mrs Llinos

Golding (Lab)
1992-97 Mrs L Golding (Lab)

1997-2001 Mrs L Golding (Lab)
2001- Paul Farrelly (Lab)

Stafford C.C.
1983-97

1983-7 Rt Hon Hugh Charles Patrick Fraser (Con) (1983-4), William NP Cash (Con) (1984-7)

1987-92 William NP Cash (Con)
1992-7 WNP Cash (Con)

STAFFORD C.C. 1983-97

STAFFORD-SHIRE MID 1983-97

Staffordshire Mid
C. C. 1983-97

1983-7 BJ Heddle (Con)
1987-92 BJ Heddle (Con)

1992-7 Michael Fabricant (Con)

339

Constituencies 1983-present

STAFFORDSHIRE MOORLANDS C.C. 1983-97

The House of Commons

Staffordshire Moorlands C.C. 1983-97

1983-7 DL Knox (Con) **1992-7** DL Knox (Con)
1987-92 DL Knox (Con)

STAFFORDSHIRE SOUTH WEST C.C. 1974-83/ SOUTH 1983-PRESENT

Staffordshire South West C.C. 1974-83

1974-9 Patrick T Cormack (Con) **1979-83** PT Cormack (Con)

Staffordshire South C.C. 1983-present

1983-7 Patrick T Cormack (Con)
1987-92 PT Cormack (Con)
1992-97 PT Cormack (Con)

1997-2001 Sir PT Cormack (Con)
2001- Sir PT Cormack (Con)

STAFFORDSHIRE SOUTH EAST C.C. 1983-97

Staffordshire South East C.C. 1983-97

1983-7 DL Lightbown (Con) (Con)
1987-92 DL Lightbown **1992-7** DL Lightbown (Con)

340

BURTON
C.C.
1997-
PRESENT

Burton C. C. 1997-present

1997-2001 Ms Janet Dean (Lab)

2001- Ms J Dean (Lab)

CANNOCK
CHASE C.C.
1997-PRESENT

Cannock Chase C.C. 1997-present

1997-2001 Dr Anthony W Wright (Lab)
2001- Dr A Wright (Lab)

LICHFIELD
C.C. 1997-
PRESENT

Lichfield C.C. 1997-present

1997-2001 Michael LD Fabricant (Con)

2001- MLD Fabricant (Con)

STAFFORD
C.C. 1997-
PRESENT

Stafford C.C. 1997-present

1997-2001 David Kidney (Lab)

2001- D Kidney (Lab)

STAFFORDSHIRE
MOORLANDS C.C.
1997-
PRESENT

Stafford-shire Moorlands C.C. 1997-present

1997-2001 Ms Charlotte Atkins (Lab)
2001- Ms C Atkins (Lab)

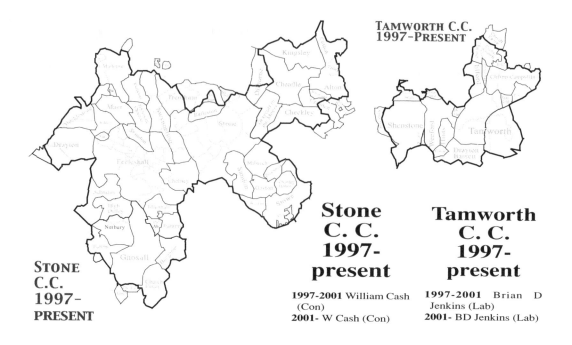

TAMWORTH C.C.
1997-PRESENT

STONE
C.C.
1997-
PRESENT

Stone C. C. 1997-present

1997-2001 William Cash (Con)
2001- W Cash (Con)

Tamworth C. C. 1997-present

1997-2001 Brian D Jenkins (Lab)
2001- BD Jenkins (Lab)

BOROUGH SEATS

Aldridge-Brownhills B.C. 1974-present

1974-9 Geoffrey Edge (Lab)
1979-83 Richard CS Shepherd (Con)
1983-7 RCS Shepherd (Con)
1987-92 RCS Shepherd (Con)
1992-7 RCS Shepherd (Con)

1997-2001 RCS Shepherd (Con)
2001- RCS Shepherd (Con)

ALDRIDGE-
BROWNHILLS
B.C.

Aston D. of Birmingham B.C. 1918-74

1918-22 Rt Hon E Cecil (Coalition Unionist)
1922-3 Rt Hon Sir E Cecil (Unionist)
1923-4 Rt Hon Sir E Cecil (Unionist)
1924-9 Rt Hon Sir E Cecil (Con)
1929-31 EJ St L Strachey (Socialist)
1931-5 Capt Hon AOJ Hope (Con)
1935-45 Capt Hon AOJ Hope (Con)
1945-50 Major W Wyatt (Lab)
1950-1 WL Wyatt (Lab)
1951-5 WL Wyatt (Lab)
1955-9 J Silverman (Lab)
1959-64 J Silverman (Lab)
1964-6 J Silverman (Lab)
1966-70 J Silverman (Lab)
1970-4 J Silverman (Lab)

Edgbaston D. of Birmingham B.C. 1885-present

1885-6 G Dixon (Lib)
1886-92 G Dixon (Lib Unionist) (unopposed)
1892-5 G Dixon (Lib Unionist) (unopposed)
1895-1900 G Dixon (Lib Unionist) (unopposed) (1895-8), FW Lowe (Con) (unopposed) (1898-1900)
1900-06 Sir FW Lowe (Con) (unopposed)
1906-10 Sir FW Lowe (Con)
1910 (Jan) Sir FW Lowe (Con)

1910 (Dec)-1918 Sir FW Lowe (Con) (unopposed)
1918-22 Sir F Lowe Bt (Coalition Unionist)
1922-3 Sir F Lowe Bt (Con) (unopposed)
1923-4 Sir F Lowe Bt (Con)
1924-9 Sir F Lowe Bt (Con)
1929-31 Rt Hon Neville Chamberlain (Con)
1931-5 Rt Hon N Chamberlain (Con)
1935-45 Rt Hon N Chamberlain (Con)
1945-50 Sir P Bennett (Con)
1950-1 Sir PFB Bennett (Con)
1951-5 Sir PFB Bennett (Con)
1955-9 Miss Edith M Pitt (Con)
1959-64 Miss EM Pitt, OBE (Con)
1964-6 Dame Edith Pitt, DBE (Con)
1966-70 Mrs Jill CJ Knight (Con)

1970-4 Mrs JCJ Knight (Con)
1974-9 Mrs JCJ Knight (Con)
1979-83 Mrs JCJ Knight (Con)
1983-7 Mrs JCJ Knight (Con)
1987-92 Dame JCJ Knight, DBE (Con)
1992-7 Dame JCJ Knight (Con)
1997-2001 Mrs Gisela Stuart (Lab)
2001- Ms G Stuart (Lab)

Handsworth D. of Birmingham B.C. 1918-83

1918-22 EC Meysey-Thompson (Coalition Unionist)
1922-3 Cdr. O Locker-Lampson (Unionist)
1923-4 Cdr. O Locker-Lampson (Unionist)
1924-9 Cdr. O Locker-Lampson (Con)
1929-31 Cdr. O Locker-Lampson (Con)
1931-5 Cdr. O Locker-Lampson (Con)
1935-45 Cdr. O Locker-Lampson (Con)
1945-50 H Roberts (Con)
1950-1 H Roberts (Con) (1950), Sir ECG Boyle

(Con) (1950-1)
1951-5 Sir ECG Boyle (Con)
1955-9 Sir ECG Boyle (Con)
1959-64 Sir ECG Boyle (Con)
1964-6 Rt Hon Sir ECG Boyle (Con)

1966-70 Rt Hon Sir ECG Boyle (Con)
1970-4 SB Chapman (Con)
1974-9 John Michael Hubert Lee (Lab)
1979-83 Mrs SRR Wright (Lab)

Ladywood D. of Birmingham B.C. 1997-present

1997-2001 Ms C Short (Lab)
2001- Rt Hon Ms C Short (Lab)

1997-present

Perry Barr D. of Birmingham B.C. 1950-present

1950-1 CC Poole (Lab)
1951-5 CC Poole (Lab)
1955-9 CA Howell (Lab)
1959-64 CA Howell (Lab)
1964-6 Dr WR Davies (Con)
1966-70 C Price (Lab)

1970-4 JR Kinsey (Con)
1974-9 Jeffrey William Rooker (Lab)
1979-83 JW Rooker (Lab)
1983-7 JW Rooker (Lab)
1987-92 JW Rooker (Lab)
1992-7 JW Rooker (Lab)
1997-2001 JW Rooker (Lab)
2001- Khalid Mahmood (Lab)

Dudley P.B., Worcs/ Staffs 1832-1974

1832-34 Sir John Campbell (Lib) (1832-4), Thomas Hawkes (Con) (1834)
1835-7 T Hawkes (Con)
1837-41 T Hawkes (Con)
1841-7 T Hawkes (Con)
1847-52 John Benbow (Con)
1852-7 John Benbow (Con) (1852-5), Sir Stafford Northcote (Lib Con) (1855-7)
1857-9 Henry B Sheridan (Lib/ Independent)
1859-65 HB Sheridan (Lib)
1865-8 HB Sheridan (Lib)
1868-74 HB Sheridan (Lib)
1874-80 HB Sheridan (Lib) (re-elected on account of an irregularity)

1885-6 HB Sheridan (Lib)
1886-92 Brooke Robinson (Con)
1892-5 Brooke Robinson (Con)
1895-1900 Brooke Robinson (Con)
1900-06 Brooke Robinson (Con)
1906-10 Arthur G Hooper (Lib)
1910 (Jan) AG Hooper (Lib)
1910 (Dec)-1918 Lt Col Sir AST Griffith-Boscawen (Con)
1918-22 Sir AST Griffith-Boscawen (Coalition Unionist) (1918-21), James Wilson (Lab) (1921-2)
1923-4 Cyril E Lloyd (Unionist)
1924-9 Cyril E Lloyd (Con)

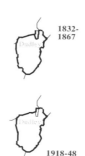

DUDLEY B.C.

1929-31 Oliver R Baldwin (Socialist)
1931-5 Dudley JB Joel (Con)
1935-45 DJB Joel (Con) (1935-41), CE Lloyd (Con) (1941-5)
1945-50 Lt-Col GEC Wigg (Lab)
1950-1 GEC Wigg (Lab)
1951-5 GEC Wigg (Lab)

1955-9 GEC Wigg (Lab)
1959-64 GEC Wigg (Lab)
1964-6 Rt Hon GEC Wigg (Lab)
1966-70 Rt Hon GEC Wigg (Lab) (1966-8), WD Williams (Con) (1968-70)
1970-4 John William Gilbert (Lab)

Dudley East B.C. 1974-97

1974-9 John William Gilbert (Lab)
1979-83 Rt Hon JW Gilbert (Lab)
1983-7 Rt Hon JW Gilbert (Lab)
1987-92 Rt Hon JW Gilbert (Lab)
1992-7 Dr J Gilbert (Lab)

DUDLEY EAST B.C.

Dudley West B.C. 1974-97

1974-9 Colin B Phipps (Lab)
1979-83 JG Blackburn (Con)
1983-7 JG Blackburn (Con)
1987-92 JG Blackburn (Con)
1992-7 JG Blackburn (Con)

Dudley North B.C. 1997-present

1997-2001 Ross F Cranston (Lab)
2001- RF Cranston (Lab)

Dudley South B.C. 1997-present

1997-2001 Ian P Pearson (Lab)
2001- IP Pearson (Lab)

DUDLEY SOUTH B.C.

344

Halesowen and Rowley Regis B.C. 1997-present

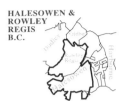

HALESOWEN &
ROWLEY
REGIS
B.C.

1997-2001 Mrs Sylvia   Heal (Lab)

2001- Ms S Heal (Lab)-

Lichfield P.B. 1302-1885

1302 Either no representation, or record

1305 Vincent de Hulton, Nicholas the clerk

1306-9 Either no representation, or record

1311-12 Nicholas de Rothewell, Reginald de Budel (in the autumn session), John de Brustow.... was sent instead of Rothwell

1312 (1) ?

1312 (2) John de Brustollia, Robert Michel

1313 (1) Reginald le Budel, William de Hampton

1313 (2) John fil. Robert de Lichfield, Adam le Parmenter

1313 (3) William de Lichfield, Richard de Lichfield

1314 (1) **-1319** Either perhaps did not meet, or no representation, or record

1320 William de Exton, William le Taverner

1321 Thomas de Pype, John de Byrmyngham

1322 (1) **-1325** Either no representation, or record

1326-7 Stephen le Blount, John de Eton

1327 Richard atte Leyes, John de Bolenhull

1328 (1) **-1337** (1) Either no representation, or record

1337 (2) (elected) Rad. de Barton, William de Eyton, Robert in le Mor

1337 (2) **-1352** (2) Either no sitting, or representation, or record

1353 Nicholas de Rotewell, Hugh de Gunston

1354-1407 Either no sitting, or representation, or record

1410 ? possibly John Delves was an MP representing the county or a borough

1411 Either no representation, or record

1413 (1) ? possibly Newport, or Robert Bapthorpe was an MP representing the county or a borough (SHC 1917-18 p175)

1413 (2) - **1547-52** No sitting, or representation, or record

1553 (1) Mark Wyrley, gent, William Fitzherbert, gent

1553 (2) Philip Draycot, miles, John Giffard, armiger

1554 Henry Vernon, esq, John Teyler, gent

1554-5 Thomas Edwardes, gent, Mark Wyrley, gent

1555 Thomas Edwardes, gent, Francis Bulstrode, gent

1558 Dr Robert Weston, Richard Cupper, gent

1559 Sir Henry Pagett, Kt, Dr Robert Weston

1563-7 Sir Henry Pagett, Kt, Michael Pulteney, Esq

1571 Edward Fitzgarret, Esq, William Tymperley, Esq

1572-83 Edward FitzGarrett, Esq, Arthur Bedell, gent

1584-5 Richard Brown, Esq, James Weston, Esq

1586-7 Richard Broughton, Esq, John Goodman, Esq

1588-9 Richard Broughton, Esq, Richard Huddlestone, Esq

1593 Sir John Wingfielde, Kt, Richard Broughton, Esq

1597-8 Joseph Oldisworth, Esq, William Fowkes, Esq

1601 Anthony Dyott, Esq, Robert Browne

1603 Anthony Dyott, Esq, Thomas Crew, Esq

1614 Sir John Egerton, Kt replaced possibly in by-election 1614 by Anthony Dyott, Esq, William Wingfield, Esq

1621-2 William Wingfield, Esq, Richard Weston, Esq

1624-5 Sir John Suckling, Kt replaced by Sir Simon Weston, Kt, William Wingfield, Esq

1625 Richard Dyott, Esq, William Wingfield, Esq

1626 Richard Dyott, Esq, William Wingfield, Esq

1628-9 Sir William Walter, Kt, Richard Dyott, Esq

1640 Sir Walter Devereux, Kt (Country), Sir Richard Dyott, Kt (Court)

1640-53 Sir Walter Devereux, Kt (Parl.) 1640-41, Michael Noble, Esq (Parl.) 1640-c48, Sir Richard Cave, Kt (Royalist) 1641-42, Michael Biddulph, Esq (Parl.) 1646-48

1653 Convention

1654-5 Thomas Minors, Esq

1656-8 Thomas Minors (sat from 1658)

1659 Jan - April - Thomas Mynors, Esq, Daniel Watson, Esq

1659 May - No Rumpers, restored.

1660 Feb - No secluded members, returned

1660 T Michael Biddulph, Esq, Daniel Watson, Esq (April-June 1660), Thomas Minors (June 1660-)

1661-79 John Lane, Esq, Sir Theophilus **1679** Sir Henry Lyttleton, Bart (Tory), Michael Biddulph, Esq (Whig)

1679-81 Daniel Finch, Esq (Tory), Michael Biddulph, Esq (Whig)

1681 T Daniel Finch, Esq (Tory), Michael Biddulph, Esq (Whig)

1685-7 Thomas Orme, Esq (Tory), Richard Leveson, Esq (Tory)

1689-90 Sir Michael Biddulph, Bart (Whig), Robert Burdett, Esq (Tory)

1690-5 Robert Burdett, Esq (Tory), Richard Dyott, Esq (Tory)

1695-8 Sir Michael Biddulph, Bart (Whig), Robert Burdett, Esq (Tory)

1698-1700 T Richard Dyott, Esq (Tory), Sir Michael Biddulph, Bart (Whig)

1701 T Richard Dyott, Esq (Tory), William Walmisley, Esq (Whig)

1701-2 Sir Michael Biddulph, Bart (Whig), Richard Dyott, Esq (Tory)

1702-5 Sir Michael Biddulph, Bart (Whig), Richard Dyott, Esq (Tory)

1705-8 Richard Dyott, Esq (Tory), Sir Henry Gough, Kt (Tory)

1708-10 John Cotes, Esq (Tory), Sir Michael Biddulph, Bart (Whig)

1710-13 T Richard Dyott, Esq (Tory), John Cotes, Esq (Tory)

1713-5 Richard Dyott, Esq (Tory), John Cotes, Esq (Tory)

1715-22 T Walter Chetwynd of Grendon, Esq (Whig) (1715-8, 1718-22), Samuel Hill, Esq (Hanoverian Tory) William Sneyd, Esq (Tory) (1718)

1722-27 T Walter Chetwynd of Grendon, Esq (Whig), Richard Plummer, Esq (Whig)

1727-34 T Walter Chetwynd of Grendon, Esq (Whig) (1727-31), Richard Plummer, Esq (Whig), George Venables Vernon, Esq (Tory) (1731-4)

1734-41 Sir Rowland Hill, Bart (Tory), George Venables Vernon, Esq (Tory)

1741-7 George Venables Vernon, Esq (Tory), Sir Lister Holt, Bart (Tory)

1747-54 T Richard Leveson Gower, Esq (Bedford Whig), Under Secretary to the Duke of Bedford (1747-53), Thomas Anson (Whig), Sir Thomas Gresley, Bart (Tory) (1753-4)T, Henry Vernon, Esq (Bedford Whig) (1754)

1754-61 T Granville Leveson Gower, Viscount Trentham (Bedford Whig) (1754-5), Thomas Anson, Esq (Whig), Henry Vernon, Esq (Bedford Whig) (1755-61)T

1761-8 T Thomas Anson, Esq (Whig), John Levett, Esq (Tory) (1761-2), Hugo Meynell, Esq (Whig) (1762-8)

1768-74 Thomas Anson Esq (Whig) (1768-70), Thomas Gilbert, Esq (Bedford Whig), George Adams, Esq (Whig) (1770-4)

1774-80 George Anson (formerly Adams), Esq (Whig), Thomas Gilbert Esq (Gower-Whig)

1780-4 George Anson, Esq (Whig), Thomas Gilbert, Esq (Gower-Whig)

1784-90 George Anson, Esq (Whig) (1784-8), Thomas Gilbert, Esq (Gower-Whig), Thomas Anson, Esq (Whig) (1788-90)

1790-96 Thomas Gilbert, Esq (Gower-Whig) (1790-5), Thomas Anson, Esq (Whig), Lord Granville Leveson Gower (Gower Whig) (1795-6)

1796-1802 T Thomas Anson (Whig), Lord Granville Leveson Gower (Gower Whig) (1796-9), Sir John Wrottesley, bart (Gower-Whig) (1799-1802)T

1802-6 Thomas Anson (Whig) (1802-6), Sir John Wrottesley, bart (Gower-Whig), Lieut-Col George Anson (Whig) (1806)

1806-7 George Granville Venables Vernon (Whig), Lieut-Col George Anson (Whig)

1807-12 George Granville Venables Vernon (Whig), Lieut-Col George Anson (Whig)

1812-18 George Granville Venables Vernon (Whig), Major-General George Anson (Whig)

1818-20 George Granville Venables Vernon (Whig), Major-General George Anson (Whig)

1820-6 George Granville Venables Vernon (Whig), Lieut-General Sir George Anson (Whig)

1826-30 T George Granville Venables Vernon (Whig), Lieut-General Sir George Anson (Whig)

1830-31 T George Granville Venables Vernon (Whig), Lieut-General Sir George Anson (Whig)

1831-2 Sir Edward Dolman Scott, bart (Whig), Lieut-General Sir George Anson (Whig)

1832-4 T Sir Edward Dolman Scott, bart (Lib), Lieut-General Sir George Anson (Lib)

1835-7 T Sir Edward Dolman Scott, bart (Lib-Whig), Sir George Anson, KCB (Lib-Whig)

1837-41 Lord Alfred Paget (Lib), Sir George Anson (Lib)

1841-7 Sir G Anson (Lib) (1841), Lord Alfred Paget (Lib) (1841-6) (1846-7) (unopposed), Lord Leveson (Lib) (1841-6) (unopposed), Hon EML Mostyn (Lib) (1846-7) (unopposed)

1847-52 Viscount Anson (Lib) (unopposed), Lord Alfred Paget (Lib) (unopposed)

1852-7 Viscount Anson (Lib) (1852-4), Lord Alfred Paget (Lib) (1852-3) (1853-7) (unopposed), Lord Waterpark (Lib) (1854-6) (unopposed), Viscount Sandon (Lib) (1856-7) (unopposed)

1857-9 Lord Alfred Paget (Lib) (unopposed), Viscount Sandon (Lib) (unopposed)

1859-65 Hon AHA Anson (Lib) (unopposed), Lord Alfred Paget (Lib) (1859) (unopposed) (1859-65) (unopposed)

1865-8 Hon AHA Anson (Lib), R Dyott (Con)

1868-74 R Dyott (Con), Hon AHA Anson (Lib)

1874-80 R Dyott (Con), C Simpson (Lib)

1880 (election declared void on petition) R Dyott (Con), Sir J Swinburne, Bt (Lib)

1880-5 TJ Levett (Con), Sir J Swinburne (Lib)

Newcastle-u-Lyme P.B. 1353-1950

-1353 Either no representation, or record

1354 John Lagowe, Richard son of Jurdan de Lavendon

1355 John de Blorton, Richard de Podmore

1357 ?

1358 William de Homersleye, Richard de Podmore

1360 William Gent, Richard de Colclough

1361 William Gent, Richard de Podmore

1362 Richard de Podmore, Thomas de Wodhull

1363 Richard de Lavndene, John de Lylsull

1365 Thomas de Wodhull, Richard de Podmore

1366 Richard de Podmore, Thomas de Wodhull

1368 ?

1369 Richard de Lavendene, Roger Letys (mayor)

1371 Roger Letys, Richard Lavendene (mayor)

1372 Edmund Toly, Thomas (vel William) Colclough

1373 Thomas de Wodhull, Roger del Castell

1376 ?

1377 (1) Richard Buntable, Thomas Thicknesse

1377 (2) Thomas de Podmore, Henry de Erdeleye

1378 Thomas de Podmore, William de Thecenes

1379 (no records)

1380 (1) John Kene, William de Thykenes

1380 (2) Returns not found

1381-2 Thomas Podmore, Thomas Hap

1382 (1) Thomas Thykenesse, John Thykenesse

1382 (2) William Thykenese, Henry de Kele

1383 (1) Thomas de Thykenese, William de Brompton

1383 (2) Thomas de Thykenes, Thomas de Podmore

1384 (1) William Thiknes, Ralf de la Hogh

1384 (2) John Colclough, William Colclough

1385 William Colclogh, Ralf del Hogh

1386 William Colclough, Ralf Hogh

1388 (1) William Thikenes, John Kene

1388 (2) William de Thikenes, Thomas de Thikenes

1390 (1) John Colclough, William Colclough

1390 (2) (no records)

1391 Thomas Thikenes, Ralf del Hogh

1392 (never met)

1393 Ralf Hogh, John Cook

1394 (no records)

1395 William Colclough, Ralf Hogh

1397 William Colclough, Thomas Thicknes

1397-8 (no records)

1399 (1) ?

1399 (2) Thomas Podmore, Thomas Thykenes

1400-1 ?

1402? (1) ? probably never met

1402 (2) John Joce, Thomas Joce

1403-4 ?

1404 ?

1406 Richard Fyton, William Lee

1407 Hugh Colclough, John Tatenhale

1410 ? possibly John Delves was an MP representing the county or a borough

1411 Thomas Thikenes, William Bowyer

1413 (1) ? possibly Newport, or Robert Bapthorpe was an MP representing the county or a borough (SHC 1917-18 p175)

1413 (2) William de Lee, Hugh Wyldeblood

1414 (1) ?

1414 (2) ?

1415 ? (no returns)

1416 (1) William Skytteby, Thomas Chamberleyn

1416 (2) ?

1417 ?

1419 John Biddulph (Bedulf), John Miners

1420 Hugo de Stanford, John Hardhed

1421 (1) John Biddulph (Bydulf), Thomas Baron

1421 (2) Hugh Stanford, Thomas Lee

1422 John Myners, Hugh Stanford

1423-4 Hugh Stanford, William Sandbache

1425 John Wode, William Hextall

1426 Robert Wodehous, Henry Lilie

1427-8 John Wode, Thomas Lee

1429-30 William Egerton, William Hextall

1431 John atte Wode, Roger Legh

1432 James Leveson, John Wood

1433 John Wood, Thomas Podmore

1435 Richard Bruyn, William Hextall

1437 Thomas Preston, Nicholas Repynghale

1439-40 ?

1442 John Nedham, William Cumberford of Cumberford

1445-6 ?

1447 John Nedham, John Cudworth

1449 John Nedham, Thomas Everdon

1449-50 Ralf Wolseley, Thomas Mayne

1450-51 Thomas Colclogh, Richard Mosley

1453-4 Thomas Colcloghe, John Spenser

1455-6 John Spenser, Richard Mosley

1459 ?

1460 ?

1461 ?

1463-5 ?

1467-8 James Norys, Robert Hille

1469 ?

1470-1 ?

1472-5 William Paston, John Wode

1477-8 William Yonge, Reynold Bray

1483 (1) ?

1483 (2) ?

1483 (3) ?

1484 ?

1485-6 ?

1487-8 ?

1489-90 ?

1491-2 Richard Harpur, Richard Blunt

1495-6 ? Sir Reynold Bray

1497 County/ or a borough - ?Richard Wrottesley, ?Humphrey Peshale, ?Humphrey Swynnerton, ?Thomas Welles

1504 (no records)

1509 ?

1512-14 ?

1515 ?

1523 ?

1529-36 John Persall (rectius Peshale), Richard Grey

1536 ?

1539-40 ?

1542-4 Harry Broke, John Smyth, yeoman

1545-7 Humphrey Wellys, armiger, Harry Broke, armiger

1547-52 James Rolston, armiger, William Stamford

by 1552 James Rolston, armiger, William Layton 'mortuus', Alexander Walker vice Layton

1553 (1) Roger Fowke, gent, John Smyth

1553 (2) Roger Fowke, James Rolston

1554 James Rolleston, gent, Francis Moore, gent

1554-5 Sir Ralph Bagnall, Kt (mayor), ?

1555 Sir Richard (rectius Nicholas) Bagnall, Richard Smyth, alderman

1558 Richard Hussey, armiger, Thomas Egerton, armiger

1559 Sir Nicholas Bagenall, Kt, Walter Blount, Esq

1563-7 Sir Ralph Bagnall, Kt, John Long, gent

1571 Sir Ralph Bagall, Ralph Bowcher

1572-83 Ralph Bouchier, Esq, Thomas Grimsdiche, Esq

1584-5 Peter Warburton, jun, Walter Chetwynd, gent

1586-7 James Colyer, Esq, Walter Chetwynd, gent

1588-9 Thomas Humphrey, Esq, Francis Angier, Esq

1593 John James, MD, Thomas Fitzherbert, Esq

1597-8 Sir Walter Leveson, Kt, John Bowyer, Esq

1601 Edward Mainwaringe, gent, Thomas Trentham, gent

1603 Walter Chetwynd, Esq, John Bowyer, Esq replaced in by-election 1605 by Rowland Cotton, Esq

1614 Edward Wymarke, Esq, Robert Needham, Esq

1621-2 Sir John Davies, Kt, Edward Kerton, Esq

1624-5 T Sir Edward Vere, Kt, Richard Leveson, Esq

1625 Edward Mainwaring, Esq, John Keeling, Esq

1626 Sir John Skeffington, Kt, John Keeling, Esq

1628-9 Sir George Gresley, Bart, Sir Rowland Cotton, Kt

1640 Sir John Merrick, Kt

(Country), Richard Lloyd, Esq (Court)

1640-53 Sir Richard Leveson, KB (Royalist) 1640-42, Sir John Merrick, Kt (Parl.) 1640-48, Samuel Terrick, Esq (Parl.) 1645-48

1653 Convention

1654-5 Edward Keeling, gent

1656-8 John Bowyer (never sat)

1659 Jan - April - Edward Keeling, Esq, Major-General Tobias Bridge

1659 May - No Rumpers, restored

1659 Feb - No Secluded members, returned

1660 * John Bowyer, Esq, Samuel Terrick, Esq

1661-79 Sir Caesar Colclough, Bart, Edward Mainwaring, Esq (1661-75), William Leveson Gower, Esq (1675-79)**T**

1679 Sir Thomas Bellot, Bart (Whig), William Leveson Gower, Esq

1679-81 Sir Thomas Bellot, Bart, William Leveson-Gower, Esq

1681 Sir Thomas Bellot, Bart (Whig), William Leveson Gower, Esq (Whig) (1681), Ralph Sneyd (Tory) (1681-)**T**

1685-7 T Edward Mainwaring, Esq (Tory), William Sneyd, jun, Esq (Tory)

1689-90 William Leveson Gower, Esq, John Lawton, Esq (Whig)

1690-5 Sir William

Leveson Gower, Bart (Tory) (1690-91), Sir Thomas Bellott, Bart (Tory), Sir John Leveson Gower, Bart (Tory) (1692-95)

1695-8 Sir John Leveson Gower, Bart (Tory), John Lawton, Esq (Whig)

1698-1700 Sir John Leveson Gower, Bart (Tory), Sir Thomas Bellott, Bart (Tory) (1698-99), Rowland Cotton, Esq (Tory) (1699-1700)**T**

1701 Sir John Leveson Gower (Tory), Rowland Cotton, Esq (Tory)

1701-2 Sir John Leveson Gower, Bart (Tory), Rowland Cotton, Esq (Tory)

1702-5 Sir John Leveson Gower, Bart (Tory) (1702-3), Rowland Cotton, Esq (Tory), John Crew Offley, Esq (Whig) (1703 T, 1704-5)

1705-8 T Sir Thomas Bellott, Bart (Tory) (1705), Rowland Cotton, Esq (Tory) (1705), Crewe Offley, Esq (Whig) (1706-8), John Lawton, Esq (Whig) (1706-8)

1708-10 T Sir Thomas Bellott, Bart (Tory) (1708-9), Rowland Cotton, Esq (Tory) (1708-9), Crew Offley, Esq (Whig) (1709-10), John Lawton, Esq (Whig) (1709-10)

1710-13 Rowland Cotton, Esq (Tory), William Burslem, Esq (Tory)

1713-5 T Rowland Cot-

ton, Esq (Tory), William Burslem, Esq (Tory)

1715-22 T Henry Vernon, Esq (Tory) (1715), Rowland Cotton, Esq (Tory) (1715), Crewe Offley (Whig) (1715-22), Sir Brian Broughton (Whig) (1715-22)

1722-27 Thomas Leveson Gower, Esq (Tory), Sir Brian Broughton, Bart (Whig) (1722-4), Sir Walter Wagstaff Bagott, Bart (Tory) (1724-7)**T**

1727-34 Baptist Leveson Gower, Esq (Tory), John Ward, Esq (Tory)

1734-41 T Baptist Leveson Gower, Esq (Tory), John Lawton, jun, Esq (Whig) (1734-40), Randle Wilbraham, Esq (Tory) (1740-1) **T**

1741-7 Baptist Leveson Gower, Esq (Tory), Randle Wilbraham, Esq (Tory)

1747-54 Baptist Leveson Gower, Esq (Bedford Whig), Thomas, Viscount Parker (Bedford Whig)

1754-61 John Waldegrave, Esq (Bedford Whig), Baptist Leveson Gower, Esq (Bedford Whig)

1761-8 General John Waldegrave (Bedford Whig) (1761-3), Henry Vernon, Esq (Bedford Whig) (1761-2), Sir Lawrence Dundas, Bart (Tory) (1762-8), Thomas Gilbert, Esq (Bedford Whig) (1763-8)

1768-74 T Captain John Wrottesley (Bedford Whig) (1768), Alexander Forrester, Esq (Bedford Whig), Dr Sir George Hay (Bedford Whig) (1768-74)

1774-80 T George Waldegrave, Viscount Chewton (Gower-Whig), Sir George Hay, Kt (Gower-Whig) (1774-9), George Granville Leveson Gower, Viscount Trentham (Gower-

Whig) (1779-80)

1780-4 George Granville Leveson Gower, Viscount Trentham (Gower-Whig), Archibald Macdonald, Esq (Gower-Whig)

1784-90 Richard Vernon (Gower-Whig), Archibald Macdonald, Esq (Gower-Whig)

1790-96 T Rear Admiral John Leveson Gower (Gower Whig) (1790-2), Sir Archibald Macdonald, Esq (Gower-Whig) (1790-3), William Egerton (Gower Whig) (1792-6) T, Sir Francis Ford, bart (Gower-Whig) (1793-6) T

1796-1802 William Egerton (Gower Whig), Edward Wilbraham Bootle (Tory)

1802-6 T Edward Wilbraham Bootle (Pittite Whig), Sir Robert Lawley, bart (Grenville Whig)

1806-7 T Edward Wilbraham Bootle (Tory), James McDonald (Whig)

1807-12 T Edward Wilbraham Bootle (Tory), James McDonald (Gower Whig)

1812-18 T George Granville, Earl Gower (Canningite) (1812-5), Sir John Fenton Fletcher Boughey, bart (Whig), Sir John Chetwode, bart (Independent Whig) (1815-8)**T**

1818-20 T William Shepherd Kinnersley (Tory), Robert John Wilmot (Canningite)

1820-6 T William Shepherd Kinnersley (Tory) (1820-3), Robert John Wilmot (Canningite), John Evelyn Denison (Canningite) (1823-6)T

1826-30 T Robert John Wilmot Horton (Canningite), Richard Borradaile (Tory)

1830-31 T Richard Borradaile (Tory), William Henry Miller

1885-1918   1918-48

NEWCASTLE-U-LYME P.B.

(Tory)

1831-2 T Edmund Peel of Bonehill (Tory), William Henry Miller (Tory)

1832-4 T Sir Henry Pollard Willoughby, Bt (Con- Whig), William Henry Miller (Con)

1835-7 T Edmund Peel (Con), William Henry Miller (Con)

1837-41 T SH de Horsey (Con), William Henry Miller (Con)

1841-7 E Buckley (Con), JQ Harris (Lib) (1841-2) (1842), JC Colquhoun

(Con) (1842-7)

1847-52 S Christy (Con) (1847) (1847-52), W Jackson (Lib)

1852-7 W Jackson (Lib), S Christy (Con)

1857-9 W Jackson (Lib), S Christy (Con)

1859-65 W Jackson (Lib) (unopposed), W Murray (Con) (unopposed)

1865-8 WS Allen (Lib), E Buckley (Con)

1868-74 WS Allen (Lib), E Buckley (Con)

1874-80 WS Allen (Lib), Sir E Buckley (Con) (1874-8), SR Edge (Lib)

(1878-80)

1880-5 WS Allen (Lib), CD Hudson (Con).

1885-6 WS Allen (Lib)

1886-92 DH Coghill (Lib Unionist)

1892-5 WS Allen junior (Gladstonian Lib)

1895-1900 WS Allen junior (Gladstonian Lib)

1900-06 Sir AS Haslam (Lib Unionist)

1906-10 Josiah C Wedgwood (Lib)

1910 (Jan) JC Wedgwood (Lib)

1910 (Dec)-**1918** JC Wedgwood (Lib)

1918-22 JC Wedgwood (Coalition Lab, then Lab) (unopposed)

1922-3 JC Wedgwood (Lab)

1923-4 JC Wedgwood (Lab)

1924-9 JC Wedgwood (Socialist)

1929-31 Rt Hon JC Wedgwood (Lab)

1931-5 Rt Hon JC Wedgwood (Lab) (unopposed)

1935-45 Rt Hon JC Wedgwood (Lab) (unopposed)

1945-50 JD Mack (Lab)

Oldbury and Halesowen B.C. 1948-74

1950-1 A Moyle (Lab)

1951-5 A Moyle (Lab)

1955-9 A Moyle (Lab)

1959-64 A Moyle, CBE

(Lab)

1964-6 J Horner (Lab)

1966-70 J Horner (Lab)

1970-4 JHR Stokes (Con)

Rowley Regis and Tipton B.C. 1948-74

1950-1 Rt Hon A Henderson (Lab)

1951-5 Rt Hon A Henderson (Lab)

1955-9 Rt Hon A Henderson, QC (Lab)

1959-64 Rt Hon A Henderson, QC (Lab)

1964-6 Rt Hon A Henderson, QC (Lab)

1966-70 PK Archer (Lab)

1970-4 PK Archer (Lab)

Smethwick B.C. 1918-74

1918-22 JE Davison (Lab) defeating Miss Christabel Pankhurst (Ind)

1922-3 JE Davison (Lab)

1923-4 JE Davison (Lab)

1924-9 JE Davison (Socialist) (1924-6),

Oswald Moseley (Lab) (1926-9)

1929-31 Sir Oswald Mosley Bt (Lab)

1931-5 AR Wise (Con)

1935-45 AR Wise (Con)

1945-50 AJ Dobbs (Lab)

1950-1 Rt Hon PC Gordon-Walker (Lab)

1951-5 Rt Hon PC Gordon-Walker (Lab)

1955-9 Rt Hon PC Gordon-Walker (Lab)

1959-64 Rt Hon PC

Gordon-Walker (Lab)

1964-6 PHS Griffiths (Con)

1966-70 AMW Faulds (Lab)

1970-4 AMW Faulds (Lab)

Stafford P.B. 1294-1918

Lost one of its two seats 1885.

-1294 Either no representation, or record

1295 William Reyner, John Beton

1298 'No return made'

1301 Richard fil. Roger de Stafford, Richard de Neuport

1305 John fil. William de Pikstok, Philip le Goldsmith

1306 Philip le Goldsmith

1307-8 Philip le Goldsmith, Simon de Neuport

1308 ?

1309 William Reyner, Simon de Stafford

1311-12 William de

Wolaston, Nicholas the Barber

1312 (1) ?

1312 (2) William Reyner, John de London

1313 (1) William Reyner, John le Mareschal

1313 (2) John de London of Stafford, Simon Trumwyne
1313 (3) John le Marshall, William Reiner
1314 (1) ? (did not meet)
1314 (2) ?
1315 Simon de Melewys, John le Somenour
1316 (1) (no records)
1316 (2) (no records)
1316 (3) (no records)
1318 (1) ?
1318 (2) Richard Sabyn, John le Somenour
1319 Simon de Mulewych, John de Hughcesdon (Hixon)
1320 John Pykestok, Richard Sabyn
1321 Simon de Melewych, Richard Sabyn
1322 (1) (no records)
1322 (2) John de Hughcesdon, Simon de Melewych
1324 (1) John de Hughcesdon, Richard de Sutton
1324 (2) (no records)
1325 William Hunfrey, Richard de Sotton
1326-7 John de Hughcesdon, Richard de Sutton
1327 Simon Trumwyne, Nicholas Reyner
1328 (1) Adam le Rotour, ____ Kneygh ___
1328 (2) Robert de Brokes (?Croftes), Simon Trumwyne
1328 (3) William Pecok, John Gilberd
1328-9 William Pecok, John Gilbert
1330 (1) Roger Wryde, William Wryde
1330 (2) John de Pykestok, Roger Wryde
1331 (no records)
1332 (1) Roger Wryde, Robert le Cartere
1332 (2) Adam le Rotour, Ralf de Falde
1332-3 (no records)
1334 (1) John de Salt of Stafford, William Dyngel of Stafford
1334 (2) John de Pykstok, William le Goldsmyth
1335 (no records)
1336 (1) William le Goldsmyth, Adam de

Hopton
1336 (2) Roger Organ, John de Salt
1337 (1) (no records)
1337 (2) (elected) Hugo de Snel, John de Salt, John de Rotor
1337 (2) (elected) John le Rotour, Hugh Snel
1338 (1) Roger Wryde, Nicholas Reyner
1338 (2) Roger Wryde, John le Rotour
1339 (1) William Dyngel, Adam de Hopton
1339 (2) Nicholas Reyner, John le Rotour
1340 (1) ?
1340 (2) John le Rotour, William de Erburton
1340 (3) ?
1340 Assembly directed to attend as merchants by Writ - Roger Wryde, John le Rotour
1341 Roger Wryde, John le Rotour
1343 (no records)
1343 Nicholas Reyner, John le Rotour
1346 Nicholas Reyner, Thomas de Alrewas
1348 (1) Nicholas Reyner, Roger de Peshale
1348 (2) Nicholas Reyner, William de Erberton
1349 No parliament sat
1351 John de Byrleye, Richard de Shelford
1352 (1) (no records)
1352 (2) (no records)
1353 Adam Rotour, Hugh Snel
1354 Adam le Rotour, Ralph del Croftes
1355 Adam Rotour, William de Homeresleye
1357 ?
1358 Ralf de Croftes, John de Croftes
1360 Hugh Snel, John de Legh
1361 John de Croftes, Ralf de Croftes
1362 Hugh Snel, Simon Organ
1363 Hugh Snel, Robert le Goldsmith
1365 Hugh Snel, William Bochard (vel Wochard)
1366 Hugh Snel, William Slindon
1368 Hugh Snel, John de

Wolaston
1369 Hugh Snel, John de Wolaston
1371 ?
1372 Robert del Mershe, John de Wolaston
1373 Hugh Snel, Nicholas Snel
1376 Hugh Snell, Nicholas Snell
1377 (1) Robert del Mershe, Henry Prest
1377 (2) Robert de Merssh, Hugh Snel
1378 John de Neuton, John le Baxter
1379 (no records)
1380 (1) Nicholas Snel, John Baxter
1380 (2) John Bougy, Thomas Jokery
1381-2 Nicholas Snel, William Broun
1382 (1) Richard de Staunford, Richard de Mor'
1382 (2) Thomas Jokery, Roger Coton
1383 (1) Thomas Jokery, John Dyngell
1383 (2) John de Croftes, John atte Assch'
1384 (1) John Ingestre, Roger de Cotes
1384 (2) John de Orewelle, John Baxtere
1385 Roger de Coton, John de Neuton
1386 Richard Staunford, Thomas Jokery
1388 (1) John Neuton, Nicholas Snel
1388 (2) John Neuton, Richard de Staunford
1390 (1) John de Neuton, John Snel
1390 (2) (no records)
1391 John de Neuton, Richard Staunford
1392 (never met)
1393 Henry Warylewe, John Baxter
1394 (no records)
1395 John Wylaston, John Baxtere
1397 John Clyfton, John Wylaston
1397-8 (no records)
1399 (1) ?
1399 (2) John Wilaston (Wolaston?)
1400-1 ?
1402? (1) ? probably never met
1402 (2) Richard Staunford, Thomas

Barbour
1403-4 Roger de Coton, Adam Heuster
1404 ?
1406 Thomas Jocary, John Huntingdon
1407 John Huntingdon, Thomas Jocary
1410 (no records)
1411 Thomas Barbour, Robert Whitgreve
1413 (1) ? possibly Newport, or Robert Bapthorpe was an MP representing the county or a borough (SHC 1917-18 p175)
1413 (2) Adam Eggeley, Thomas Barbour
1414 (1) ?
1414 (2) ?
1415 ? (no returns)
1416 (1) Robert Whitgreve, Henry Fenton
1416 (2) ?
1417 ?
1419 John Parker, John Harpur
1420 Robert Whitgreve, John Harpur
1421 (1) Robert Whitgreve, John Harpur
1421 (2) Robert Whitgreve, Adam Egglesley
1422 Robert Whitgreve, John Harpur
1423-4 Robert Whitgreve, John Harpur
1425 Robert Whitgreve, John Harpur
1426 Robert Whitgreve, William Preston
1427-8 Robert Whitgreve, John Harpur
1429-30 Robert Whitgreve, John Harpur
1431 Robert Whitgreve, William Hextall
1432 Robert Whitgreve, William Hextall
1433 Robert Whitgreve, William Barbour
1435 Robert Whitgreve, Roger Clerk, alias Tailour
1437 Robert Whitgreve, William Hextall
1439-40 ?
1442 Robert Whitgreve, Richard Broyn
1445-6 ?
1447 William Garnet, Robert Atkynson
1449 Richard Broyn,

Nicholas Assheby

1449-50 Humphrey Whitgreve, William Preston

1450-51 Humphrey Whitgreve, John Barbour

1453-4 William Barbour, John Barbour

1455-6 William Barbour, John Barbour

1459 ?

1460 ?

1461 ?

1463-5 ?

1467-8 Richard Harpour, John Preston

1469 ?

1470-1 ?

1472-5 Richard Harpour, Robert Hille

1477-8 John Eggerton, armiger, Thomas Gresley, armiger

1483 (1) ?

1483 (2) ?

1483 (3) ?

1484 ?

1485-6 ?

1487-8 ?

1489-90 ?

1491-2 William Chetwynd, Esq, Richard Pennysbye, gent

1495-6 John Ferrers, Humphrey Barbour

1497 County/ or a borough -?Richard Wrottesley, ?Humphrey Peshale, ?Humphrey Swynnerton, ?Thomas Welles

1504 (no records)

1509 ?

1512-14 ?

1515 ?

1523 ?

1529-36 Thomas Stamford (in 1530/32 he died. Mr Erdeswick elected in a bye-election) John Bykeley

1536 ?

1539-40 ?

1542-4 Walter Blount, gent, William Stamford of London, gent

1545-7 Henry Stafford, armiger, William Stamford de London, armiger

1547-52 Henry Stafford, armiger, Richard Forssett

by 1552 Henry Stafford, armiger, Richard Forsett

1553 (1) Edward Colbarne, gent, Francis Smyth, gent

1553 (2) Henry Stafford, armiger, Sir Anthony Browne/ Simon Lowe of London

1554 John Giffard, armiger, Humphrey Swynnerton, armiger

1554-5 James Rolleston, Matthew Craddock

1555 Henry Stafford, armiger, Thomas Harcourt, armiger

1558 Edward Stafford, armiger, James Fowler,gent

1559 Edward Stafford, Esq, William Twyneo

1563-7 William Twyneo Esq, Henry Goodere, gent

1571 Walter Stafford, Esq, William Knowles, Esq

1572-83 Richard Broughton, gent, Thomas Purslowe, gent

1584-5 John Stafford, Esq, Francis Craddock, gent

1586-7 John Stafford, Esq, Francis Craddock, Esq

1588-9 Francis Craddock, Esq, Henry Bourchier, Esq

1593 * Henry Bourchier, Esq, Francis Craddock, Esq

1597-8 Sir Edward Stafford, Kt, Henry Bourchier, Esq

1601 Sir Edward Stafford, Kt, William Essex, Esq

1603 Hugh Beeston, Esq replaced in by-election 1609 by Arthur Ingram, Esq, George Craddock, Esq

1614 Sir Walter Devereux, Kt, Thomas Gibbs, Esq

1621-2 Matthew Craddock, Esq, the Recorder, Richard Dyott, Esq

1624-5 T Matthew Craddock, Esq, Richard Dyott, Esq, Recorder

1625 Matthew Craddock, Esq, Sir Robert Hatton, Kt replaced in by-election by Sir John Offley, Kt

1626 Sir John Offley, Kt, Bulstrode Whitelock, Esq

1628-9 Matthew Craddock, Esq, William Wingfield, Esq

1640 Ralph Sneyd, jun, Gent (Court), Richard Weston, Esq (Court)

1640-53 Ralph Stafford, jun, esq (Royalist) 1640-43, Richard Weston, jun, Esq (Royalist) 1640-41, John Swynfen, gent (Parl.) 1645-48, Edward Leigh, Esq (Parl.) 1645-48

1653 Convention (no records)

1654-5 John Bradshawe, esq, serjt-at-law

1656-8 Martin Noel, merchant of London,

1659 Jan - April - Martin Noell, Esq, William Jessop, Esq

1659 May - Rumper, restored in May 1659:- (none)

Secluded members, returned **Feb 1660**:- John Swynfen

1660 Sir Charles Wolseley, Bart, John Swynfen, Esq

1661-79 Robert Milward, Esq (1661-74), William Chetwynd, Esq (1661-79), Walter Chetwynd, Esq (1674-79)

1679 Walter Chetwynd, Esq (Whig), Sir Thomas Armstrong, Kt (Whig)

1679-81 Sir Thomas Wilbraham, Bart, Sir Thomas Armstrong, Kt (Whig)

1681 Sir Thomas Armstrong, Kt (Whig), Edwin Skrymsher, Esq (Whig)

1685-7 Walter Chetwynd, Esq (Tory), Roland Okeover, Esq (Tory)

1689-90 Philip Foley, Esq (Whig), John Chetwynd, Esq (Tory)

1690-5 T John Chetwynd, Esq (Tory), Jonathan Cope, Esq (Tory) (1690-94), Thomas Foley, jun, Esq (Tory) (1694-95)

1695-8 Philip Foley, Esq (Mod. Tory), Thomas Foley, jun, Esq (Mod. Tory)

1698-1700 Philip Foley, Esq (Tory), Thomas Foley, jun, Esq of Witley (Tory)

1701 John Chetwynd, Esq (Tory), Thomas Foley, Esq (Tory)

1701-2 Thomas Foley, Esq (Tory), John Pershall, Esq (Whig)

1702-5 Thomas Foley, Esq (Tory), John Chetwynd, Esq (Tory)(1702), Walter Chetwynd, Esq (Godolphin Tory) (1702-5)

1705-8 Thomas Foley, Esq (Tory), Walter Chetwynd, Esq (Whig)

1708-10 Thomas Foley, Esq (Tory), Walter Chetwynd, Esq (Whig)

1710-13 T Thomas Foley, Esq (Tory) (1710-2), Walter Chetwynd, Esq (Whig) (1710-1, 1712-3), Henry Vernon, jun, Esq (Tory) (1711-3)

1713-5 Henry Vernon, jun, Esq (Tory), Walter Chetwynd, Esq (Whig)

1715-22 Walter Chetwynd, Esq (Whig), William Chetwynd, Esq (Whig)

1722-27 T Thomas Foley (Tory), John Dolphin (Tory) (1722-4), Francis Eld, Esq (Whig) (1724-5)T, Walter, Viscount Chetwynd (Whig) (1725-7)

1727-34 Walter, Viscount Chetwynd (Anti-Walpolean Whig), Joseph Gascoigne Nightingale, Esq (Tory)

1734-41 T Thomas Foley, Auditor of the Imprest (Tory) (1734-8), William Chetwynd, Master of the Mint (Anti-Walpolean Whig) John, Viscount Chetwynd (Anti-Walpolean Whig) (1738-41)

1741-7 John, Viscount Chetwynd (Patriot), William Chetwynd, Esq (Patriot)

1747-54 William Chetwynd, Esq (Bed-

STAFFORD
P.B.

---

ford Whig), John Robins (Whig)

1754-61 William Richard Chetwynd, Esq (Bedford Whig), William Chetwynd, Esq (Bedford Whig)

1761-8 William Richard Chetwynd, Esq (Bedford Whig) (1761-5), William Chetwynd, Esq (Bedford Whig), John Crewe, Esq (Whig) (1765-8)**T**

1768-74 T Richard Whitworth, Esq (Tory), William, Viscount Chetwynd (Bedford Whig) (1768-70), William Nevil Hart, Esq (Whig) (1770-4)

1774-80 T Hugo Meynell, Esq (Whig), Richard Whitworth, Esq (Tory)

1780-4 T Edward

Monckton, Esq (Whig), Richard Brinsley Sheridan, Esq (Whig)

1784-90 Edward Monckton, Esq (Whig), Richard Brinsley Sheridan, Esq (Whig)

1790-96 T Edward Monckton, Esq (Whig), Richard Brinsley Sheridan, Esq (Whig)

1796-1802 Edward Monckton (Pittite Whig), Richard Brinsley Sheridan (Whig)

1802-6 T Edward Monckton (Gower Whig), Richard Brinsley Sheridan (Whig)

1806-7 T Sir Edward Monckton (Gower Whig), Richard Mansell Philipps (Gower Whig)

1807-12 T Sir Edward Monckton (Canningite), Richard Mansell Philipps (Canningite)

1812-18 T Ralph Benson (Tory), Colonel Thomas Wilson (Tory)

1818-20 T Benjamin Benyon (Whig), Samuel Homfray (Tory)

1820-6 T George Chetwynd (Canningite),

Benjamin Benyon (Whig)

1826-30 T Richard Ironmonger (Whig) (1826), Richard Benson (Tory), Thomas Wentworth Beaumont (Whig) (1826-30)**T**

1830-31 T Thomas Gisborne (Whig), John Campbell (Whig)

1831-2 T Thomas Gisborne (Whig), John Campbell (Whig)

1832-4 T Capt William F Chetwynd (Lib), Capt Rees Howell Gronow (Lib)

1835-7 T Francis Lyttleton Holyoake Goodricke (Con) (1835), Capt William F Chetwynd (Lib -Whig), Robert Farrand (Con) (1835-7)

1837-41 T Major William F Chetwynd (Lib), Robert Farrand (Con)

1841-47 Hon ST Carnegie (Con) (1841-6, 1846-7), E Buller (Lib)

1847-52 D Urquhart (Con), T Sidney (Con)

1852-7 JA Wise(Lib), AJ Otway (Lib)

1857-9 JA Wise (Lib), Viscount Ingestre (Con)

1859-65 JA Wise (Lib) (1857-60), T Salt (Con), T Sidney (1860-5)

1865-8 MA Bass (Lib), W Meller (Con)

1868 (election declared void on petition) HD Pochin (Lib), W Meller (Con)

1869-74 T Salt (Con), Hon RAJ Talbot (Con)

1874-80 T Salt (Con), Alexander MacDonald (Lib/ Lab)

1880-5 CBB McLaren (Lib), Alexander MacDonald (Lib/ Lab) (1880-1), T Salt (Con) (1881-)

1885-6 CB McLaren (Lib)

1886-92 T Salt (Con)

1892-5 Charles Edward Shaw (Gladstonian Lib)

1895-1900 CE Shaw (Gladstonian Lib)

1900-06 CE Shaw (Lib)

1906-10 (Sir) CE Shaw (Lib)

1910 (Jan) Sir CE Shaw (Lib)

1910 (Dec)-1918 (Sir) RW Essex (Lib)

Stoke-upon-Trent P.B. 1832-1885

1832-4 T Josiah Wedgwood (Lib- Reformer), John Davenport (Con-Reformer)

1835-7 Richard Edensor Heathcote (Lib), John Davenport (Con) (1835-6), Col Hon George Anson (Lib- Whig) (1836-7)

1837-41 T WT Copeland (Con), John Davenport (Con)

1841-47 JL Ricardo

(Lib), WT Copeland (Con)

1847-52 JL Ricardo (Lib), WT Copeland (Con)

1852-7 JL Ricardo (Lib), Hon EFL Gower (Lib)

1857-9 JL Ricardo (Lib), WT Copeland (Con)

1859-65 JL Ricardo (Lib) (1859-62), WT Copeland (Con), HR Grenfell (Lib) (1862-5)

1865-8 AJBB Hope

(Con) (1865-8), HR Grenfell (Lib), G Melly (Lib) (1868)

1868-74 G Melly (Lib) (Lib) (unopposed), WS Roden (Lib) (unopposed)

1874-80 G Melly (Lib) (1874-5), R Heath (Con), EVH Kenealy (Ind) (1875-80)

1880-85 W Woodall (Lib), H Broadhurst (Lib/ Lab)

STOKE
UPON
TRENT
PARLIA-
MENTARY
BOROUGH

Stoke-upon-Trent P.B. 1885-1918

1885-6 WL Bright (Lib)

1886-92 WL Bright (Gladstonian Lib) (1886-90), GW Leveson-Gower

(Gladstonian Lib) (1890-2)

1892-5 GW Leveson-Gower (Gladstonian Lib) (1892) (1892-5)

1895-1900 Douglas Harry Coghill (Lib Unionist)

1900-06 DH Coghill (Con)

1906-10 John Ward (Lab)

1910 (Jan) J Ward (Lib)

1910 (Dec)-1918 (Lt Col) John Ward (Lib)

Hanley P.B. 1885-1918

1885-6 William Woodall (Lib)
1886-92 W Woodall (Gladstonian Lib) (un-opposed)
1892-5 W Woodall (Gladstonian Lib)

1895-1900 W Woodall (Gladstonian Lib)
1900-06 Enoch Edwards (Lab)
1906-10 Enoch Edwards (Lab)

1910 (Jan) Enoch Edwards (Lab)
1910 (Dec)-1918 Enoch Edwards (Lab) (1910-2), RL Outhwaithe (Lib) (1912-8)

Burslem D. of Stoke-on-Trent P.B. 1918-48

1918-22 Samuel Finney (Lab)
1922-3 Andrew MacLaren (Lab)

1923-4 WE Robinson (Lib)
1924-9 Andrew MacLaren (Socialist)

1929-31 Andrew MacLaren (Lab)
1931-5 W Allen (Con)

1935-45 A MacLaren (Socialist)
1945-50 AE Davies (Lab)

Hanley D of Stoke-on-Trent P.B. 1918-48

1918-22 JA Seddon (Coalition National Democratic Party)
1922-3 H Parker (Lab)
1923-4 H Parker (Lab)

1924-9 S Clowes (Socialist) (1924-8), A Hollins (Socialist) (1928-9)
1929-31 Arthur Hollins (Socialist)

1931-5 HK Hales (Con)
1935-45 A Hollins (Socialist)
1945-50 Dr B Stross (Lab)

Stoke D. of Stoke-on-Trent P.B. 1918-48

1918-22 Lt-Col John Ward (Coalition Lib) (unopposed)
1922-3 Lt-Col John Ward (National Lib)

1923-4 Lt-Col John Ward (Lib)
1924-9 Lt-Col John Ward (Constitutionalist)
1929-31 Lady Cynthia

Mosley (Socialist)
1931-5 Mrs Ida Copeland (Con), defeating Sir Oswald E Moseley (National Party)

1935-45 Ellis Smith (Socialist)
1945-50 Ellis Smith (Lab)

Stoke-on-Trent Central B.C. 1948-

1950-1 Dr B Stross (Lab)
1951-5 Dr B Stross (Lab)
1955-9 Dr B Stross (Lab)
1959-64 Dr B Stross (Lab)
1964-6 Sir B Stross (Lab)

1966-70 Robert Bowen Cant (Lab)
1970-4 RB Cant (Lab)
1974-9 RB Cant (Lab)
1979-83 RB Cant (Lab)
1983-7 Mark Fisher

(Lab)
1987-92 M Fisher (Lab)
1992-7 M Fisher (Lab)
1997-2001 M Fisher (Lab)
2001- M Fisher (Lab)

From 1948

Stoke-on-Trent North B.C. 1948-

1950-1 AE Davies (Lab)
1951-5 AE Davies (Lab)**1955-9** Mrs H Slater (Lab)

1959-64 Mrs H Slater (Lab)
1964-6 Mrs H Slater (Lab)

1966-70 John Stuart Forrester (Lab)
1970-4 JS Forrester (Lab)
1974-9 JS Forrester (Lab)

1979-83 JS Forrester (Lab)
1983-7 JS Forrester (Lab)
1987-92 Ms Joan L Walley (Lab)
1992-7 Ms JL Walley (Lab)
1997-2001 Ms JL Walley (Lab)
2001- Ms JL Walley (Lab)

Stoke-on-Trent South B.C. 1948-

1950-1 Ellis Smith (Lab)
1951-5 E Smith (Lab)
1955-9 E Smith (Lab)
1959-64 E Smith (Lab)
1964-6 E Smith (Lab)
1966-70 Jack Ashley (Lab)
1970-4 J Ashley (Lab)
1974-9 J Ashley (Lab)
1979-83 Rt Hon J Ashley, CH (Lab)
1983-7 Rt Hon J Ashley (Lab)
1987-92 Rt Hon J Ashley (Lab)
1992-7 George W Stevenson (Lab)
1997-2001 GW Stevenson (Lab)
2001- GW Stevenson (Lab)

From at least 1981

Stourbridge B.C. 1997-

1997-2001 Ms Debra Shipley (Lab)
2001- Ms D Shipley (Lab)

Sutton Coldfield B.C. 1970-

1970-4 Rt Hon GW Lloyd (Con)
1974-9 PN Fowler (Con)
1979-83 Rt Hon PN Fowler (Con)
1983-7 Rt Hon PN Fowler (Con)
1987-92 Rt Hon PN Fowler (Con)
1992-7 Rt Hon Sir N Fowler (Con)
1997-2001 Rt Hon Sir N Fowler (Con)
2001- Andrew Mitchell (Con)

Tamworth P.B. 1275-1885

1275 ?
1275-1559 Either no representation, or record
1563-7 Michael Harecourte, Esq, Robert Harcourte
1571 Edward Lewkenor, Esq, John Bullock, Esq
1572-83 Lancelot Bostock, gent, John Nuttall, gent
1584-5 John Breton, Esq, Clement Fisher, Esq
1586-7 Walter Bagot, Esq, John Ferrers, Esq
1588-9 Edward Devereux, Esq, Robert Wright, Esq
1593 John Ferrers, Esq, Thomas Smyth, gen
1597-8 George Hyde, Esq, William Temple, gent
1601 George Egeocke, Esq, Robert Burdett, Esq
1603 Sir Perceval Willoughby, Kt replaced in by-election 1604 by Sir Thomas Beaumont, Kt, Sir John Ferrers, Kt
1614 Sir Thomas Roe, Kt, Sir Perceval Willoughby, Kt
1621-2 Sir Thomas Puckering, Kt and Bart, John Ferrour, merchant of London
1624-5 John Woodford, Esq, John Wightwick, Esq
1625 Sir Thomas Puckering, Kt and Bart, Sir Richard Skeffington, Kt
1626 Sir Thomas Pucker-
ing, Kt and Bart, Sir Walter Devereux, Kt
1628-9 Sir Thomas Puckering, Kt and Bart, Sir Walter Devereux, Kt
1640 George Abbott of Caldecot, Esq (Country), Sir Simon Archer, Kt (Country)
1640-53 William Strode, Esq (Parl.) 1640 (never sat for Tamworth), Ferdinand Stanhope, Esq (Royalist) 1640-43, Henry Wilmot, Esq (Royalist) 1640-41, Sir Peter Wentworth, KB (Parl.) 1641-53, George Abbot, Esq (Parl.) 1645-48
1653 Convention
1654-5 No representation
1656-8 No representation
1659 Jan - April - John Swynfen, Esq, Thomas Fox, Esq
1659 May - Rumper restored - Sir Peter Wentworth
1660 Feb - No Secluded member, returned
1660 Richard Newdigate, Lord Chief Justice of the Upper Bench, Thomas Fox, Esq
1661-79 Amos Walrond, Esq (1661-69), John Swynfen, Esq, Charles, Lord Clifford (1669-79)T
1679 Thomas Thynne, Esq (Whig), John Swinfen, Esq (Whig)
1679-81 T Thomas

354

Thynne, Esq (Whig), Sir Andrew Hackett, Kt (Tory)

1681 Sir Thomas Thynne, Bart (Whig), John Swynfen, Esq (Whig), John Turton, Esq (Whig)

1685-7 Richard Howe, Esq (Tory), Sir Henry Gough, Kt (Tory)

1689-90 T Henry Sydney, Esq (Whig), Sir Henry Gough, Kt (Tory)

1690-5 T Sir Henry Gough, Kt (Tory), Michael Biddulph, Esq (Whig)

1695-8 Sir Henry Gough, Kt (Tory), Thomas Guy, Esq (Whig)

1698-1700 T Thomas Guy, Esq (Whig), John Chetwynd, Esq (Mod. Tory) (1698-99), Sir Henry Gough (Tory) (1699-1700)

1701 T Thomas Guy, Esq (Whig), Sir Henry Gough, Kt (Tory)

1701-2 Henry Thynne, Esq (Tory), Thomas Guy, Esq (Whig)

1702-5 Henry Thynne, Esq (Tory) (1702), Thomas Guy, Esq (Whig), Joseph Girdler, Serjeant-at-Law (Tory) (1702-5)

1705-8 T Thomas Guy, Esq (Whig), Joseph Girdler, Esq (Tory)

1708-10 T Joseph Girdler, Esq (Tory), Richard Swynfen, Esq (Whig)

1710-13 T Joseph Girdler, Esq (Tory), Samuel Bracebridge, Esq (Tory)

1713-5 T Joseph Girdler, Esq (Tory), Samuel Bracebridge, Esq (Tory)

1715-22 William Inge, Esq (Tory), Samuel Bracebridge, Esq (Tory)

1722-27 T Francis Willoughby, Esq (Tory), Samuel Bracebridge,

Esq (Tory) (1722-3), Richard Swynfen, Esq (Whig) (1723-7), Major George Compton (Tory) (1727)

1727-34 T Earl Inchiquin (Anti-Walpolean Whig), Thomas Willoughby, Esq (Tory)

1734-41 T Lord John Sackville (Whig) George Compton, Esq (Tory) (1734-5) Dr Charles Cotes (Tory) (1735-41) **T**

1741-7 T Lord John Sackville (Whig), John Floyer, Esq (Tory) (1741), Charles Cotes, Esq (Tory) (1742-7)

1747-54 Thomas Villiers, Esq (Whig), Sir Henry Harpur, Bart (Tory) (1747-8), Sir Robert Burdett, Bart (Tory) (1748-54)

1754-61 Thomas Villiers, Esq (Whig) (1754-6), Sir Robert Burdett, Bart (Tory), George Bussy, Viscount Villiers (Whig) (1756-61)**T**

1761-8 T Sir Robert Burdett, Bart (Tory), George Bussy, Viscount Villiers (Whig) (1761-5), Edward Thurlow of the Inner Temple (Bedford Whig) (1765-8)

1768-74 William de Grey, Esq (Attorney-General) (Tory) (1768), Edward Thurlow, Esq (Tory), Major-General Charles Vernon (Tory) (1768-74)

1774-80 T Thomas de Grey, jun (Gower-Whig), Edward Thurlow, Attorney-General (Tory) (1774-8), Anthony Chamier, Esq, of Epsom (Weymouth-Whig) (1778-80)

1780-4 Anthony Chamier, Esq (Weymouth-Whig) (1780),

John Courtenay, Esq (Tory), John Calvert of Albury Hall, Herts (Tory) (1780-4)

1784-90 T John Courtenay, Esq (Coalition), John Calvert, jun, of Albury Hall, Herts (Tory)

1790-96 John Courtenay, Esq (Whig), Robert Peel of Bury, Lancs (Tory)

1796-1802 Robert Peel of Bury, Lancs, and Drayton Bassett (Tory), Thomas Carter of Edgcott, Northants (Tory)

1802-6 Sir Robert Peel Bt (Tory), Major-General William Loftus (Tory)

1806-7 Sir Robert Peel Bt (Tory), Major-General William Loftus of Stifkey (Tory)

1807-12 Sir Robert Peel Bt (Tory), Major-General William Loftus of Stifkey (Tory)

1812-18 Sir Robert Peel Bt (Tory), Lord Charles Vere Ferrars Townshend (Whig)

1818-20 T Sir Robert Peel, Bt (Tory), William Yates Peel (Tory)

1820-6 Lord Charles VF Townshend (Whig), William Yates Peel (Tory)

1826-30 Lord Charles VF Townshend (Whig), William Yates Peel (Tory)

1830-31 Lord Charles VF Townshend (Whig), Rt Hon Sir Robert Peel Bt (Tory)

1831-2 Lord Charles VF Townshend (Whig), Rt Hon Sir Robert Peel Bt (Tory)

1832-4 Lord Charles VF Townshend (Lib), Rt Hon Sir Robert Peel Bt (Con)

1835-7 William Yates

TAMWORTH P.B.

Peel (Con), Rt Hon Sir Robert Peel Bt (Con)

1837-41 T Rt Hon Sir Robert Peel (Con), Capt EH a'Court (Con)

1841-7 Sir Robert Peel Bt (Con) (1841) (1841-7) (unopposed), EH a' Court (Con)

1847-52 Sir Robert Peel Bt (Con) (1847-50) (unopposed), WY Peel (Con) (1847) (unopposed), J Townshend (Lib) (1847-52) (unopposed), Sir R Peel Bt (Con) (1850-2)

1852-7 Sir R Peel Bt (Con) (1852-5) (unopposed) (1855-7), J Townshend (Lib) (1852-6) (unopposed), Viscount Rainham (Lib) (1856-7) (unopposed)

1857-9 Sir R Peel Bt (Lib) (unopposed), Viscount Rainham (Lib)(unopposed)

1859-65 Sir R Peel Bt (Lib) (1859-61) (1861-5) (unopposed), Viscount Rainham (Lib) (1859-63), J Peel (Lib) (1863-5)

1865-8 Sir R Peel Bt (Lib), J Peel (Lib)

1868-74 Sir R Peel Bt (Lib), Sir HLE Bulwer (Lib) (1868-71), J Peel (Lib) (1871-2) (unopposed), RW Hanbury (Con) (1872-4)

1874-80 Sir R Peel Bt (Lib), RW Hanbury (Con) (1874-8), HA Bass (Lib) (1878-80)

1880-5 HA Bass (Lib), JS Balfour (Lib)

Walsall P.B. 1832-1955

1832-4 T Charles Smith Forster (Con-Whig)

1835-7 Charles Smith

Forster (Con)

1837-41 T Francis Finch (Lib-Rad) (1837-41),

John Neilson Gladstone (Con) (1841)**T**

1841-7 R Scott (Lib)

1847-52 Hon ER Littleton (Lib)

1852-7 C Forster (Lib)

Warley West BC 1974-97

WALSALL P.B.

1832-1885

(unopposed)
1857-9 C Forster (Lib)
(unopposed)
1859-65 C Forster (Lib)
1865-74 C Forster (Lib)

(unopposed)
1874-80 C Forster (Lib)
1880-5 Sir C Forster Bt (Lib) (unopposed)
1885-6 Sir C Forster (Lib)
1886-92 Sir C Forster (Gladstonian Lib) (unopposed) (1886-91), ET Holden (Gladstonian Lib) (1891-2)
1892-5 Frank James (Con)

1895-1900 Sydney Gedge (Con)
1900-06 Rt Hon Sir AD Hayter (Lib)
1906-10 Major EM Dunne (Lib)
1910 (Jan) RA Cooper (Con)
1910 (Dec)-1918 (Sir) RA Cooper (Con)
1918-22 Sir RA Cooper Bt (Unionist)
1922-3 Pat Collins (Lib)

1923-4 Pat Collins (Lib)
1924-9 William Preston (Con) (1924-5, 1925-9)
1929-31 John James McShane (Lab)
1931-5 Joseph Alexander Leckie (Lib)
1935-45 JA Leckie (Lib) (1935-8),
1945-50 Major WT Wells (Lab)
1950-1 WT Wells (Lab)
1951-5 WT Wells (Lab)

Walsall North B.C. 1955-present

1955-9 WT Wells, QC (Lab)
1959-64 WT Wells , QC (Lab)
1964-6 WT Wells, QC (Lab)
1966-70 WT Wells, QC (Lab)
1970-4 WT Wells, QC (Lab)
1974-9 Rt Hon JT Stonehouse (Lab)

(1974-6), RG Hodgson (Con) (1976-9)
1979-83 David J Winnick (Lab)
1983-7 DJ Winnick (Lab)
1987-92 DJ Winnick (Lab)
1992-7 DJ Winnick (Lab)
1997-2001 DJ Winnick (Lab)
2001- DJ Winnick (Lab)

WALSALL NORTH B.C.

WALSALL SOUTH B.C.

Walsall South B.C. 1955-present

1955-9 Sir HJ d'Avigdor-Goldsmid, Bt, DSO (Con)
1959-64 Sir HJ d'Avigdor-Goldsmid (Con)
1964-6 Sir HJ d'Avigdor-

Goldsmid (Con)
1966-70 Sir HJ d'Avigdor-Goldsmid (Con)
1970-4 Sir HJ d'Avigdor-Goldsmid (Con)

1974-9 Bruce T George (Lab)
1979-83 BT George (Lab)
1983-7 BT George (Lab)
1987-92 BT George

(Lab)
1992-7 BT George (Lab)
1997-2001 BT George (Lab)
2001- Rt Hon BT George (Lab)

Warley B.C. 1997-present

1997-2001 J Spellar (Lab)
2001- Rt Hon J Spellar (Lab)

Warley East B.C. 1974-97

1974-9 AMW Faulds (Lab)
1979-83 AMW Faulds (Lab)
1983-7 AMW Faulds

(Lab)
1987-92 AMW Faulds (Lab)
1992-7 AMW Faulds (Lab)

WARLEY WEST B.C.

WEST Bromwich

WARLEY EAST B.C.

Warley West B.C. 1974-97

1974-9 PK Archer, QC (Lab)
1979-83 Rt Hon PK

Archer, QC (Lab)
1983-7 Rt Hon PK Archer, QC (Lab)

1987-92 Rt Hon RK Archer, QC (Lab)
1992-7 J Spellar (Lab)

Wednesbury P.B. 1867-1974

1868-74 A Brogden (Lib)
1874-80 A Brogden (Lib)
1880-5 A Brogden (Lib)
1885-6 Wilson Lloyd (Con)
1886-92 Hon P Stanhope (Gladstonian Lib)
1892-5 Wilson Lloyd (Con)
1895-1900 Walford Davis Green (Con)
1900-06 Walford D Green (Con)
1906-10 Clarendon G Hyde (Lib)
1910 (Jan) J Norton Griffiths (Con)

1910 (Dec)-1918 JN Griffiths (Con)
1918-22 A Short (Lab)
1922-3 A Short (Lab)
1923-4 A Short (Lab)
1924-9 A Short (Lab)
1929-31 A Short (Lab)
1931-5 Viscount Ednam (Con) (1931-2), JW Banfield (Socialist) (1932-5)
1935-45 JW Banfield (Socialist)
1945-50 SN Evans (Lab)
1950-1 SN Evans (Lab)
1951-5 SN Evans (Lab)
1955-9 SN Evans (Lab)

(1955-7), JT Stonehouse (Lab) (1957-9)
1959-64 JT Stonehouse (Lab)
1964-6 JT Stonehouse (Lab)
1966-70 JT Stonehouse (Lab)
1970-4 Rt Hon JT Stonehouse (Lab)

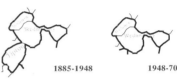

WEDNESBURY P.B.

1867-85

WEDNESBURY P.B.

1885-1948   1948-70

West Bromwich P.B. 1885-1974

1885-6 JH Blades (Lib)
1886-92 JErnest Spencer (Con)
1892-5 JE Spencer (Con)
1895-1900 JE Spencer (Con) (unopposed)
1900-06 (Sir) JE Spencer (Con) (unopposed)
1906-10 AEW Hazel (Lib)
1910 (Jan) Viscount Lewisham (Con)

1910 (Dec)-1918 Viscount Lewisham (Con) (petition and scrutiny of votes 1911)
1918-22 FO Roberts (Lab)
1922-3 FO Roberts (Lab)
1923-4 (Rt Hon) FO Roberts (Lab)
1924-9 Rt Hon FO Roberts (Socialist)
1929-31 Rt Hon FO

Roberts (Socialist)
1931-5 A Ramsay (Con)
1935-45 Rt Hon FO Roberts (Socialist)
1945-50 J Dugdale (Lab)
1950-1 Rt Hon J Dugdale (Lab)
1951-5 Rt Hon J Dugdale (Lab)
1955-9 Rt Hon J Dugdale (Lab)
1959-64 Rt Hon J

Dugdale (Lab) (1959-63), MA Foley (Lab) (1963-4)
1964-6 MA Foley (Lab)
1966-70 MA Foley (Lab)
1970-4 MA Foley (Lab)

WEST BROMWICH P.B.

West Bromwich

West Bromwich East B.C. 1974-present

1974-9 Andrew MW Faulds (Lab)
1979-83 Peter C Snape (Lab)
1983-7 PC Snape (Lab)

1987-92 PC Snape (Lab)
1992-7 PC Snape (Lab)
1997-2001 PC Snape (Lab)
2001- Tom Watson (Lab)

West Bromwich West B.C. 1974-present

1974-9 Miss Betty Boothroyd (Lab)
1979-83 Miss B Boothroyd (Lab)
1983-7 Miss B Boothroyd (Lab)
1987-92 Miss B Boothroyd (Lab)
1992-7 Rt Hon Miss B

Boothroyd (Lab), Speaker
1997-2001 Rt Hon Miss B Boothroyd (Lab), Speaker (1997-2000), Adrian Bailey (Lab) (2000-01)
2001- Adrian Bailey (Lab Co-op)

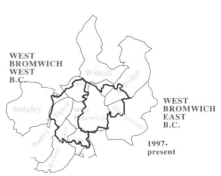

WEST BROMWICH WEST B.C.   Walsall   WEST BROMWICH EAST B.C.

Sedgley   West Bromwich   1974-1997

WEST BROMWICH WEST B.C.   Walsall   WEST BROMWICH EAST B.C.

Sedgley   Tipton   West Bromwich   1997-present

Wolverhampton P.B. 1832-1885

1832-4 T William Wolryche Whitmore (Lib- Whig), Richard Fryer (Lib- Radial Reformer)

1835-7 T Charles Pelham Villiers (Lib- Rad), Thomas Thornley (Lib-Rad)

1837-41 T Charles Pelham Villiers (Lib-Rad), Thomas Thornley (Lib- Rad)

1841-7 Hon CP Villiers (Lib) (unopposed), T Thornley (Lib) (unop-

posed)

1847-52 Hon CP Villiers (Lib) (unopposed), T Thornley (Lib) (unopposed)

1852-7 Hon CP Villiers (Lib) (1852-3) (unopposed) (1853-7) (unopposed), T Thornley (Lib) (unopposed)

1857-9 Hon CP Villiers (Lib) (unopposed), T Thornley (Lib) (unopposed)

1859-65 Hon CP Villiers (Lib) (1859) (unop-

posed) (1859-65) (unopp), Sir R Bethell (Lib) (1859) (unopposed), (1859-61) (unopp), TM Weguelin (Lib) (1861-5)

1865-8 Hon CP Villiers (Lib), TM Weguelin (Lib)

1868-74 Hon CP Villiers (Lib) (unopposed), TM Weguelin (Lib) (unopposed)

1874-80 Hon CP Villiers (Lib), TM Weguelin (Lib)

1880-5 Hon CP Villiers (Lib), HH Fowler (Lib)

Wolverhampton East B.C. 1885-1948

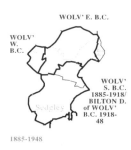

1885-6 Henry Hartley Fowler (Lib)

1886-92 Rt Hon HH Fowler (Gladstonian Lib)

1892-5 Rt Hon HH Fowler (Gladstonian Lib) (unopposed) (1892) (1892-)

1895-1900 Sir HH Fowler (Gladstonian Lib)

1900-06 Rt Hon Sir HH

Fowler (Lib) (unopposed)

1906-10 Rt Hon Sir HH Fowler (Lib) (1906-08), GR Thorne (Lib) (1908-10)

1910 (Jan) GR Thorne (Lib)

1910 (Dec)-1918 GR Thorne (Lib)

1918-22 GR Thorne (Lib)

1922-3 GR Thorne (Lib)

1923-4 GR Thorne (Lib)

1924-9 GR Thorne (Lib)

1929-31 G Le M Mander (Lib)

1931-5 G Le M Mander (Lib)

1935-45 G le M Mander (Lib)

1945-50 Capt J Baird (Lab)

Succeeded by Wolverhampton North East

Wolverhampton South B.C. 1885-1918

1885-6 Rt Hon CP Villiers (Lib) (unopposed)

1886-92 Rt Hon CP Villiers (Lib Unionist) (unopposed)

1892-5 Rt Hon CP Villiers (Lib Unionist) (unopposed)

1895-1900 Rt Hon CP Villiers (Lib Unionist) (unopposed) (1895-8),

JL Gibbons (Lib Unionist) (1898-1900)

1900-06 (Sir) Henry Norman (Lib)

1906-10 Sir H Norman (Lib)

1910 (Jan) Col TE Hickman (Con)

1910 (Dec)-1918 Brig-Gen TE Hickman (Con)

Seat renamed Bilston

Bilston D. of Wolverhampton P.B. 1918-74

1918-22 Br-Gen TE Hickman (Coalition Unionist)

1922-3 Lt Col CK Howard Bury (Unionist)

1923-4 Lt Col CK

Howard (Unionist)

1924-9 J Baker (Socialist)

1929-31 J Baker (Lab)

1931-5 Capt Geoffrey K Peto (Con)

1935-45 Ian C Hannah

The House of Commons   Wolverhampton South West BC

(Con)
1945-50 W Nally (Lab)
1950-1 W Nally (Lab)
1951-5 W Nally (Lab)
1955-9 RJ Edwards (Lab)
1959-64 RJ Edwards (Lab)
1964-6 RJ Edwards (Lab)

1966-70 RJ Edwards (Lab)
1970-4 RJ Edwards (Lab)

Succeeded by Wolverhampton South East BC

WOL' N.E. B.C.

WOLVERHAMPTON S.W. B.C.

BILSTON D. of WOL' P.B.

1955-1974

Wolverhampton West B.C. 1885-1948

1885-6 A Hickman (Con)
1886-92 Sir WC Plowden (Gladstonian Lib)
1892-5 Sir Alfred Hickman (Con)
1895-1900 Sir A Hickman (Con)
1900-06 Sir A Hickman

(Con) (unopposed)
1906-10 TF Richards (Lab)
1910 (Jan) Alfred F Bird (Con)
1910 (Dec)-1918 AF Bird (Con)
1918-22 AF Bird (Coali-

tion Unionist) (1918-22), Sir RB Bird (Unionist) (1922)
1922-3 Sir RB Bird (Con)
1923-4 Sir RB Bird (Con)
1924-9 Sir RB Bird (Con)
1929-31 WJ Brown (Socialist)

1931-5 Sir RB Bird (Con)
1935-45 Sir RB Bird (Con)
1945-50 Lt HD Hughes (Lab)

Succeeded by Wolverhampton South West

Wolverhampton North East B.C. 1948-present

1950-1 J Baird (Lab)
1951-5 J Baird (Lab)
1955-9 J Baird (Lab)
1959-64 J Baird (Lab)
1964-6 Mrs Renee Short (Lab)

1966-70 Mrs R Short (Lab)
1970-4 Mrs R Short (Lab)
1974-9 Mrs R Short (Lab)
1979-83 Mrs R Short

(Lab)
1983-7 Mrs R Short (Lab)
1987-92 Mrs MP Hicks (Con)
1992-7 Kenneth Purchase

(Lab)
1997-2001 K Purchase (Lab Co-op)
2001- K Purchase (Lab Co-op)

Wolverhampton South West B.C. 1948-present

WOLVERHAMPTON N.E. B.C.

WOLVERHAMPTON S.W. B.C.

WOLVERHAMPTON S.E. B.C.

1983-1997

1950-1 J Enoch Powell (Con)
1951-5 JE Powell (Con)
1955-9 JE Powell, MBE (Con)
1959-64 JE Powell (Con)
1964-6 JE Powell (Con)
1966-70 Rt Hon JE Powell, MBE (Con)
1970-4 Rt Hon JE Powell (Con)
1974-9 Nicholas W

Budgen (Con)
1979-83 NW Budgen (Con)
1983-7 NW Budgen (Con)
1987-92 NW Budgen (Con)
1992-7 N Budgen (Con)
1997-2001 Ms Jennifer G Jones (Lab)
2001- Robert Marris (Lab)

WOLVERHAMPTON
N.E. B.C.

WOLVERHAMPTON
S.E. B.C.

WOLVERHAMPTON
S.W. B.C.

1997-present

Wolverhampton South East B.C. 1974-present

1974-9 Robert J Edwards (Lab)
1979-83 RJ Edwards (Lab)
1983-7 R Edwards (Lab)
1987-92 Dennis Turner (Lab)
1992-7 D Turner (Lab)
1997-2001 D Turner (Lab Co-op)
2001- D Turner (Lab Co-op)

OTHER COUNTIES that took in former parts of Staffordshire: County/ Borough seats

Kidderminster D. of Worcestershire 1918-83

1918-22 Major EA Knight (Coalition Unionist)
1922-3 John S Wardlaw-Milne (Unionist)
1923-4 JS Wardlaw-Milne (Unionist)
1924-9 JS Wardlaw-Milne (Con)
1929-31 (Sir) JS Wardlaw-Milne (Con)
1931-5 Sir JS Wardlaw-Milne (Con)
1935-45 Sir JS Wardlaw-Milne (Con)
1945-50 L Tolley (Lab)
1950-1 G Nabarro (Con)
1951-5 GDN Nabarro (Con)
1955-9 GDN Nabarro (Con)
1959-64 GDN Nabarro (Con)
1964-6 Sir ETC Brinton (Con)
1966-70 Sir ETC Brinton (Con)
1970-4 Sir ETC Brinton (Con)
1974-9 James Esmond Bulmer (Con)
1979-83 JE Bulmer (Con)

North (Warwickshire) D. or Tamworth D. (or Solihull D. after 1945) of Warwickshire

1885-6 PA Muntz (Con)
1886-92 PA Muntz (Con) (unopposed)
1892-5 PA Muntz (Con) (unopposed)
1895-1900 PA Muntz (Con) (unopposed)
1900-06 (Sir) PA Muntz (Con) (unopposed)
1906-10 Sir PA Muntz (Con) (1906-09), FA Newdigate-Newdegate (Con) (unopposed) (1909-10)
1910 (Jan) FA Newdigate-Newdegate (Con)
1910 (Dec)-1918 FA Newdigate-Newdegate (Unionist) (unopposed) (1910-17), H Wilson-Fox (Unionist) (unopposed)(1917-8)
1918-22 H Wilson-Fox (Coalition Unionist) (unopposed)
1922-3 Sir PW Newson Bt (Unionist) (unopposed)
1923-4 Sir EM Iliffe (Unionist)
1924-9 Sir EM Iliffe (Con)
1929-31 Rt Hon Sir A Steel-Maitland Bt (Con) (1929-)
1931-5 Rt Hon Sir A Steel-Maitland Bt (Con) (1931-5), Sir John Mellor (Con) (unopposed) (1935)
1935-45 Sir John Mellor
(Con)
1945-50 Lt-Col M Lindsay (Con)
1950-1 M Lindsay (Con)
1951-5 MA Lindsay (Con)
1955-9 MA Lindsay, CBE, DSO (Con)
1959-64 MA Lindsay (Con)
1964-6 WP Grieve, QC (Con)
1966-70 WP Grieve, QC (Con)

EUROPEAN SEATS

1979-1984
Birmingham North EC
1979-84 ME Forth (Con)
Birmingham South EC

1979-84 Miss NF Forster (Con)
Hereford & Worcester EC
1979-84 JSR Scott-Hopkins (Con)

Salop & Stafford EC
1979-84 CJ Prout (Con)
Staffordshire EC
1979-84 RJ Moreland (Con)

Midlands West EC
1979-84 RJ Simmonds (Con)

1984-1994
Birmingham East EC
1984-89 Mrs CM Crawley (Lab)
1989-94 Mrs CM Crawley (Lab)
Birmingham West EC
1984-89 JE Tomlinson (Lab)
1989-94 JE Tomlinson (Lab)
Cheshire East EC
1984-89 T Normanton (Con)
1989-94 B Simpson (Lab)

SALOP & STAFFORD EC

STAFFORDSHIRE EC

MIDLANDS WEST EC

BIRMINGHAM NORTH EC

BIRMINGHAM SOUTH EC

HEREFORD & WORCESTER EC

Hereford & Worcester EC
1984-89 JSR Scott-Hopkins (Con)
1989-94 Sir JSR Scott-Hopkins (Con)
Midlands West EC
1984-89 TJ Pitt (Lab)
1989-94 JAW Bird (Lab co-op)
Shropshire & Stafford EC
1984-89 CJ Prout (Con)
1989-94 CJ Prout (Con)
Staffordshire East
1984-89 GW Stevenson (Lab)
1989-94 GW Steveson (Lab)

EC CONSTITUENCIES 1979-84

CHESHIRE EAST EC

SHROPSHIRE &
STAFFORD EC

STAFFORDSHIRE
EAST EC

MIDLANDS WEST EC

BIRMINGHAM WEST
EC

BIRMINGHAM EAST EC

HEREFORD &
WORCESTER EC

**EC CONSTITUENCIES
1984-94**

1994-99

**Birmingham East
EC**
1994-99 Mrs CM
Crawley (Lab)
**Birmingham West
EC**
1994-99 The Lord John
Tomlinson (Lab)
**Hereford &
Worcester EC**
1994-99 D Hallam (Lab)
Midlands West EC
1994-99 S Murphy (Lab)
Peak District EC
1994-99 Ms A McCarthy
(Lab)
**Staffordshire East
& Derby EC**
1994-99 Philip White-
head (Lab)
**Staffordshire West
& Congleton EC**
1994-99 Michael Tappin
(Lab)

1999-2009

The electoral system for
elections to the European
Parliament was changed
to the Regional Lists in
1999 by the European
Parliament Elections Act
1999 (1999 c. 1). The
constituency of West
Midlands consists of Her-
efordshire, Shropshire,
Staffordshire, Stoke-on-
Trent, Warwickshire,
West Midlands Metro-
politan County, Worces-
tershire. The Boundary
Commissions proposals
for new constituencies
were never used.

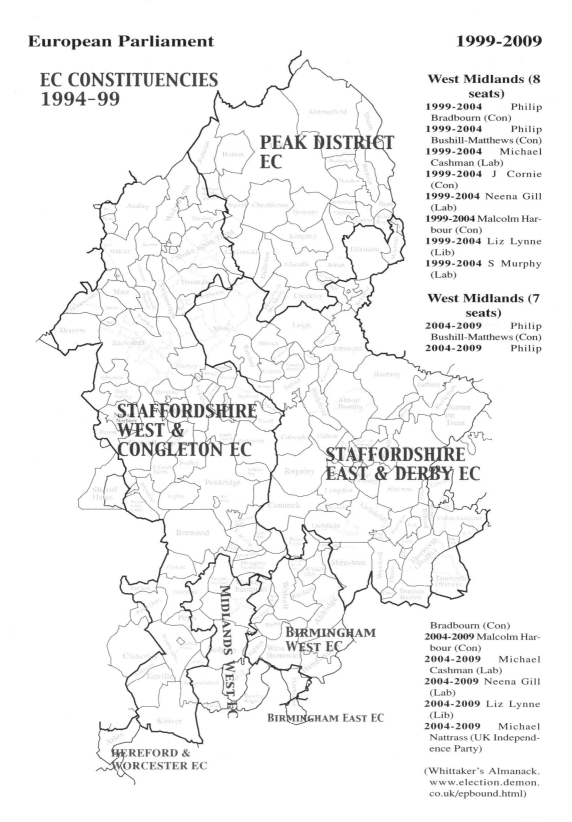

European Parliament

EC CONSTITUENCIES 1994-99

PEAK DISTRICT EC

STAFFORDSHIRE WEST & CONGLETON EC

STAFFORDSHIRE EAST & DERBY EC

MIDLANDS WEST EC

BIRMINGHAM WEST EC

BIRMINGHAM EAST EC

HEREFORD & WORCESTER EC

1999-2009

West Midlands (8 seats)
1999-2004 Philip Bradbourn (Con)
1999-2004 Philip Bushill-Matthews (Con)
1999-2004 Michael Cashman (Lab)
1999-2004 J Cornie (Con)
1999-2004 Neena Gill (Lab)
1999-2004 Malcolm Harbour (Con)
1999-2004 Liz Lynne (Lib)
1999-2004 S Murphy (Lab)

West Midlands (7 seats)
2004-2009 Philip Bushill-Matthews (Con)
2004-2009 Philip Bradbourn (Con)
2004-2009 Malcolm Harbour (Con)
2004-2009 Michael Cashman (Lab)
2004-2009 Neena Gill (Lab)
2004-2009 Liz Lynne (Lib)
2004-2009 Michael Nattrass (UK Independence Party)

(Whittaker's Almanack. www.election.demon. co.uk/epbound.html)

INDEX TO SEATS FOR PARLIAMENTARY ROLLS